BIOTECHNOLOGY AND INTERNATIONAL LAW

As with any rapid technological development, the biotechnology revolution is putting great strains on the ability of law to adapt to new challenges and threats. Although there is general agreement on the need to regulate biotechnology in many different fields of human activity (agriculture, life sciences, forensic science) domestic law remains deeply divided over the best approach to take. This book is the first attempt at covering the most pressing legal issues raised by the impact of biotechnologies on different categories of international norms. Through the contribution of a selected group of international scholars and experts from international organisations, the book addresses 1) the international status of genetic resources, both in areas of national jurisdiction and in common spaces such as the international sea bed area and Antarctica; 2) the relevance of environmental principles in the governance of modern biotechnologies; 3) the impact of biotechnologies on trade rules, including intellectual property law; 4) the human rights implications, especially in the field of human genetics; and 5) the intersection between general international law and regional systems, especially those developed in Europe and Latin America. The overall objective of the book is to provide an up-to-date picture of international law as it stands today and to stimulate critical reflection and further research on the solutions that will be required in years to come.

Volume 9 in the series, Studies in International Law

Biotechnology and International Law

Edited by

Francesco Francioni
and
Tullio Scovazzi

• HART •
PUBLISHING

OXFORD AND PORTLAND, OREGON
2006

Published in North America (US and Canada) by
Hart Publishing
c/o International Specialized Book Services
920 NE 58th Avenue, Suite 300
Portland, OR 97213-3786
USA
Tel: +1-503-287-3093 or toll-free: (1)-800-944-6190
Fax: +1-503-280-8832
E-mail: orders@isbs.com
Website: www.isbs.com

Hart Publishing, 16C Worcester Place, Oxford, OX1 2JW
Telephone: +44 (0)1865 517530 Fax: +44 (0)1865 510710
email: mail@hartpub.co.uk
Website: http//:www.hartpub.co.uk

British Library Cataloguing in Publication Data
Data Available

ISBN-13: 978-1-84113-631-8 (hardback)
ISBN-10: 1-84113-631-X (hardback)

Typeset by Compuscript, Shannon
Printed and bound in Great Britain by
TJ International Ltd, Padstow, Cornwall

Preface

This book is the product of a collective research project organised by the Editors at the University of Siena, the European University Institute of Florence and the University of Milano Bicocca in the period between 2003 and 2005. The basic question it tries to address is how international law is responding, or should be responding, to the new challenges and risks posed by the development and application of modern biotechnology.

How scientific and technological progress impacts on the law is not a new problem. Also in the past, international law has faced the challenge of its adaptation to new realities and needs posed by advances in science and technology. Its evolution in the area of the law of the sea, outer space and the control of the offensive use of weapons—to mention just a few—is witness to its capacity of timely and progressive development. In the field of biotechnology, however, the process of adaptation of the law to scientific and technological advances seems particularly problematic. First, although there is general agreement over the need for regulation in the different fields of biotechnology application such as agriculture, life sciences and forensic practices, domestic law remains deeply divided over the approach to take. Should regulation be of the 'command and control' type, or be based on flexible codes of conduct, or even left to self-regulation by relevant stakeholders? Second, ethical standards play a fundamental role in determining the limits of the permissible scope of scientific research and in directing scientific progress toward socially and morally acceptable goals, but the diversity of such standards hinder a common understanding of such limits and goals. Third, biotechnology activities are not carried out by the traditional subjects of international law, the states, but rather by private actors in science and business who are not readily amenable within the scope of application of the traditional categories of international norms which are designed to regulate state action. These are elements of a new complexity that compound the difficulty in building consensus at the international level on the development of new norms along the traditional lines of customary practice and treaty making.

This volume is an attempt at covering the most pressing legal issues raised by the impact of biotechnologies on different categories of international norms. The approach we have chosen is pluralistic in the sense of being based on critical reflections developed in the contributions of a diverse group of legal scholars and experts, with different professional and cultural backgrounds and including academics, practitioners and officials of international organisations. The contributions address: 1) the international status of genetic resources, both in areas of national jurisdiction and in common spaces, such as the international sea, the sea bed area and Antarctica; 2) the relevance of environmental principles in the governance of modern biotechnologies; 3) the impact of biotechnology products and services on trade rules, including intellectual property law; 4) the human rights implications, especially in the field of human genetics; and 5) the intersection between general international law and regional systems, especially those developed in Europe and Latin America.

The overall objective of the book is to provide an up-to-date picture of international law as it stands today and to stimulate a critical reflection and further research on the possible normative solutions that will be required in the years to come.

Francesco Francioni
European University Institute, Florence
Tullio Scovazzi
University of Milano Bicocca

This book would not have been published without the financial support of various institutions. The Editors wish to express their gratitude especially to the Italian Ministry of the University and Research for the funding of Research Project COFIN 2002 - prot. 2002121574, the European University Institute as well as Universities of Siena and Milano Bicocca, which cofinanced the research and provided support and facilities for the meetings of the participants.

Contents

Table of Cases

European Court of First Instance

European Court of Human Rights

European Court of Justice

Table of Legislation

BOLIVIA

BRAZIL

CHINA

COLOMBIA

ECUADOR

EUROPEAN COMMUNITY/EUROPEAN UNION

Decisions

Directives

Regulations

FRANCE

GERMANY

INDIA

INTERNATIONAL

ITALY

JAPAN

PERU

PHILIPPINES

SPAIN

THAILAND

UNITED KINGDOM

UNITED STATES OF AMERICA

VENEZUELA

Part I

The International Legal Regime of Biotechnology: General Aspects

1

International Law for Biotechnology: Basic Principles

FRANCESCO FRANCIONI*

I. INTRODUCTION

MORE THAN FOUR centuries ago, in the famous monologue of the Shakespearean drama, Hamlet pondered 'Whether 'tis nobler in the mind to suffer The slings and arrows of outrageous fortune, Or take arms against a sea of troubles, And by opposing end them. To die, to sleep—no more'.[1] Four centuries later, the tormenting doubts of the prince of Denmark mirror the anxieties and conflicting attitudes of the international community with regard to the regulation of modern biotechnology. Should we use, to the utmost of our ability, the power and resources of science and technology to 'take arms against a sea of troubles' and fight the unfavourable conditions of human existence, such as disease, physical disabilities, poverty, environmental degradation? Or is it 'nobler' to suffer 'the slings and arrows of outrageous fortune' and thus accept the supreme design of nature, in the name of divine providence or in the hope of a superior intelligence of the natural selection process?

As in any case of rapid and disturbing advances in science, the response to this type of questions is less than certain. At the moral level, the question of how far bio-science should be allowed to tamper with the intimate essence of nature pits the fundamental value of freedom of research against the ethical claim that application of scientific advances through specific man-made techniques must not ignore the fundamental distinction between right and wrong or between good and evil. Even if the separation between the pure 'cognitive' dimension of science and its 'technological' application is not easy to maintain, in a world where

* Professor of Law, European University Institute, Florence, and University of Siena.

[1] Hamlet, Act III, scene I.

economic and commercial interests exercise ever-growing pressure over the financing and orientation of scientific research,[2] this conceptual separation has become fertile ground for the development of the discipline of bioethics. Far from remaining confined to the value systems of national or regional legal orders, this discipline has been fully brought within the remit of universal institutions such as the UN and UNESCO, now directly engaged on the issues of human cloning[3] and the preparation of an international code of bio-ethics.[4]

At the policy level, the biotechnology revolution has generated considerable strains in the relationship between science and policy-making. A crisis of trust is currently emerging as to who should make the decisions and set the standards with regard to the application of new scientific knowledge through the use of bio-engineering techniques. Should scientists have the last word? Or should the decision be left to democratically elected officials? Should religious considerations play a role also in a secular state? How can we balance the influence of industry against the opinion and preferences of the people, as expressed through the manifold manifestations of civil society? In recent times these question have provoked very discordant answers with an increasing radicalisation of extreme positions, on either the permissive or the prohibitionist side of the issue. The result is the difficulty of dialogue between opposing camps and the consequent elusion of consensus over who has, or should have, 'authority' to set standards in the controversial uses of modern biotechnology.[5]

[2] See Krimsky, *Science in the Private Interest. Has the Lure of Profits Corrupted Biomedical Research?* (Lanham, 2003).

[3] See UN GA Declaration on Human Cloning of 17 Nov 2004 (UN doc. A.C.6/59/L.26), calling upon Member States to prohibit 'any attempt to create human life through cloning processes and any research intended to achieve that aim'.

[4] See UNESCO Universal Declaration on the Human Genome and Human Rights of 11 Nov 1997 (*infra* n 37), the UNESCO Guidelines for the Implementation of the Declaration on the Human Genome and Human Rights of 16 Nov 1999 (*infra* n 40) and the International Declaration on Human Genetic Data of 16 Oct 2003 (*infra* n 41). On 19 October 2005 UNESCO adopted the Universal Declaration on Bioethics and Human Rights, www.UNESCO.ORG/SH5/bioethics. For the work of the UN in this field, see especially: Report of the Secretary General submitted pursuant to the UN Commission on Human Rights resolution 2001/71, doc. E/CN.4/2003/98, 10 Feb 2003, with Annex; Report of the Expert Consultation on Human Rights and Biotechnology, Geneva, 24–25 Jan 2002); UN Commission on Human Rights, Sub-Commission in Prevention of discrimination and Protection of Minotities, Working Group on Indigenous Population, Human Genome Diversity Research and Indigenous Peoples, 4 June1998, doc. E/CN.4/Sub.2/AC.4/1998/4.

[5] For a balanced approach, advocating national and international regulation of biotechnologies, although within a liberal perspective, see Fukuyama, *Our Posthuman Future* (New York, 2002), especially ch 10, 11 and 12.

At the legal level this difficulty is reflected in national attempts to abrogate by popular referenda laws passed by parliaments on contested aspects of biotechnology applications,[6] and, at the international level, in the tensions surrounding attempts at establishing norms and institutions for the regulation of the most controversial aspects of biotechnologies, such as the ownership and control of genetic resources, the marketing of genetically modified seeds and food, the use of stem cells of human embryos in biomedicine. Even in Europe, where an impressive body of Community regulations has developed,[7] very different attitudes persist on the part of individual states on some key issues such as the limits of admissibility of stem cell research, genetic diagnostics and therapy, safety of genetically modified food, and environmental protection against the risk of trans-national movement of genetically modified organisms (GMO).

At the level of public international law, which is the main focus of this contribution and this book, the search for appropriate methods and regulatory approaches capable of mediating among conflicting views on biotechnology applications meets even greater difficulties. If it is true that the international legal system has demonstrated in the past the capacity to evolve as a consequence of scientific and technological developments—witness the transformation of the law of the sea as a consequence of new techniques of resource exploitation, the emergence of environmental law following massive industrialization, the development of principles governing human activities in outer space—in the field of biotechnology, the diversity and multicultural nature of the international community hinders consensus on a reasonably homogeneous core of ethical values and social interests. One manifestation of this difficulty is the current debate in the UN General Assembly with regard to the adoption of a binding legal instrument on human cloning.[8] Besides, unlike domestic law, international law is not able to respond to the challenge of rapid technological progress by way of institutional mechanisms competent to enact timely legislation by way of majority vote. The decentralised structure of the international community still relies on treaties and custom as the available tools for law-making, and at the administrative level, with the exception of some advanced regional organisation, such as the European

[6] A recent example is provided by the Italian referendum concerning the law on assisted procreation. See Lenzerini, 'Law n. 40 of 19 February 2004, in (2004) XIV *Italian Yearbook of International Law* 442.

[7] See Pavoni, *Biodiversità e biotecnologie nel diritto internazionale e comunitario* (Milan, 2004), Part II; Patterson, 'Biotechnology, Policy Regulating Risks and Risking Regulation', in Wallace and Wallace (eds), *Policy Making in the EU* (Oxford, 2000), 32 ff. See also the chapters in this volume by Poli and Sturma.

[8] See the work of the Ad Hoc Committee on an International Convention against the Reproductive Cloning of Human Beings, appointed by the UN General Assembly in 2001

Union, and of some soft law regulatory mechanisms in the field of standardisation, such as the FAO/WHO Codex Alimentarius,[9] international law cannot rely on the work of administrative agencies, or on general consensus on forms of self-regulation by private actors.[10]

More fundamentally, treaty and customs, as the typical forms of law-making in international relations, are the product of state-driven interests and have been historically concerned with the delimitation of governmental powers and state sovereignty in international relations. But biotechnologies are not directly related to governmental powers. The form of power they embody stems from the human ability to manipulate the structure of life and to develop through bio-engineering techniques new genetically modified organisms and products. This new form of technological power originates in the work of scientists and in the new knowledge which, when suitable, is privatised through the instrument of Intellectual Property Rights (IPR) and utilised by economic actors—to meet an increasing variety of market demands. This, of course, does not entail that states are powerless to control biotechnologies when they are perceived to pose unacceptable risks. They can exercise such control by way of national legislation, and, indeed, such legislation is now emerging in many states, although at a different pace and with different approaches.[11] But since national legislation is limited in scope to state jurisdiction, it cannot be very effective in relation to biotechnology activities that are developed and implemented in a transnational context. Most commercial applications of biotechnology occur in the transnational business, such as agriculture, food and pharmaceutical production, and medicine. Thus, it is clear that an international approach is necessarily based on some common understanding of what is the permissible scope of such techniques, who controls access to the biological resources necessary to their development, by whom they should be managed and overseen, who should benefit from their commercial use, and how disputes arising from their application should be resolved.[12]

(GA Res. 56/93 of 12 Dec 2001) and the draft convention text addressed to the UN Secretary General by the Government of Costa Rica on 2 Apr 2003 (UN doc. A/58/73 of 17 Apr 2003).

[9] See http://www.codexalimentarius.net/web/index_en.jsp.

[10] Even in the recent initiatives for the reform of the UN Charter on the occasion of its 60th anniversary, this issue has remained at the margin of the debate, which has mainly focused on security, terrorism and the reform of the institution. In the High Level Panel Report on Threats, Challenges and Change Level, 'A More Secure World: Our Shared Responsibility' Panel Report only a few pages are devoted to issues of environmental governance and and to issues posed by science and technology: see Francioni, 'The Role of the EU in Promoting Reform of the UN in the Field of Human Rights and Environmental Protection', Chaillot Paper n. 78 (Institute for Security Studies EU, Paris, 2005), 31 ff.

[11] Several European countries have enacted laws in this sense, including those regulating the possible uses of the human genome; see the chapter by Lenzerini, in this volume.

[12] Once the need for international regulation is recognised, the problem we have to face is how to develop specific norms and institutions to meet the new needs. Treaty negotiations

In the following discussion I will try to identify what role international law can play in providing an answer to such questions and in supporting a system of biotechnology governance that is respectful of established principles and values in international relations, including state sovereignty and the general interest of the international community as a whole. Since other contributions in this book will deal with specific treaty regimes, this chapter will address the issue of biotechnology only from the point of view of general international law. The main focus will be on the issues that have attracted most controversy in practice and literature: (1) who owns the patrimony of genetic resources that are the object of biotechnological development and application? (2) What is the relevance of general principles of international environmental law for the development and commercialisation of bio-engineered products and organisms? (3) Does international economic law provide a concept of justice applicable to the equitable sharing of benefits arising from the commercial biotechnological innovations and to trade in related products? (4) Does international law allow a human rights approach to biotechnology?[13]

II. WHO OWNS THE BIOGENETIC RESOURCES?

Available Normative Models

Since biotechnologies entail the manipulation of living organisms in order to make new products, the first question to be addressed is who owns the genetic material to which bio-engineering techniques are applied? Classical international law, since its development in the seventeenth century, has provided a simple dualist model of resource allocation. On the one hand, the physical space and the resources located therein were allocated to the spheres of national jurisdiction coinciding with the territorial sovereignty of every independent state. On the other hand, space and

and custom as traditional methods of international law-making both require some form of state consent, either by the express manifestation of the will to be bound in the former, or by the development of a consistent practice and the *opinio iuris* in the latter. It is hardly necessary to point out that these requirements entail a slow and unpredictable process of law creation that can be particularly inadequate to address the phenomenon of rapidly developing new technologies. Further, consent and *opinio iuris* can be withheld by states which have a stake in safeguarding the freedom of their economic actors in taking advantage of the global market for the commercial exploitation of their biotechnological products or services. This has become apparent in relation to the persistent refusal of some major technological players to join the Biodiversity Convention (see *infra* n 18) and the Biosafety Protocol (see *infra* n 53) in spite of the dramatic rate of biodiversity degradation the planet is undergoing.

[13] This question is the object of an ongoing research project undertaken by this writer at the European University Institute, which should lead to the preparation and publication of a second volume in 2006.

resources 'beyond national jurisdiction' were subject to the regime of freedom. This entailed equal rights of access to the resources of the high seas and the freedom to occupy and claim territories and resources that belonged to no other state. In the course of the twentieth century, this strict dualism yielded to further models of natural resources allocation and management. First, the option of enlarging the scope of national sovereignty by way of occupation of territories deemed to be *terra nullius* was precluded by the prohibition of the use of force, the elimination of colonialism and the concomitant emergence in the 1960s of the principle of permanent sovereignty over natural resources.[14] Secondly, with respect to the classical regime of the seas, the principle of freedom has undergone profound transformation as a consequence of the emergence of the new customary rules allowing states to establish the exclusive economic zone (EEZ) and the continental shelf, two legal concepts that are based on the combination of functional sovereignty of the coastal state with a residual recognition of community interests involved in their exploitation and of the traditional principle of freedom of the high seas. Thirdly, as perhaps the most radical departure from the regime of freedom, the principle of the common heritage of mankind has made the international community the title holder of the resources of the deep sea bed. An institution—the International Sea Bed Authority—has been established by the quasi-universal Law of the Sea Convention[15] and a system of prior authorisation and management has replaced the primitive principles of free access and first come, first served. Fourthly, in the second part of the last century innovative and sophisticated models of international management of resources, over which national sovereignty is absent or contested were been developed. The pre-eminent example of this model is the Antarctic Treaty System,[16] which combines freedom of access to the continent with the preservation of certain sovereignty claims and a system of international inspection, monitoring and strict environmental protection enacted and implemented by a parliament-like institution, the Antarctic Treaty Consultative Meeting.[17] Fifthly, in the last decade the new concept of 'common concern of humankind' has emerged as a legal tool designed to safeguard the general interest of the international community in the preservation of certain components of the global ecosystem, such as biodiversity and climate. Unlike the common heritage of mankind, the common concern does not purport to vest title over relevant resources, but

[14] See, in particular, GA Res. 1803 (XVII 1962), 'Permanent Sovereignty over Natural Resources', reprinted in [1963] ILM 223 (*infra*, text corresponding to n 23).

[15] See United Nations Convention on the Law of the Sea, 1982 [1982] ILM 1261, Part XI.

[16] The Antarctic Treaty System was initiated by the 1959 Antarctic Treaty (402 UNTS 71).

[17] For a general evaluation of the Antarctic Treaty system, see Francioni and Scovazzi (eds.), *International Law for Antarctica* (The Hague, 1996) and the literature cited therein.

more modestly signifies that the international community as a whole, inclusive of states and peoples, is a stakeholder in the conservation and use of such resources.

In view of this complex and quite diversified development of international law over the past half-century, the question arises which regulatory model, if any, among those examined above, is applicable to determine the status of genetic resources which today are the object of biotechnological investigation and application. Although the state of international law is still far from being settled, it is our opinion that three basic normative models now emerge in international practice.

A Modern Permanent Sovereignty Regime

The first model is what may be called the *modern permanent sovereignty regime*. By this expression we mean that biogenetic material contained in plants and animals located in the territory of a state is to be deemed subject to the sovereignty of that state. By virtue of this principle every state is free to regulate access to those resources by private or public firms operating in the field of biotechnology. However, this freedom is counterbalanced by the basic requirement that it be exercised in a manner so as to facilitate access to genetic resources for sustainable development and environmentally sound use. This rather conservative approach has been followed in Article 15(2) of the Biodiversity Convention[18] and is the result of an oscillating practice over the past 20 years. In the field of plant genetic resources, we can observe that in the mid-1980s an assertion was made under the impulse of FAO that such resources should constitute the common heritage of mankind.[19] Later on, state practice backtracked on this position under the pressure of industrial states and farmers' and breeders' associations, which were all concerned that the common heritage would pose an unacceptable threat to proprietary rights over plant varieties and their potential improvement by way of biotechnological manipulation. In parallel, less developed countries with a rich biodiversity in their territory became acutely aware of the need to secure international recognition of their entitlement to obtain some form of remuneration *vis-à-vis* the widespread practice of removal of genetic material from their territory by foreign firms. These combined pressures led to the progressive erosion of the earlier assertion of the common heritage. The FAO Conference, which had been the champion of this principle, resolved at its 26th Session in 1991,

18 See the 1992 Convention on Biological Diversity, available at http://www.biodiv.org/doc/legal/cbd-en.pdf.

19 See the 1983 FAO International Undertaking on Plant Genetic Resources, available at ftp://ext-ftp.fao.org/ag/cgrfa/iu/iutextE.pdf (see, in particular, the preambles of annexes I and II).

with an evident oxymoron, that '[t]he concept of the common heritage of mankind, as applied in the International Undertaking on Plant Genetic Resources, *is subject to the sovereignty of states over their plant genetic resources*'.[20]

The adoption of the Biodiversity Convention in 1992 confirms this return to sovereignty. The preamble to the Convention proclaims that '[s]tates have sovereign rights over their biological resources'. The same concept, in slightly different language, is expressed in Article 15(2). If we consider that the Biodiversity Convention has been ratified by the vast majority of the states,[21] that its text does not allow reservations (Article 37) capable of diminishing its normative character, and that these provisions reiterate the principle proclaimed by the FAO Conference, the reasonable conclusion is that the legal status of genetic resources cannot be founded on the common heritage principle, but rather follows the traditional rule according to which natural resources are subject to the sovereignty of the state in whose territory they are located. It is true that, following the adoption of the Biodiversity Convention, traces of the common heritage remained in the Agenda 21 programme of strengthening the FAO role as trustee of the global common represented by plant genetic resources through the FAO Global System for the Conservation and Utilisation of Plant Genetic Resources.[22] Yet, however disappointing this may be, the FAO system never succeeded in becoming the exclusive mechanism for ensuring the conservation and management of plant genetic resources. Gene banks and private networks moved in to compete in the role of collectors and custodians of plant germoplasm, and today the FAO is only one of the players in the worldwide business of potential providers of plant genetic resources.

Notwithstanding this failure in making plant genetic resources part of the common heritage, the regulatory model that emerges from the above practice significantly departs from the original concept of permanent sovereignty over natural resources as established in the well known GA Resolution 1803 of 1962.[23] First of all, the new model refers to 'sovereign rights' (see the CBD preamble) rather than sovereignty *tout court*, which in itself signals a less than absolute power of the territorial state over genetic resources. But, most important, this model can be qualified as 'modern' because it aims at reconciling the sovereignty of the territorial state with the general interest of the international community in securing conditions to facilitate access to genetic resources for environmentally

[20] Res. C 3/91, FAO Conf. 26th Sess. (emphasis added).

[21] At 30 Apr 2005 188 states were parties to the Convention; see http://www.biodiv.org/world/parties.asp.

[22] See http://www.fao.org/FOCUS/E/96/06/06-e.htm.

[23] See *supra* n 14.

sound purposes. The modernity of this approach lies in the recognised need for international cooperation in the identification, collection, evaluation and conservation of genetic resources, both *in situ* and *ex situ*. Thus, sovereignty in this area must be exercised in such a manner as to avoid unreasonable restrictions that defeat the purpose of biodiversity conservation and of sustainable use of biogenetic resources.

This conclusion is supported by the recently adopted FAO Treaty on Plant Genetic Resources for Food and Agriculture.[24] Other contributions to this volume[25] will address the complex technical innovations of this treaty. Here it is sufficient to note that its basic premise is that the recognised state's sovereignty over biological resources is to be made compatible with the overarching goal of pursuing international cooperation to ensure access to those resources for their development in the interest of the international community and in conditions of 'fair and equitable sharing of the benefits arising from their use'.

The Common Heritage Regime

(a) The sea and seabed

Although most genetic resources are located in areas subject to state sovereignty, today, an increasing variety of such resources is found in organisms which live in spaces beyond national jurisdiction. Of particular interest in this regard are the organisms which have developed in extreme environmental conditions such as those characterising the deep sea[26] and Antarctica.[27] Since in these areas there is no state sovereignty or, at least, no generally recognised sovereignty, the question arises as to what is the applicable legal regime to determine the status of genetic resources found therein. No explicit answer is provided to this question in existing treaties, such as the 1982 Law of the Sea Convention or the 1959 Antarctic Treaty.[28] However, two legal options can be found in customary international law. The first option is that of the freedom of the high seas. The second is the common heritage.

At first sight, it might appear logical to consider genetic resources of the high seas and the international seabed as equivalent to any tangible biological resources and to subject them to the regime of freedom in analogy with fishing activities. Further, since activities related to genetic resources of the sea are scientific in nature, it might be plausible to subject them to the regime of scientific research which is also covered by the principle of

24 See the 2001 International Treaty on Plant Genetic Resources for Food and Agriculture, available at ftp://ext-ftp.fao.org/ag/cgrfa/it/ITPGRe.pdf.

25 See in particular, the chapter by Footer, in this volume.

26 See the chapter by Scovazzi, in this volume.

27 See the chapters by Vigni and Guyomard, in this volume.

28 See *supra* n 16.

freedom of the sea.[29] However, such analogies with fishing and scientific research can be quite misleading when it comes to determining the status of genetic resources beyond national jurisdiction. First, fishing is concerned with harvesting living resources of the sea for human consumption or other commercial uses but has no relation whatsoever with the activity of identification, collection and possible development of the intangible patrimony of genetic resources contained in living organisms. Appropriation of the fish by the fisherman does not entail appropriation of the wealth of genetic information the catch may yield; any more than the purchase of a house designed by an architect entails the appropriation by the buyer of the talent and know-how that the architect bestowed in it. That talent, although incorporated in the house, is a separate asset with a continuing vitality and creative potential that the purchaser of the house cannot own. By the same token, also the application by analogy of the regime of freedom governing scientific research on the high seas is rather dubious. In fact, rules relating to marine scientific research are activity related, in the sense that they establish rights and obligations applicable to the conduct of science activities at sea, but in no way can such rules, those contained in Part XIII of the Law of the Sea Convention or the corresponding customary rules, be used to establish a legal status of genetic resources in the high sea and on the international sea bed. This is confirmed by Article 241 of the Law of the Sea Convention, which provides that '[m]arine scientific research activities *shall not* constitute the legal basis for any claim to any part of the marine environment or its resources'.[30]

Since the principle of freedom cannot be presumed to govern the legal status of genetic resources of the high seas and deep sea bed, and since sovereignty is excluded by definition in these areas, the logical conclusion is that these resources must be deemed to be subject to the principle of common heritage. They should therefore be placed under the jurisdiction of the existing institutional mechanisms established with the LOS Convention or under a new specialised institution to be created within the same forum. This conclusion is reinforced by the fact that the most promising repository of marine genetic material is located in the vicinity of hydrothermal vents in the sea bed, where extreme environmental conditions linked to scarcity of light and temperature variations provide precious genetic resources that science and technology are just starting to identify.[31] Since such resources are so closely linked to the physical conditions of the deep sea bed, it is unavoidable that the eventual exploitation

[29] See Part XIII of the Law of the Sea Convention, *supra* n 15.

[30] Emphasis added.

[31] See the chapter by Scovazzi in this volume, as well as the debates in the Vth Meeting of the UN open-ended informal consultative process on oceans and the law of the sea

of sea bed minerals shall have a direct impact on them. This is a further convincing reason for bringing them under the common heritage principle and for ensuring that a unified regime applies to the physical and biological environment of the international sea bed.

(b) Antarctica

As far as Antarctica is concerned, the problem of bio-prospecting is only beginning to be addressed in the context of the Antarctic Treaty Consultative Meeting (ATCM).[32] One of the principles of the Antarctic Treaty, which by way of a long and uncontested practice has acquired the status of general international law, is that activities in Antarctica must be carried out in the interest of 'all mankind' and in full respect of Antarctica as a natural reserve devoted to peace and science.[33] This principle has so far permitted access to natural resources only for scientific purposes and led in 1991 to the adoption of the well known moratorium on the exploration and exploitation of mineral resources. Bio-genetic resources do not fall within the moratorium. However, when their prospecting is carried out for gain, the related activities can be carried out within a legal framework of cooperation, exchange of information and collective solidarity of the Antarctic Treaty Consultative Parties. It is up to them to devise, if necessary, an appropriate regulatory regime for Antarctic bio-prospecting, perhaps as an annex to the Madrid Protocol on the protection of the Antarctic environment.[34]

(c) The human genome

That of genetic resources located in common spaces is not the only area where the principle of common heritage can play a role. Another important area is that of the human genome.[35] Here, it is not so much the location of the resources that makes them a global common, but rather the fact that they constitute the very essence and common patrimony of humanity. In the last decade groundbreaking research has been conducted by private and public entities in order to complete the so-called mapping of the

(UNICPOLOS), 9 June 2004, in particular the intervention by the Italian delegate Scovazzi in the panel discussion on 'New Sustainable Use of the Oceans, Including the Conservation and Management of Biological Diversity of the Seabed in Areas beyond National Jurisdiction', reprinted in *Italian Yearbook of International Law*, vol. XIV(2004), forthcoming.

32 A Resolution was adopted at the ATCM held in Stockholm in June 2005 to the effect of committing Consultative Parties to gather and exchange information and date concerning research carried out in Antarctica by their nationals and related to bio-genetic resources in view of establishing whether such research is susceptible of commercial exploitation (documents on file with the author).

33 See Preamble to the 1959 Antarctic Treaty (*supra* n 16) and art 2 of the Madrid Protocol on Environmental Protection to the Antarctic Treaty of 1991 (available at http://www.antarctica.ac.uk/About_Antarctica/Treaty/protocol.htm).

34 Further on this issue, see the chapters by Vigni and Guyomard, in this volume.

35 On this issue, see the chapter by Lenzerini, in this volume.

human genome. The results, now at an advanced stage, open up unprecedented prospects of application in life sciences, medicine, and in relation to the general goal of improving health and welfare of human beings. At the same time, the prospects of biotechnological applications to human genetic material have raised fears that human beings may be reduced to 'means' in function of technological experimentation or of commercial goals. Besides, genetic knowledge is deemed to contain the potential for conscious discrimination based on genetic patterns of individuals or groups, and on other violations of human rights. Against this problematic background, international practice over the past ten years has evolved toward the extension of the principle of common heritage from the field of economic resources to the new area of the intangible resources represented by the human genome. Thanks to the vigorous action of UNESCO, whose mandate in the field of advancement of science and culture is linked to the constitutional commitment to guarantee 'the democratic principle of the dignity, equality and mutual respect of men' (UNESCO Constitution),[36] a Universal Declaration on the Human Genome and Human Rights was adopted in 1997.[37] Article 1 of the Declaration states that '[t]he human genome underlies the fundamental unity of all members of the human family, as well as the recognition of their inherent dignity and diversity. In a symbolic sense, it is *the heritage of humanity*'.[38] Although the use of the phrase 'in a symbolic sense' may appear to weaken the legal strength of this article, the general context of the Declaration clearly confirms its intention to proclaim the human genome the common heritage of humanity. Article 4 provides that the human genome in its natural state shall not give rise to financial gains. This precludes its patenting for commercial purposes. Article 10 subjects scientific genomic research in such fields as biology and medicine to respect for human dignity and fundamental rights of individuals and peoples. Further, the Declaration requires a commitment to international cooperation in the assessment of risks and benefits deriving from genomic research and in the promotion of developing countries' capacity to carry out such research and to benefit from its technological applications.

Obviously, the Universal Declaration on the Human Genome is not a binding treaty and its text can at best reflect underlying principles of emerging international law or, at least, constitute a body of soft law designed to model the evolution of customary law around its standards. Yet, it is difficult to deny that the Declaration has affected the *opinio iuris* of the international community. Its text emanates from the UNESCO

[36] See the Preamble to the UNESCO Constitution (third sentence), available at http://www.unesco.org.

[37] See Universal Declaration on the Human Genome and Human Rights, 11 Nov 1997, available at http://www.unesco.org.

[38] Emphasis added.

General Conference, a body of universal character, where states can express their opinion and cast their votes, positive or negative; its adoption by acclamation was preceded by extensive consultations and technical preparatory work, where all currents of opinion—scientific, legal, ethical—were represented, and no objection was raised or reservation attached. After its adoption, the UN General Assembly endorsed its text by a resolution of 9 December 1998.[39] Further, the Universal Declaration has not remained an isolated act. UNESCO has followed up on the proclamation of the human genome as heritage of humanity: in 1999 it adopted implementing measures in the form of a resolution[40] prescribing guidelines for making the Declaration effective in domestic law; in October 2003 the General Conference adopted the International Declaration on Human Genetic Data,[41] a document that confirms the status of the human genome as common heritage of humanity.

The above documents have received broad support from the international community and provide principles and criteria which domestic law and regional organisations are drawing upon in developing legislation and codes of ethics for the conservation and proper use of the human genetic patrimony.[42]

(d) The common concern concept

Unlike the common heritage of mankind, the 'common concern' concept is a relatively recent development in international law. Its appearance in treaty law and practice dates back to the early 1990s, the time of the adoption of the major environmental treaties addressing global environmental problems such as biodiversity degradation and climate change. The under-lying idea of the 'common concern' is that resources of the world to which this concept applies are not 'owned' by the international community on the basis of an indivisible title, as in the case of the common heritage: on the contrary, they remain subject to the traditional regime of sovereignty or freedom, but their management requires a holistic approach that takes into account the general interest of humanity in their conservation. In this sense, such resources are an element of the general interest of humanity and the common concern serves as a legal basis for legitimising forms of intervention within the sphere of domestic jurisdiction of individual states, as well as possible limitations on the principle of

39 See A/RES/53/152 of 9 Dec 1998.

40 See 30 C/Resolution 23 of 16 Nov 1999 endorsing the Guidelines for the implementation of the Universal Declaration on the Human Genome and Human Rights.

41 See *International Declaration on Human Genetic Data*, 16 Oct 2003, available at http://www.unesco.org.

42 For an overview of domestic law on the scientific use of the human genome, cf. Commission on Human Rights, *Report on Human Rights and Bioethics*, 10 Feb 2003, UN doc. E/CN.4/2003/98.

freedom applicable to common spaces. The most direct relevance of the common concern concept is in the area of biodiversity. All genetic material, in one way or another, is related to the biological diversity of our planet. Wild plants and animals that make up the biological diversity of our planet are distributed in areas subject to sovereignty, to freedom or to the common heritage. In relation to all of them, the common concern principle may play a subsidiary role in safeguarding the general interest of the international community whenever specific regulatory models, such as the common heritage, are not applicable, or whenever the standard regime of permanent sovereignty needs to be bent to accommodate the general interest.

If we take this into account, it seems that the concept of the common concern can play a complementary role[43] in the definition of the international status of biogenetic resources. On the one hand, it is capable of reinforcing the principle of the common heritage applicable to resources located beyond the limits of national jurisdiction and to the human genome; on the other hand it serves to mitigate the exclusivity of national jurisdiction over biogenetic resources that are located within state territory. In this case, although the regime of permanent sovereignty remains applicable, the common concern provides the rational and legal foundation for the duty that every territorial state has to facilitate access to its biogenetic resources and to cooperate in view of their sustainable development.

III. BIOTECHNOLOGIES AND ENVIRONMENTAL PROTECTION

International environmental law is a relative recent development of the international legal system. Up to the second part of the last century hardly any norm could be found in this system that would significantly limit state sovereignty over national territory or state freedom in common spaces in function of the preservation of the environment. The situation has changed over the past 30 years. Now it is generally agreed in legal doctrine and in international practice that the protection of the environment has become the object of an international obligation and that such obligation entails some limits on state sovereignty over the use of natural resources in the national territory and in areas beyond national jurisdiction.[44]

[43] For a different view, according to which the common concern principle plays a primary role in this respect, see the chapter by Pavoni, in this volume.

[44] See Birnie and Boyle, *International Law and the Environment* (Oxford, 2003); Sands, *Principles of International Environmental Law* (Manchester and New York, 1995), 183 ff.; Brownlie, *Principles of Public International Law* (Oxford, 1998), 285 ff.; 'Siena Forum on the International Law of the Environment', Siena, 17–21 Apr 1990. reprinted in *Vita Italiana*, suppl. n. 1. Roma, 1990.

The first principle of international environmental law that may find useful application in the field of biotechnology is the due diligence obligation incumbent upon every state to prevent damage to the territory of other states or to common spaces as a consequence of biotechnology activities that entail release of genetically modified material into the environment. This obligation can be traced to the Stockholm Declaration,[45] Principle 21, and to the Rio Declaration,[46] Principle 2, and now forms an integral part of the International Law Commission draft articles on transfrontier damage resulting from hazardous activities (2001).[47] An express recognition of this principle in the field of biotechnology can be found in the appellate decision of the Examining Division of the European Patent Office in the well-known case of the *Onco-mouse*.[48] In this case the applicants were seeking patent registration in Europe for the Harvard 'Onco-mouse', a genetically bioengineered mouse resulting from the introduction into its genetic make-up of a specific onco gene that would make it acutely prone to develop tumours. Besides the moral considerations involved in assessing a process that entailed the intentional infliction of acute suffering upon a living creature, the Examining Division expressly referred to considerations relating to the protection of the environment as a necessary element in striking the balance between the usefulness of the invention and the protection of public order. The Division affirmed:

> There is a basic interest of mankind to remedy widespread and dangerous diseases, on the other hand the environment has to be protected against the uncontrolled dissemination of unwanted genes . . . .[49]

Finally the Division held the granting of the patent compatible with the protection of the environment on the basis of the finding that in the specific case:

> No release is intended into the general environment. Therefore the risk of an uncontrolled release is practically limited to intentional misuse or blatant ignorance on the part of the laboratory personnel carrying out the tests.[50]

It is useful to recall that, from a general point of view, the principle of prevention of transboundary environmental harm has been considered to

[45] See Stockholm Declaration on Environment and Development, 16 June 1972 [1972] ILM 1416.
[46] See Rio Declaration on Environment and Development, 14 June 1992 [1992] ILM 874.
[47] See Draft Articles on Prevention of transboundary harm from hazardous activities, 2001, available at http://www.un.org/law/ilc/texts/prevention/preventionfra.htm.
[48] *Onco-Mouse/Harvard III*, Examining Division, decision of 3 Apr 1992 [1992] *OJ EPO*, 588 ff.
[49] Para. 4.
[50] Para. 4(iv).

be part of customary international law by the International Court of Justice. In its 1996 advisory opinion on the *Legality of the Threat or Use of Nuclear Weapons* the Court affirmed that '[t]he general obligation of states to ensure that activities within their jurisdiction and control respect the environment of other states or of areas beyond national control is now part of the corpus of international law relating to the environment'.[51] Just a year after this Advisory Opinion, the International Court of Justice confirmed this finding in the well known judgment or the *Gabcikovo-Nagymaros* litigation between Hungary and Slovakia.[52]

Besides the principle of prevention, another substantive principle of international environmental law is particularly suitable for application in relation to biotechnology: that is the so-called 'precautionary approach'. In its substantive dimension, the precautionary approach requires states to adopt or tolerate the adoption of legislation or administrative measures that are necessary to forestall foreseeable risks for the environment. A radical interpretation of this principle—although still a controversial one—would entail the setting aside or cessation of an economic or technological activity that entailed a serious risk for which no reliable assessment or management method was available. In the field of biotechnology, where the implications of the release into the environment of bio-engineered organisms is still surrounded by great uncertainty, this principle can have a wide scope of application. The Bio-safety Protocol additional to the Biodiversity Convention has been inspired by the precautionary approach.[53] As we shall see in the following section, the Protocol has instituted a procedure of prior informed consent for the trade in 'living modified organisms' and permits the adoption of precautionary measures to restrict imports of such organisms when the risk they pose for the environment or health is deemed to be incompatible with the level of environmental protection and safety set by the importing state. In the case law, the reception of the precautionary approach is still patchy and rather tenuous. While specific reference was made to it by the International Tribunal for the Law of the Sea in the *Southern Bluefin Tuna* case[54] and by some individual opinions of judges of the same Tribunal in the recent *MOX Plant* case,[55] other jurisdictions have refrained from pronouncing

[51] [1996] ICJ Rep 226, 241–242, para. 29.

[52] [1997] ICJ Rep 7 41, para. 53.

[53] See Cartagena Protocol on Biosafety to the Convention on Biological Diversity, 2000 [2000] ILM 1027.

[54] *Southern Bluefin Tuna (New Zelanda v. Japan; Australia v. Japan)*, Order of 27 Aug 1999, available at http://www.itlos.org, part, para. 77 (see also the individual opinions of judges Treves and Laing).

[55] *MOX Plant (Ireland v. United Kingdom)* case, Order of 13 Nov 2001, available at http://www.itlos.org, espec. para. 84.

on the legally binding nature of the approach (*Hormones* case[56] and *Gabcikovo-Nagymaros*[57]) as either a custom or a general principle. On the other hand, this principle is well entrenched in European Union law and has been given a robust interpretation in the European judicial practice in the recent *Pfizer* case.[58] Be it as it may, it is easy to imagine that this principle, as a soft law approach or as hard law creating binding obligations, is bound to play two very important roles in relation to biotechnology. The first is a complementary role in relation to the principle of prevention examined above. Where the effect of the release of new genes into the environment can escape full scientific assessment, the precautionary approach is part and parcel of every state's due diligence obligation to see that activities within its jurisdiction or under its control do not result in environmental damage.[59] The second role is rather procedural, in the sense that it entails the appropriate use of available practices and scientific knowledge to ensure that the environmental impact of bioengineered products or services is fully evaluated before they are released into the environment. But this leads us to the procedural dimension of international environmental law.

When I speak of the 'procedural dimension' of environmental norms, I refer especially to the set of procedural obligations arising from the general principle of inter-state cooperation in preventing and minimising environmental risks. This principle entails a number of duties: the duty to provide information related to the risk posed by genetically modified organisms; the duty to consult whenever differences arise as to the nature and extent of the risk; the duty to allow civil society participation in decisions involving difficult choices between the social advantages offered by technological innovations and the risks posed by such advances; and, most important, the duty to provide an environmental impact study of the specific biotechnology upon the environment and health of the people. These different faces of the principle of cooperation have already

[56] *European Communities—Measures Concerning Meat and Meat Products (EC—Hormones)*, Report of the Appellate Body, doc. WT/DS26/AB/R-WT/DS48/AB/R of 16 Jan 1998, para. 123.

[57] See *Gabcikovo-Nagymaros Project (Hungary v. Slovakia)*, [1997] ICJ Rep 7, part. at 42, para. 54.

[58] See *Commission of the European Communities v. CEVA Santé Animale SA and Pfizer Enterprises Sàrl*, Judgement of 12 July 2005, available at http://www.europa.eu.int/eur-lex.

[59] On the issue of liability for damage caused by deliberate release of genetically modified organisms, see McGarity, 'International Regulation of Deliberate Release Biotechnologies', in Francioni and Scovazzi (eds.), *International Responsibility for Environmental Harm* (London/Dordrecht/Boston, 1991), 319 ff.; Mackenzie, 'Environmental Damage and Genetically Modified Organisms', in Bowman and Boyle (eds.), *Environmental Damage in International and Comparative Law: Problems of Definition and Valuation* (Oxford, 2002), 63 ff.

received ample recognition in international practice. In the already mentioned *MOX Plant* case,[60] the Law of the Sea Tribunal has formally recognised this principle in relation to the protection of its marine environment. In the *Gabcikovo-Nagymaros* case the International Court of Justice, in spite of its rather shy interpretation of existing norms of international environmental law, did not hesitate to consider the duty to cooperate and to provide a continuous impact assessment of technological risks as a fundamental principle binding upon the parties.[61] This practice reinforces the normative character of the principle of cooperation as enunciated in the Stockholm and Rio Declarations (Principles 24 and 7, respectively).[62]

There are other emerging principles of international environmental law that may have certain relevance to biotechnology. I am thinking particularly of sustainable development and the concept of intergenerational equity. However, these principles still remain too tenuous to be able to yield any norm-creating effects.[63] In any event, their possible relevance can be best appreciated in the context of international economic law, which is the subject of the following section.

IV. BIOTECHNOLOGIES, JUSTICE AND THE EQUITABLE SHARING OF BENEFITS

If one can speak of an 'economic constitution' of the world today, it may be defined on the basis of the post-World War II liberal project that culminated in the establishment of the WTO, following the end of the Cold War, in the development of a worldwide network of bilateral investment treaties, and the linking to intellectual property protection of the commercial advantages guaranteed by WTO. Such basic system is founded on the progressive realisation of the freedom of movement of goods and services, of capital, and to a much more limited extent, of persons seeking economic opportunities.

In relation to such framework of principles the problems raised by the application of biotechnology to economic activities can fall in a variety of legal categories as large and diverse as the multiplicity of treaty regimes ranging from trade, intellectual property rights, investments, biodiversity protections and development assistance, to mention just some examples. The issues arising in the relationship between biotechnologies and these

[60] See *supra* n 55, para. 82.

[61] See *supra* n 57, 68, para. 112 and 78, para. 140. See also the individual opinion of Vice-President Weeramantry [1997] ICJ Rep 88, at 111–113

[62] See *supra* n 45 and 46 respectively.

[63] In this sense, see Lowe, 'Sustainable Development and Unsustainable Arguments', in Boyle and Freestone (eds.), *International Law and Sustainable Development* (Oxford, 1999), 19 ff.

treaty regimes will be addressed by other contributions in this volume.[64] In the following discussion, I will address only two basic issues of general international law that today underlie the debate on the place of biotechnology in international economic law. The first is how the benefits arising from the commercial exploitation of genetic resources should be shared between potential stakeholders, primarily the biotechnological firms that have devised the methods of transforming genetic resources in new products or services, on the one hand, and the countries or communities from which the resources have originated, on the other. The second issue concerns to what extent, within the present legal framework of the world economy, states remain free to enact legislation which, on safety, health or other social grounds, restricts the access of bioengineered products to the national market.

Equitable Sharing of Benefits

As to the first problem, the adversarial relationship in which it originates and evolves is characterised by a conflicting set of arguments. The biotechnology companies and, to a certain extent, their countries of origin insist on the legitimacy and necessity of patenting of sequences of genetic material and chemical compounds combining specific genes in order to create new products. In their defence, they use the well known argument that their monopoly over the commercial use of the biotechnological processes and the high cost of the resulting products are justified as a form of equitable remuneration of their conspicuous investments in research and development. On the other hand, the source countries, and especially developing countries of the South, rich in biogenetic resources, argue that they are the title holders of genetic material and of knowledge that leads to such patents, that patents are not appropriate for life forms and that, in any event, patents make bioengineered products, even those that may be of critical need for them, too expensive for their scarce economic means.

This controversy does not find a clear-cut solution in the international regime of intellectual property rights (IPRs) protection, and the TRIPS agreement in particular. The TRIPS Agreement commits all Parties to grant protection to:

> any invention, whether products or processes, in all fields of technology, provided that they are new, involve an inventive step and are capable of industrial application [Article 27(1)].[65]

64 See, particularly, the chapters by Ullrich, Zarrilli and Petersmann, in this volume.

65 The full text of the TRIPS Agreement is available at http://www.wto.org.

However, TRIPS allows for the exclusion of IPR protection for 'plants and animals other than micro-organisms' (Article 27(3)(b)). In addition, patents may be denied on grounds of public policy or morality (Article 27(2)). Thus, states which wish to deny patent protection to gene sequences or compounds isolated from genetic material found in their jurisdiction may argue that genes are not micro-organisms within the meaning of TRIPS or that, in any event, the patenting of a form of life is contrary to *ordre public*.

This approach, however, would hardly be satisfactory. Patents for forms of life may be granted in other states, and, indeed they are granted in advanced industrial countries such as the United States and the EU. Further, the uncertainty of the international regime may make it illusory for a developing state to challenge the patent on the basis of its own view of morality. Besides, it is doubtful that the monumental task of reconciling the conflicting interests of developing and developed states in this field may be simply delegated to the technical instrument of IPR.[66]

A better approach is to proceed from the distinction we have made in the first section of this chapter between resources placed under the regime of national sovereignty—which represent the great majority of commercially developed biogenetic material—and resources found in areas beyond national jurisdiction. In the latter case, the principles of common heritage/common concern should dictate the appropriate criteria and modalities for revenue sharing pursuant to the applicable international regime, be it that of the Sea Bed Authority, the Antarctic Treaty System or other forum of international cooperation such as the FAO centres for crop genes.

In the case of genetic resources belonging to areas subject to national jurisdiction, instead, our view is that, rather than trying to re-conceive new and untested principles of international law, the correct approach is to place the matter within the scope of application of traditional rules and principles of international law governing the treatment of aliens and foreign investments. This body of international law is perfectly suitable for regulating the relationship between biotechnology investors and source countries. The development of customary international law over the past 30 years shows that the relationship between investors and capital importing states has been regulated by two fundamental principles: respect for national sovereignty of the host state of the investment, and equitable remuneration of the capital invested with the consent of the territorial state.[67] The first principle entails that biotechnology investors

[66] See the chapter by Ullrich, in this volume.

[67] For a concise and clear exposition of the law on this subject, see Conforti, *Diritto internazionale* (Naples, 2002), 230 ff.

must obtain the consent of the territorial authorities in order to obtain access to bioprospecting and commercial development of genetic resources located in a foreign state. The second principle entails that the benefits accruing from the commercial exploitation of those resources must be equitably shared with the source state. As in other areas of international law, such as delimitation of maritime areas, equity has been used by the International Court of Justice and by arbitral tribunals as a general principle capable of infusing notions of fairness and justice in areas of the law undergoing intense transformation or presenting gaps in relation to new social or technological realities. Equitable accommodation in the area under discussion entails that biotechnological applications of genetic material found within the jurisdiction of developing states cannot be placed under the exclusive control of the companies that claim patent protection over the more successful products of their research. Equity requires that, once access to genetic resources has been lawfully obtained, the benefits of the commercial exploitation of the biotechnological development must be equitably shared with the source state (or with the relevant international authority in the event of resources found beyond national jurisdiction). Such sharing of benefits may take the form of adequate monetary remuneration of the source country; but it may also take the form of technology transfers from the investing company or its home state to the source country.[68] This may be an important form of cooperation especially if the technology is suited to the territorial state's needs in the field of agriculture, medicine or environmental protection. International law does not today provide any specific normative model for giving effect to this principle of equitable sharing of benefits.[69] However, a variety of agreements, sometimes referred to as 'bio-prospecting' agreements, are rapidly developing, which provide for the payment of royalties in the event of successful exploitation, sharing of profits, and even the establishment of joint ventures.[70] As these contractual arrangements become more generalised, a practice will evolve with regard to their interpretation, implementation and settlement of related disputes. It will be in this context that the general principle of equitable sharing of benefits will play an important role, at the same time as a legitimating factor and as a limit to the contractual autonomy of the subjects involved in

[68] See, *e.g.*, art 16 and 19 of the Biodiversity Convention (*supra* n 18); art 13 of the FAO Treaty (*supra* n 24); 2002 Bonn Guidelines on Access to Genetic Resources and Fair and Equitable Sharing of the Benefits Arising out of their Utilization (available at http://www.biodiv.org/decisions/default.aspx?m=cop-06&d=24).

[69] But see the Bonn Guidelines (see previous note) and the ongoing negotiations on an international regime on access and benefit-sharing.

[70] See Putterman, 'Model Material Transfer Agreements for Equitable Biodiversity Prospecting', in Barber, Henne, Mugabe *et al* (eds.), *Access to Genetic Resources. Strategies for Sharing Benefits* (Gland, 1997), 299 ff.

the biotechnology transaction. Those who are advocating a pure and simple market-based solution to this problem, with the consequential contractualisation of the relationship between source countries and biotechnology companies, may well remember the fundamental role played by equity in the slow and difficult process of rebuilding consensus among developed and less developed states on the controversial issue of the treatment of foreign investments. In the 1980s, after bitter disputes about the legality of nationalisations of foreign property and relative standards of compensation, equity systematically shaped the outcome of investment disputes and helped the consolidation of international law on what constitutes fair treatment of the economic interests of aliens.[71]

Trade in Biotech Products

Under general international law every state is free to restrict the import or export of biotech products on grounds of safety, environmental protection or other public policy consideration. This freedom, however, is limited today by the participation of the preponderant majority of states in the WTO system, a system that requires, as a matter of treaty obligations, non-discriminatory treatment among all member states, non-discrimination between imported products and like domestic products, progressive reduction of tariffs, and the elimination of quantitative restrictions. Unlike the European Union system, where market access and economic integration are accompanied by the development of social, environmental and human rights policies, the WTO leaves the attainment of such non-economic policies to individual member states. This opens the way toward widely diverging views and regulation of biotech products or services, with considerable impact on trade. Certainly, there are instances in which trade in biotech products and services may be restricted on the basis of WTO law. The import or export of stem cells obtained from human embryos, and related therapeutic services, can fall within the moral exception of Article XX(a) GATT and Article XIV of the GATS.[72] Similarly, the import or export of biotechnological products or services to be used in offensive methods of warfare may fall within the same morality exception, and are certainly covered by the security exception (Article XXI GATT and Article XIV*bis* of the GATS). But, outside these hypotheses, there is a wide range of controversial issues arising under WTO law and related to diverging regulation of biotechnology products and services. Suffice it here to mention: (1) whether genetically modified organisms

[71] See Francioni, 'Compensation for Nationalisation of Foreign Property: The Borderland between Law and Equity', [1975] *ICLQ* 255.

[72] The full text of the GATS Agreement is available at http://www.wto.org.

and products are 'like' products within the meaning of GATT Article III; (2) whether they fall within the permissible exceptions of GATT Article XX; (3) whether identification of genetically modified products by labelling or otherwise is compatible with the relevant provisions of GATT, the Agreement on technical Barriers to Trade (TBT)[73] or the Agreement on Sanitary and Phyto-Sanitary Measures (SPS).[74] These issues have not yet attracted a set of common solutions, or even a common approach. On the contrary, they have given rise to a dispute pitting the European Union against the United States, Canada and Argentina before the WTO.[75] Other contributions in this volume will deal with the specific aspects of this trade dispute.[76] Here it is sufficient to point out that the role of general international law in addressing this type of trade-related disputes over the marketing of genetically modified products is that of resolving and minimising the conflicts between competing international norms and treaty regimes. As we have argued in other academic contributions,[77] this can be achieved by giving due consideration to multilateral environmental agreements, such as the Biodiversity Convention and its Additional Protocol on Biosafety in order to substantiate the requirement of the objective legal necessity of precautionary measures within the terms of Article XX, and for the purpose of ensuring multilateral and non-discriminatory solutions, as required by the *Chapeau* of Article XX. when taking into consideration the widespread perception that genetically modified products may pose certain risks to the health or the environment.

V. BIOTECHNOLOGY, HUMAN DIGNITY AND HUMAN LIBERTY

In addressing these questions one cannot overlook the reality that international law, and especially international human rights law, presents conflicting principles and policy goals. Biotechnology developments pit one against another; general principles of sovereignty over natural resources and principles of freedom and common heritage of humankind. At the same time, the need to preserve freedom of research and the right of everyone to benefit from the advances in science and technology may collide with the fundamental concept of human dignity and the integrity of the human person. Such antinomies are already apparent in relation to the

[73] The full text of the TBT Agreement is available at http://www.wto.org.

[74] The full text of the GATS Agreement is available at http://www.wto.org.

[75] See WT/DS291 (US), WT/DS292 (Canada), WT/DS293 (Argentina).

[76] On the procedural and substantive aspects of this dispute, see the chapter by Petersmann, in this volume.

[77] See Francioni, 'Environment, Human Rights and the Limits of Free Trade', in Francioni (ed.), *Environment, Human Rights and International Trade* (Oxford, 2001), 1 ff.

increasing medical and commercial relevance of the mapping of the human genome and of the use of stem cells of embryos in medically assisted reproduction, genetic diagnosis and therapy. Increased genomic knowledge and its technological applications may come to conflict with the fundamental value of human dignity, requiring that human beings be always treated as ends in themselves and not as means to an end. They may also come into conflict with specific human rights, such as the right not to be discriminated against on grounds of genetic traits, privacy, and the right not to know. Besides, even the rights of peoples may be endangered, especially those of vulnerable peoples who are more exposed to profit-driven genetic experimentation, and those of indigenous peoples, whose intimate knowledge of the natural properties of their habitats has become the focus of increased attention for the potential it yields in the development of new pharmaceutical products.[78]

These tensions have already spurred international efforts at making new law for an acceptable and sustainable use of biotechnology. Notable among such efforts are the Council of Europe Convention on Biomedicine,[79] with its related Protocol on Human Cloning,[80] the 1997 UNESCO Universal Declaration on the Human Genome,[81] with the related 2003 Declaration on Human Genetic Data,[82] the UN Declaration on human cloning,[83] and the 2001 FAO Treaty on Plant Genetic Resources for Food and Agriculture.[84] Specific chapters in this book will be devoted to the discussion of these legal instruments. Here it is sufficient to point out that the development of international law in the field of biotechnology cannot occur independently of a human rights approach to the problems and risks posed by this new form of technological power. First, because the respect for and protection of human rights remains one of the fundamental principles of the international community, as recognised by the UN Charter and the process of 'constitutionalisation' of such principles in customary international law. In this perspective, they represent a *prius* that must inform the process of regulation and adjudication of biotechnology issues, especially in the field of international economic law. It is a welcome step, therefore, that the UN sub-commission for the protection and

[78] For a discussion of these issues see the chapters in this book by Fraboni and Lenzerini.

[79] See Convention for the Protection of Human Rights and Dignity of the Human Being with regard to the Application of Biology and Medicine: Convention on Human Rights and Biomedicine, Oviedo, 4 Apr 1997, CETS n. 164.

[80] See Additional Protocol to the Convention for the Protection of Human Rights and Dignity of the Human Being with regard to the Application of Biology and Medicine, on the Prohibition of Cloning Human Beings, Paris, 12 Jan 1998, CETS n. 168.

[81] See *supra* n 37.

[82] See *supra* n 41.

[83] See *supra* n 3.

[84] See *supra* n 24.

promotion of human rights has appointed a rapporteur to study the interplay between international human rights and the human genome.[85] The second reason is that international human rights represent the only true universal language for communicating between increasingly extreme and radicalised ethical and religious world views and political conceptions. International human rights may provide a common ethical ground between those who are inspired by profound religious conviction and those who defend a secular role of the state and, *a fortiori*, of international law and institutions. This does not mean that international human rights have the mission of reducing or eliminating the diversity of cultures and ethical conviction in the name of an artificially constructed morality. It rather means that they may provide the framework and the needed legal space for continuing dialogue, for progress in full respect of diversity, and, hopefully, with time, for reconciliation between what today appear irreconcilable views.

[85] The Rapporteur, Motoc, of Rumania, prepared one report in 2003 (see UN doc. E/CN.4/Sub.2/2003/36 of 10 July 2003) and a second one is due to be circulated in 2005 (see UN doc. E/CN.4/Sub.2/2005/38).

2

Biodiversity and Biotechnology: Consolidation and Strains in the Emerging International Legal Regimes

RICCARDO PAVONI*

I. INTRODUCTION

THIS CONTRIBUTION DEALS with the basic legal principles and rules which may be viewed as underlying the emerging international legal regime of biodiversity and biotechnology. As its title suggests, the contribution mainly focuses on the relationship between biotechnology and biodiversity, hence on the legal issues arising from the development of plant and agricultural biotechnology.[1] However, I will endeavour to show the cross-cutting nature of certain principles and rules, that is their applicability to human genomics and genetics as well.

For a number of reasons, this exercise might be considered inappropriate or, at least, premature. As a matter of fact, this area of international law is relatively new: leaving aside soft law instruments, the first pertinent treaty, i.e. the 1992 Biodiversity Convention (CBD), is only 13 years old. At the same time, existing customary law—e.g. the duty to prevent transboundary environmental damage or the principle of permanent sovereignty over natural resources—surely applies to biodiversity and

* Associate Professor of International Law, University of Siena. This contribution reviews, expands and updates the conclusions included in my recently published book, *Biodiversità e biotecnologie nel diritto internazionale e comunitario* (Milan, 2004), 489 ff. Its cut-off date is 23 Feb 2005.

[1] The expression 'biological diversity', as well as the pertinent definition contained in Art. 2 of the CBD, also catches diversity between humans. However, it is well known that the Conference of the Parties to the CBD gave a sort of authentic interpretation of Art. 2, according to which human genetic resources fall outside the scope of the Convention: *Decision II/11 of the Conference of the Parties to the Convention on Biological Diversity*, para. 2.

biotechnology, but its operation is ostensibly limited and inadequate to address the unprecedented challenges arising in this field.[2]

Secondly, if it is true that since 1992 a huge bulk of legal instruments (treaties, declarations, resolutions, codes of conduct, and so on) has been adopted and that an increasingly high number of international organisations has taken on specific activities associated with biotechnology, the resulting legal framework nonetheless appears extremely fragmented. This makes the task of identifying the international legal regime of biotechnology particularly challenging; however, fragmentation is also an incentive to devise a coherent set of core principles and rules which may hopefully inform a future global treaty on biotechnology, to be negotiated under the aegis of the United Nations. Thirdly, the same task seems problematic as it is well-known that fragmentation in this area not only results in disconnected legal approaches, but also involves considerable tension between legal systems, such as between multilateral environmental agreements (MEAs) and WTO law. This tension, in extreme cases, may turn into veritable conflicts of norms and thus open up a Pandora's box of legal issues which only rarely are amenable to solutions in line with the need for unity and coherence of the international legal order. Fourthly, the ongoing and far-reaching scientific advances of genetics and biotechnology, as well as the uncertainty over their long-term risks and benefits, inevitably plunge this area of the law into a perpetual state of flux.

If one adds to this picture the lack of relevant international judicial decisions,[3] the perspective of this chapter may seem particularly naïve. However, the considerable amount of state practice which has rapidly accumulated in the field of biodiversity and biotechnology over the past few years cannot be underestimated. I am indeed convinced that some foundational principles and rules of an embryonic general regime of biodiversity and biotechnology may be extrapolated from this vast amount

[2] The same holds true for existing treaty law, especially the GATT 1947, subsequently incorporated into the 1994 WTO Agreement. GATT rules, indeed, apply only indirectly to biotechnology; they basically promote free trade in biotechnological products and are not meant to address the environmental and human rights challenges associated with biotechnology.

[3] At the regional level, the European Court of Justice marks an important exception to this. Leaving aside various infringement proceedings against non-compliant Member States (see, especially, and most recently, Case C–456/03, *Commission v. Italy*, judgment of 16 June 2005, not yet reported), the Court has already dealt with 6 cases directly relating to biotechnology and trade in GMOs: Case C–6/99, *Greenpeace France* [2000] *ECR* I–1651; Case C–377/98, *Netherlands v. Parliament and Council* [2001] *ECR* I–7079; Opinion 2/00 (*Cartagena Protocol on Biosafety*) [2001] *ECR* I–9713; Case C–236/01, *Monsanto Agricoltura Italia* [2003] *ECR* I–8105; Case C–316/01, *Eva Glawischnig* [2003] *ECR* I–5995; and Case C–132/03, *Ministero della Salute v. Codacons et al.*, judgment of 26 May 2005, not yet reported. Currently, other biotechnology-related cases are pending: in addition to several infringement proceedings instituted for lack of compliance with the most important EU secondary legislation in

of practice. This general regime is composed of four conceptual pillars: (a) the principle of the *common concern of humanity*; (b) the principle of *equitable benefit-sharing*; (c) the *precautionary principle*; and (d) the principle of *mutual supportiveness of environmental and trade regimes*.

II. COMMON CONCERN OF HUMANITY

The principle of the common concern of humanity has become a popular formula in the international legal arena. It has been associated with 'a consensus according to which respect for certain fundamental values is not to be left to the free disposition of States individually or *inter se* but is recognized and sanctioned by international law as a matter of concern to all States'.[4] The principle thus marks a shift from the traditional sinallagmatic conception of international legal obligations to a modern vision of rights and duties pertaining to a wider group of states or to the international community at large. Especially in the environmental field, common concern is revealed as the conceptual matrix of a number of agreements aimed at the protection of essential components of the biosphere[5] and evokes the idea of a global environmental responsibility. Biodiversity and biotechnology are no exception to this.[6] Moreover, within the area of genetics and human rights, the 1997 UNESCO Universal Declaration on the Human Genome (UDHG) is based on the premise that the human

this field (i.e., Directive 98/44 of 6 July 1998 on the legal protection of biotechnological inventions [1998] OJ L/213/13 and Directive 2001/18 of 12 March 2001 on the deliberate release into the environment of genetically modified organisms [2001] OJ L/106/1), the *Upper Austria* cases deserve particular attention: Cases C–492/03 and T–366/03 (see respectively [2004] OJ C/21/20 and [2004] OJ C/35/11). These are two parallel actions in which the Republic of Austria (before the ECJ) and the Region of Upper Austria (before the CFI) seek the annulment of a Commission decision (Decision 2003/653 of 2 Sept 2003 [2003] OJ L/230/34) rejecting draft legislation aimed at establishing a GMO-free area in Upper Austria.

It is worthwhile noting that the first international judicial decisions dealing with biotechnology issues are expected in 2006 at WTO level: *European Communities—Measures Affecting the Approval and Marketing of Biotech Products (EC—Biotech Products)*, Complaints by the United States, Canada and Argentina, Docs. WT/DS291, WT/DS292 and WT/DS293. The decisions will address the WTO legality of the EC moratorium on the marketing of GMOs which has been operative since 1998, as well as that of several EC Member States GMO trade-restrictive measures.

4 Simma, 'From Bilateralism to Community Interest in International Law' (1994) VI *Recueil des Cours de l'Académie de Droit International de la Haye* 217 at 233.

5 Reference is made to environmental treaties dealing with global environmental issues, such as especially the Framework Convention on Climate Change, the Madrid Environmental Protocol to the Antarctic Treaty, the Ozone Convention and its Montreal Protocol, the Ramsar Wetlands Convention, and the Desertification Convention.

6 Third preambular para. to the CBD; third preambular para. to the FAO Treaty on Plant Genetic Resources for Food and Agriculture (FAO Treaty); third preambular para. to Resolution 55/201 of 20 Dec 2000 of the UN General Assembly.

genome '[*i*]*n a symbolic sense, ...* is the heritage of humanity'.[7] This symbolic reference to the concurrent[8] principle of the common heritage discloses that states intended to avoid any impairment of the right to self-determination of human beings with respect to their genetic make-up. At the same time, however, it is clear that, in exercising this right, individuals do not enjoy absolute liberty, as they have to respect the principles and safeguards set out in the Declaration *vis-à-vis*, not only their state of nationality, but the whole of humanity. In other words, research and interventions concerning the human genome are a common concern of humanity.[9]

Coming back to the environmental context, I fully agree with those authors[10] who underline the normative value of the common concern principle as opposed to a purely inspirational or interpretative function, and accordingly identify precise legal implications ensuing therefrom. These implications are most commonly reconnected to the *erga omnes* status of basic environmental precepts included in the pertinent treaty regimes and to a duty to protect the domestic environment. But, before examining how such legal implications come into play with respect to biodiversity and biotechnology, a preliminary crucial issue involves the determination of what actually constitutes the general interest of humanity in this area.

The references contained in the relevant treaties are no help in this regard.[11] Nonetheless, I firmly believe that an accurate analysis of international practice clearly demonstrates that the common concern of humanity here consists in the promotion and enhancement of a rational, prudent and sustainable use of biodiversity *and biotechnology*. It would be naïve to assume that the whole rationale of international regulation in this field is to hinder or jeopardise the development of safe applications of modern

[7] Art. 1, emphasis added.

[8] Cf. *infra* in this section.

[9] The common heritage concept underlies many other instruments adopted by UNESCO. The extent to which these references are symbolic is open to debate: see most recently Francioni, 'Thirty Years On: Is the World Heritage Convention Ready for the 21st Century?' (2002) XII *Italian Ybk. of International Law* 13 at 22–24. It seems, however, a matter of common sense best to understand the same references within the context of the common concern principle. Cf., for a very similar provision to Art. 1 of the UDHG, Art. 1 of the 2001 Universal Declaration on Cultural Diversity: cultural diversity is as necessary for humankind as biodiversity is for nature. *In this sense*, it is the common heritage of humanity and should be recognized and affirmed for the benefit of present and future generations' (emphasis added).

[10] See e.g. Birnie and Boyle, *International Law and the Environment* (2nd edn., Oxford, 2002), 97 ff; Gestri, *La gestione delle risorse naturali d'interesse generale per la Comunità internazionale* (Turin, 1996), 140 ff.

[11] Cf. especially the third preambular para. to the CBD ('the *conservation of biological diversity* is a common concern of humankind') and the third preambular para. to the FAO Treaty ('*plant genetic resources for food and agriculture* are a common concern of all countries') emphasis added.

biotechnology in the name of a misplaced desire for biodiversity preservation.[12] Biotechnology is also part of the common concern due to its potential far-reaching benefits in the medical, pharmaceutical, environmental and agricultural sectors.[13] Thus, in a recent report to the UN General Assembly,[14] the UN Secretary-General stresses that '[t]he Millennium Development Goals [e.g. eradication of poverty and infectious diseases, and food security] may be more easily met with the extensive application of modern biotechnology in agriculture and health',[15] and that consequently '[i]t is in the *interest of humanity*, in developed and developing countries, that safe biotechnology applications are used as widely as possible'.[16] Such a characterisation of common concern helps one understand certain aspects of international rules in this area which at first sight might appear particularly ambiguous and disappointing from a purely environmental perspective.

(i) The example of the *limits to the sovereign management of the domestic environment* purportedly arising from regimes based on the common concern principle is an emblematic one in this regard. The 2000 Cartagena Protocol on Biosafety (BSP) is unquestionably ambitious with respect to the regulation of living modified organisms (LMOs), but only insofar as their transboundary movements (i.e. interstate transactions) are concerned. By contrast, as I have tried to show elsewhere,[17] the Protocol does not impose particularly stringent obligations and standards on the *domestic* handling of LMOs. This may be a reflection of the willful elaboration of an instrument with a focus and scope as narrow as possible, in conformity with the opportunity to lay down only those obligations that,

12 Indeed, it is well-known that the CBD is not a 'preservationist' treaty and that all its 'references to conservation of biodiversity must be read in conjunction with the sustainable use of its components': Boyle, 'The Rio Convention on Biological Diversity', in Redgwell and Bowman (eds.), *International Law and the Conservation of Biological Diversity* (The Hague, 1996), 33 ff at 38. Of course, this reasoning applies also to the common concern para., quoted above, included in the preamble to the CBD (I am very grateful to Catherine Redgwell for this remark). However, my point is that, since the adoption of the CBD and subsequent related instruments, the relationship between biodiversity and biotechnology has been depicted as an uneasy one. The impression one draws from practice is that states (including some developed, technologically advanced ones) are not fully convinced that the promotion of biotechnology serves humanity's interest and that the sustainable use of biodiversity necessarily includes bioprospecting and other biotechnology-related activities and processes.

13 Cf. the sixth preambular para. to the 2000 Cartagena Protocol on Biosafety to the Convention on Biological Diversity, and the sixth preambular para. to the UDHG.

14 *Impact of New Biotechnologies, with Particular Attention to Sustainable Development, Including Food Security, Health and Economic Productivity*, Doc. A/58/76 of 9 May 2003; cfr. GA Res. 58/200 of 23 Dec 2003 ('Science and Technology for Development'), eight preambular para. and para. 2.

15 *Ibid.*, para. 7.

16 *Ibid.*, para. 76, emphasis added.

17 Pavoni, 'Assessing and Managing Biotechnology Risk under the Cartagena Protocol on Biosafety' (2000), X *Italian Ybk. of International Law* 113 at 118–120.

while not unduly impairing the development of biotechnology, are necessary to ensure transparent and predictable international relations in the area of the export of LMOs. The 'domestic standards' set out by other international agreements, such as the CBD or the FAO Treaty, are similarly fraught with ambiguities and weaknesses. In sum, international regulation of biodiversity and biosafety does not provide convincing support for the existence of a customary rule imposing on states a duty of diligent and sustainable use of territorial natural resources that are a common concern of humanity.[18]

(ii) It is also very controversial that the basic treaty obligations existing in the area under consideration are—at least potentially—of an *erga omnes* character, namely that they are owed to the international community at large and thus legitimate, in case of a violation, the invocation of responsibility by any one state, no matter whether it is directly injured. As is well-known, the solution included in the 2001 ILC Articles on State Responsibility is not clear-cut in this respect. It retains the distinction between *erga omnes* obligations and *erga omnes partes* obligations.[19] The latter category relates to obligations 'owed to a group of States ... and ... established for the protection of a collective interest of the group'.[20] The first candidates for inclusion in this category are obligations laid down in multilateral treaties. Significantly, Special Rapporteur J Crawford, in his *Third Report on State Responsibility*,[21] has posited that obligations existing in the area of biodiversity are to be considered of an *erga omnes partes* (collective) nature.[22] Thus, if one accepts that such obligations are normally *treaty* obligations while their customary nature is exceptional and still needs evidence, the conclusion is that obligations pertaining to biodiversity are owed only as between state Parties to the relevant convention[23] and may indeed be breached only by *those* Parties to the exclusion of any

[18] As is well-known, scholars disagree in this respect. The existence of the customary rule at stake is endorsed, for instance, by Wolfrum, 'The Protection and Management of Biological Diversity', in Morrison and Wolfrum (eds.), *International, Regional and National Environmental Law* (The Hague/London/Boston, 2000), 355 at 361–363, and, though with some hesitation, by Francioni, 'Per un governo mondiale dell'ambiente: quali norme? quali istituzioni?', in Scamuzzi (ed.), *Costituzioni, razionalità, ambiente* (Turin, 1994), 431 at 445. Much more sceptical are Birnie and Boyle, *supra* n 10, at 89; Gestri, *supra* n 10, at 163–165, 399–402; and, most recently, Redgwell, 'International Environmental Law', in Evans (ed.), *International Law* (Oxford, 2003), 657 at 658.

[19] Arts. 42 and 48 of the 2001 Articles.

[20] Art. 48(1)(a).

[21] Doc. A/CN.4/507.

[22] *Ibid.*, at 47, para. 106(b).

[23] Only such Parties may thus invoke the responsibility of a wrongdoing state. They may do so as injured states, if the obligations involved are *integral* (Art. 42(a)(ii)), or as non-injured (interested) states (Art. 48) in the opposite case. The distinction between the two hypothesis entails consequences especially with regard to the right to take countermeasures *vis-à-vis* the responsible state.

third state (such as the United States, which has notoriously refrained from ratifying any of the existing biodiversity and biosafety agreements).

In addition, if one looks at the relevant primary norms, it appears problematic to associate them with schemes of collective responsibility. Once again, the Cartagena Protocol provides a paradigmatic example in this respect. The Protocol allows (precautionary) restrictions on the import of certain biotech products (so-called living modified organisms) only as long as such restrictions are meant to prevent potential damage to biodiversity 'in the Party of import'.[24] Reaction to extraterritorial damage (i.e. to the environment of other states or to global commons) is thus precluded. With regard to secondary norms, this provision may clearly imply that only directly affected *Parties* may invoke the responsibility of wrongdoing *Parties*. This should not be taken as excluding altogether the relevance of the *erga omnes* doctrine for our purposes. After all, this doctrine is crucial with respect to human genetics and biomedicine,[25] where the pertinent norms draw from existing international human rights law, but, at least in the area of biosafety, its viability presupposes evidence of state practice (which for the time being is lacking) and a consensus relating to the very content and implications of the *primary* norms composing the regime of biodiversity *and* biotechnology.

(iii) By contrast, the common concern principle considerably bears on the issue of the *status of biogenetic resources* in international law. Here, a distinction must be made between resources located within state territory and those located in areas beyond national jurisdiction (so-called global commons).[26] With respect to the former, their assimilation (most notably by the CBD and the FAO Treaty) to a common concern of humanity entails the maintenance of sovereign rights and circumvents the resistances and misunderstandings linked to the common heritage concept as originally

24 Arts. 10(6) and 11(8).

25 And, admittedly, with respect to the protection of the marine environment from harmful biotechnological activities. Here, the basic rules as codified by the UN Convention on the Law of the Sea (UNCLOS), and especially by its Arts. 192–193, are commonly said to give rise to *erga omnes* obligations.

26 I will not address here the status of human genetic resources. Suffice it to repeat, as stated at the beginning of the present section, that their assimilation to a common heritage of humanity is merely a legal fiction as long as, textually understood, this would entail an unacceptable interference with the autonomy and self-determination of human beings. At best, common heritage might apply to the sequence of the human genome that is common to the whole of humanity, but certainly not to each individual's peculiar genome (note that the human genome is not defined in the UDHG). Furthermore, patentability of isolated human genes is widely admitted by states and not excluded by the UDGH itself (Art. 4: 'The human genome *in its natural state* shall not give rise to financial gains', emphasis added). Recognition of exclusive rights, such as patent rights, vested on individuals or companies outside any form of international supervisory mechanism is notably at variance with a regime of common heritage. Cf. also ECJ, Case C–377/98, *Netherlands v. Parliament and Council*, *supra* n 3, paras. 71–75.

retained by the FAO.[27] It should also be pointed out that the frequent references to the common heritage principle seem largely misplaced in this context, as long as some of its elements have never actually materialised in the international system, such as especially a truly international institution entrusted with administering the genetic heritage. Indeed, the regime of genetic resources prior to the CBD is best characterised as one of common property, thus essentially of freedom of access and reasonable exploitation.[28] Secondly, due to the inapplicability of the common heritage principle, exclusive appropriation of genetic resources is at the disposal of the biotechnology industry for incorporation into inventions likely to be protected by patents and/or similar proprietary rights. Intellectual property rights (IPRs) are indeed an indispensable tool needed to foster the common concern associated with biodiversity *and* biotechnology. Provided such rights do respect the legitimate interests of territorial states (and especially their entitlement to a fair sharing of the benefits arising from biodiversity and biotechnology[29]), the above appropriation should not be seen as infringing the principle of permanent sovereignty over natural resources. As a matter of fact—and this brings me to the third point—common concern is not co-extensive with permanent sovereignty.[30] Sovereignty is not absolute here, as it entails common responsibilities and due regard for the general interest of humanity. Thus, prior informed consent under the CBD must not result in arbitrary and unreasonable prohibitions of access

[27] International Undertaking on Plant Genetic Resources, adopted by way of FAO Conference Resolution 8/83: 'This Undertaking is based on the universally accepted principle that plant genetic resources are a heritage of mankind and consequently should be available without restriction' (Art. 1); cf. FAO Conference Resolution 3/91 (incorporated into the Undertaking as Annex III): 'the concept of mankind's heritage, as applied in the International Undertaking on Plant Genetic Resources, is subject to the sovereignty of the states over their plant genetic resources' (first preambular para.).

[28] On the distinction between common property and common heritage, see Birnie and Boyle, *supra* n 10, at 141–144.

[29] Cf. *infra* section III.

[30] The shift from a common heritage approach to a sovereignty-based one has been criticised for the allegedly inevitable process of exclusive appropriation and commodification of biodiversity arising therefrom (as well as from IPRs related to genetic resources): see especially Footer, 'Intellectual Property and Agrobiodiversity: Towards Private Ownership of the Genetic Commons' (1999) 10 *Yearbook of International Environmental Law* 48. See also, most recently, Safrin, 'Hyperownership in a Time of Biotechnological Promise: The International Conflict to Control the Building Blocks of Life' (2004) 98 *AJIL* 641. Among many differences, what these important contributions seem to share is that they downplay the implications of the principle of the common concern relating to biogenetic resources and to their potential uses. Moreover, in looking back with regret to the system according to which genetic resources were freely accessible and exchangeable, they fail to provide a comprehensive answer to the following basic question: was that system just and equitable, especially for biodiversity-rich developing countries? What were its distortions and deficiencies? For a radically opposite view, see Mgbeoji, 'Beyond Rhetoric: State Sovereignty, Common Concern, and the Inapplicability of the Common Heritage Concept to Plant Genetic Resources' (2003) 16 *Leiden Journal of International Law* 821.

to territorial biogenetic resources likely to hinder biotechnological research with potentially far-reaching benefits for human health, food security and similar public interests. More significantly, the 2001 FAO Treaty creates a *Multilateral System of Access and Benefit-Sharing*, according to which states are obliged to *facilitate* access to a negotiated list of crops and forages. This system is explicitly deemed compatible with both the maintenance of sovereign rights and the common concern principle.[31] The preceding remarks seem to a great extent applicable also to the regime of biotechnological activities taking place within areas of the sea that are subject to national jurisdiction, especially with regard to access to the surplus of the allowable catch of living resources in the exclusive economic zone by states other than the coastal state.[32] The most debated provision here is undoubtedly Article 246(5)(a) of UNCLOS on the so-called applied scientific research[33] (an expression that certainly includes marine biotechnology) on the continental shelf and in the exclusive economic zone, wherein the power of coastal states at their discretion to withhold consent to the research activities is clearly established. I do not see, however, any particular problem in reconciling this provision with the regime of access to terrestrial biodiversity. It seems to me that the cornerstone of the UNCLOS rules at stake corresponds once again to the sharing of the benefits arising from marine scientific research: whenever the specific terms of benefit-sharing provided for by Article 249 are fulfilled, a coastal state has all the interest in granting access to its marine biodiversity.

With respect to the genetic resources located in parts of the sea beyond national jurisdiction, be they incorporated into fishery resources in the high seas or into living resources found in the vicinity of the deep sea-bed and ocean floor (the Area), I am not persuaded that they should be considered as a common heritage of humanity.[34] Freedom of access and scientific research still provide the most accurate picture of present practices and applicable law. Here, the common concern principle may operate to mitigate such freedom[35] and outlaw those practices that are ostensibly at variance with the general interest of humanity (i.e. unsustainable bioprospecting), just as it operates, in the domestic sphere, to qualify the

31 See the 14th preambular para. and Art. 10 of the Treaty.

32 Cf. Art. 62 UNCLOS.

33 That is research projects 'of direct significance for the exploration and exploitation of natural resources, whether living or non-living': Art. 246(5)(a) UNCLOS. See Farrier and Tucker, 'Access to Marine Bioresources: Hitching the Conservation Cart to the Bioprospecting Horse' (2001) 32 *Ocean Development and International Law* 213 at 222–226, and in this volume the chapters by Scovazzi and Cataldi.

34 Cf. the chapter by Francioni in this volume.

35 As is well-known, this freedom is already qualified in many respects, especially in relation to the Area, by the UNCLOS pertinent norms. See also the *Icelandic Fisheries* cases [1974] ICJ Rep 3.

power of states to grant access to the genetic resources subject to their sovereignty. Various examples of patents recognised over products derived from biological resources found in Antarctica,[36] another territory belonging (though not unquestionably) to the global commons, reinforce the impression that resources beyond the limits of national jurisdiction are in principle freely subject to appropriation. It is true that, in relation to the marine living organisms found in the Area, there are sound policy reasons and legal arguments militating in favour of extending to them the common heritage regime applicable to mineral resources. However, in view of the existing legal gap,[37] one cannot escape the conclusion that, as a matter of positive law and prevailing practices, even these resources are best characterised as a common concern of humanity.

(iv) Practice relating to biodiversity and biotechnology offers examples of further legal implications of the common concern principle. The fact that a certain treaty is grounded upon such principle leads to far-reaching interpretative consequences. At the judicial level, the most important decision is that of the European Court of Justice (ECJ) in *Netherlands v. Parliament and Council*,[38] a case dealing with an action for annulment of Directive 98/44 on the legal protection of biotechnological inventions. In its judgment of 9 October 2001, the ECJ agreed to review the legality of the Directive in light of the Biodiversity Convention, as this Convention was 'not strictly based on *reciprocal and mutually advantageous arrangements*',[39] and notwithstanding the non self-executing character of its provisions. This finding, while disposing in a welcome manner of a particularly controversial issue of EC law, emphasises the asymmetrical and multilateral (thus potentially *erga omnes partes*) nature of CBD obligations. This nature underlies the fundamental values protected by the CBD (thus, its common concern matrix) and requires that private parties and EC Member States be entitled to rely judicially on CBD provisions as a ground of illegality of inconsistent EC measures.

(v) In another topical context, that of WTO adjudication, the WTO Appellate Body (AB) has implicitly recognised the importance of regimes based on the common concern principle. In the celebrated *Shrimp/Turtle* case,[40] the AB held that GATT Article XX (general exceptions) must be read 'in the light of contemporary *concerns of the community of nations* about the protection and conservation of the environment'.[41] On the facts

[36] See the chapter by Vigni in this volume.

[37] For any further detail, see the chapter by Scovazzi in this volume.

[38] Case C–377/98, *supra* n 3.

[39] Para. 53 (emphasis added). See also para. 54.

[40] *United States—Import Prohibition of Certain Shrimp and Shrimp Products* (*US—Shrimp I*), Appellate Body Report, Doc. WT/DS58/AB/R of 12 Oct 1998.

[41] *Ibid.*, para. 129 (emphasis added).

of the case, this argument supported an evolutionary method of interpretation and the resulting conclusion, reached through an in-depth analysis of pertinent environmental instruments (CBD included),[42] that Article XX covers both living and non-living natural resources.[43]

In the more recent *Korea—Beef* case,[44] the AB substantially updated the balancing test for assessing the fulfillment of the requirement of necessity as included in some of the exceptions of GATT Article XX. The AB stated that one crucial factor in this balancing exercise is 'the relative importance of the *common interests or values* that the law or regulation ... is intended to protect',[45] and added: '[t]he *more vital or important* those common interests or values are, the easier it would be to accept as "necessary" a measure'.[46] It is self-explanatory that such an approach may be interpreted as recognising the special status in WTO dispute settlement of MEAs grounded upon the common concern principle. These agreements are indeed emanations *par excellence* of vital interests shared by humanity as a whole. If one day tested for measures implementing such agreements, the same approach might at the very least facilitate a finding of consistency with the requirement of necessity.

III. EQUITABLE BENEFIT-SHARING

A growing number of international instruments[47] dealing with biodiversity and biotechnology (including marine biotechnology[48]) requires that benefits accruing from the use of biogenetic resources and traditional knowledge associated there with (and thus *in primis* accruing from biotechnological inventions) be shared in a fair and equitable way with the states of origin of such resources, as well as with indigenous and local

42 *Ibid.*, para. 130.

43 *Ibid.*, paras. 130–131.

44 *Korea—Measures Affecting Imports of Fresh, Chilled and Frozen Beef* (*Korea—Beef*), Appellate Body Report, Doc. WT/DS161/AB/R-WT/DS169/AB/R of 11 Dec 2000.

45 *Ibid.*, para. 162 (emphasis added).

46 *Ibid.* (emphasis added). In the same sense, cf. *European Communities—Measures Affecting Asbestos and Asbestos-Containing Products* (*EC—Asbestos*), Appellate Body Report, Doc. WT/DS135/AB/R of 12 Mar 2001, para. 172.

47 Among the biodiversity instruments, see, in addition to the pertinent provisions of the CBD and the FAO Treaty, the Bonn Guidelines on Access to Genetic Resources and Fair and Equitable Sharing of the Benefits Arising out of their Utilization, a far-reaching soft law instrument adopted by the Conference of the Parties to the CBD at its sixth meeting, The Hague, 7–19 Apr 2002, decision VI/24 A, annex. See also Plan of Implementation of the World Summit on Sustainable Development (Johannesburg, 26 Aug–4 Sept 2002), para. 44(j)(n)(q). For further references, see *infra* nn 52–54, and 58.

48 Actually, the CBD and Bonn Guidelines apply also to marine genetic resources. Moreover, benefit-sharing already finds recognition within the law of the sea, not only with respect to activities conducted in the Area (Arts. 140(2) and 144 UNCLOS), but also in the context of marine scientific research at large (see especially Art. 249 UNCLOS).

communities identifiable as holders of that knowledge. A critical feature of this principle of benefit-sharing is its *cross-cutting nature*, namely its relevance to biotechnology at large, including biomedicine, human genetics and human rights.[49] Thus, according to the UNESCO International Bioethics Committee benefit-sharing constitutes 'a truly urgent and universal issue'[50] arising from advances in life sciences, while, in a similar vein, the UN High Commissioner for Human Rights' Expert Group on Human Rights and Biotechnology considers 'the linked issues of the ability to patent genetic material and the sharing of benefits deriving from commercial exploitation of that material to be the most important issues in the area of human rights and biotechnology at this time'.[51] Forms of benefit-sharing are actually envisaged by the UDHG[52] and especially by the 2003 International Declaration on Human Genetic Data (IDHGD).[53] Moreover, there is no reason to doubt that the universal instrument on bioethics, currently being elaborated by UNESCO, will incorporate the principle at stake.[54]

As I have tried to explain elsewhere,[55] equitable benefit-sharing emerges as the cornerstone of the regime of access to biodiversity and of IPRs in biotechnological inventions. In effect, any international debates and confrontations in this area—including those relating to the purported conflict between the multilateral trade system and the pertinent MEAs—are mostly focused on the necessity to devise fair mechanisms of benefit-allocation among stakeholders. I have also tried to demonstrate that the

[49] Of course, benefit-sharing in these fields involves peculiar problems and methods as compared to plant and animal biotechnology. It has a marked individualistic dimension (as opposed to a state-oriented one) as a reflection of the need to compensate the individuals who actually consented to research and clinical trials on their DNA. In the human rights context, the principle of benefit-sharing is rooted in the right of individuals to benefit from scientific progress and its applications (cf. Art. 27(1) of the Universal Declaration of Human Rights; Art. 15(1)(b) of the International Covenant on Economic, Social and Cultural Rights (ICESCR)) and in the corresponding duty of states to share scientific knowledge (Art. 15(2) ICESCR) and use scientific achievements for the benefit of humankind as a whole (see Declaration on the Use of Scientific and Technological Progress in the Interests of Peace and for the Benefit of Mankind, proclaimed by GA Res. 3384 (XXX) of 10 Nov 1975).

[50] *Report of the IBC on the Possibility of Elaborating a Universal Instrument on Bioethics*, Doc. SHS/EST/02/CIB-9/5 (Rev. 3) of 13 June 2003, para. 10.

[51] *Report of the Expert Consultation on Human Rights and Biotechnology* (Geneva, 24–25 Jan 2002), para. 17. This Report is annexed to Commission on Human Rights, Fifty-ninth session, *Human Rights and Bioethics, Report of the Secretary-General, submitted pursuant to Commission resolution 2001/71*, Doc. E/CN.4/2003/98 of 10 Feb 2003.

[52] Art. 19. See also Arts. 12(a) and 18.

[53] Adopted unanimously and by acclamation on 16 Oct 2003 by the 32nd Session of the General Conference of UNESCO: see Art. 19.

[54] Indeed, the current UNESCO draft declaration on universal norms on bioethics includes a provision that reproduces, almost *verbatim*, Art. 19 of the IDHGD: see *Elaboration of the Declaration on Universal Norms on Bioethics: Fourth Outline of a Text*, Doc. SHS/EST/04/CIB-Gred-2/4 Rev.3 of 15 Dec 2004 (see Art. 16; see also Art. 28).

[55] Pavoni, *Biodiversità e biotecnologie nel diritto internazionale e comunitario* (Milan, 2004), chapters III–IV.

duty of benefit-sharing is steadily *emerging as a rule of customary law*.[56] Practice, indeed, looks impressive. First, in addition to the already-mentioned instruments,[57] the principle at stake has been consistently recognised in various resolutions of the UN General Assembly[58] which, at the same time, has advocated[59] the negotiation of an international regime on benefit-sharing.[60] Secondly, there exist many instances of national legislation and policies endorsing benefit-sharing, the most recent (and crucial) examples being those of India[61] and the European Community.[62] Thirdly, statements and declarations made by state officials within the relevant international fora, such as the TRIPs Council or the WIPO Intergovernmental Committee on Intellectual Property and Genetic Resources, Traditional Knowledge and Folklore, constantly acknowledge the existence and importance of the principle of benefit-sharing. The only notable exception in this regard is unsurprisingly the United States, a genuine persistent objector to the emerging customary rule. The US firmly opposes the elaboration of the abovementioned international regime in the form of a *binding* instrument, since 'any initiatives in this area must fully accord access to genetic resources and respect rights and obligations under international law'.[63]

This statement highlights what the real concerns in the discourse over benefit-sharing are: the elaboration of definite, multilateral and binding standards of benefit-sharing is seen as jeopardising full access to genetic resources[64] *and* concurrent international rules. These rules are mainly to

56 For a different perspective, see the chapter in this volume by Francioni, who submits that benefit-sharing in the biotechnology context is no more than a modern variant of the well-established principle of equitable remuneration of foreign investments.

57 Cf. *supra* n 47.

58 See especially Res. 57/260 of 20 Dec 2002, third preambular para., and Res. 58/212 of 23 Dec 2003, fourth preambular para.

59 Res. 57/260, para. 8, and Res. 58/212, para. 4.

60 As originally mandated by the Johannesburg Plan of Implementation, para. 44(o). This negotiation has actually commenced within the framework of the CBD: see decision VII/19 D adopted by the seventh meeting of the Conference of the Parties to the CBD, Kuala Lumpur, 9–20 Feb 2004.

61 Biological Diversity Act 2002, reproduced in (2003) 43 *Indian Journal of International Law*, 149; see especially s 21 of the Act.

62 *The Implementation by the EC of the 'Bonn Guidelines' on Access to Genetic Resources and Benefit-Sharing under the Convention on Biological Diversity*, Communication from the Commission to the European Parliament and the Council, COM(2003) 821 fin. of 23 Dec 2003.

63 *US Interpretive Statement on the Plan of Implementation of the World Summit on Sustainable Development*, in *Report of the World Summit on Sustainable Development*, Doc. A/CONF.199/20, 148–149, para. 20.

64 It is clear that, by contrast, the essentially bilateral and contractual approach to benefit-sharing advocated by the CBD (i.e. benefit-sharing pursuant to 'mutually agreed terms', cf. e.g. Art. 15(7)) is not considered as, and indeed it is not, undermining US priorities in this area.

be found in the WTO TRIPs Agreement which recognises (*rectius*: is interpreted as recognising) the patentability of biotechnological inventions and the enjoyment of rights thereof with no exception arising from duties of benefit-sharing with, or prior informed consent of, countries of origin of genetic (raw) material. However, it should be noted that the granting of such controversial patents[65] (*once* detected) increasingly meets with protests and threats of retorsion on the part of states of origin (and at times by states not directly affected as well) which frequently lead to their revocation (or to the withdrawal of patent applications). Moreover, it is not to be taken for granted that the TRIPs Agreement allows patents incompatible with such a core principle as that of benefit-sharing. The ongoing debates within the TRIPs Council on the relationship between the CBD and TRIPs are instead testimony to the efforts of the international community to develop consensual approaches to the interpretation of the latter (or to its *reform*[66]) in line with the principle of equitable benefit-sharing.

Obviously, the outcome of the processes initiated within the WTO, WIPO and the Conference of the Parties to the CBD will be a crucial test for the crystallisation of the emerging duty of benefit-sharing. If these processes, as I hope, do not fail and rather result in unambiguously obligatory standards of benefit-sharing, it is submitted that the already-existing abundant practice may be capable of unveiling a corresponding *opinio iuris*.

IV. PRECAUTION

Much like benefit-sharing *vis-à-vis* access to genetic resources and patentability, the precautionary principle comes out as the cornerstone of biosafety, namely the regulation of risks associated with the release into the environment and marketing of genetically modified organisms (GMOs). Indeed, the most innovative aspect of this sector corresponds to the legitimation of the *right* of states to adopt, within a prior approval procedure, trade-restrictive environmental measures, even though there is substantial scientific uncertainty[67] and even though such measures are potentially inconsistent with WTO law. Other features of the biosafety regimes, such as the principles for risk assessment established by the BSP[68] or the phasing-out of antibiotic resistance genes envisaged by the EC legislation,[69] clearly reflect a precautionary logic.

65 The so-called phenomenon of biopiracy.
66 See *infra* section v.
67 Cf. especially Arts. 10(6) and 11(8) of the BSP.
68 Annex III.
69 Dir. 2001/18, *supra* n 3, Art. 4(2).

Precaution is a cross-cutting principle of the international law relating to biotechnology. It applies to biotechnological activities impacting upon terrestrial biodiversity and *a fortiori* to those affecting marine biodiversity.[70] But it also applies to the protection of human health and is thus extremely pertinent in biomedicine and human genetics. It is true that, within these fields, the principle is not as well-developed as in the environmental context and is in fact not explicitly mentioned in any of the existing instruments. However, a precautionary rationale visibly underlies various provisions of these instruments. Take the example of persons not having the capacity to consent to research affecting their genomes. According to the UDHG, such research 'may only be carried out for [the person's] direct health benefit',[71] while research that 'does not have an *expected direct health benefit* may only be undertaken *by way of exception, with the utmost restraint*, exposing the person only to a *minimal risk* and minimal burden and if the research is intended to contribute to the health benefit of other persons in the same age category or with the same genetic condition..., and provided such research is compatible with the protection of the individual's human rights'[72]. Thus, this kind of research presupposes sufficient scientific evidence showing direct health benefits to the disadvantaged person. When this evidence is absent or there is a state of scientific uncertainty, research may be carried out only in exceptional cases, pursuant to a cost-benefit analysis and if it involves *risk of the lowest degree*.[73] Conversely, if science identifies more significant (yet uncertain) risks for human health, research just *cannot* take place. It is safe to assume that, pursuant to the precautionary principle, this requirement applies generally to human genetics. Unsurprisingly, precaution is endorsed by the current draft of a UNESCO declaration on universal norms on bioethics.[74]

[70] Indeed, it is well-known that the precautionary principle first developed and is most convincingly recognised within instruments relating to the protection of the marine environment: see, for instance, the chapter by Cataldi in this volume, and, in relation to the most recent dumping conventions, Redgwell, *supra* n 18, at 688.

[71] Art. 5(e).

[72] *Ibid.*, emphasis added.

[73] It is however clear that expressions such as 'minimal risk' involve a high degree of discretion on the part of the health professionals and/or adjudicative bodies. In this context, the 2005 Additional Protocol to the Council of Europe Convention on Human Rights and Biomedicine concerning Biomedical Research is worthy of note. Art. 17 of the Protocol attempts to qualify the above mentioned discretion by giving definitions of 'minimal risk' and 'minimal burden'. This provision reads: '1. ... [I]t is deemed that the research bears a minimal risk if, having regard to the nature and scale of the intervention, it is to be expected that it will result, at the most, in a very slight and temporary negative impact on the health of the person concerned. 2. It is deemed that it bears a minimal burden if it is to be expected that the discomfort will be, at the most, temporary and very slight for the person concerned. ...'.

[74] Art. 23 of the current draft, under the misleading heading of 'risk assessment', reads: 'When scientific evidence of serious or irreversible damage to public health or human

The following conclusions and reflections on the status, components and implications of the precautionary principle are however limited to the environmental context where a considerable practice has emerged in relation to biosafety issues.

(i) The Cartagena Protocol and the pertinent EC biosafety legislation undeniably demonstrate the evolution of the role of precaution from a purely interpretive principle to a *normative* one. In other words, the principle is fully operationalised within such regimes by means of positive rights and obligations.

(ii) This normative value is not in any way adjudicative of the longstanding debate over the customary as opposed to conventional status of the principle. Rather, it is submitted that the same controversial aspects that have long been considered as affecting the customary nature of precaution show up, at least to a certain extent, in the biosafety context as well. In the first place, no international judicial decision dealing with biosafety (or contiguous issues) has so far accepted the customary status of the principle. However, this is also due to the fact that the parties to the relevant disputes never actually relied on such alleged customary status. A special reference here must be made to the notable ECJ case law on biosafety and trade in GMOs. EC Member States defending their precautionary measures in these cases[75] have refrained from invoking precaution as a principle of *international* law. They have rather posited the existence of a *general principle of EC law* without contradiction from the Court. Similarly, in the recent WTO *Japan—Apples* case,[76] the Appellate Body has pointed out the failure on the part of Japan to invoke precaution 'as a principle separate and distinct from the provisions of the *SPS* Agreement'.[77] This has probably paved the way for the rejection of the precautionary arguments raised by Japan itself.

Moreover, and perhaps more importantly, biosafety practice relating to the precautionary principle is not clear-cut. If, on the one hand, the quantity and quality of instruments and policy statements accepting precaution as their foundational and operative principle is certainly impressive, on the other, practice lacks that degree of uniformity necessary to the formation of customary law. Leaving aside the obvious example of the WTO,

welfare or the environment is not sufficient, provisional, adequate and proportionate measures shall be taken in a timely manner. ...': see *Elaboration of the Declaration on Universal Norms on Bioethics: Fourth Outline of a Text, supra* n 54.

[75] Especially in the already-mentioned *Monsanto Italia* and *Greenpeace France* cases, *supra* n 3.

[76] *Japan—Measures Affecting the Importation of Apples* (*Japan—Apples*), Appellate Body Report, Doc. WT/DS245/AB/R of 26 Nov 2003.

[77] Para. 234 of the Appellate Body Report. Likewise, it seems that the EC is not willing to invoke the precautionary principle as a self-standing argument within the pending WTO case relating to the EC moratorium on the marketing of GMOs and to the Member States GMO trade-restrictive measures (*EC—Biotech Products, supra* n 3).

even EC practice (often viewed as the most proactive with respect to precaution) looks contradictory, as long as the identification of the appropriate action to be taken in each particular case to implement the principle has invariably generated divisions and confrontations between EC institutions and Member States' authorities. The so-called *de facto* moratorium on the marketing of GMOs is an illuminating example of this. It is right to consider this moratorium as a significant manifestation of regional practice based on a far-reaching conception of the precautionary principle. At the same time, however, it is well-known that the moratorium is due to the initiative of a group of Member States only, an initiative which was (and still is) not shared by the other Members, nor by the EC institutions. The latter would rather have endorsed less radical measures deemed perfectly in line with the application of the principle at stake.

(iii) Another classical objection to the customary nature of the precautionary principle is the uncertainty over its real substance and constituent parts.[78] Again, biosafety practice is ambiguous in this respect. The Cartagena Protocol and the EC legislation endeavour to articulate the two fundamental components of precaution, namely scientific uncertainty and the seriousness of expected harm but, in the end, considerable doubts remain. On the one hand, the requirement of seriousness of harm is understated, since the above instruments envisage an apparently low threshold for invoking precaution, that is the threat of adverse effects to biodiversity *tout court*. This raises a question of coordination between the components of precaution emerging from the above instruments and those endorsed by other authoritative documents, chiefly by the 1992 Rio Declaration on Environment and Development (Principle 15).

Much more problematic, however, is the requirement of the state of scientific uncertainty. What incontestably transpires from the ECJ's case law[79] and, by way of analogy, from that of the WTO bodies[80] is that scientific uncertainty does *not* cover speculative, hypothetical or theoretical risks. On the contrary, a *prior risk assessment* capable of gathering scientific evidence (as partial and inconclusive as it may be) of a *plausible* risk of harm is a non-derogable requirement of precautionary measures. Conversely, these measures need not necessarily be based on majority scientific views; they may well conform to minority, yet recent and reliable,

[78] Until recently, this objection found support in EC law as well, given the absence of any definition of the principle in the pertinent EC legal acts (see now Art. 7 of Reg. No. 178/2002 of 28 January 2002 laying down the general principles and requirements of food law, establishing the European Food Safety Authority, and laying down procedures in matters of food safety [2002] OJ L/31/31).

[79] Case C–236/01, *supra* n 3, para. 106 (see also *ibid.*, for further references to case law).

[80] *European Communities—Measures Concerning Meat and Meat Products (EC—Hormones)*, Appellate Body Report, Doc. WT/DS26/AB/R-WT/DS48/AB/R of 16 Jan 1998, para. 186.

scientific opinions.[81] In addition, scientific evidence must be *relevant*, that is relating to specific GMOs, specific situations and specific environmental or sanitary concerns. But, finally, what is scientific uncertainty about? May it refer to the very *existence*, nature or origin of the risk? Or exclusively to its *extent*, namely to a risk which, though not exactly quantified, is nonetheless clearly characterised in its essential aspect? Although certain key provisions[82] of the Cartagena Protocol on Biosafety lend weight to the second alternative,[83] my opinion is that this must be rejected, as it would undermine the operation of the precautionary principle with respect to risks—such as, paradigmatically, those associated with GMOs—likely to be adequately appraised on a long-term basis only.[84]

(iv) The precise *nature* of legitimate precautionary measures is also controversial. Practice shows that an *a priori* categorisation of such measures is not warranted. The legitimate measure to be imposed in each particular situation is rather subject to a case-by-case review and depends on the magnitude of risks that a state is willing to prevent or minimise. Therefore, precautionary measures may correspond either to radical restrictions, such as moratoria or generalised prohibitions, or to more focused precautions, such as prohibitions targeting particularly risky GMOs or labelling, traceability and monitoring requirements. At the same time, however, states do not enjoy an unfettered discretion in the selection of measures. While in this respect the Cartagena Protocol provides for an indefinite test of *appropriateness* of precautionary measures, the ECJ has held that such measures must be reasonably sustained by the findings of a risk assessment,[85] however partial or preliminary this assessment may appear. There exists, in other words, a close relationship between the scientific assessment of risks and their political (precautionary) management, which, at the normative level, seems to introduce a requirement of *proportionality* between precautionary measures and the outcome of risk assessment. In the pertinent EC legislation, proportionality is indeed

[81] Cf. Case C–236/01, *supra* n 3, para. 113; *EC—Hormones, supra* n 80, para. 194.

[82] Arts. 10(6) and 11(8).

[83] Cf. Stoll, 'Controlling the Risks of Genetically Modified Organisms: The Cartagena Protocol on Biosafety and the SPS Agreement' (1999) 10 *Yearbook of International Environmental Law* 82 at 98–99, 116–117.

[84] The alternative is also at variance with ECJ case law: cf. the celebrated passage of the so-called *Mad Cow Disease* cases, where the Court for the first time unambiguously enunciated the precautionary principle: '[W]here there is uncertainty as to the *existence* or extent of risks to human health, protective measures may be taken without having to wait until the reality and seriousness of those risks become fully apparent': Case C–157/96, *National Farmers' Union* [1998] *ECR* I–2211, para. 63, and Case C–180/96, *UK v. Commission*, [1998] *ECR* I–2265, para. 99 (emphasis added).

[85] Case C–236/01, *supra* n 3, para. 113. This resembles the WTO requirement of a 'rational relationship between risk assessment and sanitary or phytosanitary measures': *EC—Hormones, supra* n 80, para. 193.

retained in its classic meaning, that is that precautionary measures shall not go beyond what is necessary to achieve the sanitary or environmental objectives at stake.[86]

However, the most debated issue in this context remains that of the *temporal scope* of precautionary measures. Need these measures be provisional? Or may they also be adopted for an indefinite period of time? As is well known, the first option is retained by Article 5(7) of the WTO SPS Agreement and by the safeguard clauses envisaged by the EC's GMOs legislation. It is also retained by the definition of the precautionary principle set out in Article 7 of EC Regulation No. 178/2002. Moreover, in both the SPS Agreement and the Regulation No. 178/2002, compliance with the requirement of temporariness is ensured by a duty to review precautionary measures within a reasonable period of time. What is doubtful here is the fate of measures which, after the expiry of such a reasonable period of time, still appear warranted in the light of *persistent* scientific uncertainty. If a state has in good faith undertaken periodic scientific assessments and constantly monitored the evolution of scientific knowledge, is it allowed to *maintain* the pertinent measure? Or is it obliged to repeal it?[87] In my opinion, the temporariness of precautionary measures entails no more than a *duty to assess environmental risks on a continuous basis*, a duty which has been duly recognised by the International Court of Justice in the *Gabcíkovo-Nagymaros* case.[88] The alternative view seems to a great extent capable of defeating the object and purpose of the precautionary principle. If, however, such a view were to correspond to the correct interpretation of the above SPS and EC provisions, this plainly means that these would not represent genuine examples of precautionary instruments. This finding is important for appraising the lawfulness of the several *non-provisional* moratoria and prohibitions on trade in GMOs currently in place in various national and regional contexts. In principle, such measures should be regarded as lawful, provided they are constantly updated in the light of new scientific insights.

(v) On a more general level, the precautionary principle, as adopted within the biosafety legislation, marks the distinction between *risk assessment* and *risk management*.[89] This unmistakably results in the power of

86 Art. 7(2) of Reg. No. 178/2002, *supra* n 78. It is however a matter of debate whether proportionality here also involves some kind of cost-benefit analysis pursuant to the requirement of *cost-effectiveness* contained in Principle 15 of the Rio Declaration.

87 This second alternative was most recently advocated by Spanggaard, 'The Marketing of GMOs: A Supra-national Battle over Science and Precaution' (2003) 3 *Yearbook of European Environmental Law* 79 at 109.

88 *Case Concerning the Gabcíkovo-Nagymaros Project* [1997] ICJ Rep 6 at 68, para. 112, at 78, para. 140. See also, more explicitly, the Separate Opinion of Vice-President Weeramantry, *ibid.*, 111–113.

89 See especially Arts. 15 and 16 of the BSP.

states to take risk management measures that are different from those warranted under an exclusive reliance on scientific methods and with a view to controlling uncertain risks. Yet, as already pointed out, the separation between risk assessment and risk management is not clear-cut: indeed, the latter must at the very least generate decisions that are not manifestly disproportionate to the scientific evidence ensuing from the former. More precisely, the distinction at stake sheds light on the existence of *science policies* capable of influencing the purported neutrality of (scientific) risk assessment, for instance by giving more weight to some hypotheses rather than others or by discarding a given inference.[90] Under these circumstances, it is reasonable to allow decision-makers to redress such imbalances and take measures contradicting the findings of risk assessors. The provisions of the Cartagena Protocol[91] which prescribe *precautionary* scientific methods and principles are in this respect extremely significant, as they enhance the ongoing dialogue between science and politics.

(vi) Another legal implication frequently associated with the precautionary principle is a *reversal of the burden of proof* in relation to the risks that the pertinent measures aim at averting. If one looks at the case law of the ECJ and, by analogy, that of the WTO bodies on the SPS Agreement, such far-reaching consequence ought to be excluded. Within the review of Member States' measures taken pursuant to safeguard clauses,[92] the ECJ has indeed confirmed that it is for the Member States themselves to satisfy the burden of proving the existence and nature of risks. However, in the *Monsanto Italia* case, the Court appears to have accepted a lowering of the *standard* of proof by interpreting the expression 'detailed grounds' as requiring mere 'evidence which indicates the existence of a specific risk'.[93]

Insofar as prior approval procedures of GMOs are concerned, it is true that they generally impose on producers and exporters the burden of performing a risk assessment, but I am not persuaded at all that this requirement corresponds to the full proof of absence of non-negligible risks.[94] Reversal of the burden of proof thus seems a mere aspiration not supported by practice.

[90] On these themes, cf. especially Wirth, 'The Role of Science in the Uruguay Round and NAFTA Trade Disciplines' (1994) 27 *Cornell ILJ* 817; Walker, 'Keeping the WTO from Becoming the "World Trans-science Organization": Scientific Uncertainty, Science Policy, and Factfinding in the Growth Hormones Dispute' (1998) 31 *Cornell ILJ* 251.

[91] See Annex III, points 4 and 8(f).

[92] Remember that such clauses are considered by the ECJ as the chief instrument at the disposal of Member States to implement precautionary measures.

[93] Case C–236/01, *supra* n 3, para. 109; see also *ibid.*, para. 113.

[94] See, in more detail, Pavoni, *supra* n 55 at 275–278.

(vii) Lastly, practice relating to biosafety stimulates reflections on the appropriate institutional level for implementing the precautionary principle. On the one hand, it is certainly true that states tend to perform a proactive function in this respect. They perceive themselves as the primary (if not exclusive) addressees of the right and duty to take precautionary measures. This is supported by several provisions of the Cartagena Protocol[95] and by the constant recognition in various fora (WTO *in primis*[96]) of the sovereign right of states to establish the level of environmental and sanitary protection they deem appropriate within their territory.

On the one hand, this state-centred conception of precaution is reasonable as long as state authorities are obviously best equipped to appraise the ecological, political and socio-economic peculiarities and priorities of their country. On the other hand, the absence of meaningful powers of supervision and control on the part of international institutions, such as the Meeting of the Parties to the Cartagena Protocol, entails risks of legal anarchy and proliferation of trade disputes.

This is all the more evident in particularly advanced contexts of regional economic integration like that of the European Community, given the operation of principles such as those of the indivisibility of the Single Market, fair cooperation between Member States and institutions and uniformity of application of EC law. Therefore, it is unsurprising that the main theme of the whole practice and case law of the EC relating to biosafety and trade in GMOs coincides with the sharp confrontation that during the past ten years has pitted the EC institutions against several Member States adopting radical unilateral action in the name of precaution. Reliance on the abovementioned principles and on the supervisory mechanisms established by EC law have, *to a certain extent*,[97] controlled the phenomenon of unilateral measures. In doing so, EC practice has given an important contribution to the identification of the *limits* of precautionary measures. At the same time, however, the EC institutions have on some occasions held positions not acceptable from a legalistic point of view and stretched the principles of EC law to their utmost boundary. Visibly, the objective pursued has been the abrogation of unilateral measures by all means. I believe this approach to be mistaken as long as national

[95] See e.g. Arts. 2(4) and 11(4). After all, as an author has suggested, '[t]he Protocol's system ... serves to strengthen the nation-state as the primary source of environmental governance': Falkner, 'Regulating Biotech Trade: The Cartagena Protocol on Biosafety' (2000) 76 *International Affairs* 299 at 311.

[96] Cf. e.g. Art. 3(3) of and Annex A(5) to the SPS Agreement; *EC—Hormones, supra* n 80, para. 124; *Australia—Measures Affecting Importation of Salmon* (*Australia—Salmon*), Appellate Body Report, Doc. WT/DS18/AB/R of 20 Oct 1998, para. 199.

[97] Many unilateral measures are still in place and some of them are actually challenged within the WTO: cf *EC—Biotech Products, supra* n 3.

measures may play (and have actually played) the essential role of catalysts of environmentally sound reforms of the law.

In short, it seems to me that, in light of the many outstanding uncertainties and ambiguities illustrated above, international and European practice relating to biosafety may not be seen as a real breakthrough with respect to the crystallisation of the customary nature of precaution. However, this does not deprive precaution of its crucial role in the biosafety and analogous contexts. The constant recognition of such a role in a plethora of legal instruments and state declarations does have to be taken into account. The evolution of the regime of biotechnology is rather a valuable occasion on which to refine the substance of the principle with a view to reaching a universal consensus on its status and implications.

V. MUTUAL SUPPORTIVENESS BETWEEN ENVIRONMENTAL AND HUMAN RIGHTS INSTRUMENTS ON BIOTECHNOLOGY AND THE APPLICABLE WTO AGREEMENTS

For international lawyers, the most intriguing issue arising in the context of biotechnology is probably that of the simultaneous existence of a plurality of applicable treaty regimes with a different nature, purpose and substance. This issue involves biotechnology at large. It has been mostly studied with regard to potential *inter-sectoral* conflicts as between the WTO system and (environmental) regimes on biodiversity and biosafety. But it is clear that this kind of potential conflict equally encompasses the relation of WTO law with instruments on human genetics and human rights. Moreover, there also exist *intra-sectoral* tensions, that is tensions between treaties which have important objectives in common, such as the protection of the environment. As already noted, this second type of tensions especially concerns the relationship between the CBD and the UNCLOS with respect to the regulation of marine biotechnology.

Admittedly, the problem is more acute in the former case, as it calls into question the legally and politically sensitive issue of the status of non-trade concerns in the WTO and must take into account the existence of a powerful dispute settlement system within the WTO itself. The WTO rules potentially affected by the trade-related environmental and human rights measures envisaged by the instruments on biotechnology and human genetics are wide-ranging. At the very least, one should mention the TRIPs Agreement with regard to prohibitions or limits on the granting of IPRs on genetic material (both human and non-human) and the WTO agreements relating to trade in goods (chiefly the GATT, SPS and TBT Agreements) *vis-à-vis* restrictions on the free movement of biotechnological products (such as GMOs or cloned animals) and human biological material (such as stem cells).

Particularly with respect to the environmental concerns raised by biotechnology, I suggest that the most significant development in relation to the issue at hand is associated with the steady emergence of the concept of *mutual supportiveness* of environmental treaties (so-called MEAs) and the WTO system. This concept enshrines the requirement that states are under a duty to facilitate and enhance all processes and forms of multilateral cooperation that are able to ensure the pacific co-existence of allegedly conflicting regimes and prevent potential disputes originating therefrom. The reiterated and consistent acknowledgment,[98] at all levels and in disparate institutional settings, of the duty to promote the mutual supportiveness of environmental and trade regimes warrants the idea of an *emerging* rule of customary law.

The shift from an allegedly conflicting relationship to a mutually supportive one may also be seen in the omission by the operative provisions of the most recent pertinent agreements, namely the Cartagena Protocol and the FAO Treaty, of savings clauses purporting to provide an across-the-board solution to potential conflicts arising between the agreements themselves and other international obligations (including, of course, WTO obligations) in accordance with Article 30(2) of the 1969 Vienna Convention on the Law of Treaties. These agreements rather include a more articulated formula in their *preambles*, a portion of which only may be identified with a savings clause.[99]

The same change of perspective is to be noted in relation to instruments on human genomics and genetics. The UDHG, though only in its preamble, contains a 'without prejudice' clause[100] allegedly aimed at giving

[98] See Agenda 21, para. 2(3)(b) and 2(9)(d); 1994 WTO Decision on Trade and Environment, third para. of the operative text; 2001 WTO Doha Ministerial Declaration, paras. 6 and 31; FAO Treaty, ninth preambular para.; Cartagena Protocol, ninth preambular para.; 1998 Rotterdam PIC Convention, eighth preambular para.; 2001 Stockholm POPS Convention, ninth preambular para.; Bonn Guidelines, para. 7(e); Johannesburg Plan of Implementation, paras. 44(r), 97 and 98.

[99] The preamble to the Cartagena Protocol, so far as material, reads: 'Recognizing that trade and environment agreements should be mutually supportive with a view to achieving sustainable development' (Recital 9); 'Emphasizing that this Protocol shall not be interpreted as implying a change in the rights and obligations of a Party under any existing international agreements' (Recital 10); 'Understanding that the above recital is not intended to subordinate this Protocol to other international agreements' (Recital 11). In almost identical terms, see Recitals 9–11 of the FAO Treaty. Commentators almost unanimously hold that the above recitals are cryptic and seem to contradict and neutralise each other: see e.g. Sands, *Principles of International Environmental Law* (2nd edn., Cambridge, 2003), at 654; Pauwelyn, *Conflict of Norms in Public International Law—How WTO Law Relates to Other Rules of International Law* (Cambridge, 2003), at 334. Very isolated is the view according to which Recital 10 serves the purpose of a savings clause by giving precedence to the WTO agreements over the Cartagena Protocol, *also* as between WTO Members that *are* parties to the Protocol: Safrin, 'Treaties in Collision? The Biosafety Protocol and the World Trade Organization Agreements' (2002) 96 *AJIL* 606 at 618–622. For an articulated critique of this opinion, see Pavoni, *supra* n 55, at 364–367.

[100] Third preambular para.

precedence to the treaties in the field of intellectual property, first and foremost the TRIPs Agreement. By contrast, the 2003 IDHGD, again in its preamble,[101] merely 'recalls' a number of international agreements and declarations, including the TRIPs Agreement and, most interestingly, calls upon states to regulate '*in accordance with* their domestic law and *international agreements*, the cross-border flow of human genetic data, human proteomic data and biological samples. . .'.[102] This is not a savings clause plainly accepting the primacy of international agreements,[103] but rather a reminder of the need to foster harmonious and mutually supportive relationships between the Declaration and such agreements.[104]

In the end, the only remaining genuine savings clause is Article 22 of the CBD which sets out the primacy of other international agreements, except where the exercise of the rights and obligations envisaged therein 'would cause a serious damage or threat to biological diversity'.[105] In addition, the second paragraph of the same norm addresses potential conflicts between the CBD and *inter alia* UNCLOS, by stipulating that 'Contracting Parties shall implement this Convention with respect to the marine environment *consistently* with the rights and obligations of States under the law of the sea'.[106] It is self-evident that these clauses are ambiguous in many respects and thus subject to differing interpretations. As for the relationship of the CBD and UNCLOS, it is worthwhile to add that the interaction, if any, of the two paragraphs of Article 22 is particularly controversial[107] and that the problem is further complicated by the parallel existence of a savings clause in UNCLOS itself.[108] At any rate, the most important point with respect to CBD Article 22 (and similar savings clauses) is that it is to be assimilated to a *compatibility* clause, rather than

[101] First para. Likewise, see the sixth preambular para. to the current draft of a UNESCO declaration on universal norms on bioethics (*Elaboration of the Declaration on Universal Norms on Bioethics: Fourth Outline of a Text, supra* n 54.).

[102] Art. 18(a), emphasis added.

[103] As a matter of fact, the Art. at hand adds that states should seek to ensure that the party which receives human genetic data or biological samples 'provides adequate protection in accordance with the principles set out in this Declaration'. This of course might open the way to embargoes and similar measures imposed against states that do not comply with the safeguards laid down in the Declaration.

[104] Of course, I am not formally discussing here the relationship between a declaration such as the IDHGD and international agreements according to the theory of the sources of international law. Everybody knows that agreements normally prevail over non-binding declarations, even though this is not straightforward when particular norms of a given declaration are to be considered as a codification of, or supervening, customary law (which is not to be excluded altogether in our case given the human rights nature of the IDHGD).

[105] Art. 22(1).

[106] *Ibid.*, para. (2), emphasis added.

[107] For instance, see the chapter by Cataldi in this volume.

[108] Art. 311(2). What is the legal regime of these cross-savings clauses that may contradict one with another? As already noted, however, in my opinion the conflicts between the CBD and UNCLOS are more apparent than real.

a *subordination* clause *stricto senso*. As such, it should not be considered capable of ensuring primacy to the 'saved' regimes over the conflicting rule. They should instead operate at the interpretive level by inviting a conciliatory application of both norms.[109]

Before briefly outlining the legal implications of the principle of mutual supportiveness between the instruments on biotechnology and the applicable WTO agreements, let me submit that, notwithstanding a huge bulk of scholarly debate, the general problem of the relationship between MEAs and the WTO system still appears unsettled both at the positive and theoretical levels.[110] At the positive level, all efforts undertaken so far within the WTO to reach a consensus on precise rules clarifying the relationship between MEAs and WTO law (including that between the TRIPs Agreement and the CBD) have failed.[111]

Conversely, for one reason or an other, scholarly contributions do not appear fully convincing. They can roughly be divided into two categories. The first includes those authors[112] who do not exclude the existence of genuine normative conflicts and accordingly identify solutions, generally favourable to the priority of MEAs, in line with the applicable general principles, whereas the second category encompasses those authors[113]

109 In the Italian literature, this has been convincingly demonstrated by Sciso, *Gli accordi internazionali confliggenti* (Bari, 1986), at 318–319.

110 As is well-known, there are also no pertinent international judicial decisions. The EC has timidly argued that its measures under challenge within the WTO *EC—Biotech Products* case, *supra* n 3, are in conformity with the Cartagena Protocol. It remains to be seen whether this argument will be maintained and, if so, what impact it will have on the decisions of the WTO bodies.

111 The clarification of this relationship is part of the Doha negotiating mandate. Pursuant to para. 31(i) of the Doha Declaration, the WTO Committee on Trade and Environment is carrying on negotiations on 'the relationship between existing WTO rules and specific trade obligations set out in multilateral environmental agreements (MEAs)'. Such negotiations were scheduled for completion by 1 Jan 2005, but this deadline has been missed, due to profound divisions between WTO Members on the scope and possible outcomes of the negotiations themselves. The relationship between the TRIPs Agreement and the CBD is the object of a specific analysis (though not of formal negotiations) by the TRIPs Council (see para. 19 of the Doha Declaration). For a review of the Doha provisions relating to trade and environmental issues, cf. Boisson de Chazournes and Mbengue, 'La Déclaration de Doha de la Conférence ministérielle de l'Organisation mondiale du commerce et sa portée dans les relations commerce/environnement' (2002) *Revue Générale de Droit International Public* 855.

112 Pauwelyn, *supra* n 99; Picone and Ligustro, *Diritto dell'Organizzazione mondiale del commercio* (Padua, 2002), at 623.

113 See especially, Francioni, 'Environment, Human Rights and the Limits of Free Trade', in Francioni (ed.), *Environment, Human Rights and International Trade* (Oxford, 2001), 1 at 22–24; Tarasofsky, 'Ensuring the Compatibility between Multilateral Environmental Agreements and GATT/WTO' (1996) 7 *Yearbook of International Environmental Law* 52 at 62 ff.; Marceau, 'A Call for Coherence in International Law—Praises for the Prohibition Against "Clinical Isolation" in WTO Dispute Settlement' (1999) 33 *Journal of World Trade* 87; Marceau, 'Conflicts of Norms and Conflicts of Jurisdictions—The Relationship between the WTO Agreement and MEAs and other Treaties' (2001) 35 *Journal of World Trade* 1081.

who are more inclined to explain the relationship at stake in terms of mere tensions likely to be overcome by virtue of general interpretive principles (evolutive interpretation, presumption against conflict, treaty effectiveness). The former view seems problematic for a number of technical reasons related to the principles governing the conflict of norms in international law. I will just mention that reason which, perhaps, may be considered the basic one. Is it convincingly demonstrated that there are *genuine* conflicts, that is a mutual relationship of incompatibility between norms pursuant to the definition widely accepted in international law? If one looks at the practice in the field of biodiversity and biotechnology, the answer must be in the negative. The overwhelming majority of states and pertinent international bodies and organisations rather highlight the existence of a mere interrelation,[114] interaction or intersection.

In many respects, the interpretive approach seems preferable. It is consistent with state practice and is certainly more protective of the integrity and unity of the international legal system (including the *pacta sunt servanda* rule). However, practice also shows that there are *residual* hypotheses where a considerable tension between the agreements at stake arises, if not from their textual interpretation, at least from the persistence of controversial courses of action formally justified under a given treaty. Crucially for our purposes, this is the case of the *patentability of genetic material illegally exported from the state of origin*, namely without the prior informed consent of that state as required under the CBD. The TRIPs Agreement arguably[115] allows these patents while patent offices around industrialised countries are reluctant to deny protection.[116] This phenomenon, often stigmatised as one of *biopiracy*, evidently entails the violation of the principle of equitable benefit-sharing as well.

Interpretive principles show their inherent limits here. Such practices cannot just be reconciled with the CBD. What is the way forward, then? Should the principle of mutual supportiveness of instruments on biotechnology and trade regimes be seen as a mere conceptual tool devoid of legal significance and justiciability, thus unhelpful in the situation at stake? I do not believe so. First, mutual supportiveness is contiguous with

[114] This is the expression employed by the UN General Assembly to describe the relationship between the TRIPs Agreement and the CBD: see Resolution 56/197 of 21 Dec 2001, para. 8.

[115] See most recently, Safrin, *supra* n 30, at 667, arguing that denial of patents in the case at hand entails a violation of the TRIPs Agreement. This author, however, ignores the *ordre public* and morality exceptions envisaged by Art. 27(2) of the TRIPs Agreements which might justify denial of patentability.

[116] One should also take into account that patent offices are normally either unable or unwilling to know about the legal provenance of the material incorporated into biotechnological inventions. For *de lege ferenda* proposals to improve this situation, see Safrin *supra* n 30, at 673–679.

the principle of *sustainable development*, particularly with its underlying requirement of integration between economic, environmental and social values. Therefore, mutual supportiveness may influence in a dispositive way the outcome of normative processes and judicial disputes, much as sustainable development does.[117] Secondly, mutual supportiveness is closely linked to the overarching principles of *cooperation and good faith* in international relations.[118] Thus, the conduct of a state consisting in an arbitrary and unreasoned dismissal of actions capable of safeguarding mutual supportiveness between regimes may be sanctioned as a wrongful act.

More ambitiously, could such arbitrary denial of the requirement of mutual supportiveness include the refusal to engage constructively in law-making processes aimed at amending controversial provisions of the trade system? Consider that, with respect to the problem of biotechnological patents inconsistent with the CBD outlined above, a wide-ranging group of developing countries (of enormous demographic importance) is indeed convinced that the TRIPs Agreement must be amended[119] in order to provide for the disclosure of the origin of genetic material, evidence of prior consent and benefit-sharing as conditions of patentability. This course of action goes in the same direction as other recent developments. I refer especially to the thorny issue of the relationship between intellectual property and access to essential medicines by least-developed countries, an issue which for obvious reasons is extremely pertinent in the biotechnology context. It is well-known that here the solution devised at the WTO level is the adoption of apposite waivers to the TRIPs rules concerning compulsory licences. The relevant decision[120] provides that the waivers are to apply until they are translated into corresponding *amendments* to the TRIPs Agreement.[121]

Such a development may well be explained under a perspective of mutual supportiveness between concurrent regimes (*in casu*, the human

117 See especially Lowe, 'Sustainable Development and Unsustainable Arguments', in Boyle and Freestone (eds.), *International Law and Sustainable Development: Past Achievements and Future Challenges* (Oxford, 1999) 19; Birnie and Boyle, *supra* n 10, at 96–97.

118 Note the frequent use of these general principles by the WTO dispute settlement bodies, see especially *US—Shrimp I*, *supra* n 40, para. 158; *United States—Import Prohibition of Certain Shrimp and Shrimp Products (Recourse to Article 21.5 of the DSU by Malaysia)* (*US—Shrimp II*), Appellate Body Report, Doc. WT/DS58/AB/RW of 22 Oct 2001, paras. 115–134.

119 Cf. *The Relationship between the TRIPS Agreement and the Convention on Biological Diversity and the Protection of Traditional Knowledge*, Communication from Brazil, China, Cuba, Dominican Republic, Ecuador, India, Pakistan, Thailand, Venezuela, Zambia and Zimbabwe to the TRIPs Council, Doc. IP/C/W/356 of 24 June 2002.

120 Decision of the WTO General Council of 30 Aug 2003 on the Implementation of Paragraph 6 of the Doha Declaration on the TRIPs Agreement and Public Health, Doc. WT/L/540 of 2 Sep 2003.

121 *Ibid.*, para. 11.

rights and trade regimes). Indeed, they powerfully suggest that the principle at stake *does* have normative value. In exceptional circumstances, mutual supportiveness seems to include an emerging duty to cooperate in good faith in order to facilitate amendments to trade rules likely to result in systemic conflicts with fundamental principles established by MEAs articulated around the principle of the common concern of humanity (such as the CBD and the FAO Treaty). It is remarkable that such a duty should be enforceable also against states which are not parties to the MEA in question, but are Members of the WTO.[122] To a certain extent, then, this perspective circumvents what represents the intangible aspect of international law underlying all the scholarly analyses mentioned above, namely the sanctity of the *pacta tertiis neque prosunt neque nocent* rule.

VI. CONCLUSION

The years to come will predictably be a crucial time for the elaboration of international regimes in the field of biotechnology and human genetics. Certain law-making processes are already underway and others will probably begin to address emerging issues and challenges. In this context, the most pressing question that the international community has to tackle relates to the undesirable consequences resulting from an increasingly fragmented approach to the international regulation of biotechnology. The proliferation of international bodies with biotech-related competences and of 'international regimes all addressing pieces of the biotechnology puzzle, yet ... [in]capable of addressing the problem as a whole'[123] requires streamlining, synergies and the creation of viable networks of cooperation, hopefully including relevant non-state actors and stakeholders.

The way forward could be the negotiation of a comprehensive biotechnology treaty under the aegis of the UN, laying down basic principles and procedures, addressing specific areas where consensus can be reached and, crucially, providing for a mechanism of constant updating in light of new scientific findings and advances.

In this chapter, I have attempted to provide a modest contribution to such future standard-setting exercise by focusing on some basic substantive principles of the international law of biotechnology that have emerged from the already abundant practice in this area. I am aware that some of my findings, for instance with respect to the customary nature of

[122] The underlying issue here is of course that of the unilateralism and free-riding of some states, especially the United States, with respect to the biodiversity regimes.
[123] Murphy, 'Biotechnology and International Law' (2001) 42 *Harvard ILJ* 47 at 123.

the duty of benefit-sharing, may seem particularly contentious and that other frameworks and approaches can be put forward. However, international practice is rarely clear-cut, especially in areas, such as biotechnology, that are not well-settled and are rather subject to continuing developments. In most cases, then, it is submitted that the rules extrapolated from practice deeply reflect one's own policy and value judgements and this chapter is certainly no exception. I do hope, however, that this will not be interpreted as tantamount to a lack of a positivist approach.

Part II

Biotechnology and the Protection of the Environment

3

Biotechnology, Biodiversity and Sustainable Development: Conflict or Congruence?

CATHERINE REDGWELL*

I. INTRODUCTION

WHILST ON THE one hand it is compelling to view the trinity of biotechnology,[1] biodiversity and sustainable development as mutually supportive and compatible, closer analysis of each of these three concepts, and of their interaction, reveals several areas of tension and conflict. These tensions exist at the practical level; in the extent to which biotechnology poses risks to biodiversity through, for example, the release of LMOs[2] and the consequent adulteration of natural habitat. Potential conflict plays out at the theoretical level as well, in the different dynamics of regulation of biodiversity and of biotechnology.[3] Integration of biotechnology into sustainable development concerns is a current challenge in international law in order to achieve both intragenerational equity, that is, equitable distribution of the benefits and burdens of biotechnology

* Professor of International Law, University College London.

1 Defined in Art 2 of the 1992 Convention on Biological Diversity (CBD): '"Biotechnology" means any technological application that uses biological systems, living organisms, or derivatives thereof, to make or modify products or processes for specific use'.

2 The 2000 Biosafety Protocol to the CBD uses the term 'LMO' which is defined in Art 3 thereof: '"Living Modified Organism" means any living organism that possesses a novel combination of genetic material obtained through the use of modern biotechnology'. "Modern biotechnology" means the application of in vitro nucleic acid techniques, or fusion of cells beyond the taxonomic family, 'that overcome natural physiological reproductive or recombination barriers and that are not techniques used in traditional breeding and selection'. This chapter will use 'LMO' and genetically modified organism 'GMO' interchangeably.

3 Indeed three, often disconnected, strands may be identified in GMO discourse: (i) science; (ii) economics; and (iii) socio-cultural issues. See IUCN–The World Conservation Union, *Genetically Modified Organisms and Biosafety: A background paper for decision-makers and others to assist in consideration of GMO issues* (Gland Aug 2004), at 4.

within the present generation, and intergenerational equity, which also raises questions of equitable distribution of the benefits and burdens of biotechnology, but between, rather than only within, generations, including responsibility to future generations for the conservation and sustainable use of biodiversity.[4]

In order to highlight the areas of conflict and congruence, this chapter will first analyse the development of international legal regulation of biodiversity and biotechnology principally through the pre-Rio and post-Rio process, focussing on the provisions of the 1992 Convention on Biological Diversity[5] and the 2000 Cartagena Protocol on Biosafety.[6] This is not to suggest that other instruments are not pertinent[7]—most notably the Codex Alimentarius,[8] the International Plant Protection Convention,[9] and certain of the WTO covered agreements,[10] but these are addressed in other contributions.[11] Accordingly the principal focus of this contribution is the CBD and its first progeny, the Biosafety Protocol.

II. THE DEVELOPMENT OF THE BIODIVERSITY CONCEPT

Concerns for the conservation of biological diversity, and the link with sustainable development, arose well before the Rio Conference in 1992, principally through soft law initiatives. In 1980 the IUCN/UNEP/WWF set out an ethical basis for preserving biodiversity in their World Conservation Strategy (WCS)[12] which, with its underlying theme of sustainable

[4] The Report of the CSD Secretary General on the Transfer of Environmentally Sound Technologies and the Sound Management of Biotechnology, ECOSOC E/CN.17/2001/PC/11, at 6, para. 31 raises some of these issues. This report was prepared for the Commission on Sustainable Development (CSD) in its capacity as the preparatory committee for the 2002 World Summit on Sustainable Development in Johannesburg (Rio +10).

[5] Convention on Biological Diversity, 5 June 1992, in force 29 May 1994, available at (1992) 31 818.

[6] Cartagena Protocol on Biosafety, 29 Jan 2000, available at (2000) 39 ILM 1027.

[7] In the context of agricultural biotechnology in particular, there are further linkages with, eg, the work of the UN Commission on Human Rights' Special Rapporteur on the Right to Food, and the FAO Panel of Eminent Experts in Ethics on Food and Agriculture, discussed in R Mackenzie, 'The International Regulation of Modern Biotechnology' (2002) 13 *Yearbook of International Environmental Law* 97.

[8] See http://www.codexalimentarius.net.

[9] See http://www.ipcc.int.

[10] In particular the Agreement on the Application of Sanitary and Phytosanitary Measures, 15 Apr 1994, Annex 1A, WTO Agreement, in *The Results of the Uruguay Round Multilateral Trade Negotiations: The Legal Texts* 59; the Agreement on Technical Barriers to Trade, in *ibid.*; and the General Agreement on Tariffs and Trade, in *ibid.*

[11] Such as Footer, in this volume.

[12] *World Conservation Strategy: Living Resource Conservation for Sustainable Development* (Gland, 1980), prepared by the International Union for the Conservation of Nature (IUCN), with UNEP, the WWF, FAO and UNESCO.

development, is considered to have set the 'real foundation' for the biodiversity concept in international law. To be sure, there had been some brief reference to safeguarding the natural resources of the earth, especially representative samples of natural ecosystems, in Principle 2 of the 1972 Stockholm Declaration on the Human Environment and, in Principle 4, to humankind's 'special responsibility to safeguard and wisely manage the heritage of wildlife and its habitat which are now gravely imperilled by a combination of adverse factors'. However, while of clear significance in the genesis of modern international environmental law there is little sign of the biodiversity concept as such at Stockholm. The 1980 World Conservation Strategy (WCS) does make such explicit reference to such in establishing three fundamental objectives of living resources conservation, namely: (a) to maintain essential ecological processes and life-support systems; (b) to preserve genetic diversity; and (c) to ensure the sustainable utilisation of species and ecosystems. The second of these three objectives, the preservation of genetic diversity, as it is further defined in the WCS, captures the essence of the biodiversity concept later developed. Indeed, the WCS was revised in 1991, whilst negotiation of the CBD was reaching its conclusion, and explicitly calls for the protection of biodiversity as an important element in sustainable living.[13]

This finds an echo in the 1982 World Charter for Nature[14] which provides, inter alia, for the maintenance of the 'genetic viability' of the earth, the conservation of unique areas, representative samples of ecosystems and habitats of rare or endangered species. Also stressed is the need for human management of ecosystems to achieve and maintain optimum sustainable productivity, with planning taking into account environmental impacts. We thus see the dual strands of assessment and management emerging as early as 1982, now reflected in, inter alia, Articles 15 and 16 of the Biosafey Protocol discussed further below.

Another striking feature of the 1980 WCS is the emphasis upon the practical, utilitarian values of wildlife conservation, seeking to demonstrate that environmental protection and economic development not only are reconcilable but that the former is a prerequisite for the latter.[15]

13 *Caring for the Earth: A Strategy for Sustainable Living* (Gland, 1991). Explicit linkage of biodiversity and legal principle is made in the 1987 Report of the World Commission on Environment and Development: WCED, *Our Common Future* (Oxford, 1987), the Legal Experts' Group of which proposed Legal Principles for Environmental Protection and Sustainable Development, the third of which provides: '[s]tates shall maintain ecosystems and ecological processes essential for the functioning of the biosphere, shall preserve biological diversity, and shall observe the principles of optimum sustainable yield in the use of living natural resources and ecosystems': G. Munro and D. Lammers (eds.), *Environmental Protection and Sustainable Development* (London, 1986).

14 Framed in the context of a UN General Assembly resolution adopted by 111 votes in favour 1 against, and with 18 abstentions.

15 *Supra*, n. 12.

Economic development is dependent on the continued viability of natural systems and the availability of resources, especially consumables. In other words, sustainable development, the *rapprochement* of environment and development at the heart of the 1992 Rio Conference at which the CBD was opened for signature is at the heart therefore of the CBD.[16]

III. 'FOOD.HOPE.HEALTH'[17]: AGENDA 21 AND BIOTECHNOLOGY AS A TOOL FOR SUSTAINABLE DEVELOPMENT

Perhaps the greatest congruence of the biodiversity, biotechnology and sustainable development concepts is at the level of policy and principle as expressed in Agenda 21—Earth's Action Plan—adopted at the 1992 Rio Conference on Environment and Development. Chapters 15 and 16 are devoted to conservation of biological diversity and to environmentally sound management of biotechnology, respectively.[18] Whilst cautioning that biotechnology by itself 'cannot resolve all the fundamental problems of environment and development', Chapter 16 nonetheless strikes an upbeat note in the preambular recognition that biotechnology 'promises to make a significant contribution in enabling the development of, for example, better health care, enhanced food security through sustainable agricultural practices, improved supplies of potable water, more efficient industrial development processes for transforming raw materials, suport for sustainable methods of afforestation and reforestation, and detoxification of hazardous wastes'.[19]

With relation to biodiversity, Chapter 16 of Agenda 21 explicitly acknowledges both the benefits and the risks of biotechnology development. On the one hand, biotechnology may assist with the transformation of biological resources to serve the needs of sustainable development and assist in the ex situ conservation of biological diversity.[20] The downside is the need to develop environmentally sound biotechnologies based on risk assessment and management, and to avoid developing countries in particular becoming '"testing" or "dumping" grounds for potentially harmful

[16] The objectives of which, in Art 1, have been referred to by Boyle as a trade-off between conservation and economic equity unusual for an international environmental agreement: A.E. Boyle, 'The Convention on Biological Diversity' in L. Campiglio, L. Pineschi, D. Siniscalco and T. Treves (eds.), *The Environmental After Rio* (London, Dordrecht, Boston, Mass, 1994), at 38; see also D.M. McGraw, 'The CBD—Key Characteristics and Implications for Implementation' (2002) 11:1 *RECIEL* 17.

[17] Monsanto advertisement, *The Guardian*, 16 May 1998, cited in J. Holder, 'New Age: Rediscovering Natural Law' (2000) 53 *Current Legal Problems* 151, at 155.

[18] Agenda 21, Report of the United Nations Conference on Environment and Development, Rio de Janeiro, 3–14 June 1992, UN Doc. A/CONF.151/26, Vols. I–III, 12 Aug 1992.

[19] *Ibid.*, Ch. 16, para. 16.1.

[20] *Ibid.*

technologies and products',[21] as has occurred in the past with hazardous wastes, chemicals and pesticides. Indeed, as will be discussed shortly below, the structure of the Biosafety Protocol owes much to the instruments regulating transboundary movement of hazardous wastes and pesticides,[22] as well as building on a number of soft law initiatives.[23]

IV. THE 1992 CONVENTION ON BIOLOGICAL DIVERSITY[24]

As indicated above, the Convention on Biological Diversity (CBD) was opened for signature at the Rio Conference on Environment and Development in 1992. Today it has 188 Contracting Parties bound by its terms, and thus enjoys nearly universal membership. The primary objectives of the CBD are the conservation of biological diversity, sustainable use of its components and fair and equitable sharing of the benefits arising from the utilisation of genetic resources (Article 1). Conservation obligations are reflected in the provisions on adoption of national strategies, plans or programmes (Article 6) and in the provisions on *in situ* and *ex situ* conservation (Articles 7 and 8). The reference to 'sustainable use' of the components of biological diversity is a clear indicator that this Convention is not concerned primarily with the preservation of biodiversity but 'assumes human use and benefit as the fundamental purpose for conserving biodiversity, limited only by the requirement of sustainability and the need to benefit future generations'.[25] In this sense the Convention

21 Mackenzie, *supra*, n. 7,at 97.

22 See C. Redgwell, 'Regulating Trade in Dangerous Substances: Prior Informed Consent under the 1998 Rotterdam Convention' in A. Kiss, D. Shelton and K. Ishibashi, (eds), *Economic Globalization and Compliance with International Environmental Agreements* (The Hague, 2003).

23 For example, UNEP's International Guidelines for Safety in Biotechnology (1995) and UNIDO's Voluntary Code of Conduct for the Release of Organisms into the Environment (1992).

24 On the CBD see, generally, F. McConnell, *The Biodiversity Convention: A Negotiating History* (London, The Hague, Boston, Mass, 1996); M.-A. Hermitte, 'La Convention sur la Diversité Biologique' (1992) XXXVIII *Annuaire Français de Droit International* 844 ; F. Burhenne-Guilmin and S. Casey-Lefkowitz, 'The New Law of Biodiversity' (1992) 3 *Yearbook of International Environmental Law* 43; the *Convention on Biological Diversity Handbook* (CBD Secretariat, 2001) available at http://www.biodiv.org; C. de Klemm and C. Shine, *Biological Diversity Conservation and Law* (Gland, 1993); C. Redgwell, 'The Protection of Biological Diversity' in K. Koufa, (ed.), *Protection of the Environment for the New Millenium, Thesaurus Acroasium*, (Athens, 2002), xxxi, 355–396; and two special issues of *RECIEL* (1997, Vol. 6:3 and 2002, Volume 11:1). For the wider background see, generally, M. Bowman and C. Redgwell, (eds), *The Conservation of Biological Diversity* (London, The Hague, Boston, Mass, 1991).

25 Boyle in Campiglio *et al., supra*, n. 16, at 115. 'Sustainable use' is defined in Art 2 as 'the use of components of biological diversity in a way and at a rate that does not lead to the long-term decline of biological diversity, thereby maintaining its potential to meet the needs and aspirations of present and future generations'. At COP V (2002, Decision V/24), sustainable use was adopted as a cross-cutting issue under the Convention, and at COP 7 (2004) the Addis Ababa Principles and Guidelines for the Sustainable Use of Biodiversity were adopted.

is 'philosophically closer' to environmental treaties concerned with conservation to permit sustainable human use (e.g. fisheries and migratory species) than to the preservationist concept evidenced in the Protocol to the Antarctic Treaty on Environmental Protection and in the moratorium on commercial whaling under the International Convention for the Regulation of Whaling.[26] Nonetheless the Convention constitutes an important milestone in its recognition of the intrinsic value of biodiversity and of the conservation of biodiversity as a 'common concern of humankind'.

In the 11 years since the entry into force of the CBD, the international community's approach to biodiversity has continued to evolve, with biological diversity now considered an essential part of efforts to eradicate poverty and achieve sustainable development. In the immediate run-up to the 2002 World Summit on Sustainable Development (WSSD) in Johannesburg, the 2002 Hague Ministerial Declaration of the Conference of the Parties to the CBD recognised 'that biodiversity underpins sustainable development in many ways; poverty eradication, food security, provision of fresh water, soil conservation and human health all depend directly upon maintaining and using the world's biological diversity and therefore sustainable development cannot be achieved without the conservation and sustainable use of biological diversity'.[27] Recommendation 1B of the WSSD accordingly recognises the contribution of the CBD to the sustainable development process, and to poverty eradication in particular. The need to integrate the objectives of the CBD in global, regional and national sectoral and cross-sectoral programmes and policies—the 'mainstreaming of biodiversity'—is seen both as contributing to the sustainable development process whilst also ensuring full implementation of the Convention.[28]

V. BIOSAFETY IN THE CONVENTION ON BIOLOGICAL DIVERSITY

As indicated above, Agenda 21 enthusiastically embraces the possibilities of biotechnology for sustainable development of biological and other resources in developing states in particular. In the event, two provisions of the 1992 Convention on Biological Diversity are specifically addressed to biotechnology and to biosafety, though they strike a more cautionary

[26] Boyle, *supra* n. 25.

[27] Para 5. The Declaration calls upon the World Summit on Sustainable Development to recognise and to promote these strong linkages (see para. 15(c)).

[28] Contribution of the Convention on Biological Diversity to Implementing the Outcomes of the Johannesburg Summit, *Report of the [CBD] Executive Secretary to the Commission on Sustainable Development*. The marginalization of biodiversity issues is perceived as one of the principle obstacles to full implementation of the CBD: *ibid*, para. 6.

note. The first provision is Article 8 on in situ conservation, paragraph (g) of which requires that:

> Each Contracting Party shall, as far as possible and as appropriate:
>
> . . . (g) Establish or maintain means to regulate, manage or control the risks associated with the use and release of living modified organisms resulting from biotechnology which are likely to have adverse environmental impacts that could affect the conservation and sustainable use of biological diversity, taking into account the risks to human health.

This obligation is not geographically limited, reflecting the general obligation on states to exercise diligent control over activities within their jurisdiction and control which may cause harm to the territory of other states, or to the global commons. This is made express in Article 4, which addresses the jurisdictional scope of the Convention, making it clear that the Article 8(g) obligation applies not only to components of biological diversity within the limits of national jurisdiction, but also to processes and activities, regardless of where they occur, which are carried out under state jurisdiction and control.

Transboundary movement of LMOs is addressed in Article 19(4) CBD, and requires information to be provided to another party regarding use and safety regulations in respect of the organisms, and any available information on the potential adverse impact of the specific organisms concerned to the Contracting Party where the organisms are to be introduced. Reflecting the balance indicated above, the CBD is not a prohibitionist charter, but rather an instrument based on sustainability. Thus Article 19 further recognises the need to promote and advance priority access on a fair and equitable basis, especially by developing country parties, to the results and benefits arising from biotechnologies based on their genetic resources. This is all the more compelling given the above-noted reference in Agenda 21 to the variety of purposes biotechnology might serve particularly with respect to human health, food security, and poverty alleviation.

Article 19(3) goes further and expressly contemplates consideration of the need for, and modalities of, a protocol regulating transfer and use of living modified organisms (LMOs) which may have adverse effect on the conservation and sustainable use of biological diversity.[29] This was initiated from COP I, with the adoption on 29 January 2000 of the text of the Cartagena Protocol on Biosafety. Thus the origins of the Biosafety Protocol

[29] McGraw, *supra* n. 16, at 19, refers to criticisms of this choice as reflecting an absence of 'sound science'—why not a Protocol on traditional knowledge or on alien species, for example?

may be found in the late 1980s and early 1990s; biosafety regulation in many states also predates the Biosafety Protocol, not least owing to the Article 8(g) obligation of the parent CBD indicated above.[30] Even the core decision-making principle of the Protocol—advanced informed agreement—is trailed in Article 19(3) CBD, though of course leaving much left to be negotiated in the six Biosafety Working Group meetings, the failed Extraordinary Conference of the Parties in Cartagena in 1999, informal negotiations in Montreal and Vienna, and a final extraordinary meeting of the Conference of the Parties in Montreal in January 2000 where the text of the Cartagena Protocol on Biosafety was adopted.[31]

VI. KEY PROVISIONS OF THE 2000 CARTAGENA PROTOCOL ON BIOSAFETY[32]

The focus of the Biosafety Protocol is upon the transboundary movement of LMOs which may have adverse effects on biological diversity and human health. 'Living modified organism' is defined as 'any living organism that possesses a novel combination of genetic material obtained through the use of modern biotechnology'.[33] In fact the Protocol addresses two general categories of LMO: (i) those intended for release into the environment (e.g. seeds for cultivation or animal breeding stock); and (ii) those intended for use in food or feed, or for processing (e.g. corn, cotton and soy). The latter were of particular concern to the United States as the chief exporter of genetically modified crops.[34] In the event the Protocol distinguishes between these categories, subjecting organisms intended for direct use as food or feed, or for processing, to a less onerous regime

[30] See discussion of e.g. Egypt's biosafety regime in P. Kameri-Mbote, 'The Development of Biosafety Regulation in Africa in the Context of the Cartagena Protocol: Legal and Administrative Issues' (2002) 11:1 *RECIEL* 62.

[31] It entered into force on 11 Sept 2003, and presently has 116 Parties. On the negotiation history, see *Earth Negotiations Bulletin* at http://www.iisd.ca/biodiv.html and McKenzie *et al.*, *An Explanatory Guide to the Cartagena Protocol on Biosafety*, IUCN Environmental Policy and Law Paper No. 46 (Gland, 2003).

[32] 2000 Cartagena Protocol on Biosafety to the Convention on Biological Diversity, reproduced at (2000) 39 ILM 1027. For coverage of the final negotiating session see (2000) 9 No. 137 *Earth Negotiations Bulletin* 1–11; see also http://www.iisd.ca/biodiv.html for the full negotiating history through the ENB; see also CBD, *The Cartagena Protocol on Biosafety: A Record of the Negotiations* (Montreal, 2003). On the Protocol generally, see P.E. Hagan and J.B. Weiner, 'The Cartagena Protocol on Biosafety: New Rules for International Trade in Living Modified Organisms' (2000) 12 *Georgetown Environmental Law Review* 697; S. W. Burgiel, 'The Cartagena Protocol on Biosafety: Taking the Steps from Negotiation to Implementation' (2002) 11:1 *RECIEL* 53; and R. Mackenzie *et al.*, *ibid.*

[33] Art 3(f).

[34] See further Hagen and Weiner, *supra* n. 32. Although not a party to the CBD the United States participated in the negotiation of the Protocol which, notwithstanding the compromises contained in, inter alia, Art 11, it is unlikely to participate in for the foreseeable future.

(Article 11) than that applicable to LMOs intended for direct release into the environment (Articles 7–10). This distinction in regulatory approach reflects a perception of the higher degree of risk posed by non-contained LMOs to the natural environment and, in particular, to the conservation of biological diversity, whilst not ignoring the potentially adverse effect of contained LMOs on human health and even the environment.

A marked feature of the Protocol is its overtly precautionary approach, with Article 1 making express reference to the precautionary approach contained in Principle 15 of the 1992 Rio Declaration and with implicit reference in the conditional use of 'may have an adverse effect' on biodiversity and/or human health. The chief regulatory technique employed is the 'advanced informed agreement' (AIA) procedure set out in Article 7, which is designed to ensure that Contracting Parties are provided with the information necessary to make informed decisions before agreeing to the import of LMOs into their territory. AIA marks the Protocol out from the 'prior informed consent' procedures of the 1989 Basel and 1998 Rotterdam Conventions,[35] which are based on prior multilateral agreement on the hazardous substances to be regulated and lists of which are set out in annexes. Prior informed consent has been applied where substances have already been adjudged hazardous; it is an example of an *ex ante* procedural mechanism for avoiding, managing and resolving conflict[36] which is deployed in the environmental field, particularly where the transboundary movement of hazardous and dangerous substances is involved. It is closely linked with the obligation to consult under international law, an obligation which is found in a wide range of existing environmental treaties.[37]

The primary purpose of the Biosafety Protocol is to facilitate early assessment by each Contracting Party of the potential risks in accordance with the Protocol. As Stoll observes, the Biosafety Protocol's 'unique combination between import State control and risk assessment results from the fact that it does not contain an agreed definition of materials that the

[35] The 1989 Basel Convention on the Transboundary Movement of Hazardous Wastes and their Disposal, and the 1998 Rotterdam Convention on Prior Informed Consent. The latter expressly excludes LMOs from its scope, thus eliminating the possibility of conflict arising between it and the Biosafety Protocol.

[36] For more general discussion see F.L. Kirgis, *Prior Consultation in International Law* (Washington, DC, 1983). On the function of prior informed consent in dispute avoidance, see J. Collier and V. Lowe, *The Settlement of Disputes in International Law: Institutions and Procedures* (Oxford, 1999), ch. 1 and, specifically in the environmental context, P. Sands, *Principles of International Environmental Law* (Manchester, 1995), at 607 and P. Birnie and A. Boyle, *International Law & The Environment* (Oxford, 2nd ed., 2002), at 126–29.

[37] See, eg, the 1991 Espoo Convention on Environmental Impact Assessment in a Transboundary Context and the 1992 OSPAR Convention for the Protection of the Marine Environment of the North East Atlantic.

importing State may refuse without condition or even an agreement that the substances that it regulates are "undesirable"'.[38] Indeed, the flexibility of the rules under the Protocol has led to suggestions that it represent a form of 'treaty-based environmental unilateralism'; that they are a 'prototype of minimum harmonisation legislation'.[39] They establish principles and procedures to guide national decision-making based on risk assessment and risk management, without mandating a particular outcome.

The Article 7 AIA procedure is buttressed by Articles 8–10 addressed to the notification[40] and decision procedures. The import may be approved, with or without conditions; prohibited; or additional information may be requested (Article 10(3)). Silence in response to an initial notification from the party of export does not imply consent to transboundary movement (Article 9(4)). There is also provision for review of decisions in the light of new scientific information regarding the potential adverse effects of the LMO (Article 12). Article 10(6) stresses that lack of scientific certainty due to insufficient information being available about the potential negative effects of LMOs on biodiversity, including taking into account risks to human health, will not prevent the importing/receiving state from taking decisions in respect of LMOs in order to avoid or minimise potential adverse effects. However, such decisions must be taken in accordance with the risk assessment procedure stipulated in Article 15 and Annex III.

Upward derogation is provided for in Article 2(4), which permits action more protective of biodiversity than provided for in the Protocol so long as such action is consistent both with the Protocol *and* with that Party's other obligations under international law (e.g. trade obligations).[41] The socio-economic impact of LMOs on biodiversity, especially on its value to indigenous and local communities, may also be taken into account by Contracting Parties, but again at least to the extent consistent with their other international obligations.[42] This may be compared with, for example,

[38] P.-T. Stoll, 'Controlling the Risks of Genetically Modified Organisms: The Cartagena Protocol on Biosafety and the SPS Agreement' (1999) 10 *Yearbook of International Environmental Law* 82, at 91.

[39] R. Pavoni, 'Assessing and Managing Biotechnology Risk under the Cartagena Protocol on Biosafety' (2000) X *Italian Yearbook of International Law* 113, at 115 and 116. It should be noted that Art 14 expressly provides for bilateral, regional and multilateral agreements and arrangements regarding intentional movement of LMOs so long as such arrangements do not provide a lower level of protection than that provided for by the Protocol—either equal protection or in fact a form of bilateral and/or multilateral upward derogation, and certainly precluding 'contracting out' of the Protocol's level of protection. Art 24 also envisages such agreements being concluded between Contracting Parties and non-Parties to the Protocol.

[40] Confidentiality may be preserved in accordance with Art 21.

[41] See also Art 14 ('multilateralised upward derogation'), discussed *supra* n. 39.

[42] Art 26.

the 2003 GM Food and Feed Regulation in the EU. There the legitimate objectives that may be pursued by a system of prior approval embrace not only internal market objectives and concerns for the protection of human life and health and of the environment, but also animal health and welfare and consumer interests in relation to genetically modified foodstuffs in particular.[43]

VII. AIA, BIOSAFETY AND SUSTAINABLE DEVELOPMENT

Domestic debate regarding LMOs has evidenced that consumer concerns have been as prevalent as concerns about the impact of genetically modified crops upon nature and landscape.[44] To an extent these are reflected in the CBD and Biosafety Protocol with stress upon both the environmental and the human health impacts of LMOs. During the negotiation of the Protocol there was some divergence between developed and developing states regarding the purpose of risk assessment. One of the most contentious issues was whether to include in the decision-making process the precautionary principle and socio-economic considerations. For developed states, in particular those members of the 'Miami Group' keen to facilitate LMO trade,[45] the key point was to ensure that assessments were based on the most up-to-date scientific data (what we might call the 'sound science' approach).[46] The inclusion of 'extraneous' matters such as socio-economic impact was viewed as encouraging disguised restrictions on trade.[47] Developing states considered scientific data alone to be insufficient to assess the full range of possible impacts on conservation and sustainable use of biological diversity, socio-economic factors and risks to agriculture and to human health. This broader approach necessitates a multidisciplinary approach to risk assessment,[48] the implementation of

43 For stimulating discussion of the EU regulation and 2001 Deliberate Release Directive, and WTO challenge of the 'first generation' of EU GMO regulation, see J. Scott, 'European Regulation of GMOs: Thinking About Judicial Review in the WTO' forthcoming in (2005), 58 *Current Legal Problems.*

44 Holder observes that concerns for 'self' have been as prevalent as concerns about the natural environment: see J. Holder, 'New Age: Rediscovering Natural Law' (2000) 53 *Current Legal Problems* 151, at 178.

45 Comprising Argentina, Australia, Canada, Chile, Uruguay and the US, i.e. the major actual or potential exporters of LMOs. Three of the Miami Group—Argentina, Canada and the US—launched proceedings under the WTO's dispute settlement procedure challenging the EU's biosafety regime: WT/DS292, WT/DS292 and WT/DS293, EC—Measures Affecting the Approval and Marketing of Biotech Products. See further n. 62 below.

46 Art 15 of the Biosafety Protocol provides that risk assessments 'shall be carried out in a scientifically sound manner' taking account not only of Annex III to the Protocol but also of 'recognized risk assessment techniques'—i.e. those recognised at the national, regional and international levels.

47 See Burgiel, *supra* n. 32, at 55.

48 CBD/UNEP Negotiating History, *supra* n. 32, at 51.

which requires a case-by-case approach. Arguably the flexibility to maintain a multidisciplinary case-by-case approach is provided by the Biosafety Protocol, whilst also ensuring that possible impacts on human health and on the conservation and sustainable use of biological diversity are an integral part of the risk assessment process, the 'backbone of the decision-making process' under the Protocol.[49] As we have seen, precaution is an integral part of the AIA decision-making procedure, and socio-economic concerns are catered for to an extent in the provisions permitting the taking account of the concerns of indigenous and local communities.

As for broader developing state concerns regarding implementation of the Protocol, the clearing house mechanism established under Article 20,[50] combined with the capacity-building provisions of Article 22,[51] is designed to facilitate developing states' participation in the Protocol. Scientific capacity-building at the national or regional level will, as Kameri-Mbote observes, 'go a long way in shaping the potential of the GMO revolution used to address local needs and the requirements for sustainable development'.[52] As yet, however, the biosafety CHM does not contain any data regarding decisions taken under AIA. In contrast, there are 350 entries regarding risk assessments (340 of which are from New Zealand, with Sweden, Japan and the Netherlands also present) and 406 entries under Article 11, which is the streamlined decision-making procedure in respect of LMOs for food feed and processing (showing where the real movement is for the moment).[53]

The difference in the institutional and technical capacity of states is central to the current debate under the 1998 Aarhus Convention on access to information, public participation in decision-making, and access to justice in environmental matters, regarding access to information about GMOs.

[49] Kameri-Mbote, *supra* n. 30, at 63.

[50] See www.bch.biodiv.org. This piggy-backs upon the clearing house mechanism already established under the CBD, as well as establishing a gateway to other biosafety information exchange sites such as UNIDO's Biosafety Information Network and Advisory Service (BINAS) at http://binas.unido.org/binas/ and UNEP's Information Resource for the Release of Organisms (IRRO) at http://panissi.shef.ac.uk/msdn/, as provided for in Art 20(2) of the Protocol.

[51] Which in turn is closely linked with Art 16 (access to and transfer of technology) and 18 (technical and scientific cooperation) of the CBD. Under the Protocol, capacity building is viewed as of particular importance for developing countries without domestic biosafety systems. Hence capacity-building is also linked with Art 28 of the Protocol, which is addressed to the financial mechanism and resources.

[52] *Supra* n. 30, at 73.

[53] As of 20 Dec. 2005. This is a reflection of the further function of the biosafety CHM in facilitating information exchange on LMO-FFPs under Art 11. Most of the Miami group are represented here—Argenting Australia, Canada and the US—as well as New Zealand, Lesotho, Mexico, Japan, the Czech Republic, Republic of Korea, Switzerland and the EC.

There differentiation has controversially been raised in the context of environmental impact assessment, often the principal vehicle for the risk assessment at the heart of the Biosafety Protocol's AIA procedure. Having committed the GMO Working Group to the articulation of binding principles to apply to GMOs, this Group was divided on the question whether countries not yet able to implement the existing EIA obligations contained in Article 6 of the Convention should be distinguished from those states already successfully doing so. Moreover, the utility of agreeing more rigorous guidelines for GMOs in the absence of compliance with existing EIA obligations was questioned. When Article 6 was originally concluded, decisions on GMOs were expressly excluded from its binding requirements on public participation, with the parties required to apply its terms to decisions on whether to permit the deliberate release of GMOs into the environment only 'to the extent feasible and appropriate'. This weak provision resulted from a lack of agreement on the issue between the Parties during the negotiation of the Convention, and was clearly going to be revisited once the Convention entered into force.

The Working Group reported before the second meeting of the Conference of the Parties to the Aarhus Convention in May 2005 where, after three days of 'intensive negotiations' in the run-up to the meeting, agreement was reached on an amendment to the Convention.[54] Once it enters into force, this amendment will require Parties to inform and consult the public in decision-making regarding the deliberate release and placing on the market of GMOs. The public would have the right to submit comments and public authorities would be expected to take these into account in the decision-making process. Once made, the decision taken should be publicly available, together with the reasons and considerations upon which it is based. Information associated with GMO decisions would be made available to the public, subject to the usual protection for commercially confidential information. However, confidentiality may not be extended to information on the intended uses of the release or regarding assessment of environmental risk. This is clearly to prevent abuse of the confidentiality exception, and to ensure full transparency in respect of the use and environmental impact of GMOs.[55] Upward derogation—that is, the flexibility for Parties to adopt more expansive measures for public participation and access to information in GMO decision-making[56]—is also provided for. Overall, this compromise embeds national and regional flexibility whilst establishing international minimum standards for

54 UNECE Press Release, 'Governments reach agreement on public participation in decision-making on genetically modified organisms' , Geneva, 26 May 2005, available at http://www.unece.org/press/pr2005/05env_p06e.htm.

55 An analogous proviso is contained in Art 21(6) of the Cartagena Protocol.

public participation in GMO decision-making, and seeks further to fill the biosafety regulatory gap which persists in some Central, East European and newly independent states. For states party to both the Aarhus Convention and the Biosafety Protocol (and that have also accepted the amendment and when it has entered into force), these provisions on the pubic right to participate in GMO decision-making will serve as a modest strengthening of the public awareness and participation provisions of Article 23 of the Protocol.

VIII. TRADE AND BIOSAFETY

The precautionary approach, such a key feature of the Protocol,[57] allows importing countries to ban imports because of lack of scientific certainty. Unlike under the WTO Agreement on the Application of Sanitary and Phytosanitary Measures (SPS Agreement),[58] there is no obligation to seek further information to enable a more objective, informed assessment of the risk and to review the SPS measure within a reasonable time. Thus in theory a trade-restrictive measure under the Biosafety Protocol may be of unlimited duration, or at least last until the importing country decides that scientific certainty exists regarding the effects of products on biodiversity and human health.[59] This does not, however, serve to immunise such measures from challenge elsewhere in consequence of other international legal obligations, including trade obligations under the WTO. Furthermore, as was noted above, the exercise of the AIA procedure is conditioned by the obligation of the Parties under the Protocol to act consistently with their other obligations under international law.[60]

[56] Access to justice, the third pillar of the Aarhus Convention, is not addressed in the amendment regarding GMOs, though clearly could be embraced in the exercise of such upward derogation.

[57] In addition to the preambular provisions and Art 1 cited above, see Art 10(6) and 11(8).

[58] Art 5.7 of the SPS Agreement provides that:

> 'In cases where relevant scientific evidence is insufficient, a Member may provisionally adopt sanitary and phytosanitary measures on the basis of available pertinent information, including that from relevant international organisations as well as from sanitary and phytosanitary measures applied by other Members. In such circumstances, Members shall seek to obtain the additional information necessary for a more objective assessment of risk and review the sanitary and phytosanitary measure accordingly within a reasonable period of time.'

[59] See S. Zarilli, 'International Trade in GMOs and Multilateral Negotiations: A New Dilemma for Developing Countries' in F. Francioni (ed.), *Environment, Human Rights & International Trade* (Oxford, 2001), ch. 3, esp. 57–64. See also Hagan and Weiner, *supra* n. 32, G.L. Gaston and R.S. Abate, 'The Biosafety Protocol and the World Trade Organisation: Can the Two Co-Exist?' (2000) 12 *Pace Int'l L. Rev.* 107; and Appendix, 'The Cartagena Protocol and the World Trade Organization' in R. Mackenzie *et al.*, *An Explanatory Guide to the Cartagena Protocol on Biosafey* (IUCN Environmental Policy and Law Paper No. 46, Gland, 2003).

[60] See Art 26 for example.

In respect of trade obligations, the Protocol does address its relationship with trade agreements—a contentious issue during negotiations—but only in the preamble,[61] which repeats nearly verbatim the rather unsatisfactory preambular language of the 1998 Rotterdam Convention on Prior Informed Consent in the pesticides context.[62] The Preamble to the Biosafety Protocol recognises that trade and environmental agreements should be mutually supportive[63] with a view to achieving sustainable development. It then emphasises that 'this Protocol shall not be interpreted as implying a change in rights and obligations of a Party under any existing international agreements' whilst immediately asserting that this recital "is not intended to subordinate this Protocol to other international agreement". This 'mutually-supportive, no subordination and no change in existing obligations' formula reflects the various negotiating positions taken by states on this contentious issue.[64] Given that the Protocol does not provide for any compulsory dispute settlement (in this regard it piggy-backs on Article 27 CBD) then, in the event of any conflict with trade rules, the dispute is likely to arise under the WTO, which does provide for compulsory dispute settlement. Clearly the Panels and Appellate Body are limited in their jurisdiction to hearing claims based on the covered agreements.[65] However, as the US, Canada and Argentina[66] dispute with the EU over GMO regulation current before the WTO illustrates, a moratorium on the approval of biotechnology products, as well as national marketing and import bans on such products, is susceptible to legal challenge under WTO law, in particular under the Agreement on the Application of Sanitary and Phytosanitary

[61] For thorough analysis see Stoll, *supra* n. 38, and Gaston and Abate, *supra* n. 59.

[62] As Kummer observes, '[c]ontroversy on this point appears to be inherent in multilateral environmental negotiations addressing transboundary transfer of potentially hazardous substances, since they deal with the interface of trade and environment considerations': K. Kummer, 'Prior Informed Consent for Chemicals in International Trade: The 1998 Rotterdam Convention' (1999) 8:3 *Review of European Community and International Environmental Law* 323.

[63] Mutual supportiveness of trade and environment is also addressed by Principle 12 of the 1992 Rio Declaration and in para 92 of the Plan of Implementation produced at the 2002 World Summit on Sustainable Development (available at www.johannesburgsummit.org) and in para 31 of the Doha Ministerial Declaration (available at www.wto.org).

[64] In this sense the Biosafety Protocol's relationship with the pertinent WTO covered agreements may be located within a wider debate regarding the relationship between the WTO and multilateral environmental agreements employing trade-related mechanisms, a debate which dates back a decade and more. For introductory analysis of the many complex issues, see Birnie and Boyle, 'International Law and the Environment', Ch. 14 or Sands, 'International Environmental Principles', Ch. 19, *supra* n. 36.

[65] See the Understanding on Rules and Procedures Governing the Settlement of Disputes, Appendix I, 'Agreements Covered by the Understanding', in Annex 2 to the 1994 Agreement Establishing the World Trade Organisation, available at www.wto.org.

[66] Canada and Argentina are parties to the CBD and signatories to the Protocol; the US has signed only the CBD.

Measures, the Agreement on Agriculture, the Agreement on Technical Barriers to Trade, and the General Agreement on Tariffs and Trade. As this enumeration makes clear, there is no WTO side agreement on GMOs as such; thus much will turn on judicial review[67] by the Panels and Appellate Body of national decision-making within the context of national biosafety frameworks, whether developed directly under the Biosafety Protocol or through regional regulation and implementation. How far the Biosafety Protocol, and its precautionary approach, will influence the interpretation of the covered agreements (SPS, TBT, GATT), if at all, may well be revealed in the Panel Report expected at the end of December 2005.

One of the arguments by the EU is that the interpretation of the relevant WTO agreements should be consistent with the requirements of the Biosafety Protocol, including its provisions on risk assessment and the right to take precautionary measures. This raises wider questions of the scope of judicial review under the WTO and the extent to which the external treaty obligations of Members—e.g. the Biosafety Protocol—can be taken into account in the interpretation of the WTO covered agreements.[68] We have already seen the Appellate Body in the Shrimp–Turtle dispute willing to rely on 'sustainable development' in the WTO agreement preamble in its interpretation of one of the covered agreements (GATT);[69] but how far will it step outside the WTO framework in its interpretation of the covered agreements? A narrow but widely-held view[70] is that the DSB may

[67] See J. Scott, *supra* n. 43.

[68] In *US-Import Prohibition of Certain Shrimp and Shrimp Products,* WTO Appellate Body (1998), WT/DS58/R, at paras. 171 and 174, the Appellate Body noted that the United States, though a party to the 1973 Convention on International Trade in Endangered Species, had not sought to raise the plight of sea turtles under that Convention (nor were the unilateral measures in question legally required of it under that Convention); the United States was not party to other potentially relevant instruments such as the 1982 Law of the Sea Convention and the 1992 CBD.

[69] 'We note once more that this language demonstrates a recognition by WTO negotiators that optimal use of the world's resources should be made in accordance with the objective of sustainable development. As this preambular language reflects the intentions of negotiators of the WTO Agreement, we believe it must add colour, texture and shading to our interpretation of the agreements annexed to the WTO Agreement, in this case, the GATT 1994. We have already observed that Art. XX(g) of the GATT 1994 is appropriately read with the perspective embodied in the above preamble.

We also note that since this preambular language was negotiated, certain other developments have occurred which help to elucidate the objectives of WTO Members with respect to the relationship between trade and environment. The most significant, in our view, was the Decision of Ministers at Marrakesh to establish a permanent Committee on Trade and Environment.'

US-Import Prohibition of Certain Shrimp and Shrimp Products, WTO Appellate Body (1998), WT/DS58/R, paras. 153–154.

[70] See, eg, J. Trachman, 'The Domain of WTO Dispute Resolution' (1999) 40 *Harvard International Law Journal* , 342 and M. Masushita, 'Governance of International Trade under World Trade Organisation Agreements and Other Agreements' (2004) 38 *Journal of World Trade*, 185.

apply only the rules set out in the WTO covered agreements as interpreted in accordance with customary international rules on treaty interpretation.[71] This view is based on a reading of the WTO's Dispute Settlement Understanding, which expressly authorises the Dispute Settlement Body to have recourse to customary international legal rules of treaty interpretation in the interpretation of the WTO covered agreements, whilst restraining that body from altering the obligations of the Members. In the present GMO dispute, it has been argued that the interpretation of the relevant WTO agreements should be consistent with the provisions of the Biosafety Protocol, including its provisions on risk assessment and the right to take precautionary measures—as well as taking into account the recognition of the potential risks of GMOs for human health and the environment in the standard-setting body, Codex Alimentarius. Reliance is placed on Aricle 8(g) of the Biodiversity Convention, with the argument that GM products require their own distinctive authorisation procedure and are objectively different from (i.e. not 'like') non-GM products. Inspiration may be drawn from the Appellate Body's own words in the 1998 Shrimp–Turtle case, referring to the need to take into account the 'contemporary concerns of the community of nations about the protection and conservation of the environment'.

A further question, as yet unposed directly in WTO case law, is the possibility of direct conflict between WTO agreements and external obligations of the parties, under the Biosafety Protocol, for example.[72] We have seen that the language of the Protocol is that of mutual support and accommodation with trade rules, but without subordinating the Protocol to these rules, reflecting the approach of other multilateral environmental agreements with trade-related environmental mechanisms and the 'mutually supportive' language of the Rio Declaration (Principle 12). Given the latitude for national implementation found in the Biosafety Protocol, it is highly unlikely that a direct conflict between obligations will arise—i.e. that compliance with the Biosafety Protocol necessarily implies non-compliance with WTO obligations. What is far more likely is differences in approach to the application of the precautionary principle and the exercise of national decision-making under the Protocol as compared with the covered agreements will be the subject of dispute, illustrated in part by

[71] Based on the wording of Art 3(2) of the DSU which refers to the 'customary rules of interpretation of public international law' which 'call for an examination of the ordinary meaning of the words of a treaty, read in their context, and in the light of the object and purpose of the treaty involved'. This is essentially the text embedded in Art 31(1) of the 1969 Vienna Convention on the Law of Treaties and which is widely regarded as reflecting customary international law.

[72] See, generally, J. Pauwelyn, *Conflict of Norms in Public International Law: How WTO Law Relates to other Rules of International Law* (Cambridge, 2003).

the current GMO case before the WTO. These matters are likely to continue to be played out pursuant to the compulsory dispute settlement procedures of the WTO in the absence of such compulsory procedures in multilateral environmental agreements like the Biosafety Protocol employing trade-related mechanisms.

A further interpretative question which goes beyond the trade context is the influence of the CBD and the Biosafety Protocol on interpretation in domestic implementation and enforcement. It will be recalled that the Biodiversity Convention takes the approach of ecosystem protection and that its preamble recognises the 'intrinsic value of biological diversity' as well as 'the ecological, genetic, social, economic, scientific, educational, cultural, recreational and aesthetic values of biological diversity and its components'. As Bosselman has observed, '[t]his is recognition of the distinction between (ecocentric) intrinsic values and (anthropocentric) instrument values of the environment'.[73] He suggests that with the emphasis on domestic implementation in the CBD and the Biosafety Protocol, there is a risk of a gap arising between the ecocentrism of the treaty instrument—in particular the CBD—and the more robust anthropocentrism evidenced in implementing measures under domestic law. Such gap might be bridged through, inter alia, a radical view of the polluter pays and precautionary principles.[74] The latter in particular is a key implementation principle under the Biosafety Protocol, and as such will derive buttressing support from the CBD. It provides a link to the wider concept of sustainable development.

IX. CONCLUSION

Thirteen years after the conclusion of the CBD, the ambitious prognosis in Agenda 21 of the benefits for sustainable development of biotechnology has yet fully to materialise.[75] Even where the benefits of biotechnology appear clear and unequivocal in their contribution to human health and thus, indirectly, to sustainable development and poverty alleviation, the choices are far from straightforward. An example drawn from the IUCN's 2004 Report[76] makes the point, and serves to highlight the particular

[73] K. Bosselmann, 'Human Rights and the Environment: Redefining Fundamental Principles?', University of Melbourne Environmental Justice Papers, available at www.arbld.unimelb.edu.au/envjust/papers/allpapers/bosselmann/home.htm.

[74] E.g. shifting burden of proof under the latter to the applicant: *ibid.* For discussion of the precautionary principle, see Birnie and Boyle, *supra* n. 6.

[75] In 2001 the CSD Secretary-General observed that, while the biotechnology industry had developed and become increasingly economically important in developed states, the benefits foreseen for sustainable development had not yet materialised: *supra* n. 4, at 2 para. 27.

[76] *Ibid.*, 24–25.

difficulty in reconciling intra- and inter-generational equity at the core of sustainable development:

> The single most important cause of blindness among children in developing countries is vitamin-A deficiency. This can be solved through planting rice genetically-modified to contain the required vitamins but at the cost of homogenising diet and placing reliance on a single crop. This is the short-term, 'quick' fix strategy, of immediate benefit for the present generation. A longer-term strategy is one of diversifying diet, a cheaper option that in the longer-term achieves more diverse human health benefits.

Amongst other things, the challenge remains to find the means to develop biotechnology-based public goods while maintaining incentives for private/commercial biotechnology innovation.[77] A continuing tension remains, with the breadth of opinion on LMOs ranging from a belief that they are inherently dangerous to a belief that they are the best hope for continued human survival.[78] These are the contrasting views which the Cartagena Protocol seeks to accommodate, though with 'belief' replaced by the sound science approach. The dilemma is neatly summarised in a recent CBD Report on biosafety and the environment which observes that 'future generations are likely to look back to our time and either thank us or curse us for what we do—or don't do—about GMOs and biosafety'.[79] Seeking to balancing the benefits against the risks is the principle contribution of the Cartagena Protocol where transboundary movement of LMOs is contemplated.

[77] *Ibid.*, 6 para. 30.

[78] IUCN, GMOs and Biosafety, *supra* n. 3, at 34.

[79] CBD/UNEP, *Biosafety and the Environment: An introduction to the Cartagena Protocol on Biosafety*, June 2003, at 14.

4

Bioprospecting on the Deep Seabed: a Legal Gap Requiring to be Filled *

TULLIO SCOVAZZI **

I. THERMOPHILES, HYPERTHERMOPHILES AND EXTREMOPHILES

ONLY TODAY DO we discover that the remote environment of the deep seabed supports forms of life that present unique genetic characteristics. In 1977 it was found that some animal communities live in the complete absence of sunlight on the seabed where warm water springs from tectonically active areas (so-called hydrothermal vents). Several species of micro-organisms, fish, crustaceans, polychaetes, echinoderms, coelenterates and molluscs have been found in hydrothermal vent areas. Many of them were new to science. These communities, which do not depend on plant photosynthesis for their survival, rely on specially adapted micro-organisms able to synthesise organic compounds from the hydrothermal fluid of the vents (chemosyntesis).[1]

The ability of some deep seabed organisms to survive very high temperatures (thermophiles and hyperthermophiles) and other extreme conditions (extremophiles) makes them of great interest to science and industry.[2] The possibility of using the genetic material[3] that makes

* This chapter includes, with some adjustments, parts of the report 'Some Considerations on Future Directions for the International Sea-Bed Authority', presented at the Conference for the Tenth Anniversary of the International Sea-Bed Authority (Kingston, Jamaica 25–26 May 2004).

** Professor of International Law, Faculty of Law, University of Milano-Bicocca, Milan, Italy.

1 The discovery of hydrothermal vent ecosystems has given rise to a new theory of how life originated on earth. It could have originated and evolved in association with hydrothermal vents in the primeval ocean during the early Archaean period (about 4,000 million years ago).

2 See Leary, *Bioprospecting and the Genetic Resources of Hydrothermal Vents on the High Seas – What Is the Existing Legal Position, Where Are We Heading and What Are Our Options*, Paper presented at the Workshop 'Bioprospecting in the High Seas' (Dunedin, 2003), 6.

3 As we know today, genes are the principal units of heredity: 'with genetic engineering techniques, a gene for a particular trait from one organism can be directly inserted into another, even if the two organisms are not from the same species': Glowka, Burhenne-Guilmin and Synge, *A Guide to the Convention on Biological Diversity* (Gland, 1994) 19.

hydrothermal vents species able to survive in extreme conditions opens new horizons in the field of genetic engineering and offers prospects of promising industrial and commercial implications.[4] It is reported that some biotechnology companies are currently actively involved in collaborating with public research institutions with a view to product development from derivatives of thermophiles and hyperthermophiles found around hydrothermal vents.[5]

But what is the present international regime of bioprospecting for the genetic resources found in the seabed beyond the limits of national jurisdiction, the so-called 'Area',[6] as defined by the United Nations Convention on the Law of the Sea (Montego Bay, 1982)?[7] Any tentative answer to the question has to address a number of thorny legal problems relating to both UNCLOS and the Convention on Biological Diversity (Rio de Janeiro, 5 June 1992).[8]

II. THE NOTION OF BIOPROSPECTING

The first problem to be faced is to determine what bioprospecting is and what the difference is between it and other kinds of activities. UNCLOS does not specifically address either marine genetic resources[9] or 'bioprospecting'. In a study on the relationship between the CBD the UNCLOS with regard to the conservation and sustainable use of genetic resources on the deep seabed, prepared in 2003 by the CBD Subsidiary Body on Scientific, Technical and Technological Advice (SBSTTA), bioprospecting is considered 'the exploration of biodiversity for commercially valuable genetic and biochemical resources' or 'the process of gathering information from the biosphere on the molecular composition of genetic resources for the development of new commercial products'.[10]

[4] 'Due to the species' robust nature (e.g. their enzymes can be exposed to harsh conditions and high temperature), extremophiles are being used in a number of industrial processes, ranging from liposomes for drug delivery and cosmetics, waste treatment, molecular biology, and food and agricultural processes. It appears that the commercial use of naturally occurring extremophiles is likely to increase in the near future': Report of the UN Secretary-General on Oceans and Law of the Sea, Advance unedited document of 4 Mar 2004, para. 248.

[5] Leary, *supra* n 2, 7.

[6] Hydrothermal vents may be found both in the Area and on the seabed falling within the limits of national jurisdiction (according to the definition of continental shelf given by Art 76 of UNCLOS).

[7] Hereinafter: UNCLOS.

[8] Hereinafter: the CBD.

[9] It has been remarked, as the 'deepest of ironies' that 'genetic resources may be the Area's most immediately exploitable and lucrative resource, yet they are not referred to in the convention': (Glowka, 'The Deepest of Ironies: Genetic Resources, Marine Scientific Research, and the Area' [1996] *Ocean Yearbook* 156).

[10] Doc. UNEP/CBD/SBSTTA/8/INF/3/Rev. 1 of 22 Feb 2003, para. 49. The study was prepared in response to decision II/10 taken in 1995 by the Conference of the Parties to the CBD.

Once the notion of bioprospecting is clarified, it may be asked what is the relationship between this kind of activity and other activities, which are carried out in the seas and are regulated by UNCLOS.

III. BIOPROSPECTING AND FISHING

Both fishing and bioprospecting presuppose the taking of living resources from the sea. However, what are important for fishermen are the whole bodies of the exploited resources or tangible parts of them (for example, the fin of a shark), to harvest for consumption. In most cases, fishing activities exploit large quantities of given living resources to produce the maximum yield from the target species.

The purpose of those who look for genetic material is different. Here the bodies of the species are considered receptacles of their genes. It is important to reach the functional units of heredity to determine whether and how they can be used or stored for future use. For this kind of non-consumptive and almost 'intangible' activity there is normally no need of large quantities of living resources, as quality and difference are much more significant for laboratory research than quantity and similarity. Unlike in the case of fisheries, the added value of the work on genetic material is tremendous and issues of patents and protection of intellectual property are likely to arise. While the search for, and collection of, organisms for genetic purposes may also cause a risk to the preservation of biodiversity in the deep seabed, it would be illogical to apply the rules of UNCLOS relating to fishing and conservation and management of the living resources of the high seas (Articles 116–120) to activities directed at the genetic material of the sea.

Nor is it fully convincing to consider the deep seabed organisms as 'sedentary species', as they are defined in Article 77(4) of UNCLOS ('organisms which, at the harvestable stage, either are immobile on or under the sea or are unable to move except in constant physical contact with the sea-bed or its subsoil'). Yet elements of analogy can be drawn between the regime of sedentary species of the continental shelf, which fall under the sovereign rights of the coastal state, and a future regime of the living organisms found on the Area.[11] But the notion of sedentary species, which has its own historical background,[12] is linked to the traditional

[11] The elements of analogy are developed, together with many other considerations, in a study submitted in 2004 to the Legal and Technical Commission of the International Sea-Bed Authority: Armas Pfirter, *Legal Implications Related to the Management of Seabed Living Resources in "the Area" under UNCLOS*, unpublished paper.

[12] The first precedent seems to be the regulation adopted on 9 Mar 1811 by Great Britain for the protection of His Majesty's pearl banks in Ceylon beyond the 3-mile limit of the territorial sea.

purpose of fishing for consumption and has little in common with the new and more sophisticated challenges posed by bioprospecting.[13]

IV. BIOPROSPECTING AND SCIENTIFIC RESEARCH

It is much more difficult to make a distinction between bioprospecting and marine scientific research, an activity regulated in detail, but not defined, by UNCLOS (Part XIII).

Today, because of the physical characteristics of the deep seabed and the high financial cost of exploration activities, 'very few States, including multinationals from those States, have the technical, financial and human resources to access and exploit deep marine areas'.[14] It appears that in the Area 'no single nation has the financial, technological and intellectual capacity to undertake a global programme of scientific research of the magnitude that is required'.[15] The studies which are presently being carried out 'are all essentially sectoral studies and there is no global oversight mechanism in terms of determining priorities, mobilizing the necessary political and financial commitments and sharing the benefits of such work'.[16]

As regards the notion of marine scientific research, in a widespread opinion, reflected also in the above mentioned study by SBSTTA, is based on the following assumption

> marine scientific research activities are characterized by their transparency and openness, the obligation to disseminate information and data obtained therefrom, as well as the subsequent publication of results of the research. Marine scientific research has, therefore, to be distinguished from other investigative marine activities with any kind of commercial component, such as prospecting, exploration, or fish stock assessment, which may involve confidentiality or proprietary rights. Under the United Nations Convention on the Law of the Sea, marine scientific research is primarily aimed at furthering mankind's knowledge of the marine environment, its resources and various phenomena, and is not a vehicle for searching for natural resources for commercial purpose.[17]

In other words:

> in the absence of a formal definition, marine scientific research could be defined as an activity that involves collection and analysis of information, data or

[13] It also seems uncertain whether all of the deep seabed organisms qualify for the definition of sedentary species provided by Art 77(4) of UNCLOS.

[14] Para. 1 of the doc. quoted *supra* n 10.

[15] Lodge, *Improving International Governance in the Deep Sea*, Paper presented at 'Deep Sea 2003', (Queenstown, 2003) 4.

[16] *Ibid.*

[17] Para. 39 of the study quoted *supra* n 10.

> samples aimed at increasing mankind's knowledge of the environment, and is not undertaken with the intent of economic gain. Since the object is the enhancement of knowledge, marine scientific research is characterized by openness, dissemination of data, exchange of samples, as well as publication and dissemination of research results as provided for in Part XIII.[18]

The beginning of the second passage quoted above conceals a terminological, if not logical, contradiction: if there is an 'absence of a formal definition' in UNCLOS, how can marine scientific research 'be defined' under UNCLOS? In reality, what is proposed in the SBSTTA's study is not a definition, but an interpretation of the notion of marine scientific research used in UNCLOS. This interpretation is based on the assumption of the absence of the intention of economic gain. But other interpretations may be proposed as well, considering that nowhere in UNCLOS is the condition of the absence of the intention of economic gain evoked.[19]

The widespread opinion about the UNCLOS notion of marine scientific research leaves some room for doubt. It is true that the place where UNCLOS gets closest to a notion of marine scientific research is Article 243, where 'the efforts of scientists in studying the essence of phenomena and processes occurring in the marine environment and the interrelations between them' are mentioned. But it is also true that Article 246, which applies to the exclusive economic zone and the continental shelf, makes a clear distinction between two kinds of marine scientific research projects, namely those carried out 'to increase scientific knowledge of the marine environment for the benefit of all mankind' (Paragraph 3) and those 'of direct significance for the exploration and exploitation of natural resources, whether living or non-living' (Paragraph 5(a)). This distinction provides some credibility to the opinion that, under the UNCLOS regime, research directly related to the purpose of commercial exploitation of resources also falls under the general label of 'marine scientific research'. Without trying to give any definite answer to such a difficult question here, it is sufficient to say that some doubt may exist about the content of an implicit UNCLOS notion of marine scientific research. It would follow that any kind of marine scientific research in the Area, including what is called bioprospecting, might fall under the general obligation to ensure the benefit of mankind as a whole, as required by Article 143(1).

18 *Ibid.*, para. 47.

19 Under Art 31(1) of the Vienna Convention on the Law of Treaties, a treaty 'shall be interpreted in good faith in accordance with the ordinary meaning to be given to the terms of the treaty in their context and in the light of its object and purpose'. This textual and teleological method excludes any interpretation based on the implied intention of some among the participants in a negotiation.

This provision, included in Part XI (the Area) of UNCLOS, needs further consideration. It sets out the general principle that 'marine scientific research in the Area shall be carried out exclusively for peaceful purposes and for the benefit of the mankind as a whole, in accordance with Part XIII' (Marine Scientific Research).[20] Article 143, far from being restricted to research on mineral resources, refers to any kind of marine scientific research.

The second paragraph of Article 143 provides that the International Sea-Bed Authority,[21] besides carrying out marine scientific research concerning the Area and its resources, shall promote and encourage the conduct of research and co-ordinate and disseminate the results and analysis when available.[22] Paragraph (3) of Article 143 grants to states the right to carry out scientific research in the Area and binds them to promote international co-operation in this field by:

(a) participating in international programmes and encouraging co-operation in marine scientific research by personnel of different countries and of the Authority;
(b) ensuring that programmes are developed through the Authority or other international organizations as appropriate for the benefit of developing States and technologically less developed States with a view to:
  (i) strengthening their research capabilities;
  (ii) training their personnel and the personnel of the Authority in the techniques and applications of research;
  (iii) fostering the employment of their qualified personnel in research in the Area;
(c) effectively disseminating the results of research and analysis when available, through the Authority or other international channels when appropriate.

Also this provision, far from being restricted to research on mineral resources, refers to any kind of marine scientific research in the Area.

[20] To tell the truth, UNCLOS is rather ambiguous. Art 256, which belongs to Part XIII, provides that marine scientific research shall be conducted 'in conformity with the provisions of Part XI'. Art 143, which belongs to Part XI, provides that marine scientific research shall be carried out 'in accordance with Part XIII'. If there is a conflict, which Part of the UNCLOS prevails?

[21] Hereinafter: the ISBA.

[22] The provision deals with the carrying out of 'marine scientific research concerning the Area and its resources' and, due to the narrow definition of 'resources' given by Art 133 ('all solid, liquid or gaseous mineral resources *in-situ* in the Area at or beneath the sea-bed, including polymetallic nodules'), could be interpreted as limited to mineral resources. But the provision can also be read as relating to research concerning either the Area in general or its specific mineral resources.

Yet Article 143 contradicts the easy assumption that there is an absolute freedom to carry out scientific research in the Area. In this respect, the traditional concept of freedom of the sea (a sort of 'first-come-first-served' rule) and the very innovative idea of common heritage of mankind[23] need to be harmonised in the light of the objective that marine scientific research in the Area shall be carried out for the benefit of mankind as a whole. The legal condition of the space, that is the fact that the Area is the common heritage of mankind, has an effect in granting to the ISBA a number of broad competences relating to the field of scientific research to be conducted in the Area. These competences have a cooperative, and not exclusive, character.[24]

What are particularly difficult to accept are the consequences of the widespread opinion that any intention of economic gain automatically changes the nature of a marine scientific research activity under the UNCLOS regime. It would follow that, whenever there are prospects of profit, the regime of freedom of the sea (that is the 'first-come-first-served' rule) would immediately apply to the exclusive benefit of the very few entities which have the financial and technological capacity to reach the deep seabed. Would this be, in the case of bioprospecting, 'the just and equitable international economic order which takes into account the interests and needs of mankind as a whole and, in particular the special interests and needs of developing countries', as set out in the preamble to UNCLOS? The question deserves at least some discussion.

But there is something even stranger, if it is taken for granted that any intention of economic gain automatically changes the nature of a marine scientific research activity under the UNCLOS regime. If this were the case, the role of the ISBA and states would be to cooperate in the carrying out of scientific research for the benefit of mankind as a whole, as provided for in Article 143(1) and then, of course, to disseminate information, provide the data obtained and publish the results of the research, in a spirit of full transparency and openness. At this point, the very few entities which have the financial and technological capacity to reach the deep seabed could come into play and freely start their bioprospecting activities taking advantage of the scientific knowledge gathered by others and, if their activities were successful, getting the relevant commercial profits.

[23] 'The Area and its resources are the common heritage of mankind': Art 136 of UNCLOS.

[24] As stated in the Report of the Secretary-General of the ISBA for the year 2003, 'the Authority will not only benefit from close collaboration with those who are already conducting scientific research on hydrothermal vents, but also has the potential to provide a central clearing house for exchange of information about research activities on hydrothermal vents sites and at the same time a forum for the discussion and development of principles for the better implementation of the existing legal regime for marine scientific research in the Area and the management of biodiversity in the Area': Doc. ISBA/9/A/3 of 4 June 2003, para. 63.

Would this be precisely what is intended by the expression 'benefit of mankind as whole' used in Article 143(1) of UNCLOS? Again, the question deserves at least some discussion.

V. BIOPROSPECTING AND PROTECTION OF THE MARINE ENVIRONMENT

Several provisions of UNCLOS show that the ISBA has an important role to play in relation to the protection of the marine environment in the Area.

Under Article 145, the ISBA is to adopt appropriate rules, regulations and procedures for *inter alia*:

(a) the prevention, reduction and control of pollution and other hazards to the marine environment including the coastline, and of interference with the ecological balance of the marine environment, particular attention being paid to the need for protection from harmful effects of such activities as drilling, dredging, excavation, disposal of waste, construction and operation or maintenance of installations, pipelines and other devices related to such activities;

(b) the protection and conservation of the natural resources of the Area and the prevention of damage to the flora and fauna of the marine environment.

The regulatory powers granted to the ISBA are not limited to the harmful effects of those deep seabed mining activities, which belong to the typical field of competence of this organisation. On the contrary, such powers are enlarged to encompass the protection and conservation of every kind of natural resource and all the fauna and flora which can be found in the Area.

Other provisions of UNCLOS[25] and the 1994 Agreement Relating to the Implementation of Part XI[26] confirm the competence of ISBA in the field of the protection of the marine environment. Several of the provisions included in the Regulations on Prospecting and Exploration for Polymetallic Nodules in the Area (the so-called Mining Code), approved on 13 July 2000 by the ISBA Assembly,[27] relate to the protection of the marine environment.

On 4 July 2001 the Legal and Technical Commission approved the Recommendations for the Guidance of Contractors for the Assessment of Possible Environmental Impacts Arising from Exploration for Polymetallic

[25] See Art 165(2)(e) Annex III, Art 17(1)(b)(xii).
[26] See Annex, Sect. 1, para. 5(g) Annex, Sect. 1, para. 7.
[27] Doc. ISBA/6/A/18 of 4 Oct 2000.

Nodules in the Area.[28] The Recommendations, inter alia, specify what kind of data the contractor should gather on natural conditions before exploration begins (so-called baseline data), what information should be provided by the contractor to the ISBA and what observations and measurements should be made by the contractor while performing a specific activity and after its performance.

At the 2002 meeting of the ISBA, delegates attended a seminar during which marine geologists and biologists presented the latest findings about polymetallic sulphides and cobalt-rich crusts and their environment. A biologist, Professor Juniper, told of the unique characteristics of the fauna living exclusively in the sulphur-rich waters around underwater hot springs and of the risks to which it could be exposed:

> More than 500 new animal species have been described from deep-sea hydrothermal vents since their discovery in 1977. Deep-sea vents have a high scientific value because they contain a large number of endemic and unusual species and are refuges for close relatives of ancient forms of life. Because they are visually spectacular, extreme environments, vent ecosystems have generated widespread public interest and are a resource, which can be used to inform the public about earth processes and the way in which scientists work. It is not currently possible to predict how rapidly vent sites may recover from mining operations. Some organisms will be directly killed by mining machinery, while others nearby risk smothering by material settling from plumes of particulate matter. Individuals surviving these perturbations would be subject to a radical change in habitat, and the exploited sites will have a lesser scientific and educational value. Long-lived vent fields that host the largest mineral deposits are likely to be the most ecologically stable and have the highest biodiversity. A concentration of mining activities at such sites could produce regional effects on biological processes and organisms abundance, to the point where the survival of some species could become an issue.[29]

Besides mining, threats to seabed ecosystems may derive from a number of activities, such as oil and gas exploitation, geothermal exploitation, tourism[30] and, of course, bioprospecting and marine scientific research:

> Impacts arising from scientific studies include direct impacts leading to habitat loss and organism mortality. Research activities with a negative impact on ecosystems include: the removal of chimneys and rocks for geological investigations or chemical sampling; environmental manipulation, such as drilling, which can change fluid flow pathways and shut off the supply of fluids to

[28] Doc. ISBA/7/LTC/1/Rev.1 of 10 July 2001. See also ISBA, *Deep-Seabed Polymetallic Nodule Exploration: Development of Environmental Guidelines* (Kingston, 1999).

[29] Doc. ISBA/8/A/1 of 9 May 2002, para. 19.

[30] See Korn, Friedrich and Feit, *Deep Sea Genetic Resources in the Context of the Convention on Biological Diversity and the United Nations Convention on the Law of the Sea* (Bonn, 2003), 19.

> colonies of vent organisms; the clearing of fauna, e.g. for experimental studies on recolonisation or the collecting of fauna for biodiversity or population studies; the transplanting of fauna between locations; the placement of instruments that may disturb fauna and change water flows; the deleterious effects of light on photosensitive organisms used for observation purposes; the use of manned submersible and remotely operated vehicles can damage fauna by landing on them or causing damage by the use of thrusters. These activities can cause biological effects including a decrease in population numbers; local, regional or global extinction of species; a change in community structure; the introduction of exotic species carried by underwater vehicles from another site.[31]

The unique characters of some seabed ecosystems, such as hydrothermal vents, cold water seeps, seamounts and deep water coral reefs, call for the application of Article 194(5) of UNCLOS, according to which the measures taken to protect and preserve the marine environment 'shall include those necessary to protect and preserve rare or fragile ecosystems as well as the habitat of depleted, threatened or endangered species and other forms of marine life'.[32] This obligation has a general scope of application and covers any kind of vulnerable marine ecosystems and species, wherever they are located, including the bed of the high seas.

Due to its competences, the ISBA would be in the best position to participate in the establishment of a system of marine protected areas in the seabed beyond the limits of national jurisdiction. Under Article 162(2)(x) of the UNCLOS the Council of the ISBA may disapprove areas for mining exploration in cases where substantial evidence indicates the risk of serious harm to the marine environment. The Mining Code provides that a contractor who applies for exploration rights shall propose areas to be set aside and used exclusively as impact reference zones and preservation reference zones (Regulation 31, paragraph 7).[33]

Again, the legal condition of the space had an effect in granting to the ISBA broad competences relating to the protection of the environment of the Area as a whole. The competences of the ISBA are not exclusive, as

[31] Report of the UN Secretary-General on Oceans and Law of the Sea, advance unedited document of 4 Mar 2004, para. 247.

[32] See Thiel and Koslow (eds.), *Managing Risks to Biodiversity and the Environment on the High Sea, Including Tools Such as Marine Protected Areas—Scientific Requirements and Legal Aspects* (Bonn, 2001), Gjerde and Breide (eds.), *Towards a Strategy for High Seas Marine Protected Areas* (Gland, 2003).

[33] A paper prepared by the IUCN (The World Conservation Union) to be submitted to the 2004 meeting of the UN Informal Consultative Process on Oceans and the Law of the Sea recommends that the UN General Assembly invites the ISBA 'to explore its role in identifying critical and sensitive deep seabed areas beyond national jurisdiction so that key sites are protected from minerals activities and potential operators are aware of them before they invest in minerals prospecting and exploration'. The Logatchev vent area, located on the mid-Atlantic ridge, has been proposed by the World Wide Life Fund for Nature (WWF) for designation as a protected area.

Article 209(2) also binds states to 'adopt laws and regulations to prevent, reduce and control pollution of the marine environment from activities in the Area undertaken by vessels, installations, structures and other devices flying their flag or of their registry or operating under they authority, as the case may be'. However, such national legislation shall be no less effective than 'international rules, regulations and procedures established in accordance with Part IX', that is the regime established by the ISBA. This means that the latter is granted a preferential role as regards the protection of the environment in the Area.

VI. BIOPROSPECTING AND CONSERVATION OF BIOLOGICAL DIVERSITY

As well as to UNCLOS, bioprospecting activities are also linked to the CBD. While not defining bioprospecting, the CBD refers to 'genetic material', defined as 'any material of plant, animal, microbial or other origin containing functional units of heredity', and to 'genetic resources', defined as 'genetic material of actual or potential value' (Article 2).

The CBD applies to components of biological diversity in areas within the limits of national jurisdiction of the Parties and to processes and activities carried out under the jurisdiction or control of a Contracting Party beyond the limits of national jurisdiction (Article 4(b). This includes bioprospecting activities carried out in the Area.

While some of the articles of the CBD presuppose a 'country of origin of genetic resources'[34] and consequently do not apply to areas beyond the limits of national jurisdiction, most of its provisions have a broad scope of application, which also covers the deep seabed.[35] The same can be said as regards the general objective of the CBD, namely:

> the conservation of biological diversity, the sustainable use of its components and the fair and equitable sharing of the benefits arising out of the utilization of genetic resources, including by appropriate access to genetic resources and by appropriate transfer of relevant technologies, taking into account all rights over these resources and to technologies, and by appropriate funding [Article 1][36].

34 'Country of origin of genetic resources means the country which possesses those genetic resources in *in-situ* conditions.': Art 2.

35 Including Art 8(a), which provides for the establishment of a system of protected areas where special measures need to be taken to conserve biological diversity.

36 Biological diversity is defined as 'the variability among living organisms from all sources including, *inter alia*, terrestrial, marine and other aquatic ecosystems and the ecological complexes of which they are part; this includes diversity within species, between species and of ecosystems'. Sustainable use of its components is 'the use of components of biological diversity in a way and at a rate that does not lead to the long-term decline of biological diversity, thereby maintaining its potential to meet the needs and aspirations of present and future generations': Art 2 of the CBD.

A few provisions of the CBD explicitly refer to areas beyond national jurisdiction. For example, under Article 3 states have 'the responsibility to ensure that activities within their jurisdiction or control do not cause damage to the environment . . . of areas beyond the limits of national jurisdiction'. Article 5 provides a general obligation of cooperation in the following terms:

> Each Contracting Party shall, as far as possible and as appropriate, cooperate with other Contracting Parties, directly or, where appropriate, through competent international organizations, in respect of areas beyond national jurisdiction and on other matters of mutual interest, for the conservation and sustainable use of biological diversity.[37]

The issue of the relationship between the CBD and other treaties (including, although not explicitly mentioning, UNCLOS) is addressed by Article 22 of the CBD:

> 1. The provisions of this Convention shall not affect the rights and obligations of any Contracting Party deriving from any existing international agreement, except where the exercise of those rights and obligations would cause a serious damage or threat to biological diversity.
> 2. Parties shall implement this Convention with respect to the marine environment consistently with the rights and obligations of States under the law of the sea.

A similar provision on the same issue can be found in UNCLOS (Article 237(2):

> Specific obligations assumed by States under special conventions, with respect to the protection and preservation of the marine environment, should be carried out in a manner consistent with the general principles and objectives of this Convention.

It does not seem that conflicts between the CBD and UNCLOS are likely to occur. As already remarked,[38] many provisions of UNCLOS aim at the protection of the marine environment and generally apply also to the conservation of marine biological diversity of the deep seabed. The CBD carefully avoids the expression 'common heritage of mankind' and, in the preamble, states that 'the conservation of biological diversity is a common

[37] To tell the truth, Art 5 does not say very much, being a mere invitation to cooperation. Note should be taken of the phrase 'as far as possible and as appropriate', immediately followed by another, 'where appropriate', which is a masterpiece of hortatory legal wording.

[38] *Supra* section V.

concern of humankind'.[39] But the CBD principle of 'the fair and equitable sharing of the benefits arising out of the utilization of genetic resources' goes in the same direction as the UNCLOS principle of common heritage of mankind.

VII. A GAP TO BE FILLED

While evident by themselves, some matters of fact need to be stressed.

First, there is an inextricable factual link between the protection of the deep seabed environment (including its biodiversity), marine scientific research and bioprospecting. The preservation of biological diversity and its components is a prerequisite for any future activity of marine scientific research or bioprospecting. A research endeavour organised with the intention to increase human knowledge may well result in the discovery of commercially valuable information.[40] It is impossible to establish a clear-cut distinction between one activity and the other and between one purpose and the other.

Secondly, at the time when the UNCLOS regime on marine scientific research was being drafted, very little was known about the genetic qualities of deep seabed organisms. For evident chronological reasons, the potential value of genetic resources was not considered by the UNCLOS negotiators. When they were discussing research of significance for natural resources, they had goods intended for consumption such fish, oil, polymetallic nodules and little else in mind. The lack of regulation for the search of the almost 'intangible' units of heredity of seabed organisms has arisen 'by accident rather than design'.[41] But today this kind of activity calls for a specific legal framework.

[39] 'The proposition that biological diversity should be considered as the common heritage of mankind was rejected at an early stage as inapplicable since most components of biological diversity are situated in areas under national jurisdiction': Burhenne-Guilmin-Casey-Lefkowitz, 'The Convention on Biological Diversity: A Hard Won Global Achievement', [1992] *Yearbook of International Environmental Law* 47). The expressions 'common heritage of mankind' and 'common concern of humankind' seem to be based on different assumptions. The former emphasises the profits to be shared, while the latter recalls the burdens that will be borne.

[40] 'While marine scientific research is primarily undertaken with a view to furthering knowledge of the evolutionary relationship between various organisms or of the adaptive mechanisms allowing organisms to thrive in an extreme environment with unique characteristics, some prospective activities are run to discover commercially useful information and resources for subsequent industrial, chemical, agricultural or medical purposes. However, what may have been, in the first place, an expedition with scientific purposes, where intent of economic gain was absent, may result in the genetic resources being transferred to industry for biotechnological applications. This is sometimes explicitly required under the terms of some public research grants, the primary source of funding in respect of deep seabed research': para. 101 of the SBSTTA study quoted *supra* n 10.

[41] This simple, but profound, remark has been made in doc. UNEP/CBD/SBSTTA/2/15 of 24 July 1996, *Bioprospecting of Genetic Resources of the Deep Sea-Bed*, para. 12.

Thirdly, while some general principles can be drawn from both UNCLOS and the CBD, the present gaps as regards a specific regime for the search for, and use of, seabed genetic materials need to be filled, in order to put this ever more important subject in an appropriate legal context. As remarked in a resolution approved in 1997 by the European Council of Environmental Law (ECEL):[42]

> The technical ability to conduct marine scientific research in the international area is in the hands of a limited number of actors in technologically advanced States. Some of these actors are already conducting research directed at the genetic resources in or on deep-sea vents. Some of them, having identified specific resources and their potential commercial value, have already taken out patents related to them. The trend in the applicable patent law is to ensure appropriation by patentees of all the benefits connected with the commercialization of patented substances deriving from genetic resources. This runs counter to the underlying principles of the UNCLOS and the spirit of the CBD, which aim at establishing an international legal order which will be just and equitable and enable utilization and conservation of marine living resources on a sustainable basis for the benefit of present and future generations.[43]

According to the 2004 report by the United Nations Secretary-General on oceans and law of the sea:

> as legitimate as the protection of private data and proprietary interests through intellectual property rights may be, a balance needs to be struck between private benefits and benefits to humankind as a whole through the advancement of scientific knowledge.[44]

Sooner or later the gaps left by UNCLOS and the CBD will be filled. Also in this field, it is likely that the abstract application of the principle of freedom of the sea (that is the 'first come, first served' rule[45]) would lead to hardly acceptable consequences and new cooperative schemes

[42] The ECEL is a non-governmental association based in Funchal, Portugal, and chaired by Alexandre Charles Kiss.

[43] Para. 4.1 of the resolution. 'There are at present no rules in force clearly to control and regulate the above developments. No single treaty provides for specific and precise obligations on States to control the activities of their nationals. Moreover, no State, so far as can be ascertained, has enacted national legislation for this purpose, nor, as yet, has any specific institution been designated as having responsibility for establishing even guiding principles': para. 4.2 of the resolution.

[44] Para. 260 of the 'advance, unedited document' issued on 4 Mar 2004.

[45] On the progressive erosion of the principle of freedom of the sea as an evolutionary (and very desirable) trend of present international law of the sea in the field of sustainable use of marine resources see Scovazzi, 'The Evolution of International Law of the Sea: New Issues, New Challenges', in (2000) 286 *Recueil des cours* 39.

have to be envisaged at the international level.[46] Since the final objective is to achieve a sustainable management of the deep ocean space as a whole, sectoral approaches are not likely to lead to coherent and cost-effective results. All the stakeholders should play a role in the game, including of course the ISBA, which is already entitled to exercise a broad range of preferential or cooperative responsibilities in the field of marine scientific research and protection of the environment. Once again, the legal condition of the Area, being the common heritage of mankind, may also have an effect on certain activities (though they are different from mining) which take place in that space.

This does not mean that the ISBA is to become the overarching regulatory body in the field of bioprospecting. Nor does it mean that the merits acquired by public and private entities, which have made consistent investments and developed a sophisticated technological capacity in the field of bioprospecting will be neglected. It simply means that the ISBA, the principles that it represents, as well as its already existing competences and cooperative role, need to be taken into consideration when the states and the other relevant entities decide to fill the legal gap in the regime of deep seabed genetic resources.

For the time being, in the light of its already existing responsibilities, nothing prevents the ISBA from playing a cooperative role consistent with the general principles it represents. It would be unacceptable if those involved in mining were subject, as they are, to the ISBA's regulatory powers to ensure protection of seabed biodiversity, while those involved in other activities could escape any measures. As recently pointed out by the ISBA's Secretary-General:

> it is practically impossible to distinguish between marine scientific research, including bioprospecting, and prospecting for minerals, since both may encompass the identification of biological diversity and its components. There seems little point, therefore, in trying to develop more precise definitions or in trying to create a new definition for 'bioprospecting' or 'genetic resources'. As far as environmental protection is concerned, it follows that one set of rules, protocols or practices must apply to all types of research activities. In this respect, I should mention that ISA is equipped to and could elaborate a code of conduct for marine scientific research and prospecting in the deep seabed, to include steps to protect the marine environment and its biodiversity. Such a code could well be based on the sort of voluntary code that is presently being applied by researchers.[47]

[46] In any case, the freedom of the high seas, too, far from being an absolute entitlement, has to be exercised with due regard for the rights under UNCLOS with respect to activities in the Area: Art 87(2).

[47] Nandan, *The International Seabed Authority and the Governance of High Seas Biodiversity*, Paper presented at the Workshop 'Governance of High Seas Biodiversity' (Cairns, 2003), 3.

VIII. FUTURE PROSPECTS

The 2004 report by the United Nations Secretary-General on oceans and law of the sea suggests that the legal lacuna as regards commercially-oriented research on the biological resources of the deep seabed 'should be filled in order to conserve these biological resources and provide for their sustainable use.'[48] The UN General Assembly; in Resolution 58/240 adopted on 23 December 2003, invited:

> the relevant global and regional bodies, in accordance with their mandates, to investigate urgently how to better address, on a scientific basis, including the application of precaution, the threats and risks to vulnerable and threatened marine ecosystems and biodiversity in areas beyond national jurisdiction; how existing treaties and other relevant instruments can be used in this process consistent with international law, in particular with the Convention, and with the principles of an integrated ecosystem-based approach to management, including the identification of those marine ecosystem types that warrant priority attention; and to explore a range of potential approaches and tools for their protection and management.

As regards the particular question of conservation and sustainable use of genetic resources on the deep seabed, the already mentioned study prepared in 2003 by the SBSTTA suggests three available options, namely

> (a) Maintaining the status quo;
> (b) Application of the regime under Part XI of the United Nations Convention on the Law of the Sea, currently limited to the management of mineral resources;
> (c) Application of the regime of conservation and sustainable use of genetic resources under the Convention on Biological Diversity.[49]

The study points out that the last two options are not mutually exclusive and could be integrated. It also adds that any enlargement of the mandate of the ISBA to cover marine genetic resources would require amending UNCLOS, under the procedure set out in Article 312.[50] The advantages of making use of the ISBA are summarised as follows:

[48] Report of the UN Secretary-General on Oceans and Law of the Sea, advance unedited document of 4 Mar 2004, para. 267.

[49] Para. 128 of the doc. quoted *supra* n 10.

[50] 'However, the same end might be achieved by adopting a protocol or an implementing agreement to add management of the biological resources of the Area to the mandate of the International Seabed Authority. A possible alternative could be for a meeting of the States Parties to adopt an "agreed interpretation" of the Convention stating that "resources" shall be read as including biological resources, with all the necessary consequential amendments': *ibid.*, para. 123.

Making use of the International Seabed Authority would be advantageous in two respects. The institution is already operational and has already a mandate relating to the protection and preservation of the Area's marine environment. Moreover, enlarging the institution's scope to include genetic resources would allow an integrated management of the Area, as called for under the Jakarta Mandate in respect of marine and coastal biodiversity. The institution may be granted responsibility to manage deep seabed genetic resources through modalities defined by the Parties to the Convention on Biological Diversity and the United Nations Convention on the law of the Sea, such as marine protected areas, or a licensing system for extraction and exploitation. It could also monitor activities undertaken, and act as a clearing-house for international cooperation in deep seabed scientific research through dissemination of data and research results. The mechanisms of operation and the principles according to which it is to operate would need to be clearly defined in order to accommodate all Parties to the Convention on Biological Diversity and the United Nations Convention on the law of the Sea, some of which may be Parties to one but not to the other.[51]

For the time being it is doubtful whether all states would be able to accept a proposal for such an expanded ISBA mandate. This is confirmed by the variety of views expressed on this subject at the 2004 Meeting of the United Nations Open-ended Informal Consultative Process on Oceans and the Law of the Sea (UNICPOLOS).[52] But this does not detract from the fact that the ISBA, which can rely on the very innovative ideal background of the principle of common heritage of mankind, can also call into play preferential or cooperative responsibilities in new kinds of activities taking place on the deep seabed.

The United Nations General Assembly has taken a prudent approach. By Resolution 59/24 of 4 December 2004 it decided 'to establish an Ad Hoc Open-ended informal Working Group to study issues relating to the conservation and sustainable use of marine biological diversity beyond areas of national jurisdiction'. The Working Group will convene in February 2006.

51 *Ibid.*, para. 122.

52 UN, *Report on the Work of the United Nations Open-ended Informal Consultative Process on Oceans and the Law of the Sea at its Fifth Meeting*, doc. A/59/122 of 1 July 2004, paras 90–94.

5

Biotechnology and Marine Biogenetic Resources: The Interplay between UNCLOS and the CBD

GIUSEPPE CATALDI*

I. INTRODUCTION

AN EXAMINATION OF the interplay between the United Nations Convention on the Law of the Sea (UNCLOS)[1] and the Convention on Biological Diversity (CBD)[2] is not an easy task. It has already been noted that even though both the conventions take an 'anthropocentric approach', their aims differ significantly and this difference is especially acute in respect of the provisions concerning living resources. UNCLOS provisions relating to living resources are predominantly 'exploitation oriented', while the CBD focuses on protection of species and habitat.[3]

It seems erroneous simply to compare these two conventions without considering the fact that they belong to two different generations of agreements and that we should thus interpret UNCLOS, more than 20 years after its conclusion and more than ten years after its entry into force, from the perspective of the practice of its Contracting States and according to the treaties that have completed and implemented its provisions, namely, the 1995 Agreement on Straddling Fish Stocks and Highly Migratory Species.[4]

* Professor of International Law, University of Naples 'L'Orientale'. The author wishes to thank Gemma Andreone, researcher at the Institute for International Juridical Studies, National Research Council, for her suggestions and help.

1 UNCLOS opened for signature on 10 Dec 1982, entered into force on 29 Dec 1994, (1982) 21 ILM, 1261.

2 CBD opened for signature on 5 June 1992, entered into force on 29 Dec 1993, (1992) 31 ILM, 818.

3 See Wolfrum-Matz, 'The Interplay of the United Nations Convention on the Law of the Sea and the Convention on Biological Diversity', *Max Planck Yearbook of United Nations Law*, (2000) 445–480.

4 The agreement was signed in New York in Aug 1995 and entered into force on 11 Dec 2001 (1995) 34 ILM, 1547.

If we choose this wider perspective, the differences between the two systems and legal instruments will be much less dramatic than it appears to be at first glance.

I submit a first, highly significant, example. As stated in its Preamble, the application of CBD's provisions is based on the precautionary approach. It is well known that no reference to precaution can be found in UNCLOS because, at the time of its drafting, this principle had not yet emerged in the practice of states. In fact, Article 192 refers only to a general obligation of the states parties to the agreement to protect and preserve the marine environment. Furthermore, it is precisely the Law of the Sea that defines and develops the precautionary principle, particularly with reference to the conservation and management of living resources. In 1987 the London Declaration, adopted after the second Conference on the North Sea, affirmed in the Preamble that: 'a precautionary approach is necessary which may require action to control inputs of such substances even before a causal link has been established by absolutely clear scientific evidence'. Article XVI of the Declaration also states that the duty to adopt all measures to reduce pollution exists 'even where there is no scientific evidence to prove a causal link between emission and effects (the principle of precautionary action)'.[5] This principle is also the basis for all the resolutions adopted by the United Nations General Assembly on the use of driftnets, in particular the 1991 moratorium resolution 46–215. Finally, with the entry into force of the 1995 Agreement on Straddling Stocks (11 December 2001), which, as already stated, constitutes the application of UNCLOS provisions on the conservation and management of these stocks in the Exclusive Economic Zone (EEZ), the precautionary principle becomes a conventional norm and, as such, binding on all Member States.[6] No longer devoted simply to establishing quotas, the main characteristic of the new fisheries law is a greater commitment to conservation, a perspective that is very similar to the CBD emphasis on protecting stocks to ensure preservation of marine life in general.

Notwithstanding the fact that it is doubtful that the precautionary principle has acquired the status of customary law,[7] and taking this practice into account, can we seriously maintain that the need to apply UNCLOS provisions in a specific instance authorises states to ignore this principle,

[5] See Gündling, 'The Status in International Law of the Principle of Precautionary Action', [1990] *International Journal of Estuarine and Coastal Law: special issue: The North Sea* 23.

[6] See Andreone, 'Le principe de précaution en matière de pêche après l'Accord sur les stocks chevauchants', in R. Casado Raigon (ed.), *Europe et la Mer, II Colloquium of the International Association for the Law of the Sea*, (Brussels, 2005) 87 ff.

[7] Cataldi, 'Il principio precauzionale e la protezione dell'ambiente marino', in A. Del Vecchio and A. Dal Ri Jr (eds.), *Il diritto internazionale dell'ambiente dopo il vertice di Johannesburg* (Naples, 2005) 81 ff.

already contemplated by the CBD? I believe that the answer is 'No'. The precautionary approach must be adopted in implementing the most important features shared by both systems. These are: first, the principle of the sovereign right of states to exploit their own resources; secondly, the responsibility of states to ensure that activities within their jurisdiction and control are not detrimental to the environment of other states or of areas beyond national jurisdiction; and thirdly, the principle of co-operation.

Another aspect which, in my view, cannot be over-emphasised is the general relationship between the CBD and UNCLOS regarding the law of treaties, as expressed both by customary law and by the Vienna Convention on the Law of Treaties. It has been correctly noted that Article 30 of the Vienna Convention does not provide much help in this case as it deals with overlapping treaties on the same matter, whereas the scope and primary aims of the two agreements are quite different.[8] More appropriate to this case is the general rule on interpretation provided by Article 31, which calls for the application 'in good faith in accordance with the ordinary meaning to be given to the terms of the treaty in their context and in the light of its object and purpose'. The first effect that can be deduced is the need for harmonization, to the greatest possible extent, of the two systems. This goal should be pursued primarily through the implementation of these agreements, through the national legislation of the states parties to both the CBD and UNCLOS. In my opinion, this is the best solution to the problem of the interplay between the two conventions. The new concept of 'ocean governance' may be of assistance in this case.

The positive effects of harmonisation may be attained through the competences granted to international organisations by both conventions. Obviously the institutions of these organisations, in particular those dealing with fisheries management, should bear in mind the obligation of Contracting States under the CBD. The same effects may also be attained through special agreements between adjacent states, as was accomplished by Australia and New Zealand.

The subject so far dwelled upon does not simply concern the relationship between the CBD and UNCLOS with regard to the regulation of marine scientific research. For example, it also involves UNCLOS' relationship with many other treaty regimes, such as CITES (the Convention on International Trade in Endangered Species of Wild Fauna and Flora), the WTO, GATT (General Agreement on Tariffs and Trade) or TRIPS (Trade-Related Aspects of Intellectual Property Rights Agreement). Article 311 of UNCLOS deals with the relationship with other conventions and international agreements and contains rules intended to ensure that the UNCLOS prevails over incompatible treaties. The last is, as far as

[8] See Wolfrum-Matz, *supra*, n 3, 469.

possible, to be interpreted to comply with the Law of the Sea Convention (see Article 311(2)–(4)).

As far as the CBD is concerned, since a potential conflict with other agreements, and, in particular, with the Law of the Sea, was foreseen special provisions were introduced to prevent or resolve this possibility. Among these provisions, Article 22, a rather difficult article to interpret, provides as follows:

> 1. The provisions of this Convention shall not affect the rights and obligations of any Contracting Party deriving from any existing international agreement, except where the exercise of those rights and obligations would cause a serious damage or threat to biological diversity.
> 2. Contracting Parties shall implement this Convention with respect to the marine environment consistently with the rights and obligations of States under the law of the sea.

The first paragraph is clear. It contains a clause of precedence for treaties adopted prior to the CBD. This precedence does not take place if 'serious damage or threat to biological diversity' would be caused as a consequence of the exercise of those rights and obligations. This is an evident application of the precautionary principle, open to wide interpretation as it refers not only to actual damage, but also to *threat* to biological diversity.

There are some doubts, however, concerning the meaning of the second paragraph. First of all, it does not make reference to specific international agreements, but to 'the rights and obligations of States under the law of the sea'. It must be inferred, as a consequence, that its purpose is to underscore the value of the principles of customary international law of the sea that are binding on all states. But what is really peculiar in this particular case is the absence of the limitation contained in the first paragraph, i.e., the need to apply the precautionary principle. In other words, is this an exception to the exception, in the sense that the duty to implement CBD provisions consistently with the Law of the Sea is absolute, even in the case of threat to biological diversity? I find it difficult to accept this conclusion, just as I find it difficult to understand the need to include this paragraph if we do accept this conclusion.

II. MARINE SCIENTIFIC RESEARCH AND ACCESS TO GENETIC RESOURCES

UNCLOS does not deal with marine genetic resources. Thus, the problem of access to these resources in the different marine zones may be considered only through the interpretation of pertinent provisions on different subjects, such as the exploitation and conservation of marine resources, the prevention of marine pollution, and, finally, marine research.

The use of marine genetic resources necessarily implies marine scientific research.[9] The rules concerning this subject, contained in UNCLOS, appear to be essentially inspired by two guiding principles: compliance with the sovereignty or jurisdiction of coastal states over their own maritime zones, on the one hand, and the generic right of all states, in the interest of the entire international Community, to the freedom of scientific research, on the other. Moreover, UNCLOS provisions for coastal states as well as all other states always try to conciliate economic rights with the protection of the marine environment and its resources, even though we must acknowledge the evident preference accorded to the economic uses of seas.

Even though UNCLOS does not define the expression 'scientific research', we can assume that this activity is generally related to economic activities, so that UNCLOS provisions can be applied both to pure scientific research and to research connected to industrial and commercial interests, the so-called 'applied research'.

The Law of the Sea does not consider the catch of marine genetic resources or the finding of samples and scientific data as subject to an autonomous legal regime.[10] However, these activities cannot be carried out freely in maritime zones under national sovereignty or jurisdiction, even if they are considered scientific research. For this reason UNCLOS provisions concerning scientific research make reference to a 'discretionary power' of coastal states.

In particular, Article 241 contains a prohibition on the use of marine scientific research as the legal basis for claims over the marine environment or its resources. It is a provision whose aim is to safeguard the rights of states, acting as a barrier to technologic developments that are detrimental to the rights of coastal states. This type of prohibition can also be found in other international instruments, such as the Antarctic Treaty of 1959.

Scientific research, whether of a commercial or purely scientific nature, can be conducted by any state, but always with the consent of the coastal state. In the territorial seas, this research is regulated and authorised by the coastal state (Article 245). In the EEZ and in the CS, the discretionary power of the coastal state is in a certain sense mitigated by the provision of Article 246. Though the consent of the coastal state is always necessary (Article 246(2)), there also exists a 'slight right' (what in the Italian and

9 On the regime of marine scientific research see Soons, *Marine Scientific Research and the Law of the Sea*, (The Hague, 1982) and Treves, 'Principe du consentement et nouveau régime juridique de la recherche scientifique marine', in Bardonnet and Virally (eds), *Le nouveau droit de la mer* (Paris, 1983), 286.

10 On the matter of access to the marine genetic resources see Farrier-Tucker, 'Access to Marine Bioresources: Hitching the Conservation Cart to the Bioprospecting Horse', (2001) 32 *Ocean Development and International Law* 213.

French domestic order is called a 'legitimate interest') of foreign states to obtain, in 'normal circumstances', authorisation to carry out projects of marine scientific research for the benefit of all mankind (Article 246(3)). This consent should not be unreasonably delayed or denied. But in the case of research projects specifically aimed at the exploration and exploitation of natural resources, the coastal state can exercise its discretionary power and deny its consent (Article 246(5)(a)).

Thus, it is clear that when research projects are of a commercial nature, coastal States can lawfully deny access to their national zones.

Moreover, a state wishing to undertake a research project must comply with a number of important obligations and engagements, such as the duty to ask for consent almost six months prior to the date of the project, the duty to provide the coastal state with detailed information on the project and events related to the research activity, and the duty to guarantee to the coastal state participation in the project, to be negotiated through official channels (Articles 248 and 249).

The only mitigation to these requirements is provided by Article 252 concerning the issue of implied consent. This Article decrees that it is possible to carry out research projects six months after the date upon which the necessary information has been provided, if the coastal state remains silent. At any rate, it is always possible for the coastal state to suspend or to require cessation of marine scientific research if the state or the international organisation conducting such research is considered to be in contrast with or non-observant of the requirements and obligations imposed by the UNCLOS (Article 253).

In the absence of a specific regime on the catch of resources and on the collection of data and samples for biotechnological applications, the relationship between states with a high level of technological knowledge, involved in marine research, and the states of origin of genetic resources and marine habitat remains difficult.

The activity of catching samples of resources for purposes of research or for genetic manipulation cannot be considered either as uniquely scientific nor as a uniquely fisheries related activity, for the simple reason that it is inherent to both, thus falling under the regime of each of the two activities.

Moreover, present UNCLOS provisions concerning scientific research do not pursue the issue of intellectual property rights over data, samples and scientific results. This issue is not regulated by the international law of the sea, but it has been dealt with in several international instruments, such as GATT and CITES. In general terms, the attribution of intellectual property rights and the allocation of economic benefits are regulated by national legislation and bilateral agreements between states.

In this context, it seems necessary to rethink the concept of exclusive exploitation of resources. Up to now, we have discussed the extent of the power of coastal states over exhaustible natural, biological and mineral resources; technological development now leads to new forms of economic exploitation of resources, and will do so increasingly in the future. One example is the possibility of commercialisation of products deriving from the genetic manipulation of marine species. Indeed, it remains in doubt whether economic exploitation results principally from intellectual research, with all its related consequences regarding property rights, or if it is primarily the product of the place in which such research takes place, that is rare ecosystems or important genetic resources found in national or international maritime zones. Where does the emphasis lie?

In the present law of the sea the problem of reconciling the freedom of research with the rights of coastal states over their own zones is still unsolved. Indeed, if we consider the collection and categorisation of data and samples and the study of the marine environment as exploitation of resources, the regime of scientific research would no longer be applicable and the 'slight rights' of 'researching States' would be definitely denied or limited.

With regard to the matter of access to genetic resources in the high seas,[11] we can maintain that states may, in the absence of any specific provision, freely carry out all the activities necessary to this aim, with due regard for the interests of other states and for the provisions regulating the high seas' seabed regime (Article 87 UNCLOS). The list of the freedoms of the high seas contained in this Article cannot be considered compulsory, but simply as an indication of possible human marine activities. As for research projects with economic goals to be conducted in the water column of the high seas, the provisions of Article 257 affirm the freedom of research for all states, provided that this freedom is exercised in conformity with the Convention.

Consequently, access to genetic resources of the so-called Area, to be considered like all others resources, as the common heritage of mankind, is limited by the provisions of Part XI of UNCLOS.

In the high seas all human activities, even those not mentioned in the Convention and not foreseeable at the time of its drafting, should be consistent with the provisions on the conservation of high seas resources (Articles 116–120 UNCLOS) and on the protection of the marine environment (Articles 192–196 UNCLOS). In particular, Article 196 establishes the duty of states to adopt preventive measures in the case of possible pollution of the marine environment resulting from the use of technologies under their jurisdiction or control, or from the introduction of new species into the marine environment leading to harmful changes and damage.

11 Glowka, 'The Deepest of Ironies: Genetic Resources, Marine Scientific Research, and the Area', (1996) 12 *Ocean Yearbook* 154; Glowka, 'Genetic Resources, Marine Scientific Research and the International Seabed Area', (199) 8 RECIEL, 56.

As we will see further, that provision is an important tool, since it serves as the legal basis that links to UNCLOS the restrictions on the freedom of the high seas which are the consequence of state practice implementing CBD provisions.

The CBD is an attempt to overcome the conflicts that still exist in the Law of the Sea, as it tries to harmonise the sovereign rights of coastal states over natural resources with the need to protect intellectual property rights arising from research activity relating to genetic resources.[12]

The CBD also regulates access to marine genetic resources, thus partly filling the international legal void that exists in this field. As already stated, the principle of state sovereignty over its own natural resources is confirmed in the provisions of the CBD more or less in the same terms as in UNCLOS, and so the rules on access to marine genetic resources are decided by the 'state of origin', and activities are to be conducted according to legislation of that state.

The CBD expressly recognises a link between the resources found in national maritime zones and the final product, the object of commercialisation, realised by the foreign state conducting the research. On the basis of this link, the state of origin of the data and samples of marine research has control over access to genetic resources. This control is exercised through the provisions of the coastal state's national legislation or under the bilateral or multilateral agreements concluded with the states involved in the research.

The CBD establishes the general responsibility of the states of origin of the resources (that is: the coastal states) to *facilitate* access to genetic resources for 'environmentally sound uses' (Article 15 CBD). Access is subject to the 'prior informed consent' of the state of origin of the resources (Article 15(5)) and can be conditional on the participation of the state of origin in the research activity and on the benefits deriving from the results of the research. In addition, particular attention is paid to the transfer of technology among Contracting Parties as an essential element of the facilitation of the access provided by the state of origin of resources (Article 16 CBD).

As far the states parties to both the Conventions (UNCLOS and CBD) are concerned, the provisions of Articles 15(7) and 19(2) of the CBD reinforce the rights of coastal states established by UNCLOS provisions on marine scientific research (in particular Articles 246(5)(d) and 249(2)). This guarantee of all economic rights acquired by coastal states is confirmed by the practice of states whose legislation may regulate marine scientific

[12] On the relationship between marine scientific research and intellectual property rights see Gorina-Ysern, 'Marine Scientific Research Activities as the Legal Basis for Intellectual Property Claims?', *Marine Policy* [1998] 337.

research in different ways, but always distinguishing between pure research and research applied to industry and commerce. So, in spite of the obligation to facilitate access, the most notable feature of the CBD provisions on marine scientific research is, in my view, the consolidation of a coastal state's right, according to international law, to profit from the commercial development of its own resources by other states.

III. THE RELATIONSHIP BETWEEN THE MPA (MARINE PROTECTED AREAS) SYSTEM PROVIDED BY THE CBD AND THE AIA (ADVANCED INFORMED AGREEMENT) PROCEDURE PROVIDED BY THE CARTAGENA PROTOCOL ON BIOSAFETY WITH UNCLOS PROVISIONS ON INNOCENT PASSAGE AND FREEDOM OF NAVIGATION

The CBD provides that the parties shall 'establish a system of protected areas or areas where special measures need to be taken to conserve biological diversity' (Article 8(a)). In 2003, the CBD's Subsidiary Body for Scientific, Technical and Technological Advice (SBSTTA) recognised the urgent need to establish marine protected zones beyond national jurisdiction, consistent with international law and based on scientific information, and recommended that the next Conference of Parties to the CBD convene with other international and regional bodies for the specific purpose of identifying appropriate mechanisms for the establishment and effective management of marine and protected areas beyond national jurisdiction.[13]

The problem that has been raised is reconciling the restrictions and limitations adopted as a consequence of the establishment of these areas with the traditional freedoms of navigation according to customary international law and UNCLOS provisions.[14] Thus, it becomes necessary, once again, to interpret the international law of the sea, and, in particular, UNCLOS provisions in accordance with the recent developments of states' practice. Many other international treaties or instruments contain provisions on the establishment of MPAs. What characterises the CBD's Article 8 is its broader concept regarding protection of vulnerable marine areas, based on the concept of *in situ* conservation. This possibility can be considered consistent with the general obligation to protect and preserve the marine environment that binds all states under customary international

[13] See the study on the relationship between the CBD and UNCLOS relating to the use of genetic resources of the deep seabed, carried on by the SBSTTA, Doc UNEP/CBD/SBSTTA/8/INF/3/Rev. of 22 Feb 2003.

[14] See Cataldi, 'Problèmes généraux de la navigation en Europe', in R. Casado Raigon (ed.), *Europe et la Mer, II Colloquium of the International Association for the Law of the Sea*, (Brussels, 2005) 127 ff.

law and according to Article 192 of UNCLOS. This obligation is applicable in maritime zones that are under sovereignty or jurisdiction, as well as on the high seas.

The institution of these areas also implies the duty to cooperate, a duty which, according to Article 123 UNCLOS, is particularly important in the case of closed or semi-enclosed seas. It is not by chance that regional cooperation has produced significant examples of these areas, for example in the Mediterranean.

Another UNCLOS provision, which deserves to be remembered, is Article 194(5), according to which the measures taken to protect and preserve the marine environment 'shall include those necessary to protect and preserve rare or fragile ecosystems as well as the habitat of depleted, threatened or endangered species and other forms of marine life'.

Another point I would like to emphasise is the interplay of the Advanced Informed Agreement Procedure provided by the Biosafety Protocol with UNCLOS provisions on innocent passage in the territorial sea.

The Cartagena Protocol on Biosafety to the Convention on Biological Diversity (adopted in Montreal on 29 January 2000) focuses specifically on the transboundary movement of any living modified organism resulting from modern biotechnology that may have an adverse effect on the conservation and sustainable use of biological diversity. The Protocol allows trade in these products to proceed essentially unhindered, subject to two conditions. First, the requirement for transboundary movements to be accompanied by appropriate documentation stating that LMOs not intended for intentional introduction into the environment may be contained in the shipment; secondly, detailed information to be provided, prior to the first shipment, by an exporting state to an importing state regarding any LMOs to be introduced into the environment of the latter. This is the so-called AIA procedure, which does not apply to LMOs in transit. It is really remarkable that this important step towards cooperation and transparency remains incomplete. The reason for this may be to avoid any violation of the rights of passage as contemplated by UNCLOS and by customary law. But an evolution in state practice on notification of passage has transformed the scope of states' duties consequent to the development of the international community's increasing attention to common interests and values, such as health and environmental safety. Many examples could be provided, beginning with the 1989 Basel Convention on transboundary movements of dangerous wastes, the 1996 Izmir Protocol on the same matter, and the 1998 Teheran Protocol to the 1978 Kuwait Convention on pollution.[15] There are many other examples, also in domestic systems, especially after a pollution disaster such as

[15] On this point see Cataldi, *supra* n 7.

occurred with the ship *Erika*, of legislative provisions on the obligation to notify of the passage of dangerous ships, and of the practice of exchange of this kind of information.

IV. CONCLUSION

There has been some discussion of the possibility of amending UNCLOS in order to make it more consistent with all the developments of a customary nature that have taken place in the Law of the Sea over the past 20 years, brought about by the changes occurring within the international community.

I believe it would be advisable, apart from to review UNCLOS overall, also to draft a series of implementation agreements relating to those issues that are most affected by these changes. This would prevent the emergence of any contrasts among the different Member States of UNCLOS, and even within a Member State, on 'literal' and 'extensive' interpretations of the same provisions. In the light of the considerations and observations herein submitted, I believe that the topic of this chapter is one of the sectors that would be most subject to this type of risk.

6

Antarctic Bioprospecting: Is It Compatible with the Value of Antarctica as a Natural Reserve?

PATRIZIA VIGNI*

I. INTRODUCTION

THE EFFECTS OF industrial and technological activities on the world environment have increased so much that the human impact is now perceptible even in those areas of our planet where activities are considerably limited, such as Antarctica.[1] Among such activities, bioprospecting has particularly attracted the attention of Antarctic institutions, such as the Scientific Committee on Antarctic Research (SCAR),[2] and the Antarctic Treaty Consultative Meeting (ATCM).[3] Moreover, third states and organisations with respect to the Antarctic Treaty (AT)[4] have shown some concern about the performance of bioprospecting in the Antarctic area. For example, one may mention the message of the World Parks Congress, addressed to the Conference of the Parties to the Convention on Biological Diversity (hereafter the CBD). This message

* Researcher in International Law at the Law Faculty of the University of Siena, Italy.

1 For this observation see Anton, 'Law for the Sea's Biological Diversity', (1997) 36 *Columbia Journal of Transnational Law* 350.

2 SCAR was the first international entity to raise the issue of bioprospecting in Antarctica at the XXIII Antarctic Treaty Consultative Meeting (ATCM), held in Lima in 1999, presenting a paper on this matter, XXIII ATCM/IP123.

3 The first Consultative Party that highlighted some inconsistencies between the Antarctic Treaty System (ATS) and bioprospecting activities was the UK. See XXV ATCM/WP 43, presented at the XXV ATCM, held in Warsaw in 2002 (hereafter WP 43). For an overview, see Hemmings, 'A Question of Politics: Bioprospecting and the Antarctic Treaty System', in Hemmings and Rogan-Finnemore (eds), *Antartic Bioprospecting*, Gateway Antarctica, *special publication series* (2005) (hereafter Canterbury Workshop). Only in June 2005, at the XXVIII ATCM, a resolution (a non-binding act) was adopted in order to stress the importance of bioprospecting activities carried out within the Antartic Treaty area. See Resolution 7 (2005) on biological prospecting in Antarctica.

4 The Antarctic Treaty was signed in Washington on 1 Dec. 1959, 402 UNTS 71.

states that Antarctica should be protected like other areas beyond national jurisdiction by means of the declaration of protected areas.[5]

In order to explain this worldwide interest in bioprospecting, it seems necessary to define what this activity is and, then, how it can be regulated. Some authors state that bioprospecting is the 'search for bioactive compounds in natural sources' in order to stress the fact that this type of research mainly concerns genetic resources.[6] For this reason, bioprospecting is often related to the concept of biodiversity, which includes genetic,[7] species and ecosystem diversity.[8] Thus, bioprospecting corresponds to any research activity that is somehow connected with the environment. Other legal writers emphasise the economic purpose of bioprospecting by defining this activity as 'the exploration of biodiversity for commercially valuable genetic and biochemical resources'.[9] In the present writer's view, the form of bioprospecting that deserves special attention, in particular in relation to Antarctica, includes both these characteristics. On the one hand, bioprospecting is a research activity that involves the world's nature in all its aspects and components. On the other hand, the economic character of bioprospecting is significant in order to distinguish between such activity and other types of scientific research. In fact, bioprospecting can be divided into four phases: discovery, product development, manufacturing, and marketing.[10] Nevertheless, it is not always easy to distinguish between research activities that have exclusive scientific purposes and bioprospecting. For example, a thermophilic *bacillus* that was isolated during a scientific expedition in Antarctica in 1980 was sold to a private company and commercially exploited by it.[11]

[5] International Union for the Conservation of Nature (IUCN), Durban, 2003. The Congress also adopted Recommendation 5.23, 'Protecting Marine Biodiversity and Ecosystem Processes through Marine Protected Areas beyond National Jurisdiction', that promotes the creation of protected areas in order to safeguard the environment beyond state jurisdiction: see www.iucn.org/wcpa/wpc2003.

[6] Hunter, 'Sustainable Bioprospecting: Using Private Contracts and International Legal Principles and Policies to Conserve Raw Medicinal Materials', [1997] *Boston College Environmental Affairs Law Review* 129 at n 61.

[7] Genetic resources are 'genetic materials of plant, animal and microbial or other origin containing functional units of heredity of actual or potential value', *ibid*, 170.

[8] Genetic diversity affects specimens of the same species that highlight some differences in their genes. Species diversity distinguishes different organisms. Ecosystem diversity makes a distinction between the environmental characteristics of the various areas of the planet. For this distinction, see *ibid*, 133.

[9] Glowka, 'Bioprospecting, Alien Invasive Species, and Hydrothermal Vents: Three Emerging Legal Issues in the Conservation and Sustainable Use of Biodiversity', (2000) 13 *Tulane Environmental Law Journal*, at n 2.

[10] See the paper presented by the UK and Norway at the XXVI ATCM, held in Madrid in 2003, XXVI ATCM/IP 75 that consists of a scientific work: Johnston and Lohan, 'The International Regime for Bioprospecting: Existing Policies and Emerging Issues for Antarctica', (hereafter IP 75), para. 19.

[11] *Ibid*, para. 14.

Although bioprospecting has been carried out in Antarctica for some decades, no regulation of this activity can be found in the norms of the Antarctic Treaty System (ATS). So far, bioprospecting, performed in Antarctica, has led to the discovery of new organisms or of unique characteristics for survival of already known organisms.[12] Private companies, interested in such discoveries, have immediately applied for patents in order to achieve all property rights, including intellectual property rights (hereafter IPRs). Some of these patents concern cosmetics products,[13] food conservation procedures,[14] and pharmaceuticals.[15]

Nevertheless, the IPRs deriving from Antarctic bioprospecting are recognised only at state level. Thus, even if, at the end of the 1990s, the number of applications for patents of Antarctic genetic resources increased exponentially, this race has recently stopped due to the uncertainty relating to the recognition of IPRs at international level and the possibility of commercial exploitation of Antarctic resources.[16]

Such uncertainty calls for a fresh analysis. The aim of this chapter is, therefore, to ascertain whether or not bioprospecting is compatible with ATS norms. In this respect, a distinction must be made between the AT, and the instruments originated from it, and the Convention on the Conservation of Marine Living Resources (CCAMLR).[17] Unlike the AT, the Convention permits the commercial exploitation of resources, although with some limits. Moreover, the CCAMLR applies to a larger area than the AT. This area is that located south of the Antarctic Convergence and includes zones that are subject to state jurisdiction. Therefore, some arguments that can concern the AT area, such as the doubtful applicability of the principle of state sovereignty to this area, apply to the CCAMLR only partially.

The main problems concerning the possibility of carrying out bioprospecting in Antarctica first relate to the fact that international law and, in particular, the ATS recognise the status of a natural reserve in respect of Antarctica. Secondly, the primary role, played by science in the AT and, in particular, in the Protocol on Environmental Protection (hereafter Madrid

[12] *Ibid*, para. 10.

[13] In Germany, Henkel applied for a patent relating to the green alga Prasiola, whose extracts can be used for skin treatments. See the paper 'Industry Involvement in Antarctic Bioprospecting', presented by UNEP at the XXVII ATCM, held in Cape Town in June 2004, XXVII ATCM/IP 106 (hereafter UNEP IP), 21.

[14] Unilever applied for patent in the UK for plant antifreeze proteins for use in frozen confectionery. These proteins derive from Antarctic plants such as *Nothofagus antarctica, Deschampsia antarctica and Umbilicaria antarctica*: *ibid*, 24.

[15] An enzyme deriving from *Candida Antarctica*, a type of yeast, was patented by DSM NV in the Netherlands. This enzyme can help to prepare some pharmaceuticals such as benzothiazepines: *ibid*, 26.

[16] *Ibid*, 19.

[17] Done in Canberra on 20 May 1980 [1980] ILM 827.

Protocol),[18] compels us to observe whether and to what extent bioprospecting can be regulated by the Antarctic norms relating to scientific research. Thirdly, the recognition of exclusive rights over the scientific results deriving from bioprospecting raises the problem of determining who owns the Antarctic resources that are investigated or discovered by 'bioprospectors'.

In addition, due to the lack of specific Antarctic provisions on this matter, one must examine whether and to what extent current ATS norms can be applied to bioprospecting.

Finally, in order to fill this normative lacuna, it is necessary to analyse whether other international regimes dealing with the exploitation and exploration of living resources can also be applied to Antarctica considering the peculiar geographic and legal status of this area.

II. ANTARCTICA AS A NATURAL RESERVE

Facing the increasing proliferation of bioprospecting activities in the AT area and the corresponding absence of ATS norms concerning this issue, it is necessary to ascertain whether and to what extent these activities are consistent with the existing provisions of the ATS. Among these provisions, particular importance must be given to the basic principles of the AT and its related instruments, such as the Madrid Protocol.

One of the basic principles of the ATS is set out in Article 2 of the Madrid Protocol. This Article affirms that Antarctica is a 'natural reserve, devoted to peace and science'. The fundamental aim of states parties is, therefore, to preserve this area against the harmful impacts that can be caused by human activities. For this reason, Madrid Protocol obligations are applicable to 'all activities in the Antarctic Treaty area'. Bioprospecting is not expressly contemplated, but nothing in the Protocol leads us to conclude that it should not be included. However, we must, first of all, ascertain whether an activity, which is primarily aimed at achieving economic revenues from the exploration of biological resources, can be considered compatible with the purpose of preserving a natural reserve, as Article 2 of the Madrid Protocol establishes. A clear description of the expression 'natural reserve' is provided by Article 3(1) of the Protocol. This article intends to promote the performance of those Antarctic activities that are particularly concerned with '[t]he protection of the Antarctic environment and dependent and associated ecosystems and the intrinsic value of Antarctica, including its wilderness and aesthetic values and its value as an area for the conduct of scientific research, in particular research essential to understanding the global environment'. From the

[18] Signed in Madrid on 4 Oct. 1991 [1991] ILM 1455.

wording of this Article one can easily gather that a natural reserve, like Antarctica, must be mainly preserved as such and used in the interest of the whole international community, in particular, with the purpose of providing knowledge of the global environment. In order to achieve this aim, the Madrid Protocol established a comprehensive regime for the protection of the Antarctic environment and its dependent and associated ecosystems.

The need to safeguard the global interest in preserving a natural reserve also affects state legal orders with regard to the management of national parks. As an example, one can mention the Edmonds case relating to the lawfulness of an agreement, which was concluded between the management body of Yellowstone Park, the National Park Service, and Diversa Corporation, a biotechnology company, and that concerned the collection of biological tissues for potential financial sharing.[19] The Edmonds Institute, a non-profit organisation, asked for the annulment of such agreement due to its inconsistency with the aim of the US statute that established the Park. The court that judged this case affirmed that the products deriving from the collection of the biological tissues of Yellowstone Park could not be considered and sold as research products, since such collection was not carried out for scientific reasons, but for commercial purposes. Further, the court pointed out that commercial activities have a different impact on the environment from scientific research. Thus, commercial activities cannot be allowed on the basis of the same conditions of scientific research. Notwithstanding these preliminary assumptions, the court concluded that Yellowstone Park could be considered a natural laboratory that, under US law, could be used by private operators provided that such use was consistent with the purposes for which the laboratory was created. For this reason, the agreement between the National Park Service and Diversa was declared to be consistent with the statute establishing the Park. This decision of the court was strongly influenced by the argument of the defendant according to which the financial return relating to bioprospecting activities of Yellowstone's biological tissues would be used to improve the conservation of the park's biodiversity.[20] For this reason, the agreement could be considered fully lawful and useful for the preservation of the status of Yellowstone as a natural reserve. Nevertheless, public opinion did not totally support this decision. Wood, commenting the Edmonds case, has pointed out that, in

[19] For an overview of the case see Wood, 'Are National Park Resources for Sale?: Edmonds Institute v. Babbitt' [2000] *Public Land and Resources Law Review* 201.

[20] The argument that highlights the public utility of bioprospecting is mainly based on the possibility of using biological compounds to create new medicines that can save and improve human life. This case provokes ethical conflicts concerning the question whether it is preferable to preserve biodiversity than to save human lives. For the difficulties raised by

states' heritage, there is something too special to be sold (such as Yellowstone's integrity and inaccessibility).[21]

The reasoning, assumed in the Edmonds case, could also be applied to Antarctica. In fact, first, Antarctica has been declared a natural reserve like Yellowstone Park.[22] Moreover, commercial products have been developed from the compounds of Antarctic biological resources. A number of these products such as medicines also have some public utility. Nevertheless, so far, no other public, or rather global, interest has been satisfied. No economic revenue deriving from bioprospecting activities has been used to ensure the protection of the Antarctic environment. This is due to the fact that Antarctica, unlike Yellowstone Park, is not governed by an internationally recognised institution that can use financial returns of bioprospecting activities in the interest of the international community. So, only private companies and, at least, some scientists who have sold the results of their research to such companies may have drawn profit from Antarctic bioprospecting.

In the light of the above, the solution, suggested by US judges in the Edmonds case, is not easily applicable to Antarctica. That is why some States and authors believe that research activities, carried out for commercial purposes, should be minimised in Antarctica until specific provisions relating to this matter established.[23]

One must also recall that, so far, Consultative Parties have attempted to avoid the proliferation of commercial activities of exclusive private concern in Antarctica. They have sought to deal with economic issues only once, with regard to Antarctic mineral activities, and without any success. In fact, the Convention on the Regulation of Antarctic Mineral Resource Activities (CRAMRA)[24] was set aside shortly after its adoption and Article 7 of the Madrid Protocol established a strict prohibition on mining within the Antarctic area. Moreover, one may mention the recommendation through which AT parties agreed to avoid the collection and, consequently, trade in meteorites found in the Antarctic continent.[25]

Thus, the main purpose of the ATS instruments, which are currently in force, appears to be the preservation of Antarctica as a natural reserve where the commercial exploitation of this area and its resources must be reduced as much as possible.

this kind of conflicts see Potts, 'At Least Give the Natives Glass Beads: An Examination of the Bargain made between Iceland and deCODE Genetics with Implications for Global Bioprospecting', (2002) 7 *Virginia Journal of Law and Technology* 8.

21 Wood, *supra* n 19, 218.

22 *Ibid*, 222.

23 See WP 43, *supra* n 3, para. 11.

24 Signed in Wellington on 2 June 1988 [1988] ILM 868.

25 See Resolution 3(2001), in Annex C to the Final Report of the XXIV ATCM.

III. THE STATUS OF SCIENTIFIC RESEARCH WITHIN THE ATS

Bioprospecting is undeniably a form of scientific research. Nevertheless, when bioprospecting is aimed at satisfying commercial interests, it does not seem to correspond to the form of scientific research regulated and promoted by ATS norms. In fact, Antarctic legal instruments allow a type of scientific research that is very different from the concept of 'search for bioactive compounds in natural sources for development in therapeutic or industrial applications', that defines bioprospecting.[26] The latter kind of activity is also called 'applied' research. The difference between the type of research, adopted by the ATS, and bioprospecting is the economic purpose of the latter. Therefore, in order to ascertain the compatibility of bioprospecting with the ATS, it seems necessary to make a distinction between the concepts of 'pure' research, aimed at increasing human knowledge, and 'applied' research that seeks information which can be used to satisfy interests other than scientific ones. Notwithstanding the importance of such definition and distinction for the regulation of Antarctic research, ATS norms do not provide any clarification on this matter.[27] Although both the AT and the Madrid Protocol include several provisions dealing with scientific activities, without making any distinction between 'pure' and 'applied' research, some norms are patently devoted to regulating only 'pure' research. Among these norms, one can mention Article II of the AT that establishes freedom of scientific investigation, and Article III, which promotes international cooperation; Article 3(3) of the Protocol affirms that '[a]ctivities shall be planned . . . so as to accord priority to scientific research'. Moreover, Article 7 of the Protocol prohibits '[a]ny activity related to mineral resources, other than scientific research'. It is clear that all these provisions intend to attribute special status to those activities that are carried out to satisfy the interests of the international community rather than the selfish commercial interests of states or private operators.

Actually, there was an Antarctic instrument dealing with prospecting (although it did not concern biological resources): CRAMRA. Chapter III of this convention established that sponsoring states had the power to regulate prospecting activities, although the CRAMRA Commission

26 This definition is the sum of several descriptions of bioprospecting. See Jones, 'Regulating Access to Biological and Genetic Resources in Australia: A Case Study of Bioprospecting in Queensland', [1998] *Australasian Journal of Natural Resources Law and Policy* 89 and Asebey and Kempenaar, 'Biodiversity Prospecting: Fulfill the Mandate of the Biodiversity Convention' (1995) 4 *Vanderbilt Journal of Transnational Law* 703, 706 (as quoted by Hunter, *supra* n 6, at n 61).

27 For the need to regulate these two types of research in a different manner, see also Gollin and Laird, 'Global Policies, Local Actions: The Role of National Legislation in Sustainable Biodiversity Prospecting' (1996) 2 *Boston University Journal of Science and Technology Law* 16 para 91.

could adopt measures to set the general requirements of such activities. In particular, Article 37 of CRAMRA established that data of commercial value could be excluded from the duty to exchange information[28] provided for by the Convention and the other instruments of the ATS. Despite this example of prospecting within the ATS, one must point out that the Wellington Convention has never entered into force due to the strong opposition of some Consultative Parties and third states to the too commercially-oriented character of the Convention itself. Subsequently, Consultative Parties agreed to adopt the Madrid Protocol, which is an extremely environmentally sound instrument. Thus, Chapter III of CRAMRA does not seem to express the current spirit of the ATS and, thus, cannot be used to regulate biological prospecting of commercial nature by analogy.

Nevertheless, the distinction between academic and commercially oriented research does not appear particularly effective.[29] In fact, in certain circumstances, commercial development can derive from the results of 'pure' research as the case of the thermophilic *bacillus* shows.[30] The problems that have been caused by the proliferation of bioprospecting activities in Antarctica have concrete implications that cannot be resolved simply through a linguistic operation that distinguishes between 'pure' and 'applied' research. According to an evolutive approach, one could argue that existing Antarctic provisions regulating scientific research are not suitable for application to current scientific activities considering increasing technical developments. By contrast, on the basis of a rigid approach, Consultative Parties could insist on applying ATS provisions regardless of the different regulation of research, provided for by other international regimes, in order to ensure the conservation of Antarctica as a natural reserve devoted to peace and ('pure') science. This rigid approach seems to be preferred by the AT parties that, so far, have adopted very environmentally sound legal instruments. Thus, under the ATS, Antarctic bioprospecting could be lawful only if it corresponded to scientific research as intended by the ATS itself.

[28] Art 37(12) affirms that '[t]he Sponsoring State shall ensure that basic data and information, other than interpretative data, generated by prospecting are made readily available when such data and information are not, or are no longer, of commercial value and, in any event, no later than 10 years after the year the data and information were collected, unless it certifies to the Commission that the data and information continue to have commercial value'.

[29] For the scarce usefulness of this distinction see Farrier and Tucker, 'Access to Marine Bioresources: Hitching the Conservation Cart to the Bioprospecting Horse' [2001] *Ocean Development and International Law* 227. The authors believe that all scientific research activities (in this specific case, marine research) should be considered bioprospecting due to the fact that the majority of scientific results can bring to commercial development.

[30] See *supra* Section I. For the view that academic research can also lead to the development of commercial products see Farrier and Tucker, *supra* n 29, 225.

In the light of this, Consultative Parties could consider economically oriented bioprospecting as incompatible with Antarctic norms. In fact, one of the most important obligations provided for by the AT is the duty to exchange information concerning research activities, carried out by Consultative Parties or by their nationals.[31] This obligation clashes with the fact that the results of bioprospecting, having commercial value, need confidentiality in order to preserve such value.[32] That is why private operators who have sponsored bioprospecting activities in Antarctica or bought the results of such activities have taken care to obtain a patent for the discovery of new organisms or the unique characteristics of biological resources.[33] IPRs or patents allow their owners to disseminate information in return of financial compensation.[34] Nevertheless, Antarctic norms do not establish any compensation in return for exchanged information. Thus, the imposition of such compensation could be considered inconsistent with the language and spirit of Article III of the AT.[35]

The situation is not very different if we take into account the activities that are regulated by CCAMLR. Although economic exploitation of Antarctic marine living resources, including scientific research for commercial purposes, is consistent with CCAMLR objectives, some obligations of this convention could conflict with the recognition of IPRs relating to the patented products deriving from bioprospecting. As an example, one can mention Article 20(1) of CCAMLR, which compels states to submit an annual report containing data and information about the species, harvested by states and their nationals, in order to provide information to the CCAMLR Scientific Committee and, thus, to ensure the most appropriate protection of natural species.[36] Under the obligation established by Article 20 of CCAMLR, the CCAMLR Commission has recently adopted

31 Art III(c) of the AT states: 'the Contracting Parties agree that, to the greatest extent feasible and practicable:...scientific observations and results from Antarctica shall be exchanged and made freely available'.

32 The problem of the incompatibility between Art III of the AT and the need for confidentiality of commercial data has been highlighted by WP 43, *supra* n 3, para. 13.

33 See *supra* Section I.

34 Some authors have affirmed that the recognition of such rights is the only instrument that currently encourages the exchange of scientific information of commercial value. In fact, the expectation of financial returns persuades private companies to sponsor scientific research and, thus, to increase the possibility of scientific discoveries. Moreover, the results of such discoveries can be made available for states and other private companies by means of their paying a grant to the sponsor. For this view see IP 75, *supra* n 10, para. 44.

35 This problem has been raised by Stone, 'Patent, Property Rights, and Benefit Sharing', in *Canterbury Workshop, supra* n 3.

36 Art 20(1) states: '[t]he Members of the Commission shall, to the greatest extent possible, provide annually to the Commission and to the Scientific Committee such statistical, biological and other data and information as the Commission and Scientific Committee may require in the exercise of their functions'. This problem is also highlighted by IP 75, *supra* n 10, para 52.

a measure concerning exploring fishing of *Dissostichus*.[37] Moreover, Article 24(2)(b) provides for the possibility of carrying out inspections on vessels engaged in activities, including scientific research, within the CCAMLR geographic scope. Both these provisions seem to jeopardise the confidentiality of scientific results of commercial value that are protected by IPRs.

In sum, the ATS provisions concerning scientific research seem scarcely suitable for application to 'commercial' bioprospecting, which is mainly aimed at satisfying selfish interests of private parties.

IV. THE OWNERSHIP AND BENEFIT-SHARING OF THE RESULTS OF ANTARCTIC BIOPROSPECTING

As affirmed above, it is doubtful whether the commercial purpose of bioprospecting activities is compatible with the prohibition of the economic use of Antarctica, established by the ATS. So far, the financial return, obtained from Antarctic bioprospecting, has been legitimised by state law. In fact, the recognition and transfer of the ownership of the products developed from bioprospecting took place in the territory of one of the Consultative Parties under its copyright and commercial law. In most cases, the trade involved the results of the discovery of some scientists that had carried out research activities in Antarctica. The buyers of the 'discovery' were private companies that, thanks to this discovery, manufactured and marketed new products.[38] In this case, copyrights relating to the results of scientific activities indisputably belonged to scientists. By contrast, some problems can arise when the result of bioprospecting activities consists in the extraction of some components of Antarctic living organisms. In this case, state law requires knowing to whom these organisms and, thus, their components belong in order to establish who has the right to benefit from the selling of such components. The ownership of Antarctic organisms raises several problems.[39] First of all, one must ascertain whether or not such organisms can be subject to private appropriation. In fact, if Antarctic resources were considered 'global commons' due to the nature of the natural reserve of Antarctica, the private appropriation of such resources would be excluded and the benefits deriving from

[37] Measure 41–01 (2003). *Dissostichus* (or Antarctic toothfish) is a very highly exploited species of Antarctic fish. This CCAMLR measure establishes some obligations concerning exploring fishing, which also includes scientific prospecting. The data deriving from this exploration must be made available to all CCAMLR parties.

[38] For a description of the phases of bioprospecting see *supra* Section I.

[39] For the view that bioprospecting, carried out in particular areas of the planet, raises issues of sovereignty and property rights see Cottier, 'The Protection of Genetic Resources and Traditional Knowledge: Towards More Specific Rights and Obligations in World Trade Law' [1998] *Journal of International Economic Law* 555.

bioprospecting on these resources should be shared between all the members of the international community. This view does not seem in tune with the conduct of ATS parties. In the few examples of Antarctic commercial bioprospecting that have taken already place, claimant and non-claimant states granted IPRs and patents to private operators disregarding the interests of Antarctica and the purposes of the ATS.

The problem of ownership of Antarctic resources also affects third states with respect to the AT. Since these states are not bound by ATS norms, they might assume that the regulation of Antarctic scientific activities depends on international customary and treaty law relating to the exploration of resources that are outside state jurisdiction. In order to resolve the problem of the applicability of international law to Antarctica, we must ascertain the external legitimacy and effectiveness of the ATS and its relationship with the other norms of international law. This issue will be analysed later in this chapter. At the present, it is sufficient to remember that the alternative regime for the management of Antarctica, which was proposed by third states with respect to the AT, was not based on the idea that Antarctic resources are freely available for private appropriation, but, conversely, on the assumption that Antarctica must be declared part of the common heritage of humankind.[40]

Another problem relating to the ownership of Antarctic organisms and their components concerns who has the power to grant property rights (or intellectual property rights) over such organisms. International law recognises the power of sovereign states of attributing to private persons property rights over things that are under their jurisdiction. In addition, state sovereignty entails the power of control over access to living resources. The ATS does not provide a definitive answer about who has this power in Antarctica. In the claimant states' view, the organisms that live in the territories they claim in the Antarctic should be subject to their sovereignty. Thus, claimant states may recognise property rights of private bioprospectors over the organisms in their Antarctic claimed territories. On the contrary, non-claimant states believe that Antarctica and its living resources are not subject to any state jurisdiction, but only to the ATS. ATS norms do not definitively resolve this problem. Although Article IV of the AT prohibits the denial of the existing claims to sovereignty over Antarctic territories, no ATS norm acknowledges the principle of state sovereignty as a means to regulate Antarctic activities. In fact, ATS provisions establish the same rights and duties of all states parties. The hypothesis of two different views of claimant and non-claimant states that we have just described has led some authors to believe that the performance of bioprospecting in Antarctica will raise new conflicts between these

[40] See *infra* Section VI.

groups of states.[41] Moreover, one must recall that there is a sector of the Antarctic continent that is not subject to any territorial claim and that necessarily calls for some regulation, which is not based on the principle of territorial sovereignty.

In the present writer's view, the predicted conflicts between claimant and non-claimant states do not seem to have any concrete chance of occurring. In fact, accepting the ATS norms that establish the same rights and duties of all parties, claimant States have renounced the exercise of sovereign rights in their claimed territories in the Antarctic. Moreover, in no instruments adopted under the ATS have Consultative Parties ever recognised exclusive powers of control over Antarctic resources precisely because, under the ATS, such resources must be used by all the parties for the same purposes. If claimant states tried to affirm their sovereign rights over some of these resources, they would not only cause a legal conflict with non-claimant parties, but they would, above all, deny the basic principles of the ATS itself.

Even if, hitherto, the appropriation of Antarctic living resources has been allowed for the purpose of carrying out bioprospecting, nevertheless, some problems still remain with regard to the possibility of justifying such appropriation for commercial exploitation. Article 3 of Annex II to the Madrid Protocol states that permits for the exploitation of Antarctic flora and fauna can be issued only for scientific studies and educational uses. Thus, again it appears clear that the inconsistency between bioprospecting activities and the ATS concerns the commercial purpose of such activities. The real problem relating to Antarctic bioprospecting does not affect the ownership of the resources that have been investigated, but rather the type of benefits that derive from this activity and the way in which such befits are shared between all the members of the international community. Benefit-sharing can be based on two different approaches: on the one hand, monetary returns can be shared by all the contracting states to the AT and used in the interest of preserving the Antarctic environment. On the other hand, states can recognise the IPRs and exclusive economic rights of private operators. Although, hither to, Consultative Parties have adopted the latter approach, their recent concern for the proliferation of bioprospecting activities in Antarctica makes us believe that the need to preserve the basic principles of the ATS will soon lead to the reduction of any form of commercial exploitation of Antarctica, including lucrative bioprospecting.

The problem of benefit-sharing deriving from bioprospecting also affects the CCAMLR. As affirmed above, the Canberra Convention allows

[41] See the non-paper presented by Chile at the VI Meeting of the Committee on Environmental Protection (CEP), held in Madrid in 2003, 'Notes on Bioprospecting and Antarctic Research', Non Paper VI CEP 7, para. 5 and IP 75, *supra* n 10, para. 45.

commercial exploitation of marine living resources, including exploration for economic purposes. Nevertheless, the CCAMLR regime is applied differently within the diverse zones of the CCAMLR geographic scope. While the provisions concerning the exploration of resources within the area south of the 60° South latitude and the high seas over this area impose the same rights and duties on all states parties, the obligations relating to activities carried out within the maritime areas that are subject to state jurisdiction, such as the territorial sea and the EEZ corresponding to sub-Antarctic islands, also take into account the interests of coastal states which enjoy sovereign rights over these islands. In fact, in order to enforce the obligations concerning resource exploitation in these maritime areas, coastal states can exercise sovereign powers recognised by international law and, in particular, by the law of the sea. As an example, coastal states can control the scientific activities that are carried out in their EEZ by third states or private operators, as provided for by Article 246 of UNCLOS. This Article sanctions the power of coastal states to deny their consent where scientific activities correspond to 'applied' research. Moreover, the CCAMLR establishes the duty of conservation of marine living resources that coastal states must enforce in the maritime areas that are under their jurisdiction *vis-à-vis* states and operators carrying out exploration activities. So, if bioprospecting activities, performed within the scope of the CCAMLR, are subject to different control on account of the diverse maritime areas in which they occur, the economic returns deriving from such activities will be regulated in a different manner on the basis of the same reasoning. Thus, states parties to the CCAMLR allocate the returns of the exploration activities that are carried out within the high seas, on the basis of their national law in accordance with the aims of the CCAMLR itself. By contrast, the sharing of the economic returns of bioprospecting, carried out within the CCAMLR maritime areas that are subject to state jurisdiction, needs to be regulated by an agreement between coastal states and bioprospectors. These agreements are called bioprospecting contracts. They have been adopted for almost ten years since bioprospecting activities began to proliferate. The contractual model is the most widespread means of benefit-sharing when the owner of resources is not capable of exploiting them. This model has several merits. First, it avoids bioactive resources being exploited by states-owners in their exclusive interest and by inappropriate means. Secondly, bioprospecting contracts can help to protect the environment by allowing most technologically advanced operators to cooperate with states-owners in order to carry out bioprospecting in a most environmentally concerned manner.[42] In these ways, resource exploitation will lead to joint

42 Bioprospecting contracts can provide developing states with the appropriate technologies and know-how of developed countries, while the latter can achieve the sharing of the

benefit-sharing in accordance with environmental purposes. That is why the protection of living resources under the CCAMLR regime is more effective in the areas subject to state jurisdiction than on the high seas. Nevertheless, the contractual model cannot be applied in those contexts where a party is missing. For example, in the case where bioprospecting is carried out in areas that are outside state jurisdiction, such as the high seas and Antarctica, there is no responsible entity that can conclude an agreement with bioprospectors.

In short, one must observe that, hither to, there have been no appropriate rules establishing how to share benefits deriving from bioprospecting which is carried out both in Antarctic and sub-Antarctic areas. These rules should both deal with the issue of the access to resources and establish what public or private entity is entitled to share the benefits deriving from bioprospecting. With regard to the problem of benefit-sharing, one must observe that, although bioprospecting clearly deserves compensation, such compensation does not necessarily have to result in the economic satisfaction of few people. Compensation can include support for scientific projects or institutions involved in bioprospecting activities. It may also embrace the establishment of a fund aimed at the conservation of the Antarctic environment.[43] Similarly, with regard to the recognition of IPRs, although the legal acknowledgement of the 'paternity' of a discovery is a legitimate expectation of researchers, nevertheless, one must point out that the economic advantage stemming from such acknowledgment cannot be used to disregard the interests of Antarctica.

biological resources belonging to the former. Some reasons why bioprospecting contracts are useful to preserve biological resources are described by Hunter, *supra* n 6, 171. These reasons are: (1) maintaining the continuity of control over resources exploitation; (2) preserving the interest of source states in the conservation of biological resources; (3) ensuring the accountability of the private companies that are allowed to exploit resources. The author also affirms that bioprospecting contracts can be useful to preserve the environment because contracts can either allow exchange between biological resources and environmentally sound technology or oblige one of the parties to use economic returns deriving from bioprospecting for the adoption of measures aimed at protecting the environment: *ibid*, 165. The author divides bioprospecting contracts into two categories: mutual benefit contracts that allow the exchange between access to resources and access to new technologies, and debt-for-nature-swap contracts with which developed states buy a part of the national debt of developing States obliging the latter to prohibit the overexploitation of biological resources. For the usefulness of agreements between scientists and private companies: see also Verhoosel, 'Beyond the Unsustainable Rhetoric of Sustainable Development: Transferring Environmentally Sound Technologies' (1998) 11 *Georgetown International Environmental Law Review* 76. These contracts can also improve human knowledge concerning biological organisms by remunerating the scientists that have carried out bioprospecting through the recognition of their intellectual property rights. For this view see Rubin and Fish, 'Biodiversity Prospecting: Using Innovative Contractual Provisions to Foster Ethnobotanical Knowledge, Technology, and Conservation', [1994] *Colorado Journal of International Environmental Law and Policy* 28 (as quoted by Gollin and Laird, *supra* n 27, at n 147).

[43] For the need for different forms of compensation on account of the diverse situation in which bioprospecting is carried out see Potts, *supra* n 20.

V. CONTROL OVER ANTARCTIC EXPLORING ACTIVITIES

As affirmed above, the first phase of bioprospecting implies the search for bioactive components. Such research must necessarily be carried out within the Antarctic area and, thus, bioprospectors have to comply with the same obligations that the ATS establishes *vis-à-vis* other Antarctic operators. Among such obligations, one must recall that imposing the duty to carry out a prior environmental impact assessment (EIA) of any activity that is planned in Antarctica.[44] Bioprospecting has different impacts by reason of the diverse bioactive materials that scientists intend to collect. It can require harvesting some specimens of Antarctic species. In this case, bioprospecting is directly related to the conservation of the species concerned.[45] In other circumstances, bioprospecting implies the extraction of components from the specimens of some species. In this case, the species in question are not affected by great harvesting. Sometimes, the specimens that have been investigated do not need to be killed. Nevertheless, their reintroduction into the Antarctic environment is not always possible. In fact, Article 4 of Annex II to the Madrid Protocol prohibits the introduction of alien species into Antarctica. Although Antarctic specimens, which have been investigated, are not properly alien species, genetic prospecting can modify the natural characteristics of living organisms so as to transform them into alien species with respect to their native species. Therefore, the reintroduction of genetically investigated species into the Antarctic environment might be harmful for both the other specimens of the same species and the entire ecosystem.

In addition to the procedural obligation requiring prior EIA, the ecosystem approach, adopted by Article 3 of the Madrid Protocol, compels those who carry out EIA to take into account the effects of bioprospecting, not only on the species that are subject to exploration, but also on the entire ecosystem to which such species belong.[46] In fact, ecosystems and biodiversity are not static models, but, as Arce suggests,[47] 'repeated interactions'. However, the concern for the conservation of the ecosystem seems to be justified only in those cases where bioprospecting implies the harvesting of species.

The ecosystem approach is not only a basic principle of the Madrid Protocol, but is also the primary foundation of the CCAMLR. In fact, although the Canberra Convention allows commercial exploitation of marine living resources, defining conservation as 'rational use',[48] it permits

[44] Art 8 of and Annex 1 to the Madrid Protocol.
[45] For this view see Anton, *supra* n 1, 348.
[46] See Non-paper Chile, *supra* n 41, para. 6.
[47] Arce, 'The Evolution of Heterogeneity in Biodiversity and Environmental Regimes' [2000] *Journal of Conflict Resolution* 760.
[48] Art 2(2) of CCAMLR.

such exploitation only if it is carried out in accordance with the ecosystem approach, stated by Article 1(3). Moreover, the CCAMLR regime has shown a strong conservative character from the beginning.[49] Thus, although bioprospecting seems to be fully consistent with the concept of 'rational use' of resources established by the CCAMLR, nevertheless, this activity finds a limit in the need to preserve the marine ecosystem as established by the Canberra Convention and the measures adopted by the CCAMLR Commission.

In short, the physical impact of bioprospecting activities on Antarctica seems effectively controlled through the application to such activities of the obligations established by existing Antarctic legal instruments. Ultimately, biological exploration is one of the numerous lawful activities that can be carried out within the Antarctic area.

VI. BIOPROSPECTING IN OTHER INTERNATIONAL REGIMES

The UNCLOS Provisions relating to Scientific Research

Although bioprospecting seems to need specific provisions in order to be carried out in Antarctica without prejudicing the conservation of the environment, so far, such provisions do not exist. So, one must ascertain whether and to what extent Antarctic bioprospecting can be regulated by international regimes, other than the ATS, that deal with this issue. The answer to this question is not just important for finding alternative provisions for bioprospecting while Antarctic norms are negotiated, but it is also useful to ascertain what obligations third states with respect to the ATS must comply with.

Among the international treaties that are potentially applicable to Antarctica, one must, first of all, mention UNCLOS. We will begin our analysis by taking into account bioprospecting of marine organisms and, then, examine the peculiar issue relating to scientific research activities within the Area, dealt with in Part XI of UNCLOS.

[49] For this view see Kaye, 'Legal Approaches to Polar Fisheries Regimes: A Comparative Analysis of the Convention for the Conservation of Antarctic Marine Living Resources and the Bearing Sea Doughnut Hole Convention' (1995) 26 *California Western International Law Journal* 75. By contrast, Redgwell defines CCAMLR as a resource management regime. See Redgwell, 'Protection of Ecosystems under International Law: Lessons from Antarctica', in Boyle-Freestone (eds), *International Law and Sustainable Development* (Oxford, 1999), 205. In our view, although the Convention, allowing the exploitation of marine living resources, cannot be considered a proper conservative agreement, the legal instruments that have been adopted by the Commission since its origins establish more severe obligations aimed at preserving the survival of species than other resource management agreements. This means that states parties to CCAMLR have preferred to sacrifice their possibility of exploiting marine resources in order to favour species' conservation.

The Law of the Sea Convention does not specifically regulate bioprospecting. It refers only to scientific research and living resources. Nevertheless, the evolutive interpretation of UNCLOS norms seems to allow the inclusion of the concepts of 'applied' research and 'genetic resources' in the scope of this convention.[50] The UNCLOS regime is mainly based on the principle of state sovereignty.[51] In fact, only coastal states have the power of regulating scientific research affecting living resources which belong to their territorial sea, continental shelf and EEZ.[52] UNCLOS also recognises the right of coastal states to adopt national laws 'requiring the conduct of specified fisheries research programmes and regulating the conduct of such research, including the sampling of catches, disposition of samples and reporting of associated scientific data'.[53] This right could be particularly important in allowing coastal states to intervene in bioprospecting projects that other states' nationals intend to carry out in their EEZ. Moreover, UNCLOS is the only international regime that provides for a distinction between 'pure' and 'applied' research. Article 246 of this convention recognises different powers of coastal states in the cases where third parties carry out 'pure' or 'applied' research in their EEZ or continental shelf. 'Applied' research by third states requires the consent of coastal states,[54] while consent cannot be denied for the performance of 'pure' research.[55] In addition, Article 248 establishes the duty to provide information to coastal states concerning research activities carried out in the areas subject to their jurisdiction. Even at first glance, this principle seems to highlight some inconsistencies with the need to preserve the confidentiality of bioprospecting results.

50 For a view supporting the evolutive interpretation of UNCLOS see Anton, *supra* n 1, 362.

51 For this view see Cataldi in this volume.

52 Art 19(2)(j) of UNCLOS excludes scientific research from the activities that are compatible with innocent passage in the territorial sea. Art 40 of this Convention does not allow states in transit in international straits to carry out research activities without coastal state consent. Art 54 does the same with respect to archipelagic seas. Moreover, Art 56(1)(b)(ii) affirms that '[i]n the exclusive economic zone, the coastal State has . . . jurisdiction as provided for in the relevant provisions of this Convention with regard to . . . marine scientific research'.

53 Art 62(4)(f).

54 Art 246(5)(a) states: '[c]oastal States may however in their discretion withhold their consent to the conduct of a marine scientific research project of another State or competent international organization in the exclusive economic zone or on the continental shelf of the coastal State if that project is of direct significance for the exploration and exploitation of natural resources, whether living or non-living'.

55 Art 246(3) states: '[c]oastal States shall, in normal circumstances, grant their consent for marine scientific research projects by other States or competent international organizations in their exclusive economic zone or on their continental shelf to be carried out in accordance with this Convention exclusively for peaceful purposes and in order to increase scientific knowledge of the marine environment for the benefit of all mankind.' For a description of the object and purpose of Art 246 of UNCLOS see Farrier and Tucker, *supra* n 29, 223 and Glowka, *supra* n 9, 359.

Finally, Article 249 of UNCLOS stipulates the right of coastal states to participate in the scientific activities that are carried out in their EEZ. This right is enhanced by the power to suspend such research activities, as Article 253 sanctions. From these considerable rights of coastal states one may infer that the bioprospectors acting within the EEZ must necessarily conclude bioprospecting agreements with coastal states in order to avoid impediments and unforeseen costs of their activities. Thus, in this case, benefit-sharing follows a contractual model.

As affirmed above, the principle of state sovereignty is not easily applicable to Antarctica. On the one hand, the ATS excludes the application of this principle establishing an autonomous regime through Article IV of the AT. So, states parties to both the AT and UNCLOS cannot apply to Antarctica the provisions of the Law of the Sea Convention that recognise the principle of state sovereignty. If they did so, they would breach Article IV of the AT, which is one of the fundamental rules of the ATS.[56] On the other hand, third states with respect to the ATS have never shown their intention to apply the sovereignty principle to Antarctica: few states which demonstrated their interest in establishing an alternative regime for Antarctica *vis-à-vis* the ATS at the UN General Assembly did not intend to manage Antarctica on the basis of the principle of sovereignty. Instead, they suggested declaring Antarctica as a part of the common heritage of humankind.[57] Thus, the application of the sovereignty principle to Antarctica does not seem to be legitimised either by AT parties or third states. In the light of the above, the UNCLOS norms that are based on this principle should not be applied to the Antarctic seas.

With regard to the waters that are beyond national jurisdiction, Article 87 of UNCLOS establishes freedom of scientific research and exploitation of resources as long as these activities are consistent with the duty to preserve the marine environment, as Part XII of this Convention states. According to this provision, bioprospecting activities carried out on the high seas should be equally free. Nevertheless, some UNCLOS norms, aimed at enhancing strong cooperation between states for the management of the high seas, seem to conflict with the economic and selfish aims of 'commercial' bioprospecting. For example, Article 241 affirms that '[m]arine scientific research activities shall not constitute the legal basis for any claim to any part of the marine environment or its resources'. It

[56] On the need to conciliate the ATS with the principle of sovereignty adopted by UNCLOS see Rothwell, 'Southern Ocean Bioprospecting and International Law', in *Canterbury Workshop*, *supra* n 3.

[57] In this sense see the declaration of Malaysia at the UN General Assembly Meeting of 1982, in: Doc. A/37/PV.10. More recently, Malaysia, Antigua and Barbuda, and Guinea reaffirmed that Antarctica is the common heritage of humankind at the 38th Mtg. of the First Committee during the 46th Session of the UN General Assembly, in: Doc. A/C.1/46/PV38.

means that, excluding the use of specimens caught during bioprospecting, no other form of appropriation is allowed on the high seas. This could raise some problems with respect to some forms of bioprospecting. In fact, although bioprospecting does not, in general, involve appropriation of resources, it sometimes consists of extracting some components of a species. One must recall that scientists and private companies usually apply for patents in order to enjoy the economic returns deriving from their discovery in an exclusive manner. Even though a species cannot be patented as such, it is, nevertheless, possible to patent a compound, such as some bioactive material belonging to a species which has some commercial value.[58] In this specific case, a broad interpretation of Article 241 of UNCLOS could lead to the conclusion that the recognition of IPRs of the scientists and companies that have extracted some components or compounds from marine organisms is a limit to the freedom of other scientists and companies that have to pay compensation to the discoverers in order to carry out further research relating to these compounds or components. The recognition of IPRs or other forms of exclusive economic exploitation of marine resources belonging to the high seas also seems to conflict with those provisions of UNCLOS that invite states to cooperate in order to transfer technologies.[59] This form of the duty of cooperation has been strengthened by the 1995 Agreement on Straddling and Highly Migratory Fish Stocks (hereafter Fish Stocks Agreement) which, in Article 5(k), promotes the exchange of information deriving from research and of technologies in accordance with Part XIV of UNCLOS and Annex I to the Agreement.

In short, bioprospecting cannot be banned on the high seas because UNCLOS recognises the freedom of exploration and exploitation of marine organisms. Nevertheless, since no specific norms relating to this issue exist, a cautious approach is required because several important interests are at stake. First, bioprospecting must be carried out in accordance with the duty to protect the marine environment. Secondly, the duty of cooperation, namely cooperation in exchanging information and technology, must be taken into account whenever scientists intend to carry out bioprospecting activities on the high seas. Unfortunately, the content of the duty of cooperation is too general to allow one to determine how it can be enforced against those who do not comply with it.[60] For this reason, UNCLOS provisions do not appear effectively to deal with bioprospecting within the international seas.

58 For the view that compounds can be patented since they cannot be found in nature as such see Gollin and Laird, *supra* n 27, para. 53.

59 Verhoosel affirms that the protection of intellectual property rights can be an obstacle to technology transfer: see Verhoosel, *supra* n 42, 67.

60 For the too general content of the obligations established by UNCLOS see *ibid*, 63.

As far as bioprospecting activities carried out within the Antarctic high seas are concerned, both the AT and UNCLOS seem to justify the applicability of the abovementioned norms of UNCLOS. Article VI of the AT, in fact, safeguards the rights of states on the high seas that are south of the 60° South latitude. Moreover, the UNCLOS provisions concerning scientific research, performed on the high seas, establish the same rights and duties for all states parties. These obligations are very similar to those sanctioned by the ATS, in particular, as far as the duties of cooperation and exchange of information are concerned. Nevertheless, neither Antarctic nor UNCLOS norms do seem to provide the appropriate regulation of bioprospecting activities due to the fact that such norms do not establish precise obligations on this matter.[61] Thus, the application of the UNCLOS provisions to Antarctic bioprospecting does not seem effectively to fill the normative lacuna of the ATS.

Finally, one must briefly refer to other UNCLOS norms that emphasise the need to preserve the common interest rather than selfish exigencies of states and private operators: the norms that are included in Part XI of UNCLOS and which, as is well known, concern the management of the mineral resources of the deep seabed and not of living organisms.[62] Article 143 of this part establishes that scientific research in the 'Area' must be carried out in the interest of all humankind. The principle established by this Article, together with the rules sanctioned by Part XIV of UNCLOS and the ATS relating to scientific research, leads us to the conclusion that international regimes are inclined to regulate the activities that take place within the maritime areas outside national jurisdiction in the global interest. These provisions, such as ATS norms, do not preclude the possibility of carrying out bioprospecting as such. They only establish some strict requirements that bioprospectors must respect. Moreover, most economically concerned trends can be observed in the 1994 Agreement on the Implementation of Part XI of UNCLOS (hereafter Implementing Agreement) that, in order to allow the entry into force of this Convention, adopted a benefit-sharing approach.[63] The Implementing Agreement, in fact, establishes that the approval of plans of work of private operators is subject to the fact that such operators have invested a specific amount of money in the research and exploration of an area that is suitable for exploitation.[64] Therefore, the current regime of mineral

[61] For the view that areas outside state jurisdiction are not appropriately protected by international law against unregulated harvesting of resources see Anton, *supra* n 1, 343. In the light of this, the author makes a comparison between the high seas and Antarctica: *ibid*, at n 9.

[62] For a thorough analysis of this problem see Scovazzi in this volume.

[63] For this view see Anton, *supra* n 1, 368.

[64] Para 6(a)(i) of Section 1 of the Annex to the Implementing Agreement states: 'a plan of work . . . shall be considered to have met the financial and technical qualifications necessary

prospecting of the deep seabed combines the common heritage principle, sanctioned by Part XI of UNCLOS, with the need to recognise the right to financial compensation of private investors. Similarly, the Implementing Agreement also recognises the right to financial compensation for transfers of technology by promoting the creation of joint ventures between developing countries and industrialised states.[65] So even commercial mineral prospecting seems to be permitted by the Implementing Agreement although with the abovementioned limits. Even if Part XI of UNCLOS and its Implementing Agreement cannot be applied to biological prospecting, the approach, adopted by these legal instruments, which protects both common and private interests, can provide some useful suggestions for the Consultative Parties for the future Antarctic regime of bioprospecting. In fact, private operators, who usually own best technology, need economic returns in order to be stimulated to carry out bioprospecting activities. Concurrently, some areas of the planet, such as the deep seabed or Antarctica, are of common concern and, thus, can be explored and exploited in the interest of the international community only by means of cooperation between States and private parties.

Although the comparison of the AT and its supplements with UNCLOS is interesting, the Antarctic instrument that mainly interacts with the Law of the Sea Convention is the CCAMLR. As affirmed above,[66] the Canberra Convention recognises the sovereign rights of coastal states over the territories that are within the sub-Antarctic area.[67] Thus, the applicability of the UNCLOS provisions concerning the regulation of scientific research carried out within the EEZ seems to be compatible with the CCAMLR regime, since the Law of the Sea allows coastal states to regulate scientific (in particular, 'applied') research carried out within the maritime zones subject to their jurisdiction. In the light of this power of regulation of coastal states, recognised by UNCLOS, one could argue that the parties to the the Canberra Convention could also apply, within their sub-Antarctic maritime areas, the severe norms concerning the conservation of

for approval of a plan of work if the sponsoring State or States certify that the applicant has expended an amount equivalent to at least US$ 30 million in research and exploration activities and has expended no less than 10 per cent of that amount in the location, survey and evaluation of the area referred to in the plan of work'.

65 Para 1(a) of Section 5 of the Implementing Agreement affirms that 'the Enterprise, and developing States wishing to obtain deep seabed mining technology, shall seek to obtain such technology on fair and reasonable commercial terms and conditions on the open market, or through joint-venture arrangements'. For the view that this provision permits the protection of intellectual property rights of the owners of technologies see Verhoosel, *supra* n 42, 55.

66 See *supra* Section IV.

67 Actually, the recognition of sovereign rights over sub-Antarctic islands is not sanctioned in CCAMLR, but only in the Statement of the Chairman of the Conference that led to the adoption of the Convention. For this statement see *Handbook of the Antarctic Treaty System* (US Department of State, Washington D.C., 2002), 371.

resources, which have been established within the CCAMLR regime to third states that are parties to the Law of the Sea Convention. Although this conclusion seems to be compatible with UNCLOS provisions and particularly useful to resolve the problem of uncontrolled exploitation of marine resources, the recent case law of the International Tribunal on the Law of the Sea (ITLOS) showed strong opposition to this broad application of the CCAMLR.[68] The ITLOS, in fact, considered the enforcement of the CCAMLR with respect to third states, contrary to those norms of UNCLOS that oblige coastal states to regulate the activities carried out in their EEZ in accordance with UNCLOS provisions.[69] In the ITLOS's view, the CCAMLR obligations are more severe than UNCLOS ones. With regard to the regulation of activities within the high seas the CCAMLR establishes the same rights and duties for all states parties. Thus, scientific research, including bioprospecting, is subject to the measures adopted by the CCAMLR Commission. These measures can be enforced only by flag states due to lack of other forms of control within the CCAMLR regime. In this regard, CCAMLR obligations do not seem very different from UNCLOS provisions.

In sum, with the exception of the UNCLOS provisions that are based on the principle of state sovereignty and are not suitable for application to Antarctica, the ATS and UNCLOS do not seem to establish very different obligations with regard to the regulation of scientific research and, thus, bioprospecting. The most evident characteristic of the norms of these two regimes, which emerges from our analysis, is their extremely general content that patently calls for the development of specific norms in order to ensure the effective regulation of bioprospecting.[70]

The Convention on Biological Diversity

The Convention on Biological Diversity regulates the utilisation of biological resources, including genetic resources.[71] Thus, bioprospecting is certainly one of the main activities that can be regulated by this Convention. CBD is a global agreement in terms both of geographic scope and the participation of states and international organisations. At first glance, there

[68] See Camouco and Monte Confurco cases where the ITLOS accepted the request of Panama and Seychelles, respectively, of prompt release of their vessels engaged in fishing activities of doubtful legality within the EEZ of Crozet and Kerguelen Islands, subject to French sovereignty. The *Camouco Case* (Panama v. France) [2000] ILM 666 and the *Monte Confurco Case* (Seychelles v. France), Case n. 6, available at www.itlos.org.

[69] Art 56(2) of UNCLOS states: '[i]n exercising its rights and performing its duties under this Convention in the exclusive economic zone, the coastal State shall have due regard to the rights and duties of other States and shall act in a manner compatible with the provisions of this Convention'.

[70] For this view see Anton, *supra* n 1, 371.

[71] Art 2(2) of the CBD.

are, therefore, no reasons why this convention should not be applied to Antarctica. Nevertheless, the applicability of the CBD to Antarctica must be examined in the light of some substantive requirements of this Convention, such as its object and purpose, rather than its theoretically global character. Since the purpose of the CBD is to regulate the use of biological resources, access to resources must be allowed in the areas where this convention is applied. The need to have access to resources is implicit in the concept of 'use' itself. In fact, there is no use without access.[72] If access to resources was denied in a particular area of the planet, there would be no reason why this Convention. Are Antarctic resources accessible? The answer is not as easy as it may appear. In the view of states parties to the ATS, living resources of the Antarctic continent can be exploited only for scientific purposes. Although 'access' does not exactly correspond to 'exploitation', one must point out that access to Antarctic living resources, although limited to carrying out 'pure' scientific research, frequently compels scientists to remove the specimens investigated from their original ecosystem. In fact, as affirmed above,[73] when a specimen has been subject to scientific tests, in particular genetic prospecting, it can no longer be considered a native species. In other cases, biological exploration can require the elimination of the specimens investigated. The more significant the changes in living organism, provoked by scientific exploration, are the more frequent is the need to harvest such organisms. Thus, under the ATS, access to and, thus, the use of biological resources are confined to scientific purposes. The same problem does not affect the CCAMLR since this Convention also allows both access to and exploitation of marine resources for commercial purposes. Thus, access has greater scope in the CCAMLR than in other Antarctic instruments.

Moreover, one must recall that even third states with respect to the ATS have shown their intention to minimise human activities in Antarctica in order to preserve this area in the interest of the whole of humankind. Thus, a particularly strict approach by Consultative Parties and third states could lead to preventing bioprospectors from accessing Antarctic resources for commercial purposes in order to preserve the integrity of the Antarctic ecosystem.

Next, since Antarctica can be mainly used for scientific purposes, one must ascertain whether scientific utilisation can be considered a form of access according to the CBD. Access to resources is regulated by Article 15 of the CBD. Paragraph 7 of this Article, determining the criteria for benefit-sharing, affirms that the relevant benefits are those 'arising from the commercial and other utilization of genetic resources'. Thus, scientific use

72 See Farrier and Tucker, *supra* n 29, 223.

73 See *supra* Section V.

seems to be one of the possible types of access to biological resources that are permitted by the CBD. Nevertheless, under Article 15 of the CBD, access to resources is evidently based on the principle of territorial sovereignty. This Article recognises the power of states that enjoy sovereign rights over resources to regulate access to them. As affirmed above,[74] the criterion of territorial sovereignty does not find application in the ATS. In fact, although Article IV of the AT does not exclude the existence of claims to sovereignty over Antarctic territories, ATS norms have never adopted such a criterion to attribute jurisdiction over the Antarctic continent. Thus, the reliance of the CBD on the principle of territorial sovereignty could hamper the application of this Convention to Antarctica. However, although the CBD was mainly adopted to resolve the problems concerning the management of biological resources that are under state jurisdiction, some of its norms also apply to the areas that are beyond such jurisdiction. In particular, Article 4(b) of the CBD sanctions the application of this Convention to 'processes and activities, regardless of where their effects occur, carried out under [state] jurisdiction or control, within the area of...national jurisdiction or beyond the limits of national jurisdiction'. In the light of this Article, states can exercise their control over their nationals even if they are out of state jurisdiction. Thus, a broad interpretation of the abovementioned norms of the CBD can allow the application of this Convention to Antarctic bioprospecting. Concern for the areas that are beyond national jurisdiction has recently increased in the CBD regime. The Subsidiary Body on Scientific, Technical, and Technological Advice (SBSTTA), established by Article 25 of the CBD, has suggested creating some protected areas within the high seas whose environment is particularly fragile in order to fix uniform obligations for all states and private operators.[75] The same approach could be adopted with respect to Antarctica, recognising its status of 'protected area' under the CBD regime.[76]

In order to determine to what extent the CBD can be applied to Antarctica, one must ascertain whether the purposes for which this Convention was adopted are suitable for the management of a peculiar area, such as Antarctica. The three main objectives of the CBD are the conservation of biodiversity, the sustainable use of biological resources, and the equitable sharing of benefits deriving from the exploitation of these resources.

[74] See *supra* Section VI.

[75] See VIII Meeting of the Subsidiary Body on Scientific, Technical, and Technological Advice, Mar 2003, at www.biodiv.org. In the past, the SBSTTA had highlighted only the need to accord special protection to the maritime areas that were under state jurisdiction. For an overview see Anton, *supra* n 1, 358.

[76] For this view see IP 75, *supra* n 10, para. 98 and the Message of the World Parks Congress (Durban, 2003) to the CBD Conference of the Parties, *supra* n 5.

With regard to the objective of conservation, the regimes of both the ATS and the CBD seem to establish similar rules. Such regimes allow the utilisation of resources in an environmentally sound manner. In fact, they acknowledge the power of control of states parties over their nationals and the right to adopt internal legislation implementing the general provisions of these regimes. The only conflict that can arise between the ATS and CBD concerns the extent of the utilisation of resources. On the one hand, the AT and the Madrid Protocol clearly establish a very strict regime that allows only the scientific use of Antarctic organisms. However, the CCAMLR permits the commercial exploitation of marine resources. On the other hand, the CBD does not prohibit any type of utilisation as long as it is carried out in an environmentally concerned manner. Despite this apparent inconsistency, so far, no state, either party or non-party to the ATS, has invoked the CBD in order to legitimise the commercial exploitation of the living resources of the Antarctic continent. In this regard, the possibility of a conflict between the ATS and CBD remains hypothetical. Finally, one must recall that bioprospecting seldom affects resource conservation. In fact, bioprospecting can jeopardise conservation only when it entails the harvest of living organisms.

As far as the second objective of the CBD ('sustainable use') is concerned, the most difficult task is to determine its content due to the uncertainty of this concept. Some authors have defined 'sustainable use' as 'the use of components of biological diversity in a way and at a rate that does not lead to the long-term decline of biological diversity thereby maintaining its potential to meet the needs of present and future generations'.[77] The reference to 'components' is particularly important to extend the application of the CBD and, thus, of the objective of 'sustainable use' to bioprospecting.[78] In fact, this activity frequently concerns the exploration of components of living organisms. The concept of 'sustainable use' can be interpreted in different ways in order to enhance either its environmental or commercial nature. The authors that are most environmentally concerned believe that biodiversity is a quasi-non-renewable resource. Thus, its utilisation must be severely limited.[79] For example, this approach has been adopted by Consultative Parties that have established strict limitations on the use of Antarctica through the Madrid Protocol. By contrast, most economically oriented legal writers support the idea that 'sustainable use' must be maintained by means of new technologies that are both environmentally sound and economically effective. In fact, 'sustainable use' is not an abstract concept, but must be achieved through concrete means such as, for example, technology transfer.[80] Article 16 of the CBD

[77] See Hunter, *supra* n 6, 149–150.
[78] See Glowka, *supra* n 9, 352.
[79] For this view see Hunter *supra* n 6, 143.
[80] See Glowka, *supra* n 9, 332.

regulates the issue of technology transfer on the basis of mutually agreed terms. It expressly recalls biotechnology, which is strictly linked to bioprospecting. This type of technology not only includes technological equipment, but also scientific information and know-how that, sometimes, do not belong to states.[81] Thus, the transfer of different types of technologies cannot be regulated in the same manner due to the fact that it can simultaneously affect public interests and private assets. Moreover, Verhoosel highlights that Article 16 does not regulate all types of technology transfer, but only the transfer of environmentally sound technology. A statement of the SBSTTA also specified the narrow scope of this Article. This organ interpreted the wording of Article 16 of the CBD restrictively so as to consider transfer of technology only that aimed at the conservation of biodiversity or achieving other purposes that can be useful for such conservation.[82] The ATS does not establish any provision concerning the transfer of technologies. Only Article 3(2)(c)(iv) of the Madrid Protocol compels states to ascertain whether technologies used by national operators are harmful for the conservation of the Antarctic environment. Thus, the ATS still confirms its environmentally concerned nature that is extremely restrictive with respect to the performance of those activities where technology is particularly important, such as bioprospecting.[83] The CBD provisions relating to technology transfer could be applied to Antarctica in order to specify the content of the general duty of cooperation, sanctioned by ATS instruments and inviting states to spread best available technology for the protection of the Antarctic environment.

The third objective of the CBD is benefit-sharing. As affirmed above,[84] this issue is particularly relevant to bioprospecting due to the economic purposes of this activity. The problem of benefit-sharing relating to the CBD involves the rights of both states and private operators. For this reason, the CBD establishes a form of benefit-sharing that is based on the criteria of equity and mutual agreement. While equitable sharing expresses 'distributive and inter-generational justice',[85] mutually agreed terms demonstrate the contractual nature of the CBD which is still strongly linked to the principle of state sovereignty. This contractual nature can be observed in connection with several issues: Article 15 regulates access to resources requiring mutual agreement between the countries that are 'donors' of resources and the public or private prospectors that possess the appropriate technologies and knowledge to exploit and explore such

[81] See Verhoosel, *supra* n 42, at n 68.
[82] See *ibid*, 56
[83] For the view that the CBD follows a too economic approach see Hunter, *supra* n 6, 167.
[84] See *supra* Section IV.
[85] For this expression see Cottier, *supra* n 39, at n 23.

resources; Article 16 establishes that technology transfer must be dealt with in terms of mutual agreement; finally, Article 19[86] promotes the participation of developing states in sharing the benefits deriving from biotechnologies based upon genetic resources.[87] This contractual approach patently shows that the CBD mainly deals with the cases where resources are under state jurisdiction. In fact, such approach can effectively work only when it is possible to conclude an agreement between the owner of the resources and the owner of technologies (including scientific knowledge and know-how). However, mutual benefit (or bioprospecting) agreements cannot deal with problems concerning the benefit-sharing of the resources that are beyond national jurisdiction. In fact, a party to the agreement is missing because there is no internationally recognised authority that can stand for the owner of resources that are within the areas outside state jurisdiction, such as the high seas and Antarctica.

In order to resolve the problems concerning benefit-sharing, the Conference of the Parties to the CBD adopted specific guidelines on 'Access to Genetic Resources and Fair and Equitable Sharing of Benefits Arising out of their Utilization' (hereafter the Bonn guidelines).[88] The Bonn guidelines also deal with scientific activities.[89] So, this legal instrument can also be applied to determine the equitable benefit-sharing relating to bioprospecting. In particular, paragraph 22 of these guidelines highlights the environmental concern of the CBD since it invites states to allow only national programmes that take into account the conservation of biodiversity. This environmentally sound approach of the Bonn guidelines has led some authors to believe that this instrument could offer useful suggestion to the ATS parties for the creation of their own benefit-sharing system relating to bioprospecting.[90] Although these guidelines are mainly based on the principle of state sovereignty, and, thus, are scarcely suitable for application to Antarctica, nevertheless, some of their provisions could be adapted to the peculiar status of the Antarctic area. For example, paragraphs 41–50, which define the requirement of mutual agreed terms with which benefit-sharing agreements must comply, could suggest to states

86 Art 19(2) states: '[e]ach Contracting Party shall take all practicable measures to promote and advance priority access on a fair and equitable basis by Contracting Parties, especially developing countries, to the results and benefits arising from biotechnologies based upon genetic resources provided by those Contracting Parties. Such access shall be on mutually agreed terms'.

87 The approach of the CBD provisions, based on contractual terms, is highlighted by Cottier, *supra* n 39.

88 Annex to Decision VI/24 adopted at the VI Conference of the Parties to the CBD in 2002. During the IV Conference of the Parties to the CBD, held in Bratislava in 1998, the Conference of the Parties to the CBD had established a panel of experts on access and benefit sharing, which is now a permanent working group.

89 Para 23 of Decision VI/24.

90 For this view see IP/75, *supra* n 10, para. 91.

parties to the AT how to regulate the distribution of the benefits deriving from Antarctic bioprospecting.[91] Moreover, the system of national monitoring on compliance with the environmental requirements of the Bonn guidelines, established by paragraphs 55–56, is suitable for application to the ATS. In fact, the AT and the other Antarctic instruments use monitoring as the primary form of control over operators. Finally, Section 2 of Appendix II of the Bonn guidelines provides for non-monetary benefits that can be included in bioprospecting agreements, such as the financing of training of scientists and transfer of technology that, as these guidelines specify, also includes know-how and scientific knowledge. These types of benefits seem to be the appropriate returns of bioprospecting activities, carried out in an area of common concern such as Antarctica. The applicability of the CBD regime to the Antarctic area is also shown by some recent decisions of the Conference of the Parties. For example, Decision VII/19[92] expressly establishes that the Working Group on Access and Benefit-Sharing must take into account existing international treaty systems, including the AT, in order to create an international regime regulating the distribution of benefits deriving from the exploitation and exploration of genetic resources.[93] This decision is, in fact, aimed at strengthening the application of the Bonn guidelines to domestic law, regional organisations, and at international level.

In the light of the above, one can affirm that the CBD and the legal instruments that originated from this Convention are suitable for application to Antarctic bioprospecting, with the exception of the provisions based on the principle of territorial sovereignty. However, these provisions could still be useful to regulate bioprospecting activities within the scope of the CCAMLR in the areas where state sovereignty is internationally recognised. As affirmed above, the only possible inconsistency between the CCAMLR and the CBD can affect the extent of protection of resources that these two regimes are designed to recognise. Hitherto, CCAMLR has shown a more environmentally concerned character than the CBD.[94] Nevertheless, the recent legal instruments adopted within the CBD regime seem to reduce this gap.

[91] Para 48 states: '[p]ursuant to mutually agreed terms established following prior informed consent, benefits should be shared fairly and equitably with all those who have been identified as having contributed to the resource management, scientific and/or commercial process. The latter may include governmental, non-governmental or academic institutions and indigenous and local communities. Benefits should be directed in such a way as to promote conservation and sustainable use of biological diversity'.

[92] Decision VII/19 adopted in Kuala Lumpur in 2004, at www.biodiv.org.

[93] Para (d)(xxiii) of the Annex to Decision VII/19, entitled 'Terms of Reference for the ad hoc Open-ended Working Group on Access and Benefit-Sharing'.

[94] For the new developments of the CBD regime see Redgwell in this volume.

WIPO and Genetic Discoveries

Bioprospecting also raises the issue of the recognition of intellectual property rights of scientists who made new discoveries by means of this activity. The novelty of a discovery which allows discovers to obtain intellectual property rights and patents can consist either in the finding of an unknown component of some living organisms or in the identification of some new properties of the biological components of such organisms. The economic value of a discovery, which makes it possible to enjoy exclusive rights, like IPRs and patent rights, cannot therefore be determined only on the basis of the value of the component discovered, but also by reason of the relevance of the discovery itself for its commercial exploitation.

Two main problems arise from the recognition of IPRs deriving from bioprospecting. First, such recognition clashes with the need of the international community to access resources and information concerning such resources. For this reason, IPRs are sometimes considered to obstruct the dissemination of scientific knowledge since confidentiality is the best means of protecting such rights. This feeling affects not only the ATS. Some legal instruments, adopted within the CBD regime, invite states to reduce the impact of IPRs on the exploration of genetic resources by disclosing information in applications for patents.[95] Secondly, the recognition of IPRs is usually achieved at national level. This causes lack of uniformity with regard to the extent of such rights. This problem has also been raised by the Intergovernmental Committee on Intellectual Property and Genetic Resources, Traditional Knowledge and Folklore of the World Intellectual Property Organisation (WIPO).[96]

The ATS cannot resolve either of these problems. In fact, it does not regulate IPRs arising from bioprospecting activities carried out in Antarctica. For this reason, the application to Antarctica of other international regimes, which deal with the issue of intellectual property in a specialised manner, seems to be the most viable solution until specific Antarctic provisions are established.[97] Particular importance must be given to the activity of WIPO which supervises the functioning of several international conventions, such as the Treaty on the International Recognition of the Deposit of Microorganisms for the Purposes of Patent Procedure (hereafter

[95] Section C of the Bonn guidelines concerning the 'Role of intellectual property rights in the implementation of access and benefit-sharing arrangements' and Element 3 of the Annex to Decision VII/29 that provides for the Programme of Work on Technology Transfer and Technological and Scientific Cooperation. The Annex affirms that scientific information must be disseminated as a form of technology transfer. IPRs do not have to hamper such transfer, although they need to be respected. For an overview see Stone, *supra* n 35.

[96] See IP 75, *supra* n 10, para. 102.

[97] For this view see also Guyomard in this volume.

the Budapest Treaty).[98] This Treaty is aimed at establishing a 'Union for the international recognition of the deposit of microorganisms for the purposes of patent procedure'.[99] This union is constituted by all states parties. In this regard, one might assimilate the AT Consultative Parties to a union for the management of Antarctica. In order to facilitate the functioning of the Union, the Budapest Treaty creates an institutionalised regime that includes both national and international organs. In fact, Article 6 provides for the establishment of international depositary authorities within the territory of contracting states. These authorities are the competent organs for receiving and certifying the deposit of micro-organisms. In order to be established and to exercise their function, these authorities must comply with the requirements of the Budapest Treaty. Beside these nationally based organs the Treaty creates an international structure that includes a decision-making body (the Assembly), an administrative organ (the International Bureau) and the Director General, who is the chief executive of the Union. A similar structure could also be useful within the ATS to deal with the issue of bioprospecting and related IPRs. Actually, one may assume that such structure already exists within the ATS. The Assembly corresponds to the ATCM while the functions of the International Bureau and the Director General could be exercised by the Secretariat and the Executive Secretary of the Antarctic Treaty which have recently been established and appointed. From the substantive point of view, particular importance must be given to the Regulations adopted under Article 12 of the Budapest Treaty.[100] Among such regulations, Regulation 6(4)(iii) could successfully be applied to Antarctica. [101] This regulation establishes that the deposit of micro-organisms must be refused 'where the deposit is received in a condition which clearly indicates that the microoorganism is missing or which precludes for scientific reasons the acceptance of the microorganism'. On the basis of this regulation, states parties to both the ATS and the Budapest Treaty could challenge before international tribunals the legitimacy of the granting of patents made by other contracting states to both these regimes, when such patents concern discoveries deriving from Antarctic bioprospecting activities that have been carried out in breach of ATS provisions.

Moreover, the Budapest Treaty establishes a system of benefit-sharing that can be suitable for application to cases relating to the exploitation of resources beyond national jurisdiction, including Antarctica.

[98] Done in Budapest on 28 Apr 1977, at www.wipo.int/treaties/en/registration/budapest/index.html.

[99] Art 1 of the Budapest Treaty.

[100] Regulations Under the Budapest Treaty on the International Recognition of the Deposit of Microorganisms for the Purposes of Patent Procedure, adopted on 28 Apr 1977 and amended on 20 Jan 1981 and 1 Oct 2002.

[101] For this view see IP 75, *supra* n 10, para. 104.

Thus, although the need for an uniform international regulation of intellectual property rights is growing, existing international norms may offer useful suggestions to Consultative Parties to reconcile the duty to exchange scientific information, established by the AT and its associated instruments, and the right of private operators to be rewarded for their efforts.

FAO and Genetic Resources

As affirmed above,[102] bioprospecting has also highlighted the importance of some characteristics of Antarctic organisms for purposes of food conservation. Moreover, one must recall that fisheries activities carried out within the CCAMLR geographic scope are mainly aimed at providing food. For all these reasons, the interaction between the ATS and the Food and Agriculture Organisation (FAO) seems to be quite unavoidable. In fact, Article 23(2) of the CCAMLR expressly promotes cooperation between the governing organs of the Convention (the Commission and Scientific Committee) and FAO.

Among the most recent legal instruments adopted within the FAO regime, the Treaty on Plant Genetic Resources for Food and Agriculture (hereafter FAO Treaty) appears to be particularly interesting for the innovative approach that it embraces.[103] At present, this Treaty does not seem to overlap ATS instruments due to the fact that no Antarctic species is included in the list provided for in Annex I to the FAO Treaty.[104] Nevertheless, since Article 11 of this Treaty promotes the inclusion of new species among the plant genetic resources which are in the scope of Annex I, one cannot rule out that some states will, in the future, propose adding some Antarctic plant genetic resource, in particular, some species belonging to the CCAMLR area, to such list.[105]

The FAO Treaty is important for the ATS because it can provide an effective example of equitable sharing of the benefits deriving from resources that are in the common concern of humankind.[106] In this regard, the multilateral system of access and benefit-sharing established by Part

[102] See *supra* n 14.
[103] Adopted on 3 Nov 2001 and entered into force on 29 June 2004, at www.fao.org/ag/cgrfa/itpgr.htm#text. For a thorough analysis of this treaty see Footer in this volume.
[104] Art 1(1) of the FAO Treaty states: '[t]he objectives of this Treaty are the conservation and sustainable use of plant genetic resources for food and agriculture and the fair and equitable sharing of the benefits arising out of their use'.
[105] In fact, the scope of the Treaty is quite large. Art 2 affirms that '[p]lant genetic resources for food and agriculture means any genetic material of plant origin of actual or potential value for food and agriculture'.
[106] See IP 75, *supra* n 10, para. 105.

IV of this Treaty appears to be based on some criteria and purposes that are also suitable for application to an area with a peculiar legal status, such as Antarctica. Although Part IV sets out some general concepts that are established by other international regimes,[107] such as the principle of state sovereignty over resources and the duty of cooperation particularly with developing countries, its novelty can be inferred from Article 13(2)(d)(ii). This Article obliges the recipients of plant resources, who intend to use them for commercial purposes, to pay an international authority 'an equitable share of the benefits arising from the commercialization of that product, except whenever such a product is available without restriction to others for further research and breeding'. Moreover, the FAO Treaty provides for some forms of benefit-sharing that do not have a monetary nature, such as exchange of information, access to and transfer of technology, and capacity-building.[108] In order to make its provisions most effective, this Treaty establishes the Governing Body, a decision-making organ that is competent for the supervision of the multilateral system of access and benefit-sharing provided for by Part IV. The Governing Body includes all contracting parties and is assisted by the Secretary.[109] This two-organ structure will, first of all, have to collect the payments deriving from the commercial exploitation of plant resources and take care that non-monetary benefits are shared fairly.

Since the FAO Treaty entered into force only a few months ago, it is not yet possible to ascertain its degree of effectiveness. Nevertheless, one cannot deny that this Treaty provides a good example of equitable and fair use of resources, which can be of some assistance to Consultative Parties in the establishment of a benefit-sharing regime for bioprospecting activities carried out in Antarctica.[110]

[107] The FAO Treaty also protects intellectual property rights due to the pressure of some parties that were interested in the conservation of some traditional approaches. For example, the European Community added a declaration upon approval (in fact, it is not possible to make reservations to the FAO Treaty), which states: '[t]he European Community interprets Article 12(3)(d) of the International Treaty on Plant Genetic Resources as recognising that plant genetic resources for food and agriculture or their genetic parts or components which have undergone innovation may be the subject of intellectual property rights provided that the criteria relating to such rights are met'.

[108] Article 13(2) states: '[t]he Contracting Parties agree that benefits arising from the use, including commercial, of plant genetic resources for food and agriculture under the Multilateral System shall be shared fairly and equitably through the following mechanisms: the exchange of information, access to and transfer of technology, capacity-building, and the sharing of the benefits arising from commercialization' while respecting applicable property rights and access laws, and in accordance with national capabilities.

[109] Art 19 and 20 of the FAO Treaty.

[110] The ATCM might carry out the functions of the Governing Body and be supported by the Antarctic Secretariat.

VII. CONCLUSIONS

Bioprospecting appears to be the new challenge that the ATS has to face in the future.

As highlighted by a report, published in February 2004 by the United Nations University, concerning Antarctic bioprospecting, while the physical impact of bioprospecting on the Antarctic environment is controlled by existing ATS norms, one cannot say the same with regard to the effects of the commercialisation of the results deriving from Antarctic bioprospecting. In fact, there are no specific provisions, within the ATS dealing with this issue.[111]

Although bioprospecting as a form of scientific research is a lawful activity that cannot be banned within the Antarctic area, its commercial nature seems to conflict with the character of the natural reserve of Antarctica, which is recognised by ATS instruments. Moreover, one must recall that scientific research enjoys privileged status within the ATS that could lead bioprospectors to take advantage of this favourable position with the purpose of satisfying their selfish economic interests. Therefore, even if the performance of bioprospecting is allowed in Antarctica, it must be strongly limited by the provisions of the ATS that promote the exploitation of this area in the interest of the international community as a whole. For example, the AT and, in particular, the Madrid Protocol allow the appropriation of continental biological resources only for scientific purposes. Any appropriation of such resources, justified by different reasons, might be considered an attack on the foundations of the ATS. Even the CCAMLR, which permits commercial exploitation of marine resources, adopts a conservative approach that does not unconditionally admit the possibility of carrying out bioprospecting. Moreover, the economic exploitation of bioprospecting results, which is made possible through the recognition of IPRs and patent rights, can conflict with some ATS fundamental principles. As an example, while IPRs require confidentiality, the ATS provides for the duty to exchange scientific information.

Other problems affecting the regulation of bioprospecting arise from the peculiar legal status of Antarctica. This area, like other zones beyond state jurisdiction, is not governed by any internationally recognised authority that can negotiate the terms of access to and benefit-sharing of Antarctic resources with private bioprospectors.

In short, Consultative Parties urgently need to establish specific provisions relating to the commercial aspects (in particular, with regard to benefit-sharing) of some activities carried out in Antarctica, such as bioprospecting.

111 Johnston and Lohan, *The International Regime for Bioprospecting: Existing Policies and Emerging Issues for Antarctica* (UNU, 2004). The same paper was presented by the UK at the XXVI ATCM, held in Madrid in 2003, as IP 75: see *supra* n 10.

Awaiting the adoption of specific Antarctic norms concerning bioprospecting, the application of other international provisions to Antarctica could help to fill existing normative lacunae. Nevertheless, the peculiar legal status of this area seems to hinder the effective regulation of Antarctic bioprospecting by means of such provisions. In fact, all the norms of UNCLOS or the CBD, based on the principle of territorial sovereignty, cannot be applied to Antarctica due to the fact that both Consultative Parties and third states have denied that this principle is suitable for application to this area. Moreover, UNCLOS and CBD provisions dealing with the performance of research activities within areas beyond national jurisdiction do not seem to provide an effective regulation of bioprospecting for such areas, including Antarctica. In fact, such provisions do not establish sufficiently precise obligations. They only sanction the duty of cooperation between states and the freedom of research and exploitation in accordance with environmental requirements. Thus, even international regimes other than the ATS do not seem to provide an effective regulation of Antarctic bioprospecting.

Nevertheless, some important suggestions for the creation of the future Antarctic regime on bioprospecting can be inferred from other international treaties. As affirmed above, one of the most controversial issues concerns benefit-sharing. Although the recognition of the 'paternity' of the discovery is a legitimate expectation of scientists, nevertheless, it is not reasonable to admit that a natural reserve, such as Antarctica, can be used for the exclusive advantage of private operators. Some information that results from bioprospecting can be relevant for the whole of humankind. For example, bioprospecting can lead to the production of new medicines that improve human health or to the discovery of some important characteristics of a species that allows better conservation of it. In these cases, access to the results of Antarctic bioprospecting cannot be ruled out by reason of the confidentiality of data or be conditional on the payment of monetary compensation due to the existence of patents. An equitable benefit-sharing system is necessary, and is what the CBD regime seeks to achieve.[112] Patents should be used only to hinder third parties in the commercial exploitation of a discovery. Non-commercial exploitation should be freely allowed as the FAO Treaty on Plant Genetic Resources states.[113]

Moreover, the exploitation of biological resources yields not only economic revenues, but also non-monetary benefits. Among non-monetary benefits, particular importance must be given to technology transfer and the support of scientific programmes and institutions. Moreover, some

[112] For this view see Graham, 'Environmental, Ethical and Equity Issues', in *Canterbury Workshop*, *supra* n 3.
[113] For this view see Cottier, *supra* n 39.

royalty could be established on market products[114] in order to create an international fund, managed by an international authority and aimed at enhancing the protection of the Antarctic environment.

Until states parties to the ATS adopt these specific provisions, bioprospecting activities should be minimised in Antarctica. In fact, although the absolute freedom of carrying out bioprospecting in Antarctica does not seem particularly dangerous for the Antarctic environment, however, it could seriously undermine the fragile political balance, which the ATS has preserved for 40 years and that has made it possible to manage this unique area of our planet in a peaceful and cooperative manner.

114 For this view see Hunter, *supra* n 6, 173.

7

Bioprospecting in Antarctica: A New Challenge for the Antarctic Treaty System

ANN-ISABELLE GUYOMARD*

I. INTRODUCTION

ANTARCTICA IS NO longer the last place on Earth. Since the first explorers of the eighteenth century, men have never ceased to discover new spaces in the great South. Whaling and sealing may have stopped, but there are new human pressures on the Antarctic. Amongst a lot of current activities such as station construction, drilling projects and tourism, a new one has definitely been holding our attention since the 1980s: biological prospecting.

Bioprospecting is based on the search for some form of exploitable biology. We regret the absence of an exact and definite definition of bioprospecting in international legal instruments. Nevertheless, it has been identified as 'the exploration of biodiversity for commercially valuable genetic and biochemical resources' and further defined as 'the process of gathering information from the biosphere on the molecular composition of genetic resources for the development of new commercial products'.[1] It applies to various forms of life everywhere in the world and is conducted

* This paper was prepared on the basis of recent ATCMs documents and publicly available sources for a short presentation and as a ground for discussion during the Siena Conference on "Bioprospecting and International Law". Ann-Isabelle Guyomard is a Ph. D student at the Maritime and Law of the Sea Center directed by Professor Beurier (Centre de Droit Maritime et Océanique CDMO), working on the thesis: "The New Environmental Principles in Antarctica: International and Comparative Law". University of Nantes (France). Website: www.droit.univ-nantes.fr/labos/cdmo/cdmo.htm.

1 UNEP/CBD/SBSTTA/8/INF/3/Rev.1, para.68. The term is neither defined nor used in the Convention on Biological Diversity. *The Encyclopaedia of Biodiversity* (Cambridge, Cambridge University Press, 2001, p.471) defines bioprospecting as the "systematic search

by very different bodies from the private and the public sectors. Thus, bioprospecting is a complex activity, which implies scientific research and economic interests, as well as legal and political issues.

Bioprospecting for extremophiles is currently the main focus of bioprospecting in Antarctica.[2] Consequently, two major reasons lead bioprospectors' interest in Antarctica. First, Antarctica's environmental extremes present conditions in which biota have evolved unique characteristics. Consequently, the extreme environment has led to the evolution of a range of physiological adaptations. Antarctic biological resources, particularly the large number of indigenous Antarctic micro-organisms, are seen as potentially rich sources of materials for various industries. Secondly, the lack of knowledge surrounding Antarctic biota constitutes a real opportunity to discover new organisms of potential use to biotechnology. The biota of Antarctica are still unknown, and most scientists agree that the potential for discovery of beneficial new biotechnological products is high.

However, the process of bioprospecting for Antarctic biological resources is complex. It can be subdivided into a number of phases, including the collection of samples, their isolation, their characterisation and culture, screening for pharmaceutical activity, development of products, patenting, trials, sales and marketing.[3] During this process, numerous extracts are assessed. However, perhaps only one potentially active compound will be found. Thus, bioprospecting in Antarctica involves tremendous work and is a costly and risky activity which inevitably requires investment from various sectors. To secure a return on their investment, investors will inevitably seek patent protection. Biological prospecting activities are still modest in scope. However, they are taking place in Antarctica, and in some cases have led to commercial applications which are very likely to increase in the near future.

Bioprospecting activities are carried out everywhere in the world, but they are not regulated in detail by the Convention on the Law of the Sea

for genes, natural compounds, designs, and whole organisms in wild life with a potential for product development by biological observation and biophysical, biochemical, and genetic methods, without disruption to nature". Fiji's draft sustainable development bill restricts bioprospecting to "any activity undertaken to harvest or exploit biological resources *for commercial purposes*...[including] investigative research and sampling" (emphasis added). The Philippines' Executive Order 247 is broader in defining bioprospecting as the "collection and utilization of biological and genetic resources for purposes of applying the knowledge derived therefrom to scientific and/or commercial purposes".

[2] Extremophiles inhabit diverse environments such as Alpine glaciers, alkaline soils, submarine hydrothermal vents and deep-sea sediments. They are micro-organisms living in extreme conditions such as high salt concentration and high pressure, or low pH, nutrient concentration or water availability.

[3] See an article of paramount importance for this study see J Jarbour-Green and D Nicol, 'Bioprospecting in Areas Outside National Jurisdiction: Antarctica and the Southern Ocean' (2003) 4 *Melbourne Journal of International Law* 76.

and the Convention on Biological Diversity.[4] However, and in order to avoid the 'first-come-first-served' rule,[5] Antarctica is placed under the Global Common legal regime which involves special rules and special consequences. To that end, materials coming from the Antarctic will not be subject to the same legal protection as state resources. Indeed the question of bioprospecting in Antarctica has to be contrasted with a pre-existing legal regime: the Antarctic Treaty System.[6] Since the Washington Treaty on the Antarctic (1959),[7] the Antarctic Treaty System (ATS) has evolved in order to regulate all human activities on the continent and in its ocean, and to strive for the conservation and protection of the Antarctic as a whole. The basic principles for the regulation and protection of the Antarctic are established in the Antarctic Treaty.

First, the Contracting Parties to the Antarctic Treaty agree that the freedom of scientific research and international co-operation is paramount for the good of all humanity.[8] The whole ATS is based on this concept. Indeed the very idea of Antarctica evokes pristine areas and harsh weather conditions. Even though the last place on Earth no longer exists as such, its philosophy still remains and regulates the relations between humans and this overwhelming environment. From this premise we can reasonably think that the creation of a unique legal framework for such a unique continent is more than mere chance. Consequently, the author thinks that there is a direct relationship in Antarctica between the environment and the creation of original rules. That is why it is important to bear in mind the Antarctic philosophy behind the principles of the Antarctic Treaty System. It is worth noting that the current legal framework of Antarctica has been shaped by uncommon events such as the Antarctic Treaty itself, which is not only a remarkable legal instrument, but the symbol and proof of the mutual agreement concerning Antarctica of both Soviet and American powers, right in the middle of the Cold War.[9] The Antarctic Treaty System is based on this undeniable constancy, which promotes the co-operation of all Parties each time the ATS faces new issues,

[4] Hereafter the 'CBD'.

[5] On the progressive erosion of the principle of freedom of the sea as an evolutionary trend of present international law of the sea in the field of sustainable use of marine resources see T. Scovazzi, 'The Evolution of International Law of the Sea: New Issues, New Challenges'(2000) 286 *Hague Academy of International Law Recueil des Cours* 39.

[6] The instruments of the ATS are: the Convention for the Conservation of Antarctic Seals, the Convention for the Conservation of Antarctic Marine Living Resources, the Convention on the Regulation of Antarctic Mineral Resource Activities, and the Protocol on Environmental Protection to the Antarctic Treaty.

[7] The Antarctic Treaty.

[8] Antarctic Treaty: Arts II and III.

[9] Another example is the CRAMRA reversal of the Environmental Protocol which illustrates, amongst other things, the return to the basic principles of the Antarctic Treaty System, namely peace, science, interest of mankind as a whole, wilderness and aesthetic values.

such as the exploitation of mineral resources and environmental protection. This constancy among states has become a sort of local custom in the wake of which an Antarctic regime has been developed.[10]

To emphasise the very special framework surrounding Antarctica, the Antarctic Treaty freezes the territorial claims made by the seven claimant states to various sectors of Antarctica. To that end, 'nothing in the Treaty shall be interpreted as a renunciation of asserted rights or claims to territorial sovereignty in Antarctica'.[11] However, the Treaty does not solve the problem of the existence in Antarctica of coastal zones falling within national jurisdiction. This is a consequence of the well-known 'agreement to disagree' on territorial sovereignty embodied in Article IV of the Treaty, which does not prejudice either the recognition or the non-recognition of previously asserted claims. On the one hand, the seven claimant states have not renounced their claims to the coastal zones, which are linked to territorial sovereignty, such as the territorial sea and the continental shelf. On the other, the states, which do not recognise any claim of territorial sovereignty, consider that there are no coastal zones and coastal states in Antarctica.

Consequently, this agreement to disagree allows for the construction of a comprehensive regime for the protection of the continent, notwithstanding the position of the different states having an interest in Antarctica. But the issue of territorial claims also constitutes the 'Pandora's Box' of the Antarctic Treaty System. Indeed, a lot of bioprospecting issues, such as property, patents and benefit-sharing, are linked by the question of sovereignty. Determination not to open the Pandora's Box of territorial claims has been a constant aspect of the long co-operation established by the Antarctic Treaty System since 1957. One of the fundamental elements of the ATS is surely the co-operative attitude taken by the interested states in facing common problems through the adoption of specific instruments.

However, bioprospecting in Antarctica is likely to become very controversial. Issues of ownership, access, benefit-sharing, sovereignty and jurisdiction are complicated and will need to be further discussed. As regards the development of bioprospecting in Antarctica, has the ATS reached its limits?

The ATS is, by design, dynamic, allowing the Antarctic Treaty Parties the flexibility to incorporate new regulations as the need arises.[12] The ATS has the ability to keep responsive to changing demands and the capacity

[10] The Antarctic Treaty System of laws could be perceived as an 'emotional law' system, a sort of spiritual background peculiar to Antarctica.

[11] Antarctic Treaty: Art IV.

[12] And sometimes even before the need arises! See, eg, the Convention on the Conservation of Antarctic Seals.

to monitor progress in implementing the System's decisions. All the parties (states or not) having an interest in Antarctica have always found a consensus on which they could agree to overcome the numerous issues concerning Antarctica. Bioprospecting is the new issue on which they must prove that Antarctica is definitely an incredible legal laboratory, trying to adopt the most innovative measures in order to ensure the interests of all parties and the protection of the Antarctic environment. Consequently, the Antarctic Treaty Parties should be proactive in formulating a policy for the regulation of bioprospecting in Antarctica to uphold the fundamental principles of freedom of scientific research and co-operation, and to provide added protection from unregulated resource use. Moreover, as bioprospecting is an activity involving legal, political and environmental issues, the Antarctic Treaty Parties need to set out more than a comprehensive policy position, in fact a real framework. To achieve this aim, and even in the emergency of the current situation, the Antarctic Treaty Parties must bear in mind the knowledge derived from the experience of the Antarctic Treaty System. It is indeed the most efficient legal system on Earth, concerning a whole continent and its surrounding ocean. Consequently, it is of the highest importance to regulate bioprospecting activities before they develop in an unregulated manner. An appropriate Antarctic approach is required and, fortunately, the ATS already provides an intrinsically favourable balance to innovation, however asking for transformation towards a goal of protection.

II. BIOPROSPECTING AND THE ANTARCTIC TREATY SYSTEM: AN INTRINSICALLY FAVOURABLE BALANCE TO INNOVATION

'Antarctica shall continue *forever* to be used exclusively for peaceful purposes'.[13] This quite surprising sentence in an international treaty underlines the futuristic and optimistic philosophy of the Antarctic Treaty System. Following this idea, the drafters of the Treaty established the main principles of the ATS and created a global framework on the basis of peace and freedom of scientific research in the interest of all mankind. However, in doing so in 1959, it is likely that they may not have thought about bioprospecting activities. This new issue is welcome in Antarctica because it may alleviate human suffering. Consequently, this second section demonstrates the possible insertion of bioprospecting activities into the Antarctic Treaty System and the high potential of the ATS framework as a reaction to the bioprospecting issues.

[13] Antarctic Treaty, Preamble, emphases added.

The Possible Inclusion of Bioprospecting in the Antarctic Treaty System

The inclusion of bioprospecting in the ATS seems to be, *a priori*, a very complex issue, bearing in mind Article III of the Washington Treaty. However, bioprospecting *per se* is compatible with the principles of the Antarctic Treaty System, and only its consequences may cause problems and need to be regulated in order to fulfil the aims of the ATS principles.

Compatibility between Bioprospecting and the Antarctic Treaty System

Bioprospecting leads to numerous applications. However, nothing in the Antarctic Treaty deals with the bioprospecting issue. The only prohibitions mentioned in the Treaty concern war, nuclear explosion and the disposal of radioactive waste, whereas the Madrid Protocol prohibits any activity other than scientific research relating to mineral resources. Therefore, nothing precludes bioprospecting from being compatible with the aims and objectives of the Antarctic Treaty.

Moreover, bioprospecting promotes scientific investigations for peaceful purposes. The Antarctic Treaty was created following the International Geophysical Year[14] (1957). During the Cold War period, scientific research in Antarctica was one of the few activities distant from war considerations. Consequently, the first preoccupation of the Antarctic Treaty was to preserve scientific research in spite of all opposition. To that end, Article III(3) of the Antarctic Treaty states:

> Activities shall be planned and conducted in the Antarctic Treaty area so as to accord priority to scientific research and to preserve the value of Antarctica as an area for the conduct of such research, including research essential to understanding the global environment.

Since bioprospecting is conducted by scientists and covers the same fields as scientific research, it is recognised as a scientific activity and thus may be accepted as such in Antarctica. Even with regard to the 'Pandora's Box' issue of sovereignty claims, bioprospecting still remains compatible with the Antarctic Treaty. Nothing in the Treaty shall be interpreted as:

> a) a renunciation by any Contracting Party of previously asserted rights of or claims to territorial sovereignty in Antarctica;
> b) a renunciation or diminution by any Contracting Party of any basis of claim to territorial sovereignty in Antarctica which it may have whether as a result of its activities or those of its nationals in Antarctica, or otherwise;

[14] Hereafter the 'IGY'.

c) prejudicing the position of any Contracting Party as regards its recognition or non-recognition of any other State's right of or claim or basis of claim to territorial sovereignty in Antarctica.[15]

Since bioprospecting activities are mostly conducted by public–private consortia, they are not likely to raise sovereignty questions over terrestrial or maritime areas. Nevertheless, the ownership of genetic resources and the need to ensure that they have been legitimately acquired are still unresolved issues. However, and even though issues concerning ownership are likely to arise, they are not part of bioprospecting itself, but appear only during the bioprospecting process, i.e. as a consequence of bioprospecting.

It has to be borne in mind that bioprospecting in Antarctica will mostly relate to the act of collecting and discovering novel biological resources. Even though it is ultimately for commercial purposes, bioprospecting will remain an activity that is largely scientific. Accordingly, bioprospecting activities will fall within Article III of the Washington Treaty, addressing co-operation with regard to scientific programmes, scientific personnel, scientific observations and results:

1. In order to promote international co-operation in scientific investigation in Antarctica, as provided for in Article II of the present Treaty, the Contracting Parties agree that, to the greatest extent feasible and practicable:
   a) information regarding plans for scientific programs in Antarctica shall be exchanged to permit maximum economy and efficiency of operations;
   b) scientific personnel shall be exchanged in Antarctica between expeditions and stations;
   c) scientific observations and results from Antarctica shall be exchanged and made freely available.
2. In implementing this Article, every encouragement shall be given to the establishment of co-operative working relations with those Specialized Agencies of the United Nations and other international organizations having a scientific or technical interest in Antarctica.

Consequently, the question of compatibility between bioprospecting and the ATS deserves some discussion. First, it should be borne in mind that economic gain does not have to change the nature of a scientific activity under the ATS regime. Whenever scientific research is financed by the public sector, the bioprospecting process seems to be totally compatible with the recommendations of Article III. But whenever scientific research is financed by the private sector, conclusions are much more complicated.

15 Art IV, Antarctic Treaty.

However, bioprospecting activities are mostly conducted by consortia, thus blurring the line between public- and private-sector funding.

In any case, the patenting of an application, process or product from Antarctica does not preclude the scientific information gleaned from that application etc from being in the public domain.[16] To the greatest extent feasible and practicable, information regarding plans for scientific programmes will be exchanged and made publicly available. Therefore, although bioprospecting in itself is not in breach of Article III of the Antarctic Treaty, its consequences, such as the intention to maintain 'trade secrets', would be. Indeed, the implications of bioprospecting during all its phases may be contrary to Article III and need some special regulations to fulfil the aims of the ATS principles.

The Need to Regulate Bioprospecting Consequences to Fulfil the Aims of the ATS Principles

It is worth recalling that nothing in the Antarctic Treaty precludes exploitation, with the exception of that of mineral resources, from being commercial. However, concerns have been raised about balancing the desire for commercial confidentiality with Article III of the Treaty. It is not bioprospecting itself that runs counter to the principles set out in Article III, but rather its consequences. Issues concerning access, patents and benefit-sharing have to be considered in order to promote compliance with the principles of the Treaty. Bearing in mind the potential of bioprospecting in Antarctica, it is out of the question to prohibit such activities on the basis of non-compliance with the ATS provisions. Moreover, the Antarctic Treaty provides that freedom of scientific investigation in Antarctica and co-operation toward that end, as applied during the International Geophysical Year, shall continue, subject to its provisions.[17] Therefore, it is worth considering bioprospecting as a global activity, which may find its place in the ATS.

Antarctica has not been devoted to the Common Heritage of Mankind but 'shall continue forever to be used exclusively for peaceful purposes in the interest of all mankind'.[18] It is worth noting the very innovative idea conveyed by benefit-sharing in the interest of all Mankind. This idea totally reflects the great philosophy of the Antarctic Treaty System; however it still encounters problems in its application and is likely to encounter more difficulties since bioprospecting often implies patents. At first glance, the question concerning the balance of interests between Mankind and the

[16] M. Rogan-Finnemore and A. Hemmings, 'Bioprospecting in Antarctica. An Academic Workshop', in ATCM XXVI, Information Paper, Agenda Item CEP VII, New Zealand.

[17] Art. II, Washington Treaty.

[18] Antarctic Treaty, Preamble.

patent-holder seems irreducible, but the Antarctic Treaty does not preclude the interests of both parties from being served.

Since bioprospecting is, among other things, an economic matter, it has to be borne in mind that it cannot reasonably exist without patent protection. And even though the drafters of the Treaty may not have thought about this possibility, its Preamble may be interpreted in a useful and novel way. Indeed Antarctica shall continue forever to be used exclusively for peaceful purposes in the interest of all Mankind, but this interest can be combined and balanced with other interests. Consequently, we could think about a solution to the problem of benefit-sharing in creating the most complete legal regime, which takes into account the interests of both the pharmaceutical laboratories and Mankind.[19] In practice, this could lead to the payment of a percentage of the benefit to an Antarctic *ad hoc* institution, which could redistribute it in one way or another in the interest of all Mankind.[20] If it were well established, such a system would allow bioprospecting activities in Antarctica within the ambit of the ATS principles, and prove once more the great possibilities of the ATS as an unlimited legal laboratory. But, of course, such a result would require more goodwill from the patent-holder than from Mankind.

Because bioprospecting is in itself an activity conducted for peaceful purposes, it is likely to be integrated into the Antarctic Treaty System. However, many of its consequences need in-depth consideration. Let us see how the different measures of the Antarctic Treaty System can help to regulate bioprospecting activities.

The Antarctic Treaty System: A Promising Potential Legal Framework for the Conduct of Bioprospecting Activities

In 1957, scientists from all round the world met for the International Geophysical Year. They focused a large part of their work on Antarctica and the result was such a success that they decided to negotiate the Antarctic Treaty in order to keep Antarctica away from international discord. Following this founding euphoria, the instruments of the ATS manage complementary fields. Even though none of them directly regulates bioprospecting activities in Antarctica, they constitute at least a promising potential legal framework for the conduct of bioprospecting activities in Antarctica.

19 This is also the aim of Part XI of UNCLOS: the Area.

20 The redistribution could, eg, be made in favour of the conservation of the Antarctic environment or provide subsidies for special tour operators which could allow members of developing countries to visit Antarctica. Indeed, this is a very enthusiastic view, but is not the interest of all mankind philosophy as well?

Relevant Legal Measures of the Antarctic Treaty System Instruments

The Preamble to and Articles I to IV of the Washington Treaty regulate scientific research in the respect of freedom and peaceful purposes. The Madrid Protocol on Environmental Protection[21] also finds relevance in this field. Even though the Protocol is the result of a political compromise banning all activities relating to mineral resources, the present situation reflects the founding spirit of the ATS. The Protocol protects Antarctica as 'a natural reserve devoted to peace and science'.[22] To do so, the Parties commit themselves to the 'comprehensive protection of the Antarctic environment and dependent and associated ecosystems'.[23] As for the Antarctic Treaty, the Protocol establishes a comprehensive regime in the interest of all Mankind. Moreover, in the light of the need to strengthen the ATS, the Antarctic shall 'continue forever to be used exclusively for peaceful purposes and shall not become the scene or object of international discord'.[24] The Protocol reinforces the Antarctic Treaty's provisions on co-operation, noting that Parties shall co-operate in the planning and conduct of activities; where appropriate undertake joint expeditions and share the use of stations and other facilities; and, as far as possible, share information that may be helpful in planning and conducting activities.

The environmental principles are set out in Article III of the Protocol. To this end:

> The protection of the Antarctic environment and dependent and associated ecosystems and the intrinsic value of Antarctica, including its wilderness and aesthetic values and its value as an area for the conduct of scientific research, in particular research essential to understanding the global environment, shall be fundamental considerations in the planning and conduct of all activities in the Antarctic Treaty area.

However, the most important measure concerning bioprospecting in Antarctica is set out in Article 8 of the Protocol: Environmental Impact Assessment,[25] which provides that:

> [all activities carried out in Antarctica] shall be subject to the procedures set out in Annex I for prior assessment of the impacts of those activities on the Antarctic environment or on dependent or associated ecosystems according to whether those activities are identified as having:

21 Thereafter noted as the Protocol, or PEPAT.
22 Art 2, PEPAT.
23 *Ibid.*
24 Preamble, PEPAT.
25 Hereinafter EIA.

(a) less than a minor or transitory impact;
(b) a minor or transitory impact; or
(c) more than a minor or transitory impact.

Annex I to the Protocol develops the EIA system. It sets out three different stages of EIA: the preliminary stage, the initial environmental assessment and the comprehensive environmental assessment. Since the Protocol applies to all activities in Antarctica,[26] bioprospecting activities will be subjected to the assessment. The Environmental Impact Assessment will therefore examine whether the collection of material for bioprospecting will impact on the environment and associated ecosystems. However, in the case of micro-organism samples, only small quantities are taken. Thus, the activity of collection is almost certain to cause 'less than a minor or transitory impact' on the environment.[27]

To conclude, we may say that the Antarctic Treaty and its Protocol provide a first legal framework for Antarctic bioprospecting, in organising the freedom of scientific research and co-operation in this research in the interest of all Mankind.

Moreover the Convention on Antarctic Marine Living Resources[28] is also relevant to bioprospecting activities in Antarctica. As bioprospecting is being carried out in the Southern Ocean and on the continent, the 1980 CCAMLR, which entered into force in October 1982 applies to 'the Antarctic marine living resources of the area south of 60° South latitude and to the Antarctic marine living resources of the area between that latitude and the Antarctic Convergence which form part of the Antarctic marine ecosystem'.[29] Its objective is 'the conservation of Antarctic marine living resources'.[30] Pursuant to Article II, any harvesting is to be regulated so as to prevent the decrease of harvested populations to levels below their maximum sustainable yield.[31] Although bioprospecting is unlikely to affect populations to such an extent as to fall within the scope of Article II of the CCAMLR, the Convention's requirements outlined in Article XX could include bioprospecting. To this end:

1. The Members of the Commission shall, to the greatest extent possible, provide annually to the Commission and to the Scientific Committee such

26 Scientific research programmes, tourism, governmental and non-governmental activities in the Antarctic Treaty area.

27 The situation may be different for the harvesting of biological resources for the purpose of extracting target compounds, which may have a significant impact on the environment and could therefore be subject to a higher level of environmental impact assessment.

28 Hereafter CCAMLR.

29 Art I(1), CCAMLR.

30 Art II(1), CCAMLR.

31 Art III(3), CCAMLR.

statistical, biological and other data and information as the Commission and Scientific Committee may require in the exercise of their functions.

2. The Members of the Commission shall provide, in the manner and at such intervals as may be prescribed, information about their harvesting activities, including fishing areas and vessels, so as to enable reliable catch and effort statistics to be compiled.
3. The Members of the Commission shall provide to the Commission at such intervals as may be prescribed information on steps taken to implement the conservation measures adopted by the Commission.
4. The Members of the Commission agree that in any of their harvesting activities, advantage shall be taken of opportunities to collect data needed to assess the impact of harvesting.

As noted before, ownership and rights to use are important issues. But jurisdictional questions of the Southern Ocean are made complex by reason of the various overlapping claims. Consequently, the relevance of CCAMLR to the bioprospecting question lies mainly in the requirements outlined in Article XX.

The Convention on the Regulation of Antarctic Mineral Resources Activities[32] may also be relevant to bioprospecting in Antarctica. Adopted in 1988, it is unlikely to come into force because of the subsequent entry into force of the Madrid Protocol. CRAMRA was negotiated to manage and regulate mining activities, but is worth considering in this chapter because its provisions regulate mineral resource activities, the institutional structure created by it and sovereignty issues. The objectives and general principles of CRAMRA fully respect the ATS and are designed to protect the Antarctic environment as mentioned in Article 2:

> In implementing this Convention, the Parties shall ensure that Antarctic mineral resource activities, should they occur, take place in a manner consistent with all the components of the Antarctic Treaty system and the obligations flowing therefrom.
>
> In relation to Antarctic mineral resource activities, should they occur, the Parties acknowledge the special responsibility of the Antarctic Treaty Consultative Parties for the protection of the environment and the need to:
>
> a. protect the Antarctic environment and dependent and associated ecosystems;
> b. respect Antarctica's significance for, and influence on, the global environment;
> c. respect other legitimate uses of Antarctica;
> d. respect Antarctica's scientific value and aesthetic and wilderness qualities;

[32] Hereafter CRAMRA.

e. ensure the safety of operations in Antarctica;
f. promote opportunities for fair and effective participation of all Parties; and
g. take into account the interests of the international community as a whole.

To achieve its objectives, CRAMRA establishes an institutional framework. It provides for a Commission to identify an area for exploration and development and set up a Regulatory Committee which develops regulations governing possible exploration and development activities.[33] Such institutions may be useful for a future bioprospecting framework in Antarctica.

One of the major elements in addressing the different concerns of state sovereignty was the power granted to the Commission[34] and the establishment of the Regulatory Committees which are composed of claimant and non-claimant states.[35] Prospecting activities have to be authorised by sponsoring states which must ensure that the activities are carried out in compliance with the Convention.[36] Thus, CRAMRA follows the ATS philosophy in the sense that it contributes to increasing the responsibility of states with regard to their operators. Besides, Article 16 provides that information is to be made freely available to the greatest extent feasible, whereas data of commercial value gained through prospecting may be retained by the operator in accordance with Article 37. Finally, Article 16(b) notes that regarding data and information deriving from exploration or development the Commission shall 'adopt measures relating, as appropriate, to their release and to ensure the confidentiality of data and information of commercial value'.

Consequently, CRAMRA could serve as a good example for bioprospecting activities in Antarctica. It recalls the provisions of the Antarctic Treaty, establishes an institutional framework for regulating all mineral activities in Antarctica. Even if the allocation of financial profits derived from mineral resource activities in Antarctica were not addressed by CRAMRA, the gap could be filled by the sustained action of the ATS bodies.

International co-operation is indeed one of the basic foundations of the ATS. The importance of the soft law in the Antarctic Treaty Consultative Meetings since the adoption of the Treaty is far from being the only proof of this fruitful international co-operation. The different institutions of the ATS have always promoted a sustained action and still make efforts to

33 Art 29(1), CRAMRA.
34 Art 49, CRAMRA.
35 Art 29(2), CRAMRA.
36 Art 37(2), CRAMRA

adapt the ATS to new issues such as bioprospecting. The Antarctic Treaty System is completed by different institutions which all have specific competencies. The most relevant of these to bioprospecting activities in Antarctica are the SCAR and the CEP.

The creation of SCAR follows the IGY. Though it is not an ATS institution as such, it has always played a very important role in Antarctic affairs and therefore gained true legitimacy among the Antarctic Treaty Parties. SCAR and in particular SCAR's Working Group on Biology have been alert to the issue of bioprospecting in Antarctica. In a report on Scientific Research in Antarctica,[37] it reported:

> At present there appear to be no provisions in the Antarctic Treaty to deal with exploitation of biological resources in the Antarctic, with the exception of fisheries. There have already been collections of micro-organisms for pharmaceutical purposes and a biological prospecting interest in the Antarctic is developing rapidly. The implications of biological prospecting, and the patenting of biological products, for biological research and conservation is of concern to the Working Group on Biology and the meeting agreed that these issues should be raised with SCAR and with CCAMLR.

The action of SCAR in the ATS is widely accepted and appreciated by the Antarctic Treaty Parties as it provides a scientific point of view over complex matters. Since SCAR is invited to the ATCM as a permanent observer, its contributions provide relevant developments on the bioprospecting issue.[38]

The Committee for Environmental Protection[39] was created by Article 11 of the Madrid Protocol. On the effectiveness of measures taken pursuant to the Protocol, it underlines the need to update, strengthen or otherwise improve such measures, and the need for additional measures, including for additional Annexes.[40] It gives advice and formulates recommendations to the Parties for the implementation of the Protocol.

The CEP took up the issues raised in Working Paper WP043 submitted by the UK to the XXV ATCM. Under agenda item 4(d) 'Matters covered by Annex II (Conservation of Antarctic Fauna and Flora)' of the fifth session of the CEP, the following was recorded:

> The United Kingdom presented Working Paper (XXV ATCM/WP43) on biological prospecting in Antarctica. The Meeting congratulated the United

[37] Information Paper XXIII ATCM/IP 123 SCAR (1999).

[38] The SCAR often organises workshops with the co-operation of other institutions. On this topic, see also XXVI ATCM/IP, Agenda Item CEP7, New Zealand. Subsequent to ATCM XXV, Gateway Antarctica, an institute at the University of Canterbury, NZ, held a workshop on bioprospecting in Antarctica from 7–8 Apr. 2003 in Christchurch, New Zealand.

[39] Hereafter the 'CEP'.

[40] Art12, PEPAT.

> Kingdom on their paper, which raised a series of important questions resulting from advances in biotechnology. Several delegates pointed out that the subject of biological prospecting is complex, and includes legal and political issues. Comments from members covered items such as commercial confidentiality, cross-convention aspects, the legal basis for biological prospecting, intellectual property and patents etc., as well as consistency with Article III of the Antarctic Treaty.

In conclusion, the CEP stated that the complexities and developments in this field were strong reasons for the Antarctic community to be pro-active on this issue and that biological prospecting needed to be discussed during subsequent CEP meetings.

Article IX of the Antarctic Treaty provides for meetings of the Antarctic Treaty Consultative Parties at suitable intervals and places for the exchange of information, formulation and recommendation to their governments of different measures. Since their first meeting in 1961 in Canberra, the Antarctic Treaty Consultative Parties have met 28 times[41] and have formulated numerous recommendations. These conferences are much more than formal events. They are the discussion and executive chamber of the Treaty and thus consistently fill the gaps and shortcomings of the ATS. Consequently, the role of the ATCM has increased with the emergence of new issues and will further grow with the issue of bioprospecting. The elaboration of a new regime is the responsibility of the ATCPs alone. Therefore all issues concerning bioprospecting in Antarctica will be adopted by consensus. The XXVIII ATCM recently adopted Resolution 7(2005) on the bioprospecting issue in Antarctica:

> The Representatives,
>
> Convinced of the benefits of scientific research in the field of biological prospecting for the progress of humankind;
>
> Recalling Article III(1)(c) of the Antarctic Treaty, which provides that scientific observations and results from Antarctica shall be exchanged and made freely available;
>
> Recalling the Protocol on Environmental Protection to the Antarctic Treaty, including Article 2, as well as Article 3, which provides for the regulation of activities in the Antarctic Treaty area to be planned and conducted so as to limit adverse impacts on the Antarctic environment and dependent and associated ecosystems;
>
> Bearing in mind ongoing discussions in other international fora on aspects of biological prospecting, including efforts to develop and clarify the nature and definition of such activities;
>
> Reaffirming the importance of Article III(1) of the Antarctic Treaty with regard to scientific activities relating to biological prospecting, in that, to the greatest extent feasible and practicable:

41 The XXVIII ATCM took place in Stockholm in June 2005.

(a) information regarding plans for scientific programs in Antarctica shall be exchanged to permit maximum economy and efficiency of operations;
(b) scientific personnel shall be exchanged in Antarctica between expeditions and stations;
(c) scientific observations and results from Antarctica shall be exchanged and made freely available;

Recommend that:

1) their governments draw to the attention of their national Antarctic programmes and other research institutes engaged in Antarctic biological prospecting activities the provisions of Article III(1) of the Antarctic Treaty;
2) their governments continue to keep under review the question of biological prospecting in the Antarctic Treaty Area, and exchange on an annual basis information and views relating to that question as appropriate.

Even if the wording of this resolution is still hortatory, it constitutes the very first step in the establishment of a real legal regime.

Consequently, bioprospecting in Antarctica can already rely on a set of rules with different scopes. However, it seems that these rules are still insufficient to ensure the real protection of the continent as well as the interests of all the parties involved in the bioprospecting adventure. Currently, there are only some scattered rules the objectives and applicability of which vary considerably. Notwithstanding the relevance of the ATS provisions, this pre-existing legal framework still seems unsatisfactory for the appropriate conduct of bioprospecting activities. Rather than a sector-based approach, the ATS needs a real global framework on this new issue. It is therefore of major importance for adjusting the existing ATS balance in order to integrate the bioprospecting issues into the System.

III. BIOLOGICAL PROSPECTING AND THE ANTARCTIC TREATY SYSTEM: OVERCOMING THE ATS BALANCE IN ORDER TO INTEGRATE THE BIOPROSPECTING ISSUES INTO THE SYSTEM

Since the adoption of the Madrid Protocol, the new Antarctic order has relied on the protection and conservation of the Antarctic's environment and resources.[42] However, the earlier Antarctic Treaty System is not sufficient *per se* for properly conducting bioprospecting activities. Consequently, the relevance of international law provisions, as well as the

[42] Art 2 PEPAT.

major role of the interested Parties in Antarctica, may provide useful sources of inspiration for integrating bioprospecting issues into the ATS.

The UN Convention on the Law of the Sea and the Biodiversity Convention are sources relevant to bioprospecting in Antarctica. These international conventions and related organisations find a worldwide application and thus apply to Antarctica. However, and mainly because of Antarctica's very special status, not all of these interesting measures would automatically find an application. The following study therefore briefly presents the major rules likely to govern bioprospecting activities in Antarctica and/or to inspire the drafters of the future legal instrument on bioprospecting in Antarctica.

The Relevance of the United Nations Convention on the Law of the Sea for Bioprospecting in Antarctica

UNCLOS, like the ATS, applies to an international area, including the Southern Ocean. It is particularly noteworthy that it has developed regulations on prospecting for and the exploitation of resources in this international area.

Part XI of UNCLOS (as modified by the 1994 Agreement) establishes principles applicable to the Area, which is defined as 'the sea-bed and ocean floor and subsoil thereof beyond the limits of national jurisdiction'. Thus, it applies to the Antarctic sea-bed. Consequently, the Area and its resources are identified as the Common Heritage of Mankind. It is opposed to the well-known principle of the freedom of the sea, which is a sort of 'first-come-first-served' rule and sets out the main legal parameters for the common use of the resources. Therefore states are not to claim or exercise sovereignty over the Area, and no such claims or exercise shall be recognised.[43] UNCLOS establishes the International Sea-Bed Authority to monitor the system. It organises the different activities in the Area concerned with sea-bed minerals with a view to administering its resources.[44] The Authority's responsibilities include approving exploration and exploitation activities 'on behalf of mankind as a whole'.[45] Thus, Part XI establishes that miners should submit to the Council for approval a plan of work[46] and indicate two sites. After the approval of the work plan, to ensure the proportionate sharing out of resources, the Authority's enterprise can mine one site and the miner the second. Therefore, Part XI of UNCLOS is likely to find useful application in the Antarctic ocean, with

43 Arts 136–137, UNCLOS.
44 Arts 156–157, UNCLOS.
45 Art 153(1), UNCLOS.
46 Art 153(3), UNCLOS.

respect to the different territorial claims. Moreover, the creation of an institutional body to enforce legal measures is often key to successfully achieving the objectives of a legal text. Even if the International Seabed Authority encounters difficulties, it still could manage the sea-bed minerals of Antarctica. Indeed it combines useful prerogatives in the fields of marine scientific research, the development and transfer of marine technology and polymetallic nodules.

Part XIII of UNCLOS sets out the right of all states to 'conduct marine scientific research in the territorial sea, within and beyond the exclusive economic zone and in the sea-bed and ocean floor and subsoil thereof beyond the limits of national jurisdiction'.[47] Information sharing is an important issue: 'information on proposed programmes, their objectives and resulting knowledge are [*sic*] to be made available through publication and dissemination'.[48] Moreover, states and competent international organisations 'shall actively promote the flow of data and information, and the transfer of knowledge, to developing States in particular'.[49] Under Article 242, states shall provide other states 'with a reasonable opportunity to obtain from it the information necessary to prevent damage to the health and safety of persons and to the marine environment'.

Part XIV of UNCLOS regulates the development and transfer of marine technology so that states shall co-operate in the development and transfer of marine technology on reasonable conditions. States have also to promote the development of the marine scientific and technological capacity of other states which may need technical assistance in this field. Finally, they have to favour economic and legal conditions for technology transfer on an equitable basis.[50] Article 274 provides the International Sea-Bed Authority and outlines its objectives to ensure that nationals of developing states, whether coastal, land-locked or geographically disadvantaged, shall be acceptable as members of the Authority's staff. It is also important that the technical documentation is made available to all states, in particular developing states. Moreover, adequate provision is to be made by the Authority to facilitate the acquisition of technical assistance in the field of marine technology by states, and in particular developing states, which may need and request it. States which may need technical assistance in this field, in particular developing states, should be assisted in the acquisition of the necessary equipment through any financial arrangements provided for in this Convention. Consequently, a number of measures are outlined, including the idea that Parties shall endeavour to establish programmes of technical co-operation for the effective transfer of marine

[47] Arts 238, 245–246, 256–257 UNCLOS.
[48] Art 244, UNCLOS.
[49] *Ibid.*
[50] Art 266, UNCLOS.

technology to states which need this assistance, promote the exchange of scientists, and promote favourable conditions for concluding equitable agreements under reasonable conditions.[51]

Nevertheless, all these measures are balanced by Article 267 which binds states to have 'due regard to all legitimate interests'.

Even though prospecting and exploration for polymetallic nodules is not a current activity, the following could inspire the drafters of the future legal text on bioprospecting in Antarctica. Adopted in July 2000, the Regulations on Prospecting and Exploration for Polymetallic Nodules complement the legislative regime for the international sea-bed set out in Part XI of UNCLOS. It sets out a compromise to protect freedom of scientific research, the right to conduct marine scientific research and the freedom of the high seas. Consequently, prospecting can commence only after the prospector's notification has been recorded and evaluated as causing 'no serious harm to the marine environment'.[52] Moreover, prospecting does not confer on the prospector rights to resources, but the prospector may 'recover a reasonable quantity for minerals, being the quantity necessary for testing, and not for commercial use'.[53] Nevertheless, the obligation on prospectors to notify the Authority of their activities appears weak. In fact, most of these can be carried out under the cover of marine scientific research so that no rights to the resource are granted, whereas entering into contracts for exploration does confer such rights.

Data and information submitted to the Authority and designated by the contractor as confidential shall be treated as such.[54] In August 2002, the International Seabed Authority agreed to develop a system for regulating prospecting for and the exploration of polymetallic nodules.[55]

The UNCLOS regime applies to the deep sea-bed of Antarctica notwithstanding maritime claims. It provides useful measures concerning the management of the Area and sets out an interesting process relating to access and benefit-sharing. However, nothing in UNCLOS expressly regulates bioprospecting activities. Unlike mineral resources, they do not fall within the legal framework of Part XI and are consequently not considered as Common Heritage of Mankind. Therefore, a legal gap exists and definitely needs to be filled. Also in this field, it is likely that the abstract application of the principle of freedom of the sea (that is the 'first-come-first-served' rule) would lead to hardly acceptable consequences and new co-operative schemes have to be envisaged at the

[51] Art 269, UNCLOS.

[52] Reg 2(1) and (2) of the Regulations on Polymetallic Nodules Prospecting and Exploration, ISBA/6/C/8.

[53] Reg 2(4) of *ibid*.

[54] Reg 35 of *ibid*.

[55] ISBA/8/A/5.

international level.[56] Since the final objective is to achieve sustainable management of the deep ocean space as a whole, sectoral approaches are not likely to lead to coherent and cost-effective results.[57]

The Relevance of the Convention on Biological Diversity for Bioprospecting in Antarctica

The Convention on Biological Diversity was adopted in June 1992 and entered into force in December 1993. It is the principal international legal framework concerning the conservation of biological diversity, the sustainable use of its components and the fair and equitable sharing of benefits arising from the utilisation of genetic resources. It is the first international treaty to take a global approach based on the ecosystem as a whole. The CBD is a framework instrument laying down broad goals, key objectives and general principles to be implemented by Contracting Parties through measures at the national level on the basis, *inter alia*, of the measures taken by the ATCMs. The CBD sets out two types of measures fulfilling these objectives.

The CBD contains the main international standards for bioprospecting and may apply to some extent to bioprospecting activities in Antarctica. Its Articles 15 to 21 set out provisions relating to access to genetic resources, transfer of technologies, and funding. Article 15(1) provides:

> Recognizing the sovereign rights of States over their natural resources, the authority to determine access to genetic resources rests with the national governments and is subject to national legislation.

Each state is to facilitate access to genetic resources for environmental uses by other Parties and take measures with the aim of sharing benefits with Parties providing the resources. Article 16 sets out that Parties have to provide access for and transfer to developing countries of technologies under 'fair and most favourable terms'. They are to co-operate to ensure that intellectual property rights support the CBD's objectives,[58] whereas Article 19 addresses the handling of biotechnology and the distribution of its benefits. Consequently, measures are to be adopted to provide for

[56] In any case, the freedom of the high seas, far from being an absolute entitlement, also has to be exercised with due regard for the rights under UNCLOS with respect to activities in the Area (Art 87(2)).

[57] On the future regime of biological resources of the deep marine sea-bed, see T. Scovazzi, *Some Considerations on Future Directions for the International Sea-Bed Authority*, Report presented at the Conference for the Tenth Anniversary of the International Sea-Bed Authority (Kingston, Jamaica), 25–26 May 2004).

[58] Art 16(5), CBD.

effective participation in biotechnology research by countries providing the genetic resources, and that they be given priority access to results and benefits arising from biotechnology. Besides, Parties to the CBD have developed guidelines regulating access to and benefit-sharing of genetic resources. However, and because of Article IV of the Antarctic Treaty, the question of the CBD's applicability to Antarctica remains.

As they are also Contracting Parties to the CBD, the Antarctic Treaty Consultative Parties[59] are bound by the provisions of both treaties. The difficulty in determining the applicability of the CBD to Antarctica arises from the different views about whether Antarctica lies outside the scope of national jurisdiction. The arguments about whether Article 4 of the CBD covers bioprospecting in Antarctica are complex and still unresolved:

> Subject to the rights of other Sates, and except as otherwise expressly provided in this Convention, the provisions of this Convention apply, in relation to each Contracting Party:
>
> (a) In the case of components of biological diversity, in areas within the limits of its national jurisdiction; and
> (b) In the case of processes and activities, regardless of where their effects occur, carried out under its jurisdictional control, within the area of its national jurisdiction or beyond the limits of national jurisdiction.

In conclusion, we can say that the CBD establishes a global framework for bioprospecting activities which may find application all around the world as well as in Antarctica. It provides a broad approach to biodiversity and establishes broad goals, key objectives and general principles. However, the intrinsic substance of the CBD does not seem totally to comply with the ATS principles, and we can regret the shortcomings of many of its measures. Thus, biodiversity is not protected under the Common Heritage of Mankind regime, but relies on only the common interest of mankind. [60] Moreover, even though the CBD refers to the Precautionary Principle, which is the key to the Madrid Protocol, this fundamental principle is to be reduced to a simple precautionary approach in the text of the CBD. In addition, the CBD is full of hortatory wording, such as the recurrent 'as far as possible and as appropriate', which is quite dangerous, both because the text is entirely based on the goodwill of the states parties and

[59] Except for the US.

[60] Further developments concerning marine biodiversity and international law are outlined in A.-I. Guyomard, B Guilloux and D Orabe, *L'exploitation de la biodiversité Marine et le Droit*, Report for the 'Exploitation of the Oceans' Seminar directed by Professor J-P. Beurier, in 2002–2003, available at http://www.droit.univ-nantes.fr/labos/cdmo/nept/nep27/nep27_1.pdf.

in view of the economic power of certain industries compared with the fragility of the Antarctic environment. Moreover, no institutional framework is created to ensure the enforcement of CBD measures. In any case, it is finally doubtful whether the CBD could find application in Antarctica, because of the sovereignty issues which leave the question of the sovereignty of a coastal state over its claimed sea entirely open. Consequently, it is to be hoped that the future legal regime governing bioprospecting in Antarctica will be inspired by only the best of the CBD rules, after being strengthened and adapted to the mandatory measures of the ATS.

The creation of a definite legal framework for the conduct of bioprospecting activities will take time, although bioprospecting activities are currently conducted in Antarctica. Therefore, it may be useful to create transitional legal provisions in the expectation of a complete legal framework. Considering the current development of bioprospecting activities in Antarctica, the Antarctic Treaty Parties should be proactive in taking relevant measures to supervise the main aspects of this growing industry. Even though the environmental aspect of bioprospecting is not part of the ATS, it has been tackled in the Madrid Protocol. However, the issues concerning access to and ownership of the biological resources could be discussed. At the same time, it would be of great utility to pursue the UNCLOS negotiations concerning the precise status of biological resources in the marine deep sea-bed.[61] In the case of the adoption of the Common Heritage of Mankind regime for biological resources, such an innovative idea could be extended to Antarctic biological resources, thus respecting the spirit and the very letter of the Treaty, stating that Antarctica shall continue forever to be used exclusively for peaceful purposes in the interest of all mankind.[62] Questions relating to benefit-sharing could then be tackled later. The creation of an efficient process for sharing the benefits from the exploitation of the resources equitably would, indeed, be the most difficult part of the work. However, such a question cannot be dismissed, and the creation of an *ad hoc* institution may help to find an answer.

IV. CONCLUSION

To conclude on the issue of bioprospecting in Antarctica, we should remember that international law, both at the global and the regional level, already provides a set of rules which may apply to Antarctica. However,

[61] See the Conference for the Tenth Anniversary of the International Sea-Bed Authority, above n 54.

[62] Preamble, Antarctic Treaty.

the very special Antarctic Treaty System does not always allow the direct application of those rules. In any case, they may at least serve as examples for the drafting of a future instrument concerning bioprospecting in Antarctica. Indeed, since the final objective is to achieve the sustainable management of bioprospecting activities in Antarctica, sectoral approaches are not likely to lead to coherent and environmentally protective results.

Meanwhile, this bioprospecting in Antarctica raises new issues mainly because of ethical and economical concerns. Not only does bioprospecting in Antarctica concern patent law, but also the broader horizon of the whole Antarctic Treaty System, which is entirely based on scientific and peaceful values. Thus, it is of utmost importance to determine the dividing line between freedom of scientific research and tolerance towards economic pressure. Throughout this long and difficult exercise, we will have to bear in mind that Antarctica is a natural reserve devoted to peace and science and hope that bioprospecting will never hinder the evolution of scientific discoveries. Therefore, all expectations concerning this new issue lie in the hands of the Antarctic Treaty Parties. Let us hope they will be inspired by the Antarctic philosophy to make their greatest efforts and provide adequate answers to the bioprospecting issues.

Part III

Biotechnology and International Trade Issues

8

The WTO Dispute Over Genetically Modified Organisms: Interface Problems of International Trade Law, Environmental Law and Biotechnology Law

ERNST-ULRICH PETERSMANN*

THIS CONTRIBUTION BEGINS with an overview (I) of the procedural background to the currently pending dispute in the World Trade Organization (WTO) over the EC import restrictions on genetically modified organisms (GMOs). It then discusses the main legal claims by the complainants (II), the legal defences by the EC (III), the amicus curiae submissions (IV), and some of the legal problems relating to this dispute, such as the legal relationships between the relevant WTO agreements (V), the role of science in the application of the Agreement on Sanitary and Phytosanitary (SPS) Measures (VI), and the impact of the 1992 UN Convention on Biodiversity (CBD) and its 2000 Cartagena Protocol on Biosafety on the interpretation of the relevant WTO rules (VII). The case-study illustrates, once again, how international trade creates pressures to

* Joint chair Professor of International and European Law at the European University Institute at Florence, and academic director of the Transatlantic Programme of the Robert Schuman Centre for Advanced Studies in Florence, Italy. Former legal adviser to GATT and the WTO. The author gratefully acknowledges the assistance by his doctoral student Lukasz Gruszczynski in the preparation of this Chapter. This contribution was written before the dispute settlement panel, set up by the WTO in 2003 to examine the complaints against the EC measures affecting the approval and marketing of biotech products, presented its report in 2006. As some of the legal issues (such as the definition of a '*de facto* measure', 'undue delay' actionable under WTO law) are highly fact-intensive and likely to be clarified in the WTO panel report in 2006, this chapter refrains from speculating on the legal findings in future panel and Appellate Body reports on this dispute.

reduce the fragmented regulation of the economic, environmental, technical, ethical and political dimensions of biotechnologies at national and international levels of governance in order to reduce transaction and investment costs; and why, in the absence of effective dispute settlement proceedings in multilateral environmental and biotechnology agreements, WTO dispute settlement proceedings are often in the center of the difficult interface problems of the diverse international treaty regimes and national regulatory systems.

I. INTRODUCTION AND PROCEDURAL BACKGROUND TO THE DISPUTE

Since EC Directive 90/220/EEC of 23 April 1990 on the deliberate release of genetically modified organisms [1], the European Community has enacted a large number of directives and regulations introducing approval procedures and labelling requirements for the release and marketing of GMOs, medicinal products containing or produced from GMOs, novel foods and novel food ingredients.[2] Up to October 1998, the EC had approved 18 biotech products pursuant to the procedures provided for in Directive 90/220. Between October 1998 and April 2004, however, GM products were approved only under the simplified procedure (based on 'substantial equivalence') provided for in the Novel Foods Regulation 258/97[3] but no longer under Directive 90/220 and its successor, Directive 2001/18.[4] Based on the various safeguard clauses in the EC directives and regulations, six EC Member States adopted marketing or import bans on biotech products that had previously been approved by the EC. Several EC and Member State officials spoke of a 'moratorium' pending the adoption and entry into force of new, stricter EC directives and regulations for the approval, labelling and traceability of GMOs and GM products.

[1] [1990] OJ L/117/15.

[2] For a detailed description and analysis see e.g. L. Stökl, *Der Welthandelsrechtliche Gentechnikkonflikt* (Berlin: Duncker), 2003; T. Christoforou, 'The Regulation of Genetically Modified Organisms in the EU: The Interplay of Science, Law and Politics', CML Rev 41(2004) 637; S. Zarrilli, *International Trade in GMOs and GM Products: National and Multilateral Legal Frameworks.* (UN, 2005). A GMO can be defined as an organism in which the genetic material has been altered—usually by insertion of foreign genes into the cell of the receiving organism—in a way that does not occur naturally by mating and/or natural recombination. Genes are composed of DNA (*Deoxyribonucleic Acid*) molecules that contain genetic information determining the proteins which the cell will produce. The first GMO crop was produced only in 1983 and became ready for commercialisation only in the early 1990s.

[3] [1997] OJ L/43/1.

[4] [2001] OJ L/106/1.

The change in the EC regulation of biotechnology was influenced by the entry into force of the 1992 UN Convention on Biodiversity and its 2000 Cartagena Protocol on Biosafety[5], which have prompted more than 100 countries to review or develop their national biosafety rules, often with the help of the capacity-building initiative of the Global Environment Facility of the United Nations Environment Programme (UNEP). Attitudes towards GMOs and GM products continue to vary considerably among countries depending on their biotechnological capacities, their perception of the risks and benefits of biotechnology, the level of risk they are willing to accept, their scientific risk assessment and administrative risk management capacities, their dependence on food imports, and their production and exports of GM products. Scientific risk assessments in Europe and North America have emphasised the potential advantages of GM products (e.g. in terms of increased agricultural output, higher quality food like 'vitamin A rice', protection of health and of the environment e.g. by less use of pesticides) and the apparently limited biosafety risks. The GMO regulations and risk assessments of some countries (e.g. in North America) proceed from the 'equivalence principle' relying on existing scientific evidence and substantial equivalence of GM foods with conventional products, including their equivalent safety. Other countries (notably in Europe) apply the equivalence principle to only a few categories of novel food and food ingredients and, based on a 'no risk approach' and the precautionary principle, consider GM products not only as inherently different from conventional products, but also as requiring further research and precautionary controls in view of the scientific uncertainty regarding their potential health and environmental risks. Some states (like Switzerland) have prohibited the commercial cultivation of all GMOs and all GMO imports.

In the spring of 2003, Argentina, Canada and the United States (US) requested formal dispute settlement consultations with the EC under the

[5] For the texts see e.g. D. Hunter, J. Salzman and D. Zaelke, International Environmental Law and Policy, Treaty Supplement Edition (New York: Foundation Press 2003), at 345 ff. The Biodiversity Convention has been signed by 188 contracting parties (including Argentina, Canada and the EC), but not by the US. The Biosafety Protocol was signed by more than 100 countries (including Argentina, Canada and the EC) and entered into force on 11 Sep 2003. The safe transfer, handling and use of GMOs and 'advance informed agreement' procedures for imports of GMOs are specifically regulated in the Biosafety Protocol whose Preamble also addresses the relationship between the Biosafety Protocol and other international agreements, including trade agreements, to the effect that 'this Protocol shall not be interpreted as implying a change in the rights and obligations of a Party under any existing international agreements, understanding that the above recital is not intended to subordinate this Protocol to other international agreements'. The issue of GMOs is also addressed in the Preamble to and Art 6 of the 1998 Aarhus Convention on Access to Information, Public Participation in Decision-making and Access to Justice on Environmental Matters which entered into force in Oct 2001.

WTO Dispute Settlement Understanding (DSU). The three complainants challenged the consistency of the EC's adoption of a moratorium on the approval of biotech products, as well as the national marketing and import bans on biotech products maintained by EC Member States, with the EC's obligations under WTO law, notably the SPS Agreement, the Agreement on Agriculture (AG Agreement), the Agreement on Technical Barriers to Trade (TBT Agreement) and the General Agreement on Tariffs and Trade (GATT 1994). As the consultations failed to settle the dispute, the WTO Dispute Settlement Body (DSB) established a dispute settlement panel in August 2003 with the mandate to examine the matter referred to the DSB by Argentina, Canada and the US and to make such findings as would assist the DSB in making the recommendations or in giving the rulings provided for in the relevant WTO agreements. Australia, Brazil, Chile, Colombia, India, Mexico, New Zealand and Peru reserved their rights to participate in the panel proceeding as third parties.

Following the composition of the Panel early in 2004, the first substantive meeting of the Panel with the parties and third parties took place in June 2004. In August 2004, the Panel postponed the timing of its final report from September 2004 to March 2005 and decided to seek expert advice on technical and scientific issues raised in the dispute. The hearings with the experts and the parties to the dispute took place only in February 2005. The Panel subsequently announced that its interim report would be submitted to the parties in August 2005; circulation of the final panel report was scheduled for September 2005.

II. LEGAL CLAIMS BY THE COMPLAINANTS

The main claims of the complainants are that (1) the general EC moratorium, (2) the 'product specific' EC moratoria on the approval of each of the 27 pending applications of biotech products under the EC's approval system, and (3) the national EC Member State marketing or import bans violate the SPS Agreement. Argentina and Canada also claim (4) certain violations of the TBT Agreement. In addition, all complainants claim (5) violations of GATT 1994 resulting from the national import bans. The following, brief survey summarises the main legal arguments without going into the many fact-intensive details and factual as well as legal controversies relating to the interpretation and application of the relevant WTO rules.

The General EC Moratorium Violates the SPS Agreement

Even though there is no formal EC decision on a moratorium, the complainants infer from the lack of any biotech product approvals between

October 1998 and August 2003 (i.e. the date of the establishment of the dispute settlement Panel), as well as from various statements in EC documents and by EC officials (including EC Commissioners) and EC Member State officials, that the EC practised a de facto moratorium without scientific and legal justification which delayed the 27 pending applications for placing biotech products on the market at various stages of the approval process. Many of the products had received favourable assessments from the sponsoring EC Member State as well as from the EC's Scientific Committee for Plants or the EC's Scientific Committee on Food (now part of the European Food Safety Authority); yet, since a number of EC Member States had publicly stated that they were not in a position to vote in favour of granting market authorisations for individual GM products in view of the scientific uncertainty and pending the entry into force of the new EC legislation, the EC had decided not to submit final decisions for a majority vote by the Commission or otherwise move products to a final decision in the approval process. The EC approval of GM sweetcorn in May 2004, after the entry into force of the EC's new traceability and labelling rules for biotech products in April 2004, confirmed that the EC approval process had not been held up by fact-specific problems with particular applications; this approval was not before the Panel and in no way affected the complaint that the moratorium existing up to the establishment of the Panel in August 2003 violated the EC's WTO obligations.

Even though the complainants argue that the EC failed to comply with its own approval procedures set out in its GMO Directives and Novel Food Regulation, the WTO complaints do not challenge the WTO consistency of these EC directives and regulations with the WTO. As the purpose of the EC's approval regime and moratorium is to protect human, animal or plant life or health from certain risks of GMO products, the complainants claim that the general moratorium is an SPS measure as defined in Annex A, paragraph.1(a), (b) and (d) of the SPS Agreement and affects international trade (in terms of Article 1(1) of the SPS Agreement). The general moratorium causes 'undue delay' in the EC's approval procedures and is inconsistent with the procedural requirements of Article 8 of and Annex C to the SPS Agreement, inter alia, because the EC has failed to inform the applicants of the progress of their applications. The EC has also violated Article 7 and Annex B by failing to 'publish promptly' the general moratorium. The moratorium is 'maintained without sufficient scientific evidence' in violation of Article 2(2) of the SPS Agreement, and is not 'based on' a risk assessment as required by Article 5(1); for, according to the US, there is consensus among international experts that, qualitatively, the types of risks potentially posed by products of modern biotechnology are essentially the same as those posed by similar products produced through other, more traditional technologies. The EC, it is claimed, has also applied arbitrary or unjustifiable distinctions in the levels of protection against risk (e.g. in respect of biotech products as compared to products produced using biotechnology in 'comparable situations') that have resulted in discrimination or a disguised restriction on international trade in violation of Article 5(5) of the SPS Agreement. The moratorium further arbitrarily or unjustifiably discriminates between WTO members and results in a disguised restriction on international trade in violation of Article 2(3) of the SPS Agreement.

The Product-specific Moratoria Violate the SPS Agreement

According to the complainants, the EC's failure to consider for approval each of the 27 pending applications for biotech products (= product specific moratoria) constitutes separate 'SPS measures' that (1) imposed 'undue delay' on the completion of the approval procedures, and applied approval procedures in a non-transparent manner in violation of Article 8 of the SPS Agreement; (2) failed to publish promptly the product specific moratoria in violation of Article 7; (3) failed to base the product-specific moratoria on risk assessments and scientific principles in violation of Articles 2(2) and 5(1); and (4) applied arbitrary or unjustifiable distinctions in its level of protection which resulted in discrimination or a disguised restriction on trade in violation of Articles 2(3) and 5(5) of the SPS Agreement.

The EC Member State Marketing or Import Bans Violate the SPS Agreement

According to the complainants, the Member States' bans are SPS measures affecting international trade which are 'based on' neither risk assessments as required under Article 5(1) nor on scientific principles or 'sufficient scientific evidence' as required under Article 2(2) of the SPS Agreement. None of the EC Member States' bans bore a 'rational relationship' to the only relevant risk assessments on the record in this dispute, i.e. the EC Scientific Committee's positive opinions. In the face of positive risk assessments with respect to each product subject to a Member State's ban, the EC had no basis for arguing that 'relevant scientific evidence is insufficient' and Article 5(7) of the SPS Agreement was applicable. The EC's Scientific Committee had reviewed each of the Member States' bans and had concluded that the bans were not based on 'available pertinent information'. The Member States' bans did not meet any of the four criteria necessary to bring them within the scope of Article 5(7).

Additional Violations of the TBT Agreement

According to the US, the SPS Agreement applies to all measures in the dispute, including the environmental effects of biotech plants. While the US has not made any claim under the TBT Agreement (although it reserved the right to do so), Argentina and Canada also claimed violations of the TBT Agreement (notably Articles 2(1), 2(2), 2(9) and 5) in the event that the Panel should find that the product-specific marketing bans are not SPS measures, or that those parts of the measures which do not pursue SPS objectives are covered by the TBT Agreement in addition to the SPS Agreement.

National Trade Restrictions by EC Member States in Violation of GATT 1994

According to the jurisprudence of the Appellate Body, it 'is now well established that the WTO Agreement is a 'Single Undertaking' and therefore all WTO obligations are generally cumulative and Members must comply with all of them simultaneously'.[6] However, since the General Interpretative Note to the multilateral trade agreements listed in Annex 1A of the WTO Agreement emphasises the residual nature of GATT 1994, it is well established in WTO jurisprudence that panels should first address the specific multilateral trade agreements before resorting to the residual GATT 1994 disciplines. According to the US, the Greek import ban violates Article XI(1) GATT. Argentina and Canada claim a violation also of the national treatment requirement in Article III(4) of GATT 1994.

Applicable Law

In the view of the United States, the Panel's terms of reference exclude considering the dispute in the light of the provisions of the 2000 Biosafety Protocol to the UN Convention on Biodiversity, or in the light of sources of international law other than the covered WTO agreements. The only way these other sources of international law could be pertinent to this dispute would be if, pursuant to Article 3(2) of the DSU, those other sources of law assisted the Panel in 'clarifying the existing provisions of the (covered) agreements in accordance with customary rules of interpretation of public international law'. The EC had, however, not identified how the Biosafety Protocol or a 'precautionary principle' would be of relevance to

[6] Appellate Body Report, *Korea-Dairy Safeguards*, WT/DS98/AB/R, adopted 12 Jan 2000, paras. 23, 24 and 594.

interpreting any particular WTO provision. The US noted that it strongly disagreed with the EC claim that the precautionary principle had become a rule of general international law. The Biosafety Protocol was, according to the US, not applicable in relations between the US and the EC because the US was not a party to the Biosafety Protocol.

III. LEGAL ARGUMENTS BY THE EC

The EC emphasises that its prudent GMO regulations have not adopted any general position in favour or against GMOs. Because its regulation of GMOs and GM products had remained politically controversial and scientifically complex, the EC regulations had been reviewed and amended in 1998–2001. Even though the new regulatory framework had become operational only in 2003–2004[7], some of the new requirements had already been taken into account in the approval procedures prior to the entry into force of the new rules.

There are no General or Specific Moratoria Decisions

According to the EC, the complaint of an alleged moratorium turned on the facts which the Panel had to assess in an objective manner, as required by Article 11 of the DSU. The fact not contested by the EC, i.e. that there had been no market authorisations for a given period of time other than those granted pursuant to the simplified procedure under the Novel Foods Regulation, reflected only the 'absence of a decision', but not a 'decision not to decide'. There was no EC measure which individually or collectively could be treated as a moratorium. A careful, individual consideration of each of the 43 GM product applications and approval procedures mentioned by the complainants confirmed that there had been neither any general EC decision on a formal or de facto moratorium nor any general suspension, or 'pattern of suspension', of the approval process which constituted a challengeable SPS measure.

The Delays in EC Approval Procedures Were Justified

According to the EC, individual consideration of each of the 43 GM product applications and approval procedures mentioned by the complainants also demonstrated that there had been no 'undue delay' (as defined in Annex C(1)(a) of the SPS Agreement) in individual approval procedures.

[7] Cf. e.g. EC Regulation 1829/2003 of 22 Sep 2003 on genetically modified food and feed [2003] OJ L/268/1.

As 19 out of the 43 applications had been withdrawn or abandoned by the applicants, these complaints had become moot and inadmissible. In respect of the other applications, the complainants had not met their burden of proving a prima facie case for 'undue delay' (Article 8 SPS Agreement), or that the EC had not acted 'as expeditiously as possible' (pursuant to Article 5(2)(1) of the TBT Agreement), in relation to each of their complaints.

As the classification of GM products under the SPS Agreement (e.g. its definition of 'toxin', 'additives' or a 'contaminant') required scientific expertise, the EC welcomed the Panel's decision to hear scientific and technical experts. According to the EC, only Article 8 of the SPS Agreement could be applied to the facts of this case; Articles 2(2), 2(3), 5(1), 5(5) and 5(6) of the SPS Agreement all contained obligations concerning the 'development' of an SPS measure, but not regarding its 'application'. In examining which period of time should actually be considered as a 'delay', delays caused by risk considerations falling outside the scope of the SPS Agreement, or voluntarily accepted or caused by the applicants, or due to the entry into force of new legislation with stricter requirements, could not be taken into account in determining 'undue delay' in the sense of Annex C to the SPS Agreement.

'Risk assessment' in the SPS Agreement had to be understood in the broad sense of encompassing (1) risk assessment in the narrow sense, i.e. as a 'scientifically based process'; (2) risk management and (3) risk communication. It followed from paragraphs (2) and (3) of Article 5 of the SPS Agreement that members were obliged to take into account not only scientific, but also economic and regulatory considerations. Favourable scientific opinions of the EC's Scientific Committee therefore did not inevitably mean that the EC's Regulatory Committee or the EC Commission could not take into account risk management and risk communication (e.g. labelling) considerations.

By virtue of the incorporation, by reference, of the text of Article 5(7) into Article 2(2) of the SPS Agreement, Articles 2(2) and 5(7) had to be read together. The comma after the word 'evidence' in Article 2(2) proved that the relationship between Articles 2(2) and 5(7) was one of exclusion, not exception. As the EC had applied provisional measures 'in cases where relevant scientific evidence is insufficient', the complainants had to prove prima facie that the four cumulative requirements of Article 5(7) had not been complied with. The applicability of Article 5(7) excluded the rest of Article 5 of the SPS Agreement, which was therefore not relevant to this case.

Directive 90/220 had been replaced in March 2001 by the new Directive 2001/18 which required the re-submission of applications in respect of which the procedures had not been completed by 17 October 2002 (Article 35 of Directive 2001/18). The absence of authorisations granted under these two Directives during the 1998–2003 period had been due to the change in legislation and the 'interim approach' applied by the EC. The lack of any applications to the European Court of Justice challenging any actions or alleged failure to act of the EC institutions in respect of any of these applications was further evidence that no 'undue delay' had occurred.[8] In 2004, following the entry into force of the new rules on traceability and labelling of biotech products, the EC Commission had asked the EC Council to decide on the approval of several GM products and, in July 2004 as well as in 2005, had itself approved several GM products for marketing in the EC.

Apart from those cases where actual harm to the environment through the use of certain GMOs had already been established[9], the existence of a potential threat justified the assessment of risks on a case-by-case basis and, eventually, a precautionary approach. The EC's measures, and the temporary suspensions of EC authorisations for the marketing of GM products at the level of EC Member States were in any event provisionally justified on the basis of the insufficiency of scientific evidence (Article 5(7) SPS Agreement which, according to the EC, excludes Article 5(1) and 5(5) of the SPS Agreement, rather than being an exception to it).

To the extent that the EC measures, such as the conservation of biodiversity, protected the environment they fell in whole or in part outside the SPS Agreement but were consistent with the TBT Agreement (which expressly refers to the environment e.g. in Article 2(2)) and GATT 1994. The EC approval procedures did not discriminate between GM products on grounds of origin and were, in any event, justified under GATT Article XX. In view of the EC's broad regulatory concerns, the SPS and TBT Agreements were often both applicable, so that 'mixed delays' and 'mixed risks'—meeting the requirements of both the SPS and TBT Agreements—had to be examined by the Panel. In view of this dual nature of some EC measures, a Panel finding of the inconsistency of the EC measures with SPS obligations could not justify an obligation to remove the measures if the same measure also included a TBT measure consistent with the TBT Agreement.

EC Member States' Measures

As regards the provisional EC Member States' measures, the EC considers that they are not 'technical regulations' within the meaning of the TBT Agreement and not inconsistent with the TBT Agreement. The complainants failed to take into account that the national legislator's appropriate

[8] Actions have, however, been brought against national measures in the European Court of Justice: see e.g. Case C–6/99, *Greenpeace France v. Ministry of Agriculture* [2000] ECR 1–1651; Case C–236/01, *Monsanto Italia v. Presidenza del Consiglio dei Ministri* (Case C-236/01) [2003] ECR I-8015.

[9] The EC refers e.g. to the United Kingdom field trials from 1999 to 2003 which were concluded only in Sep 2003.

level of protection (acceptable level of risk) may have been different from that of the EC Commission or EC Council. The national restrictions were consistent with both GATT and the SPS Agreement.

Applicable Law

The EC argues that the interpretation of the relevant WTO agreements should be consistent with the requirements of the Biosafety Protocol, including its provisions on risk assessments and the right to take precautionary measures. It should also take into account the recognition of the potential risks of GMOs for human health and the environment in the standard-setting work of international organisations (including e.g. the Food and Agricultural Organisation, the Codex Alimentarius Commission of the FAO and its Intergovernmental Task Force on foods derived from biotechnology, the World Health Organisation, UNEP, UNIDO, OECD). In Article 8(g) of the Biosafety Protocol, for instance, the international Community had agreed that it was necessary to:

> Establish and maintain means to regulate, manage or control the risks associated with the use and release of living modified organisms resulting from biotechnology which are likely to have adverse environmental impacts that could affect the conservation and sustainable use of biological diversity, taking into account the risks to human health.

According to the EC, the international Community had, through the Biosafety Protocol, recognised that GM products required their own, distinct authorisation procedure and were objectively different from (i.e. not 'like') non-GM products. This should be taken into account by the Panel in line with the WTO Appellate Body's finding on the need to take into account the 'contemporary concerns of the community of nations about the protection and conservation of the environment'.[10] The EC further argues that the precautionary principle has now become a fully fledged, general principle of international law that should be taken into account in the interpretation of Article 5(7) of the SPS Agreement, i.e. the autonomous right of WTO members provisionally to restrict or prohibit GMO imports in the face of scientific uncertainty.

IV. *AMICUS CURIAE* SUBMISSIONS

The WTO Dispute Settlement Understanding (DSU) contains no provision on the admissibility of *amicus curiae* briefs. In its decision in *United*

[10] *United States—Import Prohibition of Certain Shrimp and Shrimp Products* (*US—Shrimp/Turtle*), Report of the Appellate Body, 12 Oct 1998, WT/DS58/AB/R, para.129.

States—Shrimp/Turtle, the Appellate Body held that the Panel's right to seek information (Article 13 DSU) included the right to accept amicus briefs.[11] Ever since, there has been an increasing number of WTO dispute settlement panels that have received and accepted such 'friends of the court' briefs. In *United States—British Steel*[12], the Appellate Body also confirmed its own right (based on Article 17(9) of the DSU), without any duty, to consider *amicus* briefs[13]. In the Appellate Body decision in *EC—Asbestos*[14], the Appellate Body established special rules applicable for *amicus* briefs based on Rule 16(1) of its Working Procedures[15]. Even though the text of Articles 13 and 17(9) of the DSU does not mention *amicus curiae* briefs, and their admissibility continues to be challenged by many WTO Members, it has now become generally recognised in WTO dispute settlement practice that *amicus curiae* briefs may assist dispute settlement panels in their task of conducting an 'objective assessment' of the facts before a panel.[16]

In the panel proceedings concerning the EC measures affecting the approval and marketing of biotech products, three lengthy *amicus curiae* briefs were submitted to the Panel and the parties: one by an international coalition of 15 public interest groups; another by a transatlantic group of five environmental, agricultural and consumer associations; and a third by a 'group of transatlantic academics'. The first brief on behalf of the '*amicus* coalition' submits very detailed factual evidence (e.g. on the uncertain benefits of GM technology, the risks associated with GM products) as well as legal arguments in favour of the consistency with the WTO of the EC measures.

The second brief submits factual arguments for the substantial scientific uncertainty (e.g. due to unintended effects of genetic modification arising from the random nature of DNA techniques) of the human and plant impact of GMOs, as well as legal arguments why uncertainty is a critical factor in determining when scientific evidence is insufficient under

[11] *Ibid.*, paras. 100–110.

[12] *United States – Imposition of countervailing duties on certain hot-rolled lead and bismuth carbon steel products originating in the United Kingdom*, (*US—British Steel*), Report of the Appellate Body, 10 May 2000, WT/DS138/AB/R, paras. 36–42.

[13] *Ibid.*, para. 39. Art 17(9) of the DSU gives the Appellate Body the authority to adopt procedural rules, which do not conflict with any rules and procedures in the DSU or the covered agreements. The Appellate Body also held that Rule 16(1) of the Working Procedures allows it to fill in gaps in the Working Procedures by adopting new rules.

[14] *European Communities—Measures Affecting Asbestos and Asbestos-Containing Products*, (*EC-Asbestos*), Report of the Appellate Body, 12 Mar 2001, WT/DS135/AB/R.

[15] *Ibid.*, Communication from the Appellate Body (Additional Procedures), 8 Nov 2000, WT/DS135/9.

[16] The recent 'Sutherland Report' on 'The Future of the WTO: (WTO, 2004) agrees that *amicus curiae* submissions 'can in some instances improve the overall quality of the dispute settlement process' and supports the 'need to develop general criteria and procedures', at panel and appellate levels, 'to fairly and appropriately handle *amicus* submissions' (at 58).

Article 5(7) of the SPS Agreement. The 'group of transatlantic academics' argues, inter alia, that risk assessments of GMOs may legitimately vary depending on the specific national or institutional decision-making processes (e.g. differing public values regarding health and the environment, public deliberations, public confidence in regulating new food technologies); in view of the limited task of WTO panels in reviewing executive risk-assessment decisions, the alleged European moratorium should not be deemed an 'undue delay'.

V. LEGAL INTERRELATIONSHIPS BETWEEN THE RELEVANT 'MULTILATERAL AGREEMENTS ON TRADE IN GOODS'

Annex 1 A to the WTO Agreement lists 13 'multilateral agreements on trade in goods', plus six additional 'Understandings' on the interpretation of various GATT 1994 provisions and the 'Marrakesh Protocol to the GATT 1994', which—according to Article II(2) WTO Agreement—are 'integral parts of this Agreement, binding on all Members'. Article XVI(3) of the WTO Agreement prescribes that, 'in the event of a conflict between a provision of this Agreement and a provision of any of the Multilateral Trade Agreements [included in Annexes 1, 2 and 3], the provision of this Agreement shall prevail to the extent of the conflict'. The 'General interpretative note to Annex 1 A' states: '[i]n the event of a conflict between a provision of the General Agreement on Tariffs and Trade 1994 and a provision of another agreement in Annex 1A to the Agreement Establishing the World Trade Organization ..., the provision of the other agreement shall prevail to the extent of the conflict'. Several of the 13 'multilateral agreements on trade in goods' include additional provisions on how to resolve conflicts of rules. For example, according to the Agreement on Agriculture, the 'provisions of GATT 1994 and of other Multilateral Trade Agreements in Annex 1A to the WTO Agreement shall apply subject to the provisions of this Agreement' (Article 21(1)), including its 'peace clause' (Article 13) which limits recourse to WTO dispute settlement proceedings against domestic support measures and export subsidies that conform fully to the Agreement on Agriculture.

Conflict Rules in the SPS and TBT Agreements

GATT 1994 provides for general disciplines for trade in goods which, in the SPS Agreement, are supplemented by an additional 'multilateral framework of rules and disciplines to guide the development, adoption and enforcement of sanitary and phytosanitary measures in order to minimize their negative effects on trade' and 'to further the use of harmonized sanitary and phytosanitary measures between Members, on the basis of international standards, guidelines and recommendations developed by the relevant international organizations. . ., without requiring Members to change their appropriate level of protection of human, animal or plant life or health' (Preamble to the SPS Agreement). The SPS Agreement specifies that:

- the Agreement 'elaborate[s] rules for the application of the provisions of GATT 1994 which relate to the use of sanitary or phytosanitary measures, in particular the provisions of Article XX(b)' (Preamble);
- 'nothing in the Agreement shall affect the rights of Members under the Agreement on Technical Barriers to Trade with respect to measures not within the scope of this Agreement' (Article 1(4));
- 'Sanitary or phytosanitary measures which conform to the relevant provisions of this Agreement shall be presumed to be in accordance with the obligations of the Members under the provisions of GATT 1994 which relate to the use of sanitary or phytosanitary measures, in particular the provisions of Article XX(b)' (Article 2(4));
- 'Sanitary or phytosanitary measures which conform to international standards, guidelines or recommendations shall be deemed to be necessary to protect human, animal or plant life or health, and presumed to be consistent with the relevant provisions of this Agreement and of GATT 1994' (Article 3(2));
- 'The Committee on Sanitary and Phytosanitary Measures provided for in paragraphs 1 and 4 of Article 12 . . . shall develop a procedure to monitor the process of international harmonization and coordinate efforts in this regard with the relevant international organizations' (Article 3(5)).

The TBT Agreement is likewise designed 'to further the objectives of GATT 1994' and 'to ensure that technical regulations and standards, including packaging, marking and labelling requirements, and procedures for assessment of conformity with technical regulations and standards do not create unnecessary obstacles to international trade' (Preamble). The TBT Agreement recognises 'the important contribution that international standards and conformity assessment systems can make . . . by improving efficiency of production and facilitating the conduct of international trade', or by contributing 'to the transfer of technology from developed to developing countries' (Preamble). The Agreement purports 'therefore to encourage the development of such international standards and conformity assessment systems', subject to the proviso 'that no country should be prevented from taking measurers necessary to ensure the quality of its exports, or for the protection of human, animal or plant life or health, of the environment, or for the prevention of deceptive practices, at the levels it considers appropriate', or 'from taking measures necessary for the protection of its essential security interest' (Preamble). The TBT Agreement specifies that:

- 'the provisions of this Agreement do not apply to sanitary and phytosanitary measures as defined in Annex A of the Agreement on the Application of Sanitary and Phytosanitary Measures' (Article 1.5);
- 'where technical regulations are required and relevant international standards exist or their completion is imminent, Members shall use them , or the relevant parts of them, as a basis for their technical regulations except when such international standards or relevant parts would be an ineffective or inappropriate means for the fulfilment of the legitimate objectives pursued, for instance because of fundamental climatic or geographical factors or fundamental technological problems' (Article 2(4));
- 'whenever a technical regulation is prepared, adopted or applied for one of the legitimate objectives explicitly mentioned in paragraph 2, and is in accordance with relevant international standards, it shall be rebuttably presumed not to create an unnecessary obstacle to international trade' (Article 2(5));
- 'with a view to harmonizing technical regulations on as wide a basis as possible, Members shall play a full part, within the limits of their resources, in the preparation by appropriate international standardizing bodies of international standards for products for which they either have adopted, or expect to adopt, technical regulations' (Article 2(6)).

Conflict Avoidance Rules in General International Law

The above survey of the major 'conflict of law rules' in the WTO Agreements on Agriculture, SPS and TBT reflects the concern of WTO Members to limit legal conflicts resulting from the multitude of national and intergovernmental law-makers in international relations by promoting international harmonisation and reciprocal recognition of divergent regulations of trade and of technical, sanitary or phytosanitary standards. WTO Members clearly did *not* want to 'contract out' of the existing international legal system by creating a 'self-contained WTO system'. This justifies a 'presumption against conflict of norms', i.e. in favour of interpreting WTO rules in conformity with other obligations of WTO Members under international law so as to avoid 'inherent normative conflicts' (where one norm breaches the other and is illegal or ceases to exist) as well as 'conflicts in the applicable law' (where implementation of, or reliance on, one norm leads to breach of the other norm).[17]

[17] Cf. J. Pauwelyn, *Conflict of Norms in Public International Law. How WTO Law Relates to other Rules of International Law* Oxford (2003), at 488–489. There is 'conflict of norms in case one norm breaches, has led or may lead to a breach of another norm. Crucially, contradiction as between an obligation and an explicit right (be it a permission or an exemption) must also be recognized as a situation of conflict' (at 489).

The GMO dispute may require the Panel to examine—with regard to the various WTO agreements among each other as well as regarding their relationships with other worldwide agreements (like the CBD Convention, its Biosafety Protocol) and regional agreements (like EC law)—various potential conflicts of international norms and to resolve such conflicts on the basis of explicit conflict clauses (e.g. in WTO law and the Biosafety Protocol) and general international law principles (such as freedom of contract, the *lex specialis—pacta sunt servanda—pacta tertiis non nocent non prosunt*—principles). It may also require addressing conflicting obligations of 'equal legal standing' *vis-à-vis* different states (e.g. members and non-members of the Biosafety Protocol).

The Limited Jurisdiction and 'Applicable Law' in WTO Disputes

The DSU (Article 7) limits the jurisdiction of panels to examining, 'in the light of the relevant provisions in . . the covered agreement(s) cited by the parties to the dispute, the matter referred to the DSB' by the complainants in their respective documents submitted to the DSB. While the jurisdiction of WTO dispute settlement bodies is limited to claims under the covered WTO agreements only, it remains to be clarified in WTO jurisprudence whether, and to what extent, the 'applicable law' must include also other relevant rules of international law binding on the parties to the dispute. For example, examination of complaints based on WTO law may raise questions not regulated in WTO law itself (such as the admissibility of preliminary rulings by dispute settlement panels), which may be clarified only by recourse to general international law rules or to non-WTO agreements applicable in the relations between the parties to the WTO dispute. Yet, even if non-WTO rights and obligations were part of the applicable law in a WTO panel proceeding (e.g. as a valid defence against claims of breach of a WTO obligation), they could not form the basis of legal claims, and WTO panels have no jurisdiction judicially to enforce compliance with non-WTO rules.[18]

The main task of the GMO Panel will, therefore, be to examine the claims by the complainants in the light of the SPS, GATT and TBT provisions invoked by the parties, with due regard to the explicit 'conflict clauses' in these agreements as well as in general international law (like the *lex specialis* principle). As the jurisdiction of panels remains limited by the legal claims and defences of the parties to the dispute (cf. Articles 7, 11 DSU), many controversial questions relating to the relationships between GATT and SPS provisions remain outside the jurisdiction of the GMO

[18] Cf. *Ibid.*, at 491.

Panel (e.g. the different regulation of burden of proof in GATT 1994 and the SPS Agreement, the availability of 'non-violation complaints' in case of nullification of market access commitments by subsequent environmental restrictions). The need for interpreting the relevant WTO rules with due regard to the CBD Convention, the Biosafety Protocol and other rules of international law will be further discussed below (section VII).

WTO Jurisprudence on the SPS and TBT Agreements

According to the Appellate Body, 'it is now well established that the WTO Agreement is a "Single Undertaking" and therefore all WTO obligations are generally cumulative and Members must comply with all of them simultaneously'.[19] This presumption of cumulative applicability of WTO rules is subject to the specific conflict clauses in the SPS, TBT and other WTO agreements. The GMO dispute illustrates that, despite the *lex specialis* character of many SPS provisions, it may be difficult to determine whether SPS or TBT provisions may be applicable, especially with regard to multi-purpose measures pursuing health and environmental objectives simultaneously (as claimed by the EC with regard to some of its GMO measures). If a particular measure is interpreted to protect human, animal or plant life or health from the specific risks enumerated in Annex A to the SPS Agreement, it will be qualified as an SPS measure subject to the SPS Agreement; this will normally exclude simultaneous application of the TBT Agreement whose legal disciplines tend to be less demanding than the requirements of the SPS Agreement (e.g. regarding risk assessments, scientific justification of SPS measures) and recognise the *lex specialis* nature of the SPS disciplines (cf. Article 1(5) TBT Agreement).[20] Yet, the principle of cumulative application of different WTO obligations may entail that TBT provisions may remain applicable to the extent that—in the case of multi-purpose measures—an SPS regulation includes separable TBT requirements.

If the purpose of a measure is not clearly indicated in the measure itself, the legal autonomy and (quasi-) judicial tasks of WTO panels entail the right independently to review whether the pertinent claims of the defending party in the dispute are consistent with the text, content and context of the contested measure concerned. This obligation 'to make an objective assessment of the facts of the case and the applicability of and conformity with the relevant covered agreements' (Article 11 DSU) was clarified,

19 See WT/DS98/AB/R, *supra* n 6, para.74.

20 See, e.g., the Panel report on *EC—Measures Concerning Meat and Meat Products (Hormones)*, Complaint by the United States, WT/DS26/R/USA, 18 Aug 1997, para.8.29.

for instance, in the *Australia—Salmon case*, where the Appellate Body emphasised that the establishment of an appropriate level of protection 'is a prerogative of the Member concerned and not of a panel or of the Appellate Body'; however, 'in cases where a Member does not determine its appropriate level of protection, or does so with insufficient precision, the appropriate level of protection may be established by panels on the basis of the level of protection reflected in the SPS measure actually applied'.[21] Similarly, WTO dispute settlement panels cannot unilaterally rely on declarations of the defending party concerning the alleged purpose of the contested measure without making an 'objective assessment of the facts' (Article 11 DSU) and of the claims of the complaining party regarding the regulatory purpose of a contested measure by another WTO Member, which may require stricter standards of review than the judicial deference warranted under some domestic constitutional systems for review by national judges and EC judges of legislative measures.[22]

The application of the abovementioned 'conflict rules' (such as the General Interpretative Note to Annex 1A, the *lex specialis* presumptions in Articles 2(4) and 3(2) of the SPS Agreement), and of the general presumption of cumulative applicability of WTO provisions to the relationship between the SPS Agreement and GATT 1994 may leave various questions open. As GATT and SPS provisions tend to be supplementary, WTO jurisprudence has so far not established any conflicts in the narrow sense of mutually exclusive GATT and SPS obligations (where 'adherence to

[21] *Australia—Measures Affecting Imports of Salmon*, WT/DS18/AB/R, 20 Oct 1998, paras. 199, 207.

[22] In *EC-Hormones*, the Appellate Body found that 'the applicable standard is neither *de novo* review as such nor "total deference", but rather the "objective assessment of the facts"': WT/DS26/AB/R, 16 Jan 1998, para.165. *In Japan—Measures Affecting the Importation of Apples*, WT/DS245/AB/R, 26 Nov 2003, the Appellate Body confirmed that favouring 'Japan's approach to risk and scientific evidence over the views of the experts conflicts with the Appellate Body's articulation of the standard of "objective assessment of the facts"' (para. 165). Drawing the line between permissible 'objective assessment' and prohibited '*de novo* review' raises many other problems (cf. the Appellate Body report in *US—Transitional Safeguard Measures on Combed Cotton Yarn from Pakistan*, WT/DS192/AB/R, para.7, adopted in Nov 2001). WTO jurisprudence has not yet defined general standards of judicial deference similar to those applied by the ECJ: 'In a sphere in which the Community legislature is called on to undertake complex assessments based on technical and scientific information which is liable to change rapidly, judicial review of the exercise of its powers must be limited to examining whether it has been vitiated by a manifest error of assessment or a misuse of powers or whether the legislature has manifestly exceeded the limits of its discretion': Case C–127/95, *Norbrook*, [1998] ECR, 1–1531, para. 90. EC jurisprudence defines 'misuse of powers . . . as the adoption by a community institution of a measure with the exclusive or main purpose of achieving an end other than that stated or evading a procedure specifically prescribed by the Treaty for dealing with the circumstances of the case': Case C–180/96, *UK v. Commission* [1998] ECR 1—2265, para. 64).

one provision will lead to violation of the other provision'[23]). The principle of effective treaty interpretation, which has been recognised by the Appellate Body as 'one of the corollaries of the "general rule of interpretation" in the Vienna Convention'[24], requires one 'first [to] examine the claims raised under the SPS Agreement'[25] because a finding of GATT consistency would not exclude the inconsistency of the measure concerned with the SPS Agreement, and 'there is no requirement, in any provision of the SPS Agreement, that a prior violation of a GATT provision needs to be established before the SPS Agreement applies'.[26] WTO jurisprudence has also not yet clarified whether breaches of an SPS obligation may be justifiable under GATT Article XX, and whether the presumption of GATT consistency (pursuant to Article 2(4) of the SPS Agreement) of a measure in conformity with the SPS Agreement may be rebuttable.

VI. THE ROLE OF SCIENCE IN RISK REGULATION UNDER THE SPS AGREEMENT

SPS measures aim at protecting human, animal or plant life or health from specified risks of potential harm. In contrast to GATT rules and TBT rules, many SPS provisions ascribe a special role to science in the assessment and prevention of the risks, as well as in the determination of the WTO consistency of SPS measures. For instance:

- 'Members shall ensure that any sanitary or phytosanitary measure ... is based on scientific principles and is not maintained without sufficient scientific evidence, except as provided for in paragraph 7 of Article 5' (Article 2(2)).
- 'Members may introduce or maintain sanitary or phytosanitary measures which result in a higher level of sanitary or phytosanitary protection than would be achieved by measures based on the relevant international standards, guidelines or recommendations, if there is a scientific justification' (Article 3(3)).
- SPS measures must be 'based on an assessment . . . of the risks' (Article 5(1)) which 'shall take into account available scientific evidence' (Article 5(2)).
- 'In cases where relevant scientific evidence is insufficient, a Member may provisionally adopt sanitary or phytosanitary measures on the basis of available pertinent information' (Article 5(7)).

23 *Guatemala—Antidumping Investigation Regarding Portland Cement from Mexico*, WT/DS60/AB/R, 25 Nov 1998, para. 65.

24 *US-Standards for Reformulated and Conventional Gasoline*, WT/DS2/AB/R, 29 Apr 1996, para. 23.

25 See the Panel Report on EC-Hormones *supra* n 20, para. 8.29.

26 *Ibid.* para. 8.41.

Hence, even non-discriminatory SPS measures consistent with GATT rules may violate the SPS Agreement in the absence of 'sufficient scientific evidence'.

'Sufficient Scientific Evidence' as a Condition of the Lawfulness of SPS Measures

The GMO dispute illustrates that—in order to establish or refute a *prima facie* case[27] of violation of SPS obligations—WTO Members may be required to submit highly complex, scientific evidence to the WTO dispute settlement panel concerned. In order objectively to assess whether there is 'sufficient scientific evidence' (Article 2(2)) and a 'scientific justification' (Article 3(3)), WTO dispute settlement panels may decide to 'seek information from any relevant source and ... consult experts to obtain their opinion on certain aspects of the matter', including with respect to 'a factual issue concerning a scientific or other technical matter raised by a party to the dispute' (Article 13.2 DSU). The term 'scientific' was defined by the Appellate Body as 'having or appearing to have an exact, objective, factual, systematic or methodological basis' and 'relating to, or exhibiting the methods or principles of science'.[28] In the *Japan—Agricultural Products* and *Japan—Apples* cases, the Appellate Body interpreted 'sufficiency' of evidence as depending on an objective, rational relationship between the SPS measure and the scientific evidence that had to be examined on a case-by-case basis so as to take into account the particular circumstances of each case.[29] The Appellate Body acknowledged that 'the panel charged with determination ... whether "sufficient scientific evidence" exists to warrant the maintenance by a Member of a particular SPS measure, may, of course and should bear in mind that responsible, representative governments commonly act from a perspective of prudence and precaution where risks are irreversible'.[30] Yet, rationality of the relationship between the SPS measure and 'sufficient scientific evidence' may also involve some kind of proportionality requirement: In the *Japan—Apples* case, the Appellate Body upheld the panel finding that a disproportion between the risk identified by scientific evidence and an overly strict SPS measure may undermine the rationality of their relationship.[31]

[27] In *ibid.*, the Appellate Body defined a *prima facie* case as one 'which, in the absence of effective refutation by the defending party, requires a panel, as a matter of law, to rule in favor of the complaining party presenting the *prima facie* case': WT/DS26/AB/R, para.98.

[28] *Ibid.*, n 172.

[29] *Japan—Measures Affecting Agricultural Products*, WT/DS76/AB/R, 22 Feb 1999, paras. 73–74; *Japan—Apples, supra* n 22, para. 164.

[30] *EC—Hormones, supra* n 20 para. 124.

[31] *Japan—Apples, supra* n 22, para. 147.

Numerous interpretative issues, such as the interrelationships between different SPS provisions (e.g. Articles 2(2), 5(1), 5(7)), remain to be clarified in WTO jurisprudence. For example, even though an SPS measure violating Article 5(1) should be 'presumed . . . not to be based on scientific principles or to be maintained without sufficient scientific evidence'[32], an SPS measure consistent with Article 5(1) may still be found also to violate Article 2(2) (e.g. its necessity requirement).

Risk Assessment Procedures

WTO Members 'shall ensure that their sanitary or phytosanitary measures are based on an assessment, as appropriate to the circumstances, of the risks to human, animal or plant life or health, taking into account risk assessment techniques developed by the relevant international organizations' (Article 5(1) SPS Agreement). In the *EC-Hormones* case, the Appellate Body found no textual basis in the SPS Agreement that justified the Panel's strict separation between *scientific* risk assessment and *political* risk management decisions (e.g. on a Member's 'appropriate level of protection of human, animal or plant life or health').[33] Scientific and political factors may influence both risk assessment and risk management decisions. The SPS Agreement sets out (in Annex A) more stringent criteria for evaluating the 'likelihood' of 'pest and disease (quarantine) risks' than for the 'evaluation of the potential for adverse effects on human or animal health arising from the presence of additives, contaminants, toxins or disease-causing organisms in food, beverages or feedstuffs' (food-borne risks). 'In view of the very different language used in paragraph 4 of Annex A for the two types of risk assessments', the Appellate Body considered it important not to diminish the substantial differences between these two types of risk assessments'.[34]

No minimum quantity of risk needs to be demonstrated; WTO Members remain free to adopt a 'zero risk policy' (cf. Articles 3 and 5). Yet, risks need to be ascertainable and specific, as 'theoretical uncertainty is not the kind of risk which, under Article 5(1), is to be assessed'; 'the risk that is to be evaluated in the risk assessment under Article 5(1) is not only risk ascertainable in a science laboratory operating under strictly controlled conditions, but also risk in human societies as they actually exist, in other words, the actual potential for adverse effects on human health in

32 *Australia—Measures Affecting Importation of Salmon*, WT/DS18/AB/R, 20 Oct 1998, para. 137.

33 *EC—Hormones, supra* n 20, para. 181.

34 *Australia—Salmon, supra* n 32, footnote 69.

the real world where people live and work and die'.[35] While the SPS measure is to be based on a risk assessment (Article 5(1)), Members may use risk assessments carried out by another state or international organisation. As there is no procedural requirement to consider the conclusions of the risk assessment during the legislative process of enacting the SPS measure[36], it appears to be sufficient to present—during a WTO panel proceeding—scientific evidence reasonably supporting the SPS measure.

'Cases where relevant scientific evidence is insufficient' (Article 5(7))

If—as in the GMO dispute—the defending party invokes insufficiency of scientific evidence (Article 5(7)), it remains to be clarified whether provisional measures based on Article 5(7) remain subject to the disciplines of Articles 2(3), 5(5) and 5(6) of the SPS Agreement, and whether the burden of proving *prima facie* (in)consistency with Article 5(7) (as an affirmative defence) lies with the complainant[37] or the defendant.[38] According to the Appellate Body, 'relevant scientific evidence is insufficient' in terms of Article 5(7) if 'a body of available scientific evidence does not allow, in quantitative or qualitative terms, the performance of an adequate assessment of risks as required under Article 5(1)'[39]; 'insufficiency' of scientific evidence must not be equated with 'uncertainty' because 'existence of unknown and uncertain elements does not justify a departure from the requirements of Articles 5(1), 5(2) and 5(3)'.[40] The 'available pertinent information' required under Article 5(7), and its rational relationship to provisional measures under Article 5(7), may have to be specified in the GMO dispute.

Limited Role of Scientific Expert Advice in WTO Dispute Settlement Proceedings

In view of the sovereign right of WTO Members to establish their own level of protection and to base their SPS measures on scientific minority views, the role of science in risk regulation and in WTO dispute settlement

[35] *EC—Hormones supra* n 20, paras. 186–187.
[36] *Ibid.*, para. 189.
[37] The Panel in *Japan–Agricultural Products*, *supra* n 29, held 'that the United States has established a presumption that Japan did not comply with the requirements in the second sentence of Article 5.7. We also consider that Japan has not been able to rebut this presumption': WT/DS76/R, para. 8.58.
[38] In the *Japan—Apples* case, *supra* n 22, the Panel and Appellate Body assigned the burden of proof to Japan to make a prima facie case in support of its invocation of Art 5.7: WT/DS245/AB/R, para. 175.
[39] *Ibid.*, para. 179.
[40] *Australia—Salmon* para. 130; *EC—Hormones*, *supra* n 20, para. 194.

proceedings remains limited (e.g. as a device for promoting rational public discourse about risks and their control, challenging discrimination and protectionism, distinguishing lawful from illegal SPS measures). Following the hearing of experts in the GMO dispute settlement proceedings in February 2005, all parties to the dispute claimed that the experts' advice had confirmed their respective legal positions; prior to the hearing of experts, the EC's 'Supplementary Rebuttal Submission' of 15 November 2004 had emphasised the limited function of expert advice under the DSU[41] and had warned 'that such expert advice does not alter the burden of proof'; 'the Panel can only base its findings on expert advice to the extent that complainants have asserted all such facts necessary to substantiate their claims'.[42] Just as WTO rules promote international accountability of states for the 'external effects' of their national policies, so can science-based risk assessment procedures and judicial review of SPS measures promote 'deliberative democracy' and accountability of (inter)national governance across frontiers. This is also true for the challenges, in the GMO dispute, of the non-transparent EC practices delaying the applications for approval of biotech products during the 1998–2003 period without adequate, public explanation of the departures from the legally binding EC procedures.[43] Of course, 'absence of evidence of harm is not evidence of

[41] 'Expert advice under the DSU and the SPS Agreement does not have the purpose of resolving scientific controversies. Rather, expert advice is provided for assisting the Panel in its limited task of making findings in the dispute between the parties . . . Pursuant to Article 13.2 of the DSU, expert opinions may serve to clarify 'a factual issue concerning a scientific or other technical matter'. Experts enable panels to fully understand any scientific and technical facts of the case. By contrast, experts do not relieve the Panel of its duty to make an independent legal assessment of those facts . . . Expert advice on GMOs is limited to clarifying certain questions relating to scientific risks (i.e. risk assessment in the narrow sense). By contrast, expert advice cannot offer the Panel much indication as to whether certain conduct was reasonably justified from a risk management or risk communication perspective': EC rebuttal submission, p.8.

[42] The EC rebuttal submission (at.3–4) refers to the Appellate Body finding in *Japan—Agricultural Products, supra* n 29, which overruled the panel on the ground that it based itself on information not expressly asserted by the complaining party: 'in the present case, the Panel was correct to seek information and advice from experts to help it to understand and evaluate the evidence submitted and the arguments made by the United States and Japan with regard to the alleged violation of Article 5.6. The Panel erred, however, when it used that expert information and advice as the basis for a finding of inconsistency with Article 5.6, since the United States did not establish a *prima facie* case of inconsistency with Article 5.6 based on claims relating to the 'determination of absorption levels': at para. 30.

[43] See, e.g., the criticism by J. Scott, *European Regulation of GMOs: Thinking about Judicial Review in the WTO*, Jean Monnet Working Paper 04/2004, that the EC's 'executive branch—in its complex multilevel form—has departed over a long period of time from the governance precepts laid down by the legislature' (at 18). The CFI—for instance, in case T–13/99, *Pfizer*, [2002] ECR II–3305—has likewise insisted that 'a preventive measure cannot properly be based on a purely hypothetical approach to risk, founded on mere conjecture which has not been scientifically verified' (para. 143). It appears doubtful whether the objective of EC Regulation 1829/2003 on GM food and feed—i.e. to establish a 'one door—one key' procedure for the scientific assessment and authorisation of GMOs and GM food and feed

absence of harm'.[44] Yet, the EC practice (e.g. in Directive 2001/18) of placing the burden of proving 'safety' or 'lack of harm' of GM products on the applicant manufacturer may entail disproportionately restrictive results.

VII. THE IMPACT OF INTERNATIONAL LAW AND THE BIOSAFETY PROTOCOL ON WTO LAW

J. Pauwelyn[45] has claimed that—notwithstanding the limited jurisdiction of WTO dispute settlement bodies for hearing only claims based on WTO law—(1) general and conventional international law is directly applicable law in WTO dispute settlement proceedings (and not only an indirectly relevant legal context for interpreting WTO rules), and (2) many international law rules (such as human rights, environmental and labour law) may be used as defences which—due to their 'integral' compliance obligations *vis-à-vis* the community as a whole—may justify violations of reciprocal WTO obligations that may be modified bilaterally without permission of third WTO Members. While it is undisputed that general international law applies to the conduct of states unless they have effectively 'contracted out of it', the consistency of Pauwelyn's broad interpretation of the jurisdiction and applicable law in WTO dispute settlement proceedings with the explicit limitation (e.g. in Articles 3, 7, 11 DSU) of the jurisdiction and function of WTO dispute settlement bodies to the 'covered agreements' remains contested in both WTO practice (e.g. by the USA in the GMO dispute) as well as in legal literature.[46] Likewise, Pauwelyn's related views of WTO obligations as bilateral in nature and subject to mutually agreed inter se modifications, and of the higher legal rank of 'integral' *erga omnes* obligations under human rights law and environmental law, remain controversial (e.g. in view of the amendment procedures in Articles 9 and 10 of the WTO Agreement, and the inconsistency of bilaterally agreed trade restrictions with the multilateral WTO objectives of non-discriminatory conditions of competition and trade).

'resulting in a centralized, clear and transparent Community procedure where an operator is able to file a single application' (Christoforou, *supra* n 2, at 659)—has been achieved in EC practice (e.g. in view of the fact that the risk assessment opinions by the European Food Safety Authority are not legally binding on other EC and Member State institutions). Christoforou's justification of the EC's policy on GMOs as 'an attempt to follow consumer reaction to possible harm from modern biotechnology and the rapid advances in scientific research' (at 708) does not answer the criticism that the EC institutions have failed to comply with their WTO obligations to promote a science-based, well informed public discussion on GMO-related risks.

[44] UK GM Science Review Panel, First Report, July 2003, at 22, also available at www.gmsciencedebate.org.uk.

[45] See *supra* nn 17 and 18 and the related text.

[46] See e.g. the review and criticism of Pauwelyn's book by J. Trachtman, at (2004) 98 *AJIL* 855.

Neither GATT and WTO practice nor UN practice has so far identified any concrete examples of conflicts between GATT/WTO rules and general international law (e.g. the universal human rights obligations of all WTO Members). The disagreement among WTO members over the applicability of the CBD and its Biosafety Protocol in the GMO dispute may, however, induce WTO dispute settlement bodies to clarify the scope of applicable law in WTO dispute settlement proceedings.

The Cartagena Protocol on Biosafety, which entered into force in September 2003 and was accepted by more than 110 countries (Argentina, Canada and the USA have not ratified it) and the EC by the end of 2004, pursues the objective of 'ensuring an adequate level of protection in the field of the safe transfer, handling and use of living modified organisms resulting from modern biotechnology that may have adverse effects on the conservation and sustainable use of biological diversity, taking also into account risks to human health, and specifically focusing on transboundary movements' (Article 1).[47] As it was negotiated outside the WTO context as a multilateral environmental agreement focusing on the protection of biological diversity and 'biosafety', many environmental negotiators accepted international commitments (e.g. regarding 'the precautionary approach') on which trade negotiators in the WTO had failed to agree. The Protocol does not cover consumer products derived from 'living modified organisms' (= LMOs as defined in Article 3), including pharmaceuticals (Article 5). The 'Advance Informed Agreement Procedure' (AIA) as the central innovation of the Protocol applies only to LMOs 'for intentional introduction into the environment of the Party of import' (Article 7); hence, '90% of international trade in LMOs is not subject to the AIA procedure'.[48] Even though the Biosafety Protocol has not been adopted as a relevant standard by the SPS Committee, LMOs with potentially adverse effects on the environment and biodiversity are generally covered by Annex A to the SPS Agreement. Hence, the GMO Panel may have to clarify the relevance of the Biosafety Protocol for the interpretation and application of SPS provisions, including the contested scope of 'jurisdiction' and 'applicable law' in the GMO panel proceeding.

As discussed above, the legal relationships between the SPS Agreement and the Biosafety Protocol may be viewed differently depending on whether one adopts a broad 'general international law perspective' (e.g. focusing on *lex posterior* and *lex specialis* rules) or a narrow 'DSU perspective' focusing on the limited jurisdiction of WTO dispute settlement bodies. Hence, even if subsequent, specific provisions in the Biosafety Protocol should be viewed as prevailing over the earlier SPS provisions among

47 Cf. Zarrilli, *supra* n 2, at 24 ff.

48 M. Böckenförde, *Grüne Gentechnik und Welthandel. Das Biosafety-Protokoll und seine Auswirkungen auf das Regime der WTO*, (2004) at 153–160, 486.

parties to the Biosafety Protocol (such as Argentina, Canada and the EC) pursuant to the general rules of international law, the GMO Panel might find it lacked jurisdiction to apply the Biosafety Protocol if this could 'add to or diminish … the rights and obligations provided in the covered agreements' (as prohibited by Articles 3 and 19 of the DSU) by disregarding SPS provisions on grounds of general international law. If the Biosafety Protocol should be found by the GMO Panel to be 'applicable law' in the GMO dispute or relevant legal context for clarifying SPS rights and obligations, it remains to be clarified whether—and to what extent—the 'precautionary approach' in the Biosafety Protocol (e.g. Articles 10(6), 11(8)) actually exceeds the requirements in Article 5(1) and (7) of the SPS Agreement. Some of the potentially conflicting requirements of the Biosafety Protocol—such as the requirement (not provided for in the SPS Agreement) to carry out a risk assessment *before* taking a 'decision on the intentional transboundary movement' (Articles 10–12, 15), or the requirement (in Article 18(2)(a)) to include the remark 'may contain' in the documentation accompanying LMOs intended for direct use as food or feed (which may conflict with Articles 5(5) and 5(6) of the SPS Agreement)—have not been invoked by the complainants.

Given the numerous controversies relating to the jurisdiction and applicable law in WTO dispute settlement proceedings and the uncertain role of the Biosafety Protocol for interpreting and applying SPS provisions, the GMO panel may wish to reduce the risk that its panel report may be challenged as exceeding its jurisdiction and lacking legitimacy (e.g. on grounds of unwarranted 'judicial activism'). Similar to the reference to the Convention on International Trade in Endangered Species (CITES) in the US—Shrimp/Turtle case, the GMO Panel might therefore confine itself to referring to the Biosafety Protocol as an environmental agreement relevant for finding multilateral, non-discriminatory solutions as required by the *chapeau* of GATT Article XX.[49] Other difficult legal issues—such as whether LMOs and non-LMOs are 'like products' in terms of GATT Article III(4) (as claimed by Argentina and Canada based on the traditional GATT criteria, such as properties, end-uses, and tariff classification of goods) or 'unlike products' (as claimed by the EC based on the distinctions in the Biosafety Protocol, the Appellate Body findings in the Asbestos case, consumer perceptions)—may be avoided by the Panel on grounds of 'judicial economy' if recourse to GATT Article XX(b) leads to the same outcome as under the SPS Agreement.

[49] Cf. *Ibid.*, at 454–456, 491; Zarrilli supra n 1, at 38.

VIII. POSTSCRIPT : THE 2006 WTO PANEL REPORT ON THE GMO DISPUTE

On 7 February 2006, the WTO dispute settlement panel finally issued its interim report, which remains confidential until the end of the interim review procedures and subject to appellate review of the final panel report.[50] In view of its limited mandate, the Panel emphasised that it did *not* examine

- whether biotech products in general are safe or not;
- whether the biotech products at issue in this dispute are "like" their conventional counterparts;
- whether the EC has the right to require the pre-marketing approval of biotech products;
- whether the EC's approval procedures as established by Directive 90/220, Directive 2001/18 and Regulation 258/97 which provide for product-by-product assessments requiring scientific consideration of various potential risks, are consistent with the EC's WTO obligations;
- the conclusions of the relevant EC scientific committees regarding the safety evaluation of specific biotech products, which were not challenged by the complaining parties.

The legal panel findings include, *inter alia*:

- that the EC applied a general *de facto moratorium* on approvals of biotech products between June 1999 and August 2003 (the date of establishment of this Panel) which was, however, not itself an SPS measure within the meaning of the SPS Agreement;
- the general *de facto moratorium* resulted in a failure to complete individual approval procedures without undue delay, and hence gave rise to inconsistencies with Article 8 and Annex C of the SPS Agreement;
- in relation to the approval procedures with respect to 24 of the 27 specific applications identified by the complaining parties, the Panel found that there was undue delay and that the EC had breached its obligations under Article 8 and Annex C of the SPS Agreement;
- regarding the complaints against nine safeguard measures taken by Austria, Belgium, France, Germany, Italy and Luxembourg imposing SPS measures different from those of the EC as a whole, the Panel concluded that the EC member states had in no case provided an assessment of the risks to human health and/or the environment meeting

[50] WT/DS291, 292, 293/INTERIM. As this report (including 1'050 pages plus Annexes) was released only to the parties to the dispute, and only its conclusions were leaked to the public, this *Postscript* is limited to a brief summary of the main legal findings, without commenting on the still confidential reasoning of the Panel.

the requirements of the SPS Agreement, and each safeguard measure failed to meet the obligations of the EC under the SPS Agreement;
- there was no need to rule on the claims under Article III:4 of GATT 1994 and under the TBT Agreement.

The legal findings prompted the Panel to recommend the following implementing measures:

- regarding the general EC moratorium on approvals of biotech products, the Panel refrains from making recommendations pursuant to Article 19.1 of the DSU because the EC approval, in 2004, of a relevant biotech product subsequent to the establishment of the Panel "brought to an end the general moratorium on approvals which the Panel found to have existed at the time of its establishment;"
- regarding the product-specific EC measures that were found to violate Annex C(1)(a) and Article 8 of the SPS Agreement, the Panel recommends that the WTO Dispute Settlement Body (DSB) request the EC to bring these product-specific measures into conformity with its obligations under the SPS Agreement;
- regarding the Panel's legal findings relating to the nine EC member state safeguard measures in violation of the SPS Agreement (Articles 2.2, 5.1, 5.7), the Panel recommends that the DSB request the EC to bring the relevant member state safeguard measures into conformity with its obligations under the SPS Agreement.[51]

[51] In a judgment of 5 October 2005 (Joined Cases T-366/03 and T-235/04, Land Oberösterreich and *Austria v Commission* of the EC, not yet reported), the EC Court of First Instance confirmed that some of the Austrian safeguard measures also violated EC law. The EU Commission also requested other EC member states to end their national bans. The WTO dispute settlement ruling will put additional legal and political pressure on EC member states to comply with their EC and WTO obligations.

9

Traditional Knowledge, Biodiversity, Benefit-Sharing and the Patent System: Romantics v. Economics?

HANNS ULLRICH*

I. INTRODUCTION

AT ABOUT THE same time in the late 1980s early 1990s as intellectual property became the subject of world trade negotiations, which ultimately resulted in the provision by the WTO Agreement on Trade Related Aspects of Intellectual Property Rights (TRIPs Agreement) of globally available protection at internationally accepted 'adequate' conditions, which, then, contributed so much to industry's general intellectual property euphoria during the last decade, international negotiations in less industry-friendly fora of environment protection led to the development of alternative concepts of intellectual property protection. At least on their face, these seem to support some sort of counter-movement to free trade in intellectual goods. Indeed, ever since the United Nations Conference on the Environment and Development of Rio de Janeiro in 1992, the catchwords have been well-known: defence, possibly even protection of traditional knowledge, such as knowledge of nutritional or medicinal characteristics of plants, control of access to genetic resources as a matter of safeguarding biodiversity, and sharing in the benefits accruing from patents granted for biotechnological inventions which, somehow, are based on traditional knowledge and/or on genetic resources found in nature. Their common denominator is that they point to limitations of access to and use of knowledge or resources which hitherto have been considered to be in the public domain. Therefore, these

* Prof. Dr. iur., M.C.J. (N.Y.Univ.); Professor em. Universität der Bundeswehr München; professor, European University Institute, Florence. The contribution has been last up-dated in early summer 2005, for a recent overview over the subject see Van Overwalle, Protecting and sharing biodiversity and traditional knowledge:Holder and user tools, Ecological Economics 53 (2005) 585.

catchwords are generally also understood as indicating an area of basic conflict between, on the one hand, the protection of the environment (i.e. natural resources) and of the (cultural) identity of people, as well as the promotion of developing countries and, on the other, the protection of intellectual, in particular of inventive, activity, as well as the promotion of industrial innovation as part of techno-economic progress.

It is, however, precisely this broader background which invites rash value judgements on issues whose complexity and ramifications are intractable enough.[1] Therefore, rather than dealing with traditional knowledge and international intellectual property law in general, this chapter will examine only issues of biodiversity-related traditional knowledge[2] and of patent law.[3]

Biodiversity-related traditional knowledge may have a value of its own, and, being knowledge, promise of its protection may be sought under the rules of intellectual property or by analogy to these rules. In general, however, biodiversity-related traditional knowledge derives its value from the genetic resources to which it applies. As these have their own market value and are subject to rules of law of their own, the following analysis will be sub-divided accordingly in a first part on the defence or protection of traditional knowledge as such, and a second part on its activation in the context of the exploration or the exploitation of genetic resources. In both respects patents are the most important 'counterparts' as they allow for the protection of inventions based on the discovery, isolation, modification or application of genetic resources. Also patent law is

[1] A typical example of such judgement, which is even obviously circular, is the characterisation of—arguably or actually illegitimate—patenting of genetic plant resources as 'biopiracy' or 'misappropriation' (see Stenton, Biopiracy within the Pharmaceutical Industry: A Stark Illustration of How Abusive, Manipulative and Perverse the Patenting Process Can Be towards Countries of the South *European Intellectual Property Review*, [2004] 17). There can be hardly any piracy or misappropriation of subject-matter unless protection of this subject-matter by titles to property has been recognised first.

[2] Traditional knowledge may also constitute or may be akin to copyrightable subject-matter, which is protected as intellectual property proper. Proposals to make a distinction between traditional knowledge relating 'to the useful arts' (the term used by Art. 1, Sect. 8 Clause 8 of the US Constitution to determine the field of patent law) and 'traditional cultural expression' (the concept followed by the World Intellectual Property Organisation in its attempts to develop the basis for a system of protection) are not generally accepted (see Gibson, 'Intellectual Property System, Traditional Knowledge and the Legal Authority of Community' *European Intellectual Property Review* [2004] 280). For the purpose of the present chapter, however, the distinction may well serve as a working hypothesis.

[3] Thus, issues raised by plant variety protection are left aside, however important they are even in the age of gene technology (see for a clear presentation of the impact of plant variety protection and its relationship to patent protection CIPR (Commission on Intellectual Property Rights), *Integrating Intellectual Property Rights and Development Policy*, (London 2002), 59 ff); however, the problem of farmers' rights also concerns patent protection. Also related, but not dealt with here, is the protection of indications of geographical origin: see *ibid.*, at 87 ff.

both the internationally most homogenous and the systematically most clearly structured field of intellectual property, and, for this doctrinal reason alone, best suited to illustrate conflicts of traditional property protection of intellectual goods with the new concepts of narrowing the public domain by protecting traditional knowledge and the objects to which it applies.

II. THE STATUS OF TRADITIONAL KNOWLEDGE UNDER EXISTING INTERNATIONAL PATENT LAW

Defending Traditional Knowledge: Poor Romantics—Poor Economics

a) *Improper Appropriation Under the Rules for Acquisition of Patents*

At the bottom line legal literature on the safeguard of traditional knowledge approaches it as an issue of defending, according to the exclusivity rules of intellectual property protection, the inherited forms of knowledge of indigenous people—generally those living in developing countries[4]—against uncontrolled appropriation for business purposes by industry—generally from developed countries. Whilst such an approach may be too narrow in view of the need for protection from other kinds of unauthorised use of traditional knowledge of other than indigenous people,[5] it points to a minimum standard of passive protection of traditional knowledge, namely to the limits set by the rules on knowledge acquisition as provided for precisely by intellectual property law. These rules generally are intended to ensure the functionality of the system of protection. In the case of patents this functionality is directed toward stimulating the making of inventions for the sake of technological innovation. To this effect appropriable knowledge must be separated from knowledge which is,

4 These have also been the focus of WIPO (World Intellectual Property Organization), *Intellectual Property Needs and Expectations of Traditional Knowledge Holders*, Report on Fact-Finding Missions on Intellectual Property and Traditional Knowledge (1998–1999), Geneva, Apr 2021, Part 2, available at http://www.wipo.int/tk/en/tk/ffm/report/final/pdf/part2.pdf, the only exception being North America.

5 Whilst in Continental Europe traditional knowledge is abundant in many regions, specific protection is lacking. However, as regards food and wines etc. it is indirectly protected by indications of geographic origin (i.e. not against imitation as such: see Council Reg (EC) 2081/92 of 14 July 1992 on the protection of geographical indications and designations of origin for agricultural products and foodstuffs, [1992] O J L/208/1, as amended by Reg. (EC) 692/2003 of 8 April [2003], O J L/99/1, O'Connor and Kireeva, 'Overview of the EC Case Law Protecting Geographical Indications', *European Intellectual Property Review*, [2004] 313); traditional knowledge regarding medicinal methods and products, or regarding handicraft, etc., may enjoy protection under the general rules of unfair competition law (trade secrets, slavish imitation) against copying. Therefore, it must be the relationship to indigenous people which makes all the difference, and this should be reflected by the law: see *infra* 2 (c) (ii).

and which should remain, within (or should return to) the public domain.[6] Article 27 of the TRIPs Agreement internationally harmonises the relevant rules by stipulating that patent protection may be granted only to what properly may be considered inventions, and among them only to those which are new, involve an inventive activity, and are industrially applicable. The selective effect of these four conditions of patentability varies, first, according to the nature of the subject-matter for which protection is claimed, and, secondly, according to national law and practice, because TRIPs Members may implement the standards differently.

Thus, in the first respect, the concept of invention which, as regards mechanical inventions, normally is of marginal importance only, has become the crucial distinguishing factor in biotechnology. Biotechnological subject-matter may, indeed, represent a mere discovery of substances found in nature rather than an invention, the latter being defined as an instruction on how to achieve a technical result by operation of the forces of nature.[7] However, the isolation of such substances and their presentation in a form ready for use may transform the discovery into an invention.[8] Whilst the distinction may be a fine one, and may be controversial both *in concreto* and in the general context of biotechnology patenting, it raises issues of the polito-economic definition of patent protection in general, rather than of the determination of the status of traditional knowledge in particular. Therefore, it will not be dealt with here on its merits.[9]

In the second respect, however, traditional knowledge may be directly at stake. Indeed, whether traditional knowledge may be appropriated by way of taking out patents will largely depend on how national law defines the standards of novelty and inventive activity, which condition

[6] See Merges, 'Commercial Success and Patent Standards: Economic Perspectives on Innovation' (1988) 76 *Cal. L. Rev.* 803 at 806 ff.; Ullrich, *Standards of Patentability for European Inventions,* (Weinheim, 1977), 97 ff.

[7] See BGH of 27 March 1969, BGHZ 52, 74—*Red Dove;* though applying a broader concept, the famous formula of *Diamond v. Chakrabarty,* 447 US 303 (1980), ('everything under the sun that is made by man') is based on the same distinction; see geneally Mellulis, in Benkard, *Europäisches Patentübereinkommen* (Munich, 2002), Art. 52, annot. 50; Cornish and Llewelyn, *Intellectual Property: Patents, Copyright, Trademarks and Allied Rights,* (5th edn., London, 2003), 208 ff.

[8] For an illustration see BPatG of 28 July 1977, [1978] *GRUR* 238—*Antanamid*—(synthetisation of products found in nature); of 12 Dec 1983, [1985] *GRUR* 276 (*Schichtkeratotransplantat,* application-specific preparation of products found in nature, in concreto human tissue); EPO of 8 Dec 1994, Case V 8/94, [1995] *OJ EPO,* 338 C – *Relaxin* – isolation and identification of DNA-fragment coding for a human protein), but see EPO Technical Board of Appeals of 14 June 2000, Case T 241/95, [2001] *GRUR Int,* 460 (*Serotoninrezeptor/Eli Lilly*—discovery of selective linkage of compound to receptor no invention).

[9] Note, however, that the delimitation of the scope of patent protection also determines the pre-emptive or non-pre-emptive effects *vis-à-vis* the use and exploitation of traditional knowledge (see text *infra* at n. 21), and the opportunity and legitimacy of benefit sharing, see *infra* 2(c).

the grant of protection to inventions. Thus, whilst, as regards novelty, the general rule is that any prior art defeats the patentability of an invention,[10] national laws may exclude knowledge from the relevant prior art, which has not been disclosed in writing, but only orally or by use, and has been so disclosed only abroad,[11] the reason being that bringing knowledge, which is not generally available or accessible to public attention by patenting is meritorious enough.[12] Clearly, under such a national rule, foreign traditional knowledge, if not sufficiently documented in publicly available literature, may become the subject of such alienation/appropriation. And yet, it would be unwise to ask, as a matter of principle, for the modification of such 'loose' definition of prior art/novelty,[13] let alone to ask for an international harmonisation imposing a strict standard of novelty based on a broad definition of relevant prior art, since it may precisely be the developing countries that have an interest in a flexible standard of novelty.[14]

10 See eg Art. 54 of the Convention for the Grant of European Patents (European Patent Convention, available at http://www.european-patent-office.org/legal/epc/e/ar54.html #A54), which reads in relevant parts '(1) An invention shall be considered to be new if it does not form part of the state of the art. (2) The state of the art shall be held to comprise everything made available to the public by means of written or oral description, by use, or in any other way, before the date of filing of the European patent application'. This standard is adhered to throughout Europe and in most African and Latin American jurisdictions.

11 This is the case in the USA, see 35 US. C 102, which reads in relevant part:

> A person shall be entitled to a patent unless
> (a) the invention was known or used by others in this country or patented or described in a printed publication in this or a foreign country, before the invention thereof by the applicant for the patent, or
> (b) the invention was patented or described in a printed publication in this or a foreign country or in public use or on sale in this country, more than one year prior to the date of application for patent in the United States, or.......

'For a critique of Sect. 102 (b) see Bagley, 'Still Patently Unconstitutional: A Reply to Professor Nard', (2003) 88 *Minn. L. Rev.* 239 with references. Thailand, Sri Lanka, the Philippines, Peru, New Zealand, Japan, India, PR China seem to have similar rules (see Schade, *Patent-Tabelle*, (8th edn., Cologne, 2001). Utility model protection, i.e. protection of inventions by 'petty patents' (available upon mere registration) may also be obtained for inventions which are not absolutely new: see eg Sect. 3 German Gebrauchsmustergesetz of 28 Aug 1986, BGBl I 1456. However, not all subject-matter may qualify for such protection as, under some laws, processes or chemical compounds may be excluded from protection.

12 Rediscovery of prior art, which has fallen into oblivion, may equally be held meritorious enough to warrant the grant of a patent, even if it is available in (old) patent literature: see ECJ of 30 June 1988, Case 35/87, *Thetford/Fiamma* [1988] ECR 3585, (upholding the pre-1977 British limitation of patented prior art to patents granted during the last 50 years against claims of incompatibility with the Common Market's constitutive principles of free trade). New Zealand still seems to follow the old British concept: see Schade, *supra* n-11 114.

13 As suggested in strong words ('facilitates theft') by Stenton, *supra* n.1, 20.

14 Generally, the requirement of absolute novelty seems to be favoured as a matter of blocking domestic patenting by foreign applicants (see UNCTAD, *The TRIPs Agreement and Developing Countries*, (Geneva 1996), 32 ff.), but the downside of this approach is that it may inhibit domestic patenting of 'imported' knowledge. Note that the impact of limiting prior

Rather, the point to be made is another one: patent applications which are made or patents which have been granted in disrespect of novelty standards which require all knowledge to be included in prior art whether published in writing or orally or by use and regardless of the place of publication, simply are invalid or can be invalidated. Moreover, even if prior art is defined narrowly by national law, traditional knowledge may be raised to the level of relevant prior art by way of documentation, and then can be relied upon as a ground for invalidation. Actually, this is what is done now in many places.[15] To be sure, such pro-active approach to defending traditional knowledge may not always be possible, and it requires an extra effort,[16] just as opposing invalid patent applications or bringing actions for invalidation may raise issues of standing and pose problems of costs, as it does for any smaller complainant. But, at least there is a base-line of defence against acts of appropriation which lack merit. It is generally recognised and requires general respect.

However, the novelty requirement will impede patenting of inventions based on traditional knowledge only if the invention, as claimed, is identically anticipated by a teaching of traditional knowledge—most likely a rare instance given that the invention will frequently represent an adaptation or a transformation of (possibly ill-defined) traditional knowledge. By contrast, the requirement of an inventive activity or of non-obviousness of

art to publications in writing occurring anywhere and to oral disclosure or to disclosure by use, which occurs on the domestic territory, mainly depends on which market is at issue: The domestic market may always be kept free, but protection may be obtained on foreign markets (by any applicant, domestic or foreign!). Should not developing countries be more concerned with patenting conditions on their markets than with those existing on foreign markets? Note also that patenting on the basis of traditional knowledge does not normally foreclose access to markets by products of traditional knowledge (see *infra* text at n. 21); the situation is different as regards designs, trade marks, and, possibly, copyright to the extent that traditional cultural expression is appropriated.

[15] See WIPO, *Non-exhaustive Inventory of Traditional Knowledge-Related Databases*, available at http://www.wipo.int/tk/en/databases/databases.html; Ibid., 'Intellectual Property Needs and Expectations', *supra* n.4, part 2 (fact finding reports); WIPO also prepares an IP management toolkit intended to assist developing countries in the proper establishment of databases which, however, in themselves may not easily be compatible with concepts of safeguarding traditional knowledge: see Gibson, *supra* n.2, at p. 284 ff.; CIPR, *supra* n.3, 81 ff. (which also points to the important factual issue that such databases will be consulted by patent examiners only if made a mandatory element of search and examination).

[16] For frequently cited, but not necessarily typical, examples see CIPR, *supra* n.3, at 76, 81; Heath and Weidlich, 'Intellectual Property: Suitable for Protecting Traditional Medicine?'[2003] *Intellectual Property Quarterly* 69, at 77 ff. Note that in procedures before the patent offices of most jurisdictions everybody has standing to intervene in the granting procedure or to oppose the grant of patents; likewise invalidation suits may be brought by everybody. Factual barriers, however, may be high in view of the technical expertise required, the intricacies of patent law, and the expenses to be incurred.

the invention by reference to the prior art as a whole[17] should constitute the greater obstacle to undue patenting, at least in theory. In practice, however, this defence to appropriation of traditional knowledge by patenting will be available only to the extent that the 'inventive idea' of the new teaching is sufficiently related to that following from traditional knowledge. This may not be the case precisely where the particular merits or effects of the isolation, purification, synthesisation, adaptation or application of the subject-matter is claimed as its inventive characteristic.[18] Moreover, frequently it will be precisely the—possibly incremental[19] —improvement over traditional knowledge, which is claimed as a patentable invention. Therefore, other avenues for defending traditional knowledge need to be explored as well. But before turning to them, a second line of defence should be noted, which is the limitation of the scope of patents which are acquired for or on the basis of traditional biodiversity-related knowledge.

b) Limiting the Scope of Protection of Traditional Knowledge by Patents

Indeed, unless the teaching of traditional knowledge has been lawfully patented as such—which, as demonstrated, should occur in rare circumstances only[20]—reasons similar to those just mentioned normally keep traditional knowledge outside the scope of exclusivity of patents, which have been acquired for biodiversity-related inventions. This is so because the scope of their protection may not reach beyond what is claimed as a novel and non-obvious teaching. In particular, it is the very function of the claims precisely to delimit the invention from what is taught by the prior art.[21] Consequently, fears that patents based on traditional knowledge might subsequently bar the use of traditional knowledge as if they were general monopolies are unwarranted.[22] In the context of the

17 Meaning that 'inventiveness' must be assessed not by reference to specific single items of prior art, but by reference to the entire knowledge resulting from relevant prior art for the ordinary expert in the art: see *Cornish and Llewelyn, supra* n. 7, at 5 – 29 ff. at 5 – 42, 5 – 46 ff.; Jestaedt, in Benkard, *supra* n.7, Art. 55, annot. 30.

18 See references at *supra* n. 8.

19 Most patents are granted for incremental rather than only for (the few) pioneer inventions; what counts is not the advance in the art which they bring about, but whether or not they would have been produced by routine engineering, see Cornish and Llewelyn, *supra* n.7, at 5 – 34; Ullrich, *supra* n.6, 12 ff., 35 ff., 60 ff., 97 ff.

20 Conceivably this may occur with respect to secret traditional knowledge, in particular if its author/inventor is not identifiable. Violation of such secrets will not necessarily constitute a trade secret violation within the meaning of Art. 39 TRIPs Agreement, or may not be enforceable abroad or constitute a ground of patent invalidation or vindication, and possibly it may not be claimed by other than the true inventor: see Arts. 60 ff., 138 European Patent Convention.

21 See Cornish and Llewelyn, *supra* n.7, 230 ff., 236 ff.; for a comparative analysis see Scharen, in Benkard, *supra* n.7, Art. 69, annot. 3, 11, 24 ff., 65, 66 ff.

22 See WIPO, *supra* n.4, 222; misleading Stenton, *supra* n.1, 20.

patent/traditional knowledge relationship there is, therefore, also no need to rely on general exceptions from patent protection, such as prior user rights,[23] or to provide for new ones by analogy from plant variety protection, such as farmers' privileges.[24] The latter, in particular, are a concern of patent protection in general as it is extended to gene technology, regardless of where knowledge on presumed properties of genes is derived from. Therefore, it has been adopted in Europe concomitantly with such extension of protection,[25] and, if not already existent, it may be introduced by developing countries with respect to their territories in accordance with Art. 30 TRIPs Agreement.

c) Defensive Acquisition of Patents for Traditional Knowledge

The upshot of the preceding considerations then is that traditional knowledge is not so much put in jeopardy by illegitimate appropriation through patents than by economic substitution through knowledge, which has been developed more or less directly on its basis. The threat of substitution is all the greater as such derived knowledge may be more competitive in that it is—presumably most of the time—scientifically enhanced knowledge, which may be and generally is exploited industrially as regards both production and distribution. Reactions to this real threat are of various kinds.

One such reaction is to make use of the existing intellectual property system as shaped by the TRIPs Agreement. Whilst, at least in some instances of technology-related traditional knowledge, this may be a

[23] But see WIPO, *supra* n.4, 222. Under patent systems attributing the patent to the first to file (see *infra* n. 28) a new invention with the patent office (which he/she legitimately possesses), an exception of the exclusivity frequently is admitted for those who actually and legitimately practised the same invention before the application was filed, see Ss. 12 German Patent Act. The purpose of this exception is to accommodate the social costs resulting from the enforcement of absolute exclusivity, particularly in view of the legitimacy of keeping new knowledge secret (patenting is an option, not an obligation; trade secret protection for patentable knowledge is generally recognised as an alternative: see for a discussion *Kewanee Oil v. Bicron*, 416 US. 470 (1974)). However, prior user rights generally are recognised only with respect to the territory of prior use, meaning that they may benefit indigenous people only on their local markets, not abroad.

[24] See for instance Art. 14 Council Reg. 2100/94 of 2 July 1994 on Community Protection of Plant Varieties [1994] OJ L/227/1, as amended [1995]OJ L/258/3); as an exception to the exclusive right of the holder of plant variety protection, the farmers' privilege must be distinguished from farmers' rights to obtain compensation for their collective breeding efforts and achievements: see Girsberger, 'The Concept of Farmers' Rights, the Role of FAO and the TRIPS Agreement', in Cottier and Mavroidis, *Intellectual Property - Trade, Competition and Sustainable Development*, (Ann Arbor Mich, 2003), 455.

[25] See Art. 11 of Dir 98/44 of 6 July 1998 of the European Parliament and the Council on the legal protection of biotechnical inventions ([1998] OJ L/213/13); the adoption of the farmers' privilege was one of the many, but not the most, controversial issues during legislation: see Nott, 'The Proposed EC Directive on Biotechnological Inventions', [1994] *European Intellectual Property Review*, 191 at 193.

promising route as regards safeguarding the reputation of traditional knowledge by trade-marks,[26] it will generally not be available as regards protection of the substance of such knowledge. Legally speaking, frequently the very reasons that stand in the way of appropriation of traditional knowledge by non-indigenous applicants (e.g. applicants of developed countries) also impede acquisition of patent rights by the original holders of traditional knowledge. This is obvious for the novelty requirement precisely because much traditional knowledge has been more or less widely known for generations, even though only particular persons may know how (or be allowed) to practise it. Mostly this will be equally true for the requirement of inventive activity and industrial applicability. There are also additional obstacles, such as the informal, uncodified nature of traditional knowledge[27] or—at least in some jurisdictions[28]—the lack of individually attributable inventorship. No less important are the factual obstacles which beset the patent system, not just in less affluent countries, namely the costs of patent protection, and the difficulties of its procedural accessibility, in particular if protection is sought on more than the local level.[29]

26 The use of collective or of certifications marks (see Art. 64 ff. Council Reg 40/94 of 20 Dec 1993 on the Community Mark, [1994] OJ L/11/1, as last amended, [2004] OJ L/123/88), which allow the control of quality of goods sold by members of the collectivity, is frequently recommended and actually followed in practice (see CIPR, *supra* n.3, 19; WIPO. *Supra* n.4, 224; Gibson, *supra* n.2, 282 ff. summing up WIPO investigations on national laws). But the point to be made here is that such marks may also establish product fidelity and protect against reputational losses resulting from the use of the designation of traditional knowledge for derivative products, very much as trade marks are used to prolongate product fidelity after expiration of patents for pharmaceuticals.

27 The difficulty will be less for medicinal products: see the Chinese example of handling applications even for examined patents, as reported by Heath and Weidlich, *supra* n.16, 90 ff. (stressing that in China traditional medicine is a well established mainstream art); however, it may be doubtful whether it really represents traditional knowledge deserving a separate status such as indigenous knowledge: see *infra* n. 99; Generally the disclosure requirements of patent law (Art. 29 TRIPs Agreement), if handled properly in accordance with their public purpose, should pose serious hurdles for easy patenting of uncodified knowledge. The disclosure requirement represents, indeed, a part (however imperfectly put in operation) of the *quid pro quo* of the grant of exclusive rights: The exclusivity is granted to allow enterprises to abandon secrecy; the value of disclosure as a *quid pro quo* lies in the fact that it facilitates the development of both substitute knowledge and improvements: see Kraßer, *Lehrbuch des Patentrechts*, (5th edn., Munich, 2004), 34, 397; Cornish and Llewelyn, *supra* n.7, 3 – 49 ff., 5 – 84 ff.

28 Namely in those granting the patent to the 'first and true inventor' (35 USC.102(f), 115, 135) rather than to the first-to-file inventor (see Art. 60(3) European Patent Convention) because in the latter system the true inventor need not necessarily be identified, unless inventorship is claimed (see Art. 4 Paris Convention for the Protection of Industrial Property of 20 March 1883, as last amended BGBl 1984 II 799).

29 See WIPO, *supra* n.4, 222, 223; if, as will be necessary in most cases, international protection is sought, protection in Europe alone will be virtually unaffordable: see Ullrich, '*Patent Protection in Europe: Integrating Europe into the Community or the Community into Europe*', (2002) 8 *European Law Journal* 433, 440 ff., 468 ff.

d) Sui Generis Protection as a Sustainable Outer Line of Defense?

Some of these problems may be overcome by appropriate adaptation of domestic patent laws and procedure.[30] However, politically speaking, that may not even be desirable, since the availability of any "adapted" patent protection might not be for the benefit only of domestic or indigenous applicants, but also for those whom a (developing) country might wish to exclude from protection, since international convention law excludes any reservation of protection to nationals only (Article 2 of the Paris Convention).

Anyway, given the particularities of its acquisition by tradition, its definition by use, and its dependence on the cultural and ethnographic environment, traditional knowledge in essence seems to ask for specific forms of protection. Proposals for such *sui generis* regimes of protection have, indeed, been made by academics,[31] are considered within WIPO, and have been pursued by some countries.[32] However, since they must be specific to traditional knowledge in all its breadth and yet satisfy the needs of particular forms of knowledge, and since they should formally identify and protect subject-matter which may be valuable and operative only in its context of application, there is no general acceptance of legislative initiatives in the countries concerned, let alone an international consensus on what a model law should look like.[33]

Obviously also, a *sui generis* approach, however well conceived as an appropriately adapted 'full property'-regime,[34] will at best serve local trade to the extent that there is a demand for traditional subject-matter as

[30] See *supra* n. 27.

[31] See e.g. Cottier and Panizzon, 'Legal Perspectives on Traditional Knowledge. The Case for Intellectual Property Protection', (2004), 7 *Journal of International Economic Law* 371, 381 ff., 387 ff; Gupta, 'Conserving Biodiversity and Rewarding Associated Knowledge and Innovation Systems. Honey Bee Perspective', in Cottier and Mavroidis (eds.), *supra* n.24, p. 373, 382 ff.; for a broad discussion see von Hahn, *Traditionelles Wissen indigener und lokaler Gemeinschaften zwischen geistigen Eigentumsrechten und dem public domain*, (Berlin, 2004), 311 ff.

[32] See WIPO, Revised Version of Traditional Knowledge: Policy and Legal Options, WIPO/GRTKF/IC/6/4 Rev. (Document of the Secretariat for the 6th Sess. of the Intergovernmental Committee on Intellectual Property and Genetic Resources, Traditional Knowledge and Folklore, 15–19 Mar 2004 (available at www.wipo.int/documents/en/meeting/2004/igc/pdf/grtk_ic_6_4pdf); *Ibid.*, Review of Existing Intellectual Property Protection of Traditional Knowledge, WIPO/GRTKF/IC/3/7 of 6 May 2002 (available at www.wipo.int/documents/meeting/2002/igc/pdf/grtkf/ic3_7.pdf); Gibson, *supra* n.2, 283 ff.; Correa, *Traditional Knowledge and Intellectual Property—A Discussion Paper*, Geneva, 2001, at 14 ff.; Dutfield, *Protecting Traditional Knowledge and Folklore*, UNCTAD/ICTSD Issue Paper No.1, Geneva, 2003 40 ff.; as to protection schemes relating more specifically to the control of the use of genetic resources see *infra* 2b).

[33] See references *supra* n. 32 and CIPR, *supra* n.3, p. 79 ff.

[34] Meaning property carrying an obligation 'to preserve and maintain' the traditional knowledge: see the concepts discussed in WIPO, *supra* n.32, at No. 41.

such.[35] The substitution problem, however, will remain unchanged, and any hopes of conservatory effects are misplaced per se. Property titles cannot preserve knowledge that becomes obsolete or that falls into oblivion. Property is a market institution, not a conservation measure.[36] It may be based on other rationales than setting incentives and rewards.[37] But in the absence of markets, where offer and demand actually meet, it is literally worthless. More precisely, where property is supposed to operate in a museum rather than on a market, all it will produce are high individual costs and few social gains.

This, of course, is pushing the argument to its extreme. To the extent that traditional knowledge is actually traded or at least put to use as it is, available or adapted forms of intellectual property may serve a defensive purpose as a protection against acts of passing off non-genuine products or services. Possibly it may also help in codifying and formalising such knowledge, if that is compatible with its nature, and it may constitute a means of ensuring its recognition and respect.[38] In this regard, there is ample support for it also in public international law.[39] It is, however, quite revealing that it is not these aspects which ultimately have induced legislatures in at least some developing countries actually to take concrete

35 See Heath and Weidlich, *supra* n.16, 86 ff. with references.

36 For a more elaborate presentation of this basic point of industrial property law see Ullrich, 'Intellectual Property, Access to Information and Antitrust: Harmony, Disharmony and International Harmonization', in Dreyfuss, Zimmermann and First (eds.), *Expanding the Boundaries of Intellectual Property: Innovation Policy for the Knowledge Society* (Oxford, 2001) 365, at 371 ff. with references; for the historical, philosophical and economic underpinnings of patent protection in general see Granstrand, *The Economics and Management of Intellectual Property*, (Cheltenham, 1999) 17 ff., p. 55 ff.

37 At least as regards intellectual property other than patents, such as copyright in literary and artistic works proper or purely aesthetic designs, but even as regards patent law, the basis for legitimacy of granting protection for inventions is broader than merely utilitarian: see for a broad discussion Drahos, *A Philosophy of Intellectual Property*, (Aldershot, 1996), *passim* (himself defending an instrumentalist approach with the aim precisely of keeping property within the limits of functionality). It is, however, grossly misleading to pretend that protection of trade marks or of geographic indications of origin does not follow an incentive/reward rationale, but protects reputation (see for instance Downes, 'How Intellectual Property Could be a Tool to Protect Traditional Knowledge' (2000) 25 *Colorado J. Envtl. L.* 253, 259. This is simply confusing the operation of protection with its rationale, which, at least in the case of trade marks, is to encourage investment in market penetration and distribution. Likewise, indications of origin are not protected for the sake of preserving products of the past, but to allow competition on the merits in trade, i.e. investment in quality, which is to be recouped from the market. In short, intellectual property is an instrument of dynamic competition, not a standstill arrangement.

38 For an account and a juxtaposition of the arguments *on how and why to protect traditional knowledge see* WIPO, *supra* n.4, 213 ff. ; Dutfield., *supra* n.32, 25 ff., 29 ff.

39 See McClellan, 'The Role of International Law in Protecting the Traditional Knowledge and Plant Life of Indigenous Peoples', (2001)19 *Wis. Int'l L. J.* 249; Heath and Weidlich, *supra* n.16 72 ff.; Leistner, 'Traditional Knowledge', in Lewinski (ed.), *Indigenous Heritage and Intellectual Property*, (The Hague, 2004), 49 106 ff.

steps specifically to protect traditional knowledge. Rather, by limiting access to and use of traditional knowledge, in particular by attributing property-like control to communities, local authorities or eventually even the state,[40] these measures aim at elevating traditional knowledge to the level of a scarce resource for the use of which those who want to use it indirectly as a raw, material for the development, by value-adding transformation, of more readily and widely, and also more efficiently applicable knowledge should pay. The typical examples of such approaches to tapping the profit potential of innovation at its up-stream sources are presented by legislation on public and/or private 'property' over traditional medicines,[41] and, more particularly, by legislation on access to genetic resources, including traditional knowledge of their properties and applications, on disclosure of their use in the process of invention, and on sharing in the benefits of the innovation resulting therefrom.

Activating Traditional Knowledge: False Romantics—False Economics

a) The Convention on Biological Diversity

Taken mainly by developing countries,[42] such legislative measures, standing alone, would hardly be effective. It is the support, in fact the impulse,

[40] See e.g. the Thai Traditional Thai Medicinal Intelligence Act as reported by Correa, *supra* n.32, 13.

[41] See *supra* n. 40.

[42] See *supra* n. 40; as to Australia see Sherman, 'Regulating Access and Use of Genetic Resources: Intellectual Property Law and Biodiscovery', [2003] *European Intellectual Property Review*, 301 ff.; as to India see Srividhya, 'Biological Diversity: An Indian Perspective on North-South Issues', in Hill, Takenaka and Takeuchi (eds.), *Rethinking International Intellectual Property*, Proceedings of the 2000 High Technology Summit Conference, University of Washington, Seattle, 2001 (CASRIP Publication No. 6), 225 ff.; Heath and Weidlich, *supra* n.16, at 92 ff. (reporting at 94 ff. also on the Philippines); extensively see Verma, 'Access to Plant Genetic Resources and Intellectual property Rights: The Case of India', CASRIP Newsletter 2001 (Spring/Summer), 18, 23 ff.; as to Africa see for the Organisation of African Unity's Model Legislation, Kongolo, 'Biodiversity and African Countries', [2002] *European Intellectual Property Review* 579, 582 ff.; Wolson, 'Intellectual Property Rights and Biological Resources: Current Policies and Legislative Developments in South Africa', in Bellmann, Dutfield and Meléndez-Ortiz (eds.), *Development Perspectives in TRIPs, Trade and Sustainability* (London, 2003), 264, 271 ff.; Otieno-Odek, 'Towards TRIPs Compliance: Kenya's Legislative Reforms', in *ibid.*, at 277, 282; as to Latin America, see Venero Aguirre, 'The Peruvian Law on Protection of the Collective Knowledge of Indigenous Peoples Related to Biological Resources', in *ibid.*, at 285 ff.; Novak, this vol., 2.1; see also the overview by Leistner, *supra* n.39, at 120 ff., and by Hassemer, 'Genetic Resources'in *ibid.* at 151, 188 ff.; a database on national legislation has been set up by the Secretariat of the Biodiversity Convention (Database on ABS Measures, available at http://www.biodiv.org/ programmes/socio-eco/benefit/measures.aspx). It should be noted that a more or less voluntary, heterogeneous practice of contractual arrangements on access and benefit-sharing has developed between states and large corporations: see CIPR,

which they received from public international law,[43] ultimately from the Convention on Biological Diversity (CBD),[44] which makes such legislation attractive. In view of the dramatic reduction of biodiversity due to both highly selective 'industrialisation' of the exploitation of genetic resources and their substitution by derived or synthesised products,[45] the Convention seeks to control access to genetic resources on the basis of the principle that 'States have . . . the sovereign right to exploit their own resources pursuant to their own environmental policies' (Article 3). Within a rather vaguely defined framework of environmental responsibilities, such as developing conservation programmes and policies, monitoring and identifying biodiversity, establishing protected areas (*in situ* conservation) and introducing or maintaining research, training, education and awareness projects etc. (Articles 6–14), the Convention reasserts in Article 15 that, in view of their sovereign rights over their natural resources, states have the authority to determine access to genetic resources in accordance with their domestic legislation. Whilst they 'shall endeavour to create conditions to facilitate access to genetic resources for environmentally sound uses by other Contracting States and not to impose restrictions that run counter to the objectives of this Convention' (Article 15(2)), such access 'where granted, shall be on mutually agreed terms' (Article 15(4)), and 'subject to prior informed consent of the Contracting Party providing such resources' (Article 15(5)). In addition 'each Contracting Party shall take legislative, administrative or policy measures . . . with the aim of sharing in a fair and equitable way the results of research and development and the benefits arising from the commercial and other utilization of genetic resources with the Contracting Party providing such resources. Such sharing shall be upon mutually agreed terms' (Article 15(7)).

The Biodiversity Convention has its own financial resources and mechanism mainly 'to enable developing country parties to meet the agreed full incremental costs to them of implementing measures which fulfil the

supra n.3, at 77; Bell, 'The 1992 Convention on Biological Diversity: The Continuing Significance of U.S. Objections at the Earth Summit', 26 *Geo. Wash. J. Int'l. L. Ec.*, 479, 528 ff. (1993); Kneller, 'Ownership of Inventions Derived from Natural Products and Human Tissues, and Sharing of Benefits from the Communalization of Such Inventions', in Hill, Takenaka and Takeuchi (eds.), *supra* at 218, 221 ff.; Hassemer, *supra* at 205 ff.

43 See references *supra* n. 39.

44 Agreed on 5 June 1992 at Rio de Janeiro (text available at http://www.biodiv.org/default aspx); there are 188 parties (168 signatories) to the Convention, but it has not been ratified by the USA, which is the major nation in biotechnology; for the reasons of refusal, mainly related to the provisions on financing and on intellectual property see Bell, *supra* n.42 at 507 ff.

45 For a brief account of this by now generally admitted phenomenon see *ibid.*, at 483 ff.; Biber-Klemm 'Incentives to bring about Conservation and Sustainable Use of Genetic Resources in the Framework of the World Trade Order', in Cottier and Mavroidis, *supra* n.24, 481, 484 ff.

obligations of this Convention and to benefit from its provisions' (Article 20(2)).[46] It also has its own organisational structure in order to meet the long-term needs of environmental protection measures relating to biodiversity, and to take the decisions necessary to implement the provisions of the Convention (Article 23 ff). These generally are in the nature of framework rules.

The decision pertinent to the topic of this chapter is Decision VI/24 of the Conference of the Parties,[47] which adopts the so-called 'Bonn Guidelines on Access to Genetic Resources and Fair and Equitable Sharing of the Benefits Arising out of their Utilization',[48] provides for development of an 'Action Plan for Capacity-Building for Access to Genetic Resources and Benefit-Sharing', and deals with the 'Role of intellectual property rights in the implementation of access and benefit-sharing arrangements'. The—formally voluntary[49]—Bonn Guidelines more particularly 'are intended to assist Parties in developing an overall access and benefit-sharing strategy, which may be part of their national biodiversity strategy and action plan, and in identifying the steps involved in the process of obtaining access to genetic resources and sharing benefits (No. 12). To this effect they propose a complete scheme of administrative organisation and tasks, of distribution of substantive responsibilities between granting and receiving states, users and providers, of how to involve 'stakeholders', of the procedure for granting access and ensuring benefit-sharing, and of the terms and modalities of access, of prior informed consent and benefit-sharing, as well as an indicative list of mutually agreed terms' (of the arrangements between Contracting Parties). As if all this and provisions on incentives, accountability in implementing access and benefit-sharing arrangements were not enough, 'Elements for

[46] Even in view of the undisputable fact that developing countries need to be enabled to protect the environment, and that the latter is a matter of common concern of all Parties it is surprising to read Art. 20(4) of the Convention: '4. The extent to which developing country Parties will effectively implement their commitments under this Convention will depend on the effective implementation by developed country Parties of their commitments under this Convention related to financial resources and transfer of technology and will take fully into account the fact that economic and social development and eradication of poverty are the first and overriding priorities of the developing country Parties'. Given the additional claim of benefit-sharing in the commercial exploitation of the good to be protected, namely biodiversity, this provision bespeaks the ambivalence of the communitarian approach underlying the Convention.

[47] Adopted at the 6th Ordinary Meeting at the Hague, 7–19 Apr, 2002 (available at http://www.biodiv.org/decisions/defautl.aspx?m=(OP-06gid=7198glg=0), hereinafter 'Bonn Guidelines'.

[48] So called following their elaboration and adoption by an Ad hoc Open-ended Working Group on Access and Benefit-sharing in Bonn from 22–26 Oct 2001.

[49] See Bonn Guidelines, at No. 7, but remember Art. 20 (4) of the Convention (*supra* n. 46).

Material Transfer Agreements' in the form of a contract checklist are suggested, and modalities of monetary or non-monetary benefit-sharing are detailed.

(b) Intellectual Property Issues

Intellectual property comes at several points into the picture of this bureaucratic paradise.[50]

(i) Article 8(j) of the Convention extends the duties of environmental protection to traditional knowledge of indigenous and local communities, insofar as it is relevant for the conservation and sustainable use of biological diversity. The provision even establishes a duty to promote its 'wider application with the approval and involvement of the holders of such knowledge' and to 'encourage the equitable sharing of the benefits arising from the utilisation of such knowledge'. This seems to be an obligation of the Contracting Parties of its own, which must be distinguished from rules on access to and benefit-sharing as they apply when traditional knowledge is necessary for the identification and understanding of genetic resources and, therefore, is used in conjunction with the latter as 'associated traditional knowledge'.[51] Even though both kinds of traditional knowledge are not really separable on a general level, in the following text traditional knowledge will be considered only under the aspect of access to and benefit-sharing in the use or exploitation of genetic resources.

(ii) Secondly, such subjection of associated traditional knowledge under the rules governing access to and benefit-sharing in the exploitation of genetic resources primarily means compliance with the requirement of obtaining informed consent to access prior to acceding to the knowledge.[52] Whilst such prior informed consent may be relatively easy

[50] It is a paradise in permanent evolution, see Bonn Guidelines, at. No. 6; see as to the ongoing work Decision VII/19 of the Conference of the Parties (adopted at its 7th ordinary meeting, Kuala Lumpur, 9–20 and 27 Feb 2004) inviting Parties and the Executive Secretary to do further documentation work and charging the Ad hoc Open-ended Working Group on Access and Benefit-sharing with further implementation work; in addition, the Working Group has been mandated 'to elaborate and negotiate the nature, scope and elements of an international regime on access and benefit-sharing within the framework of the Convention on Biological Diversity'.

[51] See Bonn Guidelines, at No. 9, 11 lit j, 16 lit d (ii), 31; see also v. Hahn and Stoll, 'Indigenous Peoples, Indigenous Knowledge and Indigenous Resources in International Law', in v. Lewinski (ed.), *supra* n.39, 5, 28 ff., 32 ff.

[52] The concept seems to need quite some implementation as to the kind of information that is necessary to make the consent valid, and as to what prior consent means where the use made of the genetic resources is modified subsequently: see Bonn Guidelines, No. 24 ff.; Srividhy, in Hill, Takenaka and Takeuchi (eds.), *supra* n.42, at 230; according to Straus, 'Biodiversity and Intellectual Property', in *ibid.*, at 141, 148 ff. the necessity of obtaining prior informed consent and its criteria entirely depend on national law; however, it would appear that the Convention also sets limits to this requirement or else access to resources may be made unduly difficult: see Bonn Guidelines No. 26 lit. b.

to handle administratively as regards genetic resources as such,[53] in respect of traditional knowledge it will create specific practical, if not legal, difficulties. It is not easy to ask for informed consent to access to knowledge unless it is first known what the knowledge is to which access is sought.[54] Moreover, the holders of the knowledge will not always know what they are asked for, and proof of informed consent (and subsequently of the basis of benefit-sharing) will require some formalisation/codification of the knowledge. Whilst such details are a matter for further implementation of the Bonn Guidelines by Contracting Parties and/or national legislation and administration, prior informed consent clearly affords some formal extra protection to traditional knowledge,[55] and it even elevates it to the level of a proprietary asset.

(iii) This, indeed, brings up a third intellectual property issue raised by Decision VI/24 and the Bonn Guidelines in response to a general desideratum of the holders of traditional knowledge and the protagonists of its protection,[56] which is to request that the applicant for a patent should fully disclose in his patent application both the genetic resources and the traditional knowledge which, in conjunction with genetic resources or independently, constitute the subject-matter of or have been used in the development of his invention.[57] This *petitum* seems to be quite innocent as, in patent law, the description of the state of-the-art against which the invention has to be assessed is both a formal requirement and good practice, and as mentioning the contribution made by others to the

[53] Basically the consent is given via an administrative act—the prospecting permit—by the competent national authorities, but it may become more difficult when 'stakeholders', such as indigenous peoples and local communities, have to approve of prospecting. Still, it relates to the tangible 'phenotypes' of genetic resources.

[54] This vicious circle, which is noted also by Srividhy, in Hill, Takenaka and Takeuchi (eds.), *supra* n.42, at 230, is well-known from trade-secret licensing, where it is overcome by the parties first agreeing on duties of confidentiality obliging them to maintain confidentiality even in case of failure of the negotiations; breach of such agreements may be sanctioned by penalties and the grant of liquidated damages; however, this may not be a reliable mechanism in the context of bio-prospecting, where transactions may involve many and/or inexperienced people.

[55] In particular, it may protect and complement customary rules, which, in view of their proper way of functioning, their perception and precarious status cannot effectively safeguard traditional knowledge, see Bonn Guidelines No. 31, v. Hahn, *supra* n.31, at p. 209 ff., 326 ff.

[56] See Gopalakrishnan, 'TRIPS and Protection of Traditional Knowledge of Genetic Resources: New Challenges to the Patent System', [2005] *European Intellectual Property Review* 11; Sherman, *supra* n.42, at 304 ff.; Pires de Carvalho, 'Requiring Disclosure of the Origin of Genetic Resources and Prior Informed Consent in Patent Applications Without Infringing the TRIPs Agreement: The Problem and the Solution' (2000) 2 *Wash. Univ. J. L. Pol'y*, 371.

[57] See Conference of the Parties (of the CBD), Decision VI/24, *supra* n. 47, at C (Role of intellectual property rights in the implementation of access and benefit-sharing arrangements) at No. 1, 2, 3, 4 (c); Bonn Guidelines, No. 16 sub. d (ii).

invention seems simply to represent the respect due to the moral right(s) of the holder(s) of such knowledge.[58] However, the *petitum* is raised regardless of the quantum or the quality of the contribution made by traditional knowledge (or the genetic resource for that matter) to the invention[59]—it may even be public domain knowledge[60]—and it is made for much more mundane purposes: it is intended to serve as a tracking tool to control proper benefit-sharing.[61]

It is in view of this purpose too that the request for origin disclosure regarding gene-technology related inventions is considered to be a TRIPs problem: Behind the new formality lurks a problem of substance: disclosure of genetic resources, and, *a fortiori*, of traditional knowledge may not always be done easily with sufficient precision. In addition, if the informed consent has not been obtained with sufficient specificity,[62] the patent application may be invalid or the patent, as granted, invalidated. Moreover, the patent office is made the judge of whether disclosure was warranted or not in view of the quantum or the quality of the contribution made by the genetic resource or by traditional knowledge. Finally and primarily, the perspective for assessing all these new hurdles for the patent grant, which is costly and cumbersome enough,[63] risks being that

58 For an analogy see the right of the inventor to be named in the letters patent as internationally recognised by Art. 4 of Paris Convention for the Protection of Industrial Property.

59 Claims to joint inventorship are generally misplaced since the inventive activity normally does not lie in the discovery of a genetic resource or of its use, but in its isolation and presentation in purified or improved gallenic form (contra: Sherman, *supra* n.42, at 306); it is a different matter whether the grant of prior informed consent may be conditional on the acceptance of joint ownership of patents, which, though onerous enough and likely to be excessive, simply is a matter of either highhanded administrative imposition or successful negotiation of modalities of benefit-sharing: see Bonn Guidelines, Annex II (Monetary and Non-Monetary Benefits) sub. 2 q.

60 As to this problem see *infra* sect (c) (iv).

61 Decision VI/24, *supra* n. 47, at C1: 'disclosure . . . as a possible contribution to tracking compliance with prior informed consent and the mutually agreed terms on which access to those resources was granted'. Note that disclosure of origin without submission of evidence of prior informed consent would make little, if any, sense.

62 See *supra* n. 61, and note that prior informed consent is also required if, subsequent to the original consent, use to be made of the genetic resources or the traditional knowledge is changed: see Bonn Guidelines at No. 27 (c), 34 (it being an open question how detailed the indication of 'specific use[s]' must be).

63 This consideration is downplayed by Sherman, *supra* n. 42, 306; however, given that the reliability of patent granting procedures is already weak enough (see Federal Trade Commission, *To Promote Innovation: The Proper Balance of Competition and Patent Law and Policy* (Washington, DC, Oct 2003, Chapter 5), that granting procedures in Europe take 2 1/2 to 4 years on average, that on average the overall costs of a patent granted under the European Patent system are about € 30.000 over the lifetime of the patent, that protection has to be sought worldwide, and that patent agents and, subsequently, patent examiners are engineers, who are not trained to check whether prior informed consent has been duly obtained under the law(s) of one or more distant countries and from the proper owners (so that additional legal advise becomes necessary), it should become clear that the disclosure requirement raises more than simply an issue of practicality.

of benefit-sharing rather than that of the merits of the invention as a promise of an innovation that does not follow by itself from the state of the art.

The Contracting Parties to the Biodiversity Convention have asked the World Intellectual Property Organisation to submit a technical study on possible modalities and the feasibility of the disclosure requirement, a draft of which WIPO has submitted on the understanding that it does not express a policy position on the part of WIPO.[64] The lengthy paper does, however, show the extreme technical complexities and the wide array of possible approaches to a disclosure requirement. They may extend from voluntary indication of genetic resources actually implied in the invention as claimed[65] to a mandatory requirement to examine the equities of benefit-sharing based on the use of genetic resources somewhere in the process of inventing. On such a scale, making the indication of the genetic resources used for the invention a mandatory requirement of patent validity amounts to full recognition of the principle of benefit-sharing whatever its legitimacy may be in general or *in casu*, and extending such mandatory disclosure to the existence of prior informed consent would mark the transformation of the patent system from an institution for the grant of private property rights into an auxiliary instrument of administrative environment protection.[66] It is for this reason that a globally uniform disclosure rule, which reaches beyond technological information, is hard to foresee. In addition, the differences of national access regulations and of patent procedures[67] alone would seem to stand in the way of a

[64] WIPO, Draft Technical Study on Disclosure Requirements Related to Genetic Resources and Traditional Knowledge (WO/GA/30/7 Add 1 of 15 Aug 2003), circulated by the Executive Secretary of UNEP sub UNEP/CBD/COP/7/inf/17 of 15 Dec 2003 (available at http.//www.biodiv.org/doc/meetings/cop/cop-07/information/cop-inf-17-en.pdf).

[65] See recital 27 EU Dir on biotechnological inventions, *supra* n. 25, which reads: 'if an invention is based on biological material of plant or animal origin or if it uses such material, the patent application should, where appropriate, include information on the geographical origin of such material, if known; . . . this is without prejudice to the processing of patent applications or the validity of rights arising from granted patents'. Note that this is not only a non-binding, but also a rather restrictive formulation in view of the difficulties of precisely locating the origin of genetic resources, and the uncertainty where, how, and to what extent it is used in the process of invention.

[66] Much to the regret of some fervent advocates of the disclosure requirement, even India has refrained from taking this last step, and is satisfied with a technical disclosure requirement, see Gopalakrishnan, *supra* n.56, 2005, at 17 ff. After all, the prior informed consent primarily concerns the impact a request for access to genetic resources may have on bio-diversity rather than the commercial implications of the applicant's innovation project as such.

[67] The WIPO Technical Study, *supra* n. 64, has not gone into the different problems the disclosure requirement will raise, on the one hand, under an examination system (such as in the USA, in the EU or in Japan) and, on the other, under a mere registration system (such as existing in most developing countries, but also in major developed countries such as France or Italy).

patent-law supported control of the importance of the genetic resources used as a basis for the requirement of consent and benefit-sharing, of the materiality of the consent, and of the adequacy of benefit-sharing.

It is, therefore, no surprise that, at the level of the World Trade Organisation, where the same issue is debated, only little progress has been made as regards the nature and scope of a technical disclosure requirement, and even less as regards the transformation of the patent system into an instrument of environmental and developmental policy by way of an extension of the disclosure requirement to evidence of prior informed consent and, ultimately, to evidence on benefit-sharing.[68] Indeed, what is really needed is a thorough empirical economic investigation into the question of how much of an extra load can be reasonably carried by the patent system without deterring from its use.[69] Such investigation should be extended to examining the question whether the instrumentalisation of the patent system for additional, if not extraneous, purposes[70] really is efficient in view of the actual—and legitimate[71]—benefit-sharing that may reasonably be expected. After all, however important patent protection may be for biotechnology industry, the number of blockbuster patents is not likely to be greater than in other areas of chemical and pharmaceutical patenting.[72] With respect to those commercially successful inventions, however, evidence of acts of tapping genetic resources, if necessary at all, may be easier to gather *ex post* from general

[68] See para. 19 of the Declaration of the 4th Ministerial Conference held at Doha, 14 Nov 2001; for the state of play see 'TRIPs Council Update, Bridges-WTO News June 2004 (6) ; Note: 'TRIPs Council Addresses Health, Biodiversity, in Bridges-WTO/MEA News, Mar 2004 (No. 3) 12 (all available at www.ictsd.org); WTO-TRIPs Council: Communication from the European Communities and their Member States: Review of Article 27. 3 (b) of the 'TRIPs Agreement, and the Relationship between the TRIPs Agreement and the Convention on Biological Diversity (CBD) and the Protection of Traditional Knowledge and Folklore—A Concept Paper, IP/WC/383 of 17 Oct 2002; Addor, 'Industrial Property—Quo Vadis? Where now after Cancun?', Presentation made at the Conference on 'Industrial Property—Quo Vadis?', Lacco Ameno–Ischia, 5–7 Oct 2003 (available at http://www.ige.ch/E/jurinfo/pdf/Ischia.pdf); as regards requirements of evidence on prior informed consent and even on benefit-sharing as claimed by developing countries see Note, 'TRIPS Council Focuses on Benefit-Sharing for Genetic Resource, 5(5) BRIDGES BioRes of 18 Mar 2005 (available at www.ictsd.org/biores).

[69] Thus, industry may even turn to other areas of promising research: see Glaxo Smith Kline's public policy position as reported in Second Report of the European Community to the Convention on Biological Diversity, Thematic Report on Access and Benefit-Sharing, Oct 2002, Box 5 (available at http://biodiv.org/world/reportsaspx?type = abs & alpha = E).

[70] It has even been suggested that national patent offices should report to the authorities of the countries of origin on the patent applications made: see WIPO, Technical Study, *supra* n. 64 at No. 81. This is surprising not only as regards costs of such extra work, but also as regards patent law, since, within certain time limits, patent applications are made publicly available anyway.

[71] See *infra* (c) (iii).

[72] See Scherer, 'The Innovation Lottery', in Dreyfuss, Zimmerman and First (eds.), *supra* n.36, at 3 ff.

sources of information than *ex ante* via a Kafkaesque system of global bureaucratic control.

c) Systems Friction

(i) It may very well be that within WTO-TRIPs, either expressly or implicitly, much of the excess load of the biodiversity-related disclosure requirements for patent applications may be negotiated away so as to make it compatible with the proper operation and the functionality of the system of protection, and, therefore, acceptable within TRIPs.[73] This, indeed, is what happened or is likely to happen with other stumbling blocks, which developing countries and the defenders of biodiversity and traditional knowledge rolled in the way of patent-protected innovation in order to bring their interests to bear. Thus, whilst fears that exclusive rights might in turn be applied to block the use of the original plant genetic resources apparently have not been dispelled,[74] the distinction between that source and the patentable invention as such seemed to be solid enough to allow for the conclusion and, actually, the entry into force of the FAO-supported International Treaty on Plant Genetic Resources for Food and Agriculture (ITPGR).[75] Likewise, concerns mainly of the USA that the

[73] See the distinction between patent-related and patent-unrelated disclosure requirements made in the 'Additional Comments by Switzerland on its Proposals Regarding the Declaration of the Source of Genetic Resources and traditional Knowledge in Patent Applications', WIPO Document PCT/R/WG/6/11 of 21 Apr 2004, follow-up in Further Observations by Switzerland on its Proposals Regarding the Declaration of the Source of Genetic Resources and Traditional Knowledge in Patent Applications of October 26, 2004, PCT/R/WG/7, Paper No. 7 (all available at http://www.wipo.int/pct/en/meetings/reform-wg/pdf/pct_r_6_11.pdf). The EU has made it clear that it is willing to accept a mandatory technical disclosure requirement regarding the use of genetic resources for an invention, but that non-observance may not affect patent validity, and that, at any rate, the introduction of new disclosure obligations for patent applications requires a revision of the Patent Cooperation Treaty, of the Patent Law Treaty and of the European Patent Convention (which actually means delaying the introduction and its implementation for many years, if not *ad calendas graecas*): see European Community and its Member States, Disclosure of origin or source of genetic resources and associated traditional knowledge in patent applications, Proposal submitted to WIPO, 16 Dec 2004 (available at www.wipo.int/tk/en/genetic/proposals/european_community.pdf).

[74] See Bonn Guidelines No. 16 (a) (iii); COP/CBD-Decision VI/24, *supra* n. 47, C 3 (a), and see text *supra* at 1. (c), (d).

[75] See Art. 12.3 (d) of the Treaty and the Declaration made uniformously by the European Community and its Member States (available at http://www.fao.org/Legal/Treaties/033s-e.htm). The Treaty entered into force on 29 June 2004 due to the deposit of ratification instruments by the EU and all its Member States individually (thus bringing the number to 40 States; the USA and many other developed and developing having not yet ratified or even signed the Treaty). The Treaty, which contains rules on access to plant genetic resources and traditional knowledge and on benefit-sharing similar to those of the CBD, in substance follows in more concrete terms a different principle of multilateral access and benefit-sharing with respect to a limited number of specified crops (see Art. 10 ff. and Annex I). It cannot be dealt with here. As regards the recognition of farmers' rights (Art. 9) see Stoll and v. Hahn, *supra* n.51, 33 ff., and reference *supra* n. 24.

Biodiversity Convention's Article 16 on technology transfer ultimately might be used to impose rules of compulsory licensing for patented biotechnological inventions seems exaggerated in view of the flexible and limiting language of the provision.[76] At the very least, the language leaves enough room for less rigorous implementation by agreement.[77] In fact, Article 16(3) does not even appear to represent the threat that must be feared most, since the 'developing countries which provide genetic resources' and, therefore, wish to have 'access to and transfer of the technology that makes use of those resources' already possess the leverage to obtain technology access and transfer by virtue of their power to control access to the genetic resources and to request benefit-sharing in non-monetary form.[78]

(ii) The true problems of the relationship between protecting biodiversity, promoting development and protecting inventions, therefore, do not lie in the texts of the relevant conventions, agreements and statutes, but in the frictions resulting from the interaction between the regulatory systems they establish. Fortunately, discussion of these frictions is well beyond the scope of this chapter. This is obvious for the question why and how it may be expected that, by claiming participation in the benefits accruing from patent-protected innovation, precisely those effects on biodiversity may be compensated for, of which the incentive- and profit-oriented patent-competition-innovation system is accused[79]? This is a problem of environment protection, and, therefore, none of my domain. However, as a matter of logic one would expect a counter-productive result. Indeed, if there are any effects to be expected at all from this interaction, then it would appear that they take the form of some synergies in the operation of the systems, meaning that the effects will be mutually reinforcing, and, therefore, negative for the very objective of the Biodiversity Convention. Rather then contributing to the preservation of genetic diversity *in situ* as a self-sustaining and evolving common resource, the combined effects of, on the one hand, providing incentives through patents and, on the other, giving way to commercial interests of holders (and alleged protectors) of genetic resources through a promise of benefit-sharing, are likely to be technological concentration and commercial selectivity with ultimately precisely a substitution of the use of the original genetic resources and of its associated traditional knowledge by innovative 'industrial' products and processes. Whether this is desirable

76 See for US-resistance Bell, *supra* n.42, at 517 ff.; for a cautious construction Straus, in Hill, Takenaka *et al.* (eds.) *supra* n.42, at 149 ff.

77 Chen, 'Diversity and Deadlock: Transcending Conventional Wisdom on the Relationship Between Biodiversity and I.P.', in Hill, Takenaka *et al.* (eds.) *supra* n. 42, at 167, 206 ff.

78 See Bonn Guidelines No. 45 ff. and appendix II.

79 See references *supra* n. 36.

in a development perspective, and if so, how much of the associated wealth creation will occur in developing countries and actually produce general welfare again is a matter outside my expertise.

Anyway, whatever beneficial effects may occur, they obviously and precisely depend on the efficient functioning of the patent system as a form of protecting the goose which lays the golden eggs in which a share is sought. Whether the patent system can hold such promise in general is doubtful enough.[80] Certainly, however, the Biodiversity Convention's rules on access and benefit-sharing do all but improve its operation. They mistreat rather than foster the golden goose. Ideally,[81] the exclusive rights granted by patent law should allow enterprises to reap the rewards which the market offers for the inventions made through investment in the development of new and non-obvious knowledge. To this effect, the exclusivity is granted evenly for all inventions so that investors may decide freely in which inventive activity to invest. In that sense, a patent system is a policy-neutral, market-driven instrument to promote innovation in general. Framework regulations of the market, however, may influence that choice to the extent that they predetermine costs and profit potentials. Clearly, the higher the costs of an innovation, including the costs of patenting, and the more public or private taxes are levied on potential profits, the higher the profit potential itself must be.

Therefore, subjecting access to genetic resources to administrative burdens and prospecting fees, introducing onerous obligations of disclosure of genetic sources and of consent, setting restrictive standards for the making of agreements on benefit sharing,[82] and requiring such benefit-

[80] The patent system is not only struggling with itself (see Federal Trade Commission, *supra* n.63, 4, 5; Ullrich, *supra* n.29, 433 ff.; Tirole, 'Protection de la propriété intellectuelle: une introduction et quelques pistes de réflexion', in Tirole *et al.*, *Propriété intellectuelle* (Paris 2003) 11 ff., but overestimated as regards its economic effects by both its protagonists and its adversaries (see Federal Trade Commission, *supra* n.63, ch. 2; CIPR, *supra* n.3, 19 ff.; Macdonald, *Exploring the Hidden Costs of Patents*, (Geneva). Occasional Paper 4 (available at http://www.geneva.quno.info/pdf/OP4.pdf); Schalk and Täger, *Wissensverbreitung und Diffusionsdynamik im Spannungsfeld von innovierenden und imitierenden Unternehmen*, (Munich 1999), 101 ff.); and, of course, it is not perfect. But eventual changes cannot be discussed here; see with respect to its adaptation to the needs of developing countries in general CIPR, *supra* n.3, at 114 ff.; and as regards biotechnology in particular Taylor and Crayford, *American Patent Policy, Biotechnology, and African Agriculture: The Case for Policy Change* (Washington, DC 2003) 56 ff.

[81] See David, 'Intellectual Property Institutions and the Panda's Thumb: Patents, Copyrights, and Trade Secrets in Economic Theory and History', in Wallerstein (ed.), *Global Dimensions of Intellectual Property Rights in Science and Technology*, (Washington, DC 1993), 19, 32 ff.; Ullrich, *supra* n.6, at 105 ff. with references.

[82] For the complexity of contracting alone see WIPO Secretariat, Genetic Resources: Draft Intellectual Property Guidelines for Access and Benefit-Sharing Contracts (WIPO/GRTK /IC/6/5) of 3 Feb 2004 (submitted to the 6th Session of the Intergovernmental Committee on Intellectual Property and Genetic Resources, Traditional Knowledge and Folklore, 15–19 Mar 2004); Bonn Guidelines No. 41 ff. (Mutually Agreed Terms); Appendix I—Suggested Elements for Material Transfer Agreements.

sharing at both the state or regional and the local or communal levels, necessarily means that the direction of innovation becomes biased toward inventions which promise high commercial yields. To the extent, then, that such innovation depends on or at least is influenced by the availability, the quality, and the actual scope and enforceability of patent exclusivity as a means actually to realise to the profits expected, the perverse effect of a biodiversity-specific sub-system of patent protection will be, that, due to its increased costs and burdens, it will in its turn again reinforce the tendency toward selective high-yield inventive activity. Commercially promising inventions thus become specifically promoted by both the general, cost intensive regulatory regime of biodiversity-related innovation and the additional requirements which are introduced on its account into the patent system, and they are so extra-promoted to the detriment of less rewarding or more risky, but possibly more advanced or more technically/pharmaceutically valuable inventions.[83] Likewise, large enterprises, which are better equipped to handle the administrative complexities of the procedure for the grant of access, to negotiate and manage the agreements on benefit-sharing, and to take out patents in accordance with the additional disclosure requirements, are favoured over smaller enterprises.[84] The former effect obviously will not remain without its (aforementioned counterproductive) impact on biodiversity; the latter is likely to affect the attainment of the developmental objectives. It seems, indeed, that the obsession of developing countries and of many defenders of biodiversity with big business possibly has made them forget how much a policy of access control, which is focussed on benefit-sharing, actually may hurt smaller domestic industry. It is less able efficiently to handle the complex and burdensome system and to promise and actually make comparable profits on a global scale, but, nevertheless, it is subject to the same rules that apply to large foreign enterprises.[85]

(iii) This, of course, is not at all meant to deny the need to control access to genetic resources as one of the ways of safeguarding the public interest in the sustainable preservation of biodiversity. But it is to highlight the problems of its combination with developmental policies, in particular

83 At the limit, necessary inventions, such as those for orphan drugs, will not be made at all, as has been officially recognised in recital 18 to the EU Dir on biotechnological inventions, *supra* n. 25. Note also that a biodiversity-specific sub-system of patent protection may produce a technology bias towards reliance on other technologies, which may or may not be more valuable as regards the substance of the inventions.

84 As evidenced by the examples of benefit-sharing agreements typically cited: see *supra* n. 42.

85 This follows not only from the non-discrimination/national treatment-principle (see Art. 3 TRIPs Agreement), but also from the environmentalist objective of the CBO to safeguard biodiversity and its sustainable use (Art. 1): all must abide by the rules or else the objective will not be attained (see also the first recitals of the Preamble to the CBD stressing the common responsibility in the interest of humankind).

when the latter are based on a rationale of self-interested profit-making. More specifically, benefit-sharing, if required beyond the interests applicants may have in associating local industry or laboratories to their prospecting, research and exploitation activities,[86] has a weak legitimacy and easily comes into conflict with the rationale of the patent system. It is, indeed, a problematic approach to give nation states, as a matter of global interest in biodiversity, full sovereign control over the genetic resources which happen to be found within their territory, and to expect that they will exercise this control with a view to safeguarding this global interest. It is a no less problematic idea to seek to justify this approach by an analogy to sovereign control over mineral resources simply because both are natural resources.[87] Both physical and territorial control essentially concern genetic resources only as phenotypes. By contrast, such territorial control is less directly related to the genotypes which genetic resources embody, since these have a distinct value as information on genetic functions. It is, indeed, not the information support, but the genetic information as such which goes into a biotechnological invention, and it is not the preservation of genetic resources *in situ* or *ex situ*, but the inventive effort, however big or small,[88] which creates the plus value that makes the interest in protecting and exploiting the invention. Moreover, as the commercial value of the patented invention is determined by the demand which exists or which the patentee succeeds in attracting by distributional efforts on the market, there is no direct correlation between the genetic input, however direct and important, and the 'monopoly' power or the profitability of the biotechnological invention.[89] Mandatory benefit-sharing, therefore, risks not having a sufficient basis in a quid pro quo, and the more commercially successful a patented invention is.

[86] For examples see references *supra* in n. 42; such local cooperation in the very development of biodiversity-dependent innovation certainly merits to be supported as a matter of technology transfer and non-monetary *ex ante* benefit-sharing.

[87] See with a less critical undertone Straus, *supra* n. 52, at 142 ff. One should, indeed, not forget first to ask a preliminary question, which should be the inquiry into the legitimacy of exclusive territorial control over global and globally needed resources.

[88] It is undisputed that, as a rule, inventions represent incremental contributions to a cumulative process of technological progress, albeit in different ways in different industries (see Long, 'Patents and Cumulative Innovation' (2000) 2 *Wash. Univ. J. L. Ec.* 229, and references *infra* n. 94); therefore 'small' inventions should not be discriminated against. It is quite another matter whether patentability criteria, in particular the non-obviousness standard, are applied consistently and strictly enough: see Federal Trade Commission, *supra* n. 63, Ch. 4.

[89] Contra Sherman, *supra* n.42, 305 ff. Note that analogies to employer/employee relations regarding inventions are misplaced, first, because there is no universal principle as to how these relations should be regulated—to the contrary, national laws differ widely—and secondly, because the employee, by producing an invention, makes an individual, non-routine contribution to technological progress.

For all these reasons it would seem that genetic resources, which are used in the invention process, may not, as such, justify benefit-sharing, unless their utility is duly supported by associated traditional knowledge. But instead of solving the problem, access control and benefit-sharing based on the use of traditional knowledge raise additional questions. Indeed, whilst recognition of traditional knowledge as an expression of culture and identity should be as certain as is the recognition of the honour of discoverers of laws of nature or of authors of scientific theories, the claim to benefit-sharing is less convincing in all three cases, albeit for reasons which are not entirely the same.[90] In the case of traditional knowledge the connecting factor for benefit-sharing is a collective and rather diffuse merit, which typically (and literally) comes through tradition, i.e. is inherited, whereas discoveries and theories are essentially personal and innovative achievements. Benefit-sharing based on some use of traditional knowledge is unlimited in time as for as past is concerned, and also as regards the future. It will not expire as the patent lapses, but only as the profits are exhausted.[91] This means that it follows a principle of participation rather than one of incentive and reward, as is the case for patent protection. Participation as a principle is well known in intellectual property law, but only as regards copyright, which does not confer a monopoly right, either over the artistic creation or, a *fortiori*, over the idea underlying a work. It therefore, does not establish absolute and permanent dependencies. Such absolute dependencies are familiar and recurrent in patent law, but there they are limited in time and based on an inventive achievement. Introducing dependencies based on traditional knowledge, therefore, means the introduction of an element of friction and systems' incompatibility. This may be the more problematic as there is no mechanism in the protection of traditional knowledge, whether by customary law or by adapted intellectual property law,[92] which would make the

90 For the pros and cons of recognising and rewarding discoverers of laws of nature by benefit-sharing, see Beier and Straus, *Der Schutz wissenschaftlicher Forschungsergebnisse* (Weilheim, 1982); for the merits of traditional knowledge as a basis for benefitsharing see Ghidini, 'Equitable Sharing' of Biodiversity-Based Innovation: Some Reflections Under the Shadow of a Neem-Tree', [2002] *Italian Intellectual Property* 39, 40 ff., who equates traditional knowledge with know-how and argues for benefit-sharing via a local manufacturing requirement (which, however, is economically costly, contrary to the rationale of global patent protection and incompatible with the ubiquitous nature of traditional knowledge once it has been transformed into scientific knowledge).

91 The open-endedness of benefit-sharing raises many issues, such as whether benefit-sharing is still justified once the patents (which?) have expired, simply because the products are still successfully sold; should benefit-sharing also continue, if the products are sold under a trade mark (whose attractiveness is due to the marketing efforts of the enterprise), or if they are sold in competition with identical/similar, but derived generic products, and should the manufacturer/distributors of such derived generic products be included in benefit-sharing? etc.

92 See *supra* text at n. 31 ff.

knowledge-base progress. With the exception probably of some biodiversity-supportive, evolving farming methods, traditional knowledge generally is essentially retrospective and conservatory.

(iv) This systems friction is not just a philosophical one between conservation and progress, or a pecuniary one in that an additional and perpetual financial burden is laid on the patent system. Rather it affects the very rationality of promoting invention and innovation by exclusive rights which are specifically limited in time and scope. The idea underlying the patent system is that a segment may be carved out from the permanent flow of knowledge in view of the particular new use to which the inventor has brought the knowledge, but that after a while that piece of knowledge must return into generally available knowledge so as to contribute to the accumulation of human knowledge and to form part of the basis from which, by competition for inventions, new ideas may be developed for new uses.[93] The patent system, therefore, is not simply crafted like a parasite on the public domain, but symbiotically lives as much for it as it lives from it, and whilst the public domain is much broader than what inventions may contribute to it, its rationale as well goes a long way in support of technical progress. It is, indeed, based on the idea that knowledge creation is a sequential and cumulative process where the merit of new contributions is derived from prior insights, discoveries and inventions,[94] and, therefore, deserves protection by exclusivities only to the extent that, in their absence, it would not be turned, or would not sufficiently be turned, into economic value. If that risk of underinvestment in the production and exploitation of knowledge does not or does no longer exist, all knowledge—old or new—should be free in view of both its derivative nature and of its characteristics of a natural public good. As it may be used without rivalry, and as it is not subject to consumption,[95] everybody should be free to put it to its or to his or her best use.[96]

[93] The disclosure requirement of patent law (see *supra* n. 27) and the experimental use exemption from the exclusivity (see Ss. 11(2) German Patent Act; similar rules exist under all national laws, in the USA in the form of a general fair-use exception under common law see also 35 US C 271 (a) (e)) serve that very purpose; they are intended to speed up substitute innovation; for a general discussion see Eisenberg, 'Patents and the Progress of Science: Exclusive Rights and Experimental Use', (1989) 56 *U. Chi. L Rev.*, 1017; Gilat, *Experimental Use and Patents*, (Weinheim, 1995) 17 ff.

[94] For an elaboration on the famous reply by J. Newton ('if I have seen far, it is by standing on the shoulders of giants', which, in fact, repeats the same several century older insight by Bertrand of Chartres, i.e. an insight deeply rooted in our culture—and obviously one which is similar to that of traditional knowledge as a local public domain—:see Boockmann, *Wissen und Widerstand—Geschichte der deutschen Universität* (Berlin, 1999) 47, see Scotchmer, 'Standing on the Shoulders of Giants: Cumulative Research and Patent Law', (1991) 5 *J. Ec. Persp.*, 29.

[95] See David, *supra* n.81, at 25 ff., with references.

[96] For the economics of public domain knowledge and its justification see Foray, 'On the Creation of Fundamental Knowledge: Finding the Right Balance Between the Public and the Private Domain', in Granstrand (ed.), *Economics, Law and Intellectual Property* (Boston, Mass, 2003), 199: see also Eisenberg, *supra* n.93, at 1048 ff.

It is in view of this utilitarian, but longstanding and, indeed, inherited, rationale alone that knowledge should not lightly be withdrawn from the public domain,[97] and certainly not when the bounds of such withdrawal are as indefinite, if not unlimited, as they are in the case of traditional knowledge. Not only does the definition of both traditional knowledge and indigenous people or local communities, to whom it may be attributed, remain vague,[98] but the attribution itself is indefinite. The same or similar knowledge may exist elsewhere, and it may be truly public, namely propagated by uninitiated persons, or mixed with other, public knowledge. In addition, traditional knowledge in the various developing countries is of rather different quality, it is not easily separable from more or less trivial know-how or from routine craftsmanship, and it cannot properly and legitimately be distinguished from similarly 'inherited' traditional knowledge existing in various parts of developed countries.[99] If that is so, what distinctions can be made and what arguments would be left to defend against yet another extension of the access-control/benefit-sharing approach to any knowledge which, in one way or the other, may be attributed to some group or to an individual?

III. CONCLUSION

Concededly, preserving the purity of the patent system is not a principle of practical politics, nor would it be a sound guide for interpreting and applying the law. The TRIPs Agreement itself, however 'protectionist' in nature, recognises the interdependence between a market-oriented intellectual property system and market regulation in the interest of public policy. Whilst it is an open question how flexible the TRIPs Agreement really is in this regard, it will not escape claims 'for the Establishment of

[97] Contra v. Lewinski, 'Final Considerations', in v. Lewinski (ed.), *supra* n.39, at 391 ff., more convincing von Hahn, *supra* n.31, at 349 ff., who recognises the inherent dynamics of the public domain, and proposes to recognise traditional knowledge by accepting an analogy to the concept of domaine public payant.

[98] See WIPO, Secretariat, *Traditional Knowledge—Operational Terms and Definitions*, Document WIPO/GRTK/IC/3/9 of 20 May 2002 (Intergovernmental Committee on Intellectual Property and Genetic Resources, Traditional Knowledge and Folklore, 3rd Sess. Geneva, 13–21 June 2002); v. Hahn and Stoll, *supra* n.51, at 8 ff., 15 ff. (obviously, by including communal people, the concept has been extended as a matter of broadening the scope of relevant traditional knowledge, and possibly in view of an objective of environment/biodiversity protection, but at the cost of a loss of legitimacy in terms of fundamental rights and claims to non-inclusion in the public domain).

[99] It is not easy to distinguish on a conceptual level Chinese or Indian medicinal or agricultural knowledge from traditional knowledge that exists in many parts of Europe, and which relates to viniculture, beer-brewing, cheese production or, in fact, to homeopathic pharmacology; this similarity is best evidenced by proposals to grant traditional knowledge protection by indications of geographic origin, or by certification marks: see *supra* n. 26; Kur, and Kur, Knaak, in v. Lewinski, *supra* n. 39. at 63, 221 ff.

a Development Agenda' which the World Intellectual Property Organisation actually has to face.[100] The Biodiversity Convention's intellectual property rules point in the same direction. It is also to be welcomed that, within TRIPs, the various disclosure requirements which have been formulated under the CBD are not considered as a controversial issue that must be dealt with as a matter of trade policy, but as a problem of how legally to accommodate political claims which, as such, are founded in global socio-economic disparities. Such openness holds the promise of a gradual transformation of the TRIPs framework of international intellectual protection into a law-based ordering of property, as distinguished from the pressure mechanism of (bi-lateral) TRIPs-plus policies.

However, to assert that the TRIPs Agreement and the Convention on Biological Diversity may be implemented in a 'mutually supportive' way is rather misleading in view of the systemic conflicts between the exclusivity-based promotion of innovation, the privileged participation in its profit potential, and the ecologically motivated conservation of biodiversity in open nature. Given that, in addition, the developmental strategies underlying biodiversity-related patent policies of developing countries are not even consistent with their general patent policy—after all the former, to achieve purpose, require strong and broad titles of exclusivity, whereas the latter, in the interest of competitive follower strategies and of easy access to high technology, tends to favour soft and narrow protection—would it not have been more advisable to seek to achieve each policy objective separately in accordance with its proper necessities and possibilities? The specific causes and needs of safeguarding biodiversity as a matter of protecting the environment, just as the particular causes and needs of pursuing a definite developmental strategy with a view to improving socio-economic standards of living, are only loosely related to the broad reasons underlying patent protection as an incentive system for inventive activity in general. In fact, much of biodiversity-related innovation may not even meet the needs of developing countries, let alone those of indigenous people, and still be socially desirable.[101] Whilst it may not be illegitimate per se to seek to take advantage from the bargaining opportunities offered by

[100] WIPO General Assembly, Thirty-First (15th Extraordinary) Session, Geneva, 27 Sep–5 Oct 2004: Proposal by Argentina and Brazil for the Establishment of a Development Agenda for WIPO, WO/GA/31/11; see also the civil society 'Geneva Declaration on the Future of the World Intellectual Property Organization' of Oct 2004 (available at http://www.cptech.org/ip/wipo/genevadeclaration.html).

[101] See von Hahn, *supra* n. 31, at 356 ff. (pointing to the development of pharmaceuticals for diseases which do not exist in the country in question or which do not affect indigenous people).

territorial control over genetic resources or by locally existing, and generally vulnerable, associated traditional knowledge, it would seem that such legitimacy is best maintained by adequately limiting the advantages sought, and by consistently defining the means used[102] strictly in view of and by reference to the achievement of the public policy objectives that give substance to such legitimacy claims in the first place.

102 See *supra* n. 86, and also the the proposals made by von Hahn, *supra* n.31, at 358 ff. (introduction of a domaine public payant) or by Drahos, 'Indigenous Knowledge, Intellectual Property and Biopiracy: Is a Global Bio-Collecting Society the Answer?', [2000] *European Intellectual Property Review* 245.

10

International Trade in GMOs: Legal Frameworks and Developing Country Concerns

SIMONETTA ZARRILLI*

I INTRODUCTION

BIOTECHNOLOGY IS A revolutionary technology.[1] It offers humanity the power to change the characteristics of living organisms by transferring genetic information from one organism, across species boundaries, into another organism. These solutions continue the tradition of selection and improvement of cultivated crops and livestock developed over the centuries. However, modern biotechnology identifies desirable traits more quickly and accurately than conventional plant and livestock breeding and allows gene transfers across species, genera and families, impossible with traditional breeding. The use of biotechnology in sectors such as agriculture and medicine has produced a growing number of genetically modified organisms (GMOs) and products derived from them. While there is not at present a multilaterally agreed definition of GMOs, the EC has defined a genetically modified organism as follows: 'an organism, with the exception of human beings, in which the genetic material has been altered in a way that does not occur naturally by mating

* Legal Officer, Division on International Trade and Commodities, United Nations Conference on Trade and Development (UNCTAD), Geneva, Switzerland.. The author wishes to express her thanks to F. Francioni, C. Juma, V. Konde, I. Musselli, G. Stanton and R. Vossenaar for the enlightening exchanges of views on the topics addressed in this chapter. Any errors are, however, the author's, who may be contacted at: Simonetta.Zarrilli@unctad.org. This chapter is un up-dated version of the UNCTAD document UNCTAD/DITC/TNCD/2004/1. The chapter reflects the situation as at December 2005.

[1] The Convention on Biological Diversity defines biotechnology as 'any technological application that uses biological systems, living organisms, or derivatives thereof, to make or modify products or processes for specific use'.

and/or natural recombination'.[2] This definition, however, cannot be regarded as universally accepted.

Bio-technological improvements present significant opportunities for agriculture and farmers. At present, the perceived benefits of genetically modified crops are better weed and insect control, higher productivity and more flexible crop management. These 'first generation' GM crops are mainly benefiting producers, who can obtain higher yields and/or lower costs. A shift is, however, occurring from the current generation of 'agronomic' traits to the next generation of 'quality' traits, from which consumers, more than producers, would be able to benefit.

While GM crops may offer great benefits to agriculture and farmers and, potentially, to consumers, in particular to poor people in developing countries, biotechnology does not come without risks and uncertainty. Although there is not yet any definite scientific evidence of harm to human beings, animals or the environment, the public is concerned because of a history of revelations of health and environmental dangers in other fields, especially in the chemical sector. Economic preoccupations have also been voiced, the main concern being that a few large firms will enjoy monopoly power on the seed market derived from intellectual property protection. This development may change the nature, structure and ownership of food production systems and could aggravate food security problems that are allegedly caused not so much by food shortages as by inequity, poverty and concentration of food production. Moreover, the private sector invests in areas where there are hopes of a financial return; as a consequence, private science may focus on crops and innovations that are of interest to rich markets and put less emphasis on those of interest to poor countries. Finally, modern biotechnology techniques may raise ethical and religious concerns.

Country positions on agro-biotechnology depend on many factors, such as their policy awareness, the level of risk they are willing to accept, their capacity to carry out risk assessments in the sector and implement adequate legislation, their perception of the benefits they could gain from biotechnology, their dependence on agricultural exports, their reliance on food aid, and the investments they have already made in the sector. Assessments of the risks and benefits related to agro-biotechnology vary substantially between countries and regions, as do regulatory approaches (e.g. rules on GM approval, marketing, import, labelling, documentation). Diverging domestic requirements may hamper international trade and further complicate an already difficult regulatory system in the area of agricultural products.

[2] This definition is provided in Art 2(2) of Dir 2001/18/EC on the deliberate release into the environment of genetically modified organisms [2001] OJ/106/1. GMO is not actually a scientific term, nor was it coined by scientists. 'Transgenic organisms', on the other hand, is a scientific term: it refers only to organisms that have acquired genetic material from other organisms.

II. EXAMPLES OF DOMESTIC LEGISLATION ON AGRO-BIOTECHNOLOGY

According to figures from the International Service for the Acquisition of Agri-biotech Applications (ISAAA), the global area of GM crop plantation has grown 47-fold since 1996, and the estimated global GM crop area in 2004 was 81 million hectares, cultivated by approximately 8.25 million farmers in 17 countries. Herbicide-tolerant soybean was the dominant transgenic crop, followed by Bt maize[3], Bt cotton, and herbicide-tolerant canola. 14 countries grew 50,000 hectares or more of biotech crops; the eight leading biotech crop countries being the United States, representing 59 per cent of global transgenic crop area; Argentina, 20 per cent; Canada and Brazil, 6 per cent each; China, 5 per cent; Paraguay, 2 per cent; and India and South Africa, 1 per cent each. Plantings were also found in Uruguay, Australia, Romania, Mexico, Spain, the Philippines, Honduras, Colombia, and Germany. More than one-third of the global transgenic crop area in 2004 was grown in developing countries. In the same year, the global market value of GM crops was US $4.70 billion. The market value is based on the sale price of transgenic seed plus any technology fees that apply.[4]

Although continuously expanding, GM crop plantings are still confined to a rather small number of countries. Apart from suspected or scientifically proven health or environmental hazards, the reason for the restricted global uptake of GM crops may find its rationale in fear of export loss due to the political and regulatory environment in many countries outside the Americas that oppose GMOs.

GMO regulations are based on an assessment of the actual or potential risks that those products may engender. Such an assessment can be a 'conventional' risk assessment or a risk assessment based on the precautionary approach. The former is about relevant scientific evidence, which means that there will be sufficient scientific evidence for the perceived risks underlying the measure. Conversely, the 'precautionary approach' to risk assessment is concerned with scientific uncertainty, where there is no 'adequate theoretical or empirical basis for assigning possibilities to a possible set of outcomes'.[5] Three basic conditions may thus trigger application of protective measures: uncertainty, risk, and lack of proof of direct causal link.[6]

[3] Bt plants produce their own pesticide through a gene borrowed from the bacterium *Bacillus thuringiensis*.

[4] For detailed information and data, see James, *Preview, Global Status of Commercialized Transgenic Crops: 2004*, ISAAA Briefs, No. 32, 2004, available at: www.isaaa.org. ISAAA is a not-for-profit organisation with centres based in the Philippines, Kenya and the United States.

[5] Christoforou, 'The Precautionary principle in European Community Law and Science', in Tickner (ed.), *Precaution, Environmental Science, and Preventive Public Policy* (Washington, DC, 2003), 241, at 246.

[6] *Ibid.*, 243.

With respect to GMOs, the problem of defining the relationship between science and policy in risk regulation is by and large a matter of regulatory culture deeply embedded in underlying socio-economic settings. The meat hormones dispute between the EC and the United States/Canada—which shares similarities with the present GMO dispute—well illustrates diverging approaches to regulation under uncertainty.[7] It typifies trans-Atlantic differences *vis-à-vis* the relevance of the precautionary principle in risk assessment.[8]

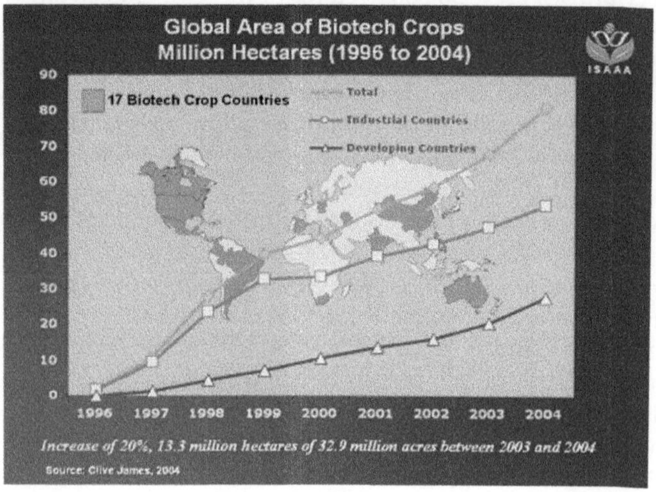

[7] WT/DS26 and WT/DS48—*European Communities—Measures Affecting Meat and Meat Products (Hormones).* The Panel dealt with a complaint by the United States and Canada against the European Communities relating to an EC prohibition of imports of meat and meat products derived from cattle to which six specific hormones had been administered for growth promotion purposes.

[8] In the view of the European Communities, the precautionary principle is already a general customary rule of international law or at least a general principle of law, the essence of which is that it applies not only in the management of a risk, but also in the assessment thereof (EC's appellant's submission, para. 91) Accordingly, the European Communities submitted, that the Panel erred in law in considering that the precautionary principle was only relevant for 'provisional measures' under Art 5(7) of the SPS Agreement. The United States rejected the claim of the European Communities that there was a generally accepted principle of international law that could be referred to as the 'precautionary principle'. In the view of the United States, the EC's invocation of a 'precautionary principle' cannot create a risk assessment where there is none, nor can a 'principle' create 'sufficient scientific evidence' where there is none (United States' appellee's submission, para. 92). The Appellate Body agreed with the finding of the Panel that the precautionary principle does not override the provisions of Art 5(1) and (2) of the SPS Agreement: the risk evaluated in a risk assessment must thus be an ascertainable risk; theoretical uncertainty is not the kind of risk which, under Art 5(1), is to be assessed.

The United States, Canada and Argentina, major agricultural exporters, have applied the conventional risk assessment approach to GMOs substantially, especially during the first years of the agro-biotechnology revolution, and have widely authorised most GM products for production and consumption. They are striving for easy and reliable access to foreign markets for their bio-engineered products. The international policy conflict over GMOs is fragmenting international markets, thereby decreasing economies of scale; producers of GMOs, however, depend on economies of scale to recoup the considerable R&D costs they incur. Moreover, the rate of technological advance in biotechnology is likely to be very rapid, meaning that the commercial life of any new GMO is likely to be short. This means that easy and quick access to foreign markets is a critical determinant for profitability.[9]

Regulators in Europe and Japan, on the other hand, have taken up a more cautious approach based on guaranteeing a very low level of risk to human health and the environment. They have therefore imposed strict control measures on approval and marketing of GMOs and GM products. They have also imposed mandatory labelling schemes. Australia and New Zealand have established processes for pre-market approval and implement mandatory labelling of GMOs. In November 2005, Switzerland passed a law on a five-year moratorium on the use of GNOs in agriculture.

Since the early 1990s, the European Communities (EC) have developed and continuously refined a rather complex legislative framework related to GMOs and GM food. Directive 2001/18,[10] which became fully applicable on 17 October 2002 and replaced Directive 90/220EEC,[11] deals with the deliberate release into the environment of GMOs for experimental purposes and with the placing of products on the Community market that consist of or contain GMOs, such as maize, tomatoes, or micro organisms. It pursues the objectives of protecting human health and the environment. To achieve its objectives, the Directive requires a case-by-case evaluation of potential risks to human health and the environment before any GMO or product consisting of or containing GMOs can be placed on the market or in any other way released into the environment within the Community. On the basis of that risk assessment, a market authorisation is either granted or refused.

The level of appropriate health and environmental protection chosen in the Directive is a level of 'no risk'. Because the authorisation for the release into the environment is to be based on the precautionary principle (as broadly applied in the EC), it is the applicant who has to demonstrate the 'safety'

9 Isaac, 'The WTO and the Cartagena Protocol: International Policy Coordination or Conflict?', *Current*, Number 4/2003, 116, at 117, available at: www.CAFRI.org.; and Phillips and Kerr, 'Alternative Paradigms—The WTO Versus the Biosafety Protocol for Trade in Genetically Modified Organisms' (2000) 34(4) *Journal of World Trade* 63 ff.

10 *Supra* n 2. Dir 2001/18 was amended by Reg 1830/2003 [2003] OJ L/268/24. See the EC website on GMOs at: http://www.europa.eu.int/comm/food/fs/gmo/gmo_index_en.html.

11 Council Dir 90/220/EEC, 23 Apr 1990 [1990] OJ L/117/15, 15 ff.

or 'lack of harm' of each individual product. The product is deemed to be dangerous until the interested manufacturer carries out the necessary scientific work and demonstrates its safety. The Directive introduces a mandatory post-marketing monitoring system of GMOs and traceability at all stages of their being placed on the market. It also establishes an advanced system for directly informing and consulting the general public during the authorisation procedure and, finally, it establishes a labelling system.[12]

In addition to 'horizontal' legislation, the EC has adopted a number of 'vertical' directives and regulations. Legislation related to novel foods and novel food ingredients deals, inter alia, with products derived from GMOs but no longer containing any GM material, such as food products like paste or ketchup derived from a GM tomato.[13] The current relevance of Regulation 258/97, which has been substantially modified by subsequent legislation, is based on the fact that food products from 13 GMOs were approved for marketing while it was in force and eight applications for GM foods are currently at different stages in the authorisation procedure. On the other hand, 18 GMOs were authorised under the 'horizontal' legislation and 22 applications are still pending. Around the mid-1990s, a number of EC Member States started raising questions on potential adverse effects of GMOs and GM products on health and the environment and raised objections to the placing on the market of new GMOs. As a result of those concerns and the negotiations on the Biosafety Protocol, no new GMOs were approved during the October 1998–April 2004 period. The authorisations that were granted have given rise to disputes within the Community.[14] The moratorium on new authorisations, on the other

[12] For a comprehensive and detailed description and analysis of the EC regulatory framework on GMOs see: Christoforou, 'The Regulation of Genetically Modified Organisms in the European Union: The Interplay of Science, Law and Politics' (2004) 41 *Common Market Law Review* 637. See also the following European Commission press releases: *Questions and Answers on the regulation of GMOs in the EU*, DN: MEMO/04/16, 28.01.2004, available at: http://europa.eu.int/rapid/start/cgi/guesten.ksh?p_action.gettxt=gt&doc=MEMO/04/16|0|RAPID&lg=EN&display=; *State of play on GMO authorizations under EU law*, DN: MEMO/04/17, 28/01/2004 available at: http://europa.eu.int/rapid/start/cgi/guesten.ksh?p_action.gettxt=gt&doc=MEMO/04/17|0|RAPID&lg=EN&display= and *GMOs: Commission takes stock of progress*, DN: IP/04/118, 28.01.2004, available at: http://europa.eu.int/rapid/start/cgi/guesten.ksh?p_action.gettxt=gt&doc=IP/04/118|0|RAPID&lg=EN&display=. This section of the chapter draws on the above-mentioned sources.

[13] Reg (EC) No. 258/97, 27 Jan 1997[1997] OJ L/43/1, 1 ff.

[14] Some Member States invoked Article 16 of Directive 90/220/EEC and Article 23 of Directive 2001/18/EC—the so-called safeguard clause—to temporarily ban the placing on the market of genetically modified maize and oilseed rape products in their territories. There are currently nine outstanding cases involving Austria, Luxembourg, France, Greece, Germany and Hungary. With the entry into force of the new legislation on biotechnology, the Commission requested, in 2003, that the above-mentioned Member States reconsider their pending safeguard clauses. Following this request, some of the Member States submitted further information in support of their bans in the first quarter of 2004. According to EC authorities, the additional information did not invalidate the original risk assessments for the products in question. No agreement was however found between the Commission and the concerned member States, therefore, the national safeguard measures are still in place.

hand, has given rise to a dispute between the EU and three of its trade partners within the WTO dispute settlement mechanism.[15]

In July 2003, Community institutions agreed on two new regulations to regulate the placing on the market and labelling of food and feed products derived from GMOs and to establish a system of traceability and labelling of GMOs and GM products. The new regulations have been in force since 18 April 2004. Regulation 1829/2003,[16] which has substantially modified Regulation 258/97, provides for Community procedures for the authorisation and supervision of GM food and feed, and includes specific provisions for their labelling. Labelling is required for foods that are delivered as such to the final consumer or mass caterers in the Community and which contain or consist of GMOs or are produced from or contain ingredients produced from GMOs. The labelling requirements are applied irrespective of the detectability of DNA or protein resulting from the genetic modification in the final product. The process or production method of the GM food or feed is now a relevant factor that justifies labelling. The presence of GM material in conventional food does not have to be labelled if it is below 0.9 per cent and if it can be shown to be adventitious and technically unavoidable. Regulation 1830/2003[17] establishes a system of traceability (i.e. the tracking of the movement of GM products through the production and distribution line) and labelling for two categories of products: products consisting of or containing GMOs; and food and feed produced from GMOs. Traceability is meant to facilitate the withdrawal of food and feed from the market if any unexpected adverse effects were to arise.

As expected, following the promulgation of the new regulations, the EC has restarted granting GM authorisations. On 9 May 2004, the European Commission authorised the placing on the market of sweetcorn from GM

15 Three complaints about EC restrictive measures affecting GMOs and GM crops were officially brought to the attention of the WTO Dispute Settlement Body by the United States, Canada and Argentina in Aug 2003. According to them, since Oct 1998 the EC had applied a *de facto* moratorium on the approval of products of agricultural biotechnology. This moratorium had allegedly restricted imports into the EC of agricultural and food products from the complaining countries and was in violation of the EC's obligations under the SPS and TBT Agreements, the Agreement on Agriculture and the GATT 1994. The complaining countries also alleged that several EC Member States had introduced bans on the importation, marketing or sale of a number of biotech products which had already been approved at Community level, thereby infringing both WTO rules and Community legislation. The report of the WTO Panel is expected in March 2006. See WTO documents: WT/DS291/23; WT/DS292/17; WT/DS293/17 dated Aug 2003. On this issue see: Brack, Falkner and Goll, *The Next Trade War? GM Products, the Cartagena Protocol and the WTO*, The Royal Institute of International Affairs, Sustainable Development Programme, Briefing Paper No. 8, Sept 2003.

16 [2003] OJ L/268/1.

17 [2003] OJ L/268/24. See also European Commission Press Release IP/03/1056, *European legislative framework for GMOs is now in place*, 22 July 2003.

maize[18], and on 26 October 2004 that of foods and food ingredients derived from GM maize NK603.[19] The two authorisations were granted in accordance with the GM Food and Feed legislation. Four products have been authorised since the entry into force of Directive 2001/18/EC.[20] It remains to be seen what impact the recent authorisations will have on the current WTO dispute related to the EC moratorium.

The United States' regulatory system relative to biotechnology products is rather different from the one in place in the EC. Based on the approach that GM products are essentially an extension of conventional products, the US government has made use of existing laws to ensure the safety of GM products. The current system was delineated under the 1986 Coordinated Framework for Regulation of Biotechnology:[21] agencies that were responsible for regulatory oversight of certain product categories or for certain product uses are also responsible for evaluating those same kinds of products developed using genetic engineering.[22] Likewise, new regulations have been formulated under existing laws[23] as needed to address genetically engineered products that have been developed.

In recent years, however, consumer resistance to GM food has also been growing in the United States, where the public is increasingly demanding

[18] The 10-year authorisation covers the specific use of canned or fresh sweet corn for imports, while an authorisation for cultivation of Bt maize is pending and has not yet been granted.

[19] According to the authorisation, it is possible to place on the market NK603 maize and derived products such as starch, oil, maize gluten feed and maize meal for food and feed use. However, the crop has to be grown and harvested outside the EU. In line with the new EU legislation on labelling, the maize and any product containing it will have to show clearly that it has been genetically modified. The Commission took the decision to authorise NK603 following the failure of the Council either to approve or reject the Commission proposal for authorisation.

[20] Monsanto NK603 GM maize was authorised in July 2004 for imports and processing for use in animal feed or for industrial purposes. GM maize MON 863 was authorised in August 2005 for import and processing as animal feed. The decision does not cover uses as human food or cultivation. The maize has been modified by Monsanto to make it resistant to the corn rootworm. GM oilseed rape known as GT73 was authorised in August 2005 for import and processing for use in animal feed or for industrial purposes. GM maize 1507 was authorised in November 2005 for import and processing for use in animal feed. The maize has been modified to make it resistant to certain pests and for tolerance to herbicides. An authorisation for use as food is still under examination. All decisions are valid for 10 years.

[21] United States Federal Register, 26 June, 1986, 51 FR 23302.

[22] The Food and Drug Administration (FDA) is responsible for food and feed safety; within the Department of Agriculture (USDA), the Animal and Plant Health Inspection Service (APHIS) is responsible for assessing the environmental safety of GM crops, and the Environmental Protection Agency (EPA) is responsible for development and release for GM plants with pest control properties.

[23] The Plant Protection Act (PPA), the Federal Food, Drug, and Cosmetic Act (FFDCA), the Federal Insecticide, Fungicide, and Rodenticide Act (FIFRA), and the Toxic Substances Control Act (TSCA).

that GM food be appropriately labelled. In May 2004, a major US producer of GM products announced that it would not try to market the GM wheat it had developed in recognition that the business opportunities for the product were not very attractive. In a recent development, the USDA has declared its intention to update and strengthen its biotechnology regulations for GMOs. Currently, companies creating new transgenic plants must submit an application to the USDA and the new GM crops must undergo field tests to ensure that they do not pose a threat to agriculture or other plants. The updated rules are likely to be broader in scope, and will encompass threats to the environment and public health. The USDA will prepare an environmental impact statement to evaluate biotechnology regulations and several possible regulation changes. This will also include a multi-tiered, risk-based permitting system to replace the current permit/notification system, as well as a more flexible process for monitoring.[24]

As for the developing countries, the major GM crops approved for commercial release are Bt cotton, which is grown commercially in China, India, South Africa, Argentina, Mexico and Columbia. China's Bt-cotton planting was officially estimated at 3.7 million hectares in 2004, corresponding to 66 per cent of the global cotton planted area. However, due to seed smuggling, the actual GM-planted area may be much bigger, and it is playing an important role in the return of production in some provinces where acreage had declined.[25] Changes in China's cotton production have the ability to affect both global cotton production and trade in textiles and apparel. The Philippines approved cultivation of Bt maize in 2002. In October 2003, Brazil authorised the planting of GM soy until the end of 2003 and the sale of GM soy crops until the end of 2004 (the authorisation was later renewed for the 2005 crop year). The law was passed as an emergency measure due to shortage of conventional soybeans and in consideration of the widespread illegal planting of GM soy in southern areas of the country. In March 2005, the Brazilian Parliament approved the new Biosafety law, clearing the way for commercial planting of GM crops. South Africa has approved GM maize, soybean and cotton for commercial release.

Many developing and least developed countries, especially in Africa, still lack, or are in the process of developing, comprehensive regulatory systems to deal with the challenges of agricultural biotechnology. Developing a regulatory framework concerning GMOs may be a costly and

24 'US to Strengthen Biotech Regulation for GMOs', *CropBiotech Update*, 6 Feb 2004, available at: http://www.isaaa.org/kc/cbtnews/bcentral/cbtupdate.htm#us.

25 MacKenzie and McLean, 'Agricultural Biotechnology: A Primer for Policymakers', in M.D. Lungo and J.D. Wash (eds), *Agriculture and the WTO—Creating a Trading System for Development*, Washington, DC, (World Bank, 2004), at 238–239.

lengthy process. Areas for regulation include: (a) R&D, e.g. conditions under which laboratory experiments take place and conditions for testing in contained facilities or in the field; (b) approval processes for commercial release, including prior scientific assessment of health and environment risks, minimum distance from organic agriculture or non-GM fields, labelling, post-commercialisation monitoring, liability; and (c) import regulations.[26] In setting up domestic legislation, developing countries seem to be paying increasing attention to international trade concerns.

Developing country preoccupations have several facets. While some developing countries produce GMOs for domestic consumption, very few export them. However, many developing countries are exporters of conventional agricultural products. Those countries find themselves in a particularly difficult situation: in order to preserve their export opportunities, especially towards markets that are sceptical about bioengineered products, they may need to be 'GM-free'. This means not only that they should not be exporters of GMOs, but also that they should not be producers of GMOs for domestic consumption and not even importers of GMOs. Losing 'GM-free' status is perceived by some countries as having negative repercussions on their export opportunities for all agricultural products. This is due to the perception that consumers, especially in Europe, may react negatively towards products that could be linked even remotely to genetic modification. Some trade-diverting effects are allegedly already taking place because of company practices to replace some inputs with others (which do not bear the risk of being genetically modified) or to use inputs coming from alternative countries, which are supposed to be 'GM-free', to avoid cumbersome documentation and traceability requirements, as well as to meet consumers' expectations.

This perception has been among the reasons why some African countries have refused food aid that includes genetically modified commodities. In 2002, Zambia declined a US offer of maize, some of which contained GM products. Main Zambian concerns related to uncertainty regarding the safety of GM maize for human consumption, as well as the possible contamination of local varieties which could allegedly imply a rejection of Zambian food exports by EC countries. The Zimbabwean government agreed in July 2002 to allow food aid into the country that contained genetically modified maize, provided it was milled immediately upon arrival to avoid any possible contamination of local varieties. Previously, Zimbabwe had rejected

[26] The International Service for National Agriculture Research (ISNAR) and FAO, in consultation with UNEP/GEF, have developed a web-based 'Decision Support Toolbox for Biosafety Implementation', which describes the key elements to be considered when developing a regulatory framework, available at: http://www.isnar.cgiar.org/ibs/biosafety/regulatory.cfm.

GM food aid due to concerns that it might supposedly threaten beef exports to the EU and local maize varieties.[27] Uganda recently announced that GM crops could be imported into the country, but that they should be used strictly for consumption and not for cultivation. At the same time, a draft law that would regulate both research into GM crops and the release of GM organisms into the environment is under consideration.[28] At the beginning of May 2004, more than 60 groups representing farmer, consumer and environmental organisations from 15 African countries sent a letter of protest to the World Food Programme (WFP). These groups were protesting against the alleged pressure exerted by the WFP and USAID on Sudan and Angola over their decisions to impose restrictions on GM food aid. Sudan has requested that food aid be certified 'GM free' (though the Sudanese government has put in place a series of temporary waivers enabling food aid shipments to the country to continue while alternatives are found) and Angola accept GM food aid only on condition that the whole GM grain is first milled. According to the organisers of this initiative, non-GM alternatives exist at national, regional and international levels and donors should make these available to Sudan and Angola.[29] According to the WFP, on the other hand, the requirement imposed by the government of Angola would imply substantial extra costs and cause shipment delays of up to two months. This decision is going further to aggravate an already serious funding situation where the WFP has received only 24 per cent of the funds it asked for under its current operation in the country. As a consequence, WFP is to halve the food rations given to the majority of the 1.9 million people it assists in Angola.[30]

In August 2003, the Southern African Development Community (SADC) approved a set of recommendations formulated by the SADC Advisory Committee on Biotechnology and Biosafety as interim measures aimed at guiding the region on those issues. The recommendations are divided into four main sections: 'Handling Food Aid', Policy and Regulations; Capacity Building; and Public Awareness and Participation. Under 'Handling Food Aid', donors providing GM food aid should comply with the Prior Informed Consent principle and with the notification requirements in accordance with Article 8 of the Biosafety Protocol. Food aid

[27] See *Bridges Trade Biores*, 11 July 2002, at http://www.ictsd.org/biores/02-07-11/inbrief.htm.

[28] 'Uganda gives cautious approval to GM food', *Science and Development Network*, 2 Mar. 2004, available at: http://www.scidev.net/News/index.cfm?fuseaction=readNews&itemid=1257&language=1.

[29] 'African countries 'forced' to accept GM food aid', Mail&Guardianonline, 5 May 2004, available at www.mg.co.za/articledirect.aspx?articleid=78580area=%2f=breaking_news% 2f breaking_news_africa%2f.

[30] *Food Rations to Be Halved in Angola Amid Funding Crisis and GM Ban*, 2 Apr 2004, World Food Programme, In Brief, available at: www.wfp.org/newsroom/in_brief/Africa/angola/angola-040402.html.

consignments containing GM grain should be milled or sterilised prior to distribution to beneficiary populations. The sourcing of food aid should be within the region, and the region should develop and adopt a harmonised transit information and management system for GM food aid designed to facilitate transboundary movement in a safe and expeditious manner. GM food aid in transit should be clearly identified and labelled in accordance with national legislation. In the absence of such a system, it is recommended that countries make use of the requirements under the African Union model law on biosafety. The recommendations encourage SADC countries to develop national biotechnology policies and strategies to exploit the benefits of biotechnology, to establish national biosafety regulatory systems, and to sign and ratify the Biosafety Protocol and the Convention on Biological Diversity.[31]

Following those recommendations, in May 2004 SADC approved guidelines on handling GM food aid. The guidelines fully endorse the recommendations of the SADC Advisory Committee on Biotechnology and Biosafety.[32]

Those developments reflect the preoccupations that several African countries have as potential importers of GMOs and GM crops. Their concerns relate both to the possible adverse effects of agro-biotechnology on human health and on the environment, and to the fact that GM imports may jeopardize exports of conventional agricultural products. These preoccupations, however, must be balanced with governments' responsibility to improve the quantity and quality of agricultural and food production made available for domestic uses: agro-biotechnology may prove an effective tool to address food shortage and malnutrition.

III. THE MULTILATERAL LEGAL FRAMEWORK

Relevant WTO rules concerning international trade in GMOs and products thereof can be found in the Agreement on the Application of Sanitary and Phytosanitary Measures (SPS Agreement), the Agreement on Technical Barriers to Trade (TBT Agreement) and the General Agreement on Tariffs and Trade (GATT) 1994. Disciplines regarding transboundary movement of GMOs, however, have also emerged from the Cartagena Protocol on Biosafety. Though most of the rules included in the different legal instruments are consistent with each other, there are a few areas where some discrepancies may be found.

[31] The Recommendations are available at the SADC web site: http://www.sadc.int/fanr.php?lang=english&path=fanr/agrres&page=sadc_biotechnology_gmo.

[32] 'SADC Sets Guidelines for Gm Food', *Zambezi Times Online*, 14 May 2004.

Cartagena Protocol on Biosafety

The Cartagena Protocol on Biosafety,[33] which was negotiated under the auspices of the Convention on Biological Diversity, was adopted on 29 January 2000 and entered into force on 11 September 2003. As of December 2005, 130 countries, including the EC, had ratified or acceded to it.[34]

The Protocol provides rules for the safe transfer, handling and use of 'living modified organisms' (LMOs). Its aim is to address the threats posed by LMOs to biological diversity, also taking into account risks to human health.

The Protocol distinguishes three categories of LMOs: LMOs for voluntary introduction into the environment (e.g. seeds for planting, live fish for release, micro-organisms for bioremediation); LMOs destined for contained use (LMOs that have limited contact with and impact on the external environment); and LMOs intended for direct use as food or feed, or for processing (LMO-FFPs). The last-named represent the large majority of internationally traded LMOs, i.e. genetically modified crops, such as soybean, maize, canola, tomato, cotton, etc. The Protocol does not cover consumer products derived from LMOs, such as corn flakes, flour, starch, seed-oil, tomato paste or ketchup. LMOs are defined by the Protocol as 'any living organism that possesses a novel combination of genetic material obtained through the use of modern biotechnology' (Article 3(g)). In many countries, the terms 'genetically modified organisms', 'genetically engineered organisms', and 'transgenic organisms' are widely used, including in domestic legislation, to describe groups of organisms that correspond to those covered by the Protocol.

The first Meeting of the Parties to the Protocol (MOP-1) was held in Malaysia in February 2004 and ended with the adoption of ten decisions. Three of them are especially significant for the actual implementation of the Protocol: (a) MOP-1 decided on the documentation that should accompany the three categories of LMOs;[35] (b) some compliance procedures and

33 In general, the term 'biosafety' describes a set of measures used to assess and manage any risk associated with GMOs.

34 This section of the chapter is not intended to analyse the Biosafety Protocol in detail, but to single out those trade-related aspects of it that exhibit some potential for tension with WTO law. For a detailed and comprehensive description and analysis of the Biosafety, Protocol see: Mackenzie *et al.*, *An Explanatory Guide to the Cartagena Protocol on Biosafety*, IUCN Environmental Policy and Law Paper No. 46, 2003.

35 For the first category, the documents should clearly identify that the shipment 'may contain LMOs' for direct use as food, feed or for processing and not intended for introduction into the environment. The accompanying documentation should also indicate the contact details of the importer, exporter or other appropriate authority. In addition, Parties decided to expand the existing requirements by urging governments to require information on the name of the organism and the transformation event or unique identifier code. While the additional information is only optional, it nevertheless marks a step beyond the requirements originally included in Art 18.2(a) of the Protocol. An expert group was given the task

mechanisms were established and a Compliance Committee was set up to hear cases of non-compliance submitted to it; (c) a working group of experts on liability and redress was set up and it was agreed that an appropriate regime would be developed by 2008. Liability and redress was perhaps the most controversial issue discussed, with developing countries, especially from Africa, pressing for MOP-1 to adopt a strong international regime. They argued, in general, that in the event of accidents where LMOs cause damage to farmers' crops, to human health or to the environment, there should be a legally binding regime to determine who is responsible and how redress or compensation can be made.[36] MOP-2 was held in Canada in May 2005. The meeting ended without agreement on the documentation requirements for bulk shipments of LMOs intended for food, feed and for processing. MOP-3 is scheduled to take place in Brazil in March 2006.

The Interface between the Biosafety Protocol and the WTO Agreements

It seems there are four aspects of the Protocol that may give rise to some overlaps and tensions with WTO law: (a) the scope for legitimate government action without conclusive scientific evidence; (b) risk assessment and risk management; (c) the socio-economic factors which may be taken into account in the decision-making process; and (d) documentation requirements.

The precautionary approach is one of the main features of the Protocol. Articles 10 and 11 include very similar language: '[L]ack of scientific certainty due to insufficient relevant scientific information and knowledge regarding the extent of the potential adverse effects of a living modified organism on the conservation and sustainable use of biological diversity in the Party of import, taking also into account risks to human health,

to further elaborate the documentation and handling requirements for these shipments. Key issues to be decided included the percentage of modified material that these shipments might contain and still be considered GMO-free and the inclusion of any additional detailed information. A decision on these matters was supposed to be agreed upon at MOP-2. For the second category of LMOs, documents accompanying them should clearly identify the LMOs, their common and scientific names, that they are destined for contained use, their commercial names and new and modified traits and characteristics. For the third category, namely LMOs meant to be introduced into the environment, the accompanying documents should clearly identify them as LMOs, specify the common, scientific and commercial names of the LMO, the transformation event code or its unique identifier code, any handling and storage requirements, contact details in the case of emergency and how the LMO is to be used.

[36] See UNEP, Convention on Biological Diversity, Press Release, *Biosafety protocol now operational as governments agree documentation rules for GMO trade*; 'Biosafety Meeting Moves on Labelling, Compliance and Liability', (2004) 4(4) *Bridges—Trade BioRes*, 5 Mar 2004, available at: http://www.ictsd.org/biores/04-03-05/story1.htm; and Khor, 'Environment: Biosafety Meet Agrees on Policy Measures on GMO Trade', *Suns* 5523, 2 Mar 2004.

shall not prevent that Party from taking a decision, as appropriate, with regard to the import of the living modified organism . . ., in order to avoid or minimize such potential adverse effects'. Importing countries can thus ban imports because of lack of scientific certainty. The ban may last until the importing country decides that it has arrived at scientific certainty about the effects of the products on biodiversity and human health. However, since the importing country is not obliged to seek the information necessary to reach scientific certainty, a trade-restrictive measure may be in force without time limits. In contrast, the SPS Agreement allows countries to adopt sanitary or phytosanitary measures provisionally when relevant scientific evidence is insufficient—this concept being different from scientific uncertainty—but obliges them to seek the additional information necessary for a more objective assessment of risk and to review the SPS measure within a reasonable period of time (Article 5(7)).

For LMOs destined for intentional introduction into the environment, the Protocol allows the exporting country to request the importing country to review a decision it has taken when a change in circumstances has occurred that may influence the outcome of the risk assessment upon which the decision was based, or additional relevant scientific or technical information has become available. The importing country must respond to such a request in writing within 90 days and set out the reasons for its decision (Article 12(2) and (3)). This provision therefore gives the exporter the right to request the importer to review its decision in the light of new information; however, the importer retains the flexibility to confirm its previous decision, but it has to justify so doing. This discipline echoes the need for review contained in the SPS Agreement when precautionary measures are used, although there are some basic differences: in the case of the SPS Agreement, the country implementing the measure is obliged to seek additional information and review the SPS measure within a reasonable period of time. In the case of the Protocol, the country implementing a restrictive measure is obliged only to consider the request made by the exporter, analyse the new circumstances or the new scientific or technical information brought to its attention, and give a justified reply within 90 days. Moreover, this rule does not apply to LMOs for direct use as food or feed or for processing.

WTO jurisprudence has addressed the issue of the precautionary principle within the SPS Agreement. In the *Japan varietals* case,[37] the Appellate Body stated that Article 5(7) sets out four cumulative requirements that must be met to adopt and maintain provisional SPS measures. A country may provisionally adopt an SPS measure if this measure is: (i) imposed in

[37] *Japan—Measures Affecting Agricultural Products*, WT/DS76/R, 27 Oct 1998, and WT/DS76/AB/R, 22 Feb 1999.

respect of a situation where relevant scientific evidence is insufficient; and (ii) adopted on the basis of available pertinent information. Such a measure may not be maintained unless the country that adopted it: (i) seeks to obtain the additional information necessary for a more objective assessment of risk; and (ii) reviews the measure accordingly within a reasonable period of time.

The more recent *Apples* case[38] seems to be particularly relevant for the analysis of the interface between the WTO rules and those of the Biosafety Protocol. The Appellate Body confirmed the need for the above-mentioned four cumulative requirements to be met in order for a WTO member country to adopt and maintain provisional SPS measures. Addressing the first criterion, i.e. a situation where 'relevant scientific evidence is insufficient', the AB stated that: 'relevant scientific evidence "will be insufficient" within the meaning of Article 5.7 if the body of available scientific evidence does not allow, in quantitative or qualitative terms, the performance of an adequate assessment of risks as required under Article 5.1 and as defined in Annex A to the SPS Agreement'.[39] The Appellate Body clarified that 'the application of Article 5.7 is triggered not by the existence of scientific uncertainty, but rather by the insufficiency of scientific evidence. The text of Article 5.7 is clear: it refers to "cases where relevant scientific evidence is insufficient", not to "scientific uncertainty". The two concepts are not interchangeable'.[40] This would seem to imply that the present inconclusiveness of scientific evidence related to the actual or potential impact of GMOs on human and animal health and on the environment cannot be regarded as a reason for taking precautionary measures under Article 5(7) of the SPS Agreement. On the other hand, Article 10(6) of the Cartagena Protocol refers to 'lack of scientific certainty due to insufficient relevant scientific information and knowledge' as the basis for taking a precautionary step. According to the Protocol, the insufficiency of scientific evidence would lead to scientific uncertainty, which, in turn, would justify a precautionary approach. Article 10(6) addresses the situation where, after carrying out the risk assessment, the Party of import concludes that there is still a lack of certainty about the potential adverse effect of LMOs on biological diversity, as well as the situation where there is insufficient information to carry out a risk assessment. Article 5(7) of the SPS Agreement, on the other hand, seems to apply only to the latter situation.

Turning to the second potential aspect of conflict between WTO rules and the Biosafety Protocol, Article 15 of the Protocol requires the importing

[38] *Japan—Measures Affecting the Importation of Apples*, WT/DS245/AB/R, 26 Nov 2003
[39] *Ibid.*, at 179.
[40] *Ibid.*, at 184.

Party to ensure that risk assessments are the basis for reaching decisions on proposed imports of LMOs for intentional release into the environment. The importing Party may carry out the risk assessment—often on the basis of the information provided by the potential exporter—or request the exporter to do so. If the risk assessment is performed by the importer, the cost can be recovered from the potential exporter. Risk assessment is also to be used for LMO-FFPs and is among the necessary information to be provided to the Biosafety Clearing House by a Party that takes a final decision regarding domestic use of LMO-FFPs that may be subject to transboundary movement. A developing country Party or a Party with an economy in transition may, in the absence of a domestic regulatory framework, declare through the Biosafety Clearing House that its decisions on the first import of LMOs-FFP will be taken in accordance with a risk assessment as set out in the Protocol and timeframe for decision-making.

In dealing with the same issue, the SPS Agreement states that SPS measures should be based on an assessment of the risks to human, animal or plant life or health. Members are free to determine the appropriate level of sanitary and phytosanitary protection (ALOP), but in doing so, they should minimise negative trade effects (Art. 5(4)). In dealing with the measures taken to achieve the ALOP, the Agreement obliges Members to ensure that the chosen measures are not more trade-restrictive than required to achieve the ALOP, taking into account technical and economic feasibility. This means that if there is an alternative measure that is equally effective in terms of achieving the appropriate level of protection that is reasonably available from a technical and economic point of view, that measure should be used. The SPS Agreement also embodies the obligation for Members to avoid arbitrary or unjustifiable distinctions in the levels of sanitary and phytosanitary protection they consider to be appropriate in different situations, if such distinctions result in discrimination or disguised restriction on international trade.

Two aspects of the discipline on risk assessment and risk management respectively developed within the Biosafety Protocol and the WTO framework may then be in tension with each other. First of all, the SPS Agreement includes reference to the restrictive trade impact that a sanitary or phytosanitary measure may have and calls for it to be minimised. In the Biosafety Protocol this preoccupation is not addressed. Secondly, while the Protocol and the SPS Agreement contain very similar obligations for the Party of import to ensure that its decision is based on a risk assessment, under the Protocol the importing country does not have to finance the underlying scientific studies to demonstrate that the product to be imported meets the level of risk that it has chosen. It may require the exporter to do so. In the case of the SPS Agreement, on the other hand, it is the importing country that usually bears the costs of the risk assessment.

Turning to the third potential aspect of conflict between WTO rules and the Biosafety Protocol, under Article 26 of the Biosafety Protocol, Parties may take into account, when deciding whether and under which conditions to allow the import of LMOs, 'socio-economic considerations arising from the impact of LMOs on the conservation and sustainable use of biological diversity, especially with regard to the value of biological diversity to indigenous and local communities'. It then appears that the Protocol would allow trade-restrictive measures justified by the fact that imports of LMOs might lead to a loss of cultural traditions, knowledge and practices, particularly among indigenous and local communities. Within the SPS framework, risk assessment can, in specific cases, take into account socio-economic considerations. According to Article 5.3, the following are regarded as relevant economic factors that can be taken into account for the assessment of risks to animal or plant life or health (the same criteria do not apply to the assessment of risks to human health): the potential damage in terms of loss of production or sales in the event of the entry, establishment or spread of a pest or disease; the costs of control or eradication in the territory of the importing Member; and the relative cost-effectiveness of alternative approaches to limiting risks. In conclusion, the kind of considerations which countries are allowed to take into account when assessing and managing the risk vary according to the two legal frameworks—the WTO agreements and the Biosafety Protocol—and the main objectives that they pursue. In an early dispute, a GATT Panel rejected trade restrictions that were solely justified on the grounds that cheap imports would undermine the traditional livelihoods of a certain minority population.[41]

Finally, Article 18 of the Biosafety Protocol sets out rules related to handling, transport, packaging and identification requirements. The rules agreed upon at the first Meeting of the Parties (MOP-1) with reference to LMOs-FFPs seem to mark a step beyond the requirements originally included in Article 18(2)(a): they urge governments to require information on the name of the organism and the transformation event or unique identifier code. Compliance with this requirement is more cumbersome than simply indicating in the accompanying documentation that the shipment 'may contain LMOs', since it implies the establishment of strict systems of identification and segregation. Documentation and labelling requirements relating to food, nutrition claims and concerns, quality and packaging regulations are normally subject to the TBT Agreement. Article 2(1) of the TBT restates the principle of non-discrimination set out in Articles I and III of the GATT 1994, as far as imported products and 'like' products of domestic origin or originating in any other country are concerned. In this context,

[41] *Japanese Measures on Imports of Leather*, GATT Panel Report BISD 31S/94, 2 Mar 1984, 44. On the issue of socio-economic considerations, see: Mackanzie *et al.*, *An Explanatory Guide to the Cartagena Protocol on Biosafety*, IUCN Environmental Policy and Law Paper No. 46 Glaud and Cambridge, (IUCN - The World Conservation Union, 2003), at 238–239.

it seems that the issue to consider is whether a genetically engineered product that sufficiently resembles a conventional product in outward characteristics would be considered substantially equivalent to the conventional product. If this were the case, the two products would therefore be regarded as equally safe and should be treated in the same way.

III. POSSIBLE GM-RELATED TRADE DISPUTES

The Preamble to the Biosafety Protocol states that it shall not be interpreted as implying a change in the rights and obligations of the parties under existing international agreements and that this is not intended to subordinate the Protocol to other international agreements. These provisions may prove not to be very helpful if a conflict arises between countries with divergent interests in the area of biotechnology. Disputes may occur between parties to the Protocol, for instance on the interpretation of the role that the precautionary approach can play in decision-making, or between parties and non-parties on such issues as import restrictions, notification and identification requirements, delays in evaluating requests and authorising imports, or on special conditions attached to the imports, such as mandatory labelling requirements.

WTO law is not very helpful either in this regard, since it does not include a conflict clause (i.e. it does not clarify its relationship with pre-existing or future treaties). Principles of international and customary law will therefore apply (see below).

On the basis of the good faith principle, states are presumed to have negotiated all their treaties in good faith, taking into account all their international law obligations. States' obligations should therefore be read together and be considered cumulative. As a consequence, WTO rules should be interpreted with a view to avoiding conflicts between them and the rules included in other international treaties, including multilateral environmental agreements (MEAs).[42]

Countries that are parties to a multilateral agreement are expected to solve their possible conflicts within the framework of the agreement they have signed and ratified.[43] However, if a party believes that in a specific circumstance its interests are better protected by WTO rules,[44] it may

[42] See Marceau, 'Conflicts of Norms and Conflicts of Jurisdiction, The relationship between the WTO Agreement and MEAs and other Treaties', [2001] *Journal of World Trade* 1081 at 1089 and 1107.

[43] The Biosafety Protocol does not contain specific provisions on the settlement of disputes arising under it, but refers back to the relevant provisions of the CBD (Art 32). Art 27 of the CBD provides for optional recourse to judicial settlement or arbitration, or a conciliation procedure that is mandatory at the request of one of the Parties to a dispute. The newly established Compliance Committee may also provide a forum for the settlement of disputes among Parties to the Protocol.

[44] Assuming that all countries involved in the dispute are Members of the WTO.

invoke those rules. In the case of the Biosafety Protocol, a party can argue that the Protocol clearly states that it shall not be interpreted as implying a change in the rights and obligations of the parties under existing international agreements. A possible conflict *between parties* may therefore be settled under the WTO dispute settlement mechanism. It flows from Article 23 of the Dispute Settlement Understanding (DSU) that any WTO Member can initiate a case in the WTO if it considers that its market access rights have been violated.

On the other hand, if a Party to the Biosafety Protocol has an interest in solving the dispute it has with another Party to the Protocol outside the WTO and according to the discipline laid down in the Protocol, it may invoke two principles of international law aimed at resolving conflicts in the applicable law: *lex posterior derogat legi priori*, meaning that a later expression of state intent should prevail over an earlier one; and *lex specialis derogat legi generali*, meaning that a special rule is more to the point than a general one and it regulates the matter more effectively than general rules do. These principles may apply when two conflicting treaties relate to the same subject matter and involve the same parties. The Biosafety Protocol could be said to reflect both a later and more specific expression of state consent than the WTO Agreements.

Finally, a country could take the option of bringing a GMO-related trade dispute before a WTO panel, but ask for its WTO obligations to be interpreted in the light of the Biosafety Protocol. The WTO legal system is linked to the rest of the international legal order and does not operate in 'clinical isolation' from existing rules of public international law.[45] First, this means that in establishing the relevant facts of a dispute and applying WTO rules to these facts, non-WTO rules may constitute proof of certain factual circumstances. The role that non-WTO rules may play as factual information (though they may not be conclusive)—for instance to prove that some items are widely regarded as dangerous for human health or for the environment or that a specific country is committed to the preservation of a certain natural resource—may be especially important to justify, within a WTO dispute, trade restrictions taken pursuant to MEAs, such as the Biosafety Protocol. Secondly, it means that non-WTO rules can be used to interpret WTO law. When interpreting WTO provisions, all

[45] In its very first report (*United States—Standards for Reformulated and Conventional Gasoline*, WT/DS2/R, 29 Jan 1996), the Appellate Body stated that GATT/WTO law is part of international law and acknowledged that the GATT 'is not to be read in clinical isolation from public international law' (at 17). In the *Korea—Government Procurement* case (*Korea—Measures Affecting Government Procurement*, WT/DS163, 19 June 2000), the panel stated that the WTO judiciary can fall back on general international law. In the US—*Shrimp* case (*United States—Import Prohibition of Certain Shrimp and Shrimp Products*, WT/DS58/AB/R, 12 Oct 1998), the Appellate Body made reference to various international conventions to interpret the term 'natural resources' and relied on a non-WTO treaty as a factual reference in its decision that the new US policy was no longer discriminatory in the sense of the *chapeau* of GATT Art. XX.

international obligations and rights of WTO Members must be taken into account. The existence of the Biosafety Protocol and the fact that the disputing parties have ratified it makes the Protocol a useful tool for interpreting WTO Members' obligations, for instance their right to resort to GATT Article XX (General Exceptions). More importantly, however, the linkages between WTO law and international law may imply that a party may invoke non-WTO rules in defence against a WTO claim. In order to do so, the essential precondition is that both disputing parties are bound by the invoked non-WTO rules, e.g. both should have ratified the MEA that is invoked. According to this approach, if a non-WTO rule is invoked, it will be for the panel and/or the Appellate Body to decide which rule—the WTO or the non-WTO rule—should prevail, in accordance with the relevant conflict rules.

While it is indisputable that the jurisdiction of WTO panels is limited (i.e. claims under WTO covered agreements only), the issue of the applicable law is controversial. Distinguished authors hold opposite views on this crucial issue: some affirm that rules of customary international law, environmental and human rights conventions or bilateral agreements to which disputing parties are bound could be invoked in defence against WTO claims and would be part of the applicable law before the panels and the Appellate Body.[46] Other commentators hold the view that the WTO covered agreements are the only law applicable in WTO dispute resolution, and if panels or the Appellate Body conclude that the WTO provision claimed to have been violated has been superseded by another non-WTO provision, they may decline jurisdiction, since no WTO provision seems applicable to the relations between the parties. According to this view, any other solution would go against the fact that panels and the Appellate Body are prohibited from reaching any conclusion that would constitute an amendment to the WTO or that would add to or diminish rights or obligations under the WTO Agreement.[47]

If a dispute occurs between *a party and a non-party* to the Protocol, the case will most likely be brought to the attention of the WTO Dispute Settlement Body, where, as mentioned before, the country party to the Biosafety Protocol may refer to it as a useful tool both for assessing the facts and for interpreting WTO obligations.

The issue of the relationship between trade rules included in MEAs and WTO rights and obligations, and in particular the issue of which rules would prevail if the trade provisions of an MEA conflicted with WTO

[46] Pauwelyn, *Conflict of Norms in Public International Law—How WTO Law Relates to Other Rules of International Law*, Cambridge Studies in International and Comparative Law, (Cambridge 2003), at ch 8.

[47] Marceau, *supra* n 42.

rules, has been discussed for several years in various international forums, without any conclusive result. A related unsolved issue is the position on non-parties to a multilateral agreement that may be affected by trade rules agreed by parties to a multilateral agreement.

Even though the trade provisions of an MEA have not yet been challenged before a WTO panel, it may be argued that there is a more concrete risk that the compatibility of the Biosafety Protocol and the WTO rules may be questioned. This is because the economic interests involved are huge, because the issue has important health, environmental and ethical implications, and because of the existence of regulatory regionalism (i.e. a deep transatlantic disagreement on the issue).[48] This is probably a field where the decision-making process has to remain with governments (through trade negotiators) and cannot be delegated to the judicial branch of the WTO system.[49] To do otherwise would reinforce the increasingly widespread perception that the dispute settlement system is becoming a surrogate for negotiations, since WTO Members are proving unable both to clarify the WTO Agreements and further to liberalise international trade through negotiations.[50] Moreover, when very sensitive issues are at stake, the use of judicial dispute settlement may be neither constructive nor likely to promote a country's goals.[51]

IV. CONCLUSIONS

Lacking conclusive scientific evidence on the actual or potential impact of agricultural biotechnology on health and on the environment, the GMO debate continues to be vocal and emotional, and countries continue to hold rather divergent views about the risks and opportunities that agro-biotechnology may bring about. Those views are reflected in domestic regulations on GMOs and GM products that vary substantially from one country to another. Divergent rules are hampering international trade in those products and may have indirect negative implications for the trans-boundary movement of conventional agricultural products.

Countries' attitudes on agro-biotechnology depend on many factors, but their positions could be classified into three main categories: (a) the

[48] Isaac, 'The WTO and the Cartagena Protocol: International Policy Coordination or Conflict?', Agriculture, Food and Resources Issues (2003) 4 *Current* 6, 116.

[49] Cottier and Oesch, 'The Paradox of Judicial Review in International Trade Regulation: Towards a Comprehensive Framework', in Cottier and Mavroidis (eds.), *The Role of the Judge in International Trade Regulation: Experience and Lessons from the WTO*, Ann Arbor Mich, Michigan press, (2003), 287.

[50] McRae, 'What is the future of WTO Dispute Settlement?' (2004) 7 *Journal of International Economic Law*, 3.

[51] Esserman and Howse, 'The WTO on Trial', *Foreign Affairs*, Jan/Feb 2003.

position of those countries that consider transgenic products by and large as equivalent to conventional products, have authorised them for production and consumption, and strive to have easy and reliable access to foreign markets; (b) the position of those countries that have mainly adopted the precautionary approach and are imposing strict rules on approval and marketing of GMOs and GM products; and finally (c) the position of those countries that are still in the first phase of evaluating the risks and benefits that agro-biotechnology may imply for them, that are striving to develop comprehensive regulatory frameworks on the issue, and whose main trade-related preoccupation at present is to prevent GM regulations and concerns having negative repercussions on their agriculture and food exports, including those of conventional products. Many developing countries fall into the third category.

While developed countries have established their national frameworks to deal with agro-biotechnology and biosafety focusing primarily on domestic priorities and strategies, most developing countries are doing so under less flexible circumstances. Instead of enjoying the freedom to assess risks and benefits that agro-biotechnology may bring about and act accordingly, developing countries seem to be increasingly expected to set up their national regulatory schemes based on the requests and expectations of their main trade partners.

As a general rule, domestic regulations are scrutinised in the light of multilaterally agreed trade rules if they are likely to have an impact on international trade. The two main legal frameworks applying to trade in agro-biotechnology products are the WTO framework—which is not specific to biotechnology and was actually developed at a time when biotechnology was not an issue—and the Biosafety Protocol which, on the contrary, is a more recent multilateral instrument specifically targeted to GMOs and GM commodities. The two legal frameworks do not seem to be fully consistent with each other. The inability of the international community to decide on how to deal with sectors that are covered by specific multilaterally agreed legal instruments but at the same time are covered by the WTO discipline is *de facto* shifting the responsibility for setting the issue from the decision-making level to the dispute settlement level, from the 'legislative' to the 'judicial' branch of the WTO system.

The lack of scientific certainty *vis-à-vis* agricultural biotechnology and the complexity of the legal framework applying to it—along with the formidable economic interests involved and the links that the sector has with health, environmental, ethical and religious concerns—make the whole issue quite prone to disputes. One was indeed brought to the attention of the WTO dispute settlement body in August 2003.

In the case of trade disputes, it is uncertain which legal arguments may prevail. The relevant WTO provisions may be interpreted in a way supporting the reasons of the claimant, as well as those of the defendant. It is very uncertain which role the Biosafety Protocol may play, since the issue of the function of non-WTO law within the WTO system, including dispute settlement, is still not settled. In any case, the Biosafety Protocol may play a role only within its scope, i.e. living organisms for intentional introduction into the environment, living organisms for contained use, and living organisms intended for direct use as food, feed or for processing, while the products thereof are not included. Whatever way present and possible future disputes are settled, the risk exists that the ruling may be regarded as lacking legitimacy and the WTO panels and Appellate Body as exceeding the scope of their mandate. The ruling may, then, create discontent not only for the country found infringing its WTO obligations, but also for civil society at large.

Biotechnology is a particularly challenging issue for developing countries. Their main concern seems to be finding the appropriate balance between pursuing their development objectives and at the same time complying with their multilaterally agreed obligations. The preoccupations that many developing countries may have as exporters of agricultural and food products must be balanced with their role as producers and their responsibility to improve the quantity and quality of agricultural and food products made available to the population, as well as with their commitment to environmental preservation. Making these goals mutually supportive is not an easy task, especially for countries that still face major difficulties in dealing with the scientific aspects of biotechnology. Additional capacity-building efforts in agro-biotechnology and biosafety therefore seem to be required, including for strengthening developing countries' ability to deal with the international trade dimension of the issue. Efforts may also be needed at the international level to set up a global strategy to deal with new phenomena in a more coherent and systemic manner and avoid ad hoc solutions. Bio-engeneering is a recent phenomenon, but the rapid evolution of science and technology will inevitably lead to new scenarios that may be challenging for all countries, but particularly for developing countries.

Part IV
Biotechnology and Human Rights

11

Agricultural Biotechnology, Food Security and Human Rights

MARY E. FOOTER*

I. INTRODUCTION

CROP GERMPLASM OR plant genetic resources for food and agriculture (PGRFA) constitute the essential raw material that farmers and plant breeders need in order to develop new varieties and thereby to contribute to the sustainable production of nutritious food for humankind. Traditional methods of farming and plant breeding have always faced natural hazards arising from climate change, pests and plant disease. In more recent times, traditional farmers and plant breeders have had to deal with new challenges arising from the modernisation of agriculture, change in diet and increasing population density.

Currently there are about 150 crops that feed most of the world's population, but only 12 of those crops provide 80 per cent of dietary energy. The key ones are rice, wheat, maize, and potato that account for some 60 percent of all staple foods. Rice alone is cultivated in 113 countries around the world and constitutes the main staple for over half the world's population.[1] Given the enormous challenges that farmers and plant breeders face in dealing with the conservation and sustainable management of essential crop germplasm in order to address issues of food security and malnutrition, particularly among some of the world's poorest nations, it

* Professor of International Economic Law, School of Law, University of Nottingham, Member of the ILA Committee on International Law and Biotechnology and the ILA International Trade Law Committee.

[1] 'Rice is Life: Increased, sustainable rice production key to global food security', Food and Agriculture Organisation Newsroom, 12 Feb 2004, available at: www.fao.org/newsroom/en/focus/2004/36887/, cited in Oldham, *Global Status and Trends in Intellectual Property Claims: Genomics, Proteomics and Biotechnology*, (ESRC Centre for Economic and Social Aspects of Genomics (CESAGen), Cardiff, 2004, 41. The UN General Assembly declared 2004 to be the International Year of Rice, UNGA, A/Res/57/162, 16 Dec 2002.

is hardly surprising to find engineered crops being used in countries as far apart as Argentina, South Africa, China, the Philippines and India.[2]

This chapter addresses the nexus between agricultural biotechnology (or agrobiotechnology), food security and human rights. It does so by asking whether the emerging international regime on agricultural biotechnology or agrobiotechnology can contribute in any meaningful way to the pressing issues of food security and the right to adequate and nutritious food. Its main aim is to explore the legal and institutional developments that have been elaborated at the international level and are relevant to the conservation and sustainable use of essential crop-germplasm, including the access and benefit-sharing mechanisms that currently exist or that are being put in place. A further aim is to address some of the broader legal and policy aspects of food security in terms of the adequate supply of basic foodstuffs, which are safe and nutritious for the world's population, and the role that agrobiotechnology may have to play in achieving this.

The chapter proceeds as follows. In section II, attention is focused on establishing some of the socio-economic aspects of the international governance of modern agrobiotechnology by defining agrobiotechnology and its relationship to food security and human rights. Section III addresses some of the flanking policy issues on food security, human rights and ethics that are receiving attention at the FAO and within the UN human rights system. Finally, section IV contains some preliminary conclusions based on the foregoing survey and offers suggestions for further research.

II. SOCIO-ECONOMIC CONCERNS IN THE INTERNATIONAL GOVERNANCE OF MODERN AGROBIOTECHNOLOGY

While the international governance of agricultural biodiversity and agrobiotechnology may appear to be of relatively recent origin, the issues underlying its regulation are not. Food and agricultural production has been with us since the dawn of humanity and so has the problem of feeding the world's population in ways that are consistent with the principles of sustainable development. If the world's food production is to increase in an environmentally sustainable fashion there is also a need to increase agricultural productivity, particularly in developing countries. While the generation of better seeds, in the form of improved crop germplasm, can be realised by expanding traditional methods of conservation and breeding, including the means of seed exchange and the development of

[2] Larson, *Trade and Development Dimension of US International Biotechnology Policy*, available at: www.usinfo.state.gov/journals/ites/0903/ijee/larson.htm.

conventional hybrids, agrobiotechnology may also have something to contribute. But what do we mean exactly when we talk about agrobiotechnology? What is the international governance structure for modern agrobiotechnology and how are cross-cutting issues of food security and the right to adequate and nutritious food being addressed within that structure?

(a) Defining Agrobiotechnology and Agrobiodiversity in their Relationship to Food Security and Human Rights

Agrobiotechnology is the application of new and promising scientific processes and techniques in the field of biotechnology[3] to crop germplasm and the novel use of plants, animals and micro-organisms for the improvement of crops and livestock in terms of yield and quality.[4] Some of the technologies currently in use in the field of agrobiotechnology include: transgenic techniques, i.e. those techniques whereby the genes of one species are inserted into another in order to develop a new plant variety; tissue culture[5] in plant breeding in order to improve productivity of a plant species;[6] techniques like marker-assisted breeding and gene sequencing that use molecular markers[7] in plants which are identifiable DNA sequences; bio-informatics[8] in order to speed up or to supplement

[3] The FAO defines biotechnology broadly as: 1. 'Any technological application that uses biological systems, living organisms, or derivatives thereof, to make or modify products or processes for specific use' (Convention on Biological Diversity). 2. 'Interpreted in a narrow sense . . . a range of different molecular technologies such as gene manipulation and gene transfer, DNA typing and cloning of plants and animals' (FAO's statement on biotechnology): *Glossary of Biotechnology for Food and Agriculture: a Revised and Augmented Edition of the Glossary of Biotechnology and Genetic Engineering* (hereinafter *FAO Glossary*), Research and Technology Paper 9, Rome, 2001, available at: http://www.fao.org/biotech/index_glossary.asp.

[4] Borlaug, 'Agriculture and Peace: The Role of Science and Technology in the 21st Century', Fourth U Thant Distinguished Lecture, United Nations University, Tokyo, 1 Oct 2002, available at: http://www.ias.unu.edu/binaries/BorlaugSpeech.pdf.

[5] Tissue culture is 'the *in vitro* culture of cells, tissues or organs in a nutrient medium under sterile conditions'; see *FAO Glossary*, *supra* n 3. It is a technique that is often used for micropropagation and for breeding purposes.

[6] Adeyemo, 'Biotechnology, in Agriculture', *Nigeria Daily Times*, 24 Oct 2002.

[7] Molecular markers are 'genetic markers' according to the *FAO Glossary*, *supra* n. 3. Essentially they comprise DNA sequences that can be associated or identified with a specific trait in a gene, e.g. tolerance to cold.

[8] Bio-informatics is: 'the use and organization of information of biological interest. In particular, concerned with organizing bio-molecular databases (particularly DNA, sequences), utilizing computers for analysing this information, and integrating information from disparate biological sources': *Glossary*, *supra* n. 3. It can also be defined as 'the relationship between genomics, proteomics and biotechnology and information technology', being 'the computer-based analysis of biological materials'; see Oldham, *supra* n. 1, 9 and 'Bio-informatics for Biodiversity' (2000) 289 *Science*, No. 5488.

conventional breeding; and bio-fortification[9] in order to develop staple crops that are rich in micronutrients. Sometimes innovative techniques are employed such as 'embryo rescue',[10] which has been used for the purposes of cross-breeding in West African rice-production in order to achieve earlier maturity, improved pest resistance, tolerance to drought and acid soils and greater height in the fields thereby making it easier for farmers to harvest by hand.[11]

Agrobiotechnologies are being used to develop low-cost disease-free PGRFA for crops such as cassava, banana and potato and to create new tools for the diagnosis and treatment of plant and animal diseases and for the measurement and conservation of genetic resources. Animal feeds and feeding practices are also being changed by agrobiotechnology in order to improve animal nutrition and to reduce environmental waste and for the production of vaccines against animal diseases.[12] Thus, it is becoming widely recognised that agrobiotechnology has the potential to reduce or eliminate major constraints to crop productivity, to improve animal welfare and to enhance food quality on a global scale.

One of the broadest definitions of agricultural biodiversity or agrobiodiversity that was endorsed by the FAO more than a decade ago is the following: 'the variety and variability of animals, plants, and micro-organisms on earth that are important to food and agriculture which result from the interaction between the environment, genetic resources and the management systems and practices used by people'. It is broad because encompassed within that definition are 'not only genetic, species and agro-ecosystem diversity and the different ways land and water resources are used for production, but also cultural diversity, which influences human interactions at all levels'. Additionally, 'it comprises the diversity of genetic resources (varieties, breeds, etc.) and species used directly or indirectly for food and agriculture (including, in the FAO definition, crops, livestock, forestry and fisheries) for the production of food, fodder, fibre, fuel and pharmaceuticals, the diversity of species that support production (soil biota, pollinators, predators, etc.) and those in the wider environment that support agro-ecosystems (agricultural, pastoral, forest

[9] Bio-fortification is 'the development of nutritionally enhanced foods'; see FAO, *The State of Food and Agriculture 2003–2004* (Rome, 2004) [hereinafter *State of Food and Agriculture*], 17.

[10] Embryo rescue is understood to mean '[a] sequence of tissue culture techniques utilised to enable a fertilised immature embryo resulting from an interspecific cross to continue growth and development, until it can be regenerated into an adult plant'; see *FAO Glossary*, *supra* n. 3.

[11] For a report on the use of embryo rescue by the West African Rice Development Association (WARDA), an international agricultural research centre or IARC, located in Côte d'Ivoire, see Keeley, *Democratizing Biotechnology: An Overview* in the series *Democratizing Biotechnology: Genetically Modified Crops in Developing Countries*, Briefing Paper 10 (Brighton, 2003); available at: www.ids.ac.uk/biotech.

[12] See *State of Food and Agriculture 2003–2004, supra* n. 9, at 9.

and aquatic), as well as the diversity of the agro-ecosystems themselves'.[13]

The concept of food security escapes easy definition. At various points over the past 30 years food security has taken on different meanings depending upon where the policy debate was taking place. In the mid-1970s policy-makers emphasised the availability of food and its supply at the global level. A decade later the emphasis had shifted to access to food and the importance of wellbeing that food security brings with it. In the 1990s food security formed part of the overall focus of policy-makers on the alleviation of poverty.[14]

In the human rights context the right to adequate food was taken up initially in Article 25 of the 1949 Universal Declaration of Human Rights (UDHR),[15] which states that 'everyone has the right to a standard of living adequate for the health and well-being of himself and of his family'. It is repeated almost verbatim in Article 11 of the 1966 Covenant on Economic, Social and Cultural Rights (ICESCR),[16] as follows: '[t]he States Parties to the present Covenant recognize the right of everyone to an adequate standard of living for himself and his family'.[17] While the term 'adequate standard of living' is not in any way defined its meaning can be understood from the context within which it is found in both of these international instruments, as including 'food, clothing, housing and medical care and necessary social services' (Article 25 UDHR) and 'adequate food, clothing and housing' (Article 11 ICESCR).[18] For more than a decade the term 'adequate food' has been considered as part of the 'minimum standard of nutrition and other basic necessities'.[19]

13 *Cultivating our Futures:* Background Paper 1: 'Agricultural Biodiversity', prepared for the FAO/Netherlands Conference on 'The Multifunctional Character of Agriculture and Land', 12–17 Sept 1990, Maastricht, The Netherlands, available at: www.fao.org/documents/show_cdr.asp?url_file=/docrep/x2775e/X2775E03.htm.

14 Scoones, *Agricultural Biotechnology and Food Security: Exploring the Debate*, IDS Working Paper (Brighton, 2002).

15 Universal Declaration of Human Rights, adopted 10 Dec 1948, GA Res. 217A (III), UN GAOR, 3rd. Sess, pt. 1, UN Doc. A/810 (1948) (hereinafter UDHR).

16 International Covenant on Economic, Social and Cultural Rights, adopted and open for signature, ratification and accession by GA Res. 2200A (XXI) of 16 Dec 1966, 21 UN GAOR Supp. (No. 16) at 49, UN Doc. A/6316 (1966), (1967) 6 ILM 360, entered into force 3 Jan 1976, 999 UNTS 3 (hereinafter ICESCR).

17 Similarly, Art 27 of the Convention on the Rights of the Child, concluded 20 Nov 1989, (1989) 28 ILM 1456, entered into force 1 Sept 1991, requires that: 'States Parties recognize the right of every child to a standard of living adequate for the child's physical, mental, spiritual, moral and social development'.

18 Eide, 'The Right to an Adequate Standard of Living including the Right to Food' in Eide, Krause and Rosas (eds.), *Economic, Social and Cultural Rights: a Textbook* (2nd rev edn., Dordrecht, 2001), 133, at 133 f.

19 *Ibid*, at 134. See also Oshaug and Eide, 'The Long Process of Giving Content to an Economic, Social and Cultural Rights: Twenty-five Years with the Case of the Right to Adequate Food' in Bergsmo (ed.) *Human Rights and Criminal Justice for the Downtrodden: Essays in Honour of Asbjørn Eide* (Leiden, 2003), 325 ff.

(b) Institutional Governance of Agrobiotechnology and its Relationship to Food Security

In this section our attention is focused on issues of institutional governance in the field of agrobiotechnology and its relationship to food security issues, with a view to examining the relevant international instruments which set out the rights or obligations of states to regulate agrobiotechnology and other institutional arrangements that exist in support thereof. We are principally concerned with the UN Convention on Biological Diversity (CBD)[20] and the FAO International Treaty on Plant Genetic Resources for Food and Agriculture (ITPGRFA or 'Seed Treaty')[21] in the matter of access to PGRFA, or crop germplasm as they relate to food security.

Besides these two major treaties, there are other institutional arrangements at work at the international level, including other instruments and processes, which may or may not be binding on their addresses and may cover such matters as policy guidelines. They include inter alia Chapter 16 of *Agenda 21*,[22] the *Plan of Implementation of the World Summit on Sustainable Development*,[23] the 1996 *World Food Summit Declaration and Plan of Action*[24] and the *Declaration of the World Food Summit: Five Years Later*,[25] all of which have been formulated within the fields of sustainable development and food agriculture, mostly under the auspices of the FAO and are relevant to this discussion.

As part of the aspirations set out in the *Declaration of the World Food Summit: Five Years Later* an Intergovernmental Working Group for the Elaboration of a Set of Voluntary Guidelines to Support the Progressive Realization of the Right to Adequate Food in the Context of National Food Security (IGWG) was established by a decision of the FAO Council in

[20] United Nations Convention on Biological Diversity, done at Nairobi, 5 June 1992, (1992) 31 ILM 818, entered into force 29 Dec 1993 (hereinafter CBD).

[21] International Treaty on Plant Genetic Resources for Food and Agriculture adopted on 3 Nov 2001 by Res. 3/01, FAO Conference, 31st Sess. (Rome, 2–13 Nov 2001), entered into force 29 June 2004; available at: www.fao.org/waicent/faoinfo/agricult/cgrfa/IU.html (hereinafter ITPGRFA or 'Seed Treaty').

[22] *Agenda 21*, Ch 16, in Robinson (ed.) *Agenda 21: Earth's Action Plan* (New York, 1993), also available at: www.un.org/esa/sustdev/agenda21text.htm.

[23] *Report of the World Summit on Sustainable Development*, Res. 2, 17th Plenary Meeting (Johannesburg, South Africa, 26 Aug–4 Sep 2002), A/CONF.199/20, *Plan of Implementation*, as Annex to the Report, para. 40, available at: www.johannesburgsummit.org.

[24] Rome Declaration on World Food Security and World Food Summit Plan of Action, adopted at the *World Food Summit*, (Rome, 13–17 Nov 1996), available at: www.fao.org/DOCREP/003/W3613E/W3613E00.HTM.

[25] *Declaration of the World Food Summit: Five Years Later*, Appendix to the *Report of the World Food Summit: Five Years Later*, (Rome, 10–13 June 2002), available at: www.fao.org/DOCREP/MEETING/005/Y7106E/Y7106E09.htm#TopOfPage.

November 2002,[26] and its guidelines on the right to food (the 'Right to Food Guidelines') were formally adopted by the FAO Committee on World Food Security and the FAO Council barely two years later.[27]

In the related field of human rights and ethics, work has been continuing under the auspices of the FAO on developing a Code of Conduct on Biotechnology,[28] and a Panel of Eminent Experts in Ethics on Food and Agriculture[29] was established at the FAO in 2000 in order to advise FAO Members on ethical issues related to agrobiotechnology in food and agriculture. The Panel of Eminent Experts has been working in close collaboration with the UN Special Rapporteur on the Right to Food[30] on matters of agrobiotechnology and food security.

It is also recognised that food safety is of central concern in any discussion concerning the role of modern biotechnology in food and agriculture and forms part of the broader concept of food security but food safety is not one of the primary objectives of the regulatory instruments addressed in this chapter.[31] Therefore, this section does not address such matters as the legal regulation of the transboundary movement of genetically modified organisms (GMOs), referred to as living modified organisms (LMOs)

26 *Establishment of an Intergovernmental Working Group for the Elaboration of a Set of Voluntary Guidelines to Support the Progressive Realization of the Right to Adequate Food in the Context of National Food Security*, Report of the FAO Council, 123rd Sess. (Rome, 28 Oct-1 Nov 2002), Doc. CL 132/22 (hereinafter IGWG). The IGWG was established pursuant to the Declaration adopted by the *World Food Summit: Five Years Later*, para 10.

27 *Report of the Chair of the Committee on World Food Security* (CFS), 30th Sess. (Rome, 20–23 Sept 2004), to the FAO Council, 27th Sess. (Rome 22–27 Nov 2004), Doc. CL 127/10-Sup. 1, including the Report of the IGWG to the CFS, 23 Sept 2004. Annex I to the aforementioned Report of the Chair of the IGWG contains the set of Voluntary Guidelines to Support the Progressive Realization of the Right to Adequate Food in the Context of National Food Security (hereinafter Right to Food Guidelines), which are also available as Doc. IGWG RTFG 4/Rep 1.

28 Request for preparation of a draft Code of Conduct on Biotechnology as it relates to Genetic Resources for Food and Agriculture, Commission on Plant Genetic Resources (CPGR), 4th Reg. Sess. (Rome, 19–23 Apr 1991), Item 10, *Biotechnology and plant genetic resources: and elements of a Code of Conduct for Biotechnology* (hereinafter draft Code of Conduct on Biotechnology), available at: www.fao.org/ag/cgrfa/biocode.htm.

29 FAO Panel of Eminent Experts in Ethics on Food and Agriculture, Report of FAO Director General to the FAO Conference, 30th Sess. (Rome, 12–23 Nov 1999), C 99/INF/22; the Director General established the Panel of Eminent Experts pursuant to Art VI:4 FAO Constitution and Rule XXXV of the General Rules of the Organisation, for a period of four years, commencing on 1 Jan 2000; for details see www.fao.org/ethics/exp_en.htm.

30 The decision to appoint a Special Rapporteur on the Right to Food was taken by the Commission on Human Rights, Resolution 2000/10, adopted at its 52nd Sess. (17 Apr 2000); for details, including the Special Rapporteur's mandate and subsequent reports to the Commission, see www.ohchr.org/english/issues/food/index.htm.

31 See, however, Mackenzie, *Globalisation and the International Governance of Modern Biotechnology: The International Regulation of Modern Biotechnology*, paper prepared for the project on *Globalisation and Poverty Programme*, Research Project R7626, Department for International Development (UK, 2003), available at www.gapresearch.org.

under the Cartagena Protocol on Biosafety (CPB),[32] the legal regime for pest control, disease and contamination in plants as provided for under the International Plant Protection Convention (IPPC),[33] nor the work of the FAO/WHO *Codex Alimentarius* Commission in elaborating standards, general principles, guidelines and recommended codes of practice in relation to food safety.[34]

Equally, the socio-economic aspects of regulating agrobiotechnology draw on a diverse cross-section of rules and standards promulgated in different *fora,* and legal and institutional developments in one forum can significantly affect the content of rules that are developed in another forum. However, disciplines relating to the international trade in food and agricultural products under the General Agreement on Tariffs and Trade or GATT 1994, the Agreement on Agriculture and the related Marrakesh Ministerial Decisions on *Measures Concerning the Possible Negative Effects of the Reform Programme on Least-Developed and Net-Food Importing Developing Countries* or *NFIDC Decision,*[35] while relevant to discussions on access and distribution of food supplies in the context of food security, including food aid, are not dealt with here. Similarly, this chapter does not cover the interface of the GATT 1994 or the Agreement on Agriculture with domestic regulatory systems involving sanitary and phytosanitary measures and technical standards under the WTO Agreements on Sanitary and Phytosanitary Measures (SPS) and on Technical Barriers to Trade (TBT) respectively, or with the intellectual property aspects of agrobiotechnology under the Agreement on Trade-Related Aspects of Intellectual Property Rights (TRIPs).[36]

[32] Cartagena Protocol on Biosafety to the Convention on Biological Diversity, adopted at Montreal on 29 Jan 2000, (2000) 39 ILM 1027, entered into force 11 Sept 2003 (hereinafter CPB).

[33] International Plant Protection Convention, adopted by FAO Conference, 6th Sess. (Rome, 6 Dec 1951), subsequently amended in 1979, entered into force 1991, later amendment of Nov 1997 not yet in force. The extant text is reproduced in a 1992 document available at www.ippc.int/servlet/CDSServlet?status=ND0zNzk1OSY2PWVuJjMzPSomMzc9a29z.

[34] For a comprehensive analysis of the ongoing process of standard-setting and rule-making by inter alia the FAO/WHO, *Codex Alimentarius* Commission (CAC) in the field of food safety see *Ad Hoc* Group on Food Safety, *Overview and Compendium of International Organisations with Food Safety Activities*, OECD, 27–28 May 2000, SG/ADHOC/FS(2000)4/FINAL and for a briefing, Suppan, *Consumers International's Decision-Making in the Global Market. Codex Briefing Paper* (Aug 2004), available at: www.tradeobservatory.org/library.cfm?RefID=36988.

[35] Ministerial Decision on Measures Concerning the Possible Negative Effects of the Reform Programme on Least-Developed and Net-Food Importing Developing Countries (the NFIDC Decision). See Footer, 'Application of the GATT, GATS and WTO Agreements to Agricultural Trade', (2001) 4 *ERA Forum* 94 at 100–101; Sensi and Werksman, 'Inside the Green Box: 'Multifunctional Agriculture and the Protection of the Environment' in McMahon (ed.) *Trade & Agriculture: Negotiating a New Agreement* (London, 2001), 463, at 480 f.

[36] However, see Footer, 'Intellectual Property and Agrobiodiversity: Towards Private Ownership of the Genetic Commons' [1999] *Yearbook of International Environmental Law,* 48 ff.; Dutfield, *Intellectual Property, Biogenetic Resources and Traditional Knowledge* (London, 2004); Pavoni, 'Accesso alle risorse fitogenetiche e diritti di proprietà intellecttuale dopo il trattato della FAO del 2001' [2003] *La Comunità Internazionale,* 369 ff.

Turning first to the institutional governance of phytogenetic resources under the CBD and the Seed Treaty, an important aspect of both framework agreements is the institutional arrangements that are foreseen in both access and benefit sharing of those resources. However, the Seed Treaty goes further than the CBD in proposing the creation of a multilateral exchange system in order to facilitate access to a range of crop plant genera and species of special interest to food security. It also specifically takes up farmers' rights for the first time in a legally binding instrument and regulates the use of extensive *ex situ* collections of PGRFA, held in national and international institutions and research centres across the globe.[37] The remainder of this section focuses on analysing the scope and structure of these two major instruments and their role in institutional governance of PGRFA, in terms of their approaches towards access and equitable sharing of the benefits of the conservation, management and utilisation of those resources.

(1) 1992 Convention on Biological Diversity (CBD)

The CBD recognises the fundamental premise of the permanent sovereignty of states over their biological resources. Its entry into force in 1993 has led to an increase in governmental authority involved in the regulation of access to genetic resources within the national jurisdictions of Parties to the Convention. However, as stated in its objectives any benefits arising out of the utilisation of genetic resources must be shared on a fair and equitable basis,[38] with appropriate guarantees on access, transfer of technology and funding, i.e. states are under an obligation to 'facilitate' access to genetic resources.

Thus, in theory the Convention provides a framework for the implementation of access to *all* genetic resources,[39] except human genetic resources and *ex situ* crop germplasm (discussed hereunder) acquired subsequent to its entry into force. The framework provisions in the CBD also make access subject to mutually agreed terms and the equitable sharing of benefits as well as the prior informed consent of the Parties.[40] Important too is the recognition that the CBD gives to the utilisation of

[37] See Footer and Opuku Awuku, 'Sustainable Agricultural Resources and Food Security: the Seed Treaty and Equitable Benefit Sharing' in Cordonier Segger and Weeramantry (eds.), *Sustainable Justice: Integrating Economic, Social and Environmental Law* (Leiden-Boston Mass, 2005), 241, at 247 ff.

[38] The relevant part of the objectives is set out in Art 1, CBD, *supra* n. 20, which states: 'fair and equitable sharing of the benefits arising out of the utilization of genetic resources, including by appropriate access to genetic resources and by appropriate transfer of relevant technologies, taking into account all rights over those resources and to technologies, and by appropriate funding'.

[39] Art15 *Ibid.*

[40] Art 15 *ibid.*

knowledge, innovations and the practices of indigenous and local communities embodying traditional lifestyles relevant for the conservation and sustainable use of biodiversity.[41] The provisions on facilitated access are also linked to others on access to and transfer of technology,[42] exchange of information,[43] technical and scientific cooperation,[44] and the handling of biotechnology and distribution of its benefits.[45]

The CBD seeks to strike a balance between a state's authority to regulate access to genetic resources and its obligation to facilitate access by others to those genetic resources.[46] In fact, states parties to the CBD enjoy a wide discretion on how to regulate access and the utilisation of those resources nationally, which does not exclude the possibility of engaging in regional measures of cooperation if they so choose. Not surprisingly, while somewhat slow, there has been a steady progression in the development of national and regional laws on access to genetic resources and benefit–sharing around the world.[47] The type of regulation that currently exists covers a broad spectrum of statutory and contractual rights (for example bioprospecting arrangements between governments and individual entities). The scope of national and regional access legislation may also extend to the regulation of traditional knowledge, including the prior consent of local and indigenous communities for access to genetic resources and their subsequent utilisation.[48]

[41] Art 8(j) *ibid.*, which states that each contracting party shall, as far as possible and as appropriate: '[s]ubject to its national legislation, respect, preserve and maintain knowledge, innovations and practices of indigenous and local communities embodying traditional lifestyles relevant for the conservation and sustainable use of biological diversity and . . . encourage the equitable sharing of the benefits arising from the utilization of such knowledge, innovations and practices'.

[42] Art 16 *ibid.*

[43] Art 17 *ibid.*

[44] Art 18 *ibid.*

[45] Art 19 (1) and (2), *ibid.*

[46] Cabrera and Garforth, 'Global Access, Local Benefits: An International Access and Benefit-Sharing Regime?' in Cordonier Segger and Weeramantry, *supra* n. 37, 219, at 221.

[47] For a brief survey of the current state of play with respect to national and regional regimes for access and benefit-sharing, see *ibid*, at 221 f. and Secretariat for the Convention on Biological Diversity, *International Regime on Access and Benefit-sharing: Proposals for an international regime on access and benefit-sharing*, Note by the Executive Secretary, to the Open-ended Inter-sessional Meeting on the Multi-year Programme of Work for the Conference of the Parties up to 2010, Montreal 17–20 Mar 2003, UNEP/CBD/MYPOW/6.

[48] See the extensive database that is currently being built up on national access and benefit-sharing schemes on the CBD's website, available at: www.biodiv.org/programmes/socio-eco/benefit/measures.aspx and which currently lists 49 measures, five of which are regional. Two examples in the latter category, both of which also deal with the rights of local and indigenous communities, include the *African Model Legislation for the Protection of the Rights of Local Communities, Farmers, Breeders and for the Regulation of Access to Biological Resources*, which was adopted by the African Union in 1998 and the Andean Pact Decision 391 on *Common Regime on Access to Genetic Resources* of 1996 which is a legislative instrument, supplemented by its *Decision 523 Estrategia regional de biodiversidad para los paises del tropico andino* of 2002, which sets out a strategy for implementation; see further Cabrera and Garforth, *supra* n. 46, at 223.

However, national access and benefit–sharing legislation does not cover *ex situ*[49] collections of genetic resources that were acquired before the entry into force of the CBD and are consequently placed beyond the jurisdictional scope of the Convention.[50] This is particularly significant for a large number of collections of plant germplasm, including the crop germplasm that is held in national agricultural research centres or NARCs, agricultural research stations, marine biological institutes, botanical gardens and so forth.

When it comes to facilitating access to genetic resources the CBD process has addressed the equitable sharing of benefits arising out of the utilisation of genetic resources in a number of ways. First, at its Fourth Meeting the Conference of the Parties (COP) to the CBD established a Panel of Experts,[51] appointed by governments but including representatives from the private and public sectors and indigenous and local communities, in order to explore all the options for access and benefit-sharing on mutually agreed terms including principles, guidelines, and codes of conduct of best practices for access and benefit-sharing arrangements.

Some of the Panel of Experts' findings in its various reports noted that: (1) national access legislation for access and benefit–sharing of plant genetic resources for food and agriculture should take into account and allow for the development of a multilateral system for facilitating access and benefit-sharing of PGRFA; (2) intellectual property rights might influence access and benefit-sharing arrangements and play a role in providing incentives for users to seek prior informed consent; (3) national access legislation often affords recognition to the rights of indigenous and local communities in deciding on access to, and utilisation of, resources on their territories, as well as to the knowledge, innovations and practices derived therefrom; and (4) many countries are adopting *sui generis* legislation that articulates those rights and makes further provisions for their protection.[52] This latter aspect is important because enhanced property rights under the CBD raise specific issues for indigenous and local communities concerning customary laws, which govern custodianship in those communities and the use and transmission of traditional knowledge and, which largely do not conform to traditional property and intellectual property regimes in the Western sense.

[49] In accordance with Art 2, *CBD, supra* n. 20, '*ex situ* conservation' means 'the conservation of components of biological diversity outside their natural habitats'.

[50] Art 15(3) *ibid*.

[51] 4th Meeting of the Conference of the Parties (COP) to the CBD (COP-4), Decision IV/8 —Access and Benefit-sharing, CBD Doc. UNEP/CBD/COP/4, available at: www.biodiv.org/cop4/pdf/cop4_decisions_e.pdf.

[52] *Report of the Panel of Experts on Access and Benefit-Sharing*, 5th Meeting of the COP of the CBD (COP-5), CBD Doc. UNEP/CB/COP/5/8. For reports of the meetings of the Panel of Experts, see www.biodiv.org/ISOC/index.html.

Secondly, the COP also established an *Ad Hoc* Open-ended Working Group[53] that was tasked with developing guidelines on inter alia the terms for prior informed consent and access to genetic resources on mutually agreed terms; the roles, responsibilities and participation of stakeholders; relevant aspects of *in situ* and *ex situ* conservation and sustainable use of genetic resources; together with mechanisms for benefit-sharing, for example through technology transfer and joint research and development. It was also charged with devising means to ensure the respect for preservation and maintenance of knowledge, innovations and the practices of indigenous and local communities that embody traditional lifestyles and that are relevant for the conservation and sustainable use of biological diversity, taking into account the work of the World Intellectual Property Organisation (WIPO) on intellectual property rights issues in the field of genetic resources.[54] A major achievement of the *Ad Hoc* Open-ended Working Group was the adoption of the Bonn Guidelines[55] on access to genetic resources and the fair and equitable sharing of the benefits arising from their utilisation at the Sixth Conference of the Parties, held in The Hague, 7–19 April 2002.[56] The Bonn Guidelines reflect all of the foregoing aspects on access and benefit–sharing of genetic resources although they have come in for criticism from some quarters, even going so far as to describe the CBD-endorsed voluntary guidelines as a global enclosure system rather than an honest attempt to create a set of guidelines on access and benefit-sharing.[57]

Since then the COP has considered other complementary approaches to the Bonn Guidelines in order to assist Parties with the implementation of the access and benefit-sharing provisions in the CBD and has adopted a

[53] At the 5th meeting of the Conference of the Parties to the CBD (COP-5), the decision was taken to establish an *Ad Hoc* Open-ended Working Group with the mandate to develop guidelines and other approaches on access to genetic resources and benefit-sharing, for submission to the 6th meeting of the Parties to the CBD (COP-6) and to assist Parties and stakeholders in addressing various elements such as prior informed consent, relevant aspects of *in situ* and *ex situ* conservation, mechanisms for benefit-sharing and so on. See Decision V/8—Access to genetic resources, *CBD* Doc. UNEP/CBD/COP/5, available at: www.biodiv.org/cop4/pdf/cop4_decisions_e.pdf.

[54] In 2000, the WIPO General Assembly established the Intergovernmental Committee(IGC) on Intellectual Property and Genetic Resources, Traditional Knowledge and Folklore (the IGC) at its 26th (12th Extraordinary) Sess. (Geneva, 25 Sept–3 Oct 2000), WO/GA/26/6 (25 Aug 2000). It has met in seven separate sessions so far, most recently from 1–5 Nov 2004, WIPO/GRTKF/IC/7, where governments appeared divided about the future work of the IGC.

[55] The meeting of the Access and Benefit-sharing Working Group, at which the Guidelines on Access to Genetic Resources and Benefit Sharing were formulated, was held in Bonn, Germany from 22–26 Oct 2001; UNEP/CBD/WG/AB/1/3 (hereinafter the Bonn Guidelines).

[56] 6th meeting of the Conference of the Parties to the CBD (COP-6) subsequently adopted the Bonn Guidelines in its Decision VI/24–Access and Benefit-sharing as related to genetic resources (Art 15); available at: www.biodiv.org/decisions/default.aspx?m=cop-06&d=24.

[57] See for example the *Communiqué* (the ETC. group, Canada), Issue 83, Jan/Feb 2004.

decision on the role of intellectual property rights in access and benefit-sharing arrangements.[58] On this last point, the COP has invited the Contracting Parties and other governments to encourage the disclosure of the country of origin of genetic resources and of related traditional knowledge, innovations and practices relevant to the conservation and sustainable use of biological diversity in applications for intellectual property rights, where the subject matter of the application concerns or makes use of genetic resources and/or traditional knowledge in its development.[59]

The *Ad Hoc* Open-ended Working Group on Access and Benefit-Sharing reported to the Seventh Conference of the Parties, held in Kuala Lumpur, Malaysia, 9–20 February 2004,[60] whereupon the Parties established the terms of reference for the negotiation of an international regime on access and benefit-sharing, or ABS, by the Working Group in collaboration with the Working Group on Article 8(j) CBD and related provisions. The terms of reference for the negotiation of an international regime on ABS, as set out in Decision VII/19, include a wide range of elements relating to inter alia research, ethics, benefit-sharing, transboundary genetic resources, respect for the human rights of indigenous peoples and local communities, consent, certification and development goals, that are intended to provide the foundation for the development of an international regime. Decision VII/19 also breaks new ground in terms of institutional governance by promoting an institutionalised process, which is both deliberative and participatory, in order to elaborate an international regime that involves not only the Parties to the CBD but also delegates of indigenous peoples and local communities, the scientific community, industry and civil society organisations.[61] The

58 *The role of intellectual property rights in access and benefit-sharing arrangements, including national and regional experiences*, Second meeting of the *Ad Hoc* Open-ended Working Group on Access and Benefit-Sharing (ABSWG 2), Item 6 of the provisional agenda (Montreal, 1–5 Dec 2003), UNEP/CBD/WG-ABS/2/3, available at: www.biodiv.org/programmes/socio-eco/benefit/regime.asp.

59 See for a parallel development in two other *fora*: WIPO's Intergovernmental Committee on Intellectual Property and Genetic Resources, Traditional Knowledge and Folklore, 4th Sess. (9–17 Dec 2002), WIPO/GRTFK/EC/4/1, available at: www.wipo.int/documents/en/meetings/2002/igc/pdf/grtkf_ic_4_11.pdf; and the WTO TRIPs Council on the issue of the relationship between the TRIPs Agreement, the CBD and the protection of traditional knowledge, with disclosure as evidence of prior informed consent; available at: www.wto.org/english/tratop_e/trips_e/art27_3b_e.htm#documents.

60 7th meeting of the Conference of the Parties to the COP to the CBD (COP-7), whereupon COP-7 adopted Decision VII/19—Access and benefit sharing as related to genetic resources (Art 15), and tasked the *Ad Hoc* Working Group with elaborating an international regime on access and benefit sharing of genetic resources, with terms of reference, as set out in the Annex to its decision, available at: http://www.biodiv.org/decisions/default.aspx?m=COP-07&id=7756&lg=0.

61 For fuller details see the Annex to section D of *ibid.*

Ad Hoc Open-ended Working Group on Access and Benefit-sharing has recently met and developed a matrix in order to identify and analyse existing gaps in international instruments and to indicate ways in which they might be addressed.[62]

(2) 2001 International Treaty on Plant Genetic Resources for Food and Agriculture (ITPGRFA)

The ITPGRFA or Seed Treaty,[63] which entered into force in June 2004, is the successor to a non-binding international instrument, the 'International Undertaking' that was adopted as a 1983 FAO Conference Resolution.[64] A fundamental revision of the International Undertaking took place from the early 1990s onwards,[65] in an attempt to harmonise it with the CBD and possibly to add it as a protocol to that treaty, in the same way as the CPB.[66]

Subsequently the (re-)negotiation of the International Undertaking became intertwined with the CBD, beginning with Resolution 3 of the 1992 Nairobi Conference, which addressed the interrelationship between the CBD and the promotion of sustainable agriculture.[67] Resolution 3 foresaw the strengthening of the FAO Global System for the Conservation and Utilisation of Plant Genetic Resources for Food and Agriculture (the FAO Global System),[68] the cornerstone of which would be a new agreement that needed to address two outstanding matters. The first was the question of access to *ex situ* collections not acquired in accordance with the CBD and the second was farmers' rights. The 1993 FAO Conference provided the framework for the revision of the International Undertaking

[62] Third meeting of the *Ad Hoc* Open-ended Working Group on Access and Benefit-Sharing (ABSWG 3), (Bangkok, 14–18 Feb 2005), available at: www.biodiv.org/meetings/abswg-03/default.shtml.

[63] ITPGRFA, *supra* n. 21.

[64] FAO, International Undertaking on Plant Genetic Resources (International Undertaking, or IU) was adopted by Res. 8/83, FAO Conference, 22nd Sess. (Rome, 5–23 Nov 1983).

[65] See Footer, *supra* n. 36, at 62 ff. for an overview of these developments.

[66] CPB, *supra* n. 32.

[67] Res. 3 of the Nairobi Conference for the Adoption of the Agreed Text of the Convention on Biological Diversity, and relating to 'The Interrelationship between the Convention on Biological Diversity and the Promotion of Sustainable Agriculture' (22 May 1992), (1992) 31 ILM 846.

[68] The FAO Global System for the Conservation and Utilisation of Plant Genetic Resources for Food and Agriculture was established by FAO Res. C 9/83, FAO Conference, 22nd Sess. (Rome, 5–23 Nov 1983) (hereinafter the 'FAO Global System'). It was originally intended that the FAO Global System should provide an intergovernmental framework for the safe conservation, promotion of unrestricted availability and sustainable utilisation of PGRFA for present and future generations. See Esquinas-Alcazar, 'The Global System on Plant Genetic Resources' [1993] *RECIEL* 152.

along these lines[69] and led to a series of negotiations under the auspices of the FAO Commission on Plant Genetic Resources, which began in 1994 and continued until the adoption of the Seed Treaty on 3 November 2001.[70]

The scope and coverage of this newest FAO treaty mark a departure from those of its predecessor, the International Undertaking, and reflect the overall orientation of the CBD. The guiding principles are the conservation and sustainable use of PGRFA in exchange for access to and equitable benefit-sharing of those resources in order to ensure sustainable agriculture and food security—a task that is particularly difficult to achieve in developing countries.[71]

Central to the Seed Treaty is the establishment for the first time in history of plant genetic resources of a multilateral system for facilitated access to a specified list of PGRFA[72] by means of the 'Multilateral System of Access and Benefit-Sharing' (the Multilateral System).[73] It represents a policy reversal in the field of plant genetic resources for food and agriculture whereby crop germplasm has effectively passed from the domain of common heritage of humankind to that of national sovereignty over biological resources in line with the CBD.[74]

The multilateral system is balanced by benefit-sharing in the areas of information exchange, technology transfer, capacity building and commercial development. It also contains a section on farmers' rights that is derived from an interpretation which was previously annexed to the

69 Res. C 7/93, FAO Conference, 27th Sess. (Rome, 6–24 Nov 1993). See generally ten Kate and Lasén Diaz, 'The Undertaking Revisited: A Commentary on the Revision of the International Undertaking on Plant Genetic Resources for Food and Agriculture' [1997] *RECIEL* 284.

70 Footer, 'Our Agricultural Heritage: Sustainability, Common Heritage and Intergenerational Equity' in Schrijver and Weiss (eds.), *International Law on Sustainable Development: Principles and Practice* (The Hague-London, 2004), 433 ff.

71 Art 1, ITPGRFA, *supra* n. 21, which is further supported by the preambular text to the Treaty (recital 4), states that: 'the conservation, exploration, collection, characterization, evaluation and documentation of plant genetic resources for food and agriculture are essential in meeting the goals of the Rome Declaration on World Food Security and the World Food Summit Plan of Action and for sustainable agricultural development for this and future generations, and that the capacity of developing countries and countries with economies in transition to undertake such tasks needs urgently to be reinforced'.

72 *Ibid* and Annex 1 to *ibid*. See further Footer, *supra* n. 70 at 444 ff.

73 Art 11, 12 and 13, *ibid*. See Fowler, 'Accessing Genetic Resources: International Law Establishes Multilateral System' [2004] *Genetic Resources and Crops Evolution* 609.

74 See Footer, *supra* n. 70, at 444 ff. Others have noted this significant departure too; see Helfer, 'Using Intellectual Property Rights to Preserve the Genetic Commons', in Reichman and Maskus (eds.), *International Public Goods and Transfer of Technology under a Globalized Intellectual* Property Regime (Cambridge, 2005 (forthcoming)). For a critique of this view, in particular the idea that the common heritage system has somehow been retained see: Mgbeoji, 'Beyond Rhetoric: State Sovereignty, Common Concern, and the Inapplicability of the Common Heritage Concept to Plant Genetic Resources' [2003] *Leiden Journal of International Law* 821.

International Undertaking,[75] but is now taken up as a separate provision in a legally-binding international instrument. [76]

2.1. Access to essential crop germplasm under the Multilateral System

Just like the provisions regulating access under the CBD, Parties to the ITPGRFA retain full authority to regulate their own crop germplasm, but where the Seed Treaty differs from the CBD is that it places strict limitations on the ability of Parties to restrict access to that crop germplasm from other states. Having said that, while the Treaty covers all genetic material for food and agriculture, Parties are under an obligation (at a minimum) to guarantee access to the genetic material of 35 crop genera and 29 forage species that are in the public domain and are considered essential for global food security and human nutrition.[77] The listing includes crops like rice, maize, wheat, cassava and potatoes which are important to agrobiodiversity and food security. One notable omission is soybean, which China managed successfully to have excluded from the basic list of food crops.[78]

It is intended that access to the Multilateral System be provided only for the purpose of utilisation and conservation of crop germplasm in pursuit of research, breeding and training for food and agriculture and that it should be accorded expeditiously, i.e. immediately without undue delay.[79] Parties to the Seed Treaty must also make available all 'passport' data and any other associated available non-confidential descriptive information.[80] There is a standstill provision which allows a developer (breeder or farmer) in a country of origin of crop germplasm the right to delay access for a period during which that crop germplasm is under development at the time when access is requested.[81]

It took seven years of protracted negotiations before the Seed Treaty was finalised. One reason for this was the controversial issue of plant genetic information and technology protected by intellectual property

[75] Para 4 of Res. C 4/89, FAO Conference, 25th Sess. (Rome, 11–29 Nov 1989) relating to plant breeders' rights recognised the contribution of farmers to the conservation and development of plant genetic resources as the 'Agreed Interpretation of the International Undertaking: Farmers Rights', but Res. C 5/89, FAO Conference, 25th sess. (the 'second interpretation') expressly recognised 'Farmers' Rights'; for details of the International Undertaking or IU, the predecessor to the ITPGRFA, see *supra* n. 64.

[76] Art 9, ITPGRFA, *supra* n. 21. On the concept of farmers' rights generally, see Girsberger, *Biodiversity and the Concept of Farmers' Rights in International Law: Factual Background and Legal Analysis* (Bern-Berlin-Brussels-Frankfurt am Main-New York, Vienna, 1999).

[77] Art 11(1) and (2), ITPGRFA. The actual listing of the 35 crop genera and 29 forage species is contained in Annex I to the Treaty.

[78] Footer, *supra* n. 70, 445, with details in n 48.

[79] Art 12 (3)(a) and (b) ITPGRFA, *supra* n. 21.

[80] Art 12 (3)(c) *ibid.*

[81] Art 12 (3)(e) *ibid.*

rights and confidentiality clauses, i.e. proprietary technologies, which divided developed and developing country governments. A compromise solution was eventually worked out that essentially favours the maintenance of essential crop germplasm in the public domain by prohibiting the grant of any intellectual property right over the accessed PGRFA. The Seed Treaty makes it clear that recipients of essential crop germplasm through the Multilateral System cannot claim intellectual property rights that might otherwise limit facilitated access to that germplasm, or their genetic parts or components, in the form received from the Multilateral System.[82]

Moreover, essential crop germplasm accessed under the Multilateral System must also be made available to other interested parties by the recipient under the conditions laid down in the Treaty.[83] This has been seen as a victory by some scientists and research institutions from countries with strong, government-backed research and breeding capabilities as well as many developing countries, but others like the US, Canada and Japan with strong life science industries remain opposed to the inclusion of such limitations on the grant of intellectual property rights, fearing that this will stifle innovation. Where PGRFA is already protected by intellectual property, or indeed any other property, rights (including communal property rights and the rights of indigenous peoples to genetic resources in some countries), access can take place only in conformity with the treaty or other statutory instruments regulating the type of property rights.[84]

2.2. Equitable Benefit sharing under the Multilateral System

The benefit-sharing provisions under the Seed Treaty form part of what some have termed a 'grand bargain',[85] by trying to redress the asymmetry in plant genetic resources and bargaining power which has developed over the centuries between the gene-rich south and the gene-hungry north, through a process of corrective equity.[86] In first instance the Multilateral System is designed to facilitate access and to ensure that all-comers receive some form of benefits. It calls for the benefits arising from use, including commercial use, of crop germplasm, which is acquired through the Multilateral System, to be shared equitably through one of

[82] Art 12 (3)(d) *ibid.* On this aspect see Helfer, *supra* n. 74, who examines the possible interpretations that could be given to this provision and some possible conflicts to which this could rise.

[83] Art 12 (3)(g) *ibid.*

[84] Art 12 (3)(f) *ibid.*

[85] ten Kate and Laird, 'Biodiversity and Business: Coming to Terms with the 'Grand Bargain', [2000] *International Affairs* 241, at 244.

[86] Franck, *Fairness in International Law and Institutions* (Oxford, 1995), where he discusses equity as a means of introducing justice into (natural) resources allocation, with examples drawn from the fields of trade and development (the Generalised System of Preferences or

four mechanisms: (i) exchange of information (catalogues and inventories, information on technologies, and the results of technical, scientific and socio-economic research); (ii) access to and transfer of technology, (iii) capacity-building (the establishment of programmes for scientific and technical education and training in conservation and sustainable use of PGRFA); and (iv) the sharing of monetary and other benefits arising from commercialisation.[87] Additionally from a sustainable development point of view, these mechanisms must take account of the priorities in the FAO's rolling Global Plan of Action,[88] which will depend on the effective implementation of the benefit-sharing provisions, and the funding strategy to be set up by the future Governing Body under the Treaty in the form of a Trust Account.[89]

It can be expected that the commercialisation aspects of benefit-sharing under the Multilateral System will attract the greatest attention. It is intended that monetary and other benefits from access to the essential crop germplasm, including those benefits arising from the involvement of the private sector in developing countries in research and technology development, will be shared with a number of beneficiaries in source countries through the mechanism of a Trust Account, which is in the process of being established. A standard Material Transfer Agreement or MTA will be used in order to facilitate access to crop germplasm through the Multilateral System, details of which are being considered by an Expert Group on the Terms of the Standard Material Transfer Agreement.[90] In its recent report the Expert Group recommended inter

GSP made possible by the GATT Decision on *Differential and More Favourable Treatment, Reciprocity and Fuller Participation of Developing Countries*, GATT Doc. L/4903 (28 Nov 1979), or 'Enabling Clause', and the eligibility of developing countries for the Stabilization of Export Earnings of STABEX funding under the Fourth ACP–EEC Convention and Final Act, 15 Dec 1989, (1990) 29 ILM 783, or Lomé IV) as well as several examples of boundary delimitations involving the continental shelf and its resources.

[87] Art 13(2) (a) to (d) ITPGRFA, *supra* n. 21.

[88] Art 14 *ibid*. The FAO Global Plan of Action for the Conservation and Sustainable Use of Plant Genetic Resources for Food and Agriculture was established in 1983 as one of the instruments in the overall FAO Global System, *supra* n. 68. It was formally adopted by 150 countries, following the adoption of the FAO, *Report on the State of the World's Plant Genetic Resources for Food and Agriculture*, prepared for the Fourth International Technical Conference on Plant Genetic Resources, Leipzig, Germany, 17–23 June 1996, and known as the 'Leipzig Declaration'. The main task of the Global Action Plan is to provide a periodic reporting system (by FAO Member governments) in order to keep track of the state of the world's plant genetic resources.

[89] Art 13 (4) and (5) in conjunction with Art 18, ITPGRFA, *supra* n. 21. See *Preparation for Consideration by the Governing Body of the Funding Strategy for the Treaty*, Second Meeting of the Commission on Genetic Resources for Food and Agriculture (CGFRA), acting as the Interim Committee for the International Treaty on Plant Genetic Resources for Food and Agriculture, Rome, 15–19 Nov 2004, CGRFA/MIC-2/04/4.

[90] An Expert Group on the Terms of the Standard Material Transfer Agreement, or MTA, charged with developing the relevant contractual basis for access and transfer of individual crop germplasm in the Multilateral System, has submitted its *Report on the Outcome of the*

alia that a Contact Group be established by the Interim Committee for the ITPGRFA in order to draft the standard MTA, which needs to include specific provisions that make it clear who benefits from the Multilateral System, and how the providers of material can receive an equitable share of the benefits arising from the commercialisation of products incorporating material accessed through the Multilateral System. A further issue that the standard MTA must address is the manner in which recipients of the material will make future payments into the Trust Account conform the Treaty and whether some categories such as small farmers in developing and transition economy countries should be excluded from payments altogether.[91] It falls to the Governing Body—the key institutional body under the Seed Treaty's governance structure—to set the level, form and manner of payment under the commercialisation provisions of Article 13(2)(d) of the Treaty, in line with commercial practice, although the matter has already attracted considerable attention, as is clear from the Report of the Expert Group on the standard MTA. [92]

2.3. *Ex situ* holdings of crop germplasm and the Multilateral System

The Multilateral System also potentially includes essential crop germplasm that is held in the *ex situ* collections of the international agricultural research centres or IARCs, which are members of the Consultative Group on International Agricultural Research or CGIAR[93] and in the *ex situ* gene bank collections of other international institutions. The number of accessions of crop germplasm considered essential for environmental sustainability and food security in these two *ex situ* source collections alone is estimated to total 660,000. (It will be recalled that the CBD does not specifically deal with such *ex situ* genetic resources.) The CGIAR collections of essential crop germplasm have historically worked on the basis of sharing resources and knowledge and have been guided by the core principle that the germplasm held in those research stations was collected from the fields and forests of farming communities in the

Expert Group on the Standard Terms for the Material Transfer Agreement to the Second Meeting of the CGFRA, acting as the Interim Committee for the International Treaty on Plant Genetic Resources for Food and Agriculture, Rome, 15–19 Nov 2004, CGRFA/IC/MTA-1/04/Rep. (hereinafter Report of the Expert Group). For details see www.fao.org/ag/cgrfa/docsic2.htm.

[91] Art 13(2)(d) (ii), first full para, in conjunction with Art 19(3)(f), ITPGRFA, *supra* n. 21.

[92] Art 13(2)(d)(ii), second full para, *ibid* and Report of the Expert Group, *supra* n. 90, paras. 25-32. See also Koo, Pardey and Wright, 'Conserving Genetic Resources for Agriculture: Counting the Cost', Brief 6 of the International Food Policy Research Institute (IFPRI) Series *Research at a Glance: Biotechnology and Genetic Resource Policies* (Washington, D.C: Jan 2003).

[93] The Consultative Group on International Agricultural Research (CGIAR) comprises an informal association of 57 public and private sector members, drawn from developed and developing countries, private foundations and development banks: see further Footer, *supra* n. 36, 56 f. for details.

developing countries of the Southern Hemisphere *and* that it is held 'in trust' for the benefit of the international community, in particular for developing countries.[94]

These *ex situ* collections of crop germplasm, which are held 'in trust' by the IARCs and similar institutions, that appear on the Annex I list and were collected *prior* to the date of entry into force of the Seed Treaty[95] will henceforth fall under the Multilateral System and will be subject to the Seed Treaty provisions.[96] They will be guided by a system of agreements to be concluded between them and the Governing Body under the Treaty. Financial benefits flowing from the exchange of germplasm in the *ex situ* collections and falling under the Multilateral System, i.e. the Annex I listings held by the IARCs and other seed banks, will accrue to the funding mechanism to be set up under the Treaty (the Trust Account), whereby such financial benefits will be applied to the conservation and sustainable use of the PGRFA in national and regional programmes located in developing countries, which are centres of genetic diversity, and least developed countries.[97]

Crop germplasm in the *ex situ* collections that does *not* appear on the Annex I list and was collected *after* the date of entry into force of the Seed Treaty will be made available on a bilateral basis, on terms mutually agreed between recipient IARCs and countries of origin, i.e. those countries that possess genetic resources *in situ* and those countries that have acquired genetic resources in accordance with the CBD (both considered as source countries under the Seed Treaty).[98]

2.4. Farmers' rights and the rights of indigenous and local communities under the ITPGRFA or Seed Treaty

Local farming communities across the globe have bred and developed their crop varieties, improved on the varieties through selective breeding and sold them locally under names which have found widespread local acceptance. The Seed Treaty goes some way to recognising the contribution of farmers to conserving and enhancing plant genetic resources for food and agriculture, but it does not define 'farmers' rights' as such.[99]

[94] Footer, *supra* n. 70, 453 ff.

[95] Art 15(1), ITPGRFA, *supra* n. 21.

[96] Art 15(1)(a) and (2), *ibid.* Crop germplasm in such *ex situ* collections, that does *not* appear on the Annex I list, for example soya, and which was collected prior to the date of entry into force of the Seed Treaty will continue to be administered through a set of FAO/CGIAR agreements (and the relevant MTA) in order to facilitate access. It is intended that the Governing Body will eventually monitor future use of the particular MTA under those agreements for a period of four years from 29 June 2004.

[97] Art 15(1)(b)(iii), *ibid.*

[98] Art 15(3), *ibid.*

[99] Art 9(1), *ibid,* simply follows the text contained in the interpretations of the earlier International Undertaking in '[recognizing] the enormous contribution that the local and

Instead, it provides broad guidelines to Parties concerning the scope of the rights to be protected but devolves overall responsibility for the realisation of those rights to the Parties themselves in a similar fashion to other economic and social rights.

According to the Seed Treaty it is the duty of national governments *inter alia* to take measures 'to protect and promote Farmers Rights' that include at a minimum the protection of traditional knowledge, farmers' entitlement to a part of benefit-sharing arrangements and the right to participate in decision-making regarding the management of plant genetic resources.[100] There is also no mention in the treaty of farmers' rights over their landraces. Instead, the only rights that are recognised are the 'residual rights' to save, use, exchange and sell farm-saved seeds. Not only does this limitation cast doubts on the ability of the Seed Treaty to offer sufficient guarantees to farmers for the protection and promotion of their rights but it also marks a significant limitation on the effective exercise by states of permanent sovereignty over their genetic resources.[101]

It is also the intention that the benefits arising from the access and benefit-sharing provisions of the Multilateral System should primarily be directed to local farmers who conserve and sustainably use crop germplasm. However, it is not clear how this will work in practice, especially since it may prove difficult to identify the 'farmers'.[102]

In addition to farmers' rights under the Seed Treaty, there is also a need to focus on recognising and protecting the rights of indigenous peoples and local communities, in the interest of food security and sustainable development.[103] While it is true that these rights may wholly or partly coincide with those of local farmers, there is no certainty that this is always the case. The World Commission on Environment and Development has stressed the importance of traditional knowledge in the sustainable development process, and observed that 'tribal and indigenous people will need special attention as the forces of economic development disrupt their traditional lifestyles'.[104] Agenda 21 recommends that governments should adopt policies and/or legal instruments that will protect intellectual and cultural property of indigenous peoples.[105]

indigenous communities and farmers of all regions of the world' make to the conservation and development of PGRFA but the provision does not contain a definition of farmers' rights.

100 Art 9(2), *ibid*.

101 Footer and Opuku Awuku, *supra* n. 37, 247 f.

102 It is also possible that similar problems may arise with respect to collaborative partnerships that are provided for in Art 13(2)(d)(i) ITPGRFA.

103 See for a preliminary discussion, Footer and Opuku Awuku, *supra* n. 37, 248 ff.

104 World Commission on Environment and Development, *Our Common Future* (Oxford, 1987) at 12.

105 Agenda 21, Ch 26.4 (b) in Robinson, *supra* n. 22, at 509.

In the context of agrobiotechnology and food security, this means that tribal and indigenous peoples may also wish to maintain control of and access to agricultural biodiversity in order to develop and sustain their farming systems as well as to benefit from biological resources and related knowledge. While the CBD recognises the utilisation of knowledge, innovations and practices of indigenous and local communities embodying traditional lifestyles relevant for the conservation and sustainable use of biodiversity,[106] no link is made to the Seed Treaty.[107] As already noted, the latter instrument does nothing more than provide for farmers' rights, which, due to the lack of specificity and recognition of those rights, may not provide sufficient guarantees to tribal and indigenous farmers, as part of local farming communities, over access and benefit-sharing crop germplasm that they may have been instrumental in developing.

Apart from this eventuality, there may be a number of other barriers that prevent both local farmers and tribal and indigenous groups in developing countries from fully achieving the benefits of modern agrobiotechnology as foreseen by the environmental and food and agricultural communities. Despite facilitated access and benefit-sharing mechanisms for genetic resources under the CBD and the Seed Treaty, both groups are often faced with inadequate regulatory procedures, poorly functioning markets, fragile seed distribution systems, weak domestic plant breeding capacity, inadequate research capacities and complex intellectual property issues that increasingly compete alongside traditional property rights, including different forms of ownership, community rights, land tenure rights, the right of usufruct and so on.[108]

Thus, a further area for consideration in the international governance of agrobiotechnology is the political economy of biotechnology, i.e. the relationships between state regulators and market actors. Meanwhile the issue of food safety, particularly the legal regulation of GMOs, has gained widespread coverage, but there are other aspects of food safety that, while not widely discussed, may merit closer analysis. Such issues include the legal regulation of pest control, disease and contamination in plant biotechnology. Equally, more research is needed into the link between patterns of production and investment in agricultural biotechnology and their relationship to the international regulation of agrobiotechnology and food safety.

[106] Art 8(j) CBD, *supra* n. 20.

[107] See, however, Decision VII/19 of COP-7, *supra* n. 60, at section D. It calls upon 'Parties, Governments, relevant organizations, indigenous and local communities, and all relevant stakeholders' to facilitate effective participation of indigenous and local communities in the process of the negotiation and elaboration of an international regime on access and benefit sharing of genetic resources.

[108] 'Biotech and Developing Countries' [2004] *Bridges*, Geneva, ICTSD, vol. 8:5. For a regime analysis of the changes in property rights brought about by interplay of the CBD, ITPGRFA

III. FOOD SECURITY, THE RIGHT TO ADEQUATE AND NUTRITIOUS FOOD AND THE LINK TO AGROBIOTECHNOLOGY

The issue of food security is one of the central tenets of the FAO. The Preamble to the FAO Constitution sets out 'raising levels of nutrition and standards of living of the peoples' as one of its purposes.[109] The definition of food security most commonly used is that of the 1996 World Food Summit Declaration when it reaffirmed the fundamental right to adequate food and defined food security as 'the right of everyone to have access to safe and nutritious food, consistent with the right to adequate food and the fundamental right of everyone to be free from hunger',[110] or, put more simply, 'access to food for a healthy life by all people at all times'.[111] The Plan of Action, attached to the Declaration, called upon FAO Members 'to clarify the content of the right to adequate food and the fundamental right of everyone to be free from hunger, as stated in the International Covenant on Economic, Social and Cultural Rights and other relevant international and regional instruments, and to give particular attention to implementation and full and progressive realization of this right as a means of achieving food security for all'.[112]

As we noted earlier the right to adequate and nutritious food has been recognised in the main human rights instruments that have formed part of the international bill of rights for several decades.[113] It has been argued that a right to a food-based approach to food security is distinct from other approaches to reducing hunger and malnutrition because it complements food security with considerations of dignity, the acknowledgment of rights, transparency and accountability and addresses concerns about empowerment.[114] However, in practice the realisation of this approach, as with other economic, social and cultural rights, is far more difficult to attain. Whereas states are under an obligation to guarantee the right to freedom from hunger as a fundamental human right (and this right is closely linked to the right to life)[115], they are required only to take

and CGIAR, together with TRIPs and UPOV, and their consequences, see Raustiala and Victor, 'The Regime Complex for Plant Genetic Resources' [2004] *International Organization* 277.

109 Fifth recital, *Constitution of the Food and Agricultural Organization of the United Nations*, Quebec, 16 Oct 1945, reproduced in *Basic Texts of the Food and Agriculture Organization of the United Nations* (Rome, 2000 edn), i and ii, available at: www.fao.org/Legal/index_en.htm.

110 Rome Declaration on World Food Security, *supra* n. 24, Objective 7.4.

111 Thrupp, *Cultivating Diversity: Agrobiodiversity and Food Security* (Washington, D.C, 1998), at 9.

112 *World Food Summit Plan of Action*, *supra* n. 24, para 61, Commitment Seven, Objective 7.4.

113 Art 25(1) UDHR and Art 11 ICESCR, *supra* n. 16 and n. 17 respectively.

114 Mechlem, 'Food Security and the Right to Food in the Discourse of the United Nations', [2004] *European Law Journal* 631.

115 Art 6 International Covenant on Civil and Political Rights, adopted and open for signature, ratification and accession by GA Res. 2200A (XXI) of 16 Dec 1966, 21 U.N. GAOR Supp. (No. 16) at 52, U.N. Doc. A/6316 (1966), (1967) 6 ILM 368, entered into force 23 Mar 1976, 99 UNTS 171 (hereinafter ICCPR).

all necessary steps possible towards the goal of full enjoyment of the right to adequate food, i.e. in accordance with the doctrine of progressive realisation of economic, social and cultural rights.[116]

According to Asbjørn Eide[117] the right to adequate food forms part of the minimum standard of nutrition and other basic necessities, and it can be broken down into a number of separate components. Thus 'adequacy of food supply' means that certain types of foodstuffs are commonly available, i.e. nationally, in local markets and per household, and that those foodstuffs are culturally acceptable, i.e. they fit the food or dietary culture prevailing in a particular community. Additionally, the overall food supply should meet nutritional needs in terms of quantity and quality, i.e. it should provide sufficient energy and essential nutrients, including micronutrients such as vitamins and iodine, and be safe, i.e. it should be free of toxins and other contaminates. The social and economic factors that underpin the right to adequate food include economic and social sustainability in terms of just income distribution and effective markets coupled with various forms of public support, for example price stabilisation mechanisms, informal support through things like solidarity networks, and safety nets in the form for example of social security schemes.

The potential role that new agricultural biotechnologies might play in improving food security, especially in the developing world, has been the subject of public policy aspirations for at least the last two decades. Such policy initiatives, which include flanking policies in the fields of agrobiotechnology and food security, account for ongoing work on food security, human rights and ethics in the FAO and the UN human rights system, either singly or through collaborative endeavours. The problem is not so much the lack of attention to issues of agrobiotechnology, food security and human rights but the number of stakeholders with interests in legal and policy outcomes and the overlap between these issues in different international *fora*.

In the field of human rights and ethics, work has been continuing since 1991 at the FAO under the auspices of the CGRFA, on developing a Code of Conduct on Biotechnology.[118] Initially, the aim was to maximise the positive effects, and minimise the possible negative effects, of biotechnology on agricultural production.[119] It covers five basic areas relating to (i) biosafety and other environmental concerns, (ii) intellectual property rights and farmers' rights, (iii) appropriate biotechnology for developing

116 Art 2(1) ICESCR, *supra* n. 17.

117 See Eide, *supra* n 19, 134 f.

118 Draft Code of Conduct on Biotechnology, *supra* n. 28.

119 *Towards an International Code of Conduct on Plant Biotechnology as it affects the Conservation and Utilization of Plant Genetic Resources*, CGRFA, 5th Sess. (Rome, 19–23 Apr 1993), CPGR/93/9.

countries, (iv) minimisation of the possible negative effects of biotechnology and (v) monitoring. The draft Code of Conduct on Biotechnology is the result of an extensive exercise involving stakeholder participation of around 400 international experts drawn from governments, the scientific community and members of the society.[120]

Work on the draft Code was temporarily suspended pending the completion of the CPB and revision of the International Undertaking that eventually led to the adoption of the Seed Treaty. Subsequently, with the completion of work on both of these international instruments, the status of the draft of the Code of Conduct on Biotechnology was reviewed by the CGRFA in October 2002,[121] with a number of FAO Members supporting continued work on the Code and suggesting a wide range of possible socio-economic issues that could be addressed. These include the socio-economic impacts of biotechnology on agricultural practices and food security, ethical issues, the substitution of traditional agricultural products, control of the global agro-food system, issues of liability and various incentives to promote biotechnologies. The CGRFA reported to the FAO Council in November 2004 on its progress to date on finalising the Code of Conduct on Biotechnology. Meanwhile, the FAO Panel of Eminent Experts in Ethics on Food and Agriculture,[122] which is responsible for raising public awareness and for advising the FAO Director-General on ethical issues related to agricultural biotechnology, has reported twice.[123]

The FAO has also continued and extended its close collaboration with the UN Special Rapporteur on the Right to Food[124] on matters of agro-biotechnology, food security and ethics in food and agriculture. The work of the UN Special Rapporteur on the Right to Food has been controversial, not least because he has been vocal in calling for an integrated approach to the right to food, international human rights law and international agricultural trade, with particular concern being expressed over the right to food in the context of modern biotechnology and related intellectual property rights. For example, he has criticised the emphasis on free trade

[120] See Bluemel, 'Separating Instrumental from Intrinsic Rights: Towards an Understanding of Indigenous Participation in International Rule-making' [2005] *American Indian Law Review* (forthcoming), for a discussion of multi-stakeholder participation that also involves civil society.

[121] *Status of the Draft Code of Conduct on Biotechnology as it relates to Genetic Resources for Food and Agriculture: Report and Survey of FAO Members and Stakeholders*, CGRFA, 9th Sess., (Rome, 14–18 Oct 2002), CGRFFA-0/02/8.

[122] See for further details on the establishment of the FAO Panel of Eminent Experts, *supra* n. 29.

[123] *Report of the Panel of Eminent Experts on Ethics in Food and Agriculture*, 1st Sess. (Rome, 26–28 Sept 2000) and *Report of the Panel of Eminent Experts on Ethics in Food and Agriculture*, 2nd Sess. (Rome, 19–22 Mar 2002); available at http://www.fao.org/ethics/exp_en.htm.

[124] The UN Commission on Human Rights adopted resolution 2000/10 of 17 Apr 2000 at its 52nd meeting, E/CN.4/Res/2000/10, para. 10, in which it appointed a Special Rapporteur on the Right to Food.

and biotechnology as key ways of reducing hunger,[125] as set out in the *Declaration of the World Food Summit: Five Years Later*,[126] stating that 'the right to food implies not only access to food, but also access to the means of producing it',[127] recommending instead that alternative policy options be explored at the international level.[128]

At the FAO, the IGWG, which was established as a subsidiary body of the Committee on World Food Security (CFS), as called for in the *Declaration of the World Food Summit: Five Years Later*,[129] was given the mandate of elaborating, within a period of two years and with a variety of stakeholders, a set of voluntary guidelines to support Members in the progressive realisation of the right to adequate food.[130] This work was recently completed, and the voluntary 'Right to Food Guidelines' were adopted by the IGWG at its September 2004 meeting.[131]

The Right to Food Guidelines take into account a variety of policy considerations and principles, such as the principles of equality and non-discrimination, considerations of participation and inclusion, accountability and rule of law, and the principle that all human rights are universal, indivisible, inter-related and interdependent.[132] The right to adequate food reflects not only access to food but also the access of individuals and groups to productive resources. Food security is understood as existing 'when all people, at all times, have physical and economic access to sufficient, safe and nutritious food to meet their dietary needs and food preferences for an active and healthy life'.[133]

The Right to Food Guidelines proceed to describe the four pillars of food security as: 'availability, stability of supply, access and utilization',[134] and clearly identify the wide range of state obligations in this respect. For example, states must respect the existing access to food and protect people from being deprived by economically powerful actors, must invest the maximum of available resources in progressively achieving the full realisation of the right to food in the context of national food security[135] and

[125] Report by the Special Rapporteur on the Right to Food to the Commission on Human Rights, UN Docs. E/CN.4/2001/53 (7 Feb 2001), para. 73 and E/CN.4/2002/58 (10 Jan 2002), paras. 108, 119 and 129.

[126] *Declaration of the World Food Summit: Five Years Later, supra* n. 25.

[127] *Report of the Special Rapporteur to the Human Rights Commission on the Right to Food*, transmitted to the UN General Assembly, U.N. Doc. A/57/356 (27 Aug 2002) para. 19.

[128] *Ibid*, paras. 25–42.

[129] *Declaration of the World Food Summit: Five Years Later, supra* n. 25, para 1.

[130] *Intergovernmental Working Group for the Elaboration of a Voluntary Guidelines Set of to Support the Progressive Realization of the Right to Adequate Food in the Context of National Food Security*, 1st Sess. (Rome, 24–26 Mar 2003), IGWG RTFG I/INF/1, established by the FAO Council, 123rd Sess. (Rome, 28 Oct–1 Nov 2002).

[131] *Right to Food Guidelines, supra* n. 27.

[132] *Ibid*, Introduction, para. 19.

[133] *Ibid*, Introduction, para 15.

[134] *Ibid*.

[135] *Ibid*, Guideline 2.1.

take immediate and targeted steps toward implementation. Although the Guidelines are voluntary in character and the application of much of their content is at the discretion of governments, they represent a significant achievement in bringing the human rights and food and agriculture communities closer together.[136]

IV. PRELIMINARY CONCLUSIONS AND SUGGESTIONS FOR FURTHER RESEARCH

The foregoing provides a brief survey of the international governance for agricultural biotechnology, food security and human rights and demonstrates how close the food and agriculture and human rights discourses have grown to one another, leading to a tangled web of differing institutional structures, operating at several levels and involving a range of stakeholders. Indeed, the current regime of plant genetic resources has been characterised as a set of overlapping international regimes or a regimes complex, which is subject to a proliferation and density of institutions and a diversity of rules and norms.[137] Similar conclusions could be drawn from the environmental, food and agriculture and human rights regimes, especially when situated around the nexus of food security. It is made only more complex by the addition of the regime for PGRFA or crop germplasm.

One preliminary conclusion is that there is an emerging problem of international governance in the overlapping fields of agricultural biotechnology, food security and human rights as a result of this multiplicity of *fora*, actors and instruments that may be difficult to contain and is leading to a plethora of competing claims on the use of resources and their effective management in respect thereof. Another preliminary conclusion is that the two flanking issues of agricultural trade reform and overlapping property regimes appear to have attracted little attention in the overall discussion of these issues. The Special Rapporteur on the Right to Food has made this point very cogently in his 2002 report to the Human Rights Commission[138] and has subsequently updated his remarks as a result of the failure of the Fifth Ministerial Meeting of the WTO, held at Cancún in 2003.[139]

136 Before and subsequent to their adoption the voluntary *Right to Food Guidelines* have also been commented upon by the Special Rapporteur on the Right to Food; see for example his report E/CN.4/2003/54 (10 Jan 2002), Part I, paras. 19–35.

137 See in particular Raustiala and Victor, *supra* n. 108, with respect to the regime complex for plant genetic resources.

138 See his remarks in his 2002 report transmitted to the UN General Assembly, U.N. Doc. A/57/356 (27 Aug 2002), *supra* n. 127.

139 Report of the Special Rapporteur on the Right to Food to the Commission on Human Rights, UN Docs. E/CN.4/2004/10 (9 Feb 2004) on trade and food security in Part I, paras. 14–23.

Obviously both of these preliminary conclusions lead to suggestions for further research into the barriers that prevent farmers, in particular local farmers from tribal and indigenous groups in developing countries, from fully achieving the benefits of modern agrobiotechnology as foreseen by the environmental and food and agricultural communities. As we noted earlier, inadequate regulatory systems, market failure, fragile distribution systems, particularly in relation to seed distribution, weak domestic plant breeding capacity, inadequate research capacities and complex intellectual property issues are competing with an intense international effort to reform agricultural trade and to make some sense out of competing claims to tangible and intangible property.

In this respect, further research into the international governance of agrobiotechnology, food security and human rights cannot ignore the political economy of biotechnology, i.e. the relationships between state regulators and market actors. At the same time, research into issues of food safety, which forms part of the broader issue of food security, should move beyond the legal regulation of GMOs and deal with the legal regulation of pest control, disease and contamination in plant biotechnology. Finally, future research should also explore the links between production and investment in agricultural biotechnology as a sub-component of ongoing research into international governance of modern agrobiotechnology and the right to food.

12

Biotechnology, Human Dignity and the Human Genome

FEDERICO LENZERINI*

I. INTRODUCTION: THE HUMAN GENOME

THE HUMAN GENOME is the map of human life (as it is known), and contains the complete genetic inheritance of a human organism or, in other words, the genetic instructions needed to develop and direct any activity performed by the organism. The complete story of any human being is 'written' in his/her genome, which is the reason of his/her uniqueness and unrepeatability.[1]

In 1990 the International Human Genome Project was launched, with the purpose of mapping and sequencing the human genome, by a public consortium composed of specialised institutions coming from several countries, namely China, France, Germany, Japan, the United Kingdom and the United States. 'Mapping' means assigning genes to specific chromosomes, that is to say discovering the location of specific biochemical

* Ph. D., International Law; Researcher, University of Siena.

1 The human genome is made of Deoxyribose Nucleic Acid (DNA), a chemical compound whose helix-shaped molecules are composed of two paired strands. Each strand is made up of four chemical units, called nucleotide bases: adenine (A), thymine (T), guanine (G) and cytosine (C). Bases on opposite strands pair specifically: an A always pairs with a T and a C always pairs with a G. The four bases may be compared to the alphabetical letters which, placed in sequence, compose an encyclopaedia. The encyclopaedia of the human genome is made up of only four letters, but contains about 3.2 billions of base pairs composed by such letters, which are organized into 23 pairs of very large molecules called chromosomes. Each chromosome contains hundreds to thousands of genes, which transmit the instructions for producing proteins by transcribing their codes into single-stranded ribonucleic acid (RNA) molecules. Except for red blood cells, which have no nucleus, the human genome is located in the nucleus of every cell of the body, and is composed of the totality of genetic material contained in the cell. The successions of the letters in the genome of any human being are very similar, but not identical: there is a difference of one letter in a thousand, which is transmitted in the proteins produced by the cells that determine the peculiar traits of the person. The diversity of any human being from all the others lies in these differences. Most of the scientific and historical information reported in the text is taken from the website of the U.S. National Human Genome Research Institute, at http://www.genome.gov (last visited on July 13, 2004).

landmarks, including genes, in chromosomes; once researchers know where the genes are located, they can ascertain when certain traits are being inherited together. The following operation, 'sequencing', means determining the exact order of the base pairs in a segment of DNA, that is to say ordering the whole succession of letters which compose the human genome. Sequencing was a main indispensable step in the road to deciphering the human genome. On 26 June 2000 the International Human Genome Sequencing Consortium announced that it had assembled a working draft of the sequence of the human genome,[2] just a couple of months after a similar announcement had been made by the private enterprise Celera Genomics (which, on 5 April 2000, announced that it had *completed* the sequence). In February 2001 the results of both the public and private researches on the human genome were published, respectively, on the journals *Nature* and *Science*. The two sequences did not appear significantly different from each other, and they were made publicly available to the scientific community. In doing this, both the public and private researchers met the relevant appeals made by the international community in the previous months. On 14 March 2000, for example, a joint declaration of the British Prime Minister Blair and the US President Clinton had urged that, 'to realize full promise of the research, raw fundamental data on the human genome including DNA sequence and its variations, should be made available to scientists everywhere'.[3]

Today the human genome may be considered, within the limits of contemporary technology, as completely sequenced. This means that it is at present as complete as it can be, in the sense that small gaps that are irrecoverable with the use of any currently known sequencing method still remain, and further research needs to be performed with the purpose of developing new technologies for filling these gaps. Anyway, the human genome may be considered as complete in virtually every way useful for scientific research, and it is publicly available.

II. 'KNOWING THE MAP': NEW PERSPECTIVES FOR HUMAN HEALTH

The knowledge of the virtually complete sequence of the human genome opens important new perspectives in the field of medicine and healthcare. Now the scientific community has all the pages of the human encyclopaedia; the problem which 'remains' to be resolved is understanding how to

[2] See 'International Human Genome Sequencing Consortium Announces "Working Draft" of Human Genome', *Science Daily*, 26, June 2000, at http://www.sciencedaily.com/releases/2000/06/000626114100.htm (last visited on July 13, 2004).

[3] See 'U.S., Britain urge free access to human genome data', CNN.com, 14 Mar 2000, at http://www.cnn.com/2000/HEALTH/03/14/human.genome03 (last visited on July 14, 2004).

read the content of these pages and how they interact one with another. In scientific terms, the accomplishment of this task would allow scientists to discover the genetic basis for health and the pathology of genetic diseases. In practical terms, it would enable medical science greatly to improve the existing diagnostic tools, to develop an enhanced approach to the preventive care of genetic diseases, as well as to grant access to new and efficient curative medicines for such diseases. The health needs of any single human being could be approached and treated on an individual basis, taking into account the unique features and peculiarities of his/her own genetic code. The first concrete outcomes of biotechnological research related to the human genome, concerning the prevention of the most common genetic diseases (*e.g.*, diabetes, cardiologic diseases and certain kinds of cancer), could be reached in a few years; these outcomes will mainly consist in the improvement of the capacity to screen individuals for the risk of being affected by such diseases, and the preventive action will be put into operation not only at the prenatal level, but also during the life of the patient.

In the medium term, the impact of the scientific knowledge relating to the human genome will concern all branches of medicine. It will be possible to know the complete sequence of events which provokes a given disease, with the consequent chance of developing medicines which are new and/or more efficient than in the past, even with the opportunity of 'personalising' such medicines according to the specific peculiarities of each individual's genome.

In the long term, when all the secrets of the human genome are definitely known, it will be possible precisely to discover the genetic composition of any human organ and tissue. Consequently, it will arguably be possible to produce human organs that will be used as perfectly compatible 'spare parts' for any individual, since they will be produced simply using a cell belonging to the person concerned. Thus, all the present problems relating to organ transplantation, i.e. the scarcity of organs and the possibility that the transplanted organ may be rejected by the patient's organism, will ultimately be resolved. Finally, the last frontier of genetic biotechnology will arguably be the development of genetic therapy, that is to say the use of genes as therapeutic devices, especially for those diseases which reveal themselves only when they have reached an advanced stage, like most cancers and degenerative diseases.

III. MANIPULATING THE HUMAN GENOME: LEGAL AND ETHICAL IMPLICATIONS

As just pointed out, the development of scientific research concerning the human genome is offering new important perspectives in the field of medical science. In particular, it is providing the tools for discovering genetic alterations that make certain families and individuals more likely than others to get diseases of a genetic nature. This raises great expectations regarding the perspective of developing treatments, also individually designed, for the prevention and/or treatment of such diseases. From this perspective, for the individuals concerned research on the human genome may fill the gap between death and life, and there is no doubt that the scientific community must invest as may resources as possible fully to take advantage of any new chance offered by genetic research.

Having said this, it is also to be noted that the improvement of medical science is not the only sector of human society which may be affected by genetics. In this sense, it is sufficient to mention the fact that the judicial machine of a large number of states currently has recourse to genetic tests for determining identities, especially in the context of criminal proceedings or paternity cases.[4] Furthermore, the impact of biogenetics on social life may be even much more invasive. For example, it may alter working relations,[5] particularly to the extent that genetic tests are used for selecting persons for employment, searching for genetic features which are thought to make them particularly fit or, on the contrary, unable to perform certain works. The genetic heritage of certain families, which makes their members more likely than the average to get certain diseases, may also alter the status of such persons in the context of welfare systems at the level both of public social security and of private insurance,[6] making their opportunities of access to welfare mechanisms more difficult than those reserved to the other members of society. Finally, it has even been reported that adoption agencies 'have refused to agree to adoptions by persons on the basis of their genetic profile'.[7]

Yet, the examples just mentioned do not represent the worst situations that, ethically speaking, could result from the influence played by biogenetics in the human society. Let's just think of human cloning, whose concrete feasibility does not seem too far from reality, not to mention the abhorrent possibility of combining human genes with genes belonging to primates for 'creating' beings intelligent enough to perform human activities but which, at the same time, given their presumed non-humanity, could be legally exploited in slavery-like conditions.

In addition, even leaving aside the possible misuse of genetic scientific knowledge, the (ethically recommendable) implementation of medical

[4] See Lenoir, 'Universal Declaration on the Human Genome and Human Rights: The First Legal and Ethical Framework at the Global Level', (1999) 30 *Columbia Human Rights Law Review* 537, at 537.

[5] *Ibid.*, 537.

[6] *Ibid.*, 537.

[7] See U.N. Sub-Commission on the Promotion and Protection of Human Rights, 'Human Rights and the Human Genome', Preliminary report submitted by the Special Rapporteur Iulia-Antonella Motoc, doc. E/CN.4/Sub.2/2004/38 of 23 July 2004, para. 10.

activities connected to the human genome also raises a number of controversial ethical and legal issues, such as those related to the nature of the informed consent that should be guaranteed to those who have a genetic test, to access to information resulting from such test, to the ownership and the possible use of such information, as well as to the possibility that the above activities result in some forms of genetic discrimination.

Taken together, all the aspects of the matter depict a nebulous future. Human history provides plenty of examples of instruments developed with the purpose of improving the quality of life and then mainly used to destroy it. For example, when in 1863 Alfred Nobel obtained his first patent on nitro-glycerine, this was classified as an industrial explosive, with the purpose of helping miners in performing their extractive activities, but, in spite of the good intentions of its inventor, it also revealed itself as the paramount tool for multiplying the destructive power of warring factions and terrorist groups.

These and other similar concerns have led to the development of a new branch of ethical and legal philosophy connected with genetics, called bioethics.

IV. THE DEVELOPMENT OF BIOETHICS IN THE LEGAL ARENA

Legally speaking, the first relevant fruits produced by bioethics have arisen at the national level, in a few developed countries, which have enacted several laws regarding organ transplantation and other bioethical issues.[8] For example, France has had a law on organ transplantation since 1976 (Law No. 76–1181 of 22 December 1976), and a comprehensive legal regime on bioethics introduced by law no. 94–654. Article 6 of Law 654 included a new provision (Article L.672–4) in the Code of Public Health which states that '*[l]e prélèvement de tissus ou de cellules ou la collecte des produits du corps humain sur une personne vivante ne peut être effectué que dans un but thérapeutique ou scientifique*'.[9] The same legal instrument, inter alia, also places precise limits on prenatal diagnostic research, especially when it is carried out on cells taken from the embryo *in vitro*, authorising such research only under exceptional circumstances and by ensuring the respect of very strict conditions, particularly that '*[l]e diagnostic ne peut avoir d'autre objet que de rechercher cette affection ainsi que les moyens de la prévenir et de la traiter*'.[10] Finally, with regard to the problem of the consent

[8] Generally on this topic see Lenoir, *supra* n. 4, 538 ff.

[9] See *Loi n° 94–654 du 29 Juillet 1994, relative au don et à l'utilisation des éléments et produits du corps humain, à l'assistance médicale, a la procréation et au diagnostic prénatal*, available at http://www.chu-rouen.fr/uchpg/LOI5.html (last visited on 21 July 2004). The relevant Arts of the French Code of Public Health are available at http://members.lycos.fr/eurosante-droit/legislat/france/themes/greffes.htm (last visited on 21 July 2004).

[10] *Ibid.*, Art 14.

of the person concerned, Article 2 of Law 94–654 asserts that *'[l]e prélèvement d'éléments du corps humain et la collecte de ses produits ne peuvent être pratiqués sans le consentement préalable du donneur. Ce consentement est révocable à tout moment'*.[11] The general approach of French law to bioethics, however, is shown by Article 2 of Law 94–653, which includes in the Civil Code a provision stating that *'[l]a loi assure la primauté de la personne, interdit toute atteinte à la dignité de celle-ci et garantit le respect de l'être humain dès la commencement de sa vie'*.[12]

Other examples of laws on bioethics are those which deal with the treatment of the human embryo and gamete, like the U.K.'s Human Fertilisation and Embryology Act of 1990.[13] Similar laws have been enacted, inter alia, by Spain in 1988,[14] Germany in 1990 (also emphasising the value of human dignity)[15] and, more recently, by Italy in 2004 (Law no. 40/2004).[16]

With regard to legislations concerning organ transplantation the Japanese situation is worth mentioning. In particular, Law no. 104 of 1997 allows transplantation of organs taken from both brain-dead and dead bodies. Nevertheless, such activity is allowed only in the respect of very strict conditions, especially that the donor has expressed his/her written consent beforehand and that the family agrees with the donation. These restrictions exist by reason of certain beliefs belonging to Japanese religious and cultural inheritance, including the reluctance to accept the notion of brain death and the idea that a cadaver cannot be interfered with before the funeral.[17] In 1999, two years after the adoption of Law 104, public acceptance of brain death as death seemed to be quite satisfactory (52 percent of the Japanese population, according to an *Ashai* poll), but the number of transplanted organs from brain dead donors was still below average.[18]

This case illustrates just one of the several situations in which bioethics law is suitable for interacting with different issues, which can actually

[11] *Ibid.*, Art 2 (corresponding to Art L.665–11 of the Code of Public Health).

[12] See *Loi n° 94–653 du 29 Juillet 1994, relative au respect du corps humain*, available at http://www.chu-rouen.fr/uchpg/LOI4.html (last visited on 21 July 2004).

[13] The full text of such act is available at http://www.hmso.gov.uk/acts/acts1990/Ukpga_19900037_en_1.htm (last visited on 21 July 2004).

[14] See *Ley 35/1988 de 22 de novembre, sobre técnicas de reproducción asistida*, available at http://cerezo.pntic.mec.es/~jlacaden/webmec12/legi_espa02.html (last visited on 21 July 2004).

[15] See *Gesetz zum Schutz von Embryonen (Embryonenschutzgesetz)*, 13 Dec 1990, [1990] I, BGBL 2746, also available at http://www.jura.uni-sb.de/BGBI/TEIL1/1990/19902746.1.HTML (last visited on 21 July 2004).

[16] See Law of 19 Feb 2004, n. 40, *Norme in materia di procreazione medicalmente assistita*, available at http://www.camera.it.parlam/leggi/040401.htm (last visited on 21 July 2004).

[17] See Lenoir, *supra* n. 4, 538.

[18] See Bagheri, 'Can the "Japan organ transplantation law" promote organ procurement from the brain dead?', in Song, Koo and Macer, *Bioethics in Asia in the 21st Century* (Tsukuba and Christchurch, Eubios Ethics Institute, 2003), 133, at 133, also available at http://www.bioltsukuba.ac.jp/~macer/ABC4/abc4133.htm (last visited on 21 July 2004).

condition and ultimately impair the correct implementation and effectiveness of such law. First, the example of Japan demonstrates how, given the particularly sensitive issues involved in the legal regulation of bioethics, which invade even the most intimate aspects of human and family life, the cultural and ethical background of a given geographical context may enter into conflict with the concrete implementation of scientifically-dictated legal rules. Also the perception and treatment of ethical aspects concerning the subject in point may greatly diverge in the different countries due to cultural reasons. By their very nature, moral and ethical issues are of relative character both in time and space, and this character is clearly reflected in the different approaches adopted by the various national legislations with regard to some core elements of bioethics. To illustrate this situation, it is sufficient to mention the fact that, even among Western European countries, which share the same cultural roots, legal regulation of embryo research varies considerably from one state to another.[19] The different approach by such countries to bioethical questions has also strongly influenced discussion on the subject in the context of European Community law, leading to a ten-year debate (mainly concentrated on ethical issues) before a directive on the protection of biotechnological inventions could be adopted.[20]

The economic aspects of the subject in point must also be considered. A few years ago a European country entrusted a private enterprise with the task of developing at the national level research on the human genome, also directly helping such company by providing considerable financial support. This country is Iceland, whose parliament in 1998 passed a bill that gave the Iceland-based US company deCODE Genetics the exclusive right to assemble a commercial centralised database of all the Icelandic peoples' genealogical, genetic, and personal medical information based on Iceland's extensive medical records. The company thus gained access to the national health records, with the purpose of searching for genes associated with over 30 diseases, partially financed by the Swiss pharmaceutical enterprise Hoffmann–LaRoche. In January 2002 deCODE Genetics announced that it had bought the US pharmaceutical company MediChem Lifesciences, which enabled the mother company to develop its own pharmacological researche in Iceland. Such operation was carried out with the help of the Icelandic government, which guaranteed a US $200 million loan to deCODE.[21] In principle, this course of action is not

[19] See Lenoir, *supra* n. 4, 543 f.

[20] See Dir 98/44/EC of the European Parliament and of the Council of 6 July 1998 on the Legal Protection of Biotechnological Inventions [1998] OJ L/213/13.

[21] The information regarding Iceland is taken from Hlodan, 'For Sale: Iceland's Genetic History', June 2000, available at http://www.actionbioscience.org/genomic/hlodan.html (last visited on 24 July 2004); Erlingsson, 'The Genomic Dream in Iceland (and elsewhere) vs. Cystic Fibrosis' 15(4) *GeneWatch*, 12 f. (also available at http://www.raunvis.hi.is/~steindor/gw.html, last visited on 24 July 2004).

immune from serious threats: governments delegate the task of developing knowledge related to extremely advanced scientific and technological issues to private entities. The more this knowledge is developed, the more the state reduces its chances of controlling the activities carried out by those private actors which, at the end of the day, could also misuse such knowledge in ways that could undermine the integrity of human dignity, escaping any kind of significant governmental control.[22] In this sense, many questions may be raised, which, as for the specific case just mentioned, have actually triggered vehement protests from the Icelandic population: who is to ensure that genetic data are not abused in ways that, for example, could violate personal privacy? What happens with data already entered in the database when the person concerned revokes his/her consent to their use? Will, and to what extent will, the donors of genetic materials share the profits of pharmaceutical companies?[23]

Finally, and most of all, globalisation of technology and scientific research has led to the absolute inadequacy of the development of national bioethics for effectively addressing the threats raised by genomic technology. As a matter of fact, enormous inconsistency of legal regulation of

[22] The concept expressed in the text is purely theoretical, and entails no explicit or implicit allusion to any private actor which has taken/is taking/will take care of any kind of activity relating to the human genome worldwide, including the companies mentioned in the text.

[23] Another country, Estonia, has recently launched a project similar to the one described in the text. In 2002 the Estonian Gene Bank (*Eesti Geenikeskus*) started the pilot phase of the Estonian Gene Project by collecting the first blood samples donated by donors who gave their prior informed consent. Learning from the lesson of the Icelandic project, in defining the characteristics of their national projects, the Estonian authorities took certain precautions which should meet the main concerns expressed after the launch of the Icelandic programme. In particular, the institution responsible for the project, the only one which is authorised to collect private data, is of public character (being appointed by the Ministry of Social Affairs) and subject to strict rules. Furthermore, an international ethics committee is entrusted with the task of monitoring the anonymity of the research. Also, any blood donor must give his/her written consent, and there is the total ban on the possibility of getting data from genetic tests of different kinds, like those used in criminal cases or for the identification of bodies. See Schümer, 'The Genetic Gold Mine', 26 Nov 2000, available at http://www.geenivaramu.ee/index.php?show=article&lang=eng&id=145&pid=3&offset=70 (last visited on 24 July 2004); 'Estonian Genome Project: First Blood Samples Received', *European Biotechnology Science & Industry News*, 10 Dec 2002, available at http://www.genomics.ee/index.php? lang=est&show=5&sub=17&level=40&nid=123 (last visited on 24 July 2004). A further example of a country which recently launched a similar programme is given by the Pacific archipelago of Tonga. In 2000 the Tongan government started a collaboration with the Australian genomics company Autogen Limited, with the purpose of isolating genes which are common to particular families located in one of the 170 islands that compose the archipelago; the Tongan situation is particularly suitable for this kind of research, since the populations of the islands have remained isolated for centuries, and there is thus less inter-racial mixture than normally (see Nicholson, 'Banking on genes', 4 Dec 2000, available at http://www.geenivaramu.ee/index.php?show=article&lang=eng&id=135&pid=3&offset=70 (last visited on 24 July 2004). Finally, Latvia, Singapore and the United Kingdom have also created national databases 'to capitalize on the knowledge of the human genome' (see doc. E/CN.4/Sub.2/2004/38, *supra* n. 7 para. 5).

genetics between the countries mentioned above and those without effective pertinent legislation encourages the transfer of practices of uncertain legality and morality to the latter countries, not so willing to enact laws similar to those adopted by developed countries in the hope of improving their level of development by importing genetic technology. At the European level this problem has been quite comprehensively approached, through the development of both legally binding instruments in the context of the Council of Europe and a framework normative instruments of EC law.

As for the Council of Europe, the Convention on Human Rights and Biomedicine (Oviedo Convention), which is also open to states not members of the Council of Europe,[24] was adopted in 1997.[25] It is a clearly human-rights-oriented treaty which, in its Preamble, besides recalling all pertinent international instruments on human rights, emphasises the fact that 'misuse of biology and medicine may lead to acts endangering human dignity'.[26] This principle is reiterated by the General Provisions of the Convention, which stress the primacy of the human being 'over the sole interest of society or science'[27] and the obligation of states parties to:

> protect the dignity and identity of all human beings and guarantee everyone, without discrimination, respect for their integrity and other rights and fundamental freedoms with regard to the application of biology and medicine.[28]

The Convention then deals with particular sensitive issues, i.e. consent, private life and right to information, the human genome, scientific research, transplantation of organs and tissues and economic issues. In addition, although quite recent, the Convention has to date been complemented by two Protocols, the first specifically dealing with the prohibition on cloning human beings (prohibiting, with no possible derogation, '[a]ny intervention seeking to create a human being genetically identical to another human being, whether living or dead')[29], and

24 See Art 34 of the Convention (*infra* n 25). A number of non-member states, particularly Australia, Canada, Japan, United States and the Holy See, also participated in the elaboration of the Convention; see Byk, 'La Convention européenne sur la biomedécine et les droits de l'homme et l'ordre juridique international' [2001] *Journal de Droit International* 47, at 55 (the author rightly emphasises the important fact that *'[h]ormis la Chine, l'ensemble des pays industrialises est concerné'*).

25 See Convention for the Protection of Human Rights and Dignity of the Human Being with regard to the Application of Biology and Medicine: Convention on Human Rights and Biomedicine, Oviedo, 4 Apr 1997, CETS n. 164. For a comprehensive analysis of the Oviedo Convention an its protocols see Byk, *supra* n. 24, *passim*; De Vel, 'Le rôle du Conseil de l'Europe en matière de bioéthique', [2003] *Revue Trimestrielle des Droits de l'Homme* 347.

26 See Preamble, 11th sentence.

27 See Art 2.

28 See Art 1.

29 See Additional Protocol to the Convention for the Protection of Human Rights and Dignity of the Human Being with regard to the Application of Biology and Medicine, on the Prohibition of Cloning Human Beings, Paris, 12 Jan 1998, CETS n. 168.

the second concerning transplantation of organs and tissues of human origin.[30] A third Protocol, concerning biomedical research, was finally adopted on 25 January 2005,[31] based on the possibly competing assumptions that 'progress in medical and biological sciences, in particular advances obtained through biomedical research, contributes to saving lives and improving quality of life', and that, given the 'paramount [importance of] the protection of the human being participating in research', 'biomedical research that is contrary to human dignity and human rights should never be carried out'.[32]

At the level of the European Union bioethics is considered to be strongly related to the right to the integrity of the person, as demonstrated by Article 3 of the Charter of Fundamental Rights of the European Union,[33] which has been incorporated as Part II of the Constitution for Europe.[34] According to such provision, in view of ensuring the integrity of the person it is indispensable that, in the field of medicine and biology:

> the following must be respected *in particular*: the free and informed consent of the person concerned, according to the procedures laid down by law; the prohibition of eugenic practices, in particular those aiming at the selection of persons; the prohibition on making the human body and its parts as such a source of financial gain; the prohibition of reproductive cloning of human beings [emphasis added].

In the context of EC legislation, the first legal instrument specifically dealing with bioethics which entered into force is the above mentioned Directive 98/44/EC.[35] As previously emphasised, the adoption process of such a directive required a very long debate, mainly due to the striking conflict between economic interests and ethical values at stake.[36] The final text was oriented towards the affirmation of ethical principles, especially by excluding the patentability of inventions linked with ethically sensitive issues. In particular, the human body and 'the simple discovery of one of its elements' (but not the 'sequence or partial sequence of a gene', which is patentable[37]), as well as processes for cloning human beings, processes for modifying the germ line genetic identity of human beings,

[30] See Additional Protocol to the Convention on Human Rights and Biomedicine concerning Transplantation of Organs and Tissues of Human Origin, Strasbourg, 24 Jan 2002, CETS n. 186.

[31] See Additional Protocol to the Convention on Human Rights and Biomedicine concerning Biomedical Research, Strasbourg, 25 Jan 2005, CETS n. 195.

[32] See Preamble, fourth, eighth and seventh sentences respectively.

[33] See [2000] OJ C/364/1.

[34] See [2004] OJ C/310/1.

[35] See *supra* n. 20.

[36] See Lenoir, *supra* n. 4, 544.

[37] See Dir 98/44/EC, *supra* n. 20, Art 5.

and uses of human embryos for industrial or commercial purposes (all practices whose exploitation is considered 'contrary to ordre public or morality'[38]), are qualified as unpatentable by the Directive. Furthermore, the 38th recital to the Preamble states that the list of unpatentable inventions included in article 6[39] is 'obviously' not exhaustive, and all processes 'the use of which offend against human dignity' are also excluded from patentability.

In spite of these provisions, ethical content of Directive 98/44 was not considered fully satisfactory by some EC Member States, as is demonstrated by the fact that in the year of its adoption it was challenged by the Netherlands, supported by Italy and Norway, before the European Court of Justice. The Netherlands argued, inter alia, that the patentability of isolated parts of the human body, provided for by Article 5(2) of the Directive, 'reduces living human matter to a means to an end, undermining human dignity', and that 'the absence of a provision requiring verification of the consent of the donor or recipient of products obtained by biotechnological means undermines the right to self-determination'.[40] The Court rejected this plea. Regarding the first part, it stated that, since '[o]nly inventions which combine a natural element with a technical process enabling it to be isolated or produced for an industrial application can be the subject of an application for a patent',[41] it follows that 'an element of the human body may be part of a product which is patentable but it may not, in its natural environment, be appropriated'.[42] In other words, according to the Court:

> the protection envisaged by the Directive covers only the result of inventive, scientific or technical work, and extends to biological data existing in their natural state in human beings only where necessary for the achievement and exploitation of a particular industrial application.[43]

The work on the sequence of human genes is used by the Court to exemplify its conclusion. In the words of the Court:

> [t]he result of such work can give rise to the grant of a patent only if the application is accompanied by both a description of the original method of sequencing which led to the invention and an explanation of the industrial application

38 *Ibid.*, Art 6.

39 See *supra* n. 38 and corresponding text.

40 See Case C-377/98 *Kingdom of the Netherlands v European Parliament and Council of the European Union*, I–07079, para. 69. On this case see Maubernard, 'Le droit fondamental à la dignité humaine" en droit communautaire: la brevetabilité du vivant à l'épreuve de la jurisprudence de la Cour de Justice des Communautés Européennes', [2003] *Revue Trimestrielle des Droits de l'Homme* 483.

41 See Case C–377/98, *supra* n. 40, para. 72.

42 *Ibid.*, para. 73.

43 *Ibid.*, para. 75.

> to which the work is to lead, as required by Article 5(3) of the Directive. In the absence of an application in that form, there would be no invention, but rather the discovery of a DNA sequence, which would not be patentable as such.[44]

In addition, according to the Court, considering the provisions of Articles 5(1)[45] and 6,[46] combined with the 38th recital to the Preamble,[47] 'the Directive frames the law on patents in a manner sufficiently rigorous to ensure that the human body effectively remains unavailable and inalienable and that human dignity is thus safeguarded'.[48]

As for the second part of the argument concerning 'the right to human integrity, in so far as it encompasses, in the context of medicine and biology, the free and informed consent of the donor and recipient',[49] the Court considered it not pertinent to the dispute, by stating that:

> [r]eliance on this fundamental right is . . . clearly misplaced as against a directive which concerns only the grant of patents and whose scope does not therefore extend to activities before and after that grant, whether they involve research or the use of the patented products.[50]

In addition to Directive 98/44, other EC legal instruments deal with bioethics, also adopting a clearly ethically-oriented approach. First, Directive 98/79/EC[51] states, in Article 1(4), that 'removal, collection and use of tissues, cells and substances of human origin shall be governed, in relation to ethics, by the principles laid down in the [Oviedo] Convention', also emphasising, at Article 19, the importance of maintaining confidentiality with regard to information obtained by the relevant actors in fulfilling tasks pertinent to the object of the Directive.

Decision 182/1999/EC (no longer in force[52]) states that all research activities conducted pursuant to the framework programme dealt with by the Decision itself, regarding research, technological development and demonstration activities for the period 1998 to 2002, 'shall be carried out in compliance with fundamental ethical principles'.[53]

[44] *Ibid.*, para. 74.
[45] See *supra* n. 37.
[46] See *supra* n. 38.
[47] See *supra,* in the text to n. 39.
[48] See Case C–377/98, *supra* n. 40, para. 77.
[49] *Ibid.*, para. 78.
[50] *Ibid.*, para. 79.
[51] See Dir n. 98/79/EC of the European Parliament and of the Council of 27 Oct 1998 on in vitro diagnostic medical devices, [1998] OJ L/331/1.
[52] See Decision 182/1999/EC of the European Parliament and of the Council of 22 Dec 1998 concerning the fifth framework programme of the European Community for research, technological development and demonstration activities (1998 to 2002) [1999] OJ L/26/1.
[53] See Art 7. Decision n. 182/1999/EC was then supplemented and implemented by Decision 1999/167/EC (Council Decision n. 1999/167/EC of 25 Jan 1999 adopting a specific programme for research, technological development and demonstration on quality of life and management of living resources (1998 to 2002), [1999] OJ L/64/1), which also shared the

Also of relevance is Directive 2001/20/EC,[54] which has the purpose of ensuring that in the implementation of clinical trials on human subjects involving medicinal products 'good clinical practice' is fully respected. 'Good clinical practice' is defined as a 'set of internationally recognised ethical and scientific quality requirements which must be observed for designing, conducting, recording and reporting clinical trials that involve the participation of human subjects'.[55] Compliance with this good practice is considered essential for ensuring 'that the rights, safety and well-being of trial subjects are protected, and that the results of the clinical trials are credible'.[56] Protection of clinical trials subjects is in the main guaranteed by requiring their prior informed consent, and special measures of protection are provided for minors and mentally handicapped adults not able to give informed legal consent.[57] Furthermore, it is worth emphasising the fact that a clinical trial may be initiated only after the authorisation of an Ethics Committee,[58] which must be established and put into operation by Member States pursuant to Article 6 of the Directive.

Finally, Directive 2004/23/EC, specifically dealing with the treatment of human tissues and cells,[59] in addition to specific provisions regarding the safeguarding of donors' rights, concerning in particular consent,[60] data protection and confidentiality,[61] emphasises its consistency with fundamental rights[62] and highlights the fact that, although it 'should not interfere with decisions made by Member States concerning the use or non-use of any specific type of human cells' (including embryonic stem cells), in the event that

> any particular use of such cells is authorised in a Member State, this Directive will require the application of all provisions necessary to protect public health,

same ethical concerns. In particular, Annex II stated that '[f]ull respect of human rights and fundamental ethical principles will be ensured throughout all activities in the specific programme in accordance with Article 6 of the European Parliament and Council Decision on the fifth framework programme'.

54 See Dir 2001/20/EC of the European Parliament and of the Council of 4 Apr 2001 on the approximation of the laws, regulations and administrative provisions of the Member States relating to the implementation of good clinical practice in the conduct of clinical trials on medicinal products for human use [20001] OJ L/121/34.

55 See Art 1 (2). The principle of 'good clinical practice' is reaffirmed by Part 4(B)(1) of Annex I to Dir 2001/83/EC of the European Parliament and of the Council of 6 Nov 2001 on the Community code relating to medicinal products for human use, [2001] OJ L/311/67.

56 *Ibid.*

57 See, respectively, Art 4 and 5.

58 See Art 3 (2).

59 See Dir 2004/23/EC of the European Parliament and of the Council of 31 Mar 2004 on setting standards of quality and safety for the donation, procurement, testing, processing, preservation, storage and distribution of human tissues and cells [2004] OJ L/102/48.

60 See Art 13.

61 See Art 14.

62 See Preamble, 22nd recital.

> given the specific risks of these cells based on the scientific knowledge and their particular nature, and *guarantee respect for fundamental rights*.[63]

In Europe, thanks to the broad regional action developed in the field of bioethics, a significant step towards an ethically satisfactory approach to the subject has been made. The same cannot be said with regard to the rest of the world; at the global level, the main problem affecting the subject is (as previously pointed out) the existence of deep inconsistencies among different national legislations, which may encourage potential bio-criminals to transfer their activities to the world's most permissive countries. As a matter of fact, such a problem has a particularly evident 'intercontinental' character, in the sense that the above inconsistencies are particularly evident when the pertinent law of Western countries is compared with the legal reality of (some) non-European developing countries. The elaboration of a common European regulation of the matter is thus not sufficient to address the problem, since it does not naturally affect extra-European countries. It follows that the solution of such problem must be searched for at a more comprehensive level. In this sense, although, perhaps, international law may not be considered a panacea for all the problems linked to bioethics, at least some of them may be overcome by developing a common regulation of the matter at the 'universal' level. Negotiations in the international arena are actually characterised by a search for mutually agreeable solutions of controversial aspects concerning a given subject, and when these solutions are finally agreed, they are appropriate to lead to the development and, eventually, the crystallisation of a common and universally valid approach to such aspects. National and regional differences may thus be overcome, to the extent that states adapt their domestic law to newly adopted international rules. This kind of action is particularly appropriate in the field of bioethics where, as already noted, the content of national laws on the subject is particularly influenced by the local environment, given the strict connection of the matter at stake with particularly sensitive aspects of social and cultural life. In recent years, the international community seems to have become conscious of this necessity, by developing legal instruments on bioethics applicable at the universal level.

V. SCIENTIFIC PROGRESS, THE HUMAN GENOME AND INTERNATIONAL LAW

International legal action for regulating bioethics has mainly taken place, at the universal level, in the framework of UNESCO, through the

[63] See Preamble, 12th recital (emphasis added).

adoption of two declarations in 1997[64] and 2003.[65] In addition, a new comprehensive Declaration on bioethics, with the purpose, inter alia of 'ensur[ing] the respect for human dignity and the protection of human rights and fundamental freedoms in [the sphere of] bioethical decision making, in accordance with human rights law',[66] is in preparation at the moment of writing (the last version currently available of the UNESCO Draft Declaration on Universal Norms on Bioethics (DDUNB) was elaborated on 27 August 2004).[67] It is natural for the international community to have become more concerned about the matter in point at a time when biogenetic research has produced its first tangible fruits, particularly on account of the new horizons opened up, not only to medical science, since the completion of the sequencing of the human genome. Nevertheless, the potentially adverse effects of technological progress had been perceived since the 1960s; in particular, point 18 of the Teheran Declaration of 1968 warned that scientific and technological progress 'may . . . endanger the rights and freedoms of individuals and will require continuing attention'.[68] Later on, in 1975, the UN General Assembly proclaimed the Declaration on the Use of Scientific and Technological Progress in the Interests of Peace and for the Benefit of Mankind.[69] Although such Declaration, being of general character, does not contain any specific reference to biogenetics, or more generally to biotechnology, a number of its provisions foresaw the possible dangers which might result from the incorrect use of biogenetic technology. First, the Preamble warns that 'while scientific and technological developments provide ever increasing opportunities to better the conditions of life of peoples and nations', at the same time, 'in a number of instances they can give rise to social problems, as well as threaten the human rights and fundamental freedoms of the individual', entailing 'dangers for the civil and political rights of the individual or of the group and for human dignity'.[70] For this reason, states are called upon to take appropriate measures 'to prevent the use of scientific and technological developments, particularly by the State organs, to limit or interfere with the

64 See Universal Declaration on the Human Genome and Human Rights, 11 Nov 1997, available in the UNESCO Web site, at http://www.unesco.org (last visited on July 24, 2004).

65 See International Declaration on Human Genetic Data, 16 Oct 2003, also available in the UNESCO website, at http://www.unesco.org (last visited on July 24, 2004).

66 See Art 2.

67 See UNESCO Doc. SHS/EST/04/CIB-2-Gred-2/4 Rev. 2 of 27 Aug 2004, available in the UNESCO website, at http://www.unesco.org (last visited on 30 August 2004).

68 See Declaration of Teheran of 13 May 1968, U.N. Doc. A/CONF.32/41, available at http://www.unhchr.ch/html/menu3/b/b_tehern.htm (last visited on 24 July 2004).

69 G. A. Res. 3384 (XXX) of 10 Nov 1975, available at http://www.unhchr.ch/html/menu3/b/70.htm (last visited on July 24, 2004).

70 See the second and fourth sentences of the Preamble.

enjoyment of the human rights and fundamental freedoms of the individual',[71] and to protect all strata of the population:

> both socially and materially, from possible harmful effects of the misuse of scientific and technological developments, including their misuse to infringe upon the rights of the individual or of the group, particularly with regard to respect for privacy and the protection of the human personality and its physical and intellectual integrity.[72]

In addition, the Declaration also places particular emphasis on the need to preserve the integrity of human dignity, by calling upon states to 'prevent and preclude the utilization of scientific and technological achievements to the detriment of human rights and fundamental freedoms and the dignity of the human person'.[73] Finally, it is opportune to emphasise that the declaration requires states 'to ensure that the utilization of scientific and technological achievements promotes the fullest realization of human rights and fundamental freedoms without any discrimination whatsoever on grounds of race, sex, language or religious beliefs'.[74] Certainly, an evolutionary interpretation of this provision would also support the inclusion among the means of discrimination provided for therein of the expression 'genetic heritage'.

The General Assembly renewed its concerns relating to the possible adverse effects of scientific and technological progress on human rights in 1993,[75] noting that 'certain advances, notably in the *biomedical* and life sciences as well as in information technology, may have potentially adverse consequences for the integrity, dignity and human rights of the individual',[76] and calling upon all member states 'to ensure that the achievements of scientific and technological progress and the intellectual potential of mankind are used for promoting and encouraging universal respect for human rights and fundamental freedoms'.[77]

As already pointed out, the first specific international legal instruments on bioethics, the Universal Declaration on the Human Genome and Human Rights (UDHGHR),[78] was adopted by UNESCO in 1997.

[71] See para. 2.
[72] See para. 6.
[73] See para. 8.
[74] See para. 7.
[75] See 'Human rights and scientific and technological progress', Doc. A/RES/48/140 of 20 Dec 1993, available at http://www.un.org/documents/ga/res/48/a48r140.htm (last visited on 24 July 2004).
[76] See Preamble, eighth sentence.
[77] See para. 1.
[78] See *supra* n. 64.

Nevertheless, in pursuance of its own institutional mandate,[79] UNESCO had already started to address the subject in the 1960s, when the work on the elaboration of a declaration on race and racial prejudice was launched. In a preparatory document, the fact that racial discrimination is normally founded on biology was stressed.[80] The document emphasises that '[racist] beliefs with regard to racial superiority relate mainly to intelligence and behaviour, and ... [attribute] the cultural backwardness of certain peoples to genetic inferiority'.[81] Although there is no explicit reference to genetic discrimination in the Declaration on Race and Racial Prejudice, adopted in 1978, it nevertheless includes a number of provisions which are implicitly pertinent to such subject.[82]

Despite the obvious lack of specific references to issues concerning biogenetics, the two declarations just described (particularly the 1975 Declaration on the Use of Scientific and Technological Progress in the Interests of Peace and for the Benefit of Mankind) seem to have foreseen the potential threats of the possible misuse of biogenetics, which could be utilised as formidable means for putting into practice delirant views based on racial discrimination and eugenics. One can only shudder when imagining what Hitler could have done had he possessed the present-day knowledge on biogenetics.

The starting point of the UDHGHR just reflects the concerns highlighted nearly 30 years before its adoption, solemnly emphasising that research on the human genome 'should fully respect human dignity, freedom and human rights, as well as the prohibition of all forms of discrimination based on genetic characteristics'.[83] The main purpose of the

[79] Art I (1) of the UNESCO Constitution (available in the UNESCO website, at http://www.unesco.org, last visited on 24 July 2004) states that '[t]he purpose of the Organization is to contribute to peace and security by promoting collaboration among the nations through education, science and culture in order to further universal respect for justice, for the rule of law and for the human rights and fundamental freedoms which are affirmed for the peoples of the world, without distinction of race, sex, language or religion, by the Charter of the United Nations'.

[80] See Hiernaux, 'Biological aspects of the racial question', in UNESCO, *Four Statements on the Race Question* (Paris, 1969), 9, at 9, available at http://unescodoc.unesco.org/images/0012/001229/122962eo.pdf (last visited on 24 July 2004)

[81] *Ibid.*, 15.

[82] See, for example, Art 1 (1) ('[a]ll human beings belong to a single species and are descended from a common stock. They are born equal in dignity and rights and all form an integral part of humanity'), Art 1 (5) ('[t]he differences between the achievements of the different peoples are entirely attributable to geographical, historical, political, economic, social and cultural factors. Such differences can in no case serve as a pretext for any rank-ordered classification of nations or peoples'), and Art 2 (1) ('[a]ny theory which involves the claim that racial or ethnic groups are inherently superior or inferior, thus implying some would be entitled to dominate or eliminate others, presumed to be inferior, or which bases value judgements on racial differentiation, has no scientific foundation and is contrary to the moral and ethical principles of humanity').

[83] See Universal Declaration on the Human Genome and Human Rights, *supra* n. 64, Preamble, last sentence.

Declaration is to set out a series of basic ethical principles of universal character to guide both states (especially their legislative action) and practitioners in their activities concerning the subject. In this perspective, Article 1 states that:

> [t]he human genome underlies the fundamental unity of all members of the human family, as well as the recognition of their inherent dignity and diversity. In a symbolic sense, it is the heritage of humanity.[84]

VI. THE HUMAN GENOME AS THE HERITAGE OF HUMANITY[85]

In evaluating the significance of Article 1 of the UDHGHR, we must first question the meaning of the term 'in a symbolic sense'. The genome is physically, tangibly appreciable, and it may be the object of material exploitation, just like the deep seabed, Antarctica or the moon (considered as common heritage of humankind). We nevertheless think that the use of the term 'symbolic' in Article 1 is not inappropriate. On the contrary, one may argue that, by using such term, the Declaration (interpreted objectively according to the meaning of its text) is intended to emphasise the fact that the significance of the human genome goes much further than its simple physical character as a sequence of molecules, and it is thus mainly considered for its potential value for human life. In other words, the human genome represents the heritage of humanity, not in its physical state, but rather in its symbolic value, which is reflected in the knowledge related to the genome itself, and especially in the complex of the scientific, medical and ethical implications attached to such knowledge, which are of great significance for humanity as a whole. Another point to be emphasised is that, in defining the human genome as 'the heritage of humanity', the drafters of the UDHGHR have not used the expression 'common heritage of humanity' but just 'the heritage of humanity'. This, in combination with the term 'in a symbolic sense', seems to indicate that the genome in its physical state is not commonly available, since only the

[84] The first part of the sentence is reproduced by the sixth sentence to the Preamble of the U. N. Commission of Human Rights Resolution n. 2003/69 of 25 Apr 2003, concerning 'human rights and bioethics'.

[85] On this topic see, in particular, Sturges, 'Who Should Hold Property Rights to the Human Genome? An Application of the Common Heritage of Humankind', (1997) 13 *American University International Law Review* 219; Spectar, 'The Fruit of the Human Genome Tree: Cautionary Tales about Technology, Investment, and the Heritage of Humankind', (2001) 23 *Loyola of Los Angeles International and Comparative Law Review* 1. See also U.N. Sub-Commission on the Promotion and Protection of Human Rights, 'Human Rights and Bioethics', expanded working paper submitted by Ms. Iulia-Antonella Motoc in accordance with Sub-Commission decision 2002/114, doc. E/CN.4/Sub.2/2003/36 of 10 July 2003, para. 7 ff.

person who is the physical 'owner' of the genome may consent to its use; the genome belonging to one individual may thus not be appropriated by anyone without his/her prior consent. At the same time, two other major consequences arise from the characterisation of the human genome as envisaged by Article 1 of the UDHGHR: first, the physical owner of the genome may consent *only* to uses of his/her own genome which are considered lawful by the international community (*rectius*: compatible with the dignity of humankind), and no unlawful use (such as reproductive cloning, prohibited by Article 11 of the UDHGHR) of the genome may be made by anyone; secondly, any benefit deriving from the research developed on the genome belonging to anyone *must* be shared with the whole of humanity.

Consistently with the approach of Article 1 of the UDHGHR, there is a series of norms in the Declaration which clearly appear to depict the human genome as the heritage of humanity. Article 12(a) states that '[b]enefits from advances in biology, genetics and medicine, concerning the human genome, *shall be made available to all*, with due regard for the dignity and human rights of each individual' (emphasis added). The same provision adds that:

> [t]he applications of research, including applications in biology, genetics and medicine, concerning the human genome, shall seek to offer relief from suffering and improve the health of individuals *and humankind as a whole* [letter (b); emphasis added].

Other provisions of the Declaration also support, although less explicitly (but not less clearly), the idea of the human genome as the heritage of humanity. Article 4, for example, states that '[t]he human genome in its natural state shall not give rise to financial gains'. Article 14 also expresses the principle of 'freedom in the conduct of research on the human genome'. Furthermore, part E of the Declaration underlines the central role of solidarity and international cooperation, by emphasising the necessity of:

> fostering the international dissemination of scientific knowledge concerning the human genome, human diversity and genetic research and, in that regard, to foster scientific and cultural co-operation, particularly between industrialized and developing countries.[86]

Article 19, in the context of international cooperation with developing countries, requires states (although using the conditional 'should') to encourage measures enabling, inter alia, 'the free exchange of scientific

[86] See Art 18.

knowledge and information in the areas of biology, genetics and medicine to be promoted'.[87]

UNESCO's perception of the human genome as the heritage of humanity, which emerges very clearly from the UDHGHR, is also confirmed by the 2003 Declaration on Human Genetic Data (DHGD),[88] whose Article 19 states that:

> benefits resulting from the use of human genetic data, human proteomic data or biological samples collected for medical and scientific research should be shared with the society as a whole and the international community.[89]

Similarly, Article 24(b) of the DDUNB asserts that 'States should foster the international dissemination of scientific information and make every effort to guarantee the free flow and sharing of scientific and technological knowledge'.[90]

It is important to emphasise that the fact that the UN General Assembly, while seeking 'to promote scientific and technical progress in the fields of biology and genetics in a manner respectful of fundamental rights and for the benefit of all',[91] has adopted the UDHGHR gives it greater solemnity and reinforces the idea of the genome as the heritage of humanity.

Apart from the two specific declarations, there are a number of international provisions on human rights which, as a matter of legal coherence, implicitly confirm the status of the human genome as the heritage of humanity. In particular, the effective implementation of all (conventional, soft law or, eventually, customary) provisions which assert the individual right to adequate standards of living and/or physical and mental health[92] would actually be impaired if dissemination of knowledge on the human genome was in any way limited. Also, it is quite clear, and thus does not require further assessment, that additional support for the idea proposed

[87] See Art. 19(iv). Art 19 also recommends states to encourage measures enabling 'the capacity of developing countries to carry out research on human biology and genetics, taking into consideration their specific problems, to be developed and strengthened' (Art 19(ii)) and "developing countries to benefit from the achievements of scientific and technological research so that their use in favour of economic and social progress can be to the benefit of all' (Art 19(iii)).

[88] See *supra* n. 65.

[89] Art 18 also confirms the principle of international cooperation as set out in Art 18 and 19 of the UDHGHR (see *supra* n. 82 and 83 and corresponding texts).

[90] See also Art 13, entitled 'Sharing of Benefits', as well as the rest of Art 24.

[91] See A/RES/53/152 of 9 Dec 1998, 'The human genome and human rights", fifth sentence of the Preamble.

[92] See, for example, Art 25 of the Universal Declaration of Human Rights (U.N. G.A. Res. 217 A (III) of 10 Dec 1948), which states that '[e]veryone has the right to a standard of living adequate for the health and well-being of himself and of his family'; similarly, Art 12(1) of the International Covenant on Economic, Social and Cultural Rights (993 UNTS 3) proclaims 'the right of everyone to the enjoyment of the highest attainable standard of physical and mental health'.

herein is supplied by those provisions, like Article 27 of the Universal Declaration of Human Rights, which proclaim that every human being 'has the right freely to ... share in scientific advancement and its benefits'.[93]

Finally, international practice also confirms that the perception of the human genome as the heritage of humanity is well entrenched in the international community. In 1993, for example, a leading international workshop on 'Legal Aspects of the Human Genome Project' was held in Bilbao, and produced the Bilbao Declaration. According to this Declaration, which also proclaimed the principles of freedom of scientific research and free dissemination of knowledge related to the human genome:

> the benefits of the Human Genome Project affect the entire world, and its results belong to the human beings of this and future generations, and not to the scientists [. . .] or to the countries supporting them.[94]

Subsequently, from the 2000 Blair/Clinton joint declaration[95] to the decision of both the public and private institutions that had completed the sequencing of the genome in 2001 to leave it publicly available to the scientific community without patenting the results of their researches,[96] relevant actors have confirmed their feeling that knowledge related to the human genome is a value which is not suitable to be appropriated by some, being a patrimony belonging to humanity as a whole.[97] In the context of such practice the United Nations Millennium Declaration emerges, in which virtually the entire international community, in the context of the

93 See *supra* n. 92. Almost identically, Art 1(b) of the International Covenant on Economic, Social and Cultural Rights (see *supra* n. 92), binds States parties to recognise the right of everyone '[t]o enjoy the benefits of scientific progress and its applications'.

94 See International Workshop on Legal Aspects of the Human Genome Project, Bilbao Declaration, Bilbao, Spain, 24–26 May 1993, cited by Spectar, *supra* n. 85, 10.

95 See *supra* n. 3 and corresponding text.

96 See *supra* section I.

97 See, inter alia, High Commissioner's Expert Group on Human Rights and Biotechnology, 'Conclusions', Geneva, 24–25 Jan 2002, available at http://www.unhchr.ch/biotech/conclusions.htm (last visited on 28 Aug 2004), para. 24 ('the enormous benefits promised by biotechnology must not be restricted to one group or society. The sharing of these benefits involves not only compensation for the contribution of genetic materials, but also the facilitation of technology transfer between developed and developing countries'); Council of Europe, Parliamentary Assembly, Recommendation 1512 (2001), adopted on 25 Apr 2001, para. 7. See also the position expressed by the Government of Cuba in a submission made to the U.N. Commission on Human Rights in 2002 (see UN doc. E/CN.4/2003/98 of 10 Feb 2003, para. 9), according to which '[s]tating that the human genome is part of common heritage of mankind, the Government [of Cuba] also expressed support for open access for both the general public and specialist personnel in every country to knowledge relating to the human genome, and opposed any form of discrimination on the basis of knowledge relating to an individual's genetic code'.

UN General Assembly, solemnly proclaimed that, inter alia, 'free access to information on the human genome sequence' had to be ensured.[98]

The human genome, which, as pointed out by a scholar, is the 'result of millions of years of evolution, a natural process caused by human adaptation and development',[99] represents the secret of human life, a life that we have inherited and that (our main mission in the world) we must transmit to future generations as custodians of a treasure which belong to humanity as a whole. It is, as such, something which cannot be owned by anyone.

VII. HUMAN GENOME AND HUMAN DIGNITY: PROBLEMATICAL ISSUES

As shown by the analysis provided in the previous sections, existing international instruments on bioethics in general, and on the human genome in particular, mainly concentrate on the problems related to human dignity which may be attached to the development and use of biogenetic knowledge. In this perspective, it is not easy exactly to select and isolate the single relevant issues which may potentially have detrimental effects on the integrity of human dignity, as well as to define the correct legal and ethical approach, both *de lege lata* and *de lege ferenda*, that should be adopted with regard to any of those issues, especially in connection with certain 'border' problems which are raised by the enormous potentialities of biogenetics. It is thus important to emphasise that this section will deal with problems raised by biogenetics relating to the dignity inherent in the individual rather than to human rights in general. This is the reason certain issues included in the area of interaction between bioethics and human rights, like that of the safeguarding of the rights of indigenous peoples over biogenetic resources, will not be dealt with here.

So as to (try to) bring systematic order to the present analysis, we will first take into account pertinent issues that have come into existence exactly as a consequence of the development of biogenetics, giving rise to new ethical problems which must be regulated by the adoption of specific legal instruments at both national and international levels. Such issues will be referred to as 'ethical issues'. We will then consider issues that, although attaining specific traits in the context of biogenetics, may be ascribed to types already regulated by international law before the advent of genetic biotechnology, and their legal regulation may thus be included in the context of existing general rules on human rights regulating the

[98] See 'United Nations Millennium Declaration', U.N. G.A. Res. 55/2 of 18 Sept 2000, para. 23.

[99] See Sturges, *supra* n. 85, 249.

'pre-existing' legal types to which they belong. This second kind of issues will be refereed to as 'legal issues'.

Ethical Issues

(a) Identification of Individuals

It is unquestionable that the development of biogenetics has resulted in outstanding benefits in the context of criminal proceedings or cases regarding paternity issues. Thanks to new technologies it is now possible to ascertain (obviously when some organic material is available) the person responsible for a given crime or whether or not an individual is the mother or the father of a child, avoiding any possibility of error. The reason for this is that it is impossible for them to be two people owning an identical genomic heritage; in other words, every individual has his/her own idiosyncratic 'genetic fingerprint'. Biogenetics, which allows scientists to identify such finger print from any kind of organic material (*e.g.* a blood track, a hair or a little piece of nail), has thus made a terrific contribution to making justice 'more just' in several countries in the world.

Nevertheless, there is another side of the coin, which raises two different problems. The first consists in the fact that, especially in criminal proceedings, the screening of the DNA of the person concerned is made (for obvious reasons) compulsorily, that is to say without his/her approval, thus derogating from the principle of consent (as well as the principle of confidentiality), which is generally considered fundamental in the context of bioethics (see below, in this section). In this regard Article 9 of the UDHGHR states that:

> in order to protect human rights and fundamental freedoms, limitations to the principles of consent and confidentiality may only be prescribed by law, for compelling reasons within the bounds of public international law and the international law of human rights.[100]

In principle, the need to avoid mistakes in the identification of people responsible for serious crimes (such as murders, rape, etc.) is certainly to be included among the compelling reasons that may justify derogations from the principles of consent and confidentiality. Nevertheless, the different perceptions of the concept of crime in the different countries raises serious risks that the collection of genetic fingerprints is used for

[100] Similarly, Art 12 of the DHGD states that '[w]hen human genetic data or human proteomic data are collected for the purposes of forensic medicine or in civil, criminal and other legal proceedings, including parentage testing, the collection of biological samples, in vivo or post-mortem, should be made only in accordance with domestic law consistent with the international law of human rights'.

illegitimate reasons. In the context of the negotiations which led to the adoption of the UDHGHR, for example, a number of delegates, mainly from developing countries, emphasised the possibility that certain governments might consider their political opponents as criminals,[101] making them the object of compulsory genetic screening. It is thus extremely important to avoid recourse to alleged and unjustified 'compelling reasons' resulting in a more or less disguised violation of fundamental human rights. In this sense, Article 26 of the Oviedo Convention is more precise than Article 9 of the UDHGHR, since it is more accurate to state that restrictions on the exercise of the rights provided for by the Convention may be imposed only when necessary 'in a democratic society in the interest of public safety, for the prevention of crime, for the protection of public health or for the protection of the rights and freedoms of others'. The use of the word 'democratic' is in principle appropriate to prevent the practice on collecting genetic data on individuals the only reason being their political ideas.

The second possible problem related to the matter in point concerns the idea of hereditary or genetic criminality. If we let our imaginations run free, we can imagine what could happen in the (near) future in the event that scientists, having studied the previously collected common genetic data of criminals, inferred that the criminal attitude of a person was caused by a particular genetic feature. At worst, it might even be possible to assume that criminality is hereditary. In this event, would the individual freedom of the people concerned be limited for the sole reason of their genetic inheritance, thus violating, inter alia, the fundamental principle of *ex post facto*? That such perspective is not simply fantastic is demonstrated by the fact that the idea that criminality derives from certain genetic characteristics has recently been put forward in certain countries, *i.e.* Canada and United States, where, inter alia, some proposals for the collection of DNA databanks of convicts have been made by governmental entities.[102]

(b) Human Cloning

Are we 'playing God'[103] or opening a new era in the field of healthcare and well-being? This is the Hamletian question which characterises the

[101] See Lenoir, *supra* n. 4, 565.

[102] See Tauer, 'International Protection of Genetic Information: The Progression of the Human Genome Project and the Current Framework of Human Rights Doctrines', (2001) 29 *Denver Journal of International Law and Policy* 209, at 220. See also Kivilcim-Forsam, 'Eugénisme et ses diverses formes', [2003] *Revue Trimestrielle des Droits de l'Homme* 515, at 524 f.

[103] See Dworkin, 'Playing God. Genes, Clones, and Luck', in Dworkin (ed.), *Sovereign Virtue* (Cambridge, 2000), 427 ff.

most controversial aspect of biogenetics, human cloning. Maybe the right answer is that we are doing both things at the same time. So, at this point the question is: is it ethically (and, *a fortiori*, legally) permissible to play God in order to improve the potentialities for medicine? At a preliminary stage, it seems important to emphasise that all the observations to be made in this section will be tempered by the awareness that, considering the cultural and ideological diversity which characterises the present world, in all probability there is not a universally valid answer to such question.

Human cloning means the laboratory production of human beings. There are two kinds of cloning: the less controversial one (in the sense that its ethical rightness and lawfulness are generally rejected) is reproductive cloning, which means laboratory creation of human embryos to be transferred into women's wombs to produce cloned human babies. The other kind (although all human cloning has a reproductive character, since a new and individual human being, at least at the embryonic stage, is produced in any case) is called therapeutic (or scientific) cloning. Therapeutic cloning involves the creation of cloned human embryos with the purpose of developing stem cells which, being 'unspecialised' and capable of dividing and renewing themselves for a long period, have the potential to develop into many different cell types in the body, serving as a sort of repairing system for the body itself. The discovery of such kind of cells has opened important new frontiers for the treatment of a number of serious diseases previously virtually incurable, as well as for the creation of 'spare-parts' human organs and tissues. The stem cells of a cloned embryo are removed in the laboratory, leading to the embryo's death. Stem cells may also be obtained without using embryos, but 'adult stem cells' are claimed to be less proficient at treating diseases than embryonic stem cells, especially for the fact that body tissue or organs created by embryonic stem cells contain exactly the same DNA as does the person from whom the clones are made, thus preventing the risk of the patient rejecting the new cells implanted into his/her body. But, as stated by Dr. Harry Griffin of the Roslin Institute of Edinburgh, which in 1996 created Dolly (the well-known cloned sheep), therapeutic cloning 'is clearly not therapeutic for the embryo'.[104] So, the problem to be overcome for establishing whether the practices in point may be considered lawful is clearly and exclusively of an ethical character: is the human embryo a person (or a human being)? In other words, must we adhere to the idealistic approach, attributing the dignity of human beings (and, *a fortiori*, the

104 Centre for Bioethics and Public Policy conference, London, 14 Nov 2000, information taken by SPUC Scotland, 'Human Cloning', 12 Aug 2004, available at http://www.spucscotland.org/education/beginningoflife/humancloning/humancloning.html (last visited on 28 August 2004).

rights attached to human dignity by international law) to the embryo, or to the pragmatic approach, according to which the embryo is a simple agglomerate of cells which, although having the potential to evolve into a human being, is actually unable to feel any human sensation, and cannot thus be considered human?

An answer to this question could be found by taking as a starting point the philosophical ideas of Plato (427 B.C.–347 B.C.). He thought that any thing or living being in the real world was nothing but an imperfect representation of a perfect model existing only in the 'world of ideas'. It follows from this perspective that any human being is, by his/her own nature, also imperfect in him/herself. At the same time, all human beings have different qualities, and these qualities make them more or less close to the ideal model they represent. Can we deny that this perspective reflects the real world? In practical terms, can we deny, for example, that St. Francis or Mahatma Gandhi is closer to the perfect idea of human being than a serial killer who spent his life raping and killing children? But, this notwithstanding, the international community and all civilised nations (in the sense of Article 38 of the Statute of the International Court of Justice) do not describe different levels of protection to individuals by reason of their different effective qualities; the serial killer is entitled to the same degree of legal protection as Mahatma Gandhi. The protection of human dignity is inherent in the human condition which qualifies any human being, irrespective of his/her status, capacities, ability to perceive sensations, etc. If we accepted the idea that the human embryo was not to be considered as entitled to human dignity due to the fact that it was unable to perceive human sensations, we would deny the idea that the human condition was valuable as such and, in addition, we would open a Pandora's box which could lead one to support the ethical goodness and legality of ideas like, *e.g.*, euthanasia or exploitation under inhumane conditions of the work of severely mentally handicapped persons who are not able to feel fatigue, or the social immorality of the form of exploitation they are suffering. Thus, to refer to Plato's philosophy again, what modern legal orders protect is the 'idea' of humanity, that is to say the dignity which is inherent in any human being. This kind of holistic approach necessarily encompasses the recognition of the dignity of the human embryo, which, although at the very first stage, is a representation of the perfect model of a human being existing only in the world of ideas. Of course, if the embryo is to be considered a human being, when he/she comes into existence he/she de facto has the same rights as any other human being, and he/she thus cannot be legally sacrificed for the benefit of another human being. This idea has recently been supported by an opinion issued on 4 February 2005 by Judge Jeffrey Lawrence of Cook County (Illinois) that 'a pre-embryo is a "human being"' and, therefore, 'a legal person', 'from the time of conception', 'whether or not it is implanted in its mother's womb'; the judge thus found that a couple, which in 2000 had stored nine embryos at a clinic for assisted human reproduction, was entitled to compensation for the fact that such embryos had been accidentally discarded by a clinic worker.[105]

On the other hand, we have thousands of people suffering and dying because of genetic diseases which could be treated by the use of therapeutic cloning. This cannot be considered merely as an utilitaristic approach: it is not humanely easy (especially for those who are directly interested) to accept the fact that the life of a 'real' person, with his/her history, with all his/her feelings, human relationships and expectations, is inescapably predestined to be lost inorder to protect a potential invisible and insensible agglomerate of cells, which, just because is the object of this kind of protection, will never come into existence, since it will simply not be produced due to the ban on its use for therapeutic reasons.[106]

Anyway, in trying to be objective as far as possible, it is especially important to ascertain the contemporary approach of the international community to the controversial issue of human cloning. As previously pointed out, while such approach is quite uniform with regard to reproductive cloning, the situation remains controversial as regards the other forms of human cloning. Article 11 of the UDHGHR points to reproductive cloning as the major example of practices contrary to human dignity which cannot be permitted. Similarly, Article 1 (1) of the 1998 Paris Protocol to the Oviedo Convention[107] states that '[a]ny intervention seeking to create a human being genetically identical to another human being, whether living or dead, is prohibited'.[108] At the EU level, as already pointed out (at section IV), reproductive human cloning is explicitly prohibited by Article 3 of the Charter of Fundamental Rights. Anyway, these instruments do not expressly mention therapeutic cloning. The Protocol to the Oviedo Convention seems to apply to human cloning in all its forms, since the very title generally refers to 'prohibition of cloning human beings', without limiting its scope to reproductive cloning. But, the text is in some way equivocal: does the term 'human being' also include the embryo? Whether therapeutic cloning is encompassed by the Protocol's ban depends on the

105 See 'Judge OKs discarded embryo lawsuit', CNN.com, 5 Feb 2005, available at http://edition.cnn.com/2005/LAW/02/05/frozen.embryo.lawsuit.ap (last visited on 7 Feb 2005); "Judge: Couple can sue over discarded embryo', Associated Press, 5 Feb 2005, available at http://msnbc.msn.com/id/6919010 (last visited on 7 Feb 2005); Patterson and Pallasch, "Destroyed embryo deemed human", *Chicago Sun-Times*, 5 Feb 2005, available at http://www.suntimes.com/output/news/cst-news-egg05.html (last visited on 7 Feb 2005).

106 On the reasons underlying the debate on both reproductive and therapeutic cloning see Frydman, 'Le clonage reproductive and thérapeutique' [2003] *Revue Trimestrielle des Droits de l'Homme* 421.

107 See *supra* n. 29.

108 Para. 2 of the same Art adds that '[f]or the purpose of this article, the term human being "genetically identical" to another human being means a human being sharing with another the same nuclear gene set'.

answer to such question, and the fact that it is not unreasonable is demonstrated by the Declaration made by the Netherlands at the time of the signature of the Protocol, according to which:

> [i]n relation to Article 1 of the Protocol, the Government of the Kingdom of the Netherlands declares that it interprets the term 'human being' as referring exclusively to a human individual, i.e. a human being who has been born.[109]

As for the Oviedo Convention, to which the Paris Protocol forms an appendix, Article 18 'takes note' of the fact that research on embryos *in vitro* may be allowed by law in some member states of the Council of Europe, providing that the embryo must be the object of adequate protection and prohibiting the creation of embryos specifically for research purposes.[110] This latter provision implies that, according to the Convention, research on embryos *in vitro* is *de facto* limited to supernumerary embryos obtained in the context of assisted insemination practices.[111] This means that, for example, the United Kingdom is not in line with Article 18 of the Oviedo Convention. In fact, on 11 August 2004, pursuant to the Human Fertilisation and Embryology Act[112] and the 2001 Human Fertilisation and Embryology (Research Purposes) Regulations,[113] the British Human Fertilisation and Embryology Authority, in authorising the Newcastle Centre for Life to develop research on therapeutic cloning, allowed the actual creation of human embryos for therapeutic purposes obtained by 'inserting the nuclei from human skin or stem cells into human eggs',[114] although all the embryos will be destroyed before reaching the fourteenth day of life and will not develop more than a minuscule agglomerate of cells. The position expressed by the European Parliament on the British approach, already articulated before the adoption by the House of Lord of the 2001 Regulations, demonstrates that the European debate on therapeutic cloning is far from reaching a solution by unanimity. In its Resolution on Human Cloning of 7 September 2000,[115] the European Parliament, having stressed that 'there is no difference between cloning

[109] See 'Declaration contained in a Note Verbale from the Permanent Representation of the Netherlands, dated 29 Apr 1998, handed to the Secretary General at the time of signature, on 4 May 1998', available at http://conventions.coe.int/Treaty/EN/cadreprincipal.htm (last visited on 28 Aug 2004).

[110] See para. 2.

[111] For a comprehensive analysis of the use of supernumerary embryos at the European and national levels see Mathieu, 'De la difficulté d'appréhender l'emploi des embryons humains en termes de droits fondamentaux' [2003] *Revue Trimestrielle des Droits de l'Homme* 387, at 389 ff.

[112] See *supra* n. 13.

[113] See http://www.legislation.hmso.gov.uk/si/si2001/20010188.htm (last visited on 28 Aug 2004).

[114] See 'HFEA grants the first therapeutic cloning licence for research', 11 Aug 2004, at http://www.hfea.gov/PressOffice/Archive/1092233888 (last visited on 28 Aug 2004).

[115] The full text of the Resolution is available at http://www.virtual-institute.de/en/hp/embryo/regional/Rhc07092000.pdf (last visited on 28 Aug 2004).

for therapeutic purposes and cloning for the purposes of reproduction'[116] and that therapeutic cloning 'poses a profound ethical dilemma, irreversibly crosses a boundary in research norms and is contrary to public policy as adopted by the European Union',[117] called 'on the UK Government to review its position on human embryo cloning'.[118] The ideological and radical repudiation by the European Parliament of therapeutic cloning (and so of any kind of human cloning) is reinforced by a further sentence in which it calls 'for human artificial insemination techniques that do not produce an excess number of embryos in order to avoid generating superfluous embryos';[119] in concrete terms, there must be no room even for scientific research on supernumerary embryos.

The position of the European Parliament is not shared by the European Group on Ethics in Science and New Technologies. The Group condemns human reproductive cloning,[120] but, at the same time, builds its idea on the assumption that '[t]he respect for different philosophical, moral or legal approaches and for diverse national culture is essential to the building of Europe'[121] and that '[i]t is not only legally difficult to seek harmonisation of national laws at Community level, but because of lack of consensus it would be inappropriate to impose one exclusive moral code'.[122] It thus emphasises the fact that '[a] clear distinction must be drawn between reproductive cloning aimed at the birth of identical individuals . . . and non-reproductive cloning, limited to the in-vitro phase'.[123] According to the Group:

> the philosophical and scientific debate on cloning is still open and it should be stressed that prohibition of a specific technique may prevent important discussions about human genetics.[124]

A similar debate characterises the matter of human cloning at the global level. In its conclusions released on 26 July 2002, the Expert Group on

116 See Preamble, letter H.
117 See para. 2.
118 See para. 3.
119 See para. 7.
120 See 'Citizens Rights and New Technologies: A European Challenge', Report of the European Group on Ethics in Science and New Technologies on the Charter of Fundamental Rights related to technological innovation as requested by President Prodi on 3 Feb 2000, Brussels, 23 May 2000, available at http://europa.eu.int/comm/european_group_ethics/docs/prodi_en.pdf (last visited on 28 Aug 2004), 18.
121 See Opinion No. 12 on 'Ethical Aspects of Research Involving the Use of Human Embryo in the Context of the 5th Framework Programme', 23 Nov 1998, available at http://europa.eu.int/comm/european_group_ethics/docs/avis12_en.pdf (last visited on 28 Aug 2004), para. 2.5.
122 *Ibid.*, para. 2.4.
123 See Opinion, No. 9 on 'Ethical Aspects Cloning Techniques', 28 May 1997, available at http://europa.eu.int/comm/european_group_ethics/gaieb/en/opinion9.pdf (last visited on 28 Aug 2004), para. 1.14.
124 See 'Citizens Rights and New Technologies: A European Challenge', *supra* n. 120, 19.

Human Rights and Biotechnology convened by the UN High Commissioner on Human Rights in January 2002 emphasised that '[h]uman cloning—for reproductive purposes in particular, is perhaps the area of biotechnology with the highest potential for controversy at the moment',[125] drawing a line between 'reproductive human cloning [and] the possibilities offered by therapeutic cloning in preventing and fighting diseases'.[126] The Experts take note that the General Assembly has decided to establish an *ad hoc* committee for the elaboration of an international convention against reproductive cloning of human beings (see below), and in this regard, while stressing the need for undertaking 'a serious and detailed human rights analysis of the issues involved in reproductive human cloning',[127] they also point out that if a treaty ban is negotiated, 'too broad a definition will result in the proscription of therapeutic techniques that appear to be essentially beneficial to humankind and are supportive of an individual's right to health and life'.[128] In stating this, they show a not too disguised support for therapeutic cloning.

Also in the context of the Ad Hoc Committee on an International Convention against the Reproductive Cloning of Human Beings, appointed by the UN General Assembly in 2001,[129] the debate on the subject has followed a similar line. Since the very first meeting of the Committee, in February 2002, while there was total unanimity of views regarding the need to ban reproductive cloning, a clear contrast between states which wanted to extend the ban to other forms of human cloning and countries that did not support such extension immediately emerged.[130] At the moment of writing, the most recent draft convention text available is that addressed to the UN Secretary General by the Government of Costa Rica on 2 April 2003.[131] It regards the prohibition of all forms of human cloning; its core provision, Article 2 (1), states that:

> [a]ny person commits an offence within the meaning of this Convention if that person intentionally engages in an action, such as somatic cell nuclear transfer

[125] See High Commissioner's Expert Group on Human Rights and Biotechnology, 'Conclusions', *supra* n. 97, para. 12.

[126] *Ibid.*, para. 13.

[127] *Ibid.*, para. 17.

[128] *Ibid.* See also para. 18, where the Experts emphasise that 'an effective way of overcoming many of the problems and shortcomings of a legal ban on cloning techniques ... would be to focus the ban on an individual's *intention* to copy genetically another human being rather than on the technique itself. Action taken to clone an embryo with the intention of creating a copy of another person would thus be the focus of the ban' (emphasis in the original text).

[129] See Res. 56/93 of 12 Dec 2001.

[130] See Nesi, 'Il divieto di clonazione di esseri umani. Recenti dibattiti in ambito Nazioni Unite', in Boschiero (ed.), *Ordine internazionale e valori etici* (Naples, 2004), 447, at 448 ff.; Shuster, 'Human Cloning: Category, Dignity, and the Role of Bioethics', [2003] *Bioethics* 517, at 525.

[131] See U.N. doc. A/58/73 of 17 Apr 2003.

or embryo-splitting, resulting in the creation of a living organism, at any stage of physical development, that is genetically virtually identical to an existing or previously existing human organism.

The draft text then includes a series of detailed provisions which place strict obligations on states parties, including the obligation of criminalising the acts provided for by Article 2 as well as the obligation *aut dedere aut judicare*. In any event, on 2 October 2003 the General Assembly decided to reconvene the Ad Hoc Committee 'in order to prepare, as a matter of urgency and if possible by the end of 2004, a draft international convention against the reproductive cloning of human beings'.[132] In the meantime, states 'that have not yet done so, pending the adoption and entry into force [of the convention] [are called] to adopt at the national level a prohibition against reproductive cloning of human beings',[133] and 'to take action to control other forms of human cloning by adopting a ban or imposing a moratorium or regulating them by means of national legislation'.[134]

Finally, the 1999 Draft World Health Organization Guidelines on Bioethics (WHO Draft Guidelines)[135] take a position similar to that of the UN High Commissioner on Human Rights' Expert Group on Human Rights and Biotechnology, stating that cloning for the replication of human individuals, as well as deliberate reproductive cloning by embryo splitting, 'is ethically unacceptable and contrary to human dignity and integrity'.[136] As regards therapeutic cloning, the Guidelines laconically point out that 'the use of embryo splitting for non-reproductive purposes in the form of biopsies, for pre-implantation genetic diagnosis of serious clinical disorders is seen as acceptable in some countries';[137] they then conclude, less laconically, that 'non-reproductive, in vitro cloning research, with the clinical objective of repairing damaged tissues and organs has important potential benefits . . . Guidelines addressing the possible involvement of human gametes or embryos must be developed'.[138]

In conclusion, while reproductive cloning is universally rejected, as contrary to human dignity, by virtually the international community as a whole,[139] the debate concerning other forms of human cloning is still

132 See U.N. doc. A/C.6/58/L.8 of 2 Oct 2003, para. 2.

133 *Ibid.*, para. 5.

134 *Ibid.*, para. 6.

135 See http://www.nature.com/wcs/b32a.html (last visited on 28 Aug 2004).

136 See paras. 26 and 27.

137 See para. 27.

138 See para. 28.

139 The Group of Eight, in its 1997 Denver Summit, also declared that '[w]e agree on the need for appropriate domestic measures and close international cooperation to prohibit the use of somatic cell nuclear transfer to create a child'; see 'Final Communique of the Denver Summit of the Eight', Denver, 22 June 1997, available at http://www.virtual-institute.de/en/hp/embryo/regional/g8final.pdf (last visited on 28 Aug 2004). See also the

open. As previously pointed out, leaving aside the precautionary approach of those states which do not support the prohibition on therapeutic cloning for ethical reasons, but rather for the risks attached to such technique, whose effects on human health have not yet been adequately tested,[140] the core question regarding the problem at stake is whether the embryo is to be considered a human being. If the answer is yes, it is clear that all rights recognised to human beings must also be attached to the human embryo, and that, *a fortiori*, even non-reproductive cloning is ethically wrong and unlawful.[141] But, in this case, the ethical implications of the matter would give rise to further problems; in particular, the problem of coherence would affect a large number of countries, because it is a fact that where abortion is lawful the embryo does not actually enjoy the rights ascribed to the human being. In other words, the maximum level of protection would be guaranteed to an embryo produced *in vitro* while the same protection would not be given to an embryo generated by two natural parents: this would be, quite frankly, a real paradox. This is absolutely not to take any position on the matter, but simply to show how ethical aspects linked to biogenetics in general and human cloning in particular are complicated and not easy to be resolved.

(c) Eugenics ('Selection' of Genetic Characters)

The word 'eugenics' was coined in 1883 by Francis Galton in his book *Inquires into the Human Faculty.* Galton, a cousin of Charles Darwin, applied Darwinian science in order to develop his own theories about the inheritance of good and noble qualities at birth. In explaining the purpose of his book, the author clarified that it did not intend to deal with 'anthropometric differences of race', but 'to touch on various topics more or less connected with that of the cultivation of race, or, as we might call it, with

U.N. Sub-Commission on the Promotion and Protection of Human Rights doc. E/CN.4/Sub.2/2003/36, *supra* n. 85, para. 15 ff. Anyway, it is wise to use the word 'virtually', since according to certain U.S. voices it should be considered as a 'protected liberty', while at the European level no objection exists on the boasts that reproductive human cloning is contrary to human dignity and thus unlawful (see Tancredi, 'Genetica umana ed altre biotecnologie nel diritto comunitario ed europeo', in Boschiero (ed.), *supra* n. 130, 381, at 400 f.).

[140] This position is particularly supported by the United States; see Tancredi, *supra* n. 139, 402 f. A similar approach is that according to which all forms of human cloning should be prohibited because in the event that therapeutic cloning was allowed it would be concretely impossible to prevent the exploitation of embryos for different (even unlawful) purposes; see Nesi, *supra* n. 130, 449.

[141] See also Ida, 'Bioethics and International Law', in Boschiero (ed.), *supra* n. 130, 365, at 370. The position according to which the embryo should be considered as an human being is supported, inter alia, by Cassiers, 'La dignité de l'embryon humain' [2003] *Revue Trimestrielle des Droits de l'Homme* 403, at 417 f., and Lahalle, 'Clonages et dignité humaine', ibid., 441 ff.

"eugenic" question'.[142] In a footnote attached to the word 'eugenic', the author further explained that:

> [t]hat is, with questions bearing on what is termed in Greek, *eugenes*, namely, good in stock, hereditarily endowed with noble qualities. This, and the allied words, *eugeneia*, etc., are equally applicable to men, brutes, and plants. We greatly want a brief word to express the science of improving stock, which is by no means confined to questions of judicious mating, but which, especially in the case of man, takes cognisance of all influences that tend in however a remote degree to give the more suitable races or strains of blood a better chance of prevailing speedy over the less suitable than they otherwise would have had. The word *eugenics* would sufficiently express the idea [Italics in the original].

Since the end of the nineteenth Century eugenics initiatives were taken throughout the world by marginalising those who were considered to have unwanted characteristics, by means of, inter alia, marriage restriction, sterilisation or custodial commitment.[143] During the very first years of the twentieth Century the doctrine of *Rassenhygiene* (race hygiene) flourished in Germany, and this in a few decades led to the adoption of a law providing for compulsory sterilisation 'for the prevention of progeny with hereditary defects'[144] (reproducing a practice common in the United States since 1907, which by 1949 led, with the blessing of the Supreme Court,[145] to the sterilisation of nearly 50.000 people, mainly foreign immigrants and African Americans[146]). This eventually led to the 'final solution' to the Jewish question, the Holocaust perpetrated by the Nazi during the Second World War. In the second half of the twentieth century a number of countries continued to put into practice national programmes of compulsory sterilisation with the object of 'purifying' the population from serious genetic infectious and mental diseases.[147] In China, the Law on Maternal and Infant Health Care, having the purpose of 'avoid[ing]

[142] See Galton, *Inquiries into Human Faculty and Its Development*, (2nd ed., London, 1907), 17 (a complete reproduction of such book is available, in PDF format, at http://www.mugu.com/galton/books/human-faculty/, last visited on 28 Aug 2004).

[143] See National Reference Center for Bioethics Literature, The Joseph and Rose Kennedy Institute of Ethics, Georgetown University, Scope Note 28, 'Eugenics', available at http://www.georgetown.edu/research/nrcbl/scopenotes/sn28.htm (last visited on 30 Aug 2004).

[144] *Ibid.* Such law was adopted in 1933 under the name of 'Eugenics in the service of public welfare'. On the eugenic practices perpetrated by Nazi Germany see also Kivilcim-Forsam, *supra* n. 102, 519 f. (referring to '[l]'*apogée de l'eugénisme*').

[145] See *Buck v. Bell*, 274 US 200 (1927).

[146] See Campiglio, 'Eugenetica e diritto internazionale', in Boschiero (ed.), *supra* n. 130, 453, at 454 f.; Kivilcim-Forsam, *supra* n. 102, 517 ff.

[147] See, for example, the case of the Scandinavian countries illustrated by Hocking, 'Confronting the Possible Eugenics of the Past Through Modern Pressures for Compensation', [2000] *Nordic Journal of International Law* 509, and by Campiglio, *supra* n. 146, 457.

new births of inferior quality and heighten[ing] the standards of the whole population',[148] requires premarital tests to determine whether both the partners carry 'genetic diseases of a serious nature', infectious diseases or 'relevant mental diseases'.[149] In the event that any such disease is detected, the marriage will be permitted only after the couple has been sterilised.[150]

Despite the few exceptions still existing (like the Chinese one just described), the practices attached to traditional eugenics are generally considered contrary to human dignity and thus unlawful;[151] some of them (like, *e.g.*, forced sterilisation or forced pregnancy) are so repugnant to the international community as a whole that they are included among *crimina juris gentium*, as lately set out in by the Rome Statute of the International Criminal Court.[152] Anyway, the advent of biogenetics has significantly changed the parameters of the problem. Thanks to the development of genetic testing and screening and gene therapy it is now possible to remove genetic malformations which are the cause of certain serious pathologies, generally otherwise untreatable, by changing the relevant gene(s) (normally at the prenatal stage). Nevertheless, serious ethical questions can be raised with regard to such eugenics too. Leaving aside problems, such as consent, information and confidentiality, which are common to virtually any aspect of biogenetics (see below), the main 'side effect' which may result from 'genetic' eugenics consists in the possibility of selecting certain characteristics (like, *e.g.*, hair or eye colour or even gender) of a child at the prenatal stage, characteristics that are not connected with the health and well-being of the individual, but reflect preferences related to aesthetic, or even discriminatory and racist considerations. This is one of the major examples of discriminatory or racist practices that may be carried out by means of biogenetics (see below). Of course, since discrimination and racism are grave offences to human dignity, when the practices in question entail discriminatory or racist behaviour, they are covered by the general prohibition of such violations of human rights provided for by general international law. This conclusion seems to be supported by relevant international practice. The UDHGHR, while not expressly mentioning eugenics, states that '[n]o one shall be

[148] See 'China to Introduce Eugenics Law', *World Tibet Network News*, 22 Dec 1993, available at http://www.tibet.ca/en/wtarchive/1993/12/22_1.html (last visited on 30 Aug 2004); see also Campiglio, *supra* n. 146, 458; Kivilcim-Forsam, *supra* n. 102, 528 f.

[149] See 'Eugenics', *supra* n. 143.

[150] *Ibid.* For other examples of eugenic practices perpetrated in some countries of the world see Campiglio, *supra* n. 146, *passim*; Kivilcim-Forsam, *supra* n. 102, *passim*.

[151] In Sweden, for example, since 1999 those who had previously suffered forced sterilisation have been able to request compensation to the government. See Campiglio, *supra* n. 146, 457, n. 10.

[152] See Rome Statute of the International Criminal Court, 1998 (1998) 37 ILM 999, Art 7 and 8.

subjected to discrimination based on genetic characteristics that is intended to infringe or has the effect of infringing human rights, fundamental freedoms and human dignity',[153] and insists on the value of diversity and uniqueness of any human being.[154]

In more specific terms, the Oviedo Convention allows the performance of both predictive genetic tests and interventions in the human genome,[155] but they may be, respectively, 'performed only for health purposes or for scientific research linked to health purposes'[156] and 'undertaken only for preventive, diagnostic or therapeutic purposes and *only if its aim is not to introduce any modification in the genome of any descendants*'.[157] In addition, a specific provision prohibits 'the use of techniques of medically assisted procreation . . . for the purpose of choosing a future child's sex, except where serious hereditary sex-related disease is to be avoided'.[158] In more radical terms Article 3 of the EU Charter of Fundamental Rights establishes 'the prohibition of eugenic practices, in particular those aiming at the selection of persons'. It seems that the use of the word 'eugenic' in this provision is to be interpreted as limited to those practices which have no therapeutic purpose. Such inference, which is coherent with the object and purpose of Article 3,[159] seems to be confirmed by the position set out in 2000 by the European Group on Ethics in Science and New Technologies, which in particular condemns traditional eugenic practices (forced sterilisation, forced pregnancies or abortions, ethnically enforced marriages) and 'genetic manipulation on human beings such as the modification of the germ line in view of enhancement, without any therapeutic aim'.[160] The Group also emphasises the fact that '*eugenics differs* from other individual practices carried out to avoid the birth of a disabled child'[161] (the Group defines the practices included in the scope of the concept of eugenics very restrictively, as is demonstrated by the fact that it does not take a

153 See Art 6.
154 See Art 2(b) and 3.
155 See, respectively, Art 12 and 13.
156 See Art 12.
157 See Art 13 (emphasis added).
158 See Art 14.
159 See Art 31(1) of the 1969 Vienna Convention on the Law of Treaties, 1155 UNTS 331. On the contrary, the interpretation of the provision in point based on the literal text of the explicative Note prepared by the *Praesidium* concerning the Charter of Fundamental Rights, which states that '[t]he reference to eugenic practices, in particular those aiming at the selection of persons, relates to possible situations in which selection programmes are organised and implemented, involving campaigns for sterilisation, forced pregnancy, compulsory ethnic marriage among others' (see Draft Charter of Fundamental Rights of the European Union, 'Note from the Praesidium', 11 Oct 2000, available at http://www.europarl.eu.int/charter/pdf/04473_en.pdf (last visited on 30 Aug 2004), Art 3) seems too much restrictive, since it would include only traditional forms of eugenics perpetrated on a wide scale as part of a programme aimed at the selection of certain characteristics at the level of a given community.
160 See Citizens Rights and New Technologies: A European Challenge", *supra* n. 120, 20.
161 *Ibid.*, 20 (emphasis added).

precise position on the genetic techniques aimed at choosing the sex of a future child, laconically stating that such question 'is at present controversial even if many national legislation exclude such practices'[162]).

Outside the European context, the 1996 Organisation of African Unity's Resolution on Bioethics[163] emphasises the need within the African Continent to promote certain 'universal rights and principles under conditions of respect for cultural social and religious values', including 'supervision of research facilities on embryos ... so as *to obviate selective eugenics by-products particularly those relating to sex considerations*'.[164]

In this writer's opinion, while practices like, e.g., predetermination of the sex of the child are clearly discriminatory, discrimination is indeed inherent in any possible modification of the physical traits of the baby which could be made at the prenatal stage, since it may have the potential of creating a generalised preference in society in favour of those who have certain physical characters. In other words, even an apparently less innocuous change, for example in eye colour, could, if generally repeated, lead to the creation of a general belief that those having a given characteristic (e.g. given eyes) are better than others, thus creating a form of discrimination to the prejudice of individuals who do not have such a characteristic.

(d) Other Ethical Issues

From the perspective of ethics the potential impact of genetic knowledge on human dignity is very broad. The issues just dealt with are only examples of a complex reality which extends its influence over a myriad of aspects of human life. It is thus quite impossible to draw up a comprehensive analysis of all the potential situations of interaction between biogenetics and human dignity. Anyway, it is worth mentioning two more problematic issues triggered by such interaction.

First, recourse to abortion is likely to increase as a result of the development of biogenetic knowledge. In the past it was impossible to know when an embryo carried a genetic disease. The existence of such disease could be known only at the moment at which it manifested itself, if this happened. So, the parents (as well as the whole of society) accepted the baby as he/she was at his/her birth, and this was favourable to the development and maintenance of the principle of solidarity. Due to

[162] *Ibid.* On the contrary, the position expressed on this matter in the WHO Draft Guidelines (see *supra* n. 135) is clearly oriented: '[s]ex is not a disease. Except for severe sex-linked genetic disorders, the use of genetic services for the purpose of sex-selection is not acceptable' (para. 21).

[163] The text of the Resolution, adopted on 8 July 1996, is available at http://www.unav.es/cdb/intoua.html (last visited on 30 Aug 2004).

[164] See para. 3.

genetic screening it is now possible to evaluate whether future children are carrying genetic defects or simply a predisposition for a disease that will develop during his/her life, without indicating when, and sometimes even whether, such event will occur. In this case, if the embryo is aborted because of such predisposition, its potential for life is denied on the sole basis of only a potential defect which could reveal itself sometimes during the life of the future individual.[165] Like eugenics, to which it is strictly related, this is a very sensitive issue. Genetic diseases not only involve the personal situation of the individual concerned or the members of his/her family, but also have public repercussions, especially in those countries where public welfare systems exist. There could thus be a sort of 'public interest' in limiting the births of people carrying such diseases, by making recourse to both eugenics and selective abortion. But, of course, the ethical implications of this course of action are self-evident.

Another ethical principle related to biogenetics is that according to which the human body and/or its parts should not as such be made a source of financial gain. Such principle is expressly stated in Article 21 of the Oviedo Convention, Article 21 of the Protocol to such Convention relating to transplantations of human organs and tissues,[166] and by Article 3 of the Charter of Fundamental Rights of the European Union. Also, according to Article 4 of the UDHGHR, the human genome (which is both a part of the human body in a physical sense and a part of the human being in a symbolic sense) 'in its natural state shall not give rise to financial gains'; with regard to the human genome in particular, such principle is indeed a natural consequence of its characterisation as the heritage of humanity. Anyway, with regard to the issue in point, certain positions which prima facie appear inconsistent with such a conclusion are also supported in the context of the international legal arena. For example, the European Group on Ethics in Science and New Technologies, in line with the position pursued by the European Union,[167] is of the view that the prohibition on trade in parts of the human body 'does not preclude the patenting of inventions derived from human elements nor the compensation for tissue bank services as far as long as [*sic.*] legal conditions and strict limits for this ... are satisfied'[168] (on this issue see below, in this section).

[165] See Tauer, *supra* n. 102, 226 f.
[166] See *supra* n. 30.
[167] See *supra* section IV, and *infra*, in this section.
[168] See 'Citizens Rights and New Technologies: A European Challenge', *supra* n. 120, 16.

Legal Issues

(a) Transplantation of Human Organs and Tissues

Genetic screening has opened up new frontiers also with regard to the issue of transplantation of organs and tissues of human origin. It is in fact possible *a priori* to obtain more precise information concerning the compatibility of the organ or tissue taken from the donor with the recipient's organism, eliminating or strongly reducing the risk that the implanted limb will be rejected.

All the principles applicable to biomedicine in general (i.e. protection of human dignity, informed consent, information, confidentiality, preservation of health and safety of the persons concerned, prohibition of financial gain[169]) are also applicable, *mutatis mutandis*, to the specific matter in question. Of course, trafficking in human organs and tissues, commonly regarded by the international community as a contemporary form of slavery,[170] is strictly prohibited in all its forms. As previously pointed out, all these aspects are the object of an *ad hoc* Protocol to the Oviedo Convention,[171] not yet in force at the time of writing.[172] The Convention itself is particularly sensitive to the issue of organ and tissue removal from living donors for transplantation purposes, stating that such removal may be allowed only 'for the therapeutic benefit of the recipient and where there is no suitable organ or tissue available from a deceased person and no other alternative therapeutic method of comparable effectiveness'.[173] Article 20 then deals with the problem of the protection of persons not able to consent to organ removal, restricting the possibilities of carrying out organ or tissue removal on such persons to only exceptional cases subject to particularly strict conditions.

In this general context, the importance of maintaining strict confidentiality in databanks of potential organ donors that may be obtained by the recourse to biogenetics is to be emphasised. As pointed out at the beginning of this section, new technologies allow the collection of data which

[169] But on this specific issue see 'Citizens Rights and New Technologies: A European Challenge', *supra* n. 120, 16, according to which 'prohibition of trade [in human organs and tissues] does not preclude the patenting of inventions derived from human elements nor the compensation for tissue bank services as far as long as legal conditions and strict limits for this in international conventions, or national laws if any, are satisfied'.

[170] See Lenzerini, 'Suppressing Slavery Under Customary International Law' [2000] *Italian Yearbook of International Law* 145, at 170 f.

[171] See *supra* n. 30. On the issue in point see also the Opinion of the European Group on Ethics in Science and New Technologies to the European Commission No. 11 of 21 July 1998, on 'Ethical Aspects of Human Tissue Banking', available at http://europa.eu.int/comm/european_group_ethics/docs/avis11_en.pdf.

[172] See http://conventions.coe.int/Treaty/EN/cadreprincipal.htm (last visited on 28 Aug 2004).

[173] See Oviedo Convention, *supra* n. 25, Art 19.

indicate, *a priori* and with extreme precision, the compatibility of each organ with the recipient. Thus, in the event that such databanks got in the hands of criminal organisations which traffick in organs around the world, such organisations would know in advance the identity of potential donors whose organs would be compatible with their customers' organism, and the very life of such donors would thus be under threat.

(b) Discrimination Based on the Genetic Heritage of the Individual

The principle of non-discrimination is well crystallised in the framework of general international law, and it is at the basis of human rights protection, being inherent to the very idea of human dignity. There are myriad provisions stating such principle in virtually all international instruments dealing with human rights protection. For example, Article 1 of the Universal Declaration of Human Rights solemnly proclaims that '[a]ll human beings are born free and equal in dignity and rights'; Article 7 adds that every individual is entitled 'without any discrimination to equal protection of the law' and 'to equal protection against any discrimination in violation of this Declaration and against any incitement to such discrimination'. Article 2 of the 1966 International Covenant on Civil and Political Rights[174] states that all such rights must be guaranteed to all individuals 'without distinction of any kind, such as race, colour, sex, language, religion, political or other opinion, national or social origin, property, birth or other status'. Equivalent provisions are contained in article 14 of the European Convention on Human Rights,[175] under the title 'Prohibition of Discrimination', and in Article 1 of the American Convention on Human Rights.[176] Also, the Preamble of the African Charter on Human and Peoples' Rights bases its very existence on, inter alia, the necessity of eliminating 'all forms of discrimination, particularly those based on race, ethnic group, color, sex, language, religion or political opinions'.[177]

Most of these provisions single out a series of specific instances of discrimination which must be particularly condemned, but the use of terms like 'such as' or 'particularly' clearly indicates that the lists are not inclusive but simply exemplificative. In other words, they are provisions of 'programmatic' character which are open to new challenges that may be come into existence in consequence of developments in human society. They thus encompass the forms of discrimination which may be perpetrated on

174 999 UNTS 171.

175 Convention for the Protection of Human Rights and Fundamental Freedoms, 4 Nov 1950, CETS n. 5.

176 American Convention on Human Rights, 22 Nov 1969, OAS Treaty Series n. 36.

177 African Charter on Human and Peoples' Rights, 1981, (1982) ILM 58, Preamble, ninth Sentence.

the basis of the genetic heritage of the individual. The possibility that new grave forms of discrimination are committed on account of individual genetic characteristics is generally perceived at the global level,[178] and may become a concrete reality in a number of sensitive contexts in human society, as is demonstrated, inter alia, by the contemporary development of new eugenic ideas (see above in this section). One of these contexts is without doubt that of employment and insurance, in which knowledge of the genetic characteristics of an individual is capable of making such person the object of discriminatory treatment with regard to access to work or availability of welfare facilities (see below in this section). Also, genetic tests could be used to exclude individuals from groups with which they are socially and spiritually linked on account of the lack of certain features in their genetic code common to the members of the relevant group.[179] Furthermore, discrimination based on gender may be intensified for genetic reasons, both on account of the reproductive role of women and in the context of eugenic practices for the selection of sex, not to mention discriminatory practices based on racial profiles.[180] Racial discrimination in particular, when based on genetic grounds, represents a sort of paradox, since the mapping of DNA has revealed a 99.9 percent genetic similarity between all human beings.[181] This fact should represent a 'powerful symbolic tool'[182] capable of sweeping away any discriminatory theory based on supposed racial differences, but, this notwithstanding, the 0.1 percent difference, or the misunderstanding of genetic knowledge, may be used as a powerful tool for racial discrimination.

In any event, as already pointed out, any discriminatory practice based on individual genetic characteristics must be considered as falling within the scope of the general prohibition on discrimination provided for by international law, and is thus unlawful. The fact that genetic discrimination is included within the ambit of such prohibition is demonstrated by the open-ended character of the international provisions which generally set out the principle of non-discrimination, as well as by the relevant

[178] See, for example, High Commissioner's Export Group on Human Rights and Biotechnology, 'Conclusions', *supra* n. 97, para. 25 ff.; 'Citizens Rights and New Technologies: A European Challenge', *supra* n. 115, 7; WHO Draft Guidelines, *supra* n. 135, para. 17.

[179] See Iles, 'The Human Genome Project: A Challenge to the Human Rights Framework', (1999) 9 *Harvard Human Rights Journal* 27, at 47.

[180] Racial discrimination is generally considered as a particularly grave form of discrimination by the international community as a whole, and it is condemned by two specific conventions of universal character, namely the 1966 International Convention on the Elimination of All Forms of Racial Discrimination, in 660 UNTS 195, and the 1973 Convention on the Suppression and Punishment of the Crime of Apartheid, (1015 UNTS 243).

[181] See High Commissioner's Export Group on Human Rights and Biotechnology, 'Conclusions', *supra* n. 97, para. 26.

[182] *Ibid.*

recent developments in international law. In this sense, Article 21 of the Charter of Fundamental Rights of the European Union, an instrument adopted when the development of biogenetics had already shown all its adverse potentialities, is of particular relevance. It states that:

> [a]ny discrimination based on any ground such as sex, race, colour, ethnic or social origin, *genetic features*, language, religion or belief, political or any other opinion, membership of a national minority, property, birth, disability, age or sexual orientation shall be prohibited.[183]

With regard to the instruments specifically dealing with bioethics, the principle set out in Article 6 of the UDHGHR[184] is reaffirmed, *mutatis mutandis*, by Article 7 of the DHGD,[185] Article 9 of the DDUNB and Article 11 of the Oviedo Convention, which asserts that '[a]ny form of discrimination against a person on grounds of his or her genetic heritage is prohibited'.

(c) Free and Informed Consent

Article 5(b) of the UDHGHR states that in all cases or research, treatment or diagnosis affecting an individual's genome, 'the prior, free and informed consent of the person concerned shall be obtained'. Such rule is also set out in Article 8 of the DHGD, Article 3 of the Charter of Fundamental Rights of the European Union, Articles 5 and 16 (with regard to scientific research) of the Oviedo Convention, and Article 14 of the Protocol concerning biomedical research to such Convention.[186] The principle of consent plays a central role in the context of biogenetics; to use the words of the European Group on Ethics in Science and New Technologies, it 'is at the very origin of modern biomedical ethics'.[187] From the legal perspective it represents an evolution of the principle of

[183] Emphasis added.

[184] See *supra* n. 153 and corresponding text. The UDHGHR also solemnly states that 'the recognition of the genetic diversity of humanity must not give rise to any interpretation of a social or political nature which could call into question 'the inherent dignity and ... the equal and inalienable rights of all members of the human family', in accordance with the Preamble to the Universal Declaration of Human Rights' (Preamble, fourth Sentence).

[185] Under the title 'Non-discrimination and non-stigmatization', Art 7 of the DHGD states that '(a) Every effort should be made to ensure that human genetic data and human proteomic data are not used for purposes that discriminate in a way that is intended to infringe, or has the effect of infringing human rights, fundamental freedoms or human dignity of an individual or for purposes that lead to the stigmatization of an individual, a family, a group or communities; (b) In this regard, appropriate attention should be paid to the findings of population-based genetic studies and behavioural genetic studies and their interpretations'.

[186] See *supra* n. 31; see also the eleventh sentence of the Preamble, which states that 'every person has a right to accept or refuse to undergo biomedical research', also adding that 'no one should be forced to undergo such research'.

[187] See 'Citizens Rights and New Technologies: A European Challenge', *supra* n. 120, 13.

international human rights law according to which 'no one shall be subjected without his free consent to medical or scientific experimentation', included among inhuman or degrading treatment by, inter alia, Article 7 of the International Covenant on Civil and Political Rights.[188] It is nevertheless indubitable that, with regard to biogenetics, the principle in question presents new relevant traits with respect to the traditional right of not being the object of medical experiments to which prior consent has not been given. Treating one's genetic heritage does not 'simply' mean making one the object of a hypothetical risk to one's health, but rather making one's intimate identity the object of deep introspection. The very identity of the person is deeply investigated, and, given the enormous implications attached to biogenetics, the consequences on his/her life may be upsetting. All the historical, familiar, environmental and cultural elements composing the identity of the individual are at stake. The cultural element, among others, may have a decisive role in such context. For example, many indigenous peoples, such as the Maori, consider their genetic heritage to be their 'life spirit', a unique individual spiritual realm made of the experience of the ancestors which will be the basis of the existence of future generations.[189] In the light of this example, the importance of free and informed consent as a prerequisite of any genetic treatment is self-evident. Among the three conditions that must be satisfied by the principle of consent, which should be prior, free and informed, that of information is of special relevance;[190] the person concerned, in particular, must be fully aware of the implications and possible consequences attached to any form of interference with his/her genetic heritage. In this regard, the problem of the protection of those who lack the capacity to consent is a particularly sensitive issue. In this respect Article 5(b) of the UDHGHR states that, when the person concerned 'is not in a position to consent, consent or authorization shall be obtained in the manner prescribed by law, guided by the person's best interest'. This principle is developed by Article 5(e), which sets out very strict conditions regarding research affecting the genome of a person not having the capacity to consent. According to the provision in question, such research may be carried out only for the direct health benefit of the person concerned:

> subject to the authorization and the protective conditions prescribed by law. Research which does not have an expected direct health benefit may only be undertaken by way of exception, with the utmost restraint, exposing the person only to a minimal risk and minimal burden and if the research is intended to contribute to the health benefit of other persons in the same age category or

[188] See *supra* n. 174.
[189] See Hamilton, 'The Human Genome Diversity Project and the New Biological Imperialism', (2001) 41 *Santa Clara Law Review* 619, at 626.
[190] In this sense see Ida, *supra* n. 141, 373.

with the same genetic condition, subject to the conditions prescribed by law, and provided such research is compatible with the protection of the individual's human rights.

The other international instruments dealing with bioethics are also particularly sensitive to the protection of persons not able to consent to the manipulation of their genetic heritage. Article 8(b) of the DHGD, as well as Article 11 of the DDUNB and Article 6 of the Oviedo Convention, requires the authorisation of the legal representative of the person concerned, who 'should have regard to [his/her] best interest'. The provisions in question also place particular emphasis on the involvement, insofar as possible, of the person concerned. In addition, the Oviedo Convention adopts a particularly restrictive approach with regard to the protection of people who have a mental disorder of a serious nature, who may be subjected, without their consent, to intervention aimed at treating their mental disorder 'only where, without such treatment, serious harm is likely to result to his or her health'.[191]

According to the two UNESCO declarations in force, limitations or exceptions to the rule of consent are acceptable for compelling reasons, only if prescribed by law and consistent with international human rights law.[192] Article 8 of the Oviedo Convention is also more restrictive, requiring that there be an emergency situation precluding the possibility of obtaining the consent of the person concerned and that the necessary intervention is carried out for the benefit of his/her health.

In addition, the DHGD expressly states that specific consent must be obtained when there is the intention of using human proteomic data and biological data for a purpose different from that for which they were originally collected,[193] as well as 'for the cross-matching of human genetic data, human proteomic data or biological samples stored for diagnostic and health care purposes and for medical and other scientific research purposes'.[194]

Finally, both Article 5 of the Oviedo Convention and Article 9 of the DHGD proclaim the right of the person concerned to withdraw consent to the treatment of his/her genetic data or materials. Such withdrawal may

191 See Art 7. See also Art 15 (in addition to the general principle expressed in the tenth sentence of the Preamble, according to which 'particular protection shall be given to human beings who may be vulnerable in the context of research') of the Protocol to the Oviedo Convention concerning biomedical research (*supra* n. 31), specifically devoted to the 'Protection of persons not able to consent to research', which contemplates particularly restrictive conditions as prerequisites for undertaking research on persons without the capacity to consent to it.

192 See Art 9 of the UDHGHR and Art 8 of the DHGD.

193 See Art 16. This is a corollary of the fact that 'consent to a specific existing research project does not imply consent to the use of genetic information for future research' (see doc. E/CN.4/Sub.2/2004/38, *supra* n. 7, para. 20).

194 See Art 22.

be exercised at any time (according to Article 5 of the Oviedo Convention), and, as stated by Article 9 of the DHGD, 'the person's genetic data, proteomic data and biological samples should no longer be used unless they are irretrievably unlinked to the person concerned'.

(d) Privacy and Confidentiality

The problem of the privacy and confidentiality of the information obtained by biogenetic screening or treatment[195] is also the object of special attention from all international instruments dealing with bioethics. Given the particularly sensitive nature of such information, it is quite natural that such attention exists, as a crucial 'projection' of the right to privacy already crystallised in the framework of international human rights law.[196] The need to maintain strict confidentiality on genetic data associated with identifiable persons is proclaimed by Article 7 of the UDHGHR, by Article 10 of the Oviedo Convention (as well as by Article 23 of its Protocol concerning transplantation of human organs and tissues and by Article 25 of the Protocol concerning biomedical research),[197] by Article 14 of the DHGD and by Article 12 of the DDUNB. This last provision, in particular, sets out a series of specific principles the respect for which may provide an important contribution to the maintenance of privacy and confidentiality with regard to human genetic data: (a) such data may be made accessible to third parties only for an important reason of public interest, 'in cases restrictively provided for by domestic law consistent with international law of human rights', or 'where the prior, free, informed and express consent of the person concerned has been obtained'; (b) human genetic data should not normally be linked to an identifiable person, except when that is necessary for carrying out research 'and provided that the privacy of the individual and the confidentiality of the data or biological samples concerned are protected in accordance with domestic law'; (c) such data 'should not be kept in a form which allows the data subject to be identified for any longer than is necessary for achieving the purposes for which they were collected or subsequently processed'.

The need to protect the confidentiality of genetic data concerning an identifiable person has also been emphasised by the Commission on Human Rights in its 2001[198] and 2003[199] resolutions on human rights and

[195] On this issue see, inter alia, Tauer, *supra* n. 102, 219 ff.; Moore, 'Owing Genetic Information and Gene Enhancement Techniques: Why Privacy and Property Rights May Undermine Social Control of The Human Genome' [2000] *Bioethics* 97, *passim*, particularly 103 ff.

[196] Such principle is expressed, inter alia, by Art 12 of the Universal Declaration of Human Rights (see *supra* n. 92) and by Art 17 of the International Covenant on Civil and Political Rights (see *supra* n. 174).

[197] See *supra* n 30 and 31 respectively.

[198] See Resolution 2001/71 of 25 Apr 2001, para. 6.

[199] See Resolution 2003/69, *supra* n. 84, para. 5.

bioethics, as well as by the UN High Commissioner on Human Rights' Expert Group on Human Rights and Biotechnology[200] and by the European Group on Ethics in Science and New Technologies, which considers personal data 'part of the identity of the individual'.[201]

There is no need to spend much more time in emphasising the importance of ensuring privacy and confidentiality with regard to human genetic data as an essential condition for the safeguarding of individual dignity. It is sufficient to remember that most violations of human dignity which are the object of this chapter may be perpetrated only if and to the extent that certain information regarding the genetic heritage of the individuals concerned is made available to potential perpetrators. Thus, maintenance of privacy and confidentiality concerning such information represents the main way of preventing the perpetration of such violations, since it eliminates one of their indispensable prerequisites.

(e) Right to Information or to Have No Information

Information deriving from genetic treatment or testing may have fundamental importance for the very life of the person concerned. On the one hand it may provide formidable tools for improving his/her existence, especially considering the potential of biogenetics in the field of healthcare. On the other hand, such information may be capable of changing the life of the individual forever in negative terms, making him/her the object of serious discriminatory practices or ruining his/her expectations for the future due to the acquired knowledge of his/her predisposition to a serious disease which may develop very soon, but which could also may never develop. It is for this reason that Article 5(c) of the UDHGHR does not simply proclaim the right of the person concerned to be informed, but asserts that the 'right of each individual to decide *whether or not* to be informed of the results of genetic examination and the resulting consequences should be respected'.[202] The same approach is followed by Article 10 of the DHGD and by Article 10(2) of the Oviedo Convention (as well as by Articles 13 and 26 of its Protocol concerning biomedical research[203]). This principle is well expressed by the WHO Draft Guidelines, according to which '[i]ndividuals have the right to retain control over their genetic material and the information derived from it',[204] where the use of the word 'control' implies, inter alia, that everyone may retain the power of deciding who, including him/herself, should become aware of such information.

200 See 'Conclusions', *supra* n. 97, para. 22(1)(ii).
201 See 'Citizens Rights and New Technologies: A European Challenge', *supra* n. 120, 26.
202 Emphasis added.
203 See *supra* n. 31.
204 See *supra* n. 135, para. 7.

The right to information is commonly depicted, in the context of biogenetics, as a corollary of the right to consent.[205] While such interpretation is undoubtedly correct, the autonomous relevance of the right at stake is to be emphasised. Unlike the right to privacy, which has a decisive role in protecting individuals from 'external' interferences (especially those of discriminatory character), the right to information (to be understood, as already pointed out, both in positive and negative terms) has mainly 'internal' relevance, in the sense that it is particularly linked with the right of the person concerned freely to determine the course of his/her own life. In other words, in positive terms the right to information is decisive for allowing the individual concerned to take decisions which may play a decisive role in improving (sometimes even 'saving') his/her own life, while in negative terms it may be crucial for permitting the person to enjoy his/her right to live the rest of his/her life with serenity, at least to the extent that it is practically possible.

(f) Social Inequality

As previously pointed out,[206] biogenetics, particularly genetic testing, may play a relevant role in the context of social life, especially in employment and insurance cover and costs. In particular, employers may use genetic testing to estimate employees' prospective productivity and suitability to perform a given task, selecting them on the basis of such testing. Similarly, insurers may ascertain the propensity of insured persons to contract a given disease and thus raise the amount of the premium due or even deprive the person concerned of the ability to be insured.[207]

The risk that such practices will flourish is well perceived by the international community. According to the UN High Commissioner on Human Rights' Expert Group on Human Rights and Biotechnology the case, for example, of an employee fired after the discovery by the employer that he has a genetic disposition to a given disease which may be relevant to his/her working capacity would be a 'clear question of discrimination'.[208] At the same time, nevertheless, the Experts state that:

> [w]hile the exercise of an individual's right to health should in no way be limited by her or his genetic characteristics, in the sphere of employment and general insurance (including life assurance), genetic characteristics may sometimes legitimately be used to discriminate between individuals in relation to the availability and, if available, the costs of insurance.[209]

[205] See Lenoir, *supra* n. 4, 564.
[206] See *supra*, section III.
[207] On this issue see Iles, *supra* n. 179, 45 ff.
[208] See High Commissioner's Export Group on Human Rights and Biotechnology, 'Conclusions', *supra* n. 97, para. 27(1).
[209] *Ibid.*, para. 29 (emphasis in the original text).

'A human rights approach', according to the Experts, simply requires that the employer demonstrate 'a legitimate occupational requirement' and the insurer 'a clear increase in probability and risk of a claim justifying a refusal to insure or a higher premium'.[210] While the whole statement of the Experts is disputable, the clearly unacceptable part is, in the opinion of the present writer, that which suggests that an individual may be left without any insurance when there are 'empirical data'[211] demonstrating his/her propensity to contract a given genetic disease. This clearly conflicts, inter alia, with Article 9 of the 1966 International Covenant on Economic Social and Cultural Rights,[212] which proclaims the right of everyone 'to social security, including social insurance' and is also quoted by the Experts themselves.[213] So, while it may be problematic to compel private insurance companies to grant a form of insurance in favour of individuals with a clear predisposition for a genetic disease, there must be within the state a public welfare system which guarantees such individuals, whether and when the disease manifests itself, the necessary assistance and economic support.

As for genetic testing in the workplace, both for the purpose of employment and testing of personnel, a specific opinion released in 2003 by the European Group on Ethics in Science and New Technologies appears particularly pertinent.[214] The Group states that, although '[e]mployers have the right to expect their employees to be capable of carrying out the work required', this may generally be done by using traditional approaches of '*curriculum vitae*, interview, aptitude tests and reference', as well as traditional medical examinations and probationary periods, with no need to have recourse to genetic tests.[215] Consequently, since '[t]he legitimate duties and rights of employers concerning the protection of health and the assessment of the ability can be fulfilled through medical examination but without performing genetic screening', such use of genetic screening 'is not ethically acceptable', and 'employers should not in general perform genetic screening nor ask employees to undergo tests'.[216] Anyway, the Group does not in absolute terms exclude the possibility of having recourse to genetic testing, but the following strict conditions must be satisfied: (a) the performance of the test is necessary for protecting the safety and health of the employee or those of third parties;

210 *Ibid.*, para. 29.
211 *Ibid.*, para. 29.
212 See *supra* n. 92.
213 See High Commissioner's Export Group on Human Rights and Biotechnology, 'Conclusions', *supra* n. 97, para. 29.
214 See Opinion No. 18, 'Ethical Aspects of Genetic Testing in the Workplace', 28 July 2003, available at http://europa.eu.int/european_group_ethics/docs/avis18EN.pdf (last visited on 30 Aug 2004).
215 *Ibid.*, para. 1.11.3.
216 *Ibid.*, para. 2.10.

(b) there is 'scientifically proved evidence' that the genetic test is valid and is the only available method of obtaining the necessary information; (c) the performance of the test 'does not prejudice the aim of improving conditions in the workplace'; (d) 'the principle of proportionality is respected regarding the motivations involved to perform the test'; (e) the principle of non-discrimination is not infringed.[217] The most important indication emerging from the opinion of the Group is that the use of genetic testing is in no way ethically permissible when performed for the purpose of ascertaining the capability of the individual to carry out the work required, but only for safeguarding human safety and health. Thus, the conclusion could be that, except in those particular cases when a certain genetic feature results in the objective inability of a person to perform given work, all genetic screening performed with the purpose of selecting employees is of discriminatory character and, as such, falls within the scope of prohibition of discrimination provided for by international human rights law, which also encompasses discrimination for genetic reasons (see above in this section). Article 6 of the International Covenant on Economic Social and Cultural Rights, by recognising 'the right to work, which includes the right of *everyone* to the opportunity to gain his living by work which he freely chooses or accepts',[218] seems implicitly to confirm the validity of such conclusion, which is also maintained by the Special Rapporteur of the UN Sub-Commission on the Promotion and Protection of Human Rights.[219] Nevertheless, the particularly controversial nature of the subject at stake cannot be denied, and it is probably impossible, in light of relevant practice, to reach a definite conclusion which may be considered generally acceptable by the international community as a whole. It is a fact that genetic testing is widely used in certain countries of the world, such as USA and United Kingdom,[220] as a means of assessing the ability of individuals to perform certain work. In addition, in the context of the European Union, the European Court of Justice has, since 1980, stated that a finding of unfitness to perform given work 'may be based not only on the existence of actual disorders but also on a medically justified prognosis of future disorders capable of jeopardizing in the foreseeable future the normal performance' of the work in question,[221] thus implicitly accepting the idea that such 'future disorders' may

[217] *Ibid.*, para. 2.12.

[218] See *supra* n. 92, Art 6 (emphasis added).

[219] See doc. E/CN.4/Sub.2/2004/38, *supra* n. 7, para. 27, according to which '[i]t should be unlawful for employers, employment agencies, labour organizations and training programmes to hire or fire anyone because of genetic information'.

[220] See 'Ethical Aspects of Genetic Testing in the Workplace', *supra* n. 214, para. 1.6.

[221] See Case 155/78 *Mlle M. v Commission of the European Communities*, [1980] ECR 1797, para. 11. The same position has also been followed by the European Court of First Instance, in Case T–18/10/93 *A. v Commission of the European Communities* [1994] ECR II–179, para. 62.

also be assessed by recourse to genetic screening. The Court of Justice has also maintained that, although a person may not be forced to undergo an AIDS screening test in the context of a pre-recruitment medical examination in view of possible recruitment as a employee of a Community institution, the 'institution cannot be obliged to take the risk of recruiting him' in the event that the person concerned withholds his consent to undertake the test.[222] This decision further supports the idea that pre-recruitment genetic tests are legitimate, although it is questionable whether the instant case, given the relatively easy transmissibility of the HIV virus, may be considered an exceptional situation in which the performance of the test was necessary for protecting the safety and health of other persons, consistently with the position expressed by the European Group on Ethics in Science and New Technologies.[223]

(g) (Intellectual) Property Rights[224]

According to the 1996 Organisation of African Unity's Resolution on Bioethics, the realisation of the principle of inalienability of the human person requires the prohibition of 'the subjection of the human body, its components particularly the human genes and the sequences thereof to commercial and property rights purposes'.[225] Following the same approach, in 1999 the Parliamentary Assembly of the Council of Europe proclaimed the principle according to which 'neither plant-, animal nor human-derived genes, cells, tissues or organs can be considered as inventions, nor be subject to monopolies granted by patents'.[226] Similarly, the UN High Commissioner on Human Rights' Expert Group on Human Rights and Biotechnology noted the serious concerns 'regarding the appropriateness of applying patent laws to genetic material and the human genome, particularly in terms of the requirements of novelty and inventiveness',[227] concluding that:

> the enormous benefits promised by biotechnology must not be restricted to one group or society. The sharing of these benefits involves not only compensation of genetic materials, but also the facilitation of technology transfer between developed and developing countries.[228]

222 See Case C–404/92, *X. v Commission of the European Communities* [1994] ECR I–4737, para. 21.

223 See *supra*, text corresponding to n. 217.

224 On this issue see, inter alia, Moore, *supra* n. 195, *passim*; Sturges, *supra* n. 85, 232 ff.

225 See *supra* n. 163, para. 3.

226 See Recommendation 1425 (1999), adopted on 20 Sept 1999, para. 12. See also Recommendation 1512 (2001), *supra* n. 97, para. 7.

227 See High Commissioner's Export Group on Human Rights and Biotechnology, 'Conclusions', *supra* n. 97, para. 23.

228 *Ibid.*, para. 24.

As a matter of legal coherence, the principle of non-patentability of human genetic material, and particularly of the human genome, constitutes an inescapable consequence of its recognition as the heritage of humanity,[229] confirmed by relevant international practice not only at the public level, but even by private actors.[230] It is also important to emphasise that, in practical terms, the application of international provisions on patentability (particularly the TRIPS Agreement) to human genetic elements would make the sharing of the benefits coming from biotechnological research much more complicated than it should be, conflicting with the right to health recognised to any human person by general international law. Recent international practice, particularly the WTO General Council decision of 30 August 2003,[231] which authorises a waiver from certain obligations set out in the TRIPS Agreement with respect to pharmaceutical products aimed at treating pandemic diseases, demonstrates that the right to health, as an essential element of human dignity, is to be considered predominant with respect to intellectual property rights. Thus, such rights should not be recognised when they may have the inescapable effect of impairing the effective enjoyment of the human right to health.

Anyway, the position just expressed is not universally shared in the international arena.[232] In this sense, it may be sufficient to refer to the fact that, while in the WHO Draft Guidelines the non-patentability of 'the genome's basic elements' is considered a natural consequence of the principle expressed by Article 4 of the UDHGHR,[233] the European Group on

[229] See *supra*, section VI. See also, in this sense, WHO Draft Guidelines, *supra* n. 135, para. 4.
[230] *Ibid.*
[231] See 'Implementation of paragraph 6 of the Doha Declaration on the TRIPS Agreement and public health', Decision of the General Council of 30 Aug 2003, WTO doc. WT/L/540 of 1 Sept 2003.
[232] As for state practice, the fact that in the USA patents on human embryonic stem cells have already been granted is to be recognised. See the Opinion of the European Group on Ethics in Science and New Technologies to the European Commission No. 16 of 7 May 2002, on 'Ethical Aspects of Inventions Involving Human Stem Cells', available at http://europa.eu.int/comm/european_group_ethics/docs/avis16_en.pdf, para. 1.17. With regard, in particular, to such cells, the Group is of the view that '[i]solated stem cells which have not been modified do not, as product, fulfil the legal requirements, especially with regard to industrial applications, to be seen as patentable ... When unmodified stem cell lines are established, they can hardly be considered as a patentable product ... Therefore only stem cell lines which have been modified by in vitro treatment or genetically modified so that they have acquired characteristics for specific industrial application, fulfil the legal requirements for patentability. As to the patentability of processes involving human stem cells, whatever their source, there is no specific ethical obstacle, in so far as they fulfil the requirements of patentability' (*Ibid.*, para 2.3). The Group also excludes the patentability 'of the process of creation of a human embryo by cloning for stem cells' (*Ibid.*, para. 2.5) and insists 'on the necessity to avoid the granting of too broad patents that would impair further research and development. ... It is therefore the opinion of [the Group] that patents shall only be granted, when the patent claim refers to a specific and a sufficiently accurately described stem cell line and its industrial application' (*Ibid.*, para. 2.7).
[233] See *supra*, text following n. 166.

Ethics in Science and New Technologies, when considering the same provision of the UDHGHR, states: '[d]oes it preclude patenting human genes? Certainly not', relying on EC Directive 98/44.[234] As previously pointed out,[235] the Directive, as interpreted by the European Court of Justice,[236] allows the patentability of the results of inventive, scientific or technical work associated with human biological data (extending to such data 'existing in their natural state in human beings only where necessary for the achievement and exploitation of a particular industrial application') and not of the elements of the human body as such. Certainly such distinction is quite sophisticated. Taking the example used by the Court to explain it,[237] regarding the sequencing of human genes it is true that, according to such position, the sequencing method, and not the DNA sequence as such, is patentable. But, at this point, a question arises: when the knowledge of a given technique is essential for obtaining certain results from human genetic materials, how can it be possible to obtain such results, and thus share the benefits of research on human genes, if it is not possible to know the technique (except, of course, on condition of payment of patent royalties, which may be unsustainable by developing countries)?[238]

VIII. CONCLUSION: THE PRIMACY OF HUMAN DIGNITY

The very recently adopted United Nations Declaration on Human Cloning solemnly states that:

> (b) Member States are called upon to prohibit all forms of human cloning inasmuch as they are incompatible with human dignity and the protection of human life; (c) Member States are further called upon to adopt the measures

234 See 'Citizens Rights and New Technologies: A European Challenge', *supra* n. 120, 18.

235 See *supra*, section IV.

236 See *supra* n. 40 and corresponding text.

237 See *supra* n. 44 and corresponding text.

238 As it may clearly appear, the answer to the final question included in the text is considered by the present writer as quite rhetorical. Anyway, there are also different opinions which are worth mentioning. In particular, according to the European Group on Ethics in Science and New Technologies the coin has two sides, in the sense that if patenting was forbidden, the consequence 'would be the major slowing of ... research [and] it would be contrary to public (and especially patients') interests' (see 'Ethical Aspects of Inventions Involving Human Stem Cells', *supra* n. 232, para. 2.1). Certainly '[o]ne ethical dilemma arises due to the fact that patents can encourage scientific progress which can be used to the benefit of better health care, and at the same time, patents can also impair access to the health care due to the need of a licence to use them and to the fees that will have to be paid to the patent holder' (*Ibid.*, para. 2.2). Therefore, the conclusion of the Group is that '[i]t is ... necessary to secure the right balance between the inventor's interests and the society's interest – in the sense that one task for the community is to secure ethical principles and values in the context of possible conflicting interests of stake-holders' (*Ibid.*, para. 2.2).

necessary to prohibit the application of genetic engineering techniques that may be contrary to human dignity. . .[239]

The same principle is stressed, in an equivalent fashion, in Article 8 of the DDUNB (stating that '[a]ny decision or practice within the scope of this Declaration shall be founded on the recognition of the primacy of the human person, which shall prevail over the [sole] interest of science or society') and Article 3 of the Protocol to the Oviedo Convention concerning biomedical research.[240] In this writer's opinion such a formula expresses the very first Commandment which should guide anyone who, in whatever position, plays a role in the field of biogenetics. The content of such provisions (the substance of which was also previously proclaimed by Article 2 of the Oviedo Convention[241]) is quite clear: the sanctity of human dignity, meant as the dignity of the individual person, prevails over both the general interest to research and scientific progress (as also expressly set out by Article 10 of the UDHGHR) and any other interest of society as a whole. In other words, the dignity of a single individual cannot be sacrificed even for the common interest of the whole of society. This rule is consistent with the very nature of contemporary international law. To use the words of the International Military Tribunal for the Former Yugoslavia (ICTY):

> [t]he essence of the whole corpus of international humanitarian law as well as human rights law lies in the protection of the human dignity of every person ... The general principle of respect for human dignity is the basic underpinning and indeed the very *raison d'être* of international humanitarian law and human rights law; indeed in modern times it has become of such paramount importance as to permeate the whole body of international law.[242]

[239] See 'General Assembly Adopts United Nations Declaration on Human Cloning by Vote of 84-34-37', U.N. Press Release GA/10333 of 8 Mar 2005; the Declaration was adopted by a vote of 84 in favour to 34 against (including Belgium, Brazil, Canada, China, Finland, France, Japan, Norway, Spain, Sweden and the United Kingdom), with 37 abstentions. The full text of the Declaration is available at http://www.macathconf.org/undeclarationcloning.htm (last visited on 25 Mar 2005).

[240] See *supra* n. 31; see also the eight sentence of the Preamble (stating that 'biomedical research that is contrary to human dignity and human rights should never be carried out') and Art 1, which proclaims the obligation of states parties to 'guarantee everyone, without discrimination, respect for the integrity and other rights and fundamental freedoms with regard to any research involving interventions on human being in the field of biomedicine'.

[241] According to Art 2 of the Oviedo Convention, entitled 'Primacy of the Human Being', '[t]he interests and welfare of the human being shall prevail over the sole interest of society or science'. See also, similarly (concerning the European Group on Ethics in Science and New Technologies), 'Ethical Aspects of Human Tissue Banking', *supra* n. 166, para. 2.1, entitled 'Ethical imperative to protect health'.

[242] See *Prosecutor v. Anto Furundzija*, Case IT-95-17/1-T, 10 Dec 1998, available at http://www.un.org/icty/furundzija/trialc2/judgement/fur-tj981210e.pdf (last visited on 30 Sept 2004).

In the context of biogenetics, this pre-eminence of human dignity evolves into a number of corollaries, inter alia: (a) all human beings must be respected in their dignity and rights regardless of their genetic characteristics;[243] (b) in particular, human beings must not be discriminated against on the basis of their genetic characteristics: existing genetic differences are not symptomatic of any disparity in the intrinsic value of individuals,[244] since they are due to the evolving nature of the human genome, which 'is subject to mutations [and] contains potentialities that are expressed differently according to each individual's natural and social environment';[245] (c) the operation of biogenetics must not involve any act or practice contrary to human dignity;[246] (d) 'genetic reductionism'[247] is also offensive to human dignity: this means that 'a person's identity should not be reduced to genetic characteristics, since it involves complex educational, environmental and personal factors and emotional, social, spiritual and cultural bonds with others and implies a dimension of freedom',[248] uniqueness and diversity;[249] (e) every individual, in the event that he/she should suffer any damage 'as a direct and determining result of an intervention' affecting his/her genetic heritage, shall have the right to just reparation.[250]

As for the 'operative' aspect is concerned, the concrete realisation of the primacy of human dignity in the context of biogenetics must first be achieved by means of the strict application of existing human rights standards as recognised by international law. Nevertheless, it would be unwise to ignore the fact that, at present, the existing framework of human rights is probably inadequate to address all threats to human dignity caused by the rapid developments of biogenetics.[251] In addition, biogenetics also has the potential to change the 'constitution' and nature of society,[252] in the sense that enthusiasm caused by the prospects of improvements in healthcare promised by biogenetic research may lead one to ignore the fact that such research, as well as the operation of its results, may be conducive to destroying human dignity, eventually bringing the general perception of intrinsically serious offences to such dignity as banal and acceptable 'side-effects' of biogenetics. For this reason, following the example of the UNESCO declarations and the Oviedo

243 See, in this sense, Art 2 of the UDHGHR.
244 See the fourth sentence of the Preamble to the UDHGHR. See also Lenoir, *supra* n. 4, 561.
245 See Art 3 of the UDHGHR.
246 See Art 11 of the UDHGHR and Art 27 of the DHGD.
247 See also Lenoir, *supra* n. 4, 566.
248 See Art 3 of the DHGH.
249 See Art 2(b) of the UDHGHR.
250 See Art 8 of the UDHGHR.
251 See Iles, *supra* n. 179, *passim*.
252 *Ibid.*, 56 f.

Convention, new specific instruments on bioethics, also of binding and universal character, should be adopted in order adequately to address all the aspects of biogenetics which may adversely impact on the integrity of human dignity. Also, it is necessary for specific mechanisms for monitoring and controlling the impact of biogenetics on human rights, with a view to prevent abuses, to be appointed both at the national and international levels.[253] This necessity is emphasised, inter alia, by Articles 16 and 24 of the UDHGHR (entrusting the International Bioethics Committee of UNESCO with the task of contributing 'to the dissemination of the principles set out in this Declaration and to the further examination of issues raised by their applications and by the evolution of the technologies in question'), Article 25 of the DHGD and Article 20 of the DDUMB (stating that '[i]ndependent, multidisciplinary and pluralist ethics committees should be established').

Finally, a new characterisation of the concept of responsibility for offences to human dignity in the context of biogenetics should be developed. In particular, in addition to the role that should be played by the state, which should, inter alia, 'provide the framework for the free exercise of Research on the human genome ..., in order to safeguard respect for human rights, fundamental freedoms and human dignity and to protect public health',[254] establish ethics committees 'to assess the ethical, legal and social issues raised by research on the human genome and its applications',[255] foster 'the international dissemination of scientific knowledge concerning the human genome',[256] promote international cooperation, provide adequate penalties in the event of malevolent use of biogenetics in a way detrimental to human dignity,[257] and ensure just reparation in favour of those who suffer injury as a result of an intervention affecting their genetic heritage,[258] other actors should bear the responsibility for misuse of biogenetics offending human dignity. In particular, applying the principle of responsibility of researchers and relevant medical personnel, who are the bearers of particularly sensitive and hardly controllable knowledge on techniques having the potential seriously to affect the integrity of human dignity, is essential to ensure adequate protection to patients and preventing offences which, by their very nature, are irreversible and not adequately remediable.[259] The recent scandals concerning HIV-contaminated blood demonstrate that national institutions may

[253] See Ida, *supra* n. 141, 379.
[254] See Art 15 of the UDHGHR.
[255] See Art 16 of the UDHGHR. See also Chapter III (Art 9–12) of the Protocol to the Oviedo Convention concerning biomedical research (*supra* n. 31).
[256] See Art 18 of the UDHGHR.
[257] See *supra*, text following n. 132.
[258] See *supra*, n. 250 and corresponding text.
[259] On this point see Byk, 'Progrès scientifique et droits de l'homme: la rupture?', [2003] *Revue Trimestrielle des Droits de l'Homme* 363, at 377 f.

hardly maintain control over hyper-specialised medical knowledge. For this reason, the classical schemes of criminal responsibility and civil liability which may be used only after the production of the damage (that in the case of biogenetics may be irreversibly harmful of the patient's dignity) are not adequate effectively to address the matter in point.[260] This concept is well expressed, inter alia, by Article 13 of the UDHGHR, which states that:

> [t]he responsibilities inherent in the activities of researchers, including meticulousness, caution, intellectual honesty and integrity in carrying out their research as well as in the presentation and utilization of their findings, should be the subject of particular attention in the framework of research on the human genome, because of its ethical and social implications. Public and private science policy-makers also have particular responsibilities in this respect.[261]

From the discovery of iron[262] to the development of biogenetics, the experience of nearly 4,000 years of human history clearly shows that any technological progress represents a coin with two well-defined sides. On the one hand there may be a potential for immense progress of humankind and general improvement in the well-being of people. This is certainly the case with biogenetics, which has opened immense new perspectives in the treatment of a number of diseases previously considered virtually incurable. On the other hand there is potential for the destruction of human dignity and the denial of basic human rights, which increases immensely when technological knowledge gets into the wrong hands. This is also the case with biogenetics, which could eventually lead to the annihilation of the very idea of humanity, through the reduction of human health to a mere economic commodity in the name of progress. For this reason, it is essential that in the context of genetic biotechnology, while making the best in view of attaining the greatest improvements in healthcare and respecting other relevant principles, such as freedom of research,[263] which may be at stake, the idea of

260 See also Lenoir, *supra* n. 4, 566.

261 See also Art 18 of the DHGD, and para. 64 of the U.N. Sub-Commission on the Promotion and Protection of Human Rights doc. E/CN.4/Sub.2/2003/36 (*supra* n. 85), according to which, since regulations adopted by governments are implemented by private actors, '[a] regulatory scheme ... should permit horizontal suits that enable people to sue other private actors to enforce State regulation. Horizontal suits would help dismantle the public and private distinction by subjecting the power arrangements and social ordering within the private sphere to scrutiny'.

262 The actual discovery of iron was probably made so early in the history of the human race that it cannot be precisely placed. Anyway, no iron objects have been found outside the area bounded by Anatolia, Mesopotamia, Egypt, and Crete before about 1600 B.C.

263 The relevance of the principle of freedom of research is asserted, inter alia, by para. 8 of the 1974 UNESCO Recommendation on the Status of Scientific Researchers (available at http://www.unesco.org, last visited on 30 Sept 2004), which recommends states to show the

the primacy of human dignity is always considered to be the leading principle informing, through the application of international norms on human rights, any concrete application of biogenetics.

POSTCRIPT

On 19 October 2005, when the editorial work for the present volume had already reached an advanced stage, the UNESCO General Conference adopted the Universal Declaration on Bioethics and Human Rights (UDBHR), based on the text of the DDUNB. Despite some changes in the wording, the provisions of the UDBHR reproduce in substance the principles previously expressed in the text of the DDUNB. However, the UDBHR has adopted a different numbering with respect to the DDUNB. In this regard, as far as the provisions quoted in the present chapter are concerned, articles 24(b), 9, 11, 12 and 8 of the DDUNB correspond, respectively to articles 24(1), 7, 9 and 3 of the UDBHR.

'utmost respect for the autonomy and freedom of research necessary to scientific progress', by Art 12(b) of the UDHGHR (stating that '[f]reedom of research, which is necessary for the progress of knowledge, is part of freedom of thought. The applications of research, including applications in biology, genetics and medicine, concerning the human genome, shall seek to offer relief from suffering and improve the health of individuals and humankind as a whole'), by the Preamble (fourteenth sentence) and by Art 1 of the DHGD. The 'importance of research on the human genome and its applications for the improvement of the health of individuals and mankind as a whole' is also emphasised by Resolution 2001/71 of the U.N. Commission of Human Rights (see *supra*, n. 198); on the other hand, the same Commission, in its Resolution n. 2003/69 (*supra* n. 84) proclaimed the principle according to which 'no research or research applications concerning the human genome ... should prevail over respect for the human rights, fundamental freedoms and human dignity of individuals' (see Preamble, seventh sentence). See also *supra*, section VI and Lenoir, *supra* n. 4, 569 ff.

13

Indigenous Peoples' Rights, Biogenetic Resources and Traditional Knowledge: The Case of the Sateré-Mawé People

MAURIZIO FRABONI AND FEDERICO LENZERINI*

I. BIOPROSPECTION OF PLANT GENETIC RESOURCES AND INDIGENOUS PEOPLES' RIGHTS

IN THE WESTERN utilitarian vision of life plant resources are basically considered as 'commodities' to be exploited for human needs. Consequently, there is nothing inappropriate in making them the object of commercial exploitation, when they have properties which make them suitable for transformation into products or services, in accordance with the rules of the globalised market. This acquisitive logic has led, mainly in the last century, to the massive exploitation of plant resources: immense forests have been completely razed to the ground, with the result that now scientists are wondering whether sufficient plants still exist to allow humanity to breath. Another consequence of this approach (which is more pertinent to the present chapter), is that, in those parts of the world that have been at the disposal of Western people (virtually the entire earth), at present there are no longer, except for rare exceptions, plants which have not been painstakingly studied and sectioned and whose properties remain unknown to scientists.

One of the rules governing the global market of Western derivation is that, when a person makes a new invention, he/she has the right, although not unlimited in time, to retain the intellectual property in such an invention. A corollary of this principle is that, when a person discovers that a plant has a given property (e.g. curative or nutritive), he/she, for a limited time retains exclusive intellectual rights to his/her invention. This matter is principally regulated by Article 27(3)(b) of the TRIPS Agreement,[1] which

* Sections I, II and III were written by Federico Lenzerini. Section IV was written by Maurizio Fraboni.

[1] The text of the TRIPS Agreement is available at http://www.wto.org.

allows state parties to exclude patentability of 'plants and animals other than micro-organisms, and essentially biological processes for the production of plants and animals other than micro-organisms', but, at the same time, states that 'Members shall provide for the protection of plant varieties either by patents or by an effective *sui generis* system or by any combination thereof'. It may be interesting to remember that this provision, as explicitly provided for by its final sentence, should have been subjected to revision four years after the date of entry into force of the WTO Agreement. At the time of writing (2005), negotiations for such revision are still underway, with any agreement on the content of the revision not yet in sight.

By contrast, the holistic vision of life that characterises indigenous peoples entails a radically different approach by human beings towards plants. Although all different peoples have their own peculiar beliefs and traditions, in general terms it is possible to observe that the earth is usually considered by indigenous communities as the mother of life, and that any creature which is on the earth, of animal, plant or inanimate character, deserves respect as an essential element of the world's divine order. The relationship of indigenous peoples with their motherland (including the resources located therein) is thus part of their very identity as peoples, and, *a fortiori*, of their souls, intended as their divine and metaphysic whole. Plants are consequently used only to the extent which is strictly indispensable for satisfying very basic human needs (i.e., basically, health, nutrition and housing), and no taking of natural resources occurs other than is strictly necessary for life. The result of this is that those (few) lands which throughout history have remained under the exclusive control of indigenous peoples, without having captured the interest of the European colonizers, have maintained their virtual virginity in their endemic biodiversity, which in most cases features plant varieties that are not available in any other part of the earth. What is more, in most cases the peoples concerned have throughout the centuries developed special knowledge concerning their endemic plant resources, a knowledge generally alien to Western scientists, and often with the strong potential of opening new perspectives in particularly sensitive fields of human life, like nutrition and health care.

The clash between these two opposite conceptions of life is strikingly evident, and it was translated into practical effects as soon as Western scientists, researchers and swashbucklers became aware of the scientific and economic potentialities of indigenous knowledge concerning plants and related resources. Indigenous ancestral lands thus became the most potentially valuable areas for bioprospection. In many cases such activity has been performed wildly, based only on the logics of profit and with no respect for indigenous peoples' rights. It has often been legally justified through recourse to a *very extensive* application of patent law, e.g., by considering as 'new', and thus patentable (since, according to Article 27(1) of the TRIPS Agreement only inventions that 'are new' may be patented), certain knowledge which has been transmitted by the indigenous peoples concerned from generation to generation. This has led indigenous peoples to make claims of 'biopiracy', consisting in the unlawful appropriation of their knowledge and resources by Western bioprospectors. Several cases of biopiracy have been recorded in recent times, all characterised by the claim of the novelty of resources, processes and/or knowledge possessed by indigenous peoples for centuries, usually without acknowledging the peoples concerned any right to share financial benefits deriving from the economic exploitation of such resources, processes and knowledge.[2] In some of these cases, however, patents previously granted were revoked after the representatives of the indigenous communities concerned had demonstrated that the process or knowledge for which patents had been accorded was in no way new or revolutionary, but was rather the usurpation of knowledge previously developed by them.[3]

In the perspective of international law it is of interest to ascertain what legal titles are 'possessed' by indigenous peoples for challenging the growing trend toward commercial usurpation of their biogenetic resources and related knowledge.

In the context of the contemporary international legal regime, indigenous rights over ancestral lands (and the resources located therein) have been increasingly recognised. Responding to the stimulus coming from a number of international bodies (e.g. the UN Commission on Human Rights, UNESCO and the World Bank)[4], most states in whose territories indigenous communities actually live have recognised a growing number of rights in favour of such communities, first at the jurisdictional level and later through specific legal (in certain cases even constitutional) provisions. This positive evolution has led to the recognition that interferences with the full ownership of the land and enjoyment and transmission to future

2 See, for example, the case of the *Pilocarpus jaborandi*, historically discovered and developed by the Guajajara tribe of Brazil (see Posey and Dutfield, *Beyond Intellectual Property: Toward Traditional Resource Rights for Indigenous Peoples and Local Communities*. (Ottawa, 1996), at 53; Hamilton, 'The Human Genome Diversity Project and the New Biological Imperialism', (2001) 41 *Santa Clara Law Review* 619, at 621 f.), or the case of Madagascar's Rosy Periwinkle (see Case Western Reserve University, 'Case Study: Rosy Periwinkle (Madagascar)', available at http://home.cwru.edu/~ijd3/autorship/rosy.html (last visited on 30 Sep 2004)).

3 See, for example, the case of the Indian Neem Tree (see Case Western Reserve University, 'Neem Seed (India)', available at http://home.cwru.edu/~ijd3/autorship/neem.html (last visited on 30 Sept 2004)), or the case of the Amazonian Cupuaçu (see 'The Cupuaçu Case', available at http://www.amazonlink.org/biopiracy/cupuacu.htm (last visited on 30 Sep 2004); 'Trademark Cupuaçu cancelled in Japan', available at http://www.amazonlink.org/biopiracy/2004_03_01.htm (last visited on 30 Sep 2004)).

4 See Lenzerini, 'Biogenetic Resources and Indigenous Peoples' Rights', forthcoming, sect. 3.

generations of their traditional uses and customs by indigenous peoples is possible only in exceptional cases and by means of measures taken by the competent governmental authorities.[5] The fact that specific provisions concerning the relationship of indigenous peoples with natural resources located in their traditional lands are included in binding international treaties is also remarkable. In particular, the 1989 ILO Convention No. 169 on Indigenous and Tribal Peoples in Independent Countries[6] entails a number of provisions which are relevant to the present issue, including, inter alia, the obligation to recognise and protect the cultures and environment of the peoples concerned,[7] as well as their social, cultural, religious and spiritual values and practices, also in the context of their relationship with their lands or territories, particularly the collective aspects of such relationship. Article 15, in particular, states that '[t]he rights of the peoples concerned to the natural resources pertaining to their lands shall be specially safeguarded. These rights include the right of these peoples to participate in the use, management and conservation of these resources'. Unlike other norms concerning land rights (included in Part II of the Convention), envisaging a full right of ownership, this provision grants indigenous peoples a simple right of participation. It entails a general principle which is *directly* applicable to biogenetic resources and related knowledge and, in stating that the rights of indigenous peoples to the natural resources located in their ancestral lands 'shall be *specially* safeguarded',[8] it presupposes an obligation upon states parties to prevent illicit appropriation of such resources. Furthermore, Article 15(2) concerns more specifically mineral and sub-surface resources located within indigenous lands which, although their ownership may be retained by the national government, cannot be the object of any programme of exploration and/or exploitation without the prior implementation of ad hoc procedures having the purpose of ascertaining 'whether and to what degree [indigenous] interests would be prejudiced' and including consultation with the peoples concerned. Such peoples are also entitled, 'wherever possible', to participate in the benefits derived from the activities performed on the resources located within their lands, as well as to receive 'fair compensation for any damages which they may sustain as a result of such activities'.

Also, in the context of environmental law, the importance of indigenous peoples for the *in situ* conservation of biodiversity is recognised by Article 8(j) of the 1992 Convention on Biological Diversity (CBD),[9] which requires

[5] *Ibid.*

[6] The full text of the Convention is available at http://www.ilo.org/ilolex/english/convdisp1.htm (last visited on 30 Sept 2004).

[7] See, in particular, art. 4, 5 and 13.

[8] Italics added.

[9] The full text of the Convention is available at http://www.biodiv.org/doc/legal/cbd-en.pdf (last visited on 30 Sept 2004).

states parties to 'respect, preserve and maintain knowledge, innovations and practices of indigenous and local communities . . . relevant for the conservation and sustainable use of biological diversity', to promote their 'wider application with the approval and involvement of [their] holders', and to encourage 'the equitable sharing of the benefits arising from the utilization of such knowledge, innovations and practices'.

Cultural rights are also of particular relevance for the present enquiry. The right of ethnic minorities (including indigenous peoples) to enjoy their own culture, contemplated by Article 27 of the International Covenant on Civil and Political Rights,[10] encompasses, according to the Human Rights Committee, 'a particular way of life associated with the use of land resources, especially in the case of indigenous peoples',[11] whose protection 'is directed towards ensuring the survival and continued development of the cultural, religious and social identity of the minorities concerned' and presupposes 'an obligation [of State parties] to ensure that the exercise of these rights is fully protected'.[12] The recently adopted UNESCO Convention for the Safeguarding of Intangible Cultural Heritage[13] provides for the specific protection of indigenous traditional knowledge, particularly 'knowledge and practices concerning nature and the universe',[14] and points out that, in acceding to intangible heritage (which by definition includes indigenous knowledge of biogenetic resources), respect for 'customary practices governing access to specific aspects of such heritage' must be ensured.[15] Furthermore, Article 15 entails a duty of states parties 'to endeavour to ensure the widest possible participation of communities ... that create, maintain and transmit' intangible cultural heritage within the framework of national safeguarding activities of such heritage, and to involve those communities 'actively in its management', thus implying that indigenous heritage and traditional knowledge may not be exploited without the active involvement of the communities concerned. However, with regard to patentability, Article 3(b) expressly states that nothing in the Convention may be interpreted as 'affecting the rights and obligations of States parties deriving from any international instruments relating to intellectual property rights (IPRs) or to the use of biological and ecological resources of which they are parties'.

10 999 UNTS 171.

11 See Human Rights Committee General Comment No. 23 of 6 Apr 1994, 'The rights of minorities (Art. 27)', available at http://www.ohchr.ch/english/bodies/hrc/comments.htm (last visited on 30 Sept 2004) para. 7.

12 *Ibid.*, para. 9.

13 The Convention was adopted by the UNESCO General Conference on 17 Oct 2003. Its text is available at http://www.unesco.org (last visited on 30 Sept 2004).

14 See the definition of 'intangible cultural heritage' provided for by Art. 2, particularly para. 2(d).

15 See Art 13(ii).

The right of indigenous peoples, as 'peoples', freely to dispose of their natural resources is also part of the principle of self-determination of peoples, proclaimed by Articles 1(2) and 55 of the Charter of the United Nations and Article 1 of both the International Covenant on Economic, Social and Cultural Rights[16] and the International Covenant on Civil and Political Rights,[17] and today part of customary international law and most likely of *jus cogens*.[18]

In sum, as regards the relationship of indigenous peoples with the natural resources located in their ancestral territories, the contemporary evolution of international law[19] leaves states no other opportunity than to recognise and respect the right of the peoples concerned to retain ownership and control of such resources and to have a substantial role in deciding about their utilisation. The infringement of such rights would entail the violation of a number of principles which today have attained the status of general international law and, in some instances, of *jus cogens*, including the right to self-determination, the right to enjoy one's own culture, the right to exist as distinct peoples, as well as the prohibition of racial discrimination (as recently recognised by the Committee on the Elimination of Racial Discrimination).[20] Only when a paramount interest of the territorial state is at stake may such rights be the object of derogation, subject to the limit of the extent to which it is strictly necessary for safeguarding such interest and to granting restitution of the resources concerned as soon as is possible or, at least, just, fair and prompt compensation for the communities affected by such derogation.

Due to the 'decentralised' character of international law, conflict between norms regulating different aspects of the international legal system is quite frequent. In the case of the apparent clash between the rights of indigenous peoples over their biogenetic resources and the system of IPRs a few observations could be developed. First, the TRIPS Agreement, adopted in 1994 and in force in 1995, is more recent than most human rights conventions, including the 1966 international covenants on human

[16] 993 UNTS 3.

[17] See *supra* n 10.

[18] See, inter alia, Conforti, *Diritto internazionale*, (Naples, 2002), 187.

[19] For a more comprehensive assessment of relevant international law, see Lenzerini, *supra* n. 4, sect. 3.

[20] See *General Recommendation XXIII (51) concerning Indigenous Peoples*, 18 Aug 1997, available at http://www.austlii.edu.au/journals.OLD/AILR/1998/6.html (last visited on 30 Sept 2004). According to para. 5, states parties to the 1966 Convention on the Elimination of All Forms of Racial Discrimination (660 UNTS 195) must 'recognise and protect the rights of indigenous peoples to own, develop, control and use their communal lands, territories and resources and, where they have been deprived of their lands and territories traditionally owned or otherwise inhabited or used without their free and informed consent, to take steps to return those lands and territories. Only when this is for factual reasons not possible, the right to restitution should be substituted by the right to just, fair and prompt compensation. Such compensation should as far as possible take the form of lands and territories'.

rights, the convention on racial discrimination and ILO Convention No. 169. In this respect it should thus be considered as a 'latter treaty' which, pursuant to the general principle codified by Article 30(3) of the Vienna Convention on the Law of Treaties (Vienna Convention),[21] should prevail over earlier treaties with respect to the incompatible provisions. Secondly, with respect to the CBD and the UNESCO Convention on Intangible Heritage, the TRIPS Agreement should prevail on account of the compatibility clauses included, respectively, in Article 22(1) CBD[22] and in Article 3(b) of the Intangible Heritage Convention.[23] Third, even assuming that the rights of indigenous peoples over natural resources located in their traditional territories have attained the status of customary law, it is well known that a treaty may lawfully derogate from customary international law with respect to the relations between parties. So, one could argue that the obligations deriving from the TRIPS Agreement prevail over the rights of indigenous peoples to their natural resources, and that states parties to the TRIPS Agreement could (rectius, would be bound to) deny the enjoyment of such rights to the peoples concerned in view of complying with their obligations pursuant to such Agreement.

Nevertheless, a more accurate assessment shows that there are at least two counter–arguments which demonstrate that such reconstruction does not correspond to the reality of the contemporary international legal regime. First, it does not correspond to state practice; in particular, with regard to the conflict between Article 27(3)(b) of the TRIPS Agreement and Article 8(j) CBD, virtually all states, in the context of both the CBD and WTO, have proclaimed their official position according to which such conflict must be resolved through the harmonisation of the two provisions in point (when they do not explicitly assert that the CBD should prevail over the TRIPS Agreement), and not through the application of the 'later in time' rule codified by Article 30(3) of the Vienna Convention.[24]

21 1155 UNTS 331.

22 Art 22(1) CBD (see *supra* n. 9) states that '[t]he provisions of this Convention shall not affect the rights and obligations of any Contracting Party deriving from any existing international agreement, except where the exercise of those rights and obligations would cause a serious damage or threat to biological diversity'. In making reference only to 'any *existing* international agreement', this provision rules out *tout court* that the Convention may be invoked for affecting the parties' rights and obligations deriving from successive treaties, even in the event that, as provided for in existing agreements, 'the exercise of those rights and obligations would cause a serious damage or threat to biological diversity'.

23 See *supra*, text following n. 15.

24 See, e.g., Grain, 'TRIPS versus Biodiversity: Options for the 1999 Review of Article 27.3(b) in the Context of CBD', Annex 1, 'Political appeals for the primacy of CBD over TRIPS', available at http://www.acts.or.ke/grain.doc (last visited on 3 Oct 2004); 'TRIPS: Reviews, Article 27.3(b) and Related Issues. Background and the Current Situation', available at http://www.wto.org/english/tratop_e/trips_e/art27_3b_background_e.htm (last visited on 3 Oct 2004), and the documents listed therein, particularly docs. IP/C/W/368 of 8 Aug 2002 ('The relationship between the TRIPS Agreement and the Convention of Biological Diversity. Summary of issues raised and points made'), IP/C/W/369 of 8 Aug

The second (and more compelling) counter–argument is that the resolution in favour of IPRs of the conflict between IPRs and indigenous rights over biogenetic resources ignores the fact that the violation of the indigenous peoples' rights in point entails the breach of some basic principles (i.e. norms on fundamental human rights) which, being included within the scope of Article 103 of the Charter of the United Nations, supersede States' obligations under 'any other international agreement'. The conclusion previously reached through the application of the 'later in time' rule is thus to be completely reversed, since the pre-eminence over IPRs of certain rights of indigenous peoples which would be breached by applying such rule is undisputable, just because these rights are included within the scope of Article 103 of the UN Charter. The fact that this is the correct conclusion is confirmed by the very first phrase of Article 30 of the Vienna Convention, according to which the validity of the provisions included in such article is '[s]ubject to Article 103 of the Charter of the United Nations', as well as by the fact that some of the norms that could be infringed through the denial of indigenous rights over their natural resources, by means of the recognition of the pre-eminence of IPRs over such rights, have attained the status of *jus cogens*, and when a conventional provision is contrary to (*rectius* not applicable in a compatible way with) a *jus cogens* norm, it is to be considered void.[25] As a consequence, in the event that the apparent clash between indigenous rights concerning biogenetic resources and IPRs was to be resolved in terms of conflict between legal norms, the inescapable conclusion would be that states were be bound to derogate from the TRIPS Agreement, pursuant to Article 103 of the UN Charter, every time the implementation of such Agreement would be suitable to produce the impairment of the rights of the indigenous communities concerned. This solution may appear too radical, but in reality it is inescapable, to the extent that indigenous peoples' rights are recognised as part of the fundamental human rights which fall within the principles of the UN Charter. However, IPRs law does not demand to be necessarily interpreted and applied in a way which is incompatible with the need to grant proper enjoyment of indigenous peoples' rights. First of all, Article 27(3)(b) of the TRIPS Agreement should soon be the object of revision,[26] and the revision could take into account the need to protect indigenous rights. In any case, even in the present state

2002 ('Review of the provisions of article 27.3(b). Summary of issues raised and points made'), and IP/C/W/370 of 8 Aug 2002 ('The protection of traditional knowledge and folklore. Summary of issues raised and points made'); see also, on the points raised by parties, docs. IP/C/W/257 (United States), IP/C/W/383 (European Union), IP/C/W/400/Rev.1 (Switzerland), IP/C/W/403 (Bolivia, Brazil, Cuba, Ecuador, India, Peru, Thailand, Venezuela) and IP/C/W/404 (The African Group).

[25] See Art 53 and 64 of the Vienna Convention, *supra* n. 21.

[26] See *supra*, section I.

of Article 27(3)(b), it is not impossible for the concrete implementation of IPRs to be carried out in a way which is compatible with the need to ensure full respect of fundamental rights, including the collective rights of indigenous peoples.

II. INDIGENOUS PEOPLES' BIOGENETIC RESOURCES AND TRADITIONAL KNOWLEDGE: TWO ELEMENTS OF A UNIQUE LEGAL VALUE

Before trying to investigate the possible 'harmonised' solution(s) to the apparent legal conflict between indigenous rights and the IPRs system, it may be useful to clarify a preliminary (but rather relevant) aspect of the matter. In dealing with the special relationship of indigenous peoples with plant genetic resources located in their ancestral lands, one must take into account that both the resources as such and traditional knowledge related to such resources are inextricably interrelated and represent two different but inseparable elements of the same legal value. Such value consists in the special holistic relationship of indigenous peoples with everything that is part of the motherland and the harmony of the universe, such relationship representing the core trait of their distinctive identity as peoples. Appropriate safeguarding of both the plant resources concerned (in their physical entity) and knowledge developed along the centuries on such resources is thus essential for ensuring the survival of most indigenous peoples as distinctive cultural entities.

In concrete terms, it is just the denial of the right of indigenous communities to exist as distinct peoples which entails the infringement of a number of fundamental principles of general international law, including (as previously seen) the right of peoples to self-determination, the prohibition of racial discrimination,[27] the right of ethnic minorities (including indigenous peoples) to enjoy their own culture,[28] the prohibition of degrading treatment (since the denial to indigenous members of the chance to live according to their lifestyle is capable of inflicting moral and spiritual pain which may actually amount to degrading treatment), and the right to life and/or dignity (since it is a fact that most indigenous members who are forced to follow the white man's lifestyle cannot integrate into Western capitalistic society, and are often led to physical death or to a kind of bodily survival which is below the level of minimum acceptable standards of human dignity). In addition, such course of action would also result in the breach of several specific treaty provisions by the states which have ratified the relevant treaties.[29] In the context of

[27] See *supra* n. 20.
[28] See *supra* n. 12 and the corresponding text.
[29] See *supra*, section I.

the subject matter of the present chapter the contextual protection of both plant resources and related knowledge is essential for preventing the violation of such international legal rules.

The possible solution(s) for reconciling indigenous rights over biogenetic resources and the international system of IPRs should thus be structured in such a way as to allow adequate protection of both the 'material' and 'spiritual' elements of the legal value which is at stake, that is the very survival of indigenous peoples as distinctive cultural and anthropological entities.

III. RECONCILING INTELLECTUAL PROPERTY AND INDIGENOUS PEOPLES' RIGHTS

In abstracto, there are four possible models suitable for granting adequate and effective safeguards to indigenous (intellectual property) rights over their biogenetic resources and related traditional knowledge: use of mechanisms of intellectual property protection that are ordinarily utilised for non-indigenous-related inventions; sharing of benefits arising from the exploitation of indigenous biogenetic resources and related knowledge; exclusion *tout court* of the 'patentability' of indigenous biogenetic resources and related traditional knowledge; use of *sui generis* systems of protection of intellectual property.

With regard to the first option, it is evident that it is in no way suitable for granting adequate safeguards of indigenous rights over biogenetic resources. First, it is based on legal notions, including the idea of 'patentability' itself, whose nature and philosophical foundations are totally extraneous to the culture and the holistic vision of life of most indigenous peoples. Second, to make a patent application by an indigenous person concretely practicable financial and technical barriers must be overcome which in practice may be virtually insuperable.[30] Thirdly, and even more importantly, there would also be practical obstacles, inherent in the very 'structure' of the IPRs system itself, which make the existing schemes of patent protection *a priori* inappropriate for the protection of indigenous biogenetic resources and related traditional knowledge. Among such obstacles one may cite the fact that patents are available only for new inventions which 'involve an innovative step',[31] and to refer to *traditional* knowledge as new would simply be unrealistic. Also, patents are generally granted to individual entities (either physical persons or legal entities),

[30] On this point see Hanning, 'An Examination of the Possibility to Secure Intellectual Property Rights for Plant Genetic Resources Developed by Indigenous Peoples of the Nafta States: Domestic Legislation Under the International Convention for Protection of New Plant Varieties', (1996) 13 *Arizona Journal of International and Comparative Law* 175, at 202.

[31] See Art 27(1) of the TRIPS Agreement.

while indigenous traditional knowledge on biogenetic resources is shared by the entire community, and is thus collective; and, no less important, patents grant exclusive rights which are limited in time, while the protection of indigenous traditional knowledge, in order to be effective, must be granted with no time limit. In sum, this option in the end would allow the unfettered appropriation by non-indigenous individuals and/or firms of indigenous plant resources and knowledge (since the application of the IPRs system could only, and not always, simply delay such appropriation), without granting to the communities concerned any form of effective protection in accordance with their own vision of life.

As for benefit-sharing, the adoption of such an option would consist in allowing industrial exploitation of indigenous biogenetic resources and related traditional knowledge by non-indigenous individuals or firms, which would be bound to grant to the communities concerned a share in the financial income derived from such exploitation. This option is the one favoured by the Conference of the Parties to the CBD,[32] and could actually be satisfactory in certain circumstances. But, altogether, it may be inadequate for at least three reasons. First, not all indigenous communities may be willing to sell for money something which, as previously emphasised, is part of their very identity as people and is thus essential for their cultural and anthropological survival. Secondly, it may be very difficult to obtain the informed consent of the communities concerned, which would be essential for the correct implementation of the option in point,[33] since such consent should be given with regard to legal concepts that are generally extraneous and hardy comprehensible for the indigenous vision of life. Thirdly, the system of benefit–sharing would be based on a patent granted and regulated according to the ordinary rules of patent protection; so, also in this case it would be a protection limited in time, which would expire after the expiry of the patent, thus leading to the definitive deprivation of the communities concerned of any exclusive right to their traditional resources and related knowledge. So, this second option also does not appear appropriate, in most cases, for ensuring adequate protection to indigenous rights over biogenetic resources and related knowledge.

The third option would be that of *tout court* excluding the patentability of biogenetic resources located in indigenous ancestral lands and related knowledge. This solution, which would prevent *a priori* any misappropriation of such resources and knowledge, could appear appropriate on

32 See Bonn Guidelines on Access to Genetic Resources and Fair and Equitable Sharing of Benefits Arising out of their Utilization, available at http://www.biodiv.org/decisions (last visited on 3 Oct 2004).

33 See Ullrich, in this volume, para. 2(b)(*ii*).

account of the fact that indigenous peoples are believed not to be generally interested in obtaining financial income from them, and often they actually do not. Nevertheless, there are two arguments which in certain cases also make this conclusion faulty. First, the term 'indigenous peoples' encompasses a large number of communities which, although generally sharing a strictly similar cultural model based on the same philosophical vision and way of life, may have different specific traits which may translate into a different practical approach to the possibility of making their traditional knowledge and related resources the object of commercial exploitation. Secondly, culture is not a static entity, and it is possible that certain indigenous communities will change their traditional approach towards biogenetic resource and traditional knowledge; this is a perfectly possible and legitimate phenomenon, the only important thing being that it is self-produced (that is to say developed in accordance with the philosophy and beliefs of the communities concerned) and not imposed by external (i.e. Western) cultures. As a consequence, to say that *all* indigenous peoples are not willing to obtain financial reward from their traditional knowledge would be misleading, as is demonstrated by the examples of indigenous communities that have already successfully developed their own systems of exploitation of their traditional knowledge concerning biogenetic resources.[34] So, the adoption of this third option would prevent indigenous communities (that are willing to do so) from ever commercialising their resources and knowledge and, at the same time, would also impair the correct implementation of IPRs law. To avoid such a distorting result, in the event that indigenous peoples are willing to make their biogenetic resources and traditional knowledge the object of commercial or industrial exploitation it is necessary for special forms of protection to be developed which are suitable to grant adequate safeguarding of their intellectual property rights concerning such resources and knowledge. These forms of protection should be shaped in such a way as to preserve the specific idiosyncratic and cultural traits characterising the communities concerned as well as the kind of traditional relationship they have developed throughout the centuries with the resources and knowledge in point. It is important to stress that such forms of protection would not necessarily be inconsistent with the present international legal regime of IPRs.

At the time of writing a strong will has emerged within the international community to resolve the tension between indigenous rights over biogenetic resources and related knowledge and the law of IPRs through the use of *sui generis* systems for the safeguarding of traditional knowledge

[34] See, for example, the case illustrated below, in section IV.

and associated resources.[35] These systems are by their own nature inherently flexible, and are thus suitable for being adapted and shaped on the basis of the concrete aspects of the cultural framework characterising the knowledge to be safeguarded. They can thus be shaped, for example, in such a way as to grant protection to rights which are of a collective nature, unlimited in time and taking into account not only the commercial and economic character attached to a given knowledge or resource, but their spiritual elements as well. Also, they can be adapted to the different peculiar traits of the different communities concerned, of the evolution of which indigenous knowledge is naturally the object in the time, as well as to the fact that the same kind of knowledge may be disseminated in different parts of the world, on account of the movements and cultural interchanges of the different indigenous communities throughout the centuries (in this sense, a model of 'cultural origin', rather than geographical origin, should generally be adopted). Of course, those indigenous communities that are not willing commercially to exploit their resources and related knowledge would retain the freedom to refuse to make them the object of any kind of such exploitation.

This solution appears to be the most suitable for reconciling the specific character of indigenous knowledge with IPRs law. The flexibility of *sui generis* systems may simply allow the grant of contextual protection of the resources concerned, in their physical status, and of the related knowledge, which, as previously pointed out,[36] are both inseparable elements of a unique legal value. At the same time, a remarkable quality of such solution is that it does not entail any legal conflict between the legal values at stake, for the simple reason that the possibility of having recourse to *sui generis* systems for plant resources is already provided by Article 27(3)(b) of the TRIPS Agreement *in its present state*. These systems could thus be legally adopted irrespective of whether the planned revision of the provision in point is achieved or not. Recent practice demonstrates that the consciousness that the provision of *sui generis* systems for the protection of traditional knowledge may actually provide the highest possible level of safeguarding such knowledge and related resources is progressively growing in the context of the international community. The Indian Biodiversity Related Community Intellectual Rights Act[37] and the African Model Legislation for the Protection of the Rights of Local Communities, Farmers and Breeders, and for the Regulation of Access to

[35] This solution is advocated, in particular, by developing countries; see WTO doc. IP/C/W/370 of 8 Aug 2002, *supra* n. 24. Among the scholars see inter alia, Cottier and Panizzon, 'Legal Perspectives on Traditional Knowledge. The Case for Intellectual Property Protection', [2004] *Journal of International Economic Law* 371, at 381 ff.

[36] See *supra*, section II.

[37] See http://www.iapad.org/publications/ppgis/legislation/in_comrightsact_94.pdf (last visited on 31 Dec 2004).

Biological Resources[38] represent two remarkable examples of such practice.

IV. CASE STUDY: THE CASE OF GUARANÀ AS INTANGIBLE CULTURAL HERITAGE OF THE SATERÉ-MAWÉ PEOPLE (BRAZIL)

Indigenous Peoples and Natural Resources under Brazilian Law

The Brazilian Constitution of 1988 represents an important change in the relationships between the Brazilian state and the indigenous peoples, who are 'all the individuals with pre-Columbian origin that identify themselves or are identified as part of an ethnic group whose cultural features distinguish them from the national society'.[39]

Until 1988, indigenous people (unless they were integrated into civil society) were considered 'inferior' and were under the wardship of a specific federal organ, the FUNAI (National Foundation for Indigenous People). In 1988, with the new Constitution, citizenship and ethnic rights were recognised to all indigenous people even if they were not fully integrated into national society.

This new and revolutionary change is sanctioned by a few lines of Article 232, which establishes that 'indigenous people, their communities and organisations are lawful parties and can appear before the Court to defend their rights'. This right is acknowledged apart from the fact that the indigenous community is recognised 'as emancipated' by a decree-law of the President of the Republic and apart from the fact that its members speak Portuguese, practise a useful activity within national society and know the habits and customs of the national community.[40]

For the rest, the specific rights of indigenous communities have their basis in Article 231 of the Constitution, which elevates some of the rules sanctioned by the Charter of Indigenous People of 1973 to constitutional law. It proclaims that 'indigenous people have the right to have their own social organisations, customs, language, beliefs and traditions' and recognises their 'original rights over the lands they traditionally inhabit' (paragraph 1). It also explains that 'the lands traditionally inhabited by natives' are all those 'permanently occupied by them'; those 'used for their productive activities'; those 'indispensable to preserve the environmental resources necessary to their wellbeing'; those 'necessary to their physical

[38] See http://www.grain.org/brl_files/oau-model-law-en.pdf (last visited on 3 Oct 2004). The Model Legislation in point has been developed by the Organization of African Unity.

[39] See the definition provided by the Charter of Indigenous People, Law 6.001 of 19 Dec 1973, art. 3(1).

[40] See Art 11 and 9 of the Charter of Indigenous People of 1973.

and cultural reproduction, according to their habits, customs and traditions'. Finally, it states (paragraph 2) that indigenous peoples have the 'exclusive usufruct of the soil, the rivers and the lakes existing in those lands'. According to a temporary constitutional law (Article 67), these lands should have been demarcated within five years from the promulgation of the Constitution. Also in this case there is the question of the elevation to constitutional law of a commitment already undertaken in the Charter of Indigenous People of 1973 (Article 65).[41] Nevertheless, 16 years later, half of the indigenous areas initially identified have not yet been demarcated.

The Andirà-Marau land, where the Saterè-Mawé people live, was one of first areas to have been recognised as 'Indigenous Land, patrimony of the Federal Union' by the Charter of Indigenous People. The fact that these territories are considered the 'patrimony of the Federal Union' and that indigenous people are not formally their owners does not in itself mean that indigenous law is weak. In the context of the full implementation of ethnic autonomy described in Article 231, this is a logical consequence of the land rights' inalienability and unavailability, and thus of the imprescriptibility of the rights over the lands sanctioned in paragraph (4). However, from the fact that these territories are considered 'patrimony of the Federal Union' there derives another rule written in paragraph (3) of Article 231 which established that 'the use of the water resources, including its energy uses, and the exploitation of the ore resources existing in the indigenous lands can be allowed only by the National Congress, after having consulted the indigenous communities and after having assured the participation to the results of the exploitation in form of law'.

In brief, the original right of usufruct (and thus of marketing) acknowledged to indigenous people is restricted to the agricultural and woodland use of the soil, and it does not include the use of the water resources (not the aquatic flora and fauna, but the water itself, and above all its potential energy use) and the subsoil resources (in particular the ore resources), which are under the control of the Congress. In fact, without the authorisation of the Congress (which is justified in the case of 'high interest for the national security and development', as provided for by Article 20 of the Charter of Indigenous People of 1973), mining is absolutely forbidden. This is valid not only for non-indigenous enterprises, but also for the enterprises belonging to the indigenous people living in those lands.

So, as far as biological resources are concerned, according to Article 231, the *Indios* in their own land can follow their traditional habits and customs. As a consequence, for indigenous producers, the ordinary legislation is valid only if their production is sold outside the communitarian trade relationships. In this case, in fact, production is regulated according

[41] See *supra* n. 39.

to the ordinary legislation and indigenous people are subjected to ordinary laws.

On the contrary, the water and subsoil resources (again considering the case of external use) belong *a priori* to the Federal Union (on the basis of Article 20 of the Constitution). Consequently, in this case the original right of the indigenous community exists, and it is a right that can be monetised under the aegis of the Congress. But the hearing of the interested indigenous community does not imply that the community can exercise a right of veto.

In the last ten years many reforms of the Charter of Indigenous People have been proposed. The current version of the Charter, in fact, is in contrast with the spirit of the Constitution, which would require a reading of Article 231 in the light of Article 232.

In particular, Title IV of the Charter is, at least in theory, absolutely inapplicable. It entrusts the management of the goods and the incomes deriving from the indigenous patrimony to the FUNAI as the protection organisation. However, according to the Constitution, the indigenous organisations have autonomous legal status and can exercise themselves all the rights sanctioned in Article 231. Besides, nowadays a large number of *indios* living in the indigenous area already exercise all those political and civil rights that were previously a prerogative of the *indios* who were integrated into the national community (Article 4 of the Charter of Indigenous People).

Aware of all this, the legislative power and the Brazilian governments (thanks also to very alert civil society) have resisted lobbying by some economic subjects. These want to sweep away the present procedural system, which requires the assent of the Congress for the exploitation of ore resources, before the approval of a new Charter of Indigenous People that assures the effectiveness of indigenous rights during negotiations.

This threat has not been averted. On the contrary, the indigenous right to enjoy the exclusive usufruct of the soil, the rivers and the lakes (settled by the Constitution) also clashes with the passive resistance of the peripheral administrations, which most of the time hamper the management of the indigenous patrimony by the communities.

But, would a new Charter of Indigenous People which includes all the conditions settled in Article 232 of the Constitutions solve the problem?

In our opinion, it would not. We have to note that Article 231 brings up the matter of how in the long term to manage the fact that the use of the soil is virtually in conflict/competition with the (industrial, commercial and military) use of the subsoil and water resources. In the Constitution, indeed, the use of the soil is considered *a priori* a matter of communitarian and infra-ethnic interest, while the use of the subsoil and water resources is considered *a priori* a matter of national-federal interest. The inadequacy of this point of view will be shown later on in our case study.

Environmental law in Brazil is based on Article 225 of the Constitution, which provides that 'everybody has the right to enjoy an ecologically balanced environment, heritage for the common use, essential for a healthy quality of life' and that 'the public power and the collectivity must preserve it for the present and the future generations'.

Most indigenous people, who, like every Brazilian citizen, benefit from the protection of this law, live and have their demarcated areas in regions that, according to paragraph IV of the same Article, are under special protection: 'the Brazilian Amazon Forest, the "Mata Atlantica", the "Serra do Mar', the 'Pantanal Mato- Grossensen" and the Coastal Zone are national patrimony. Their utilisation will be regulated by law and all the conditions that assure the protection of the environment, including those concerning the use of the natural resources, will be taken into account'.

These conditions were already explained in paragraph (I), according to which it is for the public power 'to preserve and restore the essential ecological processes and to provide for the ecological management of species and ecosystems'.

However, in recent years the discussion about the importance of Article 225 for the indigenous people has above all concerned the question of the protection of 'the indigenous traditional knowledge related to the genetic resources'. With regard to this problem, paragraph IV of Article 225 and sub-section (2) of the paragraph (I) (in which the public power is given the power 'to preserve the diversity and the integrity of the genetic patrimony of the Country and to control the institutions that carry out genetic research') find an applying regulation in PM (Provisional Measure) 2186–16 of 23 August 2001.[42]

In Article 8 (Chapter 3), the PM protects indigenous traditional knowledge related to the genetic patrimony against any illicit use or damaging action not authorised by the CGEN (Council for the Management of the Genetic Patrimony) or by an accredited institution. In particular, the PM recognises the right of indigenous communities to decide about the use of their traditional knowledge related to the genetic patrimony of the Country (paragraph 1). It also establishes that this traditional knowledge is part of the Brazilian cultural patrimony and that it can be the subject of inventory, according to the CGEN provisions and the specific legislation (paragraph 2). This, in any case, does not prejudice the indigenous communities' intellectual property rights (paragraph 4).

Besides, Article 9 settled that indigenous communities which develop, hold and protect traditional knowledge concerning the genetic patrimony have the right to: see the origin of the access to the traditional knowledge indicated in any case of publication, utilisation, exploitation and

42 The text of PM 2186–16 is available at http://www.grain.org/brl/?docid=850&lawid=1768 (last visited on 25 Sept 2004).

divulgation and to prevent any unauthorised agent from carrying out tests or research related to their traditional knowledge and from disclosing any data or information about it.

Above all, however, the PM sanctions (Article I(3)) that the indigenous communities 'have the right to a fair repartition of the benefits deriving from the exploitation of the genetic patrimony and the traditional knowledge related to it'. In fact, an entire chapter (chapter 7) is devoted to explaining the forms and the clauses of a Contract for the Utilisation of the Genetic Patrimony and for the Repartition of the Benefits among the knowledge holder, the national institution authorised to have access to it and the addressee.

The PM, which in Brazil has all the effects of a permanent law, is an important democratic conquest. It proclaims the communitarian right to veto research and to enjoy the economic benefits deriving from information expressed in a non-scientific way. Furthermore, it forces the state to protect normal daily actions and millenary practices from interference by illegal patents, a threat that is increasingly pressing today.

In spite of all this, there is an alarming aspect that we cannot disregard: the PM interprets the sentence 'to preserve the diversity and the integrity of the genetic patrimony' only in economic terms, forgetting all the cultural and moral aspects related to this question. But today the majority of public opinion thinks that the integrity of biodiversity is first a human right, and that the protection of those ecosystems, cited in paragraph IV of Article 225 as national patrimony, is a question that concerns life. Those ecosystems, in fact, are necessary to guarantee the survival of indigenous peoples, and in general the survival of human beings at the local, national and global level.

None of this is mentioned at all in the PM, even in a rhetorical reference.

In brief, the problem of the quality of environmental protection is at the heart of the indigenous question. The fact that the PM forgets this important connection leads us to suspect that, in spite of its incontestable merits, this law is far from dealing with the core of the indigenous problem, to which it is often associated.

The Guaranà as intangible cultural heritage of the Sateré-Mawé People

On the basis of their beliefs, customs, traditions and social organisation, the Sateré-Mawé people for nine years have been building an autonomous integrated project of ethnic development, by increasing the value of the most important resource of their land: the *guaranà.*

When Obadias Batista Garcia, then member of the directive council, presented the idea of the project at the General Assembly of the Tribal General Council in the *Umirituba* village, he was struck by a tale told by a venerable man, the old *tuchaua* Servo Miquilis (who is no longer with us). After listening to all the comments, Miquilis told a 'nice story' in the *Sateré* language, one of those tales handed down by word of mouth that everybody knows and that represent the cognitive paradigms for understanding the facts of life and the meaning of existence.

The story talked about Onhiàmuaçabê, a beautiful girl who lived before the beginning of human history. Onhiàmuàçabê's brothers did not want her to marry because she was an expert in medical herbs and she looked after them, but unfortunately a little snake fell in love with her. In order to woo her, the snake waited for her on the path she always used to walk along, where it touched her leg and got her pregnant. Her brothers thus became furious and they chased her and her child away from the garden of Noçoquem, where she had lived until that moment.

When the child was five years old, he secretly went back to the garden because he wanted to eat the fruit of a big tree in the middle of it, which today is called the 'Brazil nut'. His uncles had been looking forward to this for a long time. When his mother reached him it was too late; they had already killed him.

As she gathered her dead child's remains, Onhiàmuaçabê said; 'My dear son, your uncles wanted you to be a poor creature, but it will not be so!' She then plucked out his eyes, planted them in the ground and went on 'you, my son, will be the greatest power of all nature, you will go through the world to heal mankind and free people of their diseases'. She then washed his body with her saliva mixed with magic plants that she had chewed and she buried it.

The liana of the true *guaranà* sprouted from one of the child's eyes (indeed when the *guaranà* fruit is ripe, it looks very much like a human eye). In the following days, different animal species came out of the place where she had buried her child. And, in the end, his body came back to life and he became the founder of the *Mawé* indios.

At the end of the story the old *tuchaua* said that he saw in the proposed project the realisation of the Onhiàmuaçabé prophecy, because, through it, the *guaranà* would be traded all over the world under the Tribal Council's name.

What was the idea?

The Tribal General Council was a member of the COIAB (Coordination of Brazilian Amazon Indigenous Peoples), which at the same time was a member of the COICA (International Coordination of the Indigenous Peoples living in the nine Amazon Countries). The COICA was a co-founder, together with a group of European town councils that today number over 1,000, of the Climate Alliance, according to which people from the tropical forests had to be the 'forests guardians' and prevent the forests from being destroyed, while people from European countries had to reduce gas emissions.

The Sateré-Mawé people were the *guaranà* sons. They discovered *guaranà* and its properties and invented the techniques for growing it. They had always lived in the land where it is endemic, but their product was given for nothing to the *regatoes* (white traders) recognised by the FUNAI.

The project's aim was to substantiate that 'Alliance', by selling all the production at a fair price, and it took into account not only the excellent quality of the product, but also the Sateré-Mawés commitment to preserving the natural environment of native *guaranà*, in redeeming their own culture and in making sure that the social spin-offs of the project were fair.

This project was based on two assumptions: the chance for indigenous people really to organise themselve and the existence of an organised civil society of international consumers, above all European ones, interested in the product and in its social and cultural value.

Nine years later, this objective may be considered to have been achieved: about 500 producer families sell their production to their own organisation, the CGTSM (Sateré-Mawé's General Tribal Council, a complex organisation representing all the social authorities and all the agro-sylviculturists of the Andirá–Marau land) at a price three times higher than that in the regional market (State of Amazonas). The CGTSM then distributes the product within the international fair-trade network (IFAT International Federation Alternative Trade) of which it is part. The CGTSM, as a result of the *guaranà* income, is the only Brazilian indigenous organisation that does not depend on foreign aid (institutions or NGOs) for its administrative and internal transaction costs, and thus enjoys true political autonomy. The autonomous ethno-development project, with the *guaranà* income and other sub-projects, finances the inorganic waste recycling done by the indigenous women's organisation (AMISM) in all the 80 villages, and the gradual domestication, and thus protection, of the native melipona bees: all sub-projects whose aim is to seek full synergy among the social, ecological and economic objectives.

In brief, this integrated ethno-development project intends to transform the 800,000 thousand hectares of the demarcated Andirá–Marau indigenous land (the heart of the bigger Sateré-Mawé ancestral lands) into a *sateré-mawé éco ga'apypiat waraná mimotypoot sése*, which means 'ecological and cultural Sanctuary of the Sateré-Mawé's Guaranà'.

Now, the question is: can the legislative framework described in the first part of this section protect and sustain all this?

Undoubtedly, thanks to the *Sateré-Mawé's* heritage, the *guaranà*, which today is still cultivated only in Brazil, is a very profitable national resource (it is in fact a food supplement from which we obtain healthy, dietetic, cosmetic, medical and culinary products, but above all energetic and thirst-quenching drinks that are also consumed outside Brazil).

This fact is so well-known that many brands of *guaranà* use names like Sateré, Mawé, Sateré-Mawé or Andirà. This happens also in Europe, although the use of names relating to ethnic groups or geographical places is forbidden by law.

Having progressively expropriated the indigenous land for 350 years (at the beginning of the nineteenth century, Mawé producers inhabited a territory that was much larger than the current one, had a substantial monopoly over the *guaranà* production and a partial control of its trade), in 2001 the Brazilian government decided to change its policy and started to protect the traditional knowledge by establishing public control over research activities. In particular, it adopted a temporary rule according to which the traditional knowledge had to be considered 'national patrimony' and native people had the right to fair remuneration for it.

Let us focus, now, on the problem of the *guaranà* genetic patrimony, which the Sateré-Mawé people have been protecting religiously for centuries, by choosing the '*guaranà* sons' born from the 'liana mothers' in the middle of the forest and transplanting them in small clearings not far from there.

During the first meeting of the *Pagés* (shamans) organised in Manaus by the FEPI (Foundation of the Amazonas State for Indigenous Policy), a technician of the Embrapa (a Brazilian public research firm which is under the control of the Ministry of Agricultural Policies) declared that the main part of the research activity on different varieties of *guaranà* clones had been conducted on samples taken from the Sateré-Mawé communities. For this reason, the Embrapa proposed distributing for free the guaranà varieties considered most suitable for the Sateré-Mawé production to the individual Mawé producers (but not to their organisation).

The Sateré-Mawé producers refused this opportunity.

Why did they do so? And why, two years after the implementation of the PM, has the CGTSM never taken into account the possibility of compensation for the public use of the traditional knowledge? In brief, why are both of the possibilities offered by the public power considered to be terrible calamities by indigenous peoples?

First, the *guaranà* clones are not genetically differentiated, which means the Sateré-Mawé *guaranà* could not be sold on the market as native *guaranà* at the proper price. Secondly, cross-pollination, by the native bees, could drastically impoverish the last natural genetic bank of *guaranà* in the world, which the Sateré-Mawé people keep and protect in their forests. This could eliminate the principal factor on which international consumers' solidarity is based. Thirdly, the structural fragility of cloned cultivation entails the use of chemical pesticides and fertilisers, which would eliminate the biological certification and the certification of products as coming from the practice of Analog Forestry for Sateré-Mawé *guaranà*.

Finally, the traditional domestication of *guaranà* native plants represents their typical nature which justifies the premium value of this product

(Sateré-Mawé *guaranà* is the first international Slow Food presidium in Brazil). Without this individuality, nobody would be interested in sustaining the high transport cost of this Amazon forest product, because it would be virtually identical to the *guaranà* produced in Bahia do Sul.

Moreover, the impact of eventual royalties would be catastrophic from a social and cultural point of view. In May 2003, in an interview for the *Courrier International*, a journalist asked Jecinaldo Barbosa Cabral, a Sateré-Mawé *indio* and general coordinator of COIBA, whether it was not better to register a patent (in the USA or Japan) instead of trying to obtain a European quality certificate of protected origin. The answer was: 'It would mean depositing a patent on my father's head'. For the Sateré-Mawé people, *guaranà* not only has a mythological value. Indeed, in their language *guaranà* is called *warà* and means 'the origin of knowledge'. To file a patent on the origin of all knowledge, and make money from it, is inconceivable: it would be a terrible violation of the Sateré-Mawé ancestral religion.

We should also consider that all consumers who choose to buy Sateré-Mawé products are particularly sensitive to these problems. They usually criticise the unlawful use of the legislation in matters of intellectual property, and find unethical the idea of depositing a patent on living beings, including plants. Thus, earning royalties over *guaranà* patents would have disastrous economic and political consequences for the Sateré-Mawé people.

Considerable further harm to the Sateré-Mawé people could derive from the increment of dependency on external aid. In spite of the progress achieved by the *guaranà* project, food scarcity is still a widespread problem in the Antirà-Marau indigenous area, particularly during the rainy season. This is because the aid system has damaged and continuously destructured the traditional dynamics of self-sufficiency, and has undermined the autonomous exploitation of market resources. Maintaining hunger in order to increase dependency on external aid is indeed one of the methods used by the political administration (managed by local oligarchies) to obtain votes and social legitimacy, and thus to obtain power.

The huge incomes deriving from the alienation of the intellectual patrimony of their ancestors would be only another instrument for increasing the dependency of the people concerned on induced needs and a form of social integration characterised by a position of subordination.

The CGTSM is working on the construction of an indigenous society which grows rich by exercising its own economic rights autonomously, without transferring the exploitation rights to other people.

As explained above, Article 8 of the PM protects the indigenous traditional knowledge related to the genetic patrimony not only against any illicit use and exploitation but also against 'other damaging actions'.

However, it does not explain *how* such protection can be realised conversely and *what kind* of damaging actions it is talking about.

Unfortunately, in most cases, the most damaging actions are all those not well defined as 'other actions'.

For example, if we visit the AmBev's website,[43] we will discover that AmBev owns 'the biggest bank of guaranà germ-plasma in the world'.[44] This is kept safe in the Santa Helena *fazenda* in Maués: a little town of 40,000 inhabitants, world-famous for being the capital of *guaranà*. American Beverage is working, with Embrapa, the Prefecture of Maués and the IDAM (Institute for the Agro-pastoral Development of Amazonas State), on the achievement of a big project, called 'Maués Project', whose aim is to promote the 'modernisation' of *guaranà* cultivation by spreading the use of the 'genetically superior varieties' produced in the Santa Helena *fazenda* among the local farmers. In brief, AmBev owns the biggest factory for extracting *guaranà* in Brazil, the basic element of its *guaranà* drinks. The Prefecture of Maués is the only buyer of the *guaranà* harvest (in roast *guaranà* beans). It purchases at a fixed price of 7 reais per kilogrames (the price has been approved by the government of the Amazonas state for the next ten years), and requires each individual family producer to register himself as a supplier. In effect the Prefecture forces the producers to go into debt in order to buy clones, manures and pesticides, 'rationalising' their traditional production.

According to the STR of Maués (the Rural Workers' Trade Union, a local branch of CONTAG, the Brazilian Farmers' National Confederation), the banks do not finance any other project proposed by the communitarian associations unless the project is under written by the IDAM in conformity with the AmBev development plan. Moreover, credit is lavished directly in the form of technological crafts and biotechnological raw materials supplied by the firm and the producers can neither negotiate the price and the quality, nor ask for cash.

The territory has been subdivided by the Municipality into 'agricultural poles' that replace the previous producers' associations and work as the drive belt of the international buyers' monopoly.

As a consequence of all this, the family producers' condition is getting worse and worse and many spontaneous associations, individual producers and the trade union itself insistently seek the help of CGTSM.

The Prefecture of Maués is trying to introduce Ambev's clones even into the Indigenous Land which, in theory, is protected by the FUNAI. The Sateré-Mawé producers who live in the region surrounding the

43 American Beverage is a big multinational company which, through Inbev (International Beverage), controls most of the drinks production in the world.

44 See http://www.ambev.com.br/imprensa/ pressreleases/ano2002/0063 (last visited on 25 Sept 2004).

Marau River suffer the greatest pressure, because in this area federal territory overlaps the municipal.

Behaving in this way, however, the Prefecture openly ignores not only the borders of the indigenous land, but many other important things. It ignores, for instance, the existence of an autonomous integrated project of ethnic-development that involves all the Andirà-Marau land (which includes a further four municipalities) and the fact that this project participated in 2000 in the last World Exposition in Hanover, as a model project for Agenda 21 of the United Nations. It also ignores the fact that all of the about 500 families of *guaranà* producers are regularly associated within the CGTSM, and that the CGTSM is a promoter and co-owner of a social firm with a strong ethnic inclination (incubated by public power through the Manaus Free Zone Bureau—SUFRAMA): the Sapopema Itda (Society of the Peoples for the Amazon Ecodevelopment), through which it transforms its raw materials and trades in its products. It ignores the fact that the Sapopema Itda is much more than a small firm; it is a regional system of fair socio-economic trade among several indigenous and non-indigenous communities of the region (promoted by a project of international co-operation between the Brazilian government and the European Commission and co-ordinated by two Italian NGOs, ICEI and ACRA).

The Prefecture also ignores the fact that the CGTSM is carrying on its autonomous project in partnership with the INPA (National Institute of Amazon Research), and that the FAPEAM (Foundation for Sustaining Research in the Amazonas State) is financing a second project proposed by UFAM (Federal University of Amazonas) and CGTSM that employs young indigenous researchers of the CGTSM to write a rule book for *guaranà* production, to create a consortium for the protection of the original *guaranà* of the Sateré-Mawé communities and to take part in the formulation of a bill for the protection of typical products.

Another fact to be emphasised is that, in 2004, the Prefecture of Maués conducted an ideological campaign to convince indigenous producers that their *guaranà* was not native and that the Slow Food Presidium was only an instrument of the CGTSM's misleading propaganda, in this way ignoring the fact that the Presidium is sponsored by the MDA, the Brazilian Ministry for Agricultural Development.

All this is really worrying. Considering, in fact, that AmBev declares that it already controls the world's genetic bank of *guaranà in vitro* in its *Fazenda,* what could be the interest of the Maués Project agents in protecting the real genetic bank of *guaranà* of Brazil?

When, only four years ago, Marcus Barros (now president of the IBAMA—Brazilian Institute for Renewable Natural Resources—organ of the Brazilian Ministry of the Environment), during a conference in Rome about the Sateré-Mawé *guaranà*, warned against the risk represented by the multinational companies interested in the Maués area, nobody could imagine such a rapid evolution!

The 'Maués Project' is a terrible example of what is happening today in Brazil: the indigenous areas are seriously threatened by the economic interests of big multinational companies, although they represent an enormous public heritage.

This is mainly a consequence of the continuous delays in the formulation and adoption of the new Charter of Indigenous People. The old Charter, in fact, is still applied, even though it is not properly in force and it is in striking contrast to the Constitution.

This is particularly the case with Article 2, in which it is written that:

> [i]t is up to the Union, the States, the Municipalities and their administrative organs to implement, within the limits of their competences, programs and projects to protect the indigenous communities and their rights . . . These activities have to benefit the indigenous communities and *possibly have to be implemented with their collaboration*.[45]

This is a very anachronistic concept which, unfortunately, reflects reality. Many public institutions (like the FUNAI and the municipalities) ignore the indigenous organisations and do not respect their autonomy, even when (like the CGTSM) they are the direct expression of the traditional authorities, and thus the full expression of that cultural self-determination established in the Constitution of 1988.

If this is how things stand, what can be done for the Sateré-Mawé people and their *guaranà*?

The Sateré-Mawé's General Tribal Council thinks that the UNESCO Convention for the Safeguarding of Intangible Cultural Heritage[46] could be an effective instrument in this sense. If the Brazilian government acknowledged the Sateré-Mawé traditional knowledge as national cultural heritage, the integrated project of ethnic development could have a long-term perspective, and the Sateré-Mawé people could invest in long-term sustainable development without fearing that the National Congress might suddenly decide to assign their land to another public use (such as the Maués-Itaituba road, which would run right through the middle of the Sateré-Mawé land). But registration in 'the intangible cultural patrimony' within the PNPI (the Brazilian National Programme for the Intangible Patrimony, established by Decree-Law n. 3.551 of 4 August 2000) does not by itself offer all the prospects that the text of the international convention foreshadows.

Article 2 of the UNESCO Convention, in fact, establishes an indissoluble bond between culture and environment: '. . . [t]his intangible cultural

45 Emphasis added.
46 See *supra* n. 13.

heritage, transmitted from generation to generation, is constantly recreated by communities and groups in response to their environment, their interaction with nature and their history, and provides them with a sense of identity and continuity, thus promoting respect for cultural diversity and human creativity'.

This bond between culture and environment—culture and nature, culture and ecology (which in our case represents what is really at stake)—is strengthened by Article 14, which binds states parties 'to promote, with any appropriate means, education for the protection of natural spaces and places of memory whose existence is necessary for expressing the intangible cultural heritage'.

But, what is fundamental above all is the contribution of Article 15, concerning the 'participation of communities, groups and individuals', which states as follows:

> [w]ithin the framework of its safeguarding activities of the intangible cultural heritage, each State Party shall endeavour to ensure the widest possible participation of communities, groups and, in some cases, individuals that create, maintain and transmit such heritage, and to involve them actively in its management.

In other words, this Article binds national institutions to apply the subsidiary principle in the implementation of policies for the protection of the cultural heritage, and that is exactly what the Sateré-Mawé people need more than anything else. On everybody's behalf.

Part V

Biotechnology and Regional Economic Integration Systems

14

The EU Charter of Fundamental Rights and the Governance of Biotechnology in the European Union

PAVEL ŠTURMA*

I. INTRODUCTION

THERE ARE NO doubts that biotechnology has opened up many new horizons in the scientific world. However, the scientific progress which is being made in this field is also accompanied by many problematic questions from both legal and ethical points of view. A human rights approach is not the only possible way of dealing with the problem, but it has the advantage of combining of law and ethics. Several international and European instruments have tried to respond to these questions and concerns.

This Chapter will address the issue of the governance of biotechnology mainly from the point of view of the EU Charter of Fundamental Rights. It does not intend to disregard other international instruments, important as a source of inspiration and guidance on the interpretation of the relevant provisions of the Charter. Neither does it mean to exclude other instruments of EC/EU law, such as directives on some aspects of biomedicine and biotechnology. However, the Charter of Fundamental Rights has been incorporated into the recently adopted Treaty Establishing a Constitution for Europe. As such, it may become a part of the primary law of the Union if the Treaty enters into force. The rules and principles embodied in the Charter of Fundamental Rights are thus of primary—or constitutional—importance for the whole body of EC/EU legislation.

From the point of view of its structure, the Chapter is divided into three substantive parts and conclusions. In the first part, before dealing with specific rights, the general nature of the Charter and its scope of application are discussed. Next, the fundamental rights having direct impact on

* Prof. JUDr., DrSc., Faculty of Law, Charles University in Prague.

biotechnology will be analysed. The third part will clarify the scope of these rights and level of protection.

II. NATURE AND SCOPE OF APPLICATION OF THE CHARTER

Origins and Nature of the Charter

The concept of fundamental rights was first adopted in the case law of the European Court of Justice (ECJ) and only later was incorporated into the treaty instruments.[1] This is an essential difference between EU fundamental rights and the human rights standards of the Council of Europe, which always arise out of treaty instruments, although they may be interpreted by the case law of the European Court of Human Rights.

The notion of 'fundamental rights' appeared first in the treaty terminology in Article 6 of the Treaty EU (Article F(2) of the 1992 Treaty of Maastricht, as amended by the 1997 Treaty of Amsterdam. According to this provision:

> 'The Union shall respect fundamental rights, as guaranteed by the European Convention for the Protection of Human Rights and Fundamental Freedoms signed in Rome on 4 November 1950 and as they result from the constitutional traditions common to the Member States, as general principles of Community law'.

Moreover, the Treaty EU (in Article 6 F(1)) lays down that 'the Union is founded on principles of liberty, democracy, respect for human rights and fundamental freedoms, and the rule of law, principles which are common to the Member States'.

However, the general principles formulated in the case law of the ECJ are not the only source of fundamental rights in EC/EU law. Sources of fundamental rights may also be found in both primary and secondary acts of EC law and other international acts (*sui generis*).[2] They include Articles 12, 13, 136 and 141 of the EC Treaty, as well as some other provisions, in particular those on EU citizenship (Part II of the EC Treaty), complemented by copious secondary legislation, in the field of social rights and the prohibition of discrimination.

Yet another source of economic and social rights is the Charter of Fundamental Workers' Social Rights (1989),[3] which further develops prin-

[1] This concept differs from the notion of 'fundamental freedoms' set out in the EC Treaty (Arts 28, 39, 43 and 49).

[2] Cf. Šišková, *Dimenze ochrany lidských práv v EU* (Prague, 2003), p 39.

[3] [1989] OJ C/120/51. Cf. Prétot, *Le droit social européen* (Paris, 1990), p 115 ff.

ciples of the European Social Charter adopted within the Council of Europe. Although from the legal point of view it is a mere non binding declaration, the ECJ takes its content into consideration. Moreover, it is also referred to in Article 136 of the EC Treaty.

In spite of all these sources, there was no comprehensive catalogue of fundamental rights. The adoption of the Charter of Fundamental Rights of the EU has become a response to this lacuna. The document drafted by the Convention since 1999 was adopted by the European Council, Commission and Parliament at Nice on 7 December 2000. For the time being, the Charter is a political declaration, i.e. legally non-binding text.[4] By virtue of its incorporation into the adopted text of the Treaty establishing a Constitution for Europe, however, if and when the Treaty enters into force, the content of the Charter will become legally binding.

Nevertheless, the Charter is already an important document which contains the most extensive international bill of rights. It not only includes the rights already established in other international or European instruments, but also introduces some new rights which are specific to the EU and its Member States. The Charter is structured into a Preamble and seven chapters. In the Preamble, the Member States and the peoples of Europe express the will to create an ever closer union among them and an area of freedom, security and justice. Next, they reiterate the main sources of inspiration of the rights, including the case law of the ECJ and of the European Court of Human Rights.

The Charter distinguished itself among other human rights instruments not only by the unusually wide catalogue of fundamental rights but also by their new classification. Instead of the traditional division into civil and political rights on one hand and economic, social and cultural rights on the other hand, the Charter has divided rights into six chapters according to the underlying fundamental values embodied in them: dignity, freedoms, equality, solidarity, citizens' rights and justice. In a sense, the Charter thus seems to decline both the formal structure of already existing international instruments and some doctrinal concepts (e.g. generations of human rights).

Scope of application of the Charter

The Charter itself provides the answer to the question of its application. Chapter VII includes general provisions relating to the Charter as a whole, namely its scope of application, scope of guaranteed rights, level

[4] [2000] OJ C/364/1.

of protection and prohibition of abuse of rights (Articles 51 to 54). Article 51 sets out the key provision on the scope of application of the Charter:

> '1. The provisions of this Charter are addressed to the institutions and bodies of the Union with regard for the principle of subsidiarity and to the Member States only when they are implementing Union law. They shall therefore respect the rights, observe the principles and promote the application thereof in accordance with their respective powers'.

At the same time, according to Article 51 (2), the Charter does not establish any new power or duty for the Community or the Union, or modify powers and duties defined by the Treaties. Indeed, such modification would not be possible, taking into account the non-binding character of the Charter. This could be done only by the revision of existing treaties or by a new Treaty establishing a Constitution for Europe. The scope of application *ratione materiae* is thus within the scope of EC/EU law. With the extension of European law the scope of application of fundamental rights also has to be wider.

This also has impact on the scope of the Charter *ratione personae* as far as the obligatory subjects are concerned. There was no need to set any limitations on institutions and bodies of the Union. First, these institutions and bodies were established by or on the basis of the Treaties and have powers delegated to them by the Member States; therefore they may act only within their limits and on the basis of EC/EU law. Secondly, the reason for the adoption of the Charter was precisely to give to the institutions and bodies of the Union more detailed guidelines for the implementation of the principle of respect for human rights under Article 6 TEU.

On the contrary, it is fully justified to point out that the content of the Charter applies to the Member States only when they are implementing EC/EU law. It results from the case law of the ECJ that the Member States are obliged to respect fundamental rights only when they act within the framework of EC law. [5] Otherwise the Member States are bound by their constitutional rules and obligations under international treaties on human rights.

As regards beneficiaries of the fundamental rights the Charter distinguishes between (a) any person, (b) citizens of the Union, (c) any natural or legal person residing or having its registered office in a Member State, and (d) nationals of third countries. [6]

The Charter guarantees many fundamental rights to 'everyone' (every person), in particular in the field of dignity, freedoms, equality and rights relating to justice. Some other rights have been reserved only for

[5] See the judgments in Case 5/88, *Wachauf* [1989], ECR 2609; Case C–260/89, *ERT* [1991] ECR I–2925; Case C–292/97, 13 April 2000, point 37.

[6] See Pikna, *Evropská unie—vnitřní a vnější bezpečnost a ochrana základních práv* (Prague, 2002), p 175; Šišková, *supra* n. 2, p 188.

the citizens of the Union, such as the right to vote and stand as a candidate at elections to the European Parliament and at municipal elections (Articles. 39 and 40) or diplomatic and consular protection (Article 46). Yet other rights relate to 'any natural or legal person residing or having registered office in a Member State'; they include right of access to documents, right to refer to the EU Ombudsman and right to petition the European Parliament (Articles 42 to 44).

Some provisions of the Charter refer even to nationals of third states, which is *expressis verbis* in of Article 15 (3) (the right to equivalent working conditions for those who are authorised to work in the territories of the Member States). In other cases the Charter does not say so expressly but it may be assumed that the provisions refer *de facto* to nationals of third states, such as with the right to asylum and protection in the event of removal, expulsion or extradition (Articles 18 and 19 (2).[7]

III. FUNDAMENTAL RIGHTS HAVING A DIRECT IMPACT ON BIOTECHNOLOGY

Fundamental rights relating to biotechnology belong to the rights which aim at the protection of human dignity. Therefore they apply to everyone, i.e. every human being. From the point of view of our subject-matter, it is important to study the Preamble to and Article 1 and Article 3 of the Charter.

The Preamble refers to human dignity as the first of the underlying values. According to the Preamble to the Charter, 'the Union is founded on the indivisible, universal values of human dignity, freedom, equality and solidarity'. In a sense, the Preamble to the Charter follows the example of other international instruments on human rights. The 1948 Universal Declaration of Human Rights stressed the idea of human dignity mainly in its Preamble and Article 1. In the Preambles to both International Covenants of 1966 (ICCPR and ICESCR), the states parties recognise that the inalienable rights 'derive from the inherent dignity of the human person'. Similarly, the 1989 International Convention on the Rights of the Child refers to the same idea in its Preamble.

The European Convention for the Protection of Human Rights and Fundamental Freedoms (ECHR, 1950) and its additional protocols do not contain any express rules on human dignity. The ECHR refers to this idea only indirectly, as the Preamble goes back to the UN Declaration of 1948. Moreover, human dignity seems to be an underlying value for most of the rights guaranteed by the ECHR, in particular the prohibition of torture (Article 3) and the protection of private life (Article 8). As the European

[7] This is in view of the wording of Art. 18 which guarantees this right with due respect for the EC Treaty, including the Protocol on granting asylum to nationals of Member States of the EU, annexed to the Treaty of Amsterdam (1997).

Court of Human Rights pointed out in the judgment on euthanasia, 'the very essence of the Convention is respect for human dignity and human freedom'.[8]

However, the 1997 Council of Europe Convention for the Protection of Human Rights and Dignity of the Human Being with regard to the Application of Biology and Medicine—Convention on Human Rights and Biomedicine (hereafter the 'Biomedicine Convention')[9] in Article 1 (1) expressly gives as its aim 'to protect the dignity and identity of all human beings'.

Human dignity is not just the underlying value for the whole Charter and, in particular, for its Chapter I which, under the title 'Dignity', deals with the most important, absolute rights, such as the right to life, the right to the integrity of the person, the prohibition of torture and inhuman or degrading treatment or punishment, the prohibition of slavery and forced labour. It has its direct reflection in Article 1 of the Charter.

Article 1: Human Dignity

Article 1 of the Charter is a very brief provision which provides for the protection of human dignity as such. Standing alone, it is not expressly linked with other rights (for example right to the integrity). Article 1 reads as follows:

> 'Human dignity is inviolable. It must be protected and respected'.

In the Charter, unlike in other international instruments, the general recognition of human dignity takes place not only in the Preamble, but it is also pointed out in a central provision. Article 1 can be considered not only as a fundamental value but also as a guiding rule at the beginning of the Charter.

The words that human dignity 'is inviolable' stress its recognition without restriction. It means that human dignity can be neither taken away nor given up by any human being. According to the second sentence, human dignity must be 'respected and protected'. This obligation is addressed the institutions and bodies of the EU and the Member States subject to Article 51 (1) of the Charter. It involves both negative and positive obligations. The first means that an individual has the right not to be exposed to interference with his dignity from the EU institutions and the Member States. The second obligation 'to protect' means the competent

[8] ECt HR, *Pretty v. United Kingdom*, Judgment of 29 Apr 2002, [2002] III, Ref para. 65.

[9] *CETS* No. 164, in force since 1 Dec 1999. It has been ratified by 18 States, including 11 Member States of the EU.

institutions are obliged to protect people from interference with their human dignity by third parties.[10]

Article 1 of the Charter is also going to become one of the most important value statements of the new Treaty establishing a Constitution for Europe. It has rightly been described as a basic pillar of the European identity-finding development.[11]

One of the areas of protection of human dignity is related to biotechnology. It was acknowledged by the ECJ. In its decision regarding the directive on the legal protection of biotechnological inventions,[12] the Court ruled that 'it is for the Court of Justice, in its review of the compatibility of acts of the institutions with the general principles of Community law, to ensure that the fundamental right to human dignity and integrity is observed'.[13] In this connection, Advocate General Jacobs stressed that 'the right to human dignity is perhaps the most fundamental right of all "fundamental rights", and is now expressed in Article 1 of the Charter'.[14]

Therefore, Article 1 of the Charter is to be applied to the issues of biotechnology, unless more specific protection of fundamental rights is provided under another Article. The specific right should have priority in application as a *lex specialis*. The most direct link to biotechnology can be found in Article 3.

Article 3: Right to the Integrity of the Person

Article 3 of the Charter is a complex provision, involving both the traditional human right to personal integrity and the new specific principles in relation to the fields of medicine and biology. Accordingly, this Article has been divided into two paragraphs:

> 1. Everyone has the right to the respect of his or her physical and mental integrity. 2. In the fields of medicine and biology, the following must be respected in particular: the free and informed consent of the person concerned, according to the procedures laid down by law, the prohibition of eugenic practices, in particular those aiming at the selection of persons, the prohibition of making the human body and its parts as such a source of financial gain, the prohibition of the reproductive cloning of human beings.

10 Cf. Heyde, in *Commentary on the Charter of Fundamental Rights of the EU* (by the EU Network of Independent Experts on Fundamental Rights) (Brussels, 2006), Art 1.

11 Cf. Meyer, in Meyer (ed.), *Kommentar zur Charta der Grundrechte der Europäischen Union* (Baden-Baden, 2003), Preamble, 34, 30.

12 Dir of the European Parliament and of the Council 88/44, of 6 July 1998, [1998] OJ L/213/13.

13 Case C–377/98, *Netherlands v. European Parliament and Council of the European Union, C-377/98*, ECR [2001] I–07079, para. 70.

14 Opinion of 14 June 2001 (para. 197).

The main practical significance of the right to personal integrity consists in the specific limitations on medicine and biology in Article 3 (2).[15] During the drafting of the Charter and in the explanations of the Presidium it was stated that 'the principles of Article 3 of the Charter are already included in the Convention on Human Rights and Biomedicine, adopted in the framework of the Council of Europe' (CETS 164, and Additional Protocol, CETS 168). The Charter does not set out to depart from those principles. However, the development of modern techniques of medicine and biology is very dynamic. The first Additional Protocol on the Prohibition of Cloning Human Beings was adopted in 1998.[16] The second Additional Protocol on Transplantation of Organs and Tissues of Human Beings was adopted in 2002.[17]

Although the second Protocol could not yet have been taken into account during the drafting of the Charter, a dynamic interpretation of the Charter should also include a reference to the new instruments, where relevant for the fundamental right in question.[18] The wording 'in particular' in Article 3 (2) shows that the four principles expressly guaranteed therein are not exhaustive. There are also other relevant rights and principles laid down in the Biomedicine Convention and its two Protocols. Some of them are in other provisions of the Charter. For example, the right to equitable access to health care of appropriate quality (Article 3 of the Convention) is guaranteed in Article 35 of the Charter, or the prohibition of discrimination on grounds of one's genetic heritage (Article 11) is reflected in Article 21 (1) of the Charter.[19]

(a) The Principle of the free and informed consent

The first line of Article 3 (2) of the Charter points out that any intervention in the fields of medicine and biology is conditioned by the free and informed consent to it of the person concerned. This important principle has been carried over from Article 5 (1) of the Biomedicine Convention. It is not just the principle of medical ethics; it also became a legal principle by virtue of incorporation in the legally binding treaty instrument. What however is the specific normative content of this principle?

[15] Cf. Nowak, in *Commentary on the Charter of Fundamental Rights of the EU* (by the EU Network of Independent Experts on Fundamental Rights) (Brussels, 2006), Art 3.

[16] CETS No. 168, in force since 1 Mar 2001. It has been ratified by 14 states, including 10 Member States of the EU.

[17] CETS No. 186, not yet in force. It has been ratified by 3 states.

[18] Cf. the explanations of the Presidium to Art 52(3) of the Charter.

[19] Art 21: '1. Any discrimination based on any ground such as sex, race, colour, ethnic or social origin, *genetic features*, language, religion or belief, political or any other opinion, membership of a national minority, property, birth, disability, age or sexual orientation shall be prohibited' (emphasis added).

Since the provision of Article 3 (2) is a brief declaration of principles, the normative content has to be interpreted in the light of related legal instruments, in particular the Biomedicine Convention which provides more specific rules. (see below section IV.) According to Article 5 of this Convention, the person concerned is to be given appropriate information beforehand on the purpose and nature of the intervention as well as on its consequences and risks. The person concerned may also freely withdraw consent at any time.

Unlike the Charter, the Biomedicine Convention also clarifies the scope of application of the principle. It applies to every intervention in the health field, i.e not just only for preventive, diagnostic and therapeutic purposes, but also for scientific research (Article 16(v) of the Convention) and removal of organs or tissue for transplantation purposes (Article 19 (2) of the Convention and Articles 13 and 17 of Protocol No. 2).

Although the principle of free and informed consent appears to be an absolute right, it is only a general rule subject to many exceptions. Article 3 (2) of the Charter refers only to the procedures laid down by national law. However, the Biomedicine Convention is much more specific, as it contains a number of detailed provisions for the protection of persons not able to consent, such as minors, persons with a disease or mentally disabled persons (Articles 6, 7, 17 and 20). When because of an emergency situation appropriate consent cannot be obtained, any medically necessary intervention may be carried out immediately for the benefit of the health of the individual concerned (Article 8). Wishes previously expressed by a patient who is not able to express himself at the moment of the medical intervention have to be taken into consideration (Article 9).

(b) The Prohibition of eugenic practices

The prohibition of eugenic practices as such is not contained in the Biomedicine Convention. However, the prohibition was included in Article 3 (2) of the Charter at the initiative of the European Group on Ethics in Science and New Technologies. This group in June 2000 submitted a report on the draft Charter, which included the proposal for an additional article on the 'prohibition of eugenics'.[20] According to the explanation of the presidium of the Convention on Article 3 (2), the reference to eugenic practices, in particular those aiming at the selection of persons, relates to more serious situations in which selection programmes involving 'campaigns for sterilization, forced pregnancy, compulsory ethnic marriages among others are organised and implemented'. Those

[20] See Doc. CHARTE 4370/00 of 15 June 2000. Cf. also Nowak, in *Commentary on the Charter of Fundamental Rights of the EU* (by the EU Network of Independent Experts on Fundamental Rights) (Brussels, 2006), Art 3.

acts are qualified as crimes under international law by the Rome Statute of International Criminal Court. It appears that the drafters had in mind mainly the eugenic practices carried out in Nazi Germany.

This commentary calls, nevertheless, for an explanation. With due respect to the presidium, it seems that Article 3 (2) covers two different hypotheses, which are to be distinguished. The first concerns some less serious forms of eugenic practices which may occur in 'normal' peace-time situations. Their regulation is a matter of human rights law. Even though there is no specific prohibition in human rights instruments, various human rights, including the prohibition on inhuman and degrading treatment (Articles 3 ECHR and 7 ICCPR), the right to privacy and protection of the family (Articles 8 ECHR and 23 ICCPR) implies the prohibition of eugenic practices. More specifically, one may mention the principle of free and full consent in relation to the right to marry (Article 23 (3) ICCPR) or the prohibition on discrimination based on genetic features or heritage (Article 21 (1) of the Charter, Article 11 of the Biomedicine Convention). Last but not least, Article 13 makes it clear that interventions into a human genome are allowed only for diagnostic or therapeutic purposes and where they do not aim to change the genome of any child.

However, certain problems arise in this respect. First, this prohibition does not seem to be absolute, because there are some medical practices, in particular so-called predictive genetic diagnosis, which are allowed under certain conditions for medical purposes or scientific research (Article 12 of the Biomedicine Convention). Secondly, as is usual in the field of human rights, these provisions ensure the protection of individuals against measures of state. They need not to be implemented by public authorities it is enough if they are attributable to them under international law. Therefore some authors may argue that private eugenics would not fall within this prohibition.[21]

On the other hand, the most serious forms of eugenic practices are a matter of international criminal law. The practices such as forced pregnancy or enforced sterilisation, if committed as part of a widespread or systematic attack directed against any civilian population, constitute crimes against humanity. They are prohibited by Article 7 (1)(g) of the Rome Statute of the International Criminal Court (1998). The absolute prohibition and criminality of these acts applies to measures of state and non-state actors, for e.g. the practices of paramilitary forces during the internal armed conflict in the former Yugoslavia. Even an armed conflict is not necessary under Article 7 of the Rome Statute, but the threshold of 'widespread or systematic attack' has to be attained. The *mens rea* of the perpetrator must indeed include knowledge of the attack.

[21] See Borowsky, in Meyer (ed.), *supra* n. 11, 104.

Although Article 3 (2) includes the prohibition on both forms of eugenic practices, it is important to stress that only the first, research-oriented form is connected to the legal problems of biotechnology. In this field, the prohibition is subject to certain conditions laid down in legislation adopted at the international, European or national level.

(c) The Prohibition of financial gain

The next line of Article 3 (2) of the Charter provides for the prohibition on making the human body and its parts as such a source of financial gain. This brief stipulation has been taken over from Article 21 of the Biomedicine Convention. It should be read in relation to Article 22 of the Convention. When in the course of an intervention any part of a human body is removed, it may be stored and used for a purpose other than that for which it was removed only if this is done in conformity with appropriate information and consent procedures. The prohibition on financial gain has been re-affirmed and specified in Article 22 of Protocol No. 2, which contains an absolute prohibition on trafficking in human organ and tissue.

The prohibition of financial gain does not mean, however, that the human body and its parts must necessarily be *res extra dispositionem*. In other words, the human body and its parts may be an object of property rights. From the point of view of EU law, there are two major legal issues, i.e. the patentability of biotechnological inventions and the donation of human tissues and cells.

The first one is regulated by Directive 98/44/EC on the legal protection of biotechnological inventions.[22] This act makes it possible for an element isolated from the human body or otherwise produced by means of technical process, including the sequence or partial sequence of a gene, to be patentable (Article 5 (2)). However, the human body itself cannot constitute patentable inventions (Article 5 (1)). According to this Directive, only inventions which combine a natural element with a technical process enabling it to be isolated or produced for an industrial application can be the subject of an application for a patent. The Directive also provides an exception from the patentability for inventions contrary to *ordre public* or morality. According to Article 6 (2), these are (a) processes for the cloning of human beings; (b) processes for modifying the germ line identity of human beings; (c) the use of human embryos for industrial or commercial purposes; (d) processes for modifying the genetic identity of animals which are likely to cause them suffering without any substantial medical benefit to man or animals.

[22] Dir 98/44/EC of the European Parliament and of the Council of 6 July 1998 on the legal protection of biotechnological inventions, [1998] OJ L/213/13.

The European Court of Justice has already had occasion to rule on the question, raised by the Dutch government, whether the patentability of isolated human body parts would undermine human dignity and integrity. Having stressed that the human body cannot constitute a patentable invention, the Court held that 'the Directive frames the law on patents in a manner sufficiently rigorous to ensure that the human body effectively remains unavailable and inalienable and that human dignity is thus safeguarded'.[23]

The transfer of property to human organs and tissues is allowed by way of donation, subject to conditions laid down in national legislation. At the EU level, the Directive 2004/23/EC provides more detailed rules on the donation of human tissues and cells.[24] Article 12 of the Directive sets out principles governing tissue and cell donation. According to them, Member States shall endeavour to ensure voluntary and unpaid donation of tissues and cells and to ensure that the procurement of tissues and cells as such is carried out on a non-profit basis. The same Article provides that 'donors may receive compensation, which is strictly limited to making good the expenses and inconveniences related to the donation'.

(d) Prohibition on the reproductive cloning of human beings

The last sentence of Article 3 (2) of the Charter is the result of rather long and complicated discussion within the Convention and other EU bodies.[25] The European Group on Ethics in Science and New Technologies was divided on the question of cloning. It proposed either to omit any reference to the cloning of human beings or to restrict it to reproductive cloning.[26] The latter alternative was accepted and became a text of Article 3 (2). According to the explanations of the Presidium, the Charter does not set out to depart from the principles of the Biomedicine Convention (ETS 164) and Protocol No. 1 (ETS 168) and 'therefore prohibits only reproductive cloning. It neither authorises nor prohibits other forms of cloning. Thus it does not in any way prevent the legislature from prohibiting other forms of cloning'.

Although the concept of 'other forms of cloning' is not defined, it seems to refer to therapeutic cloning and cloning for the purpose of scientific research, in particular human cell research. Indeed, some controversies

[23] *Netherlands v. European Parliament and Council of the European Union, Case* C-377/98, *supra*, n. 13, paras. 69–77.

[24] Dir 2004/23/EC of the European Parliament and of the Council of 31 Mar 2004, on setting standards of quality and safety for the donation, procurement, testing, processing, preservation, storage and distribution of human tissues and cells [2004] OJ L/102/48.

[25] Cf. Nowak, *supra* n. 15.

[26] Doc. Charte 4370/00 of 15 June 2000.

remain on this subject. While some authors argue that the Charter departs from the general prohibition of cloning human beings contained in Article 1 of Protocol 1,[27] a correct interpretation of this treaty provision seems to lead to the conclusion that the prohibition concerns only cloning aimed at the creation of identical individuals. A more powerful argument may be drawn from Article 18 (2) of the Biomedicine Convention which prohibits the creation of human embryos for research purposes. Obviously, it depends on the interpretation of the term of 'human embryo'. If one interprets it in a broad sense, then any cloning of human beings for scientific research (and possibly even therapeutic cloning) might be prohibited. However, such a broad interpretation of the Biomedicine Convention would make impossible a very promising area of biomedical research (human cells research), which seems to be hardly acceptable to several EU Member States.

In our view, the compromise text of the Charter is not intended to resolve all controversies about the techniques of cloning. It rather seeks to ban only reproductive cloning as being ethically the least acceptable. Due to the lack of consent on other forms of cloning, the Charter left a margin of appreciation to the states.

Another evidence of outstanding controversies about the sensitive issues of human cloning may be seen in the recently adopted directive on the donation of human tissues and cells. Whereas the draft directive in Article 4 (4), contemplated prohibiting research on human cloning for reproductive purposes as well as research designated to create human embryos solely for research purposes or to supply stem cells,[28] the adopted text of the directive[29] avoided giving clear guidance to this effect. As pointed out in recital 22 to its preamble, this directive respects fundamental rights and observes the principles reflected in the Charter of Fundamental Rights of the EU and takes into account the Biomedicine Convention. Neither the Charter nor the Convention makes express provision for harmonisation.

Instead, its Article 4 only confirms that the directive shall not prevent a Member State from maintaining or introducing more stringent protective measures (paragraph (2)). More specifically even, 'this Directive does not affect the decisions of the Member States prohibiting the donation, procurement, testing, processing, preservation, storage, distribution or use of any specific type of human tissues or cells or cells from any specified source' (paragraph (3)). To sum up, the Member States still retain a large margin of appreciation.

[27] Cf. Nowak, *supra* n. 15.
[28] Cf. *ibid.*
[29] Dir 2004/23/EC, *supra* n. 24.

IV. SCOPE OF THE RIGHTS GUARANTEED IN ARTICLE 3 AND PROBLEMS OF IMPLEMENTATION OF THE CHARTER

Some problems of interpretation of Article 3 of the Charter, in particular its provision concerning the prohibition of the reproductive cloning of human beings, call for a thorough discussion of this provision in the light of general interpretation and limitation clauses of the Charter.

The drafters of the Charter tried to avoid the problem of double standards of human rights in Europe and, in particular, to prevent the Charter providing a lower level of protection than the European Convention on Human Rights. They considered it necessary to ensure the coexistence of two instruments, while respecting the achievements of the ECHR on the basis of its interpretation by the European Court of Human Rights. Therefore the Preamble to the Charter includes a reference to the case law of this Court.[30]

The Charter itself deals with the above problems in two provisions of the Chapter VII. According to the general clause, arising from a judgment of the ECJ,[31] in Article 52 (1):

> Any limitation on the exercise of these rights and freedoms recognised by this Charter must be provided for by law and respect the essence of those rights and freedoms. Subject to the principle of proportionality, limitations may be made only if they are necessary and genuinely meet objectives of general interest recognised by the Union or the need to protect the rights and freedoms of others.

The reference to general interest of the Union involves not only the goals cited in Article 2 but also other interests protected by special provisions of the EC Treaty (such as Article 30 or Article 39 (2)). It is worth noting that Article 52 has stressed the principle of proportionality.

Article 52 (2) specifies that rights which are based on the Community Treaties or the EU Treaty shall be exercised under the conditions and within the limits defined by those treaties. The Charter does not alter the conditions these rights.

In view of the general nature of the limitation clause in Art. 52 (1), which might appear less protective in comparison with the ECHR, the Charter has introduced an expressed reference to the ECHR in Article 52 (3):

> In so far as this Charter contains rights which correspond to rights guaranteed by the Convention for the Protection of Human Rights and Fundamental Freedoms, the meaning and scope of those rights shall be the same as those laid down by the said Convention. This provision shall not prevent Union law providing more extensive protection.

[30] Cf. Sudre, *Droit européen et international des droits de l'homme*, (6th edn., Paris, 2003), 153.
[31] See the ECJ judgment in Case C–292/97, *supra* n. 5, at 45.

By this provision, in fact, the substantive law provisions of the ECHR have been incorporated into the Charter and eventually into EC/EU law, when the Charter becomes a part of the primary law (by way of incorporation into the new Treaty establishing a Constitution for Europe).

The brief commentary by EU experts (the Presidium of the Convention) on Article 52 next enumerates the Articles of the Charter having the same meaning and scope as the corresponding Articles of the ECHR. However, some problem of interpretation may arise in cases where the Charter provisions do not have counterparts in the text of the ECHR but merely in the case law of the European Court of Human Rights. Another kind of problems concerns the Articles of the Charter which correspond neither to the text nor to the case law of the ECHR, but they have background in other treaties of the Council of Europe. This is precisely the problem of Article 3 of the Charter, as this provision seems to go far beyond the related provisions of the ECHR, namely Articles 2, 3 and 8.[32]

The effort to harmonise human rights standards under the ECHR and the Charter is to be interpreted in the light of case law of the European Court of Human Rights. To start from the principle of proportionality of concurrent fundamental rights, it follows that a broader scope of protection under the Charter is to be applied only in cases where protection of the right could not be ensured under the ECHR.

Next, the Charter includes a stand still clause.[33] According to Article 53:

> Nothing in this Charter shall be interpreted as restricting or adversely affecting human rights and fundamental freedoms as recognised, in their respective fields of application, by Union law and international law and by international agreements to which the Union, the Community or all the Member States are party, including the European Convention for the Protection of Human Rights and Fundamental Freedoms, and by the Member States' constitutions.

The purpose of this provision is to conserve the existing level of human rights protection ensured by EC/EU law, the national law of the Member States and international law. Unlike Article 52, which compares the scope of guaranteed rights with the ECHR, the last provision also takes into consideration the scope of fundamental rights achieved on a national level and of rights under other international treaties. The preeminent position is however reserved to the ECHR. It follows that the scope of rights must not go under the level of protection provided by the European Convention.

32 Cf. Byk, 'Bioéthique et Convention européenne des droits de l'homme', in Pettiti, Decaux and Imbert (eds.), *La Convention européenne des droits de l'homme. Commentaire article par article* (Paris, 1995).

33 Cf. Flauss 'Les libertés fondamentales traditionnelles: Nouvelles approches et solutions originales?', in Heusel (ed.), *The Charter of Fundamental Rights and Constitutional Development in the EU* (Cologne, 2002), 79.

However, the situation is not as clear as far as the Biomedicine Convention is concerned. Whereas this convention is the major treaty instrument in the field adopted within the Council of Europe, it is not an international agreement to which the Union, the Community or all the Member States are party. Although the explanatory note by the Presidium refers to the Biomedicine Convention and Protocol No. 1, it seems rather to be guidance for the interpretation of Article 3 of the Charter than incorporation of such treaty rules by reference. Moreover, the Charter itself and the explanations thereto could hardly forecast the post-2000 development within the Council of Europe, namely the elaboration and adoption of new protocols to the Biomedicine Convention. Of course, they may and should be taken into consideration, as far as possible, but they do not seem to control the content and scope of application of the Charter and related EU legislation.

From the institutional point of view, two different judicial bodies are competent in respect of these instruments. On the one hand, it will be for the European Court of Justice, within the limits of its power to adjudicate, to decide whether respective domestic laws are compatible with the right to personal integrity under Article 3 of the Charter. On the other hand, the European Court of Human Rights is competent to give advisory opinions on legal questions concerning the interpretation of the Biomedicine Convention (under Article 29 of this Convention). In view of the different role of the two Courts and different procedural rules, reflecting adjudication and advisory jurisdiction, a direct conflict of jurisdiction is not likely. This does not, however, preclude the fact that each Court adopts a slightly different interpretation of substantive rules, which are not necessarily identical in the Charter and the Biomedicine Convention.

V. CONCLUSIONS

Having done the above analysis, one can propose the following conclusions:

(1) there is no direct link between Article 3 (2) of the Charter and human rights guaranteed expressly by the ECHR therefore the provisions of the ECHR cannot prevail;

(2) Article 3 of the Charter must be interpreted in the light of other international agreements to which the Union, the Community or all the Member States are party;

(3) from the point of view *ratione materiae*, Article 3 (2) is closely related to the Biomedicine Convention and Protocols thereto, which however do not bind all the EU Member States;

(4) the Member States are free to apply more extensive protection of the fundamental rights if it is provided by their legislation or other international agreements to which they are party;

(5) the Member States enjoy a margin of appreciation and may also provide limitations to the above right under domestic law if they respect the essence of this right laid down in Article 3 (2) of the Charter (e.g. the prohibition on reproductive cloning of human beings);

(6) to be permissible, such limitations have to be proportional, necessary and to meet objectives of general interest recognised by the Union.

15

The EU Risk Management of Genetically Modified Organisms and the Commission's Defence Strategy in the Biotech Dispute: Are They Inconsistent?

SARA POLI*

I. INTRODUCTION

BY MARCH 2006 the Dispute Settlement Panel, appointed to rule on the compatibility of EC measures[1] affecting the approval and marketing of genetically modified organisms (GMOs) with the WTO agreements, will issue its final report. Rather than considering whether these measures are capable of breaching WTO law, or speculating on the outcome of this dispute, this chapter will focus on whether the Commission's defence strategy in the WTO 'biotech dispute',[2] as defined in the two EC written submissions[3] to the Panel, is consistent with the way the Commission enforces the EC legislation on GMOs *vis-à-vis* Member States and sub-national actors within the EU.

* Sara Poli is a research and teaching fellow in EC law and EC environmental law at the University of Trieste, Italy.

1 These measures were challenged by Argentina, Canada and USA before the WTO. In Aug 2003 these countries requested the setting up of a Dispute Settlement Panel which examined whether specific EC measures, affecting the approval and the marketing of GMOs, were compatible with the WTO agreements.

2 This is the short name used in this chapter to refer to the WTO dispute, triggered by Argentina, Canada and USA. On this trade dispute see Petersmann in this volume and Isaac and Kerr, 'Genetically Modified Organisms at the World Trade Organisation—a Harvest of Trouble' (2003) 37 *Journal of World Trade* 1083–1095.

3 See the first and second submissions by the EC, *European Communities—measures affecting the approval and marketing of biotech products* (WT/DS 291, 292, 293)', of 17 May 2004 and 19 July 2004 respectively. The first submissions can be found at the following website: http://www.trade-environment.org/output/theme/tewto/EC_submission_biotech.pdf. The second submissions have not been made public. Hereafter these submissions will be referred to as 'first EC submissions' and 'second EC submissions'.

The chapter is divided into two parts. The first shows how a few authorisation decisions on GMOs gave rise to inter-institutional and multi-level conflicts amongst different decision-makers within the EU (section II); then, it outlines the way the Commission addressed various kinds of opposition to GMOs (section III), the Commission's behaviour being crucial in the biotech dispute. The second part starts with a brief summary of the challenged measures in the biotech dispute and sketches out the line of defence presented by the Commission in the first EC submissions (section IV). Section V represents the heart of this chapter: it seeks to identify, on the one hand, the principles invoked by the Commission to defend the EC legislation on GMOs from the attacks of political actors, opposing the marketing of GMOs *within* the EU and, on the other hand, the principles relied upon by the Commission to defend the EC regulatory choices on GMOs in the written submissions. Then, these two sets of principles are compared in order to assess whether the former are consistent with the latter. Should this assessment prove that the EC defence strategy in the biotech dispute is inconsistent with the EU risk management of GMOs, the credibility of this strategy would be at stake. The concluding section VI shows that there are inconsistencies but they are justified.

II. INTER-INSTITUTIONAL AND MULTI-LEVEL CONFLICTS ON GMOS WITHIN THE EU

Looking at the way risks posed by GMOs have been managed within the EU, it is possible to note that risk decisions in this area have been affected by two sets of conflicts: *intra-institutional and multi-level conflicts*.[4] As to the first kind of conflicts, we can say that whereas the Commission's current position[5] is favourable to the marketing of GMOs, provided that this is made to comply with the relevant EC legislation, the European Parliament's position on GMOs is more cautious.[6] As to the Council, on

[4] I borrow this expression from Scott, 'European Regulation of GMOs: Thinking about "Judicial Review" in the WTO', (2004) *Jean Monnet working paper*, 4, 2.

[5] The Commission's position has been subject to an evolution, as shown in section III.

[6] For example, the Parliament supported the need for a tight authorisation regime and strict enforcement rules for GMOs. This is shown by the amendments proposed by the Parliament in the adoption of Dir 2001/18 [2001] OJ L/106/1, and of the 2003 regulations: see *infra* n. 17. In both cases the Parliament advocated a stricter authorisation regime and a more comprehensive scope of the EC legislation. Moreover, the Parliament supported the adoption of specific liability rules for environmental damage provoked by GMOs. Finally, it should be noted that a Parliamentary committee considered national bans on the cultivation of GMOs appropriate in certain circumstances. In a report, it stated that 'Community coexistence rules must allow Member States the right to prohibit completely the cultivation of GMOs in geographically restricted areas so as to safeguard coexistence'. See Report on coexistence between genetically modified crops and conventional and organic crops, A5-0465/2003 of 4 Dec 2003, para. 14.

more than one occasion, this institution has been divided as to whether an authorisation to market a GMO could be given, as will be shown below.[7]

Multi-level conflicts on the management of GMOs within the EU can also be identified. These conflicts concern actors at different levels of government, in particular the Commission on the one hand, and Member States' national authorities or sub-national authorities (such as *Länder*, Regions) on the other. Multilevel conflicts have taken place between 1997 and the present time in the course of the authorisation procedure and after this procedure was completed. The first notorious example of multilevel conflict, which occurred while the 'first generation of GMOs legislation'[8] was in force, concerns an application to market the genetically modified maize 'L. Zea'. During the authorisation procedure for this GMO, the regulatory committee, set up by Directive 1990/220,[9] was asked to assess the above mentioned application;[10] however, it did not adopt an opinion favourable to the marketing of such GMO, nor could the Council reach a qualified majority to reject the Commission's proposal for authorisation. Eventually, the GMO concerned was approved[11] but the following individual applications for the marketing of other GMOs were very closely scrutinised[12] and, as a result, no authorisation decisions on the basis of Directive 1990/200 had been taken as of October 1998.[13] After the GMO concerned was authorised, a few Member States adopted safeguard measures[14] suspending the release of authorised GMOs, on the basis of Article 16 of Directive 1990/220 (Austria, Greece, Luxembourg, Germany, the UK) and Article 12 of Regulation 258/97 (Italy).[15]

[7] See *infra*, especially n 21.

[8] By 'first generation of EC legislation on GMOs' is meant Dir 1990/220 on the deliberate release into the environment of genetically modified organisms [1990] OJ L/117/15, and Reg 258/97 on novel food and novel food ingredients [1997] OJ L/43/1. The former was repealed by Dir 2001/18 and the latter is still in force even if Reg 1829/2003 almost completely replaced the provisions of the 1997 Reg.

[9] *Supra* n. 8.

[10] Under the authorisation procedure of Dir 1990/220, the regulatory committee was to be consulted each time Member States' national authorities raised objections to individual applications to place GMOs on the market. These objections were raised by Member States very often. For details see first EC submissions, paras. 202–284.

[11] See Commission Dec 97/98, [1997] OJ L/31/69.

[12] See the next section.

[13] The complainants in the biotech dispute hold that, as from Oct 1998, the EC suspended the consideration of applications for, or granting of, approval of biotech products. See *infra*.

[14] These are measures enabling Member States to suspend the marketing of authorised GMOs when the latter threaten certain public interests such as the protection of human health or the environment.

[15] These measures are described in paras. 339–359 of the first EC submissions. The Commission consulted its scientific committees and asked whether the safeguard measures adopted by Member States were scientifically justified. The negative opinions of these committees are listed in the first submission by the USA, *European Communities-measures affecting the approval and marketing of biotech products* (WT/DS 291, 292, 293)', 21 Apr 2004, in particular see nn. 140 (Austria), 142 (France), 144 (Luxembourg), 146 (Germany), 149 (Italy), 151 (Greece). The complainants in the biotech dispute consider Member States' safeguard measures tantamount to illegal marketing and import bans. See *infra*.

The second generation of EC legislation in this field, heralded by the 'new framework Directive' 2001/18 (horizontal legislation)[16] and completed by Regulations 1829/2003 and 1830/200317 (sector-specific legislation), was supposed to equip the European Community with the most stringent rules on genetically modified organisms and derivatives. However, the authorisation procedure for the marketing of GMOs continued to be problematic; moreover few Member States invoked the safeguard clauses included in the newly enacted legislation.

In 2004 three individual applications for the marketing of a novel food[18] and two GMOs[19] also did not receive favourable opinions from the regulatory committees[20] involved in the authorisation procedure. Moreover, the Council could not approve the Commission's decision authorising the placing on the market of the three products,[21] this automatically made it possible for the Commission to take the final decision and eventually two products (the novel food sweetcorn Bt-11[22] and the genetically modified maize NK 603[23]) were authorised.

As already mentioned, in 2004 some Member States confirmed the safeguard measures originally enacted when the first generation of EC legislation on GMOs was in force. For example, Austria reiterated its safeguard measures against genetically modified maize lines Bt176, MON 810 and T25, under Article 23 of Directive 18/2001. So did Greece with respect

[16] Member States did not promptly implement this Dir. Therefore, the Commission started infringement procedures against 14 Member States for failure to transpose this Dir into their national legal orders. See *XXth Annual Report on the application and control of EC law* (2002), in COM(2003) 699, 49.

[17] Reg 1829/2003 on genetically modified food and feed [2003] OJ L/268/1 and Reg 1830/2003 concerning the traceability and labelling of genetically modified organisms and the traceability of food and feed products produced from genetically modified organisms and amending Dir 18/2001, [2003] OJ L/268/24 . See for a comment Christoforou, 'The Regulation of Genetically Modified Organisms in the European Union: The Interplay of Science, Law and Politics' (2004) 41 *Common Market Law Review* 637; Poli, 'The Overhaul of the European Legislation on GMOs, Genetically Modified Food and Feed: Mission Accomplished. What Now?' (2004) 11 *Maastricht Journal of European and Comparative Law* 1, 13.

[18] This is genetically modified maize BT-11.

[19] These are genetically modified maize NK 603 and GT73 oilseed rape.

[20] With respect to sweetcorn BT-11, the Standing Committee on food chain and animal health (a regulatory committee under Reg. 258/97) did *not* adopt a positive opinion on the Commission's draft proposal authorising the marketing of this product. See document 8341/04 of 7 Apr 2004. As for genetically modified maize NK 603 and GT73 oilseed rape, in both cases the regulatory committee, set up by Art. 30 of Dir 18/2001, could not vote in favour of the authorisation. See document 11068/2004 of 1 July 2004 and document 12343/04 of 10 Sept 2004, published in the public register of the Council.

[21] The Council could not achieve qualified majority in the voting procedure on the Commission's proposals for authorisation to place genetically modified maize Bt-11, genetically modified maize NK 603 and the GT 73 oilseed rape on the market.

[22] Commission Dec 2004/657 [2004] OJ L/300/48.

[23] Commission Dec 2004/643, [2004] OJ L/295/35.

to the genetically modified spring oilseed rape line, Topas 19/2. In February and March 2004, the two countries provided the Commission with additional information to support the adoption of the above mentioned measures. The Commission asked the European Food Safety Authority (hereafter 'EFSA') to evaluate whether the new information, provided by Austria and Greece to support their respective safeguard measures, proved that the concerned GMOs constituted a risk to human health or the environment. The EFSA issued two scientific opinions in which it stated that there was no new scientific evidence which invalidated the risk assessments of the authorised GMOs; hence, the safeguard measures concerned were not considered to be scientifically justified.[24]

The final example of multilevel conflict on GMOs concerns a sub-national authority and the Commission. In 2003 the *Land* of Upper Austria requested from the Commission the authorisation to enact a regional ban on the cultivation of GMOs, in derogation from Directive 2001/18. However, this request, submitted under Article 95(5) of the EC Treaty, was rejected.[25] The negative Commission Decision was unsuccessfully challenged by the Land of Upper Austria before the Court of First Instance.[26]

The above mentioned Austrian Land is not the only sub-national entity wishing to adopt regional bans on GMOs: a few regions adopted legislation banning the use of GMOs,[27] without informing the Commission. In other cases, Member States or sub-national actors notified the Commission of draft measures strongly limiting the use of GMOs.[28]

It is now necessary to look more closely at the way in which the Commission reacted to national authorities or sub-national actors' various attempts to oppose the marketing of GMOs. As will be shown later, the challenging countries in the biotech dispute consider, inter alia, the Commission's behaviour, both during the authorisation procedure and after it was completed, illegal in the light of WTO law.

24 On the Austrian safeguard measures, see the European Food Safety Authority's (hereafter EFSA) opinion released on 8 July 2004 and published in (2004) 78 *EFSA Journal* 1–13; on the Greek safeguard measures see the EFSA opinion of 8 July 2004 and published in (2004) *EFSA Journal* 1–8.

25 See Commission Dec 2003/653, [2003] OJ L/230/34.

26 Cases T–366/03 and T–235/04 *Land Oberösterriech*, 5 Oct. 2005, not yet reported.

27 10 regions in Austria, Italy, France Greece, Germany and Spain formed a network of 'GMO-free' regions. See (2003) 3 *BRIDGES-Trade Biores* 20.

28 It should be noted that instead of national bans on GMOs, Member States may be allowed to enact measures ensuring the coexistence of different forms of agriculture, an area in which Member States retain competence. See the Commission's recommendation 2003/556 on guidelines for the development of national strategies and best practices to ensure the coexistence of genetically modified crops with conventional and organic farming, [2003] OJ L/189/86. The Commission is currently evaluating whether these draft 'coexistence' measures are compatible with the EC Treaty and secondary legislation. Notifications of draft measures were made by the *Land* of Salzburg, the *Land* of Carinthia, the Land of Burgenland, Denmark, Luxembourg and Germany.

III. THE WAY THE COMMISSION ADDRESSED MEMBER STATES AND SUB-NATIONAL AUTHORITIES' OPPOSITION TO GMOS: SCIENTIFIC EVIDENCE AS A 'FLEXIBLE YARDSTICK'?

First, we will look at the way in which the Commission reacted when individual applications for the marketing of GMOs met an obstacle in the authorisation procedure. Here, an evolution in the Commission's behaviour between the time the first generation of GMO legislation was in force and the time the 2003 Regulations entered into force[29] can be noted. In the first lapse of time, which, by the way, is the only relevant in the biotech dispute,[30] the Commission did not take a definite position on individual applications and, as a result, the authorisation procedure was not concluded. The reasons[31] preventing the Commission from proceeding were different: in some cases, the Commission failed to take a definite position on individual applications when national authorities raised objections and the regulatory committee, involved in the procedure, could not take a favourable opinion on the marketing of the GMOs concerned. Facing these 'procedural obstacles,' the Commission did not go on with the authorisation, even after the EC scientific committees, consulted by the Commission, released an opinion maintaining that the concerned GMO did not raise health or environmental concerns.[32] In these cases, scientific evidence was not considered enough to take the authorisation decision. In other cases, the Commission did not complete the authorisation procedure because the applicant's notification was incomplete (and had to be completed) or required additional information. Finally, in the remaining cases no authorisation decisions were taken because the applicants withdrew their application.[33] Obviously, these 'obstacles,' which are regarded as justified by the Commission and as unjustified by the complainants in

[29] Reg 1829/2003 and 1830/2003, *supra* n. 17, entered into force in Apr 2003.

[30] The complainants in the biotech dispute are challenging EC measures on the approval of GMOs which were taken between 1997 and the day the complainants requested consultations with the EC on the subject of the above mentioned EC measures (17 Mar 2003).

[31] It is not the purpose of this chapter to decide whether the reasons put forward by the Commission to justify its behaviour are convincing or not. It is however possible to criticise the Commission for the lack of transparency in the authorisation procedure; this might have contributed to generating the impression in the public opinion that GMOs were unsafe.

[32] This is the case for the following individual applications: *Bayer oilseed rape (FALCON GS40/90), Bayer hybrid oilseed rape (MS8/RF3), Trifolium/Monsanto/Danisco Roundup Ready fodder beat (A5/15), Monsanto Bt Cotton (531), Monsanto Roundup Ready cotton (RRC1445), Amylogene Starch potato, Syngenta156 glufosinate tolerant and Bt resistant (Bt-11) corn (stack), Pioneer/Dow AgroSciences Bt corn Cry1F (1507), Pioneer/Dow AgroSciences Bt corn Cry1F (1507).* See first EC submissions, section D. In a few of these cases, regulatory committees also failed to adopt an opinion either in favour or against the granting of an authorisation. See EC second submissions, paras. 164, 168, 176, 179 and 184.

[33] See first EC submissions, paras. 285–297.

the biotech dispute, prevented the completion of the authorisation procedure for all applications.[34]

After the reformed EC legislation on GMOs came into force, at least two authorisations decisions were taken by the Commission,[35] and both of them were positive, although, as already said, the relevant regulatory committee and the Council did not vote in favour of these applications for authorisation.[36]

The second issue which it is necessary to examine is how the Commission evaluated safeguard measures enacted by Member States after a given GMO was authorised. Changes in the Commission's behaviour before and after the entry into force of the reformed EC legislation on GMOs can be noted. In the first period, the Commission refrained from taking action when Member States did not withdraw their safeguard measures,[37] considered illegal by the scientific committees[38] of the Commission. After the amended EC legislation came into effect, Austria and Greece reiterated their safeguard measures,[39] providing the Commission with additional information to support the adoption of such measures. However, the EFSA did not consider these measures justified.[40] If the Commission's failure to act before the entry into force of the amended EC legislation on GMOs was understandable in the light of the special circumstances in which the Commission was required to act,[41] by contrast, for the Community executive was more difficult to justify a failure to take action

34 The complainants in the biotech dispute consider the failure by the EC to examine for approval applications for specific biotech products (called 'product specific delays') illegal in WTO law. See *infra*.

35 These concern the sweetcorn Bt-11 and roundup ready corn (NK 603). See above nn. 22 and 23.

36 The relevant regulatory committee and the Council did not explicitly vote in favour of these applications. See *supra* nn. 20 and 21.

37 In one case, the Commission did not make the safeguard measures adopted by Italy under Art. 12 of Reg. 258/97 subject to review.

38 These are the EC Scientific Committee for Plants and the EC Scientific Committee for Food.

39 Austria confirmed its safeguard measures, under Art. 23 of Dir 2001/18, against genetically modified maize lines Bt176, MON 810 and T25. So did Greece with respect to genetically modified spring oilseed rape line, Topas 19/2.

40 The Commission asked the EFSA to evaluate whether the new information provided by Austria and Greece proved that the GMOs concerned constituted a risk to human health or the environment. This Authority issued two scientific opinions in which it stated that there was no new scientific evidence which invalidated the risk assessments of the GMOs concerned. See *supra* n. 24.

41 At the time the Commission should have taken action against the Member States which refused to withdraw the safeguard measures, the EC legislation containing such clauses was under revision to be made stricter; therefore the opening of infringement proceedings could be inappropriate before the revision of the EC legislation was completed. Moreover, it is submitted that the Commission's hesitation was due to the fact that no scientific body, capable of providing scientific and independent advice, was available at the time the safeguard measures were enacted. The situation has changed with the setting up of the EFSA.

against Greece and Austria, after the EFSA's positive opinion was released and in the absence of any special circumstances. Probably, this is why the Commission eventually decided to consider the opinion of scientific bodies sufficient to justify the withdrawal of scientifically unfounded measures. Proposals aimed at the withdrawal of the safeguard measures taken by certain Member States (Austria, France, Germany Greece and Luxembourg) against several transgenic plant varieties were submitted to the Council. However, the latter voted against these proposals at the meeting of the environmental Council of 24 June 2005.

The Commission's decision on Upper Austria's request to enact a regional ban on the cultivation of GMOs stands out in the Commission's enforcement of the EC legislation on GMOs. Indeed, in this case the Commission was firm in opposing sub-national authorities' attempts to impose outright bans on the use of GMOs in breach of the EC legislation. The Commission's position was clear-cut: the scientific evidence provided by Upper Austria to support its request for derogation from Directive 2001/18 did not provide any new information which specifically concerned the environment.[42] Moreover, reliance on the precautionary principle was not possible because the notified measure was based, as the Court of First Instance put it in the *Alpharma* case,[43] on 'a purely hypothetical approach to the risk, founded on mere conjecture, which ha[d] not yet been scientifically verified'.[44]

The lack of (new) scientific evidence supporting the regional ban was at the heart of the Commission Decision; socio-economic reasons, such as the need to safeguard organic agricultural products from possible GMO contamination,[45] were not considered relevant to justify the setting up of 'GMO-free areas.' The lessons to be learnt from Upper Austria's unsuccessful request for derogation is that the Commission is very strict in evaluating measures pursuing a higher level of environmental protection than that pursued by the EC legislation (Directive 2001/18) if these measures put in jeopardy the functioning of the internal market.

The analysis of the Commission's way of addressing measures opposing the marketing of GMOs revealed that whereas the Commission considers scientific evidence as a yardstick for assessing a sub-national measure in the framework of Article 95(5) of the EC Treaty, by contrast, scientific evidence is only one of the factors evaluated by the Commission

[42] See para. 66 of Commission Dec 2003/653, *supra* n. 25. The Commission adhered to the EFSA's negative opinion which had been asked to review the scientific evidence provided by Upper Austria.

[43] Case T–13/99 *Pfizer Animal Health SA v. Council of the European Union* and T-70/99 *Alpharma Inc. v. Council of the European Union* [2002] ECR, II–3305.

[44] Para. 156 of *Alpharma* .

[45] Para. 61 of Commission's Dec 2003/653, *supra* n. 25.

in the authorisation procedure of transgenic products and the evaluation of Member States' safeguard measures.

IV. THE COMMISSION'S DEFENCE STARTEGY IN THE EC SUBMISSION

In biotech disputes the challenged measures are of a different nature from those which were the object of other trade disputes. Here the complainants do not challenge a piece of EC legislation as they did, for example, in the hormones-in-beef dispute;[46] by contrast, they contest the way the EC legislation was applied. In particular, the measures covered by the request to set up a Panel are:

(a) the suspension by the EC of consideration of applications for, or granting of, approval of biotech products (the 'alleged moratorium');[47]
(b) the failure by the EC to consider for approval applications for specific biotech products ('product specific delays');[48]
(c) national marketing and import bans maintained by Member States ('Member States' safeguard measures').[49]

The Commission's defence strategy of the EU regulatory choices in the written submissions focuses on the following points:

(a) there is no *en bloc* behaviour against GMOs in the EU since no evidence of this has been provided by the complainants; in any case 'this repeated pattern in similar responses to applications'[50] is not a challengeable measure under the WTO law.
(b) both product-specific delays and Member States' safeguard measures come within the SPS Agreement *only in part* because they pursue objectives (i.e. the protection of biodiversity) which are different from those falling within the scope of the SPS Agreement.[51] Where product-specific measures have an objective which falls within the SPS Agreement, they do not breach the obligations of the SPS Agreement. Indeed, they do not amount to 'undue delay' within the meaning of this term in the SPS Agreement[52] and, in any event, they

46 See *EC-hormones*, WT/DS26/AB/R and WT/DS48/AB/R of 16 Jan 1998.
47 These measures are dealt with by section D of the first EC submissions and section B of the second EC submissions.
48 These measures are dealt with by section C of the first EC submission.
49 These measures are dealt with by section E of the first EC submission.
50 See first EC submissions, para. 542.
51 This argument is developed in section B of the first EC submissions.
52 Art. 8 and Annex C point 1(a) of the SPS agreement.

are *provisionally* justified on the basis of the insufficiency of scientific evidence. Neither product-specific measure breaches TBT or GATT.

(c) As to Member States' safeguard measures, they are 'provisional measures pending a full assessment at EC level which will eventually lead either to a modification of the Community-wide authorisation or a termination of the national safeguard measures'.[53] These measures, to the extent that they fall with the scope of the SPS Agreement, are justified by Article 5(7) of the SPS Agreement. Moreover, they do not come within the term of the TBT Agreement and are consistent with Article III.4 of GATT.

V. THE INCONSISTENCIES OF THE COMMISSION'S DEFENCE OF THE EU MEASURES ON GMOS IN THE EC WRITTEN SUBMISSIONS

The purpose of this section is to highlight whether there is consistency between the way the Commission managed risks posed by GMOs within the EU and the way the same institution defended the EC's position on GMOs from the attacks of Argentina, Canada and USA. In order to answer this question, I chose to compare on the one hand, the principles underlying the way the Commission acted against national and sub-national authorities, threatening the application of the EC legislation on GMOs, and the principles/arguments raised by the Commission in defending the EU regulatory measures on GMOs in the written submissions, on the other hand. One would expect these two sets of 'principles', those applied domestically and those invoked at WTO level, to be consistent with each other and to go hand in hand; if this is not so, an explanation should be given.

In order to single out these principles, three questions will be addressed in this chapter.[54] The first is: what is the meaning of 'individual assessment' in risk management decisions on GMOs? In the written submissions the Commission shows that both product-specific measures and Member States' safeguard measures were subject to 'individual (risk) assessments'.[55] This assessment encompasses three different aspects: (1) risk assessment in the narrow sense, i.e. as a 'scientifically based process', (2) risk management, and (3) risk communication.[56] Thus, 'scientific but

[53] See first EC submissions, para. 572.

[54] It should be noted that in order to decide whether or not the principles underlying the EU risk management process are consistent with those invoked by the Commission in the written submissions, a number of methods could be used. This chapter chooses to look at the above mentioned problem by raising three issues which are only a selection of all possible issues that could be chosen to carry out the enquiry of this chapter.

[55] See second EC submissions, para. 291.

[56] See second EC submissions, para. 21.

also economic and regulatory considerations'[57] are taken into consideration in making this assessment. An example of the application of this broad notion of 'individual assessment' is the Commission's political decision, taken before the reform of the GMOs legislation, not to ask Member States who enacted safeguard measures considered scientifically unjustified, to repeal them. Another example is the decision of the Commission not to authorise the marketing of a GMO, even if there was no scientific evidence proving that it was dangerous.

However, the Commission did not give individual assessment such a broad meaning after the reform of the GMOs legislation and in the assessment of the Upper Austria's request for derogation, under Article 95(5) of the EC Treaty. This Article requires the derogating Member States to provide new scientific evidence, under the assumption that only scientific evidence can be the 'neutral arbiter'[58] for assessing barriers to Community trade. In the evaluation of Upper Austria's request, the Commission bases its decision on the EFSA's negative scientific assessment of the regional ban on GMOs. No factors other than scientific evidence were taken into consideration in this Decision. The conclusion can be drawn that the Commission's refusal to authorise Upper Austria to ban the cultivation of GMOs in the light of the absence of new scientific evidence supporting this ban can be considered in contrast to the Commission's claim in the first EC submissions that 'scientific knowledge may not be sufficient to clearly identify the risk'[59] and with the above mentioned decisions taken by the Commission with respect to GMOs.[60]

The second question is: what is the role of the precautionary principle in the management of risks posed by GMOs? In the written submissions, the Commission affirms that measures related to GMOs taken by the EC institutions or by single Member States were prudent and reasonable and in compliance with Article 5(7) of the SPS Agreement, which is considered by many to be an expression of the precautionary principle. The Commission gives three examples of these measures.[61] At EU level, both

57 See second EC submissions, para. 23.

58 This expression is taken from Walker, 'The Myth of Science as a "Neutral Arbiter" for Triggering Precautions', (2003) 26 *Boston College International & Comparative Law Review*, 184.

59 See second EC submissions, para 26.

60 As mentioned, these decisions are the refusal to authorise the marketing of a GMO even if scientific committees reassured on the risks posed by the GMO concerned and the decision not to ask Member States to repeal their safeguard measures after the EU scientific committees (and later the EFSA) considered these measures not to be scientifically founded.

61 First, the EC as a whole adopted the precautionary principle when in 2000 it decided to put in place more stringent framework legislation on GMOs. Secondly, Member States' safeguard measures are an expression of the precautionary principle and were taken in a situation of scientific uncertainty. They are considered provisional or temporary, within the meaning of Art. 5(7) of the SPS Agreement, pending the Community assessment. The third example is the Member States' decision within the Council (1999) to apply the precautionary approach to individual applications for authorisation to market GMOs.

the EU institutions and Member States are allowed to invoke the precautionary principle. However, Member States can rely on this principle to justify national measures departing from EC legislation, provided that the risk is not 'merely hypothetical'[62] and that decisions, taken on the basis of this principle, are reviewed at EC level so as to avoid their being used as a barrier to Community trade.[63] Therefore, reliance on this principle is very much constrained within the EU.[64] It can be concluded that the precautionary principle is invoked in the written submissions to justify specific EU measures/positions on GMOs and it also applies at EU level. However, whereas in the EU context the conditions for Member States to be able to rely on this principle are interpreted very strictly—to the effect that only in exceptional cases[65] were Member States authorised to make use of this principle and the ability to rely on this principle was denied in Upper Austria's decision[66]—by contrast, in the first EC submissions, the Commission is not so strict in relying on the precautionary principle when it is necessary to justify EC as well as Member States' measures.

The third problem addressed concerns the following issue: does a measure restricting free trade/the functioning of the internal market in order to protect the environment need be justified in the light of scientific evidence? It is submitted that the answer to this question is negative in the written submissions and positive under EU law, as showed by the rejection of Upper Austria's request for derogation.

In the written submissions, the Commission claims, amongst others, that Directive 1990/220 aims at protecting the environment; in fact GMOs of the first generation addressed environmental concerns.[67] However, since these concerns fall outside the SPS Agreement,[68] EC measures taken

[62] See Cases T–13/99 and T–70/99, *supra* n. 43, para. 146. For a comment, see Vos, (2004) 11 *Maastricht Journal of European and Comparative Law* 187.

[63] Guidelines on the way the precautionary principle should be applied in the GMOs authorisation procedure can be found in the provisions (safeguard clauses) of the EC legislation in this area and in the following EC case law: See Cases C–6/99 *Greenpeace France and others*, [2000] ECR, I–1651, paras 44–46 and C–236/01 *Monsanto Agricoltura Italia SpA and Others v. Presidenza del Consiglio dei ministri and Others* [2003] ECR I–8105, para. 111, and C–132/03 *Ministero della Salute and Codacons* of 26 May 2005, not yet reported, paras. 56–64.

[64] For example, invoking the precautionary principle 'in a vague and general manner' is prohibited, as is stated in the Upper Austria decision. See para. 72 of Dec 2003/653, *supra* n. 25.

[65] See Commission Dec 549/2003 [2003] OJ L/187/27, and 2004/1, [2004] OJ L/1/20. For a comment see Poli and Notaro, 'Environmental Law (2002–2003),' (2004) 23 *YEL*, 383, especially at 391–394.

[66] See para. 73 of Commission Dec 2003/653, *supra* n. 25.

[67] See first EC submissions, paras. 416, 418.

[68] The EC admits that steps taken by the EC to protect interests different from environmental protection (such as human health, animal health, plant life or health) fall within the scope of this agreement. However, the SPS is not infringed because such steps are provisionally justified on the basis of the insufficiency of scientific evidence.

to protect the environment do not breach the SPS Agreement.[69] The same conclusion can be drawn in relation to Member States' safeguard measures aiming *in part* at protecting biodiversity.[70] These measures need be assessed by reference to other WTO agreements (the TBT and GATT) and all WTO agreements should be interpreted and applied in the light of the Biosafety Protocol, which is considered a relevant source of interpretation for these agreements.[71]

Therefore, the result of the Commission's position is that the obligations of the SPS Agreement, in particular, the principal requirement of this agreement, i.e. to give SPS measures 'science and risk assessment justifications,'[72] are side-stepped because the EC measures aim in part at protecting the environment/biodiversity. The implication of this position of the Commission is that trade-restrictive measures aiming at protecting the environment escape the requirement to be scientifically based.[73] This principle conflicts with the principle, applied at EU level and embodied by Article 95(5) of the EC Treaty, whereby only (new) scientific evidence only can justify a trade restrictive measure, limiting the circulation of GMOs, for environmental reasons.

VI. JUSTIFICATIONS OF INCONSISTENCIES

The previous section showed that there are a number of discrepancies between the principles underlying the Commission's defence of the European regulatory approach on GMOs in the biotech dispute and the principles enshrined in the EC Treaty and applied by the Commission in the management of GMOs within the EU. Essentially the Commission's defence strategy appears inconsistent with the principles of the TEC and with those underlying the management of risks posed by GMOs in the EU. This is because, on the one hand, the Commission does not allow Member States or national authorities to rely on the precautionary principle or to seek environmental protection greater than that pursued at the EC level if they threaten the application of the EC legislation on GMOs, ensuring the functioning of the internal market. Individual risk assessments based on scientific evidence *only* are demanded from national authorities seeking to adopt national measures which are more stringent

69 See first EC submissions, paras. 418, 433.

70 See second EC submissions, paras. 58–59.

71 See first EC submissions, paras. 457 and 386.

72 Motaal, 'The "Multilateral Scientific Consensus" and the World Trade Organisation' (2004) 38 *Journal of World Trade* 856.

73 The Commission's position is tantamount to affirming that no scientific evidence is necessary to justify a measure that aims at protecting the environment.

than the EC ones. On the other hand, in the written submissions, the Commission argues that the EC contested measures are justified by the precautionary principle; these measures should not be assessed exclusively in the light of scientific evidence; finally, to the extent that these SPS measures aim at protecting the environment, they escape the obligation of the SPS agreement to be based on scientific principles.

Can these inconsistencies be justified? It is submitted that the answer to this question is positive and, as a result, the credibility of the EC submissions in the biotech dispute is not undermined.

First, the reason the meaning given to 'individual assessment' and the scope of the precautionary principle are different within the EU and in the written submissions is that these two organisations have different objects and purposes.[74] The EC pursues a high level of market integration and the Commission is entrusted with the role of ensuring the functioning of the internal market. Therefore, it is logical that Article 95(5)[75] of the TEC enables the Commission to scrutinise Member States' unilateral measures in the light of scientific evidence *only* (with the exclusion of any other economic and regulatory factors) because these measures clearly affect the internal market. The ability of Member States to invoke the precautionary principle is accordingly interpreted narrowly because this principle could be used as a 'defence'[76] to raising barriers to Community trade.

The fact that the Commission attributes a narrow meaning to 'individual assessment' in the Upper Austria Decision and a broad meaning in the first EC submissions when it has to justify safeguard measures or individual applications is not an inconsistency in the Commission's policy. Indeed, the Commission cannot evaluate safeguard measures or the behaviour of national authorities in the authorisation procedure by reference to scientific evidence only: the former measure and the latter procedure, unlike the Upper Austria request for derogation, concern not only the internal market but also environmental and health protection. These are areas of shared competence and therefore the subsidiarity principle needs to be taken into consideration: in examining the safeguard measures or individual applications, the Commission cannot use the same yardstick it used in assessing Upper Austria's request for derogation because whereas the subsidiarity principle operates for the former set of

[74] Scott, 'International Trade and environmental Governance: Relating Rules (and Standards) in the EU and the WTO' (2004) 15 *European Journal International Law* 307.

[75] The Commission attached exclusive importance to scientific evidence in evaluating Upper Austria's request for derogation because this is required by Art. 95(5) of the TEC. By contrast, the Commission certainly took into consideration factors other than science when it did not act against those Member States refusing to withdraw safeguard measures, found scientifically unjustified by the Scientific Committee or, more recently, by the EFSA.

[76] Peel, 'Risk Regulation under the WTO SPS Agreement: Science as International Normative yardstick?' (2004) *Jean Monnet working paper*, 2, 38–39.

measures it cannot be taken into consideration for a national request for derogation under Article 95 (5).

The WTO agreements have the purpose of removing (tariff and non-tariff) barriers to international trade without requiring proof of discrimination;[77] at the same time, WTO members are empowered to pursue the level of protection that they deem appropriate for their citizens, subject to a broad notion of individual risk assessment and 'to some trade-based requirements but not to any (explicitly) science-based criteria'.[78] The principle of the appropriate level of protection gives WTO members considerable leeway to the extent that non-trade concerns (i.e. the need to protect the environment) can be used by WTO members to justify their SPS or TBT measures. Moreover, Article 5(7) of the SPS Agreement allows WTO members to take provisional measures in a situation of scientific uncertainty.

Finally, the fact that measures aimed at protecting the environment need be scientifically justified in the EU has to be reconciled with the Commission's argument in the first EC submissions that measures aimed at protecting the environment escape the obligation to be scientifically justified. Whereas within the EU, Member States' freedom to adopt measures seeking a higher level of environmental protection than that of the EC legislation on GMOs is curtailed by the existence of harmonisation measures.[79] No such measures[80] limiting the ability of WTO members to take GMO trade-restrictive measures for environmental or other purposes are in place at WTO level.[81] Therefore, whereas scientific evidence is considered a neutral yardstick in respect of which environmental measures

[77] Hudec, 'Science and Post-discriminatory WTO Law', (2003) 26 *Boston College International & Comparative Law Review* 184, 187–188.

[78] Peel, *supra* n. 76, 14.

[79] For example, the existence of the harmonisation Dir 2001/18 was crucial to the Commission's negative evaluation of the Upper Austria's request for derogation.

[80] Neither the *Codex Alimentarius* Commission nor other standardisation bodies have provided international standards on this issue as yet. This does not mean that international standards of the *Codex Alimentarius* Commission or other international standard-setting organisations are not relevant at all in the biotech dispute. As the EC points out, the Codex definition of 'contaminant' is a 'standard' (Codex Standard 193, rev 1, 1995) which is relevant in the light of Art 3(3) SPS Agreement. See second EC submissions, para. 38.

[81] The *Codex Alimentarius* Commission has not yet provided international standards on GMOs, this organisation is active in promoting the adoption of standards relating to genetically modified food/feed. For example, recently it has adopted standards on the definition of 'traceability' of GMOs and a discussion on the labelling of foods and food ingredients obtained through certain techniques of genetic modification/genetic engineering was held within the *Codex* Committee on Food Labelling. See the newsletter (2004) 4/10 *Bridges- trade Biores*. See generally on the relationship between the European Community and the *Codex Alimentarius* Commission, Poli, 'The European Community and the Adoption of International Food Standards within the Codex Alimentarius Commission' (2004) 10 *European Law Journal* 613.

which go beyond the protection afforded by harmonised measures can be assessed, there is no need to base environmental measures on scientific evidence within the WTO because here, in the absence of these standards, WTO members enjoy an extended degree of freedom in taking measures addressing environmental risks.

The thoughts illustrated above support the conclusion that the credibility of the EC submissions is not undermined by the fact that the notion of 'individual assessment' and the precautionary principle have a different meaning and scope according to the context in which they are relied upon.[82] This is justifiable in the light of the different constraints to which the EC Member States are subject in the EC and in the WTO. The credibility of the EC submissions is not even undermined by the different importance attached to scientific evidence as a support for environmental measures in the EU and in the mentioned submissions. This difference is justified by the absence of harmonisation measures in the WTO.

Because the WTO agreements and the EC have different objects and purposes, it is submitted that the Panel should maintain a 'vertical deference in respect of member state regulatory choices'[83] and should not require the EC to change its regulatory measures on GMOs.[84] This is especially true in an area in which no harmonisation measures exist,[85] and harmonisation of risk assessment methodology is still in its infancy.[86]

[82] This does not mean the Commission's defence is convincing in all parts. This point will not be developed here due to space constraints.

[83] Scott, *supra* n. 74, 313.

[84] Along these lines, an author argues that 'The WTO must be less interventionist in judging its Members than the ECJ is when judging its Member States. The EU's goals are far loftier than those of the WTO, and in the EU, Member States have explicitly accepted some limitations of their sovereignty so that such goals may be achieved. Meanwhile, the WTO's goals are humbler, and WTO Members have steadfastly refused any encroachment on their sovereignty. Finally, the WTO does not—yet—have the legitimacy of the EU and its institutions.' See McNelis, 'the role of the Judge in the EC and WTO: Lessons from the BSE and Hormones Cases,' (2001) 4 *Journal of International Economic Law* 205–207, quoted by Slotboom, 'Do Public Health Measures Receive Similar Treatment in European Community and World Trade Organization Law?' (2003) 37 *Journal of World Trade* 553, 587.

[85] It should be noted that there are authors who are in favour of this 'less interventionist approach' even in disputes concerning areas in which harmonisation measures exist. 'In any dispute involving breach of WTO agreements, when the Panel evaluates regulatory measures which breach the WTO harmonisation obligations—such as in the *EC—hormones* and *EC—sardines*—it should apply a less stringent and intrusive standard of review than that it applies when the breach of WTO agreements concerns a non discrimination obligation. See V. Heiskanen, 'The regulatory philosophy of international trade law': (2003) 38 *Journal of World Trade* 35.

[86] The *Codex Alimentarius* Commission has just started to work on biotechnology issues. See *supra* n. 81.

16

Biotechnology and Regional Integration Systems: Legislation and Practices in the Andean Community Countries

FABIAN NOVAK*

I. INTRODUCTION

SCIENTIFIC AND TECHNOLOGICAL innovation based on biological diversity[1] commonly known as biotechnology, has always depended on access to biological material. In the past, access to biological material (including genetic material) was free, as it was considered the heritage of all humankind. For that reason, transnational companies and the large investigation centres, which used these resources had free access to them, with no need to share the benefits derived from their use with the suppliers. However, this changed during the 1990s when, since the approval of the Agreement on Biological Diversity, the principle of sovereignty of states over their own natural and genetic resources has been recognised.[2]

As of that time, developing countries which possessed these resources (among them, the Andean countries) began the debate related to access to genetic resources and the knowledge associated with them, setting out the

* Director of the International Studies Institute (IDEI) of the Pontificia Universidad Católica of Peru. Professor of International Law of the Universidad Católica (Catholic University) and the University of Lima. Associate of the Hispano-Luso-Americano Institute of International Law (IHLADI).

I would like to thank Luz Maria Ramirez, Investigator at the International Studies Institute (IDEI), for her invaluable support and contribution in the search for and selection of bibliographical references necessary for the elaboration of this work, as well as for her interesting opinions and reflections on its configuration.

1 Refers to the application of technology to any kind of living organisms (vegetable, animal, micro-organisms), for the purpose of creating new products on specific purposes.

2 Caillaux, 'The Debate on Biotechnology in the Andean Region: Now and in the Future' in *Peruvian Environmental Law Association (The Debate on Biotechnology in the Andean Region: Now and in the future,* Lima: Peruvian Environmental Law Association, 1999) 1–2.

need for technologically advanced countries' access to be subject to a fair distribution of the benefits derived from their use and commercialisation.

Developing countries, particularly the Andean countries, do not have their own biotechnological industries. Therefore, the quickest, most direct possibility of being part of the technological revolution applied to biodiversity necessarily involves taking advantage of their biological diversity, allowing the developed countries access to it and the knowledge associated with it, in exchange for monetary and non-monetary benefits, which has caused certain tension between the two groups of countries.

This supposed tension between the states possessing technology and the states possessing biological resources should lead to imaginative solutions which benefit both parties in the end. To be precise, in the Andean sub-region, diverse regulatory alternatives which facilitate access to biological resources by the countries which possess technology but at the same time distribute the benefits derived from their use among the suppliers, are currently being proposed.

The following is the existing Andean regulation related to these topics, as well as the internal legislation of the Andean countries, which allows us to come to certain conclusions.

1.1. Importance of Biotechnology and Biosecurity to the Andean Countries

It is interesting to begin this study by analysing what concerns motivate the Andean countries to elaborate legislation which allows the development of modern biotechnology in the sub-region as well as biosecurity mechanisms aimed at preventing the health risks and damage to the environment that comes with such technology. In this sense, it can be said that there are two fundamental concerns of the Andean countries:

1.1.1. The Biological Diversity of the Andean Region

There can be no doubt that one of the main reasons that justifies the importance of biotechnology and biosecurity for the Andean region is the great wealth and biological diversity that the five Andean countries possess.

In effect, 25 percent of the biodiversity of the planet is concentrated in these five countries, which form part of the 17 countries with the greatest biodiversity in the world. Likewise, the Tropical Andes constitute an ecoregion considered by international experts to be the 'epicentre of biodiversity', since the area is first in the world in diversity of vascular plants, birds, amphibians and total vertebrates (without considering fish). Additionally, important Andean–Amazonian phitogenetic resources, which provide about 35 percent of the world's agro-industrial and nutritional production, have their origin in the Andean tropics.[3] As if that were not enough, 16.8 percent of the birds, 10.5 percent of the amphibians and 10.3 percent of the mammals in the entire world are concentrated in the sub-region. In the case of Colombia alone, it is estimated that 50,000 species of superior plants exist, 5,000 of those endemic. This country also has the greatest diversity of birds in the world—1,754 species—73 of which are endemic; it is also one of the countries with the largest number of mammals in the world—359 known species—and has one of the greatest proportions of reptiles with 386 known species, 104 of which are considered endemic; and it is the country with the second highest number of amphibians with 585 known species, 141 of them endemic. Of the 114,178,800 hectares of continental Colombian territory, 53.2 million are covered by natural forests, 21.6 million by other types of vegetation in savannahs, dry areas and humid areas, and at least 38.4 million are used for agriculture and colonisation.

This Andean mega-diversity is possible thanks to the convergence of a set of geographic and climatic factors that favour the existence of a large variety of biomes, ecosystems and habitats.[4]

Considering the foregoing, it is easy to infer that for the Andean countries the possession of this biological diversity represents important economic potential, not only for the growing interest in tourism due to activities related to the environment, but also—regarding biotechnology—for the value that these resources currently have for the pharmaceutical and food industries, among others. It should not be forgotten that 40 percent of world trade comes from biological products and processes, that the world market for biological resources has reached over US$900 billion in recent years,[5] and that, in 2000, the pharmaceutical industry of the countries in the northern hemisphere had revenues of $47,000 million dollars from medicinal plants of South American origin, where two thirds of the world's medicinal plants are concentrated.[6] Consequently, it is evident that the biodiversity of the Andean countries more than justifies their interest in biotechnology, to the extent that they are the suppliers of resources for the more developed countries, which obtain large profits by technologically transforming these resources. Consider, for example, the

[3] Andean Community. *Decision 523–Annex:Regional Biodiversity Strategy for the Tropical Andean Countries* (Andean Community Law) 10. See Tréllez Solís. *Legal Protection of the Biodiversity in the Andean Countries. Volume I: Biodiversity and its Protection in the Andean Community* (Buenos Aires, 1998), 25.

[4] Andean Community. *Geo Andino 2003. Environmental Perspectives* (Lima, 2003), 73.

[5] 68% of plant seeds, 85% of genetic animal resources and 86% of samples of micro-organisms (fungus, bacteria), which come from developing countries are stored in the genetic banks of the industrialised countries. See Romero, 'The Economic Valuation of Biodiversity', *Socialism and Participation* 105.

[6] *Ibid.*, 104.

contribution of the Andean countries to genetic resources for the world agro-industrial and nutritional production in 2003.[7]

Table 1:
Contribution of the main regions of the world in genetic resources for agro-industrial and nutritional production

Region	Agricultural Production (% De production)	Industrial crops (% Area covered)
China–Japan	12.9	2.1
Western Central Asia	30.0	10.8
Indochina	7.5	13.7
Mediterranean	1.4	18.2
Africa	4.0	8.3
Andes–Amazon	35.6	34.5
North America	0.0	10.5

However, the lack of technological development in the sub-region impedes the Andean countries from successfully participating in the economic benefits of biotechnology. The Regional Biotechnology Programme in Latin America and the Caribbean (Spanish acronym PRB) estimates that the investment in investigation and development related to biotechnology is 100 times less in Latin America than in the United States, where the annual government investment in this field is over 4,000 million dollars. In addition, there is a lack of specialised scientists to carry out the planning and development of biotechnology in the region. These deficiencies of capital and human resources do not allow the region to take advantage of advances in the field.[8]

The foregoing is particularly serious because if the developing countries in general—including the Andean countries—do not participate in the international commerce of the bio-economy, a 'genetic division, which increases the disparities between rich and poor nations' could result.[9] In effect, as the industrialised countries are the ones which have the capacity to develop and apply new biotechnology, it is feared that their production will displace the products for export from poor countries and diminish their participation in the global economy. In other words: [10]

[7] Andean Community. *supra* n. 4, 23.

[8] Estrada, 'Biotechnology and Engineering in Latin America' in Andean Commission of Technology Co-Ordination *Biotechnology, Recursos Fitogenéticos y Agricultura en los Andes (Biotechnology, Phitogenic Resources and Agriculture in the Andes).* (Lima, 1993) 153.

[9] Cruz Zamorano, 'Biotechnology: Challenges and Opportunities for the Developing Countries' (2003) 53 *International Commerce* 494.

[10] *Ibid.*

Biotechnology has contributed to a worsening of the already deteriorated economic relations between the industrialized world and the rest of the nations. If the latter are not guaranteed participation in the biotechnology market, the distortion could be greater.

If traditional technology has created a situation in which 20% of the wealthiest population of the world accumulates 82.7% of the income and the poorest 20% accumulates 1.4% of the world's income, the imbalance will be greater when the futures business revolves around products, which are complex to manufacture.

For these reasons, it is vitally important that the developing countries[11] (including the Andean countries) establish strategic alliances among themselves, as well as between the public and private sectors, which allow them to achieve greater industrial integration, the transfer of technology, financial support, formation of human capital, and so on, nationally.[12] In other words, it is very important that the Andean countries take advantage of their biological diversity to participate, directly or indirectly, in biotechnology and its benefits. On this last issue, it is worth pointing out that, currently, the Andean agricultural industry is using an improved generation of seeds, for example, based on native varieties and techniques to combat epidemics using natural control mechanisms. Likewise, the value of Andean exports of plants used in perfumes, medicines or insecticides grew steadily during the last decade, as shown in the following table:[13]

Table 2:

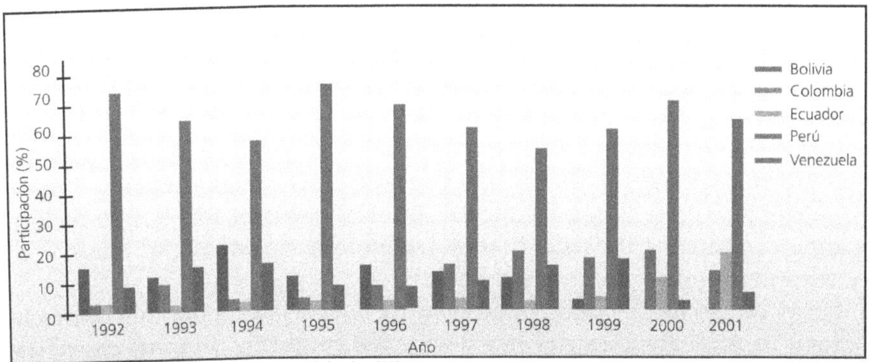

Fuente: Sistema Integrado de Comercio Exterior de la Comunidad Andina, 2003

11 As is the case of the Group of Likeminded Mega diverse Countries which was created by the Declaration of Cancun on 18 February 2002 for the purpose of creating a common agenda on the conservation and sustainable use of biodiversity. It is composed of: *Bolivia*, Brazil, China, *Colombia*, Costa Rica, *Ecuador*, Philipines, India, Indonesia, Kenya, Malaysia, Mexico, *Peru*, South Africa and *Venezuela*.

12 Cruz Zamorano, *supra* n. 9, 494.

13 Andean Community, *supra* n. 4, 73.

In general terms, this natural capital which the Andean countries possess puts them in a privileged position due to the development of biotechnology. Proof of that is that in 2002 the value of exports of biodiversity represented 37 percent of the exports of Ecuador, while for Bolivia, Colombia and Peru it fluctuated at between 23 and 28 percent.[14] See the following figure.

Figure 1 Participation in the biodiversity of Andean exports

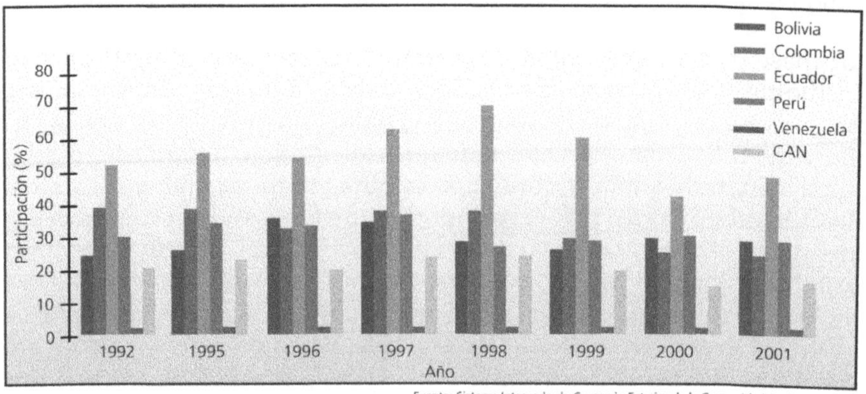

Fuente: Sistema Integrado de Comercio Exterior de la Comunidad Andina, 2003

However, beyond these advances, the fact is that the Andean countries have not reached the optimum level of participation in biotechnology and its benefits; in the first place, because they have not managed to develop their own biotechnology (due to a lack of capital and human resources) and, secondly, because their participation as mere suppliers of biological resources does not obtain the corresponding economic benefits (for lack of international legislation to protect these resources and their related knowledge).

Finally, given that the Andean countries—as we have already pointed out—form a sub-region that is characterised by its mega-diversity,[15] these countries also have a logical concern about biosecurity, that is, about eliminating or reducing the risks that biotechnology can create for biodiversity, the environment and human health.

However, so far the policies on security as it relates to modern biotechnology in Andean countries has developed modestly. In most cases, the policies are a response to external factors (requests from transnational companies to free modified organisms), which contrasts with the speed at which the proportion surface of the earth occupied by transgenic crops is growing.

[14] *Ibid.*, 76.

[15] Brañes and Rey. *Politics, Law and Administration of Biotechnological Security in Latin America and the Caribbean* (Santiago de Chile, 2001), 22.

While it is true that exploitation of this type has hither to been rare in the Andean countries, in bordering countries such as Argentina, Brazil and Chile, the increase in transgenic crops has been significant. For that reason, the Andean countries have started to pass certain internal biosecurity laws to regulate this activity,[16] for the purpose of attenuating socio-economic, institutional and ecological imbalances, which can be caused by the application of biotechnology in the region.

1.1.2. Traditional Andean knowledge

Secondly, the so-called traditional knowledge regarding biodiversity (that is, the knowledge which is developed collectively, in an informal way, over time), which exists in the Andean sub-region, plays an important role in the field of biotechnology. It is estimated that 80 percent of the population of developing countries treats illnesses on the basis of its knowledge of medicinal plants; at the same time, the North American pharmacopoeia includes 150 drugs which come from plants known to the natives of the Andean region, whose traditional knowledge was vital in their preparation.[17] Likewise, other plants and the knowledge associated with them, such as quinoa, ayahuascar, sangre de grado (also known as dragon's blood), maca, coloured cotton, etc. are being used by the European pharmaceutical industry, with no benefit to the indigenous communities.

It can therefore be deduced that traditional Andean knowledge is very important to the developed countries which use it in the field of modern biotechnology, and also to the Andean countries, which could obtain significant economic benefits from it, if they profited from allowing developed countries access to it. Unfortunately, the practice of bio-piracy has permitted access to and the use of traditional knowledge without the consent or approval of those who possessed it, or adequate compensation for its use. The legal situation of the knowledge of indigenous peoples is in contrast with the situation of modern or scientific knowledge. Therefore:[18]

> While modern, occidental intellectual effort ... which results in an invention, a biotechnological product or a plant variety, for example, can be protected by the intellectual property system through patents, acquirer's rights, industrial secrets, trademarks, etc., an important sector of the intellectual output and the effort made by indigenous groups is not protected or supported.[19]

16 Andean Community. *supra* n. 3, 84: Although they have basic differences and differences in their legal hierarchy, Peru and Venezuela have a law, Bolivia has a Supreme Decree, Colombia has a Resolution and Ecuador has a Proposed Law.

17 Romero, *supra* n. 5, 104–105.

18 Ruiz Muller, *Sui Géneris Protection of Indigenous Knowledge in the Amazon Region.* (Lima, 2002), 39.

19 *Ibid.*, 39–40: And this for multiple reasons: the system is costly and formal, the difficulty in finding one innovator (in the indigenous context) and its monopolistic and private nature.

Precisely because of the aforementioned, seeking adequate regulation of traditional knowledge, which would permit them to obtain the benefits of biotechnology through profits that could be obtained by permitting access to that knowledge, constitutes a priority issue for the Andean countries.

In summary, the possession of biological mega-diversity and ample traditional knowledge related to biodiversity makes the Andean region an attractive area for the countries highly developed in science and technology, since such countries need precisely these resources and knowledge for the development of biotechnology. At the same time, these resources and knowledge have generated interest in participating in the benefits of biotechnology in the Andean countries, as well as concern about adopting measures that eliminate, or at least reduce, the implicit risk involved.

II. REGULATION OF BIOTECHNOLOGY AND BIOSECURITY IN THE ANDEAN COMMUNITY

Although the development achieved in the Andean region regarding biotechnology and biosecurity is moderate, it is interesting to do a follow-up on it which allows us to find out not only the principal factors which motivate the Andean countries in relation to both issues, but also the internal regulation which is being developed in each of these countries.

2.1. Andean Regulation of Biotechnology

2.1.1. Andean Definition

Before discussing the Andean juridicial treatment of biotechnology, it is necessary to agree on certain basic concepts. Therefore, we should start by mentioning that in relation to the concept of 'biotechnology', the Andean countries use two definitions.

The first definition is contained in Article 2 of the United Nations Framework Convention on Biodiversity of 1992, in which all the Andean countries participate.[20] This Article sets out that:

> By 'biotechnology' we mean all technological applications, which use biological systems and living organisms or their derivatives for the creation or modification of products or processes for specific uses.

A second definition—very similar to the first—is included in Article 1 of Decision 391 of the Andean Community, which states:

[20] Bolivia (since 3 Oct 1994), Colombia (since 28 Nov 1994), Ecuador (since 23 Feb 1993), Peru (since 7 June 1993) and Venezuela (since 13 Sept 1994).

BIOTECHNOLOGY: All technological applications which use biological systems or organisms, parts of them or their derivatives, for the creation or modification of derived products, away from their *in site* conditions. [21]

As one can see, the two definitions coincide almost completely. In effect, beyond the expression 'away from their *in site* conditions', included in Decision 391, referring to the modification of genetic resources which is done outside their natural ecosystems and environment, there is no major difference between one and the other.[22] In any case, based on this last definition, the Andean Community will propose certain basic regulatory principles.

2.1.2. *Principles of the Andean community regarding biotechnology*

In 1989 the 'Andean Biotechnology Programme' was launched by the Andean Fomentation Corporation (Spanish acronym, CAF) for the purpose of contributing to the development of biotechnology in the sub region by supporting the applied investigation sectors and stimulating the creation of structures that incorporate the results of the investigations in productive activity.[23] However, a short time later, in 1991, this programme was cancelled and not replaced.

Within the Andean sub-region, only Colombia and Peru have developed legislation regarding biotechnology. In effect, Colombia was the first country to create a National Biotechnical Programme in 1985. This programme, which the National Biotechnology Council is in charge of, is financed by the Colombian Scientific Investigations Fund (Spanish acronym, COLCIENCIAS) and puts emphasis on agriculture, to which 80 percent of its funds go.

Among the priorities of the Colombian programme we have: (a) the formation of qualified, first-rate investigators; (b) the consolidation of the national biotechnological community; (c) the strengthening of ties between investigators and the productive sector; (d) the development of a legislative system that regulates intellectual property, biological security and the use of germoplasm; and (e) the development of the capacity to follow up scientific and industrial activity in biotechnological areas.[24]

21 Andean Community, *Decision 391–Rules on Common Access to Genetic Resources*, adopted 2 June 1996 and published in the Gaceta Oficial on 17 July of the same year.

22 Trellez Solís, 102; Falconi, 'Financing of Agricultural Biotechnology in Peru: A profitable investment', in *Transformation of the Priorities into Feasible Programs (Actas del Seminario de Política Biotecnológica Agrícola para América Latina)* (Lima, 6–10 October 1996) 129.

23 Andean Fomentation Corporation, *Andean Biotechnology Program*, (Caracas, 1988), 24–43.

24 Komen, 'Introduction to the Seminar', in: *Transformación de las Prioridades en Programas Viables* (Actas del Seminario de Política Biotecnológica Agrícola para América Latina), Lima: ISNAR, 6–10 Oct 1996, 6.

Regarding Peru, we have the National Genetic Resources and Biotechnology Programme, which the National Institute of Agrarian Investigation (Spanish acronym, INIA) is in charge of, financed by funds of the institute itself and universities, as well as the National Science and Technology Council (Spanish acronym, CONCYTEC). This programme has established three priority areas for action: (a) conservation, characterization, development and exploitation of genetic resources through the use of biotechnology; (b) integrated control of epidemics and diseases, focusing on crops and agricultural products for export; (c) strengthening the data bases, networks and information systems that facilitate the development of the aforementioned areas.[25]

The foregoing notwithstanding, beyond these national biotechnology programmes which are being implemented in the Andean sub-region, it is a fact that the level of expense for biotechnology and investigation, in the public sector as well as in the private sector, have not yet reached significant sums in the sub-region. Likewise, the number of professionals in biotechnology as well as physical resources for its development, is still very small.

Conscious of this reality, in 2002, by means of Decision 523, the Andean Community approved the 'Regional Strategy for Biodiversity', in which, regarding biotechnology, a development strategy based on four basic principles, detailed below, was set out.

2.1.2.1. Sovereignty over biological resources

As we know, until the 1990s, genetic resources were considered the heritage of all humankind, with no recognition of the sovereignty of any state over them. During the 1970s the FAO initiated the debate on this issue, concluding that these resources were 'the heritage of all mankind' and therefore, freely accessible and available.[26] Later, in the 1980s, negotiations began on an International Compromise on Phitogenetic Resources which, among other things, reaffirmed the conception of these resources as the heritage of all mankind, establishing that they should be freely available.[27]

However, the paradigm changed in 1992 with the approval of the Convention on Biodiversity, in which the principle of national sovereignty over natural resources and genetic resources was reaffirmed.[28] That

[25] *Ibid*. For the background on this programme, see National Council on Science and Technology (CONCYTEC). *Andean Biotechnology Program*, 'Biotechnology in Peru National Seminar. Bases for a Governmental Policy' (Lima, 1987); Bazinet and Aguirre Bastos, 'Biotechnology in the Andean Group' in *Para una Perspectiva de la sub. region Andina* (Sucre, 1994).

[26] Peruvian Environmental Law Association 'Intellectual Property and its Implications in Negotiations of the ALCA', *Series of Politics and Environmental Law*. No. 12 (Lima, 2005) 3.

[27] *Ibid*.

[28] *Ibid*.

meant a radical change in the way these resources were considered, modifying access conditions and their availability, to the benefit of their legitimate owners.

Due to the great wealth and biological diversity of the member countries of the Andean community, these countries agreed to support this position, not only ratifying the Convention but also affirming their sovereignty over their natural and genetic resources, considering Decision 523 of the CAN, which states:

> CONSIDERING . . .
> That the Member Countries have sovereign rights over their own biological resources, in accordance with the Convention on Biological Diversity,[29] particularly over those resources which have their origin in those countries.

This principle was later reaffirmed by Article 5 of Decision 391, and by the five member countries of the CAN, in the Declaration of Johannesburg of 2002 on Conservation and Sustainable Use of Biodiversity, drafted in relation to the World Summit on Sustainable Development.[30] As mega-diverse countries, the Andean countries 'reaffirmed their sovereign rights over their own biological resources', thereby establishing a clear starting point for access to and the availability of these resources, fundamentally for biotechnology.

2.1.2.2. Access to biological (genetic) resources in exchange for a fair and equitable distribution of the benefits obtained from them

Regarding *access* to genetic resources, three divergent positions exist in the region. The first sustains the need to establish national regulations on access to restricted genetic resources, tending to control the flow of and international traffic in resources and obtain the benefits resulting from their use. The second is more sceptical regarding the viability of effectively regulating access to genetic resources and obtaining benefits; while the third position proposes the establishment of flexible regulatory systems based on modern contractual formulas that allow the user countries access to these resources on the one hand, and protect the interest of the supplier countries on the other hand, guaranteeing a fair and equitable distribution of the benefits.[31]

This last position is the one that was finally adopted by the Andean Community in Decision 391. In effect, on 2 July 1996, the Andean

[29] In its preamble, this Convention states: 'Reaffirming that the States have sovereign rights over their own biological resources...'.

[30] Johannesburg, South Africa, 3 Sept 2002.

[31] Ruiz Muller, Manuel, 'Among the Access to Genetic Resources, Intellectual Property Rights and the Protection of Traditional Knowledge of Indigenous and Local Communities', in Peruvian Environmental Law Association, *Programa de Biodiversity, Serie Política y Derecho Ambiental*, no. 2 (Lima, Oct 1997), 1.

Community Commission approved Decision 391—Common Regulations on Access to Genetic Resources, reaching a very important milestone on the regional and international level, as this was the first regional and global juridical instrument which set out specific regulations and principles on how and under what conditions it is possible to access and use components of the biological and genetic patrimony of the sub-region.[32]

This ruling begins by defining 'access' as the attainment and use of genetic resources kept in *ex site* and *in site* conditions of the products derived from them, or as the case may be, of their intangible components, for the purpose of investigation, biological prospecting, conservation, industrial application or commercial exploitation, among others';[33] after which—as previously indicated—it establishes the sovereignty of the Andean countries in the use and exploitation of their genetic resources, the products derived from them and related knowledge as a basic consideration,[34] declaring such resources inalienable and not subject to seizure. Likewise, in accordance with the Convention on Biological Diversity,[35] it recognises the Andean countries' authority to regulate access to genetic resources, without imposing unnecessary restrictions. In this sense, regulations are then established for the attainment and use of Andean genetic resources, products derived from them or their intangible components, for the purpose of investigation, prospecting, conservation, industrial application or commercial exploitation. This set of regulations is a juridical-administrative system, which has as its main objective the fair and equitable distribution of the benefits (monetary and non monetary) derived from the use of genetic resources, indicating the procedure to follow to use these resources of the member countries of the CAN.[36]

In this sense, based on the principle established by the Biological Diversity Convention, that 'access to genetic resources will be subject to the previous founded consent of the Contracting Party that supplies the resources',[37] Decision 391 distinguishes several types of contracts: the *access contract* between the state of origin and the solicitors (Article 16–40); the *accessory contract* between the solicitor and the owner of the genetic resource (Article 41–47), etc.; as well as limits on access and sanctions in case of infringement of this procedure.

[32] Ruiz Muller, 'Is a New Juridical Framework for Bioprospecting in the Andean Region Necessary? Brief Critical Review of Decision 391' in Peruvian Environmental Law Association, *Serie Política y Derecho Ambiental*, no. 14 (Lima, Feb 2003), 1.

[33] See Art 1.

[34] See Art 5 and 6(2) of Decision 391. Foy, Novak, Namihas and Vera. *International Environmental Law* (Lima, 2003) 127; Caillaux and Ruiz. *Access to Genetic Resources. Proposal and Juridical Instruments* (Lima, 1999).

[35] See Art 15, annexes 1 and 2 of the Biological Diversity Convention.

[36] Andean Community, 28.

[37] See Art 15(5) of the Biological Diversity Convention. In the same sense, see number 3 of the Johannesburg Declaration of 2002.

In effect, according to Decision 391, all procedures related to access to genetic resources in the Andean sub-region are to begin with a request to the competent national authority that, in addition to other information, must contain the identification of the solicitor and the supplier of genetic resources. This request will be inscribed in the corresponding registers, published in a widely circulated means of communication and evaluated by the authority that will finally issue a technical and legal decision on the procedure requested. If it is approved, negotiation and drafting of the access contract between the competent national authority (representing the state) and the access solicitor can begin. Where access to genetic resources with an intangible (traditional knowledge) component is requested, the contract will include an annex providing that 'fair and equitable distribution of the benefits arising from the use of said component' is considered, with nullification as the sanction for incompliance.[38]

Finally, the signing of accessory contracts to the access contract between the solicitor and the owner, holder or administrator of the location where the biological resource is located is permitted for the purpose of carrying out activities related to access to these resources.[39]

However, if we evaluate the application of Decision 391 in the Andean sub-region, we will encounter some legal and institutional difficulties.

In the first place, the procedure for access to genetic resources is excessively cumbersome and complex, discouraging access to these resources by following the rules and encouraging their attainment outside the law. In effect, Decision 391 establishes—as we can see—a complex contractual system in which diverse parties participate: the State, the interested party, the indigenous community which owns and stands to benefit from the resource,[40] which makes entering into and complying with the contract difficult.

Secondly, the emphasis put on the role of the State as the principal negotiator of access is difficult to understand. It could well be a private or public university, or a scientific institution, which carried out this negotiation, safeguarding the interests of the state and avoiding scaring off potential investors.[41]

Thirdly, there is no clarity among member countries of CAN regarding the field of influence and scope of this decision, nor about some of its definitions.[42] Fourthly, Decision 391 has made no distinction between the different methods of bioprospecting,[43] which could have important

38 See Art 16, 26, 27, 28, 29, 30, 32, 35 and 39 of CAN Decision 391.
39 See Art 41 of CAN Decision 391.
40 Ruiz Muller, *supra* n. 31, 3.
41 *Ibid.*
42 *Ibid.*
43 We mean the various forms and modalities of exploring and using natural and biological resources.

consequences for its effective implementation.[44] Finally, Decision 391 does not take into account the transaction costs, which appear to be greater than the benefits to be obtained from it, that its proper implementation within the CAN member countries implies.[45]

Therefore, an amendment to the aforementioned Decision is needed, which implies: (a) a better definition of the field of influence of the norm and greater precision in its definition, for the purpose of facilitating its effective and uniform application; (b) the consolidated existence of integrated governmental mechanisms that allow its uniform implementation and compliance with it; (c) an increase in the scientific capacity of the member countries; (d) specific financial support; (e) a system for registering technical information and documentation for the member countries, regarding the issue of access to genetic resources; (f) a system of adequate incentives that promote bioprospecting, since the control and sanction mechanisms by themselves are not likely to be successful, among other issues.[46]

As if that were not enough, with respect to Decision 391—relative to *access* to genetic resources—the Andean countries are in different stages of implementation. Bolivia has Supreme Decree No. 24679 of 21 June 1997, which regulates access to genetic resources that have Bolivia as their place of origin, their derivatives, their associated intangible components and the genetic resources of migratory species which, because of natural causes, are found in national territory (Article 2). This norm regulates—in accordance with Decision 391—the internal procedure for presenting a request for access to genetic resources (Article 17) as well as for entering into the access contracts referred to in the aforementioned Decision (Article 36). Likewise, this norm establishes the Ministry of Sustainable Development and Planification as the competent authority, through the Vice Minister of Sustainable Development and the Environment (Article 6).[47]

Colombia has not translated this Decision into national law, but applies it directly through the national competent authority: the Ministry of the Environment, which by means of Resolution 0620 of 7 July 1997, has delegated the functions contained in Decision 391 to two authorities: (a) the Vice Minister, for the evaluation of the request and the supervision of the contracts which are entered into (Article 1), and (b) the Juridical Office, to process the request, the creation and maintenance of the public registry of

[44] Ruiz Müller, 4. See also Ruiz Müller, 'Regulating Bioprospecting and Protecting Indigenous Peoples Knowledge in the Andean Community: Decision 391 and its Overall Impacts in the Region'. *Expert Meeting on Traditional Knowledge* (Ginebra 2000), 5.

[45] Ruiz Müller, *supra* n. 32,4.

[46] *Ibid.*

[47] Trellez Solís, *supra* n. 3, 93.

access to genetic resources, the juridical support to evaluate and follow up on the contracts, etc. (Article 2).[48]

Peru currently has two access systems: one for biological resources (basically wild flora and fauna) contained in the Forestry Law regulations, and another one for genetic resources, derived from Decision 391.

Lastly, through a Ministry of the Environment and Renewable Natural Resources Committee, Venezuela analyses the access requests and processes the contracts, indicating the conditions, which must be included in them.[49]

In any case, beyond the problems presented by CAN Decision 391 and the speed at which it is being implemented within the Andean countries, what is certain is that, regarding access to genetic resources, the position of the Andean sub-region is clear: access should be given as long as a fair and equitable distribution of the benefits (monetary and non-monetary) obtained from the use of these resources is guaranteed.

Regarding the *distribution* of the benefits from genetic resources, the CAN member countries approach the issue from a common analysis of the situation, according to which there is an unequal distribution of the benefits of biodiversity. Therefore, the developing countries with low levels of industrialisation, regardless of the fact that the major part of the biodiversity of the planet is concentrated in them, receive few benefits from biodiversity, in contrast to the industrialised countries with high scientific and technological capacity and a high consumption capacity that receive greater benefits by reason of biotechnology.[50] That is not only paradoxical but unjust, if we take into account that the developing countries also assume the high social and economic costs of conserving the biodiversity.

Because of that, the Biological Diversity Convention commits the states parties to it to adopt legislative, administrative or political measures to distribute and/or share equitably the benefits derived from access to genetic resources, as well as those from the utilisation of traditional knowledge, innovations and the practice of conservation of biological diversity.[51]

Precisely in accordance with this Convention, the aforementioned CAN Decision 391 aims to achieve the fair and equitable distribution of the benefits derived from access to genetic resources.[52] However, it has not been

[48] *Ibid.*
[49] *Ibid.*, 93–94.
[50] Andean Community, *supra* n. 3, 30.
[51] Art 15(7) and Art 19(2) of the Biological Diversity Convention.
[52] It should be noted that this same principle of fair and equitable distribution of the benefits derived from biotechnology is included in point 3 of the Johannesburg Declaration of 2002 on Conservation and Sustainable Use of Biodiversity; in the Cuzco Declaration on Access to Genetic Resources, Traditional Knowledge and Intellectual Property Rights of the Likeminded Mega-diverse Countries of 29 Nov 2002, in which five Andean countries

successful. In the first place, because Decision 391 itself does not define what is understood as 'fair and equitable distribution'; secondly, the agreements entered into between those who require access to genetic resources and/or traditional knowledge and those who provide those resources do not tend to maintain that equity. Likewise, Decision 391 has not been able to impede the illegal transfer of these resources. All of this gives cause for criticism and even claims on the part of the indigenous communities.[53]

For these reasons, there is a need to give CAN more effective instruments which facilitate equitable *access to and* distribution of the benefits derived from the exploitation of biological diversity. In this sense, in August 2002, the CAN launched a 'Regional Biodiversity Strategy' that in the area of access and equitable distribution of genetic resources sets out the need to:

(a) confirm a new set of regulations on access to genetic resources that is clear and simple, for the purpose of guaranteeing juridical security to all interested parties;
(b) make the access regulations flexible, in the sense that they must cover different types of contracts that in turn allow for different modalities of bioprospectiong;
(c) identify key categories (resources) of exploitation around which efforts will be centered for an aggressive agenda of international negotiation and internal regulation of the Andean countries, which permit an equitable distribution of the benefits;
(d) identify the benefits that can be obtained for each category or resource, the time in which they can be achieved, the parties that will participate, the role the national authorities will play, etc;
(e) stimulate the scientific development and technology of the member countries for the purpose of directly exploiting these resources and knowledge, as well as the preparation of the parties involved. The year 2010 has been set as the date by which these objectives should be achieved.[54]

Lastly, it is pointed out that the benefits to be obtained by the Andean countries for allowing access to genetic resources and the knowledge associated with them can come in different forms (monetary and non-monetary[55]). Among the monetary benefits are quotas on bioprospecting,

participated; as well as in the Code of Conduct on Biotechnology of the FAO. See Gonzalez, 'Meeting of Likeminded Mega-diverse Countries, Environmental Legislation on Genetic Resources, Traditional Knowledge and Intellectual Propery', available at http://www.prodiversitas.bioteca.org/doc8-2.htm.

[53] Andean Community, *supra* n. 3,31

[54] *Ibid.*, 32 and 42.

[55] Office of the Secretary of the Environment and Natural Resources of Mexico, 'Access to Genetic Resources and the Fair and Equitable Distribution of Benefits, Making a Common

quotas for collecting samples, a percentage of the investigation budget, a percentage of the royalties, etc. Among the non-monetary benefits, the following can be said to be obligations of the acquirer: (a) to share the scientific information obtained as a result of the project; (b) to contribute economically to a national fund oriented toward promoting investigative activities; (c) to strengthen the capacity of national institutions through courses or training programmes for scientists and technical personnel; (d) to deposit of samples in national collections; (e) to carry out joint investigations that permit the participation of national investigators; (f) to have access to the products derived or invented; etc.[56]

2.1.2.3. Development and transfer of technology (biotechnology) in the sub-region

As we know, the Biological Diversity Convention sets out the transfer of technology as one of its basic principles. While Article 16(1) calls for only the appropriate transfer of 'pertinent' technology—thereby limiting the quality of technology to be transferred (that is, only that which is pertinent to the conservation of the environment)—Article 12 is more extensive, leaving open the possibility of transferring technology developed from biological resources of the country of origin.[57] In any case, this agreement leaves clearly established the obligation of the Member States to adopt legislative, administrative or political measures to facilitate access to technology (including biotechnology) for the developing countries (among them, the Andean countries), 'under fair conditions and in the most favorable terms, including preferential conditions and concessionaires established by common agreement'.[58]

Following what was stated in the Biological Diversity Convention, the Andean countries, in Decision 391[59] as well as in their 'Regional Biodiversity Strategy' (Decision 523) petition for the transfer of scientific knowledge and financial resources from countries with developed technology, to allow them (as countries of origin) to convert the biological raw

Agenda', in *Mega diverse. Memoria de la Primera Reunión Ministerial de Países Megadiversos Afines sobre Conservación y Uso Sustentable de la Diversidad Biológica*, 16–18 Feb, 2002 (Cancún, 2002 26.)

[56] Ruiz Müller, *supra* n. 31, 5. See also Office of the Secretary of the Environment and Natural Resources of Mexico, *supra* n. 55, 26.

[57] Mayorga Zárate, 'Industrial Property within the Framework of the Biological Diversity Convention' in *Seminar*, Cuzco: Peruvian Environmental Law Association, Oct, 1995, 5–6.

[58] See Art 16(2)(3) and (4) of the Convention on Biological Diversity. In this sence, see point 5 of the Johannesburg Declaration of 2002; point 4 of the Presidential Declaration of Guayaquil related to the World Summit on Sustainable Development of the South American Countries, of 27 July 2002; Resolution 58/200 of 23 Dec 2003, approved by the General Assembly of the UN; and the Final Declaration of the Global Biotechnology Forum, held in Concepción, Chile, 2–5 Mar 2004.

[59] See art 8 and 9 of the CAN.

materials which they possess into higher value products, in exchange for allowing the developed countries access to the biodiversity.[60] Beyond the apparent weakness that this position may project, the Andean countries feel that it is not only fair, but also realistic, because genetic technology, as opposed to the chemistry of natural compounds, does not depend on large investments in laboratory equipment.[61]

On the other hand, Decision 391 and the 'Regional Biodiversity Strategy' (Decision 523) of the Andean countries is not limited to proposing the transfer of technology on the part of developed countries; it covers the promotion of national investigations in priority areas in biotechnology matters, for which it proposes the articulation of the public and private sectors, promoting strategic alliances for the development of scientific knowledge, innovation and technology within the sub-region, as web as the creation of investment funds for development.[62] Unfortunately, in the Andean countries, very little is invested in technology these days. To cite just one example, we have the case of Peru, where the annual budget for implementing its national biotechnology plan during 2003 was US$ 32,228.[63] To be precise, this decision is intended to be repealed by Decision 523.

Concerning the priority investigations into biotechnology matters, the Andean Community understands that large transnational companies have dedicated their efforts to the biotechnological investigation of traditional products, among them commodities (soybeans, corn, wheat), and not so much to products and processes in the field of the Andean sub-region, such as is the case with Andean crops and species (tubers, grains, fruit, and many animal species). In this sense, the need arises for the Andean countries to apply technological transformation processes to these resources for the purpose of giving them added value to obtain great advantages in their commercialisation in the market.[64]

From all this, it can be deduced that the current Andean strategy on matters related to technology applied to biodiversity consists of fomenting the transfer of technology from the more developed countries in favour of the Andean countries, but also encouraging the development of their own technology.

[60] Sittenfeld, 'Biotechnology, Prospecting of Biodiversity and Access to Genetic Resources: Questions for Latin America' ISNAR (International Service for National Agricultural Research, *Transformación de las Prioridades en Programas Viables*, Minutes of the Seminar on Agricultural Biotechnological Politics for Latin America: ISNAR, 1996, 21. See also Andean Community *supra* n. 3, 47–48.

[61] Sittenfeld, *supra* n. 60, 21.

[62] Andean Community, *supra* n. 3, 64. See action line 14.

[63] See http://ap.concytec.gob.pe/oficinas/administ/web/tplan1.htm.

[64] Andean Community, *supra* n. 3, 65.

The five Andean countries in the Johannesburg Declaration of 2002 have even confirmed this strategy.[65] Likewise, at the level of internal legislation, the Andean countries have signed both components of the proposal. To cite just one example, in the case of Peru we have Law no. 26821—Organic Law for the Sustainable Exploitation of Natural Resources, of 27 June 1997, in which not only the need to promote the transfer of technology and biotechnology, but also the development of their own biotechnology, is set out (Article 9).

2.1.2.4. *Sui generis* protection of knowledge, innovations and traditional practices of the indigenous communities

(A) Definition of knowledge, innovations and traditional practices of the indigenous communities Before going into the analysis of the protection to be given to traditional knowledge related to biodiversity of the Andean indigenous, agreeing on certain basic concepts is fundamental. In this sense, it is of major importance to reach a definition of 'indigenous communities', since, just as in the traditional system of intellectual property in which a clearly identifiable individual or legal entity is the beneficiary of the protection, these communities must also be identifiable for the purpose of assigning a defined entitlement to the right to be conceded.[66] It is also fundamental to define 'knowledge, innovations and traditional practices', since each of these three concepts can signify a distinct type of protection, with diverse instruments.[67]

In this sense, it is worth indicating that Article 1 of Andean Community Decision 391 defines *indigenous or local community*, as the 'human group whose social, cultural and economic conditions distinguish it from other sectors of the national collectivity, which is ruled partially or totally by its own customs or traditions or by special legislation, and that regardless of its juridical situation, maintains its own social, economic, cultural and political institutions, or part of them'. Likewise, it defines *intangible component* (*traditional knowledge*) as 'all knowledge, innovation or individual or collective practices, with real or potential value, associated with a genetic resource, or its derivative products or the biological resources it contains, protected or not by intellectual property regulations'.

However, there are still some gaps. For example, Decision 391 does not specifically define 'knowledge', 'innovation' or 'practice'. Ruiz Müller proposes that 'knowledge' be understood as what is known and the intellectual

65 See points 5 and 6 of the Johannesburg Declaration of 3 Sep, 2002.
66 Ruiz, *supra n.* 35.
67 *Ibid.*, 36 and 37.

construction related to something, that is, the knowledge itself that the communities possess and maintain about their environment and certain resources therein; the 'innovations' would be the material products resulting from the application of the aforementioned knowledge; while the 'practices' would be the processes or procedures that the communities come up with from the application of the knowledge.[68] In any case, each of these three concepts must be regulated, for the purpose of achieving an 'integrated protection system'.

(B) Economic importance of this knowledge With the emergence of modern biotechnology, genetic resources and the traditional knowledge associated with them have acquired a growing economic, scientific, and commercial value.[69] Specifically, in relation to the importance of traditional knowledge, this is due to: (1) its permitting us to become familiar with certain techniques for the conservation of biological diversity, and (2) its offering us indications of what could be a use or an eventual industrial or commercial application of medicinal plants and edible plants.[70] For those reasons, they have significant economic value. Therefore, it is estimated that the annual value in the global market of products derived from genetic and biological resources reaches sums, which vary between US$500 and 800 trillion per year.[71] If making a very conservative estimate, it is assumed that only 10 percent of this amount is derived from resources for which original indigenous knowledge exists, we would have a result that, at least, 'products plus indigenous knowledge have an approximate value of 50 trillion dollars annually'.[72] Other data in this sense are that at least 25 percent of the medical prescriptions in the United States contain medicine that comes directly or indirectly from Andean medicinal plants, the same ones that were traditionally used by indigenous communities in different Andean countries.[73] In the following table, the situation of certain Andean medicinal plants can be seen:

[68] *Ibid.*, 36 and 90.

[69] National Institute of Ecology of Mexico, 'Traditional Knowledge Associated with Biodiversity, Conservation, and Distribution of Benefits' in Secretary of the Environmental and Natural Resource of Mexico, *Megadiversos. Memoria de la Primera Reunión Ministerial de Países Mega diversos Afines sobre Conservación y Uso Sustentable de la Biological diversity Común*: (Office of the Secretary of the Environment and Natural Resources of Mexico, Mexico City, 16–18 Feb 2002), 43.

[70] Peruvian Environmental Law Association, 'Perspectives on the Negotiations of the ALCA' in Peruvian Environmental Law Association, *Series de Política y Derecho Ambiental*, No 12 (Lima, 2003) 4.

[71] *Ibid.*

[72] Ruiz, *supra* n. 18, 26.

[73] Peruvian Environmental Law Association, *supra* n. 70, 4. See also Romero, *supra* n. 5, 104–105.

Table 3
Medicinal Plants of the Amazon Jungle Used by Amazonian Communities and Their Current Situation

Resource	Composition and Use	Situation
Curare (*Chondodendron tomento zum*)	D'tubocurarina, used as a muscle relaxant	The pharmaceutical industry is experimenting with muscle relaxant drugs
Quinine (*Chinchona sp.*)	Quinine, anti-malaria	Base of pharmaceutical derivatives (Medications such as Chloroquine and Primaquine; Novartis)
Coca (*Erytroxylum coca*)	Cocaine, local anesthetic and stimulant	
Uña de gato or Cat's claw (*Uncaria tomentosa*)	Anti-inflammatory, contra-conceptive, cancerostatic	It is sold in lyophilised form mainly in Latin American and US markets
Sangre de Grado (*Croton lecheri*)	Coagulant, antidiarrhetic, cancerostatic	Shaman Botanicals commercialises SB-Normal Stool Formula

Prepared by: SPDA, 2001.

This table shows the commercialisation and industrialisation of certain products, where the indigenous intellectual contribution made possible their initial identification, their conservation and improvement, and their later investigation and development.[74] Therefore, there is tangible proof of the valuable economic contribution that traditional knowledge means and can mean in the future for the CAN member countries.

However, much information about the characteristics of medicinal plants and crops used by indigenous communities has already been published and is available for industrial or commercial exploitation, without fair and equitable compensation (and sometimes no payment at all) having been made in their favour. Even today, there are several examples of crops used ancestrally by indigenous communities[75] that are now found in markets or about to be introduced, with no payment for the intellectual, moral and economic interest of the indigenous. For example:

[74] Ruiz, *supra* n. 18, 27.
[75] *Ibid.*, 29.

> An indigenous variety of potatoes from Brazil (Polo variety) is being used to create new commercial varieties in Europe; yams or sweet potatoes from the Andean sub region are being evaluated for their incorporation in the snack market in the U.S.; two varieties of wild tomatoes from Peru contribute US$ 5 million a year to tomato processors in the U.S.; varieties of colored cotton from Peru have been improved in the U.S. and submitted for plant patents (the owners are negotiating with Levi Strauss Inc.), among other cases.[76]

All of this reveals the need to protect the traditional indigenous knowledge of the Andean countries, which in turn should be included within the developed countries' framework of interest in extending intellectual property law to the entire world.[77] On this point, reference is made to the following section.

(C) Elements of a set of regulations for *sui generis* protection Once again the Biological Diversity Convention broke new ground by recognising the importance of traditional knowledge, since before 1992 (the date it was approved), the value of this knowledge was limited to the academic field. Currently, the Biological Diversity Convention commits the states that are parties to it to respect, preserve and maintain the knowledge, innovations and practices of those indigenous and local communities that have traditional lifestyles favourable for the conservation and sustainable use of biodiversity, to promote their wider application and to foment the understanding that the benefits derived from their use are to be shared equitably.[78]

This same recognition can be seen in the Andean Community Decision 391, Article 7, which states:

> The Member Countries, in conformity with this Decision and their complementary national legislation, recognize and value the faculty of the indigenous communities, local and Afro-American, to make decisions about their knowledge, innovations and traditional practices associated with genetic resources and their derivative products.

In this context, there are many reasons for protecting the traditional knowledge of the indigenous communities. Among them, doctrine highlights the following: (1) that this is about fundamental human rights, a collective right in this case (and sometimes shared with other communities) and transgenerational by nature, constitutes a fundamental part of the integrity and existence of the indigenous community as a people; (2) that it has economic value, because of the income that can be obtained

[76] *Ibid.*, 29–30.
[77] *Ibid.*, 30.
[78] See art 8(1) of the Biological Diversity Convention.

from its commercialisation; (3) that it has cultural value, in that it forms a substantial part of the cultural identity of each group of people; (4) that its equitable, since the communities should also receive benefits from the commercialization of their knowledge by third parties; (5) the need to avoid piracy or claims of monopolistic rights or patents on knowledge which belongs only to the community, among other reasons.[79]

However, to date, the indigenous communities (including the Andean communities) have not had a set of effective regulations for the protection of their traditional knowledge. This is due, in the first place, to the fact that the classic intellectual property systems such as patents for inventions, acquirer's rights, trade marks, and others do not seem to be adequate for protecting these interests. It should be kept in mind that this is not about individual rights, but collective rights that are handed down from one generation to the next in a community. Likewise, that traditional knowledge is more than a series of economic rights; it should be considered as heritage and implies the responsibility of caring for the natural resource.[80] As Daes points out:

> The traditional guardians act as caretakers of the interests of the entire community and only enjoy the privileges and prestige of that job while they work for the benefit of the greater interests of the community. The collective right to administer their heritage is fundamental to the identity, survival and development of each indigenous society.[81]

More specifically, Aguilar points out that the intellectual property rights system does not suit the needs of indigenous peoples for several reasons, among which the following stand out:[82]

- Indigenous peoples cannot afford the cost of registering intellectual property rights.
- The concession of intellectual property right is not extended to material that is found in the public domain, and much indigenous knowledge is already in the public domain.
- The criteria for obtaining patents as novelties, invention, reproductivity and industrial application, or for obtaining acquirers' certificates as novelty,

[79] De la Cruz and Enrique Sánchez, 'Reasons to Protect Traditional Knowledge' in Workshop; *Protection Instruments of Indigenous Systems about Biodiversity Knowledge CAF-CAN* (Santa Cruz, 2003 5–6.

[80] Office of the Secretary of the Environment and Natural Resources of Mexico, *supra* n. 55, 23.

[81] *Ibid.*

[82] G. Aguilar, 'Intellectual Property Rights, Access to Genetic Resources and Traditional Knowledge', *De Rio a Johannesburgo: Perspectivas del Derecho Ambiental en Latinoamérica*, (Regional office for Latin America and the Caribbean (UNEP)—World Union for Nature (UICN), Mexico City, 2002) 185.

distinction, homogeneity, and stability are not relevant for the protection of traditional knowledge.[83]

— They do not include the possibility of collective rights, among them past or future generations. In this sense, the possibility of conceding protection is excluded when the inventor is not identified, impeding protection of the collective innovation achieved over many years by indigenous and local communities.

— They do not take into account common law already in existence in relation to property rights among indigenous people and local communities.

— As they offer monopolistic systems for a certain period, the collective property would cease to exist when the period expires, affecting the collective property of future generations.

— Intellectual property rights, especially according to ADPIC, recognise knowledge and innovation only when they generate economic benefits, not only when they solve social needs. It is for the genetic resources industry and not for the minor players of society.

Secondly, neither would it be possible to accept that this regulation of indigenous knowledge be carried out by means of codes of conduct—as some developed countries propose—since protection based totally on the willingness of states would not be effective. Thirdly, the protection mechanisms for this knowledge, which already exist, are insufficient.

Therefore, we can conclude that the traditional knowledge of the indigenous communities (including the Andean communities) is virtually unprotected. This is particularly serious if we take into account the growth in recent years of bio-piracy, by which some people obtain biological resources and the knowledge associated with them, without the consent of the owners or adequate compensation for their use.

Precisely, in answer to this serious situation, currently there are protective instruments or measures for the traditional knowledge being applied in the Andean sub-region that are worth noting.

[83] Peruvian Environmental Law Association, *supra* n. 70, 4. In the case of patents, it is necessary that the knowledge to be protected be new, which is not the case with traditional knowledge that dates back to times no-one can remember. Additionally, the burden of Proof system was designed for the indigenous or local people, for whom it would be impossible to prove that a patented product and the procedure are not new. For example, this is the case with the *ayahuasca* plant which the people of the Peruvian and Colombian Amazon Jungle have used longer than anyone can remember as medicine or for religious purposes and which was patented by the North American company, Plant Medicine Corporation, alleging that it had altered the plant and had discovered its medicinal properties for the first time. Both indigenous organisations which have lodged complaints are having serious difficulties proving that they have known the properties of this plant for many years. The same thing is happening with the species uncaria tormentosa, known is Peruvian as *uña de gato'* or *cat's claw*, patented in the United States and with *Lepidium Meyenii*, also patented in the United States, has resulted in claims by Peru to the respective WIPO Committee, as well as the prohibition of the exportation of botanic seeds, vegetative, specimens, products, and sub products of maca (Supreme Decree No. 039–2003–AG, of 5 Dec 2003).

First, we have the *registers of traditional knowledge*, administered by the state or by the communities themselves, the purpose of which is to avoid the loss of information and/or traditional knowledge (preservation of knowledge),[84] as well as the granting of patents on it and protecting the rights that may be derived from them in favour of those who register such knowledge. In that regard, Tréllez states:

> Support for the development of traditional knowledge [implies] its collection, registration and systemization, aimed as much at encouraging the advancement of knowledge, as at systematizing and registering it, seeking the classification of the existing knowledge, of who possesses it, as well as the means to protect that knowledge that should constitute scientific or production secrets.[85]

For that, it is of vital importance that these registers be easily accessible, with better communication between the patent offices and offices for access to genetic resources. Likewise, these registers should contain precise information on: (a) the community that requests registration, (b) the identification of its representative, (c) the identification of the biological resource which the knowledge is related to, (d) indication of the use to which the resource in question will be put, (e) a proper description of the collective knowledge, and (f) the act which contains the agreement of the community to proceed with this registration.[86]

This mechanism, which is also being discussed at the WIPO level,[87] has been put into practice in Venezuela, for example, with the Biozulua Register which incorporates all the ethno-botanical information on the traditional knowledge of the Amazonian communities of that country; and in Peru, with the local registers of the Potato Park in Cuzco, where the registration of traditional information and knowledge has been worked on with the indigenous communities.[88]

For these reasons, the Andean countries, by means of Decision 486, have ruled out the possibility of patenting plants and animals, applying Art 27(3)(b) of the Agreement on Aspects of Intellectual Property Rights Related to Commerce (ADPIC or TRIPS), which so permits. See Aguilar, 175–178; Valente da Costa, 'Genetic Resources and Intellectual Property Rights' in *Megadiversos*, (Cancún 2002) 38–39.

84 Ruiz Müller, 'Initial Scope of Register of Knowledge, Innovations and Practices of Indigenous Communities Associated with Biodiversity' in *Serie de Política y Derecho Ambiental*, No. 6 (Lima, 2001), 1.

85 Tréllez Solís, *supra* n. 3, 122.

86 Ruiz Müller, *supra* n. 84, 3.

87 Peruvian Environmental Law Association, *supra* n. 70, 6. Recently, the Conference of the Parties (COP) to the Biological Diversity Convention sent the WIPO a request to define a system to identify the origin of genetic resources and their associated knowledge. See WIPO. *Comité Intergubernamental sobre Propiedad Intelectual, Recursos Genéticos, Traditional knowledge and Folklore*. Sixth session, Geneva, 15–19, Mar 2004, WIPO/GRTKF/IC/6/13.

88 It should be pointed out that some communities express their fear of using this type of register, since they could not maintain the necessary confidentiality, passing some knowledge to the public and making it impossible to protect it as intellectual property. Likewise,

Secondly, the need arises to add certain *form requirements in the requests for patents on inventions* 'to require that whoever wants to obtain intellectual property rights show the legal origin of the knowledge the knowledge that could be incorporated in certain inventions'.[89] It is made clear that this is not a new requirement for patentability, but a simple requirement that guarantees the interests of the indigenous groups. This measure is already considered in Article 3 of CAN Decision 487—Common Set of Regulations on Industrial Property 2000,[90] which enables the national authorities to require those seeking patents on inventions to show the origin of the knowledge used for the invention, presenting a copy of the document that awards the licence or authorisation for the use of traditional knowledge.[91] While it is true that this requirement is discretionary and limited to the field of biotechnology, Article 75 (h) enables the national competent authority to annul the grant of a patent if it is proven that this requirement was not fulfilled. Other than that, this same resolution can be seen in the second and third complementary resolutions of CAN Decision 391 of 1996, as well as in the Andean national legislation, such as Law No. 27811 on the Regulations on the Protection of the Collective Knowledge of the Indigenous Peoples in relation with biological resources in Peru.[92]

Lastly, there is a need to *design a* sui generis *protection system*, by means of a *special law* that not only includes the two preceding points, but also protects this knowledge in a comprehensive and coordinated manner,[93] by means of an adaptation of the intellectual property rights already in existence (collective frameworks and denominations of origin[94]) and the creation of other mechanisms of a different nature. This is the position

there may be discord when one community receives protection of its intellectual property rights and another one does not: Aguilar, *supra* n. 70, 178.

[89] Peruvian Environmental Law Association, *supra* n. 70, 7.

[90] It should be pointed out that this Decision, of 14 Sep 2000, includes a series of norms on the protection of traditional knowledge of the indigenous communities, relating the Intellectual Property Rights, established in the Agreement on Aspects of Intellectual Property Rights related to Commerce (ADPIC or TRIPS) with the Biological Diversity Convention.

[91] Peruvian Environmental Law Association, *supra* n. 70, 7.

[92] In effect, in Peru we have the Law on Conservation and Sustainable Exploitation of Biological Diversity of 1997 which establishes that traditional knowledge is the cultural heritage of the rural and native communities and is vitally important for the sustainable use of biological diversity. It is complemented by the General Law on Industrial Property (Decree Law No. 26017) of 1996, which establishes that 'inventions related to biotechnology and vegetable varieties will be governed by specific norms' which to date have not been passed, only the National Regulations on the Protection of the Rights of the Acquirers of Vegetables, See Falconi, *supra* n. 91, 133.

[93] *Ibid.*

[94] As for intellectual property rights, it has been proposed that the patent systems be reformed so that the communities themselves can request patent and have them in their name, or have a certificate of acceptance of the community of origin together with the patent request; or the use of the 'trade secrets' concept to protect traditional knowledge: *Ibid.*, 23–24.

taken by the five Andean countries in the Johannesburg Declaration of 2002,[95] in the Cuzco Declaration of the same year[96] and in the eighth transitory resolution of CAN Decision 391.

While it is true that the majority of national studies aimed precisely at developing this *sui géneris protection system* has already been completed, a common, comprehensive norm has yet to be approved.[97] In any case, in their 'Regional Biodiversity Strategy' of 2002 (Decision 523), the CAN member countries agreed to establish a common policy (by means of an Andean norm) for the protection of the knowledge and traditional practices referred to as biodiversity, with the participation and consultation of the indigenous communities (line of action 11 of the Andean Strategy). For that purpose, a working group made up of experts, representatives of each state and representatives of the communities has been formed to elaborate the Andean norm.

Likewise, in 2002 Decision 524 institutionalised the Table on the Rights of Indigenous People in the Andean countries for the purpose of allowing them to participate in community management. Similarly, as a result of Decision 435 of 11 June 1998, progress was made with the creation of the Andean Committee of Environmental Authorities (Spanish acronym, CAAAM), based in Lima, that will be in charge of follow-up, application and compliance for the 'Andean Biodiversity Strategy'; while Decision 391 has created the Andean Committee on Genetic Resources, which promotes the issue.

In any case, it should be kept in mind that the success of the future Andean norm on traditional knowledge will depend on international recognition (Result 11.3 of the Andean Strategy); for that reason, it is essential to promote this type of reform, in the World Trade Organization (TRIPS agreement)[98] as well as the World Intellectual Property

95 Para 4 of this Declaration states: 'Promote the development of a set of sui generis regulations for the protection of the traditional knowledge associated with biological diversity, based on different types of instruments and mechanismsado, and that it be duly taken into account in the evaluation of the requests for Intellectual Property Rights'.

96 See the Cuzco Declaration on Access to Genetic Resources, Traditional Knowledge and Intellectual Property Rights of the Like-Minded Megadiverse Countries of 29 Nov 2002.

97 By means of Decision 345—Common Set of Regulations for the Protection of Rights of Acquirers of Vegetable Varieties, made at Santa Fe de Bogotá, 21 Oct 1993 and published the 29th of the same month and year in the oficial newspaper, the CAN has established a legal framework recognising the acquire's who have created new vegetables. For that purpose, 'vegetable variety' is understood as that distinguished by mophological, physiological, citological, chemical characterisics and can be perpetuated by reproduction, multiplication or propagation; while it will be 'new' when the material reproduced or multiplied, or a product of its harvest, has not been sold or delivered illicitly to third parties by the acquirer or his representative for the purpose of commercial exploitation of the variety (art 8). However, this norm is not only a partial regulation but leaves out the indigenous peoples and their traditional knowledge.

98 It should be noted that art 27 (3)(b) of the Agreement on Aspects of Intellectual Property Rights related to Commerce (TRIPS), establishes a protection system by means of patents or

Organisation (WIPO), where the Intergovernmental Committee on Intellectual Property and Genetic Resources, Traditional Knowledge and Folklore is analysing the issue. For that purpose, it is considered fundamental that alliances with the rest of the mega-diverse countries be created to strengthen the Andean position.[99]

In that regard, the 'Andean Regional Biodiversity Strategy' indicates that regulation for the protection of Andean traditional knowledge is based on three basic principles:[100]

1. affirming collective intellectual property rights[101] related to traditional knowledge, on behalf of the owners (indigenous communities) of such knowledge, even in cases in which it is in the public domain.
2. establishing that a condition for third parties to obtain access to this knowledge is the attainment of the prior consent of the corresponding indigenous community. For that purpose, it must be determined, within the communities, who are authorised to approve access to the resources or related traditional knowledge. Correspondingly, for the concession of patents on inventions or acquirers' certificates, the requirement of showing that the knowledge or resource to be patented was obtained legally must be fulfilled.
3. an equitable share of the benefits (monetary or non-monetary), which may be derived from the use of traditional knowledge. For that purpose, there could be joint ventures with scientific institutions and transnational companies, or juridical related contracts that are adjudicable in national courts, by means of which permission or concessions

a *sui generis system* for all vegetable acquisitions,which has been seen by some indigenous communities as a threat of monopoly or privatisation of their resources and traditional knowledge. However, the same Art permits the member states to exclude plants and animals from patentability (which has already been done in the Andean subregion). Additionally, it is pointed out that in reality this Art opens a window for the Andean countries when it sets out the possibility of creating a *sui generis* system for the protection of traditional knowledge that, added to art 1 of this Agreement, which establishes that countries can increase the scope of protection beyond that established in the Agreement itself, can mean having a space to introduce the protection of traditional knowledge in the negotiations of the WTO.

[99] Caillaux and Ruiz, 'Legislative Experiences with Access to Genetic Resources and Options for Megadiverse Countries', in Secretary of that Environment and National Resources of Mexico, *Megadiversos. Memoria de la Primera Reunión Ministerial de Países Megadiversos Afines.* (Cancún, 2002) 83.

[100] De la Cruz, 'The Position of the Indigenous Peoples and Organizations on the Regional and Global Debate'in *Taller Regional Andino: Herramientas de Protection of los Sistemas Indígenas de Knowledge sobre la Biodiversity CAF-CAN*, Santa Cruz: CAF, 20–21 of Sep 2003, 8–17. The Andean countries express themselves in the same way in the Cuzco Declaration of Likeminded Megadiverse Countries of 2002.

[101] See Salazar, 'Structural Bases for an Andean Decision on the Protection of Knowledge, Innovations and Traditional Practices of the Indigenous, Afroamerican and Local Communities' in CAN, BID and INTAL, *V Programa de Formación en Integración Andina*, Lima: CAN/BID/INTAL, 2001, 107.

for use—and not ownership—of traditional knowledge are given, since the collective property of the community must be recognised as inalienable, unprescribable and not susceptible to appropriation by third parties.[102]

Lastly, it is worth mentioning that in relation to traditional knowledge, the Andean countries now have their own internal regulations that fully comply with the Andean strategy previously described.

In the case of Ecuador, the Political Constitution of 1998 recognises 'the collective intellectual property of their ancestral knowledge; its valuation, use and development in accordance with the law' (Article 84, point 9). While the Regulations Project on Decision 391, written by the National Working Group on Biodiversity, includes the concept of informed prior consent to gain access to genetic resources as well as the need to obtain a letter of commitment to provide the genetic resource or indigenous knowledge from the indigenous community (Article 22).[103]

In the case of Bolivia, its Constitution of 1994 recognises indigenous peoples as legal entities, which can be owners of collective intellectual property rights. Likewise, the regulations on Decision 391 (Supreme Decree 24676 of 21 June 1997) designate the Minister of Sustainable Development and the Environment, through the Office of the National Secretary of Natural Resources, to oversee compliance with the aforementioned Decision, establishing the absence of the annex certifying the authorisation of the indigenous community (Article 40 ff) as a cause for the resolution and nullity of the contract for access to the genetic resource. In the same way, there is a need to ensure in contract the fair and equitable distribution of the benefits obtained by third parties by the exploitation of this knowledge.[104]

Regarding Colombia, this country has a Proposal for the Protection of Collective Knowledge of 2000, which includes: (a) the recognition of the collective ownership of the indigenous communities of their intellectual cultural heritage, (b) the creation of a national registration system for traditional knowledge, (c) the creation of a modified patent system, (d) the creation of a fund for the benefit of the indigenous communities and (e) informed prior consent as a requirement for gaining access to genetic resources (Article 5, points 3, 6 and 7).[105]

In the case of Peru, there is Law No. 27811—Set of Regulations for the Protection of the Collective Knowledge of the Indigenous Peoples in

[102] See Aguilar, *supra* n. 18, 179.

[103] Ruiz Müller, *supra* n. 18, 71–72.

[104] *Ibid.*, 70–71. See Curichacón, 'Regulatory Protection of Biodiversity in Bolivia', in Tréllez Solís, *supra* n. 3, 178–180.

[105] Ruiz Müller, *supra* n. 18, 65–69.

relation to biological resources, of 8 August 2002, which establishes: (a) the recognition of the right of indigenous peoples to make decisions about their collective knowledge (Article 1), (b) the affirmation that indigenous knowledge is collective by nature, possible pertaining to several national or foreign communities at the same time (Article 10), (c) the possibility of negotiating compensation for the use of traditional knowledge, for which a contract can be entered into or a license to use the knowledge issued (*know-how* licences) (Articles 7 and 20),[106] (d) the creation of a national register of traditional knowledge, which must be protected by the national authorities (Articles 15 to 20),[107] and, (e) the creation of a fund for the development of the indigenous peoples to be obtained from the profits from allowing access to genetic resources (Articles 8 and 37).[108]

Additionally, it is worth mentioning Supreme Decree 008-96-ITNCI of 3 May 1996, which regulates Decision 345 and its Article 15 establishes that prior to the concession of an acquirer's certificate, the requestor must indicate not only the genetic content of the variety to be protected, but the indigenous knowledge from which it may have originated, been obtained, or been developed.[109]

Lastly, in the case of Venezuela, the Constitution of 1999 'guarantees and protects the collective intellectual property of knowledge, technology and innovations of the indigenous peoples. The registration of patents on these resources and ancestral knowledge is prohibited' (Article 124). This prohibition is also included in Article 82 of its Law on Biological Diversity. Finally, the National Office of Biological Diversity of the Ministry of the Environment and Natural Resources is in charge of coordinating and supervising compliance with Decision 391.[110]

2.2. Andean Regulation on Biosecurity

2.2.1. Andean definition

While it is true that modern biotechnology offers us a set of advantages and possibilities, it also implies a set of risks, which require regulation.

106 In 1999 a contract was entered into for licence to use traditional knowledge, by which the Confederation of Amazon Nationalities of Peru, representing the Aguarunas communities, has provided its knowledge to the subsidiary of the pharmaceutical company, SEARLE, regarding medicinal plants collected.

107 Currently, in Peru there is a Register of Collective Knowledge of the Indigenous Peoples administered by the National Institute for the Defense of Competition and Intellectual Property (Spanish acronym, INDECOPI).

108 Ruiz Müller, *supra* n. 18, 49–51.

109 Pajares, Erick. 'Regulatory Protection of Biodiversity in Peru' in Tréllez Solis, *supra* n. 3, 439.

110 Ruiz Müller, *supra* n. 18, 55–60.

Precisely, biosecurity establishes a set of measures to control these risks, safeguarding biological diversity and human life.[111] In this sense, biological security or biosecurity can be defined as:

> [The set of procedures or] measures to regulate, administer or control the risks derived from the use and liberation of modified living organisms as a result of biotechnology, which have probable adverse environmental repercussions that affect the conservation and sustainable use of biological diversity, also taking into account the risks for human health.[112]

This definition—which corresponds to the Biological Diversity Convention—is shared with very slight variation by other international and internal instruments, which regulate the issue,[113] as is the case with the Cartagena Protocol on Security of Biotechnology of 2000 drafted within the framework of the aforementioned Convention,[114] or that of Decision 523 of the Andean Community of 2002. In this last case, biotechnology is understood to be:

> Security measures aimed at minimizing the risk implied by the transfer, handling, use and liberation of these of these MODIFIED LIVING ORGANISM and their products, for the sustainability of the environment, biological diversity, human health and socioeconomic structure.[115]

Given this definition, let us examine the main principles of biosecurity in the Andean region.

2.2.2. *Principles of the Andean Community regarding biosecurity*

There are diverse instruments in the international field that in one way or another have to do with the issue of biosecurity, starting with the previously mentioned Biological Diversity Convention, the International Convention on Phitosanitary Protection, the International Convention for the Protection of Plants, the International Convention for the Protection of New Vegetable Varieties, the Convention for the Protection of World Cultural and Natural Heritage, and the Convention on International

111 Foy *et al.*, *supra* n. 34, 126.

112 Art 8(g) of the Biological Diversity Convention.

113 Trellez Solís, *supra* n. 3, 118–119.

114 Art 1 of the Protocol establishes: 'In accordance with the cautionary approach in Principle 5 of the Declaration of Rio on the Environment and Development, the objective of this Protocol is to help guarante an adequate level of protection in the sphere of the safe transfer, manipulation, and utilization of modified living organisms resulting from modern biotechnology that can have adverse effects on the conservation and sustainable use of biological diversity, also taking into account the risks to human health, and centering concretely on cross-border activity'.

115 See Annex to Decision 523 of the CAN (2.7.1).

Trade in Endangered Species of Wild Flora and Fauna, among others. Likewise, we have GATT 1994 and the Agreement on Sanitary and Phitosanitary Measures.[116] Additionally, it is worth mentioning that other instruments that bring together the world-wide consensus on this issue, such as the International Code of Conduct for the Distribution and Use of Pesticides of the FAO, the Technical Guidelines on Biotechnological Security of the PNUMA, the Code of Voluntary Conduct for the Liberation of Genetically Modified Organisms in the Environment of the ONUDI, the Code of Conduct related to Vegetable Biotechnology of the FAO, etc.[117]

However, beyond those instruments, the Cartagena Protocol on Biotechnological Security of 2000 stands out, which, although it does not regulate all aspects of biosecurity (it is limited exclusively to regulating cross-border movement of modified living organisms), it is a fundamental document, as no other has approached such complex issues as this Protocol does.[118]

The Cartagena Protocol approved in Montreal on 29 January 2000, which almost all of the countries of the Andean Community have signed up to,[119] constitutes development of the Biological Diversity Convention of 1992.

Regarding its contents, the Protocol establishes a set of measures aimed at avoiding the risks derived from the use, handling and transfer of modified living organisms, such as: (a) the evaluation of the risk that each member country should perform before importing a modified living organism, (b) the obligation to report any decision on national use or introduction to the market of modified living organisms to the Centre for the Exchange of Information on Biotechnological Security, (c) the obligation to report any involuntary liberation of modified living organisms which occurs in the national territory, (d) security regulations for handling, transporting and packaging these organisms, (e) measures against illegal transportation and transfer of modified living organisms, and (f) laws aimed at raising consciousness and public participation, among others.

For the countries of the Andean region, the approval of this Protocol lays down a legislative challenge, since the existing legislation in those countries does not cover all the aspects that the Protocol covers.[120]

[116] Brañes and Rey, *supra* n. 15, 24.
[117] *Ibid.*
[118] *Ibid.*, 130.
[119] As is the case with Bolivia, Colombia, Ecuador and Venezuela which have been parties to this Protocol since 11 Sep 2003. In Peru's case, this country has signed the Protocol, but has not yet ratified it.
[120] Brañes and Orlando Rey, *supra* n. 15, 130.

However, it should be pointed out that on the level of the Andean Community, Decision 391 establishes in its seventh transitory rule that CAN member countries must adopt a common set of regulations on biosecurity, precisely within the framework of the Biological Diversity Convention, which has yet to be implemented.

This notwithstanding, in the 'Regional Biodiversity Strategy' (Decision 523 of the CAN) it is established that the Andean regulation on biosecurity matters must include at least two basic principles:[121]

a) The Andean countries must carry out joint investigation projects that permit the determination of the risks to the environment and human health that could result from the introduction of modified living organisms to the environment, in order to make a decision whether or not to introduce a product on a technical basis. The results of these investigations must also be incorporated in a common database to facilitate the other member countries' access to this information.
b) The Andean countries must establish a set of preventive measures in relation to the modified living organism introduced, such as: its labelling; the registration of the person or legal entity in charge of its introduction, use, commercialisation, transportation or handling; the follow-up of the modified living organism for a period of time; the possibility of withdrawing the modified living organism introduced as a preventative or definitive measure, etc.

On the other hand, among CAN member countries it is possible to observe the existence of internal legislation on biosecurity matters, which is within the framework of the Andean principles previously described, although with significant differences relating to their hierarchy and scope. Peru and Venezuela have a Law, Bolivia has a Supreme Decree, Colombia has two Resolutions of the Colombian Fish Farming Institute (ICA) on agricultural and fish farming biosecurity, whereas Ecuador has a proposed Law. However, their objectives are basically the same.[122]

So, in general, these norms require the elimination or reduction of the risks to biological diversity, the environment, and human health, which are applicable to all activity with modified living organisms, whether plants, animals or micro-organisms, which have been obtained by manipulation of DNA (except in the specific case of Colombia, where the activity with these organisms must be related to fish farming activities).[123]

121 See Annex to Decision 523 (Actino Line 7).
122 Andean Community, *supra* n. 3, 37.
123 *Ibid.* See also Artunduaga, 'The Impact of Biotechnology in Latin America and the Caribbean' (2002) 391 *Revista Nacional de Agricultura* 53.

In effect, Resolution C 3492 of the Colombian Fish Farming Institute of 22 December 1998 regulates and establishes the procedure for the introduction, production, liberation and commercialisation of modified living organisms, specifically vegetables which have been deliberately altered by the introduction of genetic material or by the manipulation of its genomes, thereby not applying to the plants obtained by traditional techniques (Articles 1 and 2). Likewise, the Resolution establishes obligatory registration for persons or legal entities that are dedicated to the introduction, transport, production, handling, confined use, liberation and commercialisation of modified living organisms for agricultural use (Article 5).[124] According to the Colombian Resolution, once the request is received, it must be analysed, evaluating the risk relating to the effects that the modified living organism could have on the production of fish farms and agricultural ecosystems (Articles 12, 13 and 14). In the same way, it requires that the imported modified living organism be visibly identified by means of labels. It also sets out that a three-year follow-up of the modified living organism be done once it has been introduced, for the purpose of determining its effects. The Colombian Fish Farming Institute (ICA), as a Colombian authority, is authorised to withdraw liberated materials from the market as a preventive measure, with no indemnity rights.[125] Lastly, a list of actions constituting an infraction, such as hiding or falsifying information, not promptly reporting a risk or imminent danger to ICA, not applying the mitigation measures provide for emergencies, interfering with the follow-up performed by ICA, etc. (Articles 23 and 24).[126]

In the case of Bolivia we have Supreme Decree No. 24676, of 21 June 1997, which regulates the introduction, investigation, manipulation, production, utilisation, transport, storage, conservation, commercialisation, use and liberation of modified living organisms, for the purpose of minimising risks and preventing environmental impact that is detrimental to human health, the environment and biological diversity derived from the activities previously described (Articles 2 and 3). For that purpose, the competent authority to ensure compliance with this norm is the Ministry of Sustainable Development and Environment through the Vice Minister of Natural Resources, Environment and Forestry Development.[127]

Regarding Venezuela, we have the Biological Diversity Law of 24 May 2000, for which regulations have not yet been established. This norm regulates the investigation, development, production, utilisation, liberation

[124] Brañes and Rey, *supra* n. 15, 48.
[125] *Ibid.*, 49.
[126] *Ibid.*
[127] Andean Community, *supra* n. 4, 135.

or introduction of any element of the modified or exotic biological diversity to avoid damage, in addition to regulating commerce in modified organisms, their by-products or technology. The Ministry of the Environment and Natural Resources, through the National Office of Biological Diversity, is in charge of overseeing compliance with this law, to avoid real or potential dangers to biological diversity and human beings.[128]

In the case of Peru, Law No. 27104 on Prevention of Risks Derived from the Use of Biotechnology of 12 May 1999 is applicable to the investigation, production, introduction, manipulation, transportation, storage, conservation, exchange, commercialisation, confined use and liberation of modified living organisms, under controlled conditions; in addition to any activity involving the manipulation of DNA or the utilisation of modified living organisms as vector, receptor, or parental organisms (Article 3). All that is to: (a) protect human health, the environment and biological diversity, (b) promote security in the investigation and development of biotechnology, (c) regulate, manage and control the risks derived from the confined use and liberation of modified living organisms, and (d) regulate the exchange and commercialisation, inside and outside the country of the modified living organisms. For compliance with this norm, the sectorial institutions are the competent authorities, under the coordination of the National Council on the Environment (Article 2).[129]

Lastly, in Ecuador, currently there is no regulation on the matter, but only a proposed Law on Conservation and Sustainable Use of Biodiversity, aimed at regulating propagation in the environment, experimentation, use, commercialisation and importation of modified living organisms.[130]

III. CONCLUSIONS

It is possible to draw the following conclusions from the foregoing:

1. The interest of the Andean countries in biotechnology and biosecurity is derived from the great wealth and biological diversity that they possess (25 percent of the biodiversity of the planet) as well as the traditional knowledge associated with it. However, the Andean countries have not yet reached an optimum level of participation in the benefits of biotechnology; first, because they have not developed their own biotechnology (due to a lack of capital and human resources)

[128] *Ibid.*
[129] *Ibid.*
[130] *Ibid.*

and, secondly, because their participation as mere providers of biological resources does not obtain the corresponding economic benefits, due to the absence of international legislation that protects these resources and its associated knowledge.

2. Because of the foregoing, the Andean countries have drafted a 'Regional Biodiversity Strategy' (Decision 523) that includes a strategy for developing biotechnology in the sub-region, based on four basic principles:
   2.1. First, the Andean countries ratify their sovereignty over the natural and genetic resources existing in their respective territories.
   2.2. Secondly, the Andean countries seek access to the genetic resources of the sub-region on the part of the developed countries, by means of different types of contracts, in exchange for a fair and equitable distribution of the monetary and non-monetary benefits obtained from the use or exploitation of such resources.
   2.3. Thirdly, the Andean countries set out the need to promote in their favour the transfer of technology on the part of the developed countries as well as the development of their own technology, which would permit them to convert the biological raw materials which they possess in products of greater value.
   2.4. Fourthly, the Andean countries request *sui generis* protection regulations for their traditional knowledge that would permit them to determine the eventual use or industrial or commercial application of medicinal and edible plants they possess. They start out affirming that the intellectual property rights system in force does not fit the characteristics of this knowledge, which makes it necessary to create an ad hoc protection system, characterised by the recognition of the collective intellectual property rights of indigenous Andean communities in relation to their traditional knowledge; regarding which they can enter into concessions for their use in exchange for monetary or no monetary benefits.
3. However, the Andean strategy regarding biotechnology previously described has serious limitations for its proper implantation, such as: the lack of capital to finance it, the lack of human resources to sustain it and the absence of a majority consensus that would permit a more widespread incorporation of this strategy, as in the case of the WIPO or the WTO.
4. Consequently, it is necessary to prioritise sectors and establish alliances with the rest of the mega-diverse countries, for the purpose of making the proposal viable so it can materialise, allowing the Andean countries to benefit at last from biotechnology.

Index

www.ingramcontent.com/pod-product-compliance
Ingram Content Group UK Ltd.
Pitfield, Milton Keynes, MK11 3LW, UK
UKHW021033041026
15470UKWH00018B/1843/J

9 781841 136318